55·34
econ 1150

These chapters describe the forces that in the long run determine key real variables, including growth in GDP, saving, investment, real interest rates, and unemployment.

The monetary system is crucial in determining the long-run behaviour of the price level, the inflation rate, and other nominal variables.

A nation's economic interactions with other nations are described by its trade balance, net foreign investment, and exchange rate.

A long-run model of the open economy explains the determinants of the trade balance, the real exchange rate, and other real variables.

The model of aggregate demand and aggregate supply explains short-run economic fluctuations, the short-run effects of monetary and fiscal policy, and the short-run linkage between real and nominal variables.

A capstone chapter presents both sides of five major debates over economic policy.

PRINCIPLES OF
MACROECONOMICS

SECOND CANADIAN EDITION

PRINCIPLES OF
MACROECONOMICS

N. Gregory Mankiw
Harvard University

Ronald D. Kneebone
University of Calgary

Kenneth J. McKenzie
University of Calgary

Nicholas Rowe
Carleton University

THOMSON
NELSON

Australia   Canada   Mexico   Singapore   Spain   United Kingdom   United States

THOMSON

NELSON

Principles of Macroeconomics
Second Canadian Edition

by N. Gregory Mankiw, Ronald D. Kneebone, Kenneth J. McKenzie, and Nicholas Rowe

Editorial Director and Publisher:
Evelyn Veitch

Acquisitions Editor:
Anthony Rezek

Developmental Editor:
Klaus G. Unger

Production Editor:
Emily Ferguson

Production Coordinator:
Renate McCloy

Copy Editor:
Claudia Kutchukian

Proofreader:
Cathy Fraccaro

Creative Director:
Angela Cluer

Cover Design:
Sonya V. Thursby, Opus House Incorporated

Cover Image:
Mall by Brian Kipping.
© Brian Kipping. 19 cm x 22 cm, mixed media on wood. Reproduced with permission of the artist and Bau-Xi Gallery, Toronto.

Compositor:
Brian Lehen • Graphic Design Ltd.

Printer:
Quebecor World

Canadian Cataloguing in Publication Data

Main entry under title:
    Principles of macroeconomics

2nd Canadian ed.
Includes bibliographical references and index.
ISBN 0-03-034059-4

    1. Macroeconomics. I. Mankiw, N. Gregory

HB172.5.P744 2002   339
C2001-903630-2

About the cover painting: *Mall* by Brian Kipping shows people in a modern mall, epitomizing the authors' approach to economics as social interaction in the ordinary business of life. At the same time, the painting's structured set-up makes for a subtle representation of the scientific side of economics and its clear lucid structure.

About the interior illustrations: The interior illustrations are the work of Fort Worth artist Lamberto Alvarez. Each illustration brings to life economic markets and activities that are associated with chapter topics presented in the book. Alvarez, an award-winning illustrator and artist, is primarily known for his extensive magazine and newspaper work, some of which is syndicated through Pen Tip International Features. He is currently coauthoring and self-publishing an illustrated novel, *Muñeca*, with friend Michael H. Price.

Statistics Canada information is used with permission of the Minister of Industry, as minister responsible for Statistics Canada. Information on the wide range of data from Statistics Canada can be obtained from Statistics Canada regional offices, its World Wide Web site at http://www.statcan.ca, and its toll-free access number 1-800-263-1136.

To Catherine, Nicholas, and Peter,
my other contributions to the next generation

To our parents
and
Cindy,
Kathleen and Janetta,
Muriel and Julia
Thanks for your support and patience

N. Gregory Mankiw is Professor of Economics at Harvard University. As a student, he studied economics at Princeton University and MIT. As a teacher, he has taught various courses, including macroeconomics, microeconomics, statistics, and principles of economics. He even spent one summer long ago as a sailing instructor on Long Beach Island.

Professor Mankiw is a prolific writer. His work has been published in academic journals, such as the *American Economic Review, Journal of Political Economy,* and *Quarterly Journal of Economics,* and in more popular forums, such as *The New York Times, The Financial Times,* and *The Wall Street Journal.* He has been a columnist for *Fortune* magazine and is author of the best-selling intermediate-level textbook *Macroeconomics* (Worth Publishers). In addition to his teaching, research, and writing, Professor Mankiw has served as director of the Monetary Economics Program at the National Bureau of Economic Research, a nonprofit think tank in Cambridge, Massachusetts, and as an adviser to the Federal Reserve Bank of Boston and the Congressional Budget Office.

Professor Mankiw lives in Wellesley, Massachusetts, with his wife, Deborah, and their children, Catherine, Nicholas, and Peter.

Ronald D. Kneebone is Professor of Economics at the University of Calgary. He received his PhD from McMaster University. Professor Kneebone has taught macroeconomics from principles through to the PhD level, as well as courses in public finance, and is a regular nominee for teaching awards. Research interests are primarily in the areas of public finance and fiscal federalism. His academic journal articles cover topics such as government budget financing, and fiscal and monetary relations. He shares with Kenneth McKenzie the Douglas Purvis Memorial Prize for the best published work in Canadian public policy in 1999.

Kenneth J. McKenzie is Professor of Economics at the University of Calgary. He received his PhD from Queen's University. Specializing in public economics, with an emphasis on taxation and political economy, Professor McKenzie has published extensively in these areas. He is the winner of the 1996 Harry Johnson Prize (with Herb Emery) for the best article in the *Canadian Journal of Economics*, the 1999 Douglas Purvis Memorial Prize (with Ronald Kneebone) for a published work relating to Canadian public policy, and the 2000 Faculty of Social Sciences Distinguished Researcher Award at the University of Calgary. He has taught microeconomics and public economics from the principles to the graduate level, and has received several departmental teaching awards.

Nicholas Rowe is Associate Professor of Economics at Carleton University. He received his PhD from the University of Western Ontario. He has twenty years' experience in teaching economics, at various levels, in Canada, Cuba, and Australia. Professor Rowe's research interests are in the area of monetary policy, more specifically inflation targeting by central banks. For the 2001–2002 academic year, Nicholas Rowe will be on sabbatical, visiting the Bank of Canada's research department.

FOREWORD

During my 20-year career as a student, the course that excited me most was the two-semester sequence on the principles of economics that I took during my freshman year in college. It is no exaggeration to say that it changed my life.

I had grown up in a family that often discussed politics over the dinner table. The pros and cons of various solutions to society's problems generated fervent debate. But, in school, I had been drawn to the sciences. Whereas politics seemed vague, rambling, and subjective, science was analytic, systematic, and objective. While political debate continued without end, science made progress.

My freshman course on the principles of economics opened my eyes to a new way of thinking. Economics combines the virtues of politics and science. It is, truly, a social science. Its subject matter is society—how people choose to lead their lives and how they interact with one another. But it approaches the subject with the dispassion of a science. By bringing the methods of science to the questions of politics, economics tries to make progress on the challenges that all societies face.

I was drawn to write this book in the hope that I could convey some of the excitement about economics that I felt as a student in my first economics course. Economics is a subject in which a little knowledge goes a long way. (The same cannot be said, for instance, of the study of physics or the Japanese language.) Economists have a unique way of viewing the world, much of which can be taught in one or two semesters. My goal in this book is to transmit this way of thinking to the widest possible audience and to convince readers that it illuminates much about the world around them.

I firmly believe that everyone should study the fundamental ideas that economics has to offer. One purpose of general education is to inform people about the world and thereby make them better citizens. The study of economics, as much as any discipline, serves this goal. Writing an economics textbook is, therefore, a great honor and a great responsibility. It is one way that economists can help promote better government and a more prosperous future. As the great economist Paul Samuelson put it, "I don't care who writes a nation's laws, or crafts its advanced treaties, if I can write its economics textbooks."

It is tempting for a professional economist writing a textbook to take the economist's point of view and to emphasize those topics that fascinate him and other economists. I have done my best to avoid that temptation. I have tried to put myself in the position of someone seeing economics for the first time. My goal is to emphasize the material that *students* should and do find interesting about the study of the economy.

One result is that this book is briefer than many books used to introduce students to economics. As a student, I was (and unfortunately still am) a slow reader. I groaned whenever a professor gave the class a 1000-page tome to read. Of course, my reaction was not unique. The Greek poet Callimachus put it succinctly: "Big book, big bore." Callimachus made that observation in 250 B.C., so he was probably not referring to an economics textbook, but today his sentiment is echoed around the world every semester when students first see their economics assignments. My goal in this book is to avoid that reaction by skipping the bells, whistles, and extraneous details that distract students from the key lessons.

Another result of this student orientation is that more of this book is devoted to applications and policy—and less to formal economic theory—than is the case with many other books written for the principles course. Throughout, I have tried to return to applications and policy questions as often as possible. Most chapters include case studies illustrating how the principles of economics are applied. In addition, "In the News" boxes (most of which are new to this edition) offer excerpts from newspaper articles showing how economic ideas shed light on current issues facing society. After students finish their first course in economics, they should think about news stories from a new perspective and with greater insight.

I am delighted that versions of this book are (or will soon be) available in many of the world's languages. Currently scheduled translations include Chinese (in both standard and simple characters), Czech, French, German, Greek, Indonesian, Italian, Japanese, Korean, Portuguese, Romanian, Russian, and Spanish. In addition, adaptations of the book for Canadian and Australian students are also available. Instructors who would like more information about these books should contact Nelson Thomson Learning.

A special thanks go to Karen Dynan, Douglas Elmendorf, and Dean Croushore, who drafted many of the problems and applications presented at the end of each chapter. Yvonne Zinfon, my secretary at Harvard, as usual went beyond the call of duty and helped me proofread the entire book.

The team of editors that worked on this book improved it tremendously. Jane Tufts, developmental editor, provided truly spectacular editing—as she always does. Mike Roche, publisher, did a splendid job of overseeing the many people involved in such a large project. Amy Ray and Amy Porubsky, developmental editors, assembled an excellent team to write the supplements while managing beautifully the thousands of related details. Lois West, production manager, and Charlie Dierker, project editor, had the patience and dedication necessary to turn my manuscript into this book. Scott Baker, art director, gave this book its clean, friendly look. Michele Gitlin, copyeditor, refined my prose; Sheryl Nelson, proofreader, scrutinized all of the page proofs; and Alexandra Nickerson, indexer, prepared a careful and thorough index. Marketing strategists Kathleen Sharp and Janet Morey, and field editorial specialist Dave Theisen, worked long hours getting the word out to potential users of this book. The rest of the Harcourt team was also consistently professional, enthusiastic, and dedicated: Linda Blundell, photo and permissions editor; Kimberly Dolejsi, manufacturing manager; C.J. Jasieniecki, project editor; Michelle Graham, editorial assistant; Megan McDaniel, marketing coordinator; and Marlon Rison, marketing assistant.

I must also thank my "in house" editor—Deborah Mankiw. As the first reader of almost everything I write, she continued to offer just the right mix of criticism and encouragement.

Finally, I am grateful to my children, Catherine, Nicholas, and Peter. Their unpredictable visits to my study offered welcome relief from long spans of writing and rewriting. Although now they are only eight, five, and one and a half years old, someday they will grow up and study the principles of economics. I hope this book provides its readers some of the education and enlightenment that I wish for my own children.

N. Gregory Mankiw
July 2000

PREFACE TO THE SECOND CANADIAN EDITION

As soon as we got our hands on the first U.S. edition of *Principles of Macroeconomics,* it was clear to us that "this one is different." If other first-year economics textbooks are encyclopedias, Gregory Mankiw's is a handbook.

Between the three of us, we have many years of experience teaching first-year economics. Like many instructors, we found it harder and harder to teach with each new edition of the thick, standard texts. It was simply impossible to cover all of the material. Of course, we could have skipped sections, boxes, or whole chapters, but then, apart from the sheer hassle of telling students which bits to read and not to read, and worries about the consistency and completeness of the remaining material, we ran the risk of leaving students with the philosophy that what matters is only what's on the exam.

We do not believe that the writers of these books set out with the intention of cramming so much material into them. It is a difficult task to put together the perfect textbook—one that all instructors would approve of and all students would enjoy using. Therefore, to please all potential users, most of the books end up covering a wide range of topics. And so the books grow and grow.

Professor Mankiw made a fresh start in the first U.S. edition. He included all of the important topics and presented them in order of importance. And in the second U.S. edition, he has resisted the temptation to add more and more material. We have, in adapting the text for Canadian students, taken a minimalist approach: "If it isn't broken, don't fix it!" While the book is easily recognizable as Professor Mankiw's, we have made changes that increase its relevance to Canadian students. Some of these changes reflect important differences between the Canadian and U.S. economies. For example, the Canadian economy is much smaller and more open than the U.S. economy, and this fact is explicitly recognized in this edition. Other changes reflect important institutional differences between the two countries, including the structure of the tax system and the nature of competition policy. Finally, the Canadian edition focuses on issues and includes examples that are more familiar and relevant to a Canadian audience.

We would not have agreed to participate in the Canadian edition if we were not extremely impressed with the U.S. edition. Professor Mankiw has done an outstanding job of identifying the key concepts and principles that every first-year student should learn.

It was truly a pleasure to work with such a well-thought-out and well-written book. We have enjoyed teaching from the first Canadian edition. We look forward again to using the second Canadian edition, and we hope you do too.

WHAT'S NEW IN THE SECOND CANADIAN EDITION?

Much has changed in the world since we wrote the first edition of this book: The Internet has become a central part of Canadian life, the federal government's budget has gone from deficit to surplus, the U.S. Justice Department has brought a landmark antitrust suit against Microsoft, the stock market has experienced a historic boom, technology stocks have crashed, Europe has adopted a common currency, and Wayne Gretzky has retired from hockey. Because the teaching of economics has to stay current with an ever-changing world, this new edition includes dozens of new case studies and boxes.

In addition to updating the book, we have refined its coverage and pedagogy with input from many users of the first edition. Several topics appear in this edition that were missing from the first, including cross-price elasticity of demand and the debate over predatory pricing. We have also expanded the treatment of some topics, such as the computation of elasticity and the various concepts of firms' costs.

All of the changes that we made, and the many others that we considered, were evaluated in light of the benefits of brevity. Like most things that we study in economics, a student's time is a scarce resource. We always keep in mind a dictum from the great novelist Robertson Davies: "One of the most important things about writing is to boil it down and not bore the hell out of everybody."

HOW IS THIS BOOK ORGANIZED?

To write a brief and student-friendly book, we had to consider new ways to organize familiar material. What follows is a whirlwind tour of this text. The tour will, we hope, give instructors some sense of how the pieces fit together.

Introductory Material

Chapter 1, "Ten Principles of Economics," introduces students to the economist's view of the world. It previews some of the big ideas that recur throughout economics, such as opportunity cost, marginal decision making, the role of incentives, the gains from trade, and the efficiency of market allocations. Throughout the book, we refer regularly to the *Ten Principles of Economics* in Chapter 1 to remind students that these principles are the foundation for most economic analysis. A building-blocks icon in the margin calls attention to these references.

Chapter 2, "Thinking Like an Economist," examines how economists approach their field of study. It discusses the role of assumptions in developing a theory and introduces the concept of an economic model. It also discusses the role of economists in making policy. The appendix to this chapter offers a brief refresher course on how graphs are used and how they can be abused.

Chapter 3, "Interdependence and the Gains from Trade," presents the theory of comparative advantage. This theory explains why individuals trade with their neighbours, as well as why nations trade with other nations. Much of economics is about how market forces coordinate many individual production and consumption decisions. As a starting point for this analysis, students see in this chapter why specialization, interdependence, and trade can benefit everyone.

The Fundamental Tools of Supply and Demand

The next three chapters introduce the basic tools of supply and demand. Chapter 4, "The Market Forces of Supply and Demand," develops the supply curve, the demand curve, and the notion of market equilibrium. Chapter 5, "Elasticity and Its Application," introduces the concept of elasticity and uses it to analyze events in three different markets. Chapter 6, "Supply, Demand, and Government Policies," uses these tools to examine price controls, such as rent-control and minimum-wage laws, and tax incidence.

Chapter 7, "Consumers, Producers, and the Efficiency of Markets," extends the analysis of supply and demand using the concepts of consumer surplus and producer surplus. It begins by developing the link between consumers' willingness to pay and the demand curve and the link between producers' costs of production and the supply curve. It then shows that the market equilibrium maximizes the sum of the producer and consumer surplus. Thus, students learn early about the efficiency of market allocations.

The next two chapters apply the concepts of producer and consumer surplus to questions of policy. Chapter 8, "Application: The Costs of Taxation," shows why taxation results in deadweight losses and what determines the size of those losses. Chapter 9, "Application: International Trade," considers who wins and who loses from international trade and presents the debate over protectionist trade policies.

Macroeconomics

Our overall approach to teaching macroeconomics is to examine the economy in the long run (when prices are flexible) before examining the economy in the short run (when prices are sticky). We believe that this organization simplifies learning macroeconomics for several reasons. First, the classical assumption of price flexibility is more closely linked to the basic lessons of supply and demand, which students have already mastered. Second, the classical dichotomy allows the study of the long run to be broken up in several, more easily digested pieces. Third, because the business cycle represents a transitory deviation from the economy's long-run growth path, studying the transitory deviations is more natural after the long-run equilibrium is understood. Fourth, the macroeconomic theory of the short run is more controversial among economists than the macroeconomic theory of the long run. For these reasons, most upper-level courses in macroeconomics now follow this long-run-before-short-run approach; our goal is to offer introductory students the same advantage.

Returning to the detailed organization, we start the coverage of macroeconomics with issues of measurement. Chapter 10, "Measuring a Nation's Income," discusses the meaning of gross domestic product and related statistics from the national income accounts. Chapter 11, "Measuring the Cost of Living," discusses the measurement and use of the consumer price index.

The next three chapters describe the behaviour of the real economy in the long run. Chapter 12, "Production and Growth," examines the determinants of the large variation in living standards over time and across countries. Chapter 13, "Saving, Investment, and the Financial System," discusses the types of financial institutions in our economy and examines their role in allocating resources. Chapter 14, "Unemployment and Its Natural Rate," considers the long-run determinants of the unemployment rate, including job search, minimum-wage laws, the market power of unions, and efficiency wages.

Having described the long-run behaviour of the real economy, the book then turns to the long-run behaviour of money and prices. Chapter 15, "The Monetary System," introduces the economist's concept of money and the role of the central bank in controlling the quantity of money. Chapter 16, "Money Growth and Inflation," develops the classical theory of inflation and discusses the costs that inflation imposes on a society.

The next two chapters present the macroeconomics of open economies, maintaining the long-run assumptions of price flexibility and full employment. Chapter 17, "Open-Economy Macroeconomics: Basic Concepts," explains the relationship among saving, investment, and the trade balance, the distinction between the nominal and real exchange rate, and the theory of purchasing-power parity. Chapter 18, "A Macroeconomic Theory of the Open Economy," presents a classical model of the international flow of goods and capital. The model sheds light on various issues, including the link between budget deficits and trade deficits and the macroeconomic effects of trade policies. Because instructors differ their emphasis on this material, these chapters are written so that they can be used in different ways. Some may choose to cover Chapter 17 but not Chapter 18; others may skip both chapters; and still others may choose to defer the analysis of open-economy macroeconomics until the end of their courses.

After fully developing the long-run theory of the economy in Chapters 12 through 18, the book turns to explaining short-run fluctuations around the long-run trend. This organization simplifies teaching the theory of short-run fluctuations because, at this point in the course, students have a good grounding in many basic macroeconomic concepts. Chapter 19, "Aggregate Demand and Aggregate Supply," begins with some facts about the business cycle and then introduces the model of aggregate demand and aggregate supply. Chapter 20, "The Influence of Monetary and Fiscal Policy on Aggregate Demand," explains how policymakers can use the tools at their disposal to shift the aggregate-demand curve. Chapter 21, "The Short-Run Tradeoff between Inflation and Unemployment," explains why policymakers who control aggregate demand face a tradeoff between inflation and unemployment. It examines why this tradeoff exists in the short run, why it shifts over time, and why it does not exist in the long run.

The book concludes with Chapter 22, "Five Debates over Macroeconomic Policy." This capstone chapter considers five controversial issues facing policymakers: the proper degree of policy activism in response to the business cycle, the choice between rules and discretion in the conduct of monetary policy, the desirability of reaching zero inflation, the importance of reducing the government's debt, and the need for tax reform to encourage saving. For each issue, the chapter presents both sides of the debate and encourages students to make their own judgments.

LEARNING TOOLS

The purpose of this book is to help students learn the fundamental lessons of economics and to show how such lessons can be applied to the world in which they live. Toward that end, we have used various learning tools that recur throughout the book.

- ◆ **Chapter Objectives** Every chapter begins with a list of primary objectives to give students a sense of where it is heading. Each list is brief to help students stay focused on the four or five key lessons presented in the chapter.
- ◆ **Case Studies** Economic theory is useful and interesting only if it can be applied to understanding actual events and policies. This book, therefore, contains numerous case studies that apply the theory that has just been developed.
- ◆ **"In the News" Boxes** One benefit students gain from studying economics is a new perspective and greater understanding of news from around the world. To highlight this benefit we have included excerpts

from many newspaper articles, some being opinion columns written by prominent economists. These articles, together with our brief introductions, show how basic economic theory can be applied. Most of the boxes are new to this edition.

◆ **"FYI" Boxes** The "FYI" boxes provide additional material "for your information." Some of them offer a glimpse into the history of economic thought. Others clarify technical issues. Still others discuss supplementary topics that instructors might choose either to discuss or skip in their lectures.

◆ **Definitions of Key Concepts** When key concepts are introduced in the chapter, they are presented in bold type. In addition, their definitions are placed in the margin. This treatment should aid students in learning and reviewing the material.

◆ **Quick Quizzes** After each major section, students are offered a "quick quiz" to check their comprehension of what they have just learned. If students cannot readily answer these quizzes, they should stop and reread material before continuing.

◆ **Chapter Summaries** Each chapter ends with a brief summary that reminds students of the most important lessons that they have just learned. Later in their study it offers an efficient way to review for exams.

◆ **Key Concepts** A list of key concepts at the end of each chapter offers students a way to test their understanding of the new terms that have been introduced. Page references are included so that students can review the terms that they do not understand.

◆ **Questions for Review** At the end of each chapter are questions for review that cover the chapter's primary lessons. Students can use these questions to check their comprehension and to prepare for exams.

◆ **Problems and Applications** Each chapter also contains a variety of problems and applications that ask students to apply the material that they have learned. Some professors may use these questions for home-work assignments. Others may use them as a starting point for classroom discussion.

SUPPLEMENTS

For the Instructor

Teaching the principles of economics can be a demanding job. Often, classes are large and teaching assistants are in short supply. The supplements designed for the instructor make the job less demanding and more fun.

◆ **Computerized Test Bank/Test Bank** Ronald D. Kneebone (University of Calgary) has prepared the Canadian edition of a computerized test bank for PC and Macintosh users. Consisting of 3900 true–false, multiple-choice, short-answer, and critical-thinking questions, the CTB has many features that facilitate test preparation, scoring, and grade recording. It also offers great flexibility. The order of test questions can be altered to create different versions of any given test, and it is easy to modify questions and reproduce any of the graphing questions to meet the instructor's needs. For the instructor's convenience, every question is identified according to the chapter learning objective that it covers, the chapter section in which the material is covered, the level of difficulty, and the type of question (true–false, multiple-choice, short-answer, or critical-thinking). Answers are also provided. The same material is available as a paper test bank.

◆ **Instructor's Resource Manual with Adjunct and Teaching Assistant Guide** Sigrid Ewender (Kwantlen University College) has written the Canadian edition of an instructor's manual aimed at helping both experienced and novice instructors prepare their lectures. Lecture notes for each chapter briefly summarize the text material and provide additional examples and applications. The Adjunct and Teaching Assistant Guide offers extensive outlines of every chapter, even more examples, and classroom warm-up activities to help introduce chapter topics.

◆ **Solutions Manual** Véronique Flambard (Grant MacEwan Community College) has written the Canadian edition of a solutions manual that contains complete solutions for all of the Questions for Review and Problems and Applications found in the text.

◆ **PowerPoint Presentation and Overhead Transparencies** Brian VanBlarcom (Acadia University) has developed the Canadian edition of a computer-based PowerPoint presentation that can save instructors time as they prepare for class. This supplement covers all of the essential topics presented in each chapter of the book. Graphs, tables, lists, and concepts are developed sequentially, much as one might develop them on a blackboard. Additional examples and applications are used to reinforce major lessons. The slides are crisp, clear, and colourful. Instructors may adapt or add slides to customize their lectures.

   The overhead transparencies consist of graphic slides from the PowerPoint presentation, allowing instructors to build images into their lectures. Some of the more complex transparencies are layered to show what happens graphically when curves shift.

◆ **Web Site** A Web site has been developed to accompany this text. To appreciate this resource, we invite you to visit the site at http://www.mankiw.nelson.com. The Web site is both a teaching and an economic research tool, with separate areas for students and instructors. Students visiting this page can learn from tutorials featuring interactive graphs, access a page of economic indicators, follow links relevant to each chapter, find out about career opportunities, and test their knowledge with our on-line quizzes. Instructors will be able to search a bank of news summaries and comprehension questions, download sample chapters of the instructor's resource material, and view an on-line classroom activities guide.

◆ **Classroom Activities, Demonstrations, and Games** Charles A. Stull (Kalamazoo College) has written a supplement that helps instructors interested in incorporating cooperative learning and learning by experiment exercises in their courses. This supplement contains over 50 games, classroom experiments, in-class demonstrations, and take-home and in-class assignments. Each activity is linked to a specific text chapter and lists the type of activity, topics covered, materials list, time required for completion, and classroom limitations. Thorough directions are provided for the instructor. For the instructor's convenience, all pages are designed for easy overhead use and photocopying.

◆ **"Ten Principles" Video Set**   Ten video segments illustrate the *Ten Principles of Economics* introduced in Chapter 1. Instructors can show these videos as an interesting and visually appealing introduction to topics.

For the Student

A supplement is available for students who are studying the principles of economics. This supplement reinforces the basic lessons taught in the book and offers opportunities for additional practice and feedback.

◆ **Student Study Guides**   Shahram Manouchehri (Grant MacEwan College) and Peter Fortura (Algonquin College) have written the Canadian edition of the macroeconomics study guide, which provides students with a useful summary and review of the important concepts presented in the text. Each study guide chapter includes a chapter overview and helpful hints. Students can test their understanding of the material with self-testing questions and practice problems. Solutions to all study guide questions and problems follow each chapter.

ACKNOWLEDGEMENTS

We would like to acknowledge the comments and feedback offered by numerous reviewers. Without exception, their suggestions were thoughtful and relevant, and the book is much better for them. Although we were not able to address all the comments, we did our best. Individuals who read and commented on portions of the manuscript include

Keith Baxter (*Bishop's University*)
Martin Dooley (*McMaster University*)
Ernie Jacobson (*Northern Alberta Institute of Technology*)
Chris McDonnell (*Malaspina University-College*)
Stephen Rakoczy (*Humber College*)
Maurice Tugwell (*Acadia University*)

The success of the first edition of this textbook was due in part to the many reviewers who helped us shape the manuscript. We continue to be grateful for their comments:

Nancy Churchman, *Carleton University*
Kevin Clinton, *Bank of Canada*
Herb Emery, *University of Calgary*
Pierre Fortin, *University of Quebec at Montreal*
David Gray, *University of Ottawa*
Robin Neill, *University of Prince Edward Island* and *Carleton University*
Costas Nicolau, *University of Manitoba*
Gregor Smith, *Queen's University*

A special thanks goes to Bill Scarth of McMaster University, who offered invaluable advice regarding the structure and emphasis of the Canadian editions of the book. Dr. Scarth is an award-winning teacher and author, and to ignore his advice would have been perilous indeed. His extensive comments were instrumental in helping us formulate our approach to the Canadian editions.

We would also like to thank our colleagues at the University of Calgary and Carleton University who provided invaluable informal input and useful examples and applications. We, of course, bear full responsibility for any misinterpretations and remaining errors.

Canadianizing this book has been a team effort from the very start. We would like to acknowledge the editorial, production, and marketing teams at Harcourt Canada (which, while the second edition was being written, became part of Nelson Thomson Learning) for their professionalism, advice, and encouragement throughout the process. Deserving of special mention in this regard are Joan Langevin and Anthony Rezek, our acquisitions editors, for successfully steering the second edition through the difficulties of mergers and acquisitions; Klaus Unger, who replaced Martina van de Velde as developmental editor seamlessly in midstream, for making sure the three of us handed in our work (nearly) on time; and Claudia Kutchukian, copy editor, for her thorough editing.

Finally, we are grateful to our families for their indulgence and encouragement throughout the researching and writing process. Their patience and understanding are greatly appreciated.

Ronald D. Kneebone
Kenneth J. McKenzie
Nicholas Rowe
October 2001

PREFACE TO THE STUDENT

"Economics is a study of mankind in the ordinary business of life." So wrote Alfred Marshall, the great nineteenth-century economist, in his textbook *Principles of Economics*. Although we have learned much about the economy since Marshall's time, this definition of economics is as true today as it was in 1890, when the first edition of his text was published.

Why should you, as a student at the beginning of the twenty-first century, embark on the study of economics? There are three reasons.

The first reason to study economics is that it will help you understand the world in which you live. Many questions about the economy might spark your curiosity. Why are apartments so hard to find in New York City? Why do airlines charge less for a round-trip ticket if the traveller stays over a Saturday night? Why is Jim Carrey paid so much to star in movies? Why are living standards so meagre in many African countries? Why do some countries have high rates of inflation while others have stable prices? Why are jobs easy to find in some years and hard to find in others? These are just a few of the questions that a course in economics will help you answer.

The second reason to study economics is that it will make you a more astute participant in the economy. As you go about your life, you make many economic decisions. While you are a student, you decide how many years to stay in school. Once you take a job, you decide how much of your income to spend, how much to save, and how to invest your savings. Someday you may find yourself running a small business or a large corporation, and you will decide what prices to charge for your products. The insights developed in the coming chapters will give you a new perspective on how best to make these decisions. Studying economics will not by itself make you rich, but it will give you some tools that may help in that endeavour.

The third reason to study economics is that it will give you a better understanding of the potential and limits of economic policy. As a voter, you help choose the policies that guide the allocation of society's resources. When deciding which policies to support, you may find yourself asking various questions about economics. What are the burdens associated with alternative forms of taxation? What are the effects of free trade with other countries? What is the best way to protect the environment? How does a government budget deficit affect the economy? These and similar questions are always on the minds of policymakers in government offices.

Thus, the principles of economics can be applied in many of life's situations. Whether the future finds you reading the newspaper, running a business, or running the country, you will be glad that you studied economics.

N. Gregory Mankiw
Ronald D. Kneebone
Kenneth J. McKenzie
Nicholas Rowe
October 2001

BRIEF CONTENTS

TABLE OF CONTENTS

PART ONE
INTRODUCTION   1

**PART TWO
SUPPLY AND DEMAND I:
HOW MARKETS WORK   63**

Handwritten notes:
ch 6 , 7 , 13
price controls'
taxes
cs, ps,
TS
cost + profits
up to page 274

PART THREE
SUPPLY AND DEMAND II: MARKETS AND WELFARE   139

PART FOUR
THE DATA OF
MACROECONOMICS   203

PART FIVE
THE REAL ECONOMY
IN THE LONG RUN   237

CHAPTER 14

UNEMPLOYMENT AND ITS NATURAL RATE   289

**PART SIX
MONEY AND PRICES
IN THE LONG RUN   317**

**PART SEVEN
THE MACROECONOMICS
OF OPEN ECONOMIES   369**

CHAPTER 18

A MACROECONOMIC THEORY OF
THE OPEN ECONOMY   397

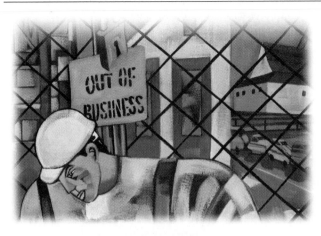

**PART EIGHT
SHORT-RUN ECONOMIC
FLUCTUATIONS   421**

CHAPTER 21

THE SHORT-RUN TRADEOFF BETWEEN INFLATION AND UNEMPLOYMENT   499

PART NINE
FINAL THOUGHTS   529

One

INTRODUCTION

1

TEN PRINCIPLES
OF ECONOMICS

IN THIS CHAPTER
YOU WILL . . .

*Learn that
economics is about
the allocation of
scarce resources*

*Examine some of the
tradeoffs that people
face*

*Learn the meaning of
opportunity cost*

*See how to use
marginal reasoning
when making
decisions*

*Discuss how
incentives affect
people's behaviour*

*Consider why trade
among people or
nations can be good
for everyone*

*Discuss why markets
are a good, but not
perfect, way to
allocate resources*

*Learn what
determines some
trends in the overall
economy*

The word *economy* comes from the Greek word for "one who manages a house-hold." At first, this origin might seem peculiar. But, in fact, households and economies have much in common.

A household faces many decisions. It must decide which members of the household do which tasks and what each member gets in return: Who cooks dinner? Who does the laundry? Who gets the extra dessert at dinner? Who gets to choose what TV show to watch? In short, the household must allocate its scarce resources among its various members, taking into account each member's abilities, efforts, and desires.

Like a household, a society faces many decisions. A society must decide what jobs will be done and who will do them. It needs some people to grow food, other people to make clothing, and still others to design computer software. Once society has allocated people (as well as land, buildings, and machines) to various

3

jobs, it must also allocate the output of goods and services that they produce. It must decide who will eat caviar and who will eat potatoes. It must decide who will drive a Porsche and who will take the bus.

The management of society's resources is important because resources are scarce. **Scarcity** means that society has limited resources and therefore cannot produce all the goods and services people wish to have. Just as a household cannot give every member everything he or she wants, a society cannot give every individual the highest standard of living to which he or she might aspire.

scarcity
the limited nature of society's resources

economics
the study of how society manages its scarce resources

Economics is the study of how society manages its scarce resources. In most societies, resources are allocated not by a single central planner but through the combined actions of millions of households and firms. Economists therefore study how people make decisions: how much they work, what they buy, how much they save, and how they invest their savings. Economists also study how people interact with one another. For instance, they examine how the multitude of buyers and sellers of a good together determine the price at which the good is sold and the quantity that is sold. Finally, economists analyze forces and trends that affect the economy as a whole, including the growth in average income, the fraction of the population that cannot find work, and the rate at which prices are rising.

Although the study of economics has many facets, the field is unified by several central ideas. In the rest of this chapter, we look at *Ten Principles of Economics*. These principles recur throughout this book and are introduced here to give you an overview of what economics is all about. You can think of this chapter as a "preview of coming attractions."

HOW PEOPLE MAKE DECISIONS

There is no mystery to what an "economy" is. Whether we are talking about the economy of Vancouver, Canada, or of the whole world, an economy is just a group of people interacting with one another as they go about their lives. Because the behaviour of an economy reflects the behaviour of the individuals who make up the economy, we start our study of economics with four principles of individual decision making.

PRINCIPLE #1: PEOPLE FACE TRADEOFFS

The first lesson about making decisions is summarized in the adage "There is no such thing as a free lunch." To get one thing that we like, we usually have to give up another thing that we like. Making decisions requires trading off one goal against another.

Consider a student who must decide how to allocate her most valuable resource—her time. She can spend all of her time studying economics, she can spend all of her time studying psychology, or she can divide her time between the two fields. For every hour she studies one subject, she gives up an hour she could have used studying the other. And for every hour she spends studying, she gives up an hour that she could have spent napping, bike riding, watching TV, or working at her part-time job for some extra spending money.

Or consider parents deciding how to spend their family income. They can buy food, clothing, or a family vacation. Or they can save some of the family income for retirement or the children's university education. When they choose to spend an extra dollar on one of these goods, they have one less dollar to spend on some other good.

When people are grouped into societies, they face different kinds of tradeoffs. The classic tradeoff is between "guns and butter." The more we spend on national defence to protect our shores from foreign aggressors (guns), the less we can spend on consumer goods to raise our standard of living at home (butter). Also important in modern society is the tradeoff between a clean environment and a high level of income. Laws that require firms to reduce pollution raise the cost of producing goods and services. Because of the higher costs, these firms end up earning smaller profits, paying lower wages, charging higher prices, or some combination of these three. Thus, while pollution regulations give us the benefit of a cleaner environment and the improved health that comes with it, they have the cost of reducing the incomes of the firms' owners, workers, and customers.

Another tradeoff society faces is between efficiency and equity. **Efficiency** means that society is getting the most it can from its scarce resources. **Equity** means that the benefits of those resources are distributed fairly among society's members. In other words, efficiency refers to the size of the economic pie, and equity refers to how the pie is divided. Often, when government policies are being designed, these two goals conflict.

efficiency
the property of society getting the most it can from its scarce resources

equity
the property of distributing economic prosperity fairly among the members of society

Consider, for instance, policies aimed at achieving a more equal distribution of economic well-being. Some of these policies, such as the welfare system or employment insurance, try to help those members of society who are most in need. Others, such as the individual income tax, ask the financially successful to contribute more than others to support the government. Although these policies have the benefit of achieving greater equity, they have a cost in terms of reduced efficiency. When the government redistributes income from the rich to the poor, it reduces the reward for working hard; as a result, people work less and produce fewer goods and services. In other words, when the government tries to cut the economic pie into more equal slices, the pie gets smaller.

Recognizing that people face tradeoffs does not by itself tell us what decisions they will or should make. A student should not abandon the study of psychology just because doing so would increase the time available for the study of economics. Society should not stop protecting the environment just because environmental regulations reduce our material standard of living. The poor should not be ignored just because helping them distorts work incentives. Nonetheless, acknowledging life's tradeoffs is important because people are likely to make good decisions only if they understand the options that they have available.

PRINCIPLE #2: THE COST OF SOMETHING IS WHAT YOU GIVE UP TO GET IT

Because people face tradeoffs, making decisions requires comparing the costs and benefits of alternative courses of action. In many cases, however, the cost of some action is not as obvious as it might first appear.

Consider, for example, the decision whether to go to university. The benefit is intellectual enrichment and a lifetime of better job opportunities. But what is the cost? To answer this question, you might be tempted to add up the money you spend on tuition, books, room, and board. Yet this total does not truly represent what you give up to spend a year in university.

The first problem with this answer is that it includes some things that are not really costs of going to university. Even if you quit school, you would need a place to sleep and food to eat. Room and board are costs of going to university only to the extent that they are more expensive at university than elsewhere. Indeed, the cost of room and board at your school might be less than the rent and food expenses that you would pay living on your own. In this case, the savings on room and board are a benefit of going to university.

The second problem with this calculation of costs is that it ignores the largest cost of going to university—your time. When you spend a year listening to lectures, reading textbooks, and writing papers, you cannot spend that time working at a job. For most students, the wages given up to attend school are the largest single cost of their education.

opportunity cost
whatever must be given up to obtain some item

The **opportunity cost** of an item is what you give up to get that item. When making any decision, such as whether to attend university, decision makers should be aware of the opportunity costs that accompany each possible action. In fact, they usually are. University-age athletes who can earn millions if they drop out of school and play professional sports are well aware that their opportunity cost of university is very high. It is not surprising that they often decide that the benefit is not worth the cost.

PRINCIPLE #3: RATIONAL PEOPLE THINK AT THE MARGIN

Decisions in life are rarely black and white but usually involve shades of grey. When it's time for dinner, the decision you face is not between fasting or eating like a pig, but whether to take that extra spoonful of mashed potatoes. When exams roll around, your decision is not between blowing them off or studying 24 hours a day, but whether to spend an extra hour reviewing your notes instead of watching TV.

marginal changes
small incremental adjustments to a plan of action

Economists use the term **marginal changes** to describe small incremental adjustments to an existing plan of action. Keep in mind that "margin" means "edge," so marginal changes are adjustments around the edges of what you are doing.

In many situations, people make the best decisions by thinking at the margin. Suppose, for instance, that you asked a friend for advice about how many years to stay in school. If he were to compare for you the lifestyle of a person with a PhD with that of a high-school dropout, you might complain that this comparison is not helpful for your decision. You have some education already and most likely are deciding whether to spend an extra year or two in school. To make this decision, you need to know the additional benefits that an extra year in school would offer (higher wages throughout life and the sheer joy of learning) and the additional costs that you would incur (tuition and the forgone wages while you're in school). By comparing these *marginal benefits* and *marginal costs*, you can evaluate whether the extra year is worthwhile.

As another example, consider an airline deciding how much to charge passengers who fly standby. Suppose that flying a 200-seat plane across the country costs the airline $100 000. In this case, the average cost of each seat is $100 000/200, which is $500. One might be tempted to conclude that the airline should never sell a ticket for less than $500. In fact, however, the airline can raise its profits by thinking at the margin. Imagine that a plane is about to take off with ten empty seats, and a standby passenger is waiting at the gate willing to pay $300 for a seat. Should the airline sell it to him? Of course it should. If the plane has empty seats, the cost of adding one more passenger is minuscule. Although the *average* cost of flying a passenger is $500, the *marginal* cost is merely the cost of the bag of peanuts and can of soda that the extra passenger will consume. As long as the standby passenger pays more than the marginal cost, selling him a ticket is profitable.

As these examples show, individuals and firms can make better decisions by thinking at the margin. A rational decision maker takes an action if and only if the marginal benefit of the action exceeds the marginal cost.

PRINCIPLE #4: PEOPLE RESPOND TO INCENTIVES

Because people make decisions by comparing costs and benefits, their behaviour may change when the costs or benefits change. That is, people respond to incentives. When the price of an apple rises, for instance, people decide to eat more pears and fewer apples, because the cost of buying an apple is higher. At the same time, apple orchards decide to hire more workers and harvest more apples, because the benefit of selling an apple is also higher. As we will see, the effect of price on the behaviour of buyers and sellers in a market—in this case, the market for apples—is crucial for understanding how the economy works.

Public policymakers should never forget about incentives, for many policies change the costs or benefits that people face and, therefore, alter behaviour. A tax on gasoline, for instance, encourages people to drive smaller, more fuel-efficient cars. It also encourages people to take public transportation rather than drive and to live closer to where they work. If the tax were large enough, people would start driving electric cars.

When policymakers fail to consider how their policies affect incentives, they can end up with results that they did not intend. For example, consider public policy regarding auto safety. Today all cars have seat belts, but that was not true 40 years ago. In the late 1960s, Ralph Nader's book *Unsafe at Any Speed* generated much public concern over auto safety. Parliament responded with laws requiring car companies to make various safety features, including seat belts, standard equipment on all new cars.

How does a seat belt law affect auto safety? The direct effect is obvious. With seat belts in all cars, more people wear seat belts, and the probability of surviving a major auto accident rises. In this sense, seat belts save lives.

But that's not the end of the story. To fully understand the effects of this law, we must recognize that people change their behaviour in response to the incentives they face. The relevant behaviour here is the speed and care with which drivers operate their cars. Driving slowly and carefully is costly because it uses the driver's time and energy. When deciding how safely to drive, rational people compare the marginal benefit from safer driving with the marginal cost. They drive more slowly and carefully when the benefit of increased safety is high. This explains why people drive more slowly and carefully when roads are icy than when roads are clear.

HOCKEY STARS LIKE JOE SAKIC UNDERSTAND OPPORTUNITY COST AND INCENTIVES. THE COST OF GOING TO UNIVERSITY IS TOO GREAT IF THEY GIVE UP A HIGHER-PAYING CAREER IN THE NHL.

IN THE NEWS

Paying the Stork Worked in Quebec

THIS ARTICLE ILLUSTRATES JUST HOW widely Principle #4 can be applied!

Couples Responded to Bonus for Babies

BY INGRID PERITZ

During its nine-year existence, Quebec's controversial policy of giving couples cash to have babies was described as many things—but fruitful was never one of them.

Critics derided the "bébé bonus" as patronizing. Some said governments were playing Santa Claus in exchange for votes. And Quebec's current Minister for the Family, whose government scrapped the bonuses in 1997, called them an abject failure.

But recent studies suggest that offering couples money to procreate works. And during the period Quebec implemented the policy, it brought the province's abysmal birthrate almost in line with the rest of Canada's.

"People respond to incentives," said Kevin Milligan, a University of Toronto economics doctoral candidate who completed a study on Quebec's baby bonus. "If a couple is on the edge, saying 'Should we have a child or not,' this kind of thing would push them over the edge."

Mr. Milligan's study, called Subsidizing the Stork, found that the bonuses had a "strong, positive and robust" impact on Quebeckers' fertility: It grew overall by 12 percent.

And the bigger the cash offer, the more frequent the trips to the maternity ward—the $8000 bonus for a third child drove up fertility 25 percent, he concluded.

The findings suggest that thousands of Quebec children owe their existence to a government cheque, and that cold calculations play a role in a couple's decision to bring up the baby or not.

Pierre Lefebvre, an economics professor at the University of Quebec at Montreal, said similar studies carried out in his department have confirmed the findings.

"There's nothing shocking about this. We have children because they bring us pleasure. We're ready to make sacrifices for that," he said.

"But having a child also involves major direct costs, and that makes some people hesitate. [The baby bonuses] have a positive effect on the birthrate."

Mr. Milligan compared the birthrate in Quebec and the other Canadian provinces, which had no baby bonuses, between 1988 and 1997. During that time, the gap in the birthrates nearly closed. He took into account other influencing factors such as family income and education, and held those factors constant.

The bonuses went from $500 for a first baby up to $8000 for a third.

SOURCE: *The Globe and Mail*, January 31, 2001. Available http://www.globeandmail.ca, January 31, 2001.

Now consider how a seat belt law alters the cost–benefit calculation of a rational driver. Seat belts make accidents less costly for a driver because they reduce the probability of injury or death. Thus, a seat belt law reduces the benefits of slow and careful driving. People respond to seat belts as they would to an improvement in road conditions—by faster and less careful driving. The end result of a seat belt law, therefore, is a larger number of accidents.

How does the law affect the number of deaths from driving? Drivers who wear their seat belts are more likely to survive any given accident, but they are also more likely to find themselves in an accident. The net effect is ambiguous. Moreover, the reduction in safe driving has an adverse impact on pedestrians (and on drivers who do not wear their seat belts). They are put in jeopardy by the law because they are more likely to find themselves in an accident but are not protected by a seat belt. Thus, a seat belt law tends to increase the number of pedestrian deaths.

At first, this discussion of incentives and seat belts might seem like idle speculation. Yet, in a 1975 study, economist Sam Peltzman showed that the auto-safety laws have, in fact, had many of these effects. According to Peltzman's evidence, these laws produce both fewer deaths per accident and more accidents. The net result is little change in the number of driver deaths and an increase in the number of pedestrian deaths.

Peltzman's analysis of auto safety is an example of the general principle that people respond to incentives. Many incentives that economists study are more straightforward than those of the auto-safety laws. No one is surprised that people drive smaller cars in Europe, where gasoline taxes are high, than in Canada, where gasoline taxes are low. Yet, as the seat belt example shows, policies can have effects that are not obvious in advance. When analyzing any policy, we must consider not only the direct effects but also the indirect effects that work through incentives. If the policy changes incentives, it will cause people to alter their behaviour.

QUICK QUIZ: List and briefly explain the four principles of individual decision making.

HOW PEOPLE INTERACT

The first four principles discussed how individuals make decisions. As we go about our lives, many of our decisions affect not only ourselves but also other people. The next three principles concern how people interact with one another.

PRINCIPLE #5: TRADE CAN MAKE EVERYONE BETTER OFF

You have probably heard on the news that Americans are our competitors in the world economy. In some ways, this is true, for Canadian and American firms do produce many of the same goods. Nortel and Lucent compete for the same customers in the market for telecommunications. Brights and Gallo compete for the same customers in the market for wine.

Yet it is easy to be misled when thinking about competition among countries. Trade between Canada and the United States is not like a sports contest, where one side wins and the other side loses. In fact, the opposite is true: Trade between two countries can make each country better off.

To see why, consider how trade affects your family. When a member of your family looks for a job, he or she competes against members of other families who are looking for jobs. Families also compete against one another when they go shopping, because each family wants to buy the best goods at the lowest prices. So, in a sense, each family in the economy is competing with all other families.

Despite this competition, your family would not be better off isolating itself from all other families. If it did, your family would need to grow its own food, make its own clothes, and build its own home. Clearly, your family gains much from its ability to trade with others. Trade allows each person to specialize in the activities he or she does best, whether it is farming, sewing, or home building. By

THE WALL STREET JOURNAL

ENGLEMAN

"For $5 a week you can watch baseball without being nagged to cut the grass!"

trading with others, people can buy a greater variety of goods and services at lower cost.

Countries as well as families benefit from the ability to trade with one another. Trade allows countries to specialize in what they do best and to enjoy a greater variety of goods and services. The Americans, as well as the Japanese and the Egyptians and the Brazilians, are as much our partners in the world economy as they are our competitors.

PRINCIPLE #6: MARKETS ARE USUALLY A GOOD WAY TO ORGANIZE ECONOMIC ACTIVITY

The collapse of communism in the former Soviet Union and Eastern Europe may be the most important change in the world during the past half century. Communist countries worked on the premise that central planners in the government were in the best position to guide economic activity. These planners decided what goods and services were produced, how much was produced, and who produced and consumed these goods and services. The theory behind central planning was that only the government could organize economic activity in a way that promoted economic well-being for the country as a whole.

market economy

an economy that allocates resources through the decentralized decisions of many firms and households as they interact in markets for goods and services

Today, most countries that once had centrally planned economies have abandoned this system and are trying to develop market economies. In a **market economy,** the decisions of a central planner are replaced by the decisions of millions of firms and households. Firms decide whom to hire and what to make. Households decide which firms to work for and what to buy with their incomes. These firms and households interact in the marketplace, where prices and self-interest guide their decisions.

At first glance, the success of market economies is puzzling. After all, in a market economy, no one is looking out for the economic well-being of society as a whole. Free markets contain many buyers and sellers of numerous goods and services, and all of them are interested primarily in their own well-being. Yet, despite decentralized decision making and self-interested decision makers, market economies have proven remarkably successful in organizing economic activity in a way that promotes overall economic well-being.

In his 1776 book *An Inquiry into the Nature and Causes of the Wealth of Nations,* economist Adam Smith made the most famous observation in all of economics: Households and firms interacting in markets act as if they are guided by an "invisible hand" that leads them to desirable market outcomes. One of our goals in this book is to understand how this invisible hand works its magic. As you study economics, you will learn that prices are the instrument with which the invisible hand directs economic activity. Prices reflect both the value of a good to society and the cost to society of making the good. Because households and firms look at prices when deciding what to buy and sell, they unknowingly take into account the social benefits and costs of their actions. As a result, prices guide these individual decision makers to reach outcomes that, in many cases, maximize the welfare of society as a whole.

There is an important corollary to the skill of the invisible hand in guiding economic activity: When the government prevents prices from adjusting naturally to supply and demand, it impedes the invisible hand's ability to coordinate the millions of households and firms that make up the economy. This corollary explains

FYI

Adam Smith and the Invisible Hand

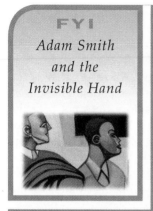

Adam Smith's great book, *An Inquiry into the Nature and Causes of the Wealth of Nations*, published in 1776, promoted a point of view that was prevalent at the time—that individuals are usually best left to their own devices, without the heavy hand of government guiding their actions. This political philosophy provides the intellectual basis for the market economy, and for free society more generally.

Why do decentralized market economies work so well? Is it because people can be counted on to treat one another with love and kindness? Not at all. Here is Adam Smith's description of how people interact in a market economy:

> Man has almost constant occasion for the help of his brethren, and it is vain for him to expect it from their benevolence only. He will be more likely to prevail if he can interest their self-love in his favor, and show them that it is for their own advantage to do for him what he requires of them. . . . It is not from the benevolence of the butcher, the brewer, or the baker that we expect our dinner, but from their regard to their own interest. . . .

> Every individual . . . neither intends to promote the public interest, nor knows how much he is promoting it. . . . He intends only his own gain, and he is in this, as in many other cases, led by an invisible hand to promote an end which was no part of his intention. Nor is it always the worse for the society that it was no part of it. By pursuing his own interest he frequently promotes that of the society more effectually than when he really intends to promote it.

ADAM SMITH

Smith is saying that participants in the economy are motivated by self-interest and that the "invisible hand" of the marketplace guides this self-interest into promoting general economic well-being.

Many of Smith's insights remain at the centre of modern economics. Our analysis in the coming chapters will allow us to express Smith's conclusions more precisely and to analyze fully the strengths and weaknesses of the market's invisible hand.

why taxes adversely affect the allocation of resources: Taxes distort prices and thus the decisions of households and firms. It also explains the even greater harm caused by policies that directly control prices, such as rent control. And it explains the failure of communism. In communist countries, prices were not determined in the marketplace but were dictated by central planners. These planners lacked the information that gets reflected in prices when prices are free to respond to market forces. Central planners failed because they tried to run the economy with one hand tied behind their backs—the invisible hand of the marketplace.

PRINCIPLE #7: GOVERNMENTS CAN SOMETIMES IMPROVE MARKET OUTCOMES

Although markets are usually a good way to organize economic activity, this rule has some important exceptions. There are two broad reasons for a government to intervene in the economy: to promote efficiency and to promote equity. That is, most policies aim either to enlarge the economic pie or to change how the pie is divided.

market failure
a situation in which a market left on its own fails to allocate resources efficiently

externality
the impact of one person's actions on the well-being of a bystander

market power
the ability of a single economic actor (or small group of actors) to have a substantial influence on market prices

The invisible hand usually leads markets to allocate resources efficiently. Nonetheless, for various reasons, the invisible hand sometimes does not work. Economists use the term **market failure** to refer to a situation in which the market on its own fails to allocate resources efficiently.

One possible cause of market failure is an externality. An **externality** is the impact of one person's actions on the well-being of a bystander. The classic example of an external cost is pollution. If a chemical factory does not bear the entire cost of the smoke it emits, it will likely emit too much. Here, the government can raise economic well-being through environmental regulation. The classic example of an external benefit is the creation of knowledge. When a scientist makes an important discovery, she produces a valuable resource that other people can use. In this case, the government can raise economic well-being by subsidizing basic research, as in fact it does.

Another possible cause of market failure is market power. **Market power** refers to the ability of a single person (or small group of people) to unduly influence market prices. For example, suppose that everyone in town needs water but there is only one well. The owner of the well has market power—in this case a *monopoly*—over the sale of water. The well owner is not subject to the rigorous competition with which the invisible hand normally keeps self-interest in check. You will learn that, in this case, regulating the price that the monopolist charges can potentially enhance economic efficiency.

The invisible hand is even less able to ensure that economic prosperity is distributed fairly. A market economy rewards people according to their ability to produce things that other people are willing to pay for. The world's best hockey player earns more than the world's best chess player simply because people are willing to pay more to watch hockey than chess. The invisible hand does not ensure that everyone has sufficient food, decent clothing, and adequate health care. A goal of many public policies, such as the income tax and the welfare system, is to achieve a more equitable distribution of economic well-being.

To say that the government *can* improve on markets outcomes at times does not mean that it always *will*. Public policy is made not by angels but by a political process that is far from perfect. Sometimes policies are designed simply to reward the politically powerful. Sometimes they are made by well-intentioned leaders who are not fully informed. One goal of the study of economics is to help you judge when a government policy is justifiable to promote efficiency or equity and when it is not.

▌ QUICK QUIZ: List and briefly explain the three principles concerning economic interactions.

HOW THE ECONOMY AS A WHOLE WORKS

We started by discussing how individuals make decisions and then looked at how people interact with one another. All these decisions and interactions together make up "the economy." The last three principles concern the workings of the economy as a whole.

PRINCIPLE #8: A COUNTRY'S STANDARD OF LIVING DEPENDS ON ITS ABILITY TO PRODUCE GOODS AND SERVICES

The differences in living standards around the world are staggering. In 1999 the average Canadian had an income of about $28 000. In the same year, the average Mexican earned about $12 000, and the average Nigerian earned about $1500. Not surprisingly, this large variation in average income is reflected in various measures of the quality of life. Citizens of high-income countries have more TV sets, more cars, better nutrition, better health care, and a longer life expectancy than citizens of low-income countries.

Changes in living standards over time are also large. In Canada, incomes have historically grown about 2 percent per year (after adjusting for changes in the cost of living). At this rate, average income doubles every 35 years. Over the past century, average income has risen about eightfold.

What explains these large differences in living standards among countries and over time? The answer is surprisingly simple. Almost all variation in living standards is attributable to differences in countries' **productivity**—that is, the amount of goods and services produced from each hour of a worker's time. In nations where workers can produce a large quantity of goods and services per unit of time, most people enjoy a high standard of living; in nations where workers are less productive, most people must endure a more meagre existence. Similarly, the growth rate of a nation's productivity determines the growth rate of its average income.

productivity
the amount of goods and services produced from each hour of a worker's time

The fundamental relationship between productivity and living standards is simple, but its implications are far-reaching. If productivity is the primary determinant of living standards, other explanations must be of secondary importance. For example, it might be tempting to credit labour unions or minimum-wage laws for the rise in living standards of Canadian workers over the past century. Yet the real hero of Canadian workers is their rising productivity. As another example, some commentators have claimed that increased competition from Japan and other countries explains the slow growth in Canadian incomes over the past 30 years. Yet the real villain is not competition from abroad but flagging productivity growth in Canada.

The relationship between productivity and living standards also has profound implications for public policy. When thinking about how any policy will affect living standards, the key question is how it will affect our ability to produce goods and services. To boost living standards, policymakers need to raise productivity by ensuring that workers are well educated, have the tools needed to produce goods and services, and have access to the best available technology.

In the 1980s and 1990s, for example, much debate in Canada centred on the government's budget deficit—the excess of government spending over government revenue. As we will see, concern over the budget deficit was based largely on its adverse impact on productivity. When the government needs to finance a budget deficit, it does so by borrowing in financial markets, much as a student might borrow to finance a college education or a firm might borrow to finance a new factory. As the government borrows to finance its deficit, therefore, it reduces the quantity of funds available for other borrowers. The budget deficit thereby reduces investment both in human capital (the student's education) and physical capital (the firm's factory). Because lower investment today means lower productivity in the future, government budget deficits are generally thought to depress growth in living standards.

PRINCIPLE #9: PRICES RISE WHEN THE GOVERNMENT PRINTS TOO MUCH MONEY

inflation

an increase in the overall level of prices in the economy

In Germany in January 1921, a daily newspaper cost 0.30 marks. Less than two years later, in November 1922, the same newspaper cost 70 000 000 marks. All other prices in the economy rose by similar amounts. This episode is one of history's most spectacular examples of **inflation,** an increase in the overall level of prices in the economy.

Although Canada has never experienced inflation even close to that of Germany in the 1920s, inflation has at times been an economic problem. During the 1970s, for instance, the overall level of prices more than doubled. By contrast, inflation in the 1990s was about 1.5 percent per year; at this rate it would take nearly 50 years for prices to double. Because high inflation imposes various costs on society, keeping inflation at a low level is a goal of economic policymakers around the world.

What causes inflation? In almost all cases of large or persistent inflation, the culprit turns out to be the same—growth in the quantity of money. When a government creates large quantities of the nation's money, the value of the money falls. In Germany in the early 1920s, when prices were on average tripling every month, the quantity of money was also tripling every month. Although less dramatic, the economic history of Canada points to a similar conclusion: The high inflation of the 1970s was associated with rapid growth in the quantity of money, and the low inflation of the 1990s was associated with slow growth in the quantity of money.

"Well it may have been 68 cents when you got in line, but it's 74 cents now!"

PRINCIPLE #10: SOCIETY FACES A SHORT-RUN TRADEOFF BETWEEN INFLATION AND UNEMPLOYMENT

If inflation is so easy to explain, why do policymakers sometimes have trouble ridding the economy of it? One reason is that reducing inflation is often thought to cause a temporary rise in unemployment. The curve that illustrates this tradeoff between inflation and unemployment is called the **Phillips curve,** after the economist who first examined this relationship.

The Phillips curve remains a controversial topic among economists, but most economists today accept the idea that there is a short-run tradeoff between inflation and unemployment. This simply means that, over a period of a year or two, many economic policies push inflation and unemployment in opposite directions. Policymakers face this tradeoff regardless of whether inflation and unemployment both start out at high levels (as they were in the early 1980s), at low levels (as they were in the late 1990s), or someplace in between.

Why do we face this short-run tradeoff? According to a common explanation, it arises because some prices are slow to adjust. Suppose, for example, that the government reduces the quantity of money in the economy. In the long run, the only result of this policy change will be a fall in the overall level of prices. Yet not all prices will adjust immediately. It may take several years before all firms issue new catalogues, all unions make wage concessions, and all restaurants print new menus. That is, prices are said to be *sticky* in the short run.

Because prices are sticky, various types of government policy have short-run effects that differ from their long-run effects. When the government reduces the quantity of money, for instance, it reduces the amount that people spend. Lower spending, together with prices that are stuck too high, reduces the quantity of goods and services that firms sell. Lower sales, in turn, cause firms to lay off workers. Thus, the reduction in the quantity of money raises unemployment temporarily until prices have fully adjusted to the change.

The tradeoff between inflation and unemployment is only temporary, but it can last for several years. The Phillips curve is, therefore, crucial for understanding many developments in the economy. In particular, policymakers can exploit this tradeoff using various policy instruments. By changing the amount that the government spends, the amount it taxes, and the amount of money it prints, policymakers can, in the short run, influence the combination of inflation and unemployment that the economy experiences. Because these instruments of monetary and fiscal policy are potentially so powerful, how policymakers should use these instruments to control the economy, if at all, is a subject of continuing debate.

QUICK QUIZ: List and briefly explain the three principles that describe how the economy as a whole works.

Phillips curve
a curve that shows the short-run tradeoff between inflation and unemployment

---

CONCLUSION

You now have a taste of what economics is all about. In the coming chapters we will develop many specific insights about people, markets, and economies. Mastering these insights will take some effort, but it is not an overwhelming task. The field of economics is based on a few basic ideas that can be applied in many different situations.

Throughout this book we will refer back to the *Ten Principles of Economics* highlighted in this chapter and summarized in Table 1-1. Whenever we do so, a building-blocks icon will be displayed in the margin, as it is now. But even when that icon is absent, you should keep these building blocks in mind. Even the most sophisticated economic analysis is built using the ten principles introduced here.

Table 1-1

TEN PRINCIPLES OF ECONOMICS

HOW PEOPLE MAKE DECISIONS	#1:	People Face Tradeoffs
	#2:	The Cost of Something Is What You Give Up to Get It
	#3:	Rational People Think at the Margin
	#4:	People Respond to Incentives
HOW PEOPLE INTERACT	#5:	Trade Can Make Everyone Better Off
	#6:	Markets Are Usually a Good Way to Organize Economic Activity
	#7:	Governments Can Sometimes Improve Market Outcomes
HOW THE ECONOMY AS A WHOLE WORKS	#8:	A Country's Standard of Living Depends on Its Ability to Produce Goods and Services
	#9:	Prices Rise When the Government Prints Too Much Money
	#10:	Society Faces a Short-Run Tradeoff between Inflation and Unemployment

Summary

♦ The fundamental lessons about individual decision making are that people face tradeoffs among alternative goals, that the cost of any action is measured in terms of forgone opportunities, that rational people make decisions by comparing marginal costs and marginal benefits, and that people change their behaviour in response to the incentives they face.

♦ The fundamental lessons about interactions among people are that trade can be mutually beneficial, that markets are usually a good way of coordinating trade among people, and that the government can potentially improve market outcomes if there is some market failure or if the market outcome is inequitable.

♦ The fundamental lessons about the economy as a whole are that productivity is the ultimate source of living standards, that money growth is the ultimate source of inflation, and that society faces a short-run tradeoff between inflation and unemployment.

Key Concepts

scarcity, p. 4
economics, p. 4
efficiency, p. 5
equity, p. 5
opportunity cost, p. 6

marginal changes, p. 6
market economy, p. 10
market failure, p. 12
externality, p. 12
market power, p. 12

productivity, p. 13
inflation, p. 14
Phillips curve, p. 15

Questions for Review

1. Give three examples of important tradeoffs that you face in your life.

2. What is the opportunity cost of seeing a movie?

3. Water is necessary for life. Is the marginal benefit of a glass of water large or small?

4. Why should policymakers think about incentives?

5. Why isn't trade among countries like a game with some winners and some losers?

6. What does the "invisible hand" of the marketplace do?

7. Explain the two main causes of market failure and give an example of each.

8. Why is productivity important?

9. What is inflation, and what causes it?

10. How are inflation and unemployment related in the short run? 通货膨胀　　失业　　有关连～
   P15.

Problems and Applications

1. Describe some of the tradeoffs faced by the following:
   a. a family deciding whether to buy a new car
   b. a member of Parliament deciding how much to spend on national parks
   c. a company president deciding whether to open a new factory
   d. a professor deciding how much to prepare for class

2. You are trying to decide whether to take a vacation. Most of the costs of the vacation (airfare, hotel, forgone wages) are measured in dollars, but the benefits of the vacation are psychological. How can you compare the benefits with the costs?

3. You were planning to spend Saturday working at your part-time job, but a friend asks you to go skiing. What is the true cost of going skiing? Now suppose that you had been planning to spend the day studying at the library. What is the cost of going skiing in this case? Explain.

4. You win $100 in a hockey pool. You have a choice between spending the money now or putting it away for a year in a bank account that pays 5 percent interest. What is the opportunity cost of spending the $100 now?

5. The company that you manage has invested $5 million in developing a new product, but the development is not quite finished. At a recent meeting, your salespeople report that the introduction of competing products has reduced the expected sales of your new product to $3 million. If it would cost $1 million to finish development and make the product, should you go ahead and do so? What is the most that you should pay to complete development?

6. Three managers of the Magic Potion Company are discussing a possible increase in production. Each suggests a way to make this decision.

   HARRY: We should examine whether our company's productivity—litres of potion per worker—would rise or fall.

   RON: We should examine whether our average cost—cost per worker—would rise or fall.

   HERMIONE: We should examine whether the extra revenue from selling the additional potion would be greater or smaller than the extra costs.

   Who do you think is right? Why?

7. The Old Age Security program provides income for people over age 65. If a recipient of Old Age Security decides to work and earn some income, the amount he or she receives in Old Age Security benefits is typically reduced.
   a. How does the provision of Old Age Security affect people's incentive to save while working?
   b. How does the reduction in benefits associated with higher earnings affect people's incentive to work past age 65?

8. Proposed changes to Canada's Employment Insurance (EI) program would increase the number of weeks that unemployed workers in some regions could collect EI benefits.
   a. How does this change affect the incentives for working?
   b. How might this change represent a tradeoff between equity and efficiency?

9. Your roommate is a better cook than you are, but you can clean more quickly than your roommate can. If your roommate did all of the cooking and you did all of the cleaning, would your chores take you more or less time than if you divided each task evenly? Give a similar

example of how specialization and trade can make two countries both better off.

10. Suppose Canada has adopted central planning for its economy, and you are the chief planner. Among the millions of decisions that you need to make for next year are how many compact discs to produce, what artists to record, and who should receive the discs.
    a. To make these decisions intelligently, what information would you need about the compact disc industry? What information would you need about each of the people in Canada?
    b. How would your decisions about CDs affect some of your other decisions, such as how many CD players to make or cassette tapes to produce? How might some of your other decisions about the economy change your views about CDs?

11. Explain whether each of the following government activities is motivated by a concern about equity or a concern about efficiency. In the case of efficiency, discuss the type of market failure involved.
    a. regulating cable TV prices
    b. providing free prescription drugs for people on welfare
    c. prohibiting smoking in public places
    d. preventing mergers between major banks
    e. imposing higher personal income tax rates on people with higher incomes
    f. instituting laws against driving while intoxicated

12. Discuss each of the following statements from the standpoints of equity and efficiency:

    a. "Everyone in society should be guaranteed the best health care possible."
    b. "When workers are laid off, they should be able to collect Employment Insurance until they find a new job."

13. In what ways is your standard of living different from that of your parents or grandparents when they were your age? Why have these changes occurred?

14. Suppose Canadians decide to save more of their incomes. If banks lend this extra saving to businesses, which use the funds to build new factories, how might this lead to faster growth in productivity? Who do you suppose benefits from the higher productivity? Is society getting a free lunch?

15. Suppose that when everyone wakes up tomorrow, they discover that the government has given them an additional amount of money equal to the amount they already had. Explain what effect this doubling of the money supply will likely have on the following:
    a. the total amount spent on goods and services
    b. the quantity of goods and services purchased if prices are sticky
    c. the prices of goods and services if prices can adjust

16. Imagine that you are a policymaker trying to decide whether to reduce the rate of inflation. To make an intelligent decision, what would you need to know about inflation, unemployment, and the tradeoff between them?

2

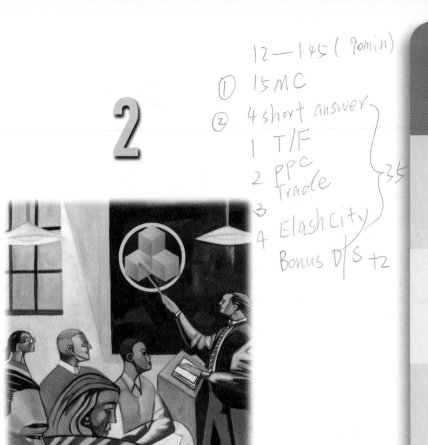

Handwritten note:
12—1:45 (90min)
① 15 MC
② 4 short answer
1 T/F
2 PPC
Trade
3
4. Elash city
Bonus D/S +2
35

THINKING LIKE
AN ECONOMIST

Every field of study has its own language and its own way of thinking. Mathematicians talk about axioms, integrals, and vector spaces. Psychologists talk about ego, id, and cognitive dissonance. Lawyers talk about venue, torts, and promissory estoppel.

Economics is no different. Supply, demand, elasticity, comparative advantage, consumer surplus, deadweight loss—these terms are part of the economist's language. In the coming chapters, you will encounter many new terms and some familiar words that economists use in specialized ways. At first, this new language may seem needlessly arcane. But, as you will see, its value lies in its ability to provide you with a new and useful way of thinking about the world in which you live.

The single most important purpose of this book is to help you learn the economist's way of thinking. Of course, just as you cannot become a mathematician, psychologist, or lawyer overnight, learning to think like an economist will take some time. Yet with a combination of theory, case studies, and examples of economics in the news, this book will give you ample opportunity to develop and practise this skill.

Before delving into the substance and details of economics, it is helpful to have an overview of how economists approach the world. This chapter, therefore, discusses the field's methodology. What is distinctive about how economists confront a question? What does it mean to think like an economist?

THE ECONOMIST AS SCIENTIST

Economists try to address their subject with a scientist's objectivity. They approach the study of the economy in much the same way a physicist approaches the study of matter and a biologist approaches the study of life: They devise theories, collect data, and then analyze these data in an attempt to verify or refute their theories.

To beginners, it can seem odd to claim that economics is a science. After all, economists do not work with test tubes or telescopes. The essence of science, however, is the *scientific method*—the dispassionate development and testing of

"I'm a social scientist, Michael. That means I can't explain
electricity or anything like that, but if you ever want to know
about people I'm your man."

theories about how the world works. This method of inquiry is as applicable to studying a nation's economy as it is to studying the earth's gravity or a species' evolution. As Albert Einstein once put it, "The whole of science is nothing more than the refinement of everyday thinking."

Although Einstein's comment is as true for social sciences such as economics as it is for natural sciences such as physics, most people are not accustomed to looking at society through the eyes of a scientist. Let's therefore discuss some of the ways in which economists apply the logic of science to examine how an economy works.

THE SCIENTIFIC METHOD: OBSERVATION, THEORY, AND MORE OBSERVATION

Isaac Newton, the famous seventeenth-century scientist and mathematician, allegedly became intrigued one day when he saw an apple fall from an apple tree. This observation motivated Newton to develop a theory of gravity that applies not only to an apple falling to the earth but to any two objects in the universe. Subsequent testing of Newton's theory has shown that it works well in many circumstances (although, as Einstein would later emphasize, not in all circumstances). Because Newton's theory has been so successful at explaining observation, it is still taught today in undergraduate physics courses around the world.

This interplay between theory and observation also occurs in the field of economics. An economist might live in a country experiencing rapid increases in prices and be moved by this observation to develop a theory of inflation. The theory might assert that high inflation arises when the government prints too much money. (As you may recall, this was one of the *Ten Principles of Economics* in Chapter 1.) To test this theory, the economist could collect and analyze data on prices and money from many different countries. If growth in the quantity of money were not at all related to the rate at which prices are rising, the economist would start to doubt the validity of his theory of inflation. If money growth and inflation were strongly correlated in international data, as in fact they are, the economist would become more confident in his theory.

Although economists use theory and observation like other scientists, they do face an obstacle that makes their task especially challenging: Experiments are often difficult in economics. Physicists studying gravity can drop many objects in their laboratories to generate data to test their theories. By contrast, economists studying inflation are not allowed to manipulate a nation's monetary policy simply to generate useful data. Economists, like astronomers and evolutionary biologists, usually have to make do with whatever data the world happens to give them.

To find a substitute for laboratory experiments, economists pay close attention to the natural experiments offered by history. When a war in the Middle East interrupts the flow of crude oil, for instance, oil prices skyrocket around the world. For consumers of oil and oil products, such an event depresses living standards. For economic policymakers, it poses a difficult choice about how best to respond. But for economic scientists, it provides an opportunity to study the effects of a key natural resource on the world's economies, and this opportunity persists long after the wartime increase in oil prices is over. Throughout this book, therefore, we consider many historical episodes. These episodes are valuable to study because they give us insight into the economy of the past and, more important, because they allow us to illustrate and evaluate economic theories of the present.

THE ROLE OF ASSUMPTIONS

If you ask a physicist how long it would take for a marble to fall from the top of a ten-storey building, she will answer the question by assuming that the marble falls in a vacuum. Of course, this assumption is false. In fact, the building is surrounded by air, which exerts friction on the falling marble and slows it down. Yet the physicist will correctly point out that friction on the marble is so small that its effect is negligible. Assuming the marble falls in a vacuum greatly simplifies the problem without substantially affecting the answer.

Economists make assumptions for the same reason: Assumptions can make the world easier to understand. To study the effects of international trade, for example, we may assume that the world consists of only two countries and that each country produces only two goods. Of course, the real world consists of dozens of countries, each of which produces thousands of different types of goods. But by assuming two countries and two goods, we can focus our thinking. Once we understand international trade in an imaginary world with two countries and two goods, we are in a better position to understand international trade in the more complex world in which we live.

The art in scientific thinking—whether in physics, biology, or economics—is deciding which assumptions to make. Suppose, for instance, that we were dropping a beach ball rather than a marble from the top of the building. Our physicist would realize that the assumption of no friction is far less accurate in this case: Friction exerts a greater force on a beach ball than on a marble. The assumption that gravity works in a vacuum is reasonable for studying a falling marble but not for studying a falling beach ball.

Similarly, economists use different assumptions to answer different questions. Suppose that we want to study what happens to the economy when the government changes the number of dollars in circulation. An important piece of this analysis, it turns out, is how prices respond. Many prices in the economy change infrequently; the newsstand prices of magazines, for instance, are changed only every few years. Knowing this fact may lead us to make different assumptions when studying the effects of the policy change over different time horizons. For studying the short-run effects of the policy, we may assume that prices do not change much. We may even make the extreme and artificial assumption that all prices are completely fixed. For studying the long-run effects of the policy, however, we may assume that all prices are completely flexible. Just as a physicist uses different assumptions when studying falling marbles and falling beach balls, economists use different assumptions when studying the short-run and long-run effects of a change in the quantity of money.

ECONOMIC MODELS

High-school biology teachers teach basic anatomy with plastic replicas of the human body. These models have all the major organs—the heart, the liver, the kidneys, and so on. The models allow teachers to show their students in a simple way how the important parts of the body fit together. Of course, these plastic models are not actual human bodies, and no one would mistake the models for real people. These models are stylized, and they omit many details. Yet despite this lack of realism—indeed, because of this lack of realism—studying these models is useful for learning how the human body works.

Economists also use models to learn about the world, but instead of being made of plastic, they are most often composed of diagrams and equations. Like a biology teacher's plastic model, economic models omit many details to allow us to see what is truly important. Just as the biology teacher's model does not include all of the body's muscles and capillaries, an economist's model does not include every feature of the economy.

As we use models to examine various economic issues throughout this book, you will see that all of the models are built with assumptions. Just as a physicist begins the analysis of a falling marble by assuming away the existence of friction, economists assume away many of the details of the economy that are irrelevant for studying the question at hand. All models—in physics, biology, or economics— simplify reality in order to improve our understanding of it.

OUR FIRST MODEL: THE CIRCULAR-FLOW DIAGRAM

The economy consists of millions of people engaged in many activities—buying, selling, working, hiring, manufacturing, and so on. To understand how the economy works, we must find some way to simplify our thinking about all of these activities. In other words, we need a model that explains, in general terms, how the economy is organized and how participants in the economy interact with one another.

Figure 2-1 presents a visual model of the economy, called a **circular-flow diagram.** In this model, the economy has two types of decision makers: households and firms. Firms produce goods and services using inputs, such as labour, land, and capital (buildings and machines). These inputs are called the *factors of production*. Households own the factors of production and consume all the goods and services that the firms produce.

Households and firms interact in two types of markets. In the *markets for goods and services*, households are buyers and firms are sellers. In particular, households buy the output of goods and services that firms produce. In the *markets for the factors of production*, households are sellers and firms are buyers. In these markets, households provide firms with the inputs that the firms use to produce goods and services. The circular-flow diagram offers a simple way of organizing all the economic transactions that occur between households and firms in the economy.

The inner loop of the circular-flow diagram represents the flows of goods and services between households and firms. The households sell the use of their labour, land, and capital to the firms in the markets for the factors of production. The firms then use these factors to produce goods and services, which in turn are sold to households in the markets for goods and services. Hence, the factors of production flow from households to firms, and goods and services flow from firms to households.

The outer loop of the circular-flow diagram represents the corresponding flow of dollars. The households spend money to buy goods and services from the firms. The firms use some of the revenue from these sales to pay for the factors of

circular-flow diagram
a visual model of the economy that shows how dollars flow through markets among households and firms

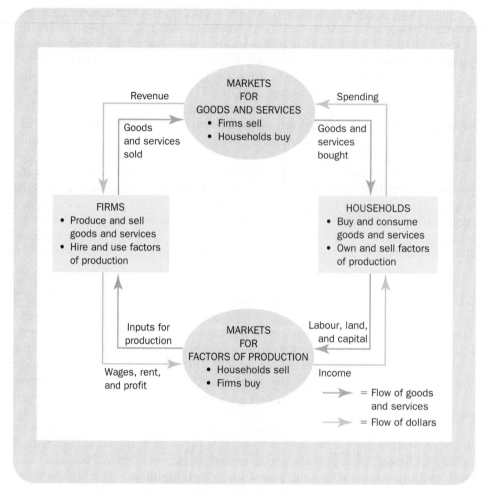

Figure 2-1

THE CIRCULAR FLOW.   This diagram is a schematic representation of the organization of the economy. Decisions are made by households and firms. Households and firms interact in the markets for goods and services (where households are buyers and firms are sellers) and in the markets for the factors of production (where firms are buyers and households are sellers). The outer set of arrows shows the flow of dollars, and the inner set of arrows shows the corresponding flow of goods and services.

production, such as the wages of their workers. What's left is the profit of the firm owners, who themselves are members of households. Hence, spending on goods and services flows from households to firms, and income in the form of wages, rent, and profit flows from firms to households.

Let's take a tour of the circular flow by following a dollar bill as it makes its way from person to person through the economy. Imagine that the dollar begins at a household, sitting in, say, your wallet. If you want to buy a cup of coffee, you take the dollar to one of the economy's markets for goods and services, such as your local Starbucks coffee shop. There you spend it on your favorite drink. When the dollar moves into the Starbucks cash register, it becomes revenue for the firm. The dollar doesn't stay at Starbucks for long, however, because the firm uses it to buy inputs in the markets for the factors of production. For instance, Starbucks might use the dollar to pay rent to its landlord for the space it occupies or to pay the wages of its workers. In either case, the dollar enters the income of some household and, once again, is back in someone's wallet. At that point, the story of the economy's circular flow starts once again.

The circular-flow diagram in Figure 2-1 is one simple model of the economy. It dispenses with details that, for some purposes, are significant. A more complex and realistic circular-flow model would include, for instance, the roles of government and international trade. Yet these details are not crucial for a basic understanding of how the economy is organized. Because of its simplicity, this circular-flow diagram is useful to keep in mind when thinking about how the pieces of the economy fit together.

OUR SECOND MODEL: THE PRODUCTION POSSIBILITIES FRONTIER

Most economic models, unlike the circular-flow diagram, are built using the tools of mathematics. Here we consider one of the simplest such models, called the production possibilities frontier, and see how this model illustrates some basic economic ideas.

Although real economies produce thousands of goods and services, let's imagine an economy that produces only two goods—cars and computers. Together the car industry and the computer industry use all of the economy's factors of production. The **production possibilities frontier** is a graph that shows the various combinations of output—in this case, cars and computers—that the economy can possibly produce given the available factors of production and the available production technology that firms can use to turn these factors into output.

Figure 2-2 is an example of a production possibilities frontier. In this economy, if all resources were used in the car industry, the economy would produce 1000 cars and no computers. If all resources were used in the computer industry, the economy would produce 3000 computers and no cars. The two endpoints of

production possibilities frontier
a graph that shows the combinations of output that the economy can possibly produce given the available factors of production and the available production technology

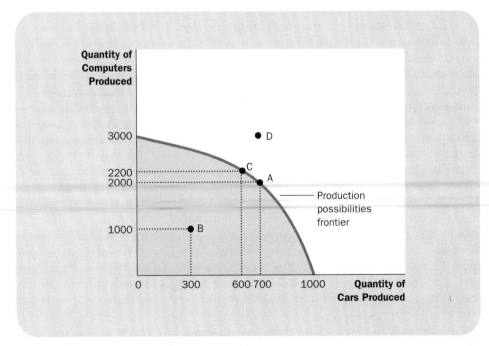

Figure 2-2

THE PRODUCTION POSSIBILITIES FRONTIER.   The production possibilities frontier shows the combinations of output—in this case, cars and computers—that the economy can possibly produce. The economy can produce any combination on or inside the frontier. Points outside the frontier are not feasible given the economy's resources.

the production possibilities frontier represent these extreme possibilities. If the economy were to divide its resources between the two industries, it could produce 700 cars and 2000 computers, shown in the figure by point A. By contrast, the outcome at point D is not possible because resources are scarce: The economy does not have enough of the factors of production to support that level of output. In other words, the economy can produce at any point on or inside the production possibilities frontier, but it cannot produce at points outside the frontier.

An outcome is said to be *efficient* if the economy is getting all it can from the scarce resources it has available. Points on (rather than inside) the production possibilities frontier represent efficient levels of production. When the economy is producing at such a point, say point A, there is no way to produce more of one good without producing less of the other. Point B represents an *inefficient* outcome. For some reason, perhaps widespread unemployment, the economy is producing less than it could from the resources it has available: It is producing only 300 cars and 1000 computers. If the source of the inefficiency were eliminated, the economy could move from point B to point A, increasing production of both cars (to 700) and computers (to 2000).

One of the *Ten Principles of Economics* discussed in Chapter 1 is that people face tradeoffs. The production possibilities frontier shows one tradeoff that society faces: Once we have reached the efficient points on the frontier, the only way of getting more of one good is to get less of the other. When the economy moves from point A to point C, for instance, society produces more computers but at the expense of producing fewer cars.

Another of the *Ten Principles of Economics* is that the cost of something is what you give up to get it. This is called the *opportunity cost.* The production possibilities frontier shows the opportunity cost of one good as measured in terms of the other good. When society reallocates some of the factors of production from the car industry to the computer industry, moving the economy from point A to point C, it gives up 100 cars to get 200 additional computers. In other words, when the economy is at point A, the opportunity cost of 200 computers is 100 cars.

Notice that the production possibilities frontier in Figure 2-2 is bowed outward. This means that the opportunity cost of cars in terms of computers depends on how much of each good the economy is producing. When the economy is using most of its resources to make cars, the production possibilities frontier is quite steep. Because even workers and machines best suited to making computers are being used to make cars, the economy gets a substantial increase in the number of computers for each car it gives up. By contrast, when the economy is using most of its resources to make computers, the production possibilities frontier is quite flat. In this case, the resources best suited to making computers are already in the computer industry, and each car the economy gives up yields only a small increase in the number of computers.

The production possibilities frontier shows the tradeoff between the production of different goods at a given time, but the tradeoff can change over time. For example, if a technological advance in the computer industry raises the number of computers that a worker can produce per week, the economy can make more computers for any given number of cars. As a result, the production possibilities frontier shifts outward, as in Figure 2-3. Because of this economic growth, society might move production from point A to point E, enjoying more computers and more cars.

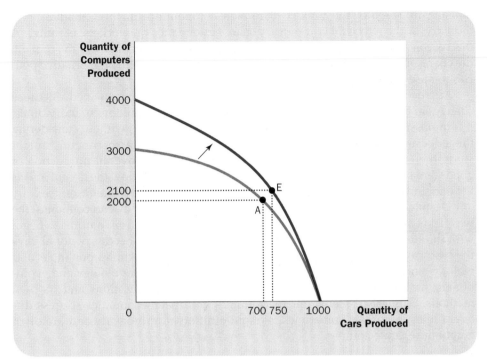

Figure 2-3

A Shift in the Production Possibilities Frontier.   An economic advance in the computer industry shifts the production possibilities frontier outward, increasing the number of cars and computers the economy can produce.

The production possibilities frontier simplifies a complex economy to highlight and clarify some basic ideas. We have used it to illustrate some of the concepts mentioned briefly in Chapter 1: scarcity, efficiency, tradeoffs, opportunity cost, and economic growth. As you study economics, these ideas will recur in various forms. The production possibilities frontier offers one simple way of thinking about them.

MICROECONOMICS AND MACROECONOMICS

Many subjects are studied on various levels. Consider biology, for example. Molecular biologists study the chemical compounds that make up living things. Cellular biologists study cells, which are made up of many chemical compounds and, at the same time, are themselves the building blocks of living organisms. Evolutionary biologists study the many varieties of animals and plants and how species change gradually over the centuries.

Economics is also studied on various levels. We can study the decisions of individual households and firms. Or we can study the interaction of households and firms in markets for specific goods and services. Or we can study the operation of the economy as a whole, which is just the sum of the activities of all these decision makers in all these markets.

The field of economics is traditionally divided into two broad subfields. **Microeconomics** is the study of how households and firms make decisions and how they interact in specific markets. **Macroeconomics** is the study of economy-wide phenomena. A microeconomist might study the effects of rent control on

microeconomics
the study of how households and firms make decisions and how they interact in markets

macroeconomics
the study of economy-wide phenomena, including inflation, unemployment, and economic growth

housing in Toronto, the impact of foreign competition on the Canadian auto industry, or the effects of compulsory school attendance on workers' earnings. A macroeconomist might study the effects of borrowing by the federal government, the changes over time in the economy's rate of unemployment, or alternative policies to raise growth in national living standards.

Microeconomics and macroeconomics are closely intertwined. Because changes in the overall economy arise from the decisions of millions of individuals, it is impossible to understand macroeconomic developments without considering the associated microeconomic decisions. For example, a macroeconomist might study the effect of a cut in the federal income tax on the overall production of goods and services. To analyze this issue, she must consider how the tax cut affects the decisions of households about how much to spend on goods and services.

Despite the inherent link between microeconomics and macroeconomics, the two fields are distinct. In economics, as in biology, it may seem natural to begin with the smallest unit and build up. Yet doing so is neither necessary nor always the best way to proceed. Evolutionary biology is, in a sense, built upon molecular biology, since species are made up of molecules. Yet molecular biology and evolutionary biology are separate fields, each with its own questions and its own methods. Similarly, because microeconomics and macroeconomics address different questions, they sometimes take quite different approaches and are often taught in separate courses.

QUICK QUIZ: In what sense is economics like a science? ◆ Draw a production possibilities frontier for a society that produces food and clothing. Show an efficient point, an inefficient point, and an infeasible point. Show the effects of a drought. ◆ Define *microeconomics* and *macroeconomics*.

THE ECONOMIST AS POLICY ADVISER

Often economists are asked to explain the causes of economic events. Why, for example, is unemployment higher for teenagers than for older workers? Sometimes economists are asked to recommend policies to improve economic outcomes. What, for instance, should the government do to improve the economic well-being of teenagers? When economists are trying to explain the world, they are scientists. When they are trying to help improve it, they are policy advisers.

POSITIVE VERSUS NORMATIVE ANALYSIS

To help clarify the two roles that economists play, we begin by examining the use of language. Because scientists and policy advisers have different goals, they use language in different ways.

For example, suppose that two people are discussing minimum-wage laws. Here are two statements you might hear:

POLLY: Minimum-wage laws cause unemployment. P

NORMA: The government should raise the minimum wage. N

Ignoring for now whether you agree with these statements, notice that Polly and Norma differ in what they are trying to do. Polly is speaking like a scientist: She is making a claim about how the world works. Norma is speaking like a policy adviser: She is making a claim about how she would like to change the world.

In general, statements about the world are of two types. One type, such as Polly's, is positive. **Positive statements** are descriptive. They make a claim about how the world *is*. A second type of statement, such as Norma's, is normative. **Normative statements** are prescriptive. They make a claim about how the world *ought to be*.

A key difference between positive and normative statements is how we judge their validity. We can, in principle, confirm or refute positive statements by examining evidence. An economist might evaluate Polly's statement by analyzing data on changes in minimum wages and changes in unemployment over time. By contrast, evaluating normative statements involves values as well as facts. Norma's statement cannot be judged using data alone. Deciding what is good or bad policy is not merely a matter of science. It also involves our views on ethics, religion, and political philosophy.

Of course, positive and normative statements may be related. Our positive views about how the world works affect our normative views about what policies are desirable. Polly's claim that the minimum wage causes unemployment, if true, might lead us to reject Norma's conclusion that the government should raise the minimum wage. Yet our normative conclusions cannot come from positive analysis alone. Instead, they require both positive analysis and value judgements.

As you study economics, keep in mind the distinction between positive and normative statements. Much of economics just tries to explain how the economy works. Yet often the goal of economics is to improve how the economy works. When you hear economists making normative statements, you know they have crossed the line from scientist to policy adviser.

positive statements
claims that attempt to describe the world as it is

normative statements
claims that attempt to prescribe how the world should be

ECONOMISTS IN OTTAWA

U.S. President Harry Truman once said that he wanted to find a one-armed economist. When he asked his economists for advice, they always answered, "On the one hand, . . . On the other hand, . . . "

Truman was right in realizing that economists' advice is not always straightforward. This tendency is rooted in one of the *Ten Principles of Economics* in Chapter 1: People face tradeoffs. Economists are aware that tradeoffs are involved in most policy decisions. A policy might increase efficiency at the cost of equity. It might help future generations but hurt current generations. An economist who says that all policy decisions are easy is an economist who is not to be trusted.

The government of Canada, like other governments, relies on the advice of economists. Economists at the Department of Finance help design tax policy. Economists at Industry Canada help design and enforce Canada's antimonopoly laws. Economists at the Department of Foreign Affairs and International Trade help negotiate trade agreements with other countries. Economists at Human Resources Development Canada analyze data on workers and on those looking for work to help formulate labour-market policies. Economists at Environment Canada help design environmental regulations. The Canadian International Development Agency employs economists, both on staff and as consultants, to give advice on

"Let's switch. I'll make the policy, you implement it, and he'll explain it."

overseas development projects. Statistics Canada employs economists to collect the data analyzed by other economists to give policy advice. The Bank of Canada, the quasi-independent institution that sets Canada's monetary policy, employs about 200 economists to analyze financial markets and macroeconomic developments.

Economists outside the government also give policy advice. The C.D. Howe Institute, The Fraser Institute, and other independent organizations publish reports by economists that analyze current issues such as poverty, unemployment, and the deficit. These reports try to influence public opinion and give advice on government policies. Table 2-1 lists the Web sites of some of these organizations.

Table 2-1

WEB SITES. Here are the Web sites of some of the organizations that hire economists and influence economic policy.

Statistics Canada	http://www.statcan.ca
Environment Canada	http://www.ec.gc.ca
Department of Finance Canada	http://www.fin.gc.ca
Industry Canada	http://www.ic.gc.ca
Department of Foreign Affairs and International Trade	http://www.dfait.gc.ca
Human Resources Development Canada	http://www.hrdc.gc.ca
Bank of Canada	http://www.bank-banque-canada.ca
C.D. Howe Institute	http://www.cdhowe.org
The Fraser Institute	http://www.fraserinstitute.ca
Institute for Research on Public Policy	http://www.irpp.org

The influence of economists on policy goes beyond their role as advisers: Their research and writings often affect policy indirectly. Economist John Maynard Keynes offered this observation:

> The ideas of economists and political philosophers, both when they are right and when they are wrong, are more powerful than is commonly understood. Indeed, the world is ruled by little else. Practical men, who believe themselves to be quite exempt from intellectual influences, are usually the slaves of some defunct economist. Madmen in authority, who hear voices in the air, are distilling their frenzy from some academic scribbler of a few years back.

Although these words were written in 1935, they remain true today. Indeed, the "academic scribbler" now influencing public policy is often Keynes himself.

QUICK QUIZ: Give an example of a positive statement and an example of a normative statement. ◆ Name three parts of government that regularly rely on advice from economists.

WHY ECONOMISTS DISAGREE

"If all economists were laid end to end, they would not reach a conclusion." This quip from George Bernard Shaw is revealing. Economists as a group are often criticized for giving conflicting advice to policymakers. U.S. President Ronald Reagan once joked that if the game Trivial Pursuit were designed for economists, it would have 100 questions and 3000 answers.

Why do economists so often appear to give conflicting advice to policymakers? There are two basic reasons:

◆ Economists may disagree about the validity of alternative positive theories about how the world works.

◆ Economists may have different values and, therefore, different normative views about what policy should try to accomplish.

Let's discuss each of these reasons.

DIFFERENCES IN SCIENTIFIC JUDGEMENTS

Several centuries ago, astronomers debated whether the earth or the sun was at the centre of the solar system. More recently, meteorologists have debated whether the earth is experiencing "global warming" and, if so, why. Science is a search for understanding about the world around us. It is not surprising that as the search continues, scientists can disagree about the direction in which truth lies.

Economists often disagree for the same reason. Economics is a young science, and there is still much to be learned. Economists sometimes disagree because they have different hunches about the validity of alternative theories or about the size of important parameters.

For example, economists disagree about whether the government should levy taxes based on a household's income or its consumption (spending). Advocates of a switch from the current income tax to a consumption tax believe that the change would encourage households to save more, because income that is saved would not be taxed. Higher saving, in turn, would lead to more rapid growth in productivity and living standards. Advocates of the current income tax believe that household saving would not respond much to a change in the tax laws. These two groups of economists hold different normative views about the tax system because they have different positive views about the responsiveness of saving to tax incentives.

DIFFERENCES IN VALUES

Suppose that Peter and Paul both take the same amount of water from the town well. To pay for maintaining the well, the town taxes its residents. Peter has income of $50 000 and is taxed $5000, or 10 percent of his income. Paul has income of $10 000 and is taxed $2000, or 20 percent of his income.

Is this policy fair? If not, who pays too much and who pays too little? Does it matter whether Peter's high income is due to a large inheritance or to his willingness to work long hours at a dreary job? Does it matter whether Paul's low income is due to a medical disability or to his decision to pursue a career in acting?

These are difficult questions on which people are likely to disagree. If the town hired two experts to study how the town should tax its residents to pay for the well, we would not be surprised if they offered conflicting advice.

This simple example shows why economists sometimes disagree about public policy. As we learned earlier in our discussion of normative and positive analysis, policies cannot be judged on scientific grounds alone. Economists give conflicting advice sometimes because they have different values. Perfecting the science of economics will not tell us whether it is Peter or Paul who pays too much.

PERCEPTION VERSUS REALITY

Because of differences in scientific judgements and differences in values, some disagreement among economists is inevitable. Yet one should not overstate the amount of disagreement. In many cases, economists do offer a united view.

Table 2-2 contains ten propositions about economic policy. In a survey of economists in business, government, and academia, these propositions were endorsed by an overwhelming majority of respondents. Most of these propositions would fail to command a similar consensus among the general public.

The first proposition in the table is about rent control. For reasons we will discuss in Chapter 6, almost all economists believe that rent control adversely affects the availability and quality of housing and is a very costly way of helping the most needy members of society. Nonetheless, some provincial governments choose to ignore the advice of economists and place ceilings on the rents that landlords may charge their tenants.

The second proposition in the table concerns tariffs and import quotas. For reasons we will discuss in Chapter 3 and more fully in Chapter 9, almost all economists oppose such barriers to free trade. Nonetheless, over the years, Parliament has chosen to restrict the import of certain goods. The 1988 federal election was fought on the issue of whether Canada should sign the Free Trade Agreement, which would reduce barriers to trade between Canada and the United States. Despite the overwhelming support of economists, the agreement was opposed by many voters and by the Liberal and New Democratic parties. The Progressive Conservative Party eventually won the election and signed the agreement, but only after a closely fought race. In this case, economists did offer united advice, but many voters and politicians chose to ignore it.

Why do policies such as rent control and import quotas persist if the experts are united in their opposition? The reason may be that economists have not yet convinced the general public that these policies are undesirable. One purpose of this book is to make you understand the economist's view of these and other subjects and, perhaps, to persuade you that it is the right one.

Table 2-2

TEN PROPOSITIONS ABOUT WHICH MOST ECONOMISTS AGREE

PROPOSITION (AND PERCENTAGE OF ECONOMISTS WHO AGREE)

1. A ceiling on rents reduces the quantity and quality of housing available. (93%)
2. Tariffs and import quotas usually reduce general economic welfare. (93%)
3. Flexible and floating exchange rates offer an effective international monetary arrangement. (90%)
4. Fiscal policy (e.g., tax cut and/or government expenditure increase) has a significant stimulative impact on a less than fully employed economy. (90%)
5. If the federal budget is to be balanced, it should be done over the business cycle rather than yearly. (85%)
6. Cash payments increase the welfare of recipients to a greater degree than do transfers-in-kind of equal cash value. (84%)
7. A large federal budget deficit has an adverse effect on the economy. (83%)
8. A minimum wage increases unemployment among young and unskilled workers. (79%)
9. The government should restructure the welfare system along the lines of a "negative income tax." (79%)
10. Effluent taxes and marketable pollution permits represent a better approach to pollution control than imposition of pollution ceilings. (78%)

SOURCE: Richard M. Alston, J.R. Kearl, and Michael B. Vaughn, "Is There Consensus among Economists in the 1990s?" *American Economic Review* (May 1992): 203–9.

QUICK QUIZ: Why might economic advisers to the prime minister disagree about a question of policy?

LET'S GET GOING

The first two chapters of this book have introduced you to the ideas and methods of economics. We are now ready to get to work. In the next chapter we start learning in more detail the principles of economic behaviour and economic policy.

As you proceed through this book, you will be asked to draw on many of your intellectual skills. You might find it helpful to keep in mind some advice from the great economist John Maynard Keynes:

> The study of economics does not seem to require any specialized gifts of an unusually high order. Is it not . . . a very easy subject compared with the higher branches of philosophy or pure science? An easy subject, at which very few excel! The paradox finds its explanation, perhaps, in that the master-economist must possess a rare *combination* of gifts. He must be mathematician, historian, statesman, philosopher—in some degree. He must understand symbols and speak in words. He must contemplate the particular in terms of the general, and touch abstract and concrete in the same flight of thought. He must study the present in the light of the past for the purposes of the future. No part of man's nature or his institutions must lie entirely outside his regard. He must be purposeful and disinterested in a simultaneous mood; as aloof and incorruptible as an artist, yet sometimes as near the earth as a politician.

It is a tall order. But with practice, you will become more and more accustomed to thinking like an economist.

Summary

- Economists try to address their subject with a scientist's objectivity. Like all scientists, they make appropriate assumptions and build simplified models in order to understand the world around them. Two simple economic models are the circular-flow diagram and the production possibilities frontier.

- The field of economics is divided into two subfields: microeconomics and macroeconomics. Microeconomists study decision making by households and firms and the interaction among households and firms in the marketplace. Macroeconomists study the forces and trends that affect the economy as a whole.

- A positive statement is an assertion about how the world *is*. A normative statement is an assertion about how the world *ought to be*. When economists make normative statements, they are acting more as policy advisers than scientists.

- Economists who advise policymakers offer conflicting advice either because of differences in scientific judgements or because of differences in values. At other times, economists are united in the advice they offer, but policymakers may choose to ignore it.

Key Concepts

circular-flow diagram, p. 23
production possibilities frontier, p. 25

microeconomics, p. 27
macroeconomics, p. 27

positive statements, p. 29
normative statements, p. 29

Questions for Review

1. How is economics like a science?

2. Why do economists make assumptions?

3. Should an economic model describe reality exactly?

4. Draw and explain a production possibilities frontier for an economy that produces milk and cookies. What happens to this frontier if disease kills half of the economy's cow population?

5. Use a production possibilities frontier to describe the idea of "efficiency."

6. What are the two subfields into which economics is divided? Explain what each subfield studies.

7. What is the difference between a positive and a normative statement? Give an example of each.

8. What is the Bank of Canada?

9. Why do economists sometimes offer conflicting advice to policymakers?

Problems and Applications

1. Describe some unusual language used in one of the other fields that you are studying. Why are these special terms useful?

2. One common assumption in economics is that the products of different firms in the same industry are indistinguishable. For each of the following industries, discuss whether this is a reasonable assumption:
   a. steel
   b. novels
   c. wheat
   d. fast food

3. Draw a circular-flow diagram. Identify the parts of the model that correspond to the flow of goods and services and the flow of dollars for each of the following activities:
   a. Sam pays a storekeeper $1 for a litre of milk.
   b. Sally earns $6.50 per hour working at a fast-food restaurant.
   c. Serena spends $7 to see a movie.
   d. Stuart earns $10 000 from his 10 percent ownership of Acme Industrial.

4. Imagine a society that produces military goods and consumer goods, which we'll call "guns" and "butter."
   a. Draw a production possibilities frontier for guns and butter. Explain why it most likely has a bowed-out shape.
   b. Show a point that is impossible for the economy to achieve. Show a point that is feasible but inefficient.
   c. Imagine that the society has two political parties, called the Hawks (who want a strong military) and the Doves (who want a smaller military). Show a point on your production possibilities frontier that the Hawks might choose and a point the Doves might choose.
   d. Imagine that an aggressive neighbouring country reduces the size of its military. As a result, both the Hawks and the Doves reduce their desired production of guns by the same amount. Which party would get the bigger "peace dividend," measured by the increase in butter production? Explain.

5. The first principle of economics discussed in Chapter 1 is that people face tradeoffs. Use a production possibilities frontier to illustrate society's tradeoff between a clean environment and high incomes. What do you suppose determines the shape and position of the frontier? Show what happens to the frontier if engineers develop an automobile engine with almost no emissions.

6. Classify the following topics as relating to microeconomics or macroeconomics:
   a. a family's decision about how much income to save
   b. the effect of government regulations on auto emissions
   c. the impact of higher national saving on economic growth
   d. a firm's decision about how many workers to hire
   e. the relationship between the inflation rate and changes in the quantity of money

7. Classify each of the following statements as positive or normative. Explain.

a. Society faces a short-run tradeoff between inflation P and unemployment.
b. A reduction in the rate of growth of money will P reduce the rate of inflation.
c. The Bank of Canada should reduce the rate of N growth of money.
d. Society ought to require welfare recipients to look N for jobs.
e. Lower tax rates encourage more work and more P saving.

8. Classify each of the statements in Table 2-2 as positive, normative, or ambiguous. Explain.

9. If you were prime minister, would you be more interested in your economic advisers' positive views or their normative views? Why?

10. The C.D. Howe Institute and The Fraser Institute regularly publish reports containing economic commentary and policy recommendations. Find a recent publication from either of these organizations at your library (or from their Web sites http://www.cdhowe.org and http://www.fraserinstitute.ca), and read about an issue that interests you. Summarize the discussion of this issue and the author's proposed policy.

11. Who is the current governor of the Bank of Canada? Who is the current minister of finance?

12. Look up one of the Web sites listed in Table 2-1. What recent economic trends or issues are addressed there?

13. Would you expect economists to disagree less about public policy as time goes on? Why or why not? Can their differences be completely eliminated? Why or why not?

GRAPHING: A BRIEF REVIEW

Many of the concepts that economists study can be expressed with numbers—the price of bananas, the quantity of bananas sold, the cost of growing bananas, and so on. Often these economic variables are related to one another. When the price of bananas rises, people buy fewer bananas. One way of expressing the relationships among variables is with graphs.

Graphs serve two purposes. First, when developing economic theories, graphs offer a way to visually express ideas that might be less clear if described with equations or words. Second, when analyzing economic data, graphs provide a way of finding how variables are in fact related in the world. Whether we are working with theory or with data, graphs provide a lens through which a recognizable forest emerges from a multitude of trees.

Numerical information can be expressed graphically in many ways, just as a thought can be expressed in words in many ways. A good writer chooses words that will make an argument clear, a description pleasing, or a scene dramatic. An effective economist chooses the type of graph that best suits the purpose at hand.

In this appendix we discuss how economists use graphs to study the mathematical relationships among variables. We also discuss some of the pitfalls that can arise in the use of graphical methods.

GRAPHS OF A SINGLE VARIABLE

Three common graphs are shown in Figure 2A-1. The *pie chart* in panel (a) shows how total income in Canada is divided among the sources of income, including wages and salaries, corporation profits, and so on. A slice of the pie represents each source's share of the total. The *bar graph* in panel (b) compares the population of various regions in Canada. The height of each bar represents the population in each region. The *time-series graph* in panel (c) traces the rising productivity in the Canadian economy over time. The height of the line shows output per hour in each year. You have probably seen similar graphs presented in newspapers and magazines.

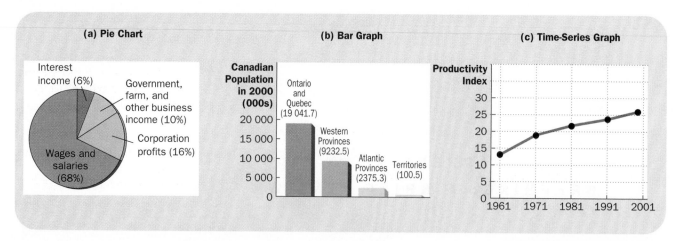

(a) Pie Chart

Interest income (6%)

Government, farm, and other business income (10%)

Corporation profits (16%)

Wages and salaries (68%)

(b) Bar Graph

Canadian Population in 2000 (000s)

Ontario and Quebec (19 041.7)

Western Provinces (9232.5)

Atlantic Provinces (2375.3)

Territories (100.5)

20 000
15 000
10 000
5 000
0

(c) Time-Series Graph

Productivity Index

30
25
20
15
10
5
0

1961 1971 1981 1991 2001

TYPES OF GRAPHS. The pie chart in panel (a) shows how Canadian national income is derived from various sources. The bar graph in panel (b) compares the population in four Canadian regions. The time-series graph in panel (c) shows the growth in productivity of the Canadian economy from 1961 to 1999.

Figure 2A-1

SOURCES: National income data from Statistics Canada, CANSIM database, matrices 9465 and 9480; population data from Statistics Canada, "Estimates of Population," CANSIM II, Table 051-0010; productivity data from Statistics Canada.

GRAPHS OF TWO VARIABLES: THE COORDINATE SYSTEM

Although the three graphs in Figure 2A-1 are useful in showing how a variable changes over time or across individuals, such graphs are limited in how much they can tell us. These graphs display information only on a single variable. Economists are often concerned with the relationships between variables. Thus, they need to be able to display two variables on a single graph. The *coordinate system* makes this possible.

Suppose you want to examine the relationship between study time and grade point average. For each student in your class, you could record a pair of numbers: hours per week spent studying and grade point average. These numbers could then be placed in parentheses as an *ordered pair* and appear as a single point on the graph. Albert E., for instance, is represented by the ordered pair (25 hours/week, 3.5 GPA), while his "what-me-worry?" classmate Alfred E. is represented by the ordered pair (5 hours/week, 2.0 GPA).

We can graph these ordered pairs on a two-dimensional grid. The first number in each ordered pair, called the *x-coordinate,* tells us the horizontal location of the point. The second number, called the *y-coordinate,* tells us the vertical location of the point. The point with both an *x*-coordinate and a *y*-coordinate of zero is known as the *origin.* The two coordinates in the ordered pair tell us where the point is located in relation to the origin: *x* units to the right of the origin and *y* units above it.

Figure 2A-2 graphs grade point average against study time for Albert E., Alfred E., and their classmates. This type of graph is called a *scatterplot* because it plots scattered points. Looking at this graph, we immediately notice that points farther to the right (indicating more study time) also tend to be higher (indicating

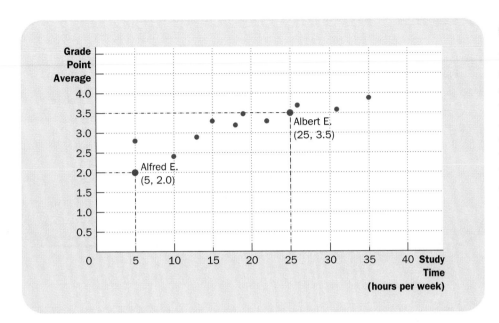

Figure 2A-2

USING THE COORDINATE SYSTEM. Grade point average is measured on the vertical axis and study time on the horizontal axis. Albert E., Alfred E., and their classmates are represented by various points. We can see from the graph that students who study more tend to get higher grades.

a better grade point average). Because study time and grade point average typically move in the same direction, we say that these two variables have a *positive correlation*. By contrast, if we were to graph party time and grades, we would likely find that higher party time is associated with lower grades; because these variables typically move in opposite directions, we would call this a *negative correlation*. In either case, the coordinate system makes the correlation between the two variables easy to see.

CURVES IN THE COORDINATE SYSTEM

Students who study more do tend to get higher grades, but other factors also influence a student's grade. Previous preparation is an important factor, for instance, as are talent, attention from teachers, even eating a good breakfast. A scatterplot like Figure 2A-2 does not attempt to isolate the effect that study has on grades from the effects of other variables. Often, however, economists prefer looking at how one variable affects another holding everything else constant.

To see how this is done, let's consider one of the most important graphs in economics—the *demand curve*. The demand curve traces out the effect of a good's price on the quantity of the good consumers want to buy. Before showing a demand curve, however, consider Table 2A-1, which shows how the number of novels that Emma buys depends on her income and on the price of novels. When novels are cheap, Emma buys them in large quantities. As they become more expensive, she borrows books from the library instead of buying them or chooses to go to the movies instead of reading. Similarly, at any given price, Emma buys more novels when she has a higher income. That is, when her income increases, she spends part of the additional income on novels and part on other goods.

Table 2A-1

NOVELS PURCHASED BY EMMA. This table shows the number of novels Emma buys at various incomes and prices. For any given level of income, the data on price and quantity demanded can be graphed to produce Emma's demand curve for novels, as in Figure 2A-3.

	INCOME		
PRICE	$20 000	$30 000	$40 000
$10	2 novels	5 novels	8 novels
9	6	9	12
8	10	13	16
7	14	17	20
6	18	21	24
5	22	25	28
	Demand curve, D_3	Demand curve, D_1	Demand curve, D_2

Figure 2A-3

DEMAND CURVE.   The line D_1 shows how Emma's purchases of novels depend on the price of novels when her income is held constant. Because the price and the quantity demanded are negatively related, the demand curve slopes downward.

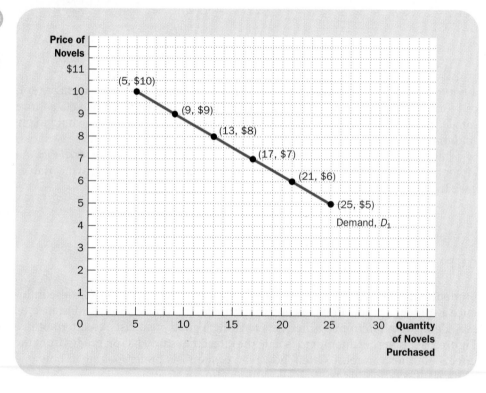

We now have three variables—the price of novels, income, and the number of novels purchased—which is more than we can represent in two dimensions. To put the information from Table 2A-1 in graphical form, we need to hold one of the three variables constant and trace out the relationship between the other two. Because the demand curve represents the relationship between price and quantity demanded, we hold Emma's income constant and show how the number of novels she buys varies with the price of novels.

Suppose that Emma's income is $30 000 per year. If we place the number of novels Emma purchases on the *x*-axis and the price of novels on the *y*-axis, we can graphically represent the middle column of Table 2A-1. When the points that represent these entries from the table—(5 novels, $10), (9 novels, $9), and so on—are connected, they form a line. This line, pictured in Figure 2A-3, is known as Emma's demand curve for novels; it tells us how many novels Emma purchases at any given price. The demand curve is downward sloping, indicating that a higher price reduces the quantity of novels demanded. Because the quantity of novels demanded and the price move in opposite directions, we say that the two variables are *negatively related.* (Conversely, when two variables move in the same direction, the curve relating them is upward sloping, and we say the variables are *positively related.*)

Now suppose that Emma's income rises to $40 000 per year. At any given price, Emma will purchase more novels than she did at her previous level of income. Just as earlier we drew Emma's demand curve for novels using the entries from the middle column of Table 2A-1, we now draw a new demand curve using the entries from the right-hand column of the table. This new demand curve (curve D_2) is pictured alongside the old one (curve D_1) in Figure 2A-4; the new curve is a similar line drawn farther to the right. We therefore say that Emma's demand curve for novels *shifts* to the right when her income increases. Likewise, if Emma's income were to fall to $20 000 per year, she would buy fewer novels at any given price and her demand curve would shift to the left (to curve D_3).

In economics, it is important to distinguish between *movements along a curve* and *shifts of a curve.* As we can see from Figure 2A-3, if Emma earns $30 000 per year and novels cost $8 apiece, she will purchase 13 novels per year. If the price of

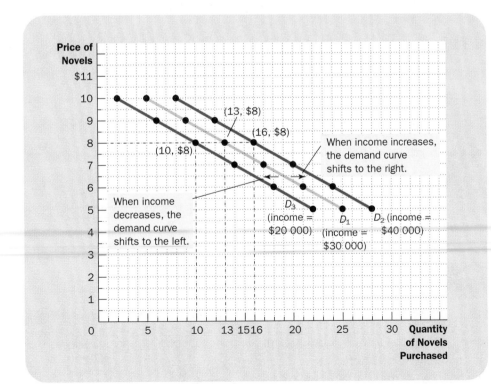

Figure 2A-4

SHIFTING DEMAND CURVES. The location of Emma's demand curve for novels depends on how much income she earns. The more she earns, the more novels she will purchase at any given price, and the farther to the right her demand curve will lie. Curve D_1 represents Emma's original demand curve when her income is $30 000 per year. If her income rises to $40 000 per year, her demand curve shifts to D_2. If her income falls to $20 000 per year, her demand curve shifts to D_3.

novels falls to $7, Emma will increase her purchases of novels to 17 per year. The demand curve, however, stays fixed in the same place. Emma still buys the same number of novels at *each price*, but as the price falls she moves along her demand curve from left to right. By contrast, if the price of novels remains fixed at $8 but her income rises to $40 000, Emma increases her purchases of novels from 13 to 16 per year. Because Emma buys more novels *at each price*, her demand curve shifts out, as shown in Figure 2A-4.

There is a simple way to tell when it is necessary to shift a curve. When a variable that is not named on either axis changes, the curve shifts. Income is on neither the *x*-axis nor the *y*-axis of the graph, so when Emma's income changes, her demand curve must shift. Any change that affects Emma's purchasing habits besides a change in the price of novels will result in a shift in her demand curve. If, for instance, the public library closes and Emma must buy all the books she wants to read, she will demand more novels at each price, and her demand curve will shift to the right. Or, if the price of movies falls and Emma spends more time at the movies and less time reading, she will demand fewer novels at each price, and her demand curve will shift to the left. By contrast, when a variable on an axis of the graph changes, the curve does not shift. We read the change as a movement along the curve.

SLOPE

One question we might want to ask about Emma is how much her purchasing habits respond to price. Look at the demand curve pictured in Figure 2A-5. If this curve is very steep, Emma purchases nearly the same number of novels regardless

Figure 2A-5

CALCULATING THE SLOPE OF A LINE.   To calculate the slope of the demand curve, we can look at the changes in the *x*- and *y*-coordinates as we move from the point (21 novels, $6) to the point (13 novels, $8). The slope of the line is the ratio of the change in the *y*-coordinate (−2) to the change in the *x*-coordinate (+8), which equals −1/4.

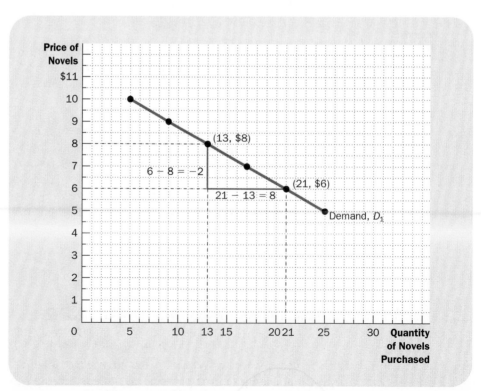

of whether they are cheap or expensive. If this curve is much flatter, Emma purchases many fewer novels when the price rises. To answer questions about how much one variable responds to changes in another variable, we can use the concept of *slope*.

The slope of a line is the ratio of the vertical distance covered to the horizontal distance covered as we move along the line. This definition is usually written out in mathematical symbols as follows:

$$\text{slope} = \frac{\Delta y}{\Delta x},$$

where the Greek letter Δ (delta) stands for the change in a variable. In other words, the slope of a line is equal to the "rise" (change in y) divided by the "run" (change in x). The slope will be a small positive number for a fairly flat upward-sloping line, a large positive number for a steep upward-sloping line, and a negative number for a downward-sloping line. A horizontal line has a slope of zero because in this case the y-variable never changes; a vertical line is defined to have an infinite slope because the y-variable can take any value without the x-variable changing at all.

What is the slope of Emma's demand curve for novels? First of all, because the curve slopes down, we know the slope will be negative. To calculate a numerical value for the slope, we must choose two points on the line. With Emma's income at $30 000, she will purchase 21 novels at a price of $6 or 13 novels at a price of $8. When we apply the slope formula, we are concerned with the change between these two points; in other words, we are concerned with the difference between them, which lets us know that we will have to subtract one set of values from the other, as follows:

$$\text{slope} = \frac{\Delta y}{\Delta x} = \frac{\text{first } y\text{-coordinate} - \text{second } y\text{-coordinate}}{\text{first } x\text{-coordinate} - \text{second } x\text{-coordinate}} = \frac{6-8}{21-13} = \frac{-2}{8} = \frac{-1}{4}.$$

Figure 2A-5 shows graphically how this calculation works. Try computing the slope of Emma's demand curve using two different points. You should get exactly the same result, $-1/4$. One of the properties of a straight line is that it has the same slope everywhere. This is not true of other types of curves, which are steeper in some places than in others.

The slope of Emma's demand curve tells us something about how responsive her purchases are to changes in price. A small slope (a number close to zero) means that Emma's demand curve is relatively flat; in this case, she adjusts the number of novels she buys substantially in response to a price change. A larger slope (a number farther from zero) means that Emma's demand curve is relatively steep; in this case, she adjusts the number of novels she buys only slightly in response to a price change.

CAUSE AND EFFECT

Economists often use graphs to advance an argument about how the economy works. In other words, they use graphs to argue about how one set of events *causes* another set of events. With a graph like the demand curve, there is no doubt about cause and effect. Because we are varying price and holding all other variables constant, we know that changes in the price of novels cause changes in the quantity Emma demands. Remember, however, that our demand curve came from a hypothetical example. When graphing data from the real world, it is often more difficult to establish how one variable affects another.

The first problem is that it is difficult to hold everything else constant when measuring how one variable affects another. If we are not able to hold variables constant, we might decide that one variable on our graph is causing changes in the other variable when actually those changes are caused by a third *omitted* variable not pictured on the graph. Even if we have identified the correct two variables to look at, we might run into a second problem—*reverse causality*. In other words, we might decide that A causes B when in fact B causes A. The omitted-variable and reverse-causality traps require us to proceed with caution when using graphs to draw conclusions about causes and effects.

Omitted Variables To see how omitting a variable can lead to a deceptive graph, let's consider an example. Imagine that the government, spurred by public concern about the large number of deaths from cancer, commissions an exhaustive study from Big Brother Statistical Services, Inc. Big Brother examines many of the items found in people's homes to see which of them are associated with the risk of cancer. Big Brother reports a strong relationship between two variables: the number of cigarette lighters that a household owns and the probability that someone in the household will develop cancer. Figure 2A-6 shows this relationship.

What should we make of this result? Big Brother advises a quick policy response. It recommends that the government discourage the ownership of cigarette lighters by taxing their sale. It also recommends that the government require warning labels: "Big Brother has determined that this lighter is dangerous to your health."

In judging the validity of Big Brother's analysis, one question is paramount: Has Big Brother held constant every relevant variable except the one under consideration? If the answer is no, the results are suspect. An easy explanation for Figure 2A-6 is that people who own more cigarette lighters are more likely to smoke cigarettes and that cigarettes, not lighters, cause cancer. If Figure 2A-6 does not hold constant the amount of smoking, it does not tell us the true effect of owning a cigarette lighter.

Figure 2A-6

GRAPH WITH AN OMITTED VARIABLE. The upward-sloping curve shows that members of households with more cigarette lighters are more likely to develop cancer. Yet we should not conclude that ownership of lighters causes cancer because the graph does not take into account the number of cigarettes smoked.

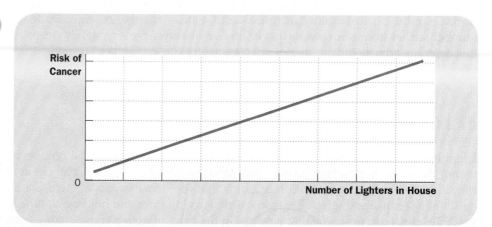

This story illustrates an important principle: When you see a graph being used to support an argument about cause and effect, it is important to ask whether the movements of an omitted variable could explain the results you see.

Reverse Causality   Economists can also make mistakes about causality by misreading its direction. To see how this is possible, suppose the Association of Canadian Anarchists commissions a study of crime in Canada and arrives at Figure 2A-7, which plots the number of violent crimes per thousand people in major cities against the number of police officers per thousand people. The anarchists note the curve's upward slope and argue that because police increase rather than decrease the amount of urban violence, law enforcement should be abolished.

If we could run a controlled experiment, we would avoid the danger of reverse causality. To run an experiment, we would set the number of police officers in different cities randomly and then examine the correlation between police and crime. Figure 2A-7, however, is not based on such an experiment. We simply observe that more dangerous cities have more police officers. The explanation for this may be that more dangerous cities hire more police. In other words, rather than police causing crime, crime may cause police. Nothing in the graph itself allows us to establish the direction of causality.

It might seem that an easy way to determine the direction of causality is to examine which variable moves first. If we see crime increase and then the police force expand, we reach one conclusion. If we see the police force expand and then crime increase, we reach the other. Yet there is also a flaw with this approach: Often people change their behaviour not in response to a change in their present conditions but in response to a change in their *expectations* of future conditions. A city that expects a major crime wave in the future, for instance, might well hire more police now. This problem is even easier to see in the case of babies and minivans. Couples often buy a minivan in anticipation of the birth of a child. The minivan comes before the baby, but we wouldn't want to conclude that the sale of minivans causes the population to grow!

There is no complete set of rules that says when it is appropriate to draw causal conclusions from graphs. Yet just keeping in mind that cigarette lighters don't cause cancer (omitted variable) and minivans don't cause larger families (reverse causality) will keep you from falling for many faulty economic arguments.

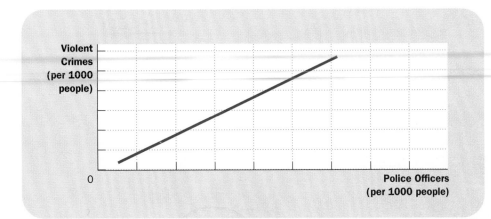

Figure 2A-7

GRAPH SUGGESTING REVERSE CAUSALITY.   The upward-sloping curve shows that cities with a higher concentration of police are more dangerous. Yet the graph does not tell us whether police cause crime or crime-plagued cities hire more police.

3

INTERDEPENDENCE AND THE
GAINS FROM TRADE

**IN THIS CHAPTER
YOU WILL . . .**

*Consider how
everyone can benefit
when people trade
with one another*

*Learn the meaning of
absolute advantage
and comparative
advantage*

*See how comparative
advantage explains
the gains from trade*

*Apply the theory of
comparative
advantage to
everyday life and
national policy*

Consider your typical day. You wake up in the morning, and you pour yourself juice from oranges grown in Florida and coffee from beans grown in Brazil. Over breakfast, you watch a news program broadcast from Toronto on your television made in Japan. You get dressed in clothes made of cotton grown in Georgia and sewn in factories in Thailand. You drive to class in a car made of parts manufactured in more than a dozen countries around the world. Then you open up your economics textbook written by authors living in Massachusetts, Alberta, and Quebec, published by a company located in Ontario, and printed on paper made from trees grown in New Brunswick.

Every day you rely on many people from around the world, most of whom you do not know, to provide you with the goods and services that you enjoy. Such interdependence is possible because people trade with one another. Those people who provide you with goods and services are not acting out of generosity or concern for your welfare. Nor is some government agency directing them to make what you want and to give it to you. Instead, people provide you and other consumers with the goods and services they produce because they get something in return.

In subsequent chapters we will examine how our economy coordinates the activities of millions of people with varying tastes and abilities. As a starting point for this analysis, here we consider the reasons for economic interdependence. One of the *Ten Principles of Economics* highlighted in Chapter 1 is that trade can make everyone better off. This principle explains why people trade with their neighbours and why nations trade with other nations. In this chapter we examine this principle more closely. What exactly do people gain when they trade with one another? Why do people choose to become interdependent?

A PARABLE FOR THE MODERN ECONOMY

To understand why people choose to depend on others for goods and services and how this choice improves their lives, let's look at a simple economy. Imagine that there are two goods in the world—meat and potatoes. And there are two people in the world—a cattle rancher and a potato farmer—each of whom would like to eat both meat and potatoes.

The gains from trade are most obvious if the rancher can produce only meat and the farmer can produce only potatoes. In one scenario, the rancher and the farmer could choose to have nothing to do with each other. But after several months of eating beef roasted, boiled, broiled, and grilled, the rancher might decide that self-sufficiency is not all it's cracked up to be. The farmer, who has been eating potatoes mashed, fried, baked, and scalloped, would likely agree. It is easy to see that trade would allow them to enjoy greater variety: Each could then have a hamburger with french fries.

Although this scene illustrates most simply how everyone can benefit from trade, the gains would be similar if the rancher and the farmer were each capable of producing the other good, but only at great cost. Suppose, for example, that the potato farmer is able to raise cattle and produce meat, but that he is not very good at it. Similarly, suppose that the cattle rancher is able to grow potatoes, but that her land is not very well suited for it. In this case, it is easy to see that the farmer and the rancher can each benefit by specializing in what he or she does best and then trading with the other.

The gains from trade are less obvious, however, when one person is better at producing *every* good. For example, suppose that the rancher is better at raising cattle *and* better at growing potatoes than the farmer. In this case, should the rancher or the farmer choose to remain self-sufficient? Or is there still reason for them to trade with each other? To answer this question, we need to look more closely at the factors that affect such a decision.

PRODUCTION POSSIBILITIES

Suppose that the farmer and the rancher each work 8 hours a day and can devote this time to growing potatoes, raising cattle, or a combination of the two. Table 3-1

	AMOUNT PRODUCED IN 1 HOUR (IN KILOGRAMS):		AMOUNT PRODUCED IN 8 HOURS (IN KILOGRAMS):	
	MEAT	POTATOES	MEAT	POTATOES
FARMER	1	1	8	8
RANCHER	8	2	64	16

Table 3-1

THE PRODUCTION OPPORTUNITIES OF THE FARMER AND THE RANCHER

shows the amount of each good each person can produce in one hour. The farmer can produce 1 kg of meat per hour or 1 kg of potatoes per hour. The rancher, who is more productive in both activities, can produce 8 kg of meat per hour or 2 kg of potatoes per hour.

Panel (a) of Figure 3-1 illustrates the amounts of meat and potatoes that the farmer can produce. If the farmer devotes all 8 hours of his time to potatoes, he produces 8 kg of potatoes and no meat. If he devotes all of his time to meat, he produces 8 kg of meat and no potatoes. If the farmer divides his time equally between the two activities, spending 4 hours on each, he produces 4 kg of potatoes and 4 kg of meat. The figure shows these three possible outcomes and all others in between.

This graph is the farmer's production possibilities frontier. As we discussed in Chapter 2, a production possibilities frontier shows the various mixes of output that an economy can produce. It illustrates one of the *Ten Principles of Economics* in Chapter 1: People face tradeoffs. Here the farmer faces a tradeoff between producing meat and producing potatoes. You may recall that the production possibilities frontier in Chapter 2 was drawn bowed out; in this case, the tradeoff between the two goods depends on the amounts being produced. Here, however, the farmer's technology for producing meat and potatoes (as summarized in Table 3-1) allows him to switch between one good and the other at a constant rate. In this case, the production possibilities frontier is a straight line.

Panel (b) of Figure 3-1 shows the production possibilities frontier for the rancher. If the rancher devotes all 8 hours of her time to potatoes, she produces 16 kg of potatoes and no meat. If she devotes all of her time to meat, she produces 64 kg of meat and no potatoes. If the rancher divides her time equally, spending 4 hours on each activity, she produces 8 kg of potatoes and 32 kg of meat. Once again, the production possibilities frontier shows all the possible outcomes.

If the farmer and the rancher choose to be self-sufficient, rather than to trade with each other, then each consumes exactly what he or she produces. In this case, the production possibilities frontier is also the consumption possibilities frontier. That is, without trade, Figure 3-1 shows the possible combinations of meat and potatoes that the farmer and the rancher can each consume.

Although these production possibilities frontiers are useful in showing the tradeoffs that the farmer and the rancher face, they do not tell us what the farmer and the rancher will actually choose to do. To determine their choices, we need to know the tastes of the farmer and the rancher. Let's suppose they choose the combinations identified by points A and B in Figure 3-1: The farmer produces and consumes 4 kg of potatoes and 4 kg of meat, while the rancher produces and consumes 8 kg of potatoes and 32 kg of meat.

Figure 3-1

THE PRODUCTION POSSIBILITIES FRONTIER. Panel (a) shows the combinations of meat and potatoes that the farmer can produce. Panel (b) shows the combinations of meat and potatoes that the rancher can produce. Both production possibilities frontiers are derived from Table 3-1 and the assumption that the farmer and the rancher each work 8 hours a day.

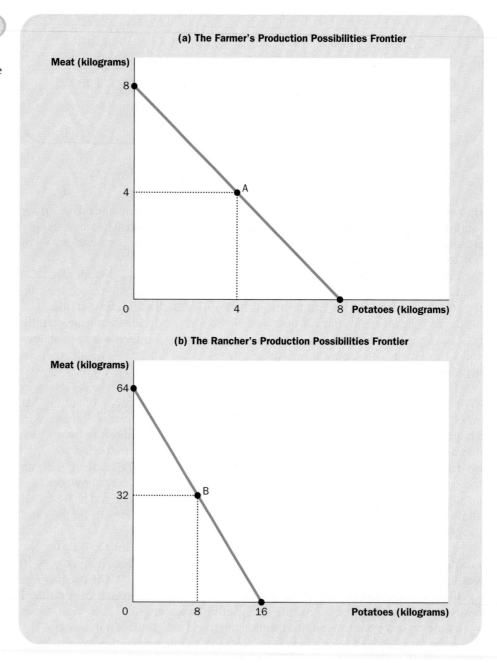

(a) The Farmer's Production Possibilities Frontier

(b) The Rancher's Production Possibilities Frontier

SPECIALIZATION AND TRADE

After several years of eating combination B, the rancher gets an idea and goes to talk to the farmer:

RANCHER: Farmer, my friend, have I got a deal for you! I know how to improve life for both of us. I think you should stop producing meat altogether and devote all your time to growing potatoes. According to my calculations, if you work 8 hours a day growing potatoes, you'll produce 8 kg of potatoes. If you give me 3 of those 8 kg, I'll give you 6 kg of meat in return. In the end, you'll get to eat 5 kg of potatoes and

6 kg of meat every week, instead of the 4 kg of potatoes and 4 kg of meat you now get. If you go along with my plan, you'll have more of *both* foods. [To illustrate her point, the rancher shows the farmer panel (a) of Figure 3-2.]

FARMER: *(sounding skeptical)* That seems like a good deal for me. But I don't understand why you are offering it. If the deal is so good for me, it can't be good for you too.

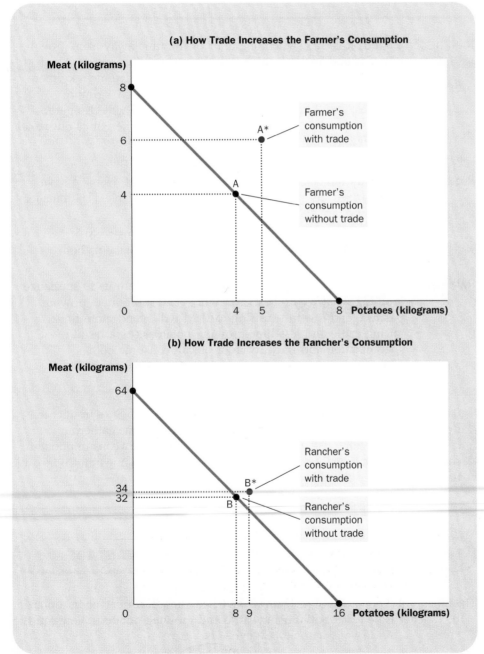

(a) How Trade Increases the Farmer's Consumption

Meat (kilograms)

Farmer's consumption with trade → A*

Farmer's consumption without trade ← A

Potatoes (kilograms)

(b) How Trade Increases the Rancher's Consumption

Meat (kilograms)

Rancher's consumption with trade → B*

Rancher's consumption without trade ← B

Potatoes (kilograms)

Figure 3-2

HOW TRADE EXPANDS THE SET OF CONSUMPTION OPPORTUNITIES. The proposed trade between the farmer and the rancher offers each of them a combination of meat and potatoes that would be impossible in the absence of trade. In panel (a), the farmer gets to consume at point A* rather than point A. In panel (b), the rancher gets to consume at point B* rather than point B. Trade allows each to consume more meat and more potatoes.

	WITHOUT TRADE:	WITH TRADE:			
	PRODUCTION AND CONSUMPTION	PRODUCTION	TRADE	CONSUMPTION	GAINS FROM TRADE
FARMER	4 kg meat 4 kg potatoes	0 kg meat 8 kg potatoes	Gets 6 kg meat for 3 kg potatoes	6 kg meat 5 kg potatoes	2 kg meat 1 kg potatoes
RANCHER	32 kg meat 8 kg potatoes	40 kg meat 6 kg potatoes	Gives 6 kg meat for 3 kg potatoes	34 kg meat 9 kg potatoes	2 kg meat 1 kg potatoes

Table 3-2

THE GAINS FROM TRADE: A SUMMARY

RANCHER: Oh, but it is! If I switch one hour of my time away from growing potatoes and spend it raising cattle instead, I'll produce 2 kg less potatoes and 8 kg more meat. But when you give me 3 kg more potatoes in exchange for 6 kg of meat, I'll have 1 kg more potatoes, and 2 kg more meat. So in the end, I will also get to consume more of both foods than I do now. [She points out panel (b) of Figure 3-2.]

FARMER: I don't know. . . . This sounds too good to be true.

RANCHER: It's really not as complicated as it seems at first. Here—I have summarized my proposal for you in a simple table. [The rancher hands the farmer a copy of Table 3-2.]

FARMER: *(after pausing to study the table)* These calculations seem correct, but I am puzzled. How can this deal make us both better off?

RANCHER: We can both benefit because trade allows each of us to specialize in doing what we do best. You will spend more time growing potatoes and less time raising cattle. I will spend more time raising cattle and less time growing potatoes. As a result of specialization and trade, each of us can consume both more meat and more potatoes without working any more hours.

QUICK QUIZ: Draw an example of a production possibilities frontier for Robinson Crusoe, a shipwrecked sailor who spends his time gathering coconuts and catching fish. Does this frontier limit Crusoe's consumption of coconuts and fish if he lives by himself? Does he face the same limits if he can trade with natives on the island?

THE PRINCIPLE OF COMPARATIVE ADVANTAGE

The rancher's explanation of the gains from trade, though correct, poses a puzzle: If the rancher is better at both raising cattle and growing potatoes, how can the farmer ever specialize in doing what he does best? The farmer doesn't seem to do anything best. To solve this puzzle, we need to look at the principle of *comparative advantage.*

As a first step in developing this principle, consider the following question: In our example, who can produce potatoes at lower cost—the farmer or the rancher? There are two possible answers, and in these two answers lie both the solution to our puzzle and the key to understanding the gains from trade.

ABSOLUTE ADVANTAGE

One way to answer the question about the cost of producing potatoes is to compare the inputs required by the two producers. The rancher needs only 30 minutes to produce a kilogram of potatoes, whereas the farmer needs 1 hour. Based on this information, one might conclude that the rancher has the lower cost of producing potatoes.

Economists use the term **absolute advantage** when comparing the productivity of one person, firm, or nation to that of another. The producer that requires a smaller quantity of inputs to produce a good is said to have an absolute advantage in producing that good. In our example, the rancher has an absolute advantage both in producing potatoes and in producing meat, because she requires less time than the farmer to produce a unit of either good.

absolute advantage
the comparison among producers of a good according to their productivity

OPPORTUNITY COST AND COMPARATIVE ADVANTAGE

There is another way to look at the cost of producing potatoes. Rather than comparing inputs required, we can compare the opportunity costs. Recall from Chapter 1 that the **opportunity cost** of some item is what we give up to get that item. In our example, we assumed that the farmer and the rancher each spend 8 hours a day working. Time spent producing potatoes, therefore, takes away from time available for producing meat. As the rancher and the farmer change their allocations of time between producing the two goods, they move along their production possibility frontiers; in a sense, they are using one good to produce the other. The opportunity cost measures the tradeoff that each of them faces.

opportunity cost
whatever must be given up to obtain some item

Let's first consider the farmer's opportunity cost. Producing 1 kg of potatoes takes him 1 hour of work. When the farmer spends that hour producing potatoes, he spends 1 hour less producing meat. Since he produces 1 kg of meat per hour, he produces 1 kg of meat less for every extra 1 kg of potatoes he produces. Hence, the farmer's opportunity cost of 1 kg of potatoes is 1 kg of meat. The farmer's production possibilities frontier reflects this opportunity cost. The downward-sloping production possibilities frontier in panel (a) of Figure 3-1 has a slope ("rise over run") equal to 1.

Now consider the rancher's opportunity cost. Every hour she spends producing potatoes instead of meat, she produces 2 kg more potatoes and 8 kg less meat. And so every half-hour she spends producing potatoes, she produces 1 kg more potatoes and 4 kg less meat. Hence, the rancher's opportunity cost of 1 kg of potatoes is 4 kg of meat. The rancher's production possibilities frontier in panel (b) of Figure 3-1 reflects this opportunity cost by having a slope equal to 4.

Table 3-3

THE OPPORTUNITY COST OF
MEAT AND POTATOES

	OPPORTUNITY COST OF 1 KG OF	
	MEAT (IN TERMS OF POTATOES GIVEN UP)	POTATOES (IN TERMS OF MEAT GIVEN UP)
FARMER	1	1
RANCHER	1/4	4

comparative advantage

the comparison among producers of a good according to their opportunity cost

Table 3-3 shows the opportunity cost of meat and potatoes for the two producers. Notice that the opportunity cost of meat is the inverse of the opportunity cost of potatoes. Because 1 kg of potatoes costs the rancher 4 kg of meat, 1 kg of meat costs the rancher 0.25 kg of potatoes. Similarly, because 1 kg of potatoes costs the farmer 1 kg of meat, 1 kg of meat costs the farmer 1 kg of potatoes.

Economists use the term **comparative advantage** when describing the opportunity cost of two producers. The producer who has the smaller opportunity cost of producing a good is said to have a comparative advantage in producing that good. In our example, the farmer has a lower opportunity cost of producing potatoes than the rancher (1 kg versus 4 kg of meat). The rancher has a lower opportunity cost of producing meat than the farmer (0.25 kg versus 1 kg of potatoes). Thus, the farmer has a comparative advantage in growing potatoes, and the rancher has a comparative advantage in producing meat.

Notice that it would be impossible for the same person to have a comparative advantage in both goods. Because the opportunity cost of one good is the inverse of the opportunity cost of the other, if a person's opportunity cost of one good is relatively high, his or her opportunity cost of the other good must be relatively low. Comparative advantage reflects the relative opportunity cost. Unless two people have exactly the same opportunity cost, one person will have a comparative advantage in one good, and the other person will have a comparative advantage in the other good.

COMPARATIVE ADVANTAGE AND TRADE

Differences in opportunity cost and comparative advantage create the gains from trade. When each person specializes in producing the good for which he or she has a comparative advantage, total production in the economy rises, and this increase in the size of the economic pie can be used to make everyone better off. In other words, as long as two people have different opportunity costs, each can benefit from trade by obtaining a good at a price lower than his or her opportunity cost of that good.

Consider the proposed deal from the viewpoint of the farmer. The farmer gets 6 kg of meat in exchange for 3 kg of potatoes. In other words, the farmer buys each kilogram of meat for a price of 0.5 kg of potatoes. This price of meat is lower than his opportunity cost of meat, which is 1 kg of potatoes. Thus, the farmer benefits from the deal because he gets to buy meat at a good price.

Now consider the deal from the rancher's viewpoint. The rancher buys each kilogram of potatoes for a price of 2 kg of meat. This price of potatoes is lower than her opportunity cost of potatoes, which is 4 kg of meat. Thus, the rancher benefits because she gets to buy potatoes at a good price.

These benefits arise because each person concentrates on the activity for which he or she has the lower opportunity cost: The farmer spends more time growing potatoes, and the rancher spends more time producing meat. As a result, the total production of potatoes and the total production of meat both rise, and the farmer and the rancher share the benefits of this increased production. The moral of the story of the farmer and the rancher should now be clear: *Trade can benefit everyone in society because it allows people to specialize in activities in which they have a comparative advantage.*

QUICK QUIZ: Robinson Crusoe can gather 10 coconuts or catch 1 fish per hour. His friend Friday can gather 30 coconuts or catch 2 fish per hour. What is Crusoe's opportunity cost of catching 1 fish? What is Friday's? Who has an absolute advantage in catching fish? Who has a comparative advantage in catching fish?

APPLICATIONS OF COMPARATIVE ADVANTAGE

The principle of comparative advantage explains interdependence and the gains from trade. Because interdependence is so prevalent in the modern world, the principle of comparative advantage has many applications. Here are two examples, one fanciful and one of great practical importance.

SHOULD JOE SAKIC MOW HIS OWN LAWN?

Joe Sakic is a great athlete. Considered by many the greatest hockey player in the NHL today, he can make plays and shoot better than most other people. Most likely, he is better at other activities too. For example, Sakic can probably mow his lawn faster than anyone else. But just because he *can* mow his lawn fast, does this mean he *should*?

To answer this question, we can use the concepts of opportunity cost and comparative advantage. Let's say that Sakic can mow his lawn in 2 hours. In that same 2 hours, he could film a television commercial for hockey skates and earn $10 000. By contrast, Jennifer, the girl next door, can mow Sakic's lawn in 4 hours. In that same 4 hours, she could work at McDonald's and earn $20.

In this example, Sakic's opportunity cost of mowing the lawn is $10 000, and Jennifer's opportunity cost is $20. Sakic has an absolute advantage in mowing lawns because he can do the work in less time. Yet Jennifer has a comparative advantage in mowing lawns because she has the lower opportunity cost.

The gains from trade in this example are tremendous. Rather than mowing his own lawn, Sakic should make the commercial and hire Jennifer to mow the lawn. As long as he pays her more than $20 and less than $10 000, both of them are better off.

IN THE NEWS
Who Has a Comparative Advantage in Producing Lamb?

A COMMON BARRIER TO FREE TRADE among countries is tariffs, which are taxes on the import of goods from abroad. In the following opinion column, economist Douglas Irwin discusses a recent example of their use.

Lamb Tariffs Fleece U.S. Consumers

BY DOUGLAS A. IRWIN

President Clinton dealt a serious blow to free trade last Wednesday, when he announced that the U.S. would impose stiff import tariffs on lamb from Australia and New Zealand. His decision undercuts American leadership and makes a mockery of the administration's claims that it favours free and fair trade.

U.S. sheep producers have long been dependent on government. For more than half a century, until Congress enacted farm-policy reforms in 1995, they received subsidies for wool. Having lost that handout, saddled with high costs and inefficiencies, and facing domestic competition from chicken, beef, and pork, sheep producers sought to stop foreign competition by filing for import relief.

Almost all U.S. lamb imports come from Australia and New Zealand, major agricultural producers with a crushing comparative advantage. New Zealand has fewer than 4 million people but as many as 60 million sheep (compared with about 7 million sheep in the U.S.). New Zealand's farmers have invested substantial resources in new technology and effective marketing, making them among the most efficient producers in the world. New Zealand also eliminated domestic agricultural subsidies in the free-market reforms of the 1950s, and is a free-trading country, on track to eliminate all import tariffs by 2006.

Rather than emulate this example, the American Sheep Industry Association, among others, filed an "escape clause" petition under the Trade Act of 1974, which allows temporary "breathing space" protection to import-competing industries. Under the escape-clause provision, a petitioning industry is required to present an adjustment plan to ensure that it undertakes steps to become competitive in the future. The tariff protection is usually limited and scheduled to be phased out.

The U.S. International Trade Commission determines whether imports are a cause of "serious injury" to the domestic industry and, if so, proposes a remedy, which the president has full discretion to adopt, change, or reject. In February, the ITC did not find that the domestic industry had suffered "serious

SHOULD CANADA TRADE WITH OTHER COUNTRIES?

Just as individuals can benefit from specialization and trade with one another, as the farmer and rancher did, so can populations of people in different countries. Many of the goods that Canadians enjoy are produced abroad, and many of the goods produced in Canada are sold abroad. Goods produced abroad and sold domestically are called **imports**. Goods produced domestically and sold abroad are called **exports**.

To see how countries can benefit from trade, suppose there are two countries, Canada and Japan, and two goods, food and cars. Imagine that the two countries produce cars equally well: A Canadian worker and a Japanese worker can each produce 1 car per month. By contrast, because Canada has more and better land, it is better at producing food: A Canadian worker can produce 2 tonnes of food per month, whereas a Japanese worker can produce only 1 tonne of food per month.

The principle of comparative advantage states that each good should be produced by the country that has the smaller opportunity cost of producing

imports
goods and services that are produced abroad and sold domestically

exports
goods and services that are produced domestically and sold abroad

injury," but rather adopted the weaker ruling that imports were "a substantial cause of threat of serious injury." The ITC did not propose to roll back imports, only to impose a 20 percent tariff (declining over four years) on imports above last year's levels.

The administration at first appeared to be considering less restrictive measures. Australia and New Zealand even offered financial assistance to the U.S. producers, and the administration delayed any announcement and appeared to be working toward a compromise. But these hopes were completely dashed with the shocking final decision, in which the administration capitulated to the demands of the sheep industry and its advocates in Congress.

The congressional charge was led by Sen. Max Baucus (D., Mont.), a member of the Agriculture Committee whose sister, a sheep producer, had appeared before the ITC to press for higher tariffs. The administration opted for . . . [the following:] On top of existing tariffs, the president imposed a 9 percent tariff on *all* imports in the first year (declining to 6 percent and then 3 percent in years two and three), and a whopping 40 percent tariff on imports above last year's levels (dropping to 32 percent and 24 percent). . . .

The American Sheep Industry Association's president happily announced that the move will "bring some stability to the market." Whenever producers speak of bringing stability to the market, you know that consumers are getting fleeced.

The lamb decision, while little noticed at home, has been closely followed abroad. The decision undercuts the administration's free-trade rhetoric and harms its efforts to get other countries to open up their markets. Some import relief had been expected, but not so clearly protectionist as what finally materialized. The extreme decision has outraged farmers in Australia and New Zealand, and officials there have vowed to take the U.S. to a WTO dispute settlement panel.

The administration's timing could not have been worse. The decision came right after an Asia Pacific Economic Cooperation summit reaffirmed its commitment to reduce trade barriers, and a few months before the World Trade Organization's November meeting in Seattle, where the WTO is to launch a new round of multilateral trade negotiations. A principal U.S. objective at the summit is the reduction of agricultural protection in Europe and elsewhere.

In 1947, facing an election the next year, President Truman courageously resisted special interest pressure and vetoed a bill to impose import quotas on wool, which would have jeopardized the first postwar multilateral trade negotiations due to start later that year. In contrast, Mr. Clinton, though a lame duck, caved in to political pressure. If the U.S., whose booming economy is the envy of the world, cannot resist protectionism, how can it expect other countries to do so?

SOURCE: *The Wall Street Journal*, July 12, 1999, p. A28.

that good. Because the opportunity cost of a car is 2 tonnes of food in Canada but only 1 tonne of food in Japan, Japan has a comparative advantage in producing cars. Japan should produce more cars than it wants for its own use and export some of them to Canada. Similarly, because the opportunity cost of a tonne of food is 1 car in Japan but only 1/2 car in Canada, Canada has a comparative advantage in producing food. Canada should produce more food than it wants to consume and export some of it to Japan. Through specialization and trade, both countries can have more food and more cars.

In reality, of course, the issues involved in trade among nations are more complex than this example suggests, as we will see in Chapter 9. Most important among these issues is that each country has many citizens with different interests. International trade can make some individuals worse off, even as it makes the country as a whole better off. When Canada exports food and imports cars, the impact on a Canadian farmer is not the same as the impact on a Canadian auto worker. Yet, contrary to the opinions sometimes voiced by politicians and political commentators, international trade is not like war, in which some countries win and others lose. Trade allows all countries to achieve greater prosperity.

FYI

The Legacy of Adam Smith and David Ricardo

Economists have long understood the principle of comparative advantage. Here is how the great economist Adam Smith put the argument:

It is a maxim of every prudent master of a family, never to attempt to make at home what it will cost him more to make than to buy. The tailor does not attempt to make his own shoes, but buys them of the shoemaker. The shoemaker does not attempt to make his own clothes but employs a tailor. The farmer attempts to make neither the one nor the other, but employs those different artificers. All of them find it for their interest to employ their whole industry in a way in which they have some advantage over their neighbours, and to purchase with a part of its produce, or what is the same thing, with the price of part of it, whatever else they have occasion for.

This quotation is from Smith's 1776 book, *An Inquiry into the Nature and Causes of the Wealth of Nations,* which was

a landmark in the analysis of trade and economic interdependence.

Smith's book inspired David Ricardo, a millionaire stockbroker, to become an economist. In his 1817 book, *Principles of Political Economy and Taxation,* Ricardo developed the principle of comparative advantage as we know it today. His defence of free trade was not a mere academic exercise. Ricardo put his economic beliefs to work as a member of the British Parliament, where he opposed the Corn Laws, which restricted the import of grain.

DAVID RICARDO

The conclusions of Adam Smith and David Ricardo on the gains from trade have held up well over time. Although economists often disagree on questions of policy, they are united in their support of free trade. Moreover, the central argument for free trade has not changed much in the past two centuries. Even though the field of economics has broadened its scope and refined its theories since the time of Smith and Ricardo, economists' opposition to trade restrictions is still based largely on the principle of comparative advantage.

QUICK QUIZ: Suppose that the world's fastest typist happens to be trained in brain surgery. Should he do his own typing or hire a secretary? Explain.

CONCLUSION

The principle of comparative advantage shows that trade can make everyone better off. You should now understand more fully the benefits of living in an interdependent economy. But having seen why interdependence is desirable, you might naturally ask how it is possible. How do free societies coordinate the diverse activities of all the people involved in their economies? What ensures that goods and services will get from those who should be producing them to those who should be consuming them?

In a world with only two people, such as the rancher and the farmer, the answer is simple: These two people can directly bargain and allocate resources between themselves. In the real world with billions of people, the answer is less obvious. We take up this issue in the next chapter, where we see that free societies allocate resources through the market forces of supply and demand.

Summary

◆ Each person consumes goods and services produced by many other people both in our country and around the world. Interdependence and trade are desirable because they allow everyone to enjoy a greater quantity and variety of goods and services.

◆ There are two ways to compare the ability of two people in producing a good. The person who can produce the good with the smaller quantity of inputs is said to have an *absolute advantage* in producing the good. The person who has the smaller opportunity cost of producing the good is said to have a *comparative advantage*. The gains

from trade are based on comparative advantage, not absolute advantage.

◆ Trade makes everyone better off because it allows people to specialize in those activities in which they have a comparative advantage.

◆ The principle of comparative advantage applies to countries as well as to people. Economists use the principle of comparative advantage to advocate free trade among countries.

Key Concepts

absolute advantage, p. 53
opportunity cost, p. 53

comparative advantage, p. 54
imports, p. 56

exports, p. 56

Questions for Review

1. Explain how absolute advantage and comparative advantage differ.

2. Give an example in which one person has an absolute advantage in doing something but another person has a comparative advantage.

3. Is absolute advantage or comparative advantage more important for trade? Explain your reasoning, using the example in your answer to Question 2.

4. Will a nation tend to export or import goods for which it has a comparative advantage? Explain.

5. Why do economists oppose policies that restrict trade among nations?

Problems and Applications

1. Consider the farmer and the rancher from our example in this chapter. Explain why the farmer's opportunity cost of producing 1 kg of meat is 1 kg of potatoes. Explain why the rancher's opportunity cost of producing 1 kg of meat is 0.25 kg of potatoes.

2. Maria can read 20 pages of economics in an hour. She can also read 50 pages of sociology in an hour. She spends 5 hours per day studying.
   a. Draw Maria's production possibilities frontier for reading economics and sociology.
   b. What is Maria's opportunity cost of reading 100 pages of sociology?

3. Canadian and Japanese workers can each produce 4 cars a year. A Canadian worker can produce 10 tonnes of grain a year, whereas a Japanese worker can produce 5 tonnes of grain a year. To keep things simple, assume that each country has 100 million workers.
   a. For this situation, construct a table similar to Table 3-1.
   b. Graph the production possibilities frontier of the Canadian and Japanese economies.
   c. For Canada, what is the opportunity cost of a car? Of grain? For Japan, what is the opportunity cost of a car? Of grain? Put this information in a table similar to Table 3-3.

d.   Which country has an absolute advantage in producing cars? In producing grain?

e.   Which country has a comparative advantage in producing cars? In producing grain?

f.   Without trade, half of each country's workers produce cars and half produce grain. What quantities of cars and grain does each country produce?

g.   Starting from a position without trade, give an example in which trade makes each country better off.

4.   Pat and Kris are roommates. They spend most of their time studying (of course), but they leave some time for their favourite activities: making pizza and brewing root beer. Pat takes 4 hours to brew a litre of root beer and 2 hours to make a pizza. Kris takes 6 hours to brew a litre of root beer and 4 hours to make a pizza.

a.   What is each roommate's opportunity cost of making a pizza? Who has the absolute advantage in making pizza? Who has the comparative advantage in making pizza?

b.   If Pat and Kris trade foods with each other, who will trade away pizza in exchange for root beer?

c.   The price of pizza can be expressed in terms of litres of root beer. What is the highest price at which pizza can be traded that would make both roommates better off? What is the lowest price? Explain.

5.   Suppose that there are 10 million workers in Canada, and that each of these workers can produce either 2 cars or 30 tonnes of wheat in a year.

a.   What is the opportunity cost of producing a car in Canada? What is the opportunity cost of producing a tonne of wheat in Canada? Explain the relationship between the opportunity costs of the two goods.

b.   Draw Canada's production possibilities frontier. If Canada chooses to consume 10 million cars, how much wheat can it consume without trade? Label this point on the production possibilities frontier.

c.   Now suppose that the United States offers to buy 10 million cars from Canada in exchange for 20 tonnes of wheat per car. If Canada continues to consume 10 million cars, how much wheat does this deal allow Canada to consume? Label this point on your diagram. Should Canada accept the deal?

6.   Consider a professor who is writing a book. The professor can both write the chapters and gather the needed data faster than anyone else at his university. Still, he pays a student to collect data at the library. Is this sensible? Explain.

7.   England and Scotland both produce scones and sweaters. Suppose that an English worker can produce 50 scones per hour or 1 sweater per hour. Suppose that a Scottish worker can produce 40 scones per hour or 2 sweaters per hour.

a.   Which country has the absolute advantage in the production of each good? Which country has the comparative advantage?

b.   If England and Scotland decide to trade, which commodity will Scotland trade to England? Explain.

c.   If a Scottish worker could produce only 1 sweater per hour, would Scotland still gain from trade? Would England still gain from trade? Explain.

8.   Consider once again the farmer and rancher discussed in the chapter.

a.   Suppose that a technological advance makes the farmer better at producing meat, so that he now can produce 6 kg of meat per hour. What is his opportunity cost of meat and potatoes now? Does this alter his comparative advantage?

b.   Is the deal that the rancher proposes—2 kg of meat for 1 kg of potatoes—still good for the farmer? Explain.

c.   Propose another deal to which the farmer and rancher might now agree.

9.   The following table describes the production possibilities of two cities in the country of Hockeya:

	No. of Blue Sweaters per Worker per Hour	No. of Red Sweaters per Worker per Hour
Toronto	3	3
Montreal	2	1

a.   Without trade, what is the price of red sweaters (in terms of blue sweaters) in Toronto? What is the price in Montreal?

b.   Which city has an absolute advantage in the production of each colour sweaters? Which city has a comparative advantage in the production of each colour sweater?

c.   If the cities trade with each other, which colour sweater will each export?

d.   What is the range of prices at which trade can occur?

10. Suppose that all goods can be produced with fewer worker hours in Germany than in France.
    a. In what sense is the cost of all goods lower in Germany than in France?
    b. In what sense is the cost of some goods lower in France?
    c. If Germany and France traded with each other, would both countries be better off as a result? Explain in the context of your answers to parts (a) and (b).

11. Are the following statements true or false? Explain in each case. *gains from trade are based on the*
    a. "Two countries can achieve gains from trade even if one of the countries has an absolute advantage in the production of all goods." T *concept of comparative advantage*
    b. "Certain very talented people have a comparative advantage in everything they do." F
    c. "If a certain trade is good for one person, it can't be good for the other one." F *not absolut*

11.
b. It is not possible for an individual for an individual to have a comparative advantage in everything

c. False   trade can be final for all trading partner individaivl.

7. 11 C. Yes, both countries will still gain

7.
F
S

Scones   Sweather
give up
5 0 (1) 1/50   1 (50)
4 0 (2) 1/20   2 (20)

PEARS 1.29 lb.

SUPPLY AND DEMAND I:
HOW MARKETS WORK

4

THE MARKET FORCES OF SUPPLY AND DEMAND

When a cold snap hits Florida, the price of orange juice rises in supermarkets throughout Canada. When the weather turns warm in Quebec every summer, the price of hotel rooms in the Caribbean plummets. When a war breaks out in the Middle East, the price of gasoline in Canada rises, and the price of a used Cadillac falls. What do these events have in common? They all show the workings of supply and demand.

Supply and *demand* are the two words that economists use most often—and for good reason. Supply and demand are the forces that make market economies work. They determine the quantity of each good produced and the price at which it is sold. If you want to know how any event or policy will affect the economy, you must think first about how it will affect supply and demand.

This chapter introduces the theory of supply and demand. It considers how buyers and sellers behave and how they interact with one another. It shows how supply and demand determine prices in a market economy and how prices, in turn, allocate the economy's scarce resources.

MARKETS AND COMPETITION

market

a group of buyers and sellers of a particular good or service

The terms *supply* and *demand* refer to the behaviour of people as they interact with one another in markets. A **market** is a group of buyers and sellers of a particular good or service. The buyers as a group determine the demand for the product, and the sellers as a group determine the supply of the product. Before discussing how buyers and sellers behave, let's first consider more fully what we mean by a "market" and the various types of markets we observe in the economy.

COMPETITIVE MARKETS

Markets take many forms. Sometimes markets are highly organized, such as the markets for many agricultural commodities. In these markets, buyers and sellers meet at a specific time and place, where an auctioneer helps set prices and arrange sales.

More often, markets are less organized. For example, consider the market for ice cream in a particular town. Buyers of ice cream do not meet together at any one time. The sellers of ice cream are in different locations and offer somewhat different products. There is no auctioneer calling out the price of ice cream. Each seller posts a price for an ice-cream cone, and each buyer decides how much ice cream to buy at each store.

Even though it is not organized, the group of ice-cream buyers and ice-cream sellers forms a market. Each buyer knows that there are several sellers from which to choose, and each seller is aware that his or her product is similar to that offered by other sellers. The price of ice cream and the quantity of ice cream sold are not determined by any single buyer or seller. Rather, price and quantity are determined by all buyers and sellers as they interact in the marketplace.

competitive market

a market in which there are many buyers and many sellers so that each has a negligible impact on the market price

The market for ice cream, like most markets in the economy, is highly competitive. A **competitive market** is a market in which there are many buyers and many sellers so that each has a negligible impact on the market price. Each seller of ice cream has limited control over the price because other sellers are offering similar products. A seller has little reason to charge less than the going price, and if he or she charges more, buyers will make their purchases elsewhere. Similarly, no single buyer of ice cream can influence the price of ice cream because each buyer purchases only a small amount.

In this chapter we examine how buyers and sellers interact in competitive markets. We see how the forces of supply and demand determine both the quantity of the good sold and its price.

COMPETITION: PERFECT AND OTHERWISE

We assume in this chapter that markets are *perfectly competitive*. Perfectly competitive markets are defined by two primary characteristics: (1) the goods being offered for sale are all the same, and (2) the buyers and sellers are so numerous that no single buyer or seller can influence the market price. Because buyers and sellers in perfectly competitive markets must accept the price the market determines, they are said to be *price takers.*

There are some markets in which the assumption of perfect competition applies perfectly. In the wheat market, for example, there are thousands of farmers who sell wheat and millions of consumers who use wheat and wheat products. Because no single buyer or seller can influence the price of wheat, each takes the price as given.

Not all goods and services, however, are sold in perfectly competitive markets. Some markets have only one seller, and this seller sets the price. Such a seller is called a *monopoly.* Your local cable television company, for instance, may be a monopoly. Residents of your town probably have only one cable company from which to buy this service.

Some markets fall between the extremes of perfect competition and monopoly. One such market, called an *oligopoly,* has a few sellers that do not always compete aggressively. Airline routes are an example. If a route between two cities is serviced by only two or three carriers, the carriers may avoid rigorous competition to keep prices high. Another type of market is *monopolistically competitive;* it contains many sellers, each offering a slightly different product. Because the products are not exactly the same, each seller has some ability to set the price for its own product. An example is the restaurant industry. Many restaurants compete with one another for customers, but every restaurant is different from every other and has its own list of prices.

Despite the diversity of market types we find in the world, we begin by studying perfect competition. Perfectly competitive markets are the easiest to analyze. Moreover, because some degree of competition is present in most markets, many of the lessons that we learn by studying supply and demand under perfect competition apply in more complicated markets as well.

QUICK QUIZ: What is a market? ◆ What does it mean for a market to be competitive?

DEMAND

We begin our study of markets by examining the behaviour of buyers. Here we consider what determines the **quantity demanded** of any good, which is the amount of the good that buyers are willing to purchase. To focus our thinking, let's keep in mind a particular good—ice cream.

quantity demanded
the amount of a good that buyers are willing to purchase

WHAT DETERMINES THE QUANTITY AN INDIVIDUAL DEMANDS?

Consider your own demand for ice cream. How do you decide how much ice cream to buy each month, and what factors affect your decision? Here are some of the answers you might give.

law of demand
the claim that, other things equal, the quantity demanded of a good falls when the price of the good rises

Price   If the price of ice cream rose to $20 per scoop, you would buy less ice cream. You might buy frozen yogurt instead. If the price of ice cream fell to $0.20 per scoop, you would buy more. Because the quantity demanded falls as the price rises and rises as the price falls, we say that the quantity demanded is *negatively related* to the price. This relationship between price and quantity demanded is true for most goods in the economy and, in fact, is so pervasive that economists call it the **law of demand:** Other things equal, when the price of a good rises, the quantity demanded of the good falls.

Income   What would happen to your demand for ice cream if you lost your job one summer? Most likely, it would fall. A lower income means that you have less to spend in total, so you would have to spend less on some—and probably most—goods. If the demand for a good falls when income falls, the good is called a **normal good.**

normal good
a good for which, other things equal, an increase in income leads to an increase in demand

Not all goods are normal goods. If the demand for a good rises when income falls, the good is called an **inferior good.** An example of an inferior good might be bus rides. As your income falls, you are less likely to buy a car or take a cab, and more likely to ride the bus.

inferior good
a good for which, other things equal, an increase in income leads to a decrease in demand

Prices of Related Goods   Suppose that the price of frozen yogurt falls. The law of demand says that you will buy more frozen yogurt. At the same time, you will probably buy less ice cream. Because ice cream and frozen yogurt are both cold, sweet, creamy desserts, they satisfy similar desires. When a fall in the price of one good reduces the demand for another good, the two goods are called **substitutes.** Substitutes are often pairs of goods that are used in place of each other, such as hot dogs and hamburgers, sweaters and sweatshirts, and movie tickets and video rentals.

substitutes
two goods for which an increase in the price of one leads to an increase in the demand for the other

Now suppose that the price of hot fudge falls. According to the law of demand, you will buy more hot fudge. Yet, in this case, you will buy *more* ice cream as well, because ice cream and hot fudge are often used together. When a fall in the price of one good raises the demand for another good, the two goods are called **complements.** Complements are often pairs of goods that are used together, such as gasoline and automobiles, computers and software, and skis and ski lift tickets.

complements
two goods for which an increase in the price of one leads to a decrease in the demand for the other

Tastes   The most obvious determinant of your demand is your tastes. If you like ice cream, you buy more of it. Economists normally do not try to explain people's tastes because tastes are based on historical and psychological forces that are beyond the realm of economics. Economists do, however, examine what happens when tastes change.

Expectations   Your expectations about the future may affect your demand for a good or service today. For example, if you expect to earn a higher income next month, you may be more willing to spend some of your current savings buying ice cream. As another example, if you expect the price of ice cream to fall tomorrow, you may be less willing to buy an ice-cream cone at today's price.

THE DEMAND SCHEDULE AND THE DEMAND CURVE

We have seen that many variables determine the quantity of ice cream a person demands. Imagine that we hold all these variables constant except one—the price. Let's consider how the price affects the quantity of ice cream demanded.

Table 4-1 shows how many ice-cream cones Catherine buys each month at different prices of ice cream. If ice cream is free, Catherine eats 12 cones. At $0.50 per cone, Catherine buys 10 cones. As the price rises further, she buys fewer and fewer cones. When the price reaches $3.00, Catherine doesn't buy any ice cream at all. Table 4-1 is a **demand schedule,** a table that shows the relationship between the price of a good and the quantity demanded. (Economists use the term *schedule* because the table, with its parallel columns of numbers, resembles a train schedule.)

Figure 4-1 graphs the numbers in Table 4-1. By convention, the price of ice cream is on the vertical axis, and the quantity of ice cream demanded is on the

demand schedule
a table that shows the relationship between the price of a good and the quantity demanded

---

Table 4-1

CATHERINE'S DEMAND SCHEDULE. The demand schedule shows the quantity demanded at each price.

PRICE OF ICE-CREAM CONE	QUANTITY OF CONES DEMANDED
$0.00	12
0.50	10
1.00	8
1.50	6
2.00	4
2.50	2
3.00	0

Figure 4-1

CATHERINE'S DEMAND CURVE. This demand curve, which graphs the demand schedule in Table 4-1, shows how the quantity demanded of the good changes as its price varies. Because a lower price increases the quantity demanded, the demand curve slopes downward.

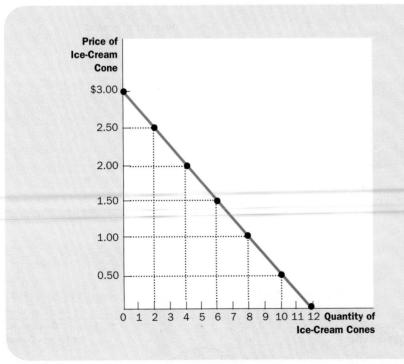

demand curve

a graph of the relationship between the price of a good and the quantity demanded

horizontal axis. The downward-sloping line relating price and quantity demanded is called the **demand curve.** A demand curve may be curved, or it may be a straight line, as in this simple example.

CETERIS PARIBUS

Whenever you see a demand curve, remember that it is drawn holding many things constant. Catherine's demand curve in Figure 4-1 shows what happens to the quantity of ice cream Catherine demands when only the price of ice cream varies. The curve is drawn assuming that Catherine's income, tastes, expectations, and the prices of related products are not changing.

ceteris paribus

a Latin phrase, translated as "other things being equal," used as a reminder that all variables other than the ones being studied are assumed to be constant

Economists use the term *ceteris paribus* to signify that all the relevant variables, except those being studied at that moment, are held constant. The Latin phrase literally means "other things being equal." The demand curve slopes downward because, *ceteris paribus*, lower prices mean a greater quantity demanded.

Although the term *ceteris paribus* refers to a hypothetical situation in which some variables are assumed to be constant, in the real world many things change at the same time. For this reason, when we use the tools of supply and demand to analyze events or policies, it is important to keep in mind what is being held constant and what is not.

MARKET DEMAND VERSUS INDIVIDUAL DEMAND

So far we have talked about an individual's demand for a product. To analyze how markets work, we need to determine the *market demand*, which is the sum of all the individual demands for a particular good or service.

Catherine's Demand

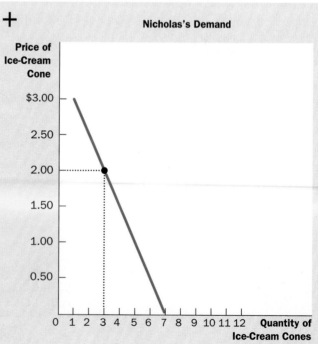

Nicholas's Demand

Table 4-2 shows the demand schedules for ice cream of two individuals—Catherine and Nicholas. At any price, Catherine's demand schedule tells us how much ice cream she buys, and Nicholas's demand schedule tells us how much ice cream he buys. The market demand is the sum of the two individual demands.

Because <u>market demand is derived from individual demands, it depends on all those factors that determine the demand of individual buyers.</u> Thus, market demand depends on buyers' incomes, tastes, and expectations, and the prices of related goods. It also depends on the number of buyers. (If Peter, another consumer of ice cream, were to join Catherine and Nicholas, the quantity demanded in the market would be higher at every price.) The demand schedules in Table 4-2 show what happens to quantity demanded as the price varies while all the other variables that determine quantity demanded are held constant.

Figure 4-2 shows the demand curves that correspond to these demand schedules. Notice that we sum the individual demand curves *horizontally* to obtain the

PRICE OF ICE-CREAM CONE	CATHERINE		NICHOLAS		MARKET
$0.00	12	+	7	=	19
0.50	10		6		16
1.00	8		5		13
1.50	6		4		10
2.00	4		3		7
2.50	2		2		4
3.00	0		1		1

Table 4-2

INDIVIDUAL AND MARKET DEMAND SCHEDULES.   The quantity demanded in a market is the sum of the quantities demanded by all the buyers.

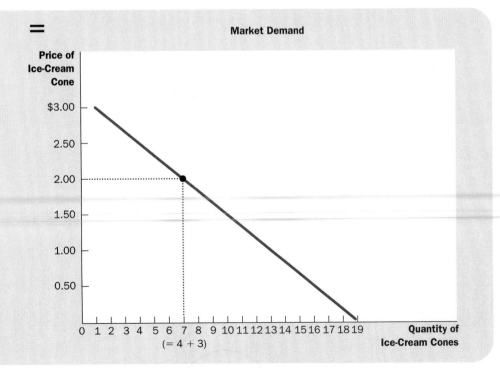

Figure 4-2

MARKET DEMAND AS THE SUM OF INDIVIDUAL DEMANDS.   The market demand curve is found by adding horizontally the individual demand curves. At a price of $2, Catherine demands 4 ice-cream cones and Nicholas demands 3 ice-cream cones. The quantity demanded in the market at this price is 7 cones.

market demand curve. That is, to find the total quantity demanded at any price, we add the individual quantities found on the horizontal axis of the individual demand curves. Because we are interested in analyzing how markets work, we will work most often with the market demand curve. The market demand curve shows how the total quantity demanded of a good varies as the price of the good varies.

SHIFTS IN THE DEMAND CURVE

Suppose that the Canadian Medical Association suddenly announces a new discovery: People who regularly eat ice cream live longer, healthier lives. How does this announcement affect the market for ice cream? The discovery changes people's tastes and raises the demand for ice cream. At any given price, buyers now want to purchase a larger quantity of ice cream, and the demand curve for ice cream shifts to the right.

Whenever any determinant of demand changes, other than the good's price, the demand curve shifts. As Figure 4-3 shows, any change that increases the quantity demanded at every price shifts the demand curve to the right. Similarly, any change that reduces the quantity demanded at every price shifts the demand curve to the left.

Table 4-3 lists the variables that determine the quantity demanded in a market and how a change in the variable affects the demand curve. Notice that price plays a special role in this table. Because price is on the vertical axis when we graph a demand curve, a change in price does not shift the curve but represents a movement along it. By contrast, when there is a change in income, the prices of related goods, tastes, expectations, or the number of buyers, the quantity demanded at each price changes; this is represented by a shift in the demand curve.

Figure 4-3

SHIFTS IN THE DEMAND CURVE. Any change that raises the quantity that buyers wish to purchase at a given price shifts the demand curve to the right. Any change that lowers the quantity that buyers wish to purchase at a given price shifts the demand curve to the left.

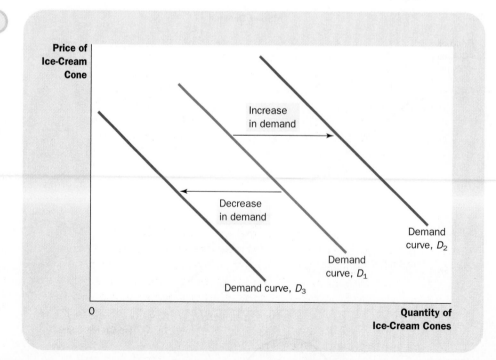

Table 4-3

VARIABLES THAT AFFECT QUANTITY DEMANDED	A CHANGE IN THIS VARIABLE . . .
Price	Represents a movement along the demand curve
Income	Shifts the demand curve
Prices of related goods	Shifts the demand curve
Tastes	Shifts the demand curve
Expectations	Shifts the demand curve
Number of buyers	Shifts the demand curve

THE DETERMINANTS OF QUANTITY DEMANDED.   This table lists the variables that can influence the quantity demanded in a market. Notice the special role that price plays: A change in the price represents a movement along the demand curve, whereas a change in one of the other variables shifts the demand curve.

In summary, *the demand curve shows what happens to the quantity demanded of a good when its price varies, holding constant all other determinants of quantity demanded. When one of these other determinants changes, the demand curve shifts.*

CASE STUDY   TWO WAYS TO REDUCE THE QUANTITY OF SMOKING DEMANDED

Public policymakers often want to reduce the amount that people smoke. There are two ways that policy can attempt to achieve this goal.

One way to reduce smoking is to shift the demand curve for cigarettes and other tobacco products. Public service announcements, mandatory health warnings on cigarette packages, and the prohibition of cigarette advertising on television are all policies aimed at reducing the quantity of cigarettes demanded at any given price. If successful, these policies shift the demand curve for cigarettes to the left, as in panel (a) of Figure 4-4.

Alternatively, policymakers can try to raise the price of cigarettes. If the government taxes the manufacture of cigarettes, for example, cigarette companies pass much of this tax on to consumers in the form of higher prices. A higher price encourages smokers to reduce the numbers of cigarettes they smoke. In this case, the reduced amount of smoking does not represent a shift in the demand curve. Instead, it represents a movement along the same demand curve to a point with a higher price and lower quantity, as in panel (b) of Figure 4-4.

How much does the amount of smoking respond to changes in the price of cigarettes? Economists have attempted to answer this question by studying what happens when the tax on cigarettes changes. They have found that a 10 percent increase in the price causes a 4 percent reduction in the quantity demanded. Teenagers are found to be especially sensitive to the price of cigarettes: A 10 percent increase in the price causes a 12 percent drop in teenage smoking.

A related question is how the price of cigarettes affects the demand for illicit drugs, such as marijuana. Opponents of cigarette taxes often argue that tobacco and marijuana are substitutes, so that high cigarette prices encourage marijuana use. By contrast, many experts on substance abuse view tobacco as a "gateway drug" leading the young to experiment with other harmful substances. Most studies of the data are consistent with this view: They find that lower cigarette prices are associated with greater use of marijuana. In other words, tobacco and marijuana appear to be complements rather than substitutes.

WHAT IS THE BEST WAY TO STOP THIS?

Figure 4-4

SHIFTS IN THE DEMAND CURVE VERSUS MOVEMENTS ALONG THE DEMAND CURVE.   If warnings on cigarette packages convince smokers to smoke less, the demand curve for cigarettes shifts to the left. In panel (a), the demand curve shifts from D_1 to D_2. At a price of $2 per pack, the quantity demanded falls from 20 to 10 cigarettes per day, as reflected by the shift from point A to point B. By contrast, if a tax raises the price of cigarettes, the demand curve does not shift. Instead, we observe a movement to a different point on the demand curve. In panel (b), when the price rises from $2 to $4, the quantity demanded falls from 20 to 12 cigarettes per day, as reflected by the movement from point A to point C.

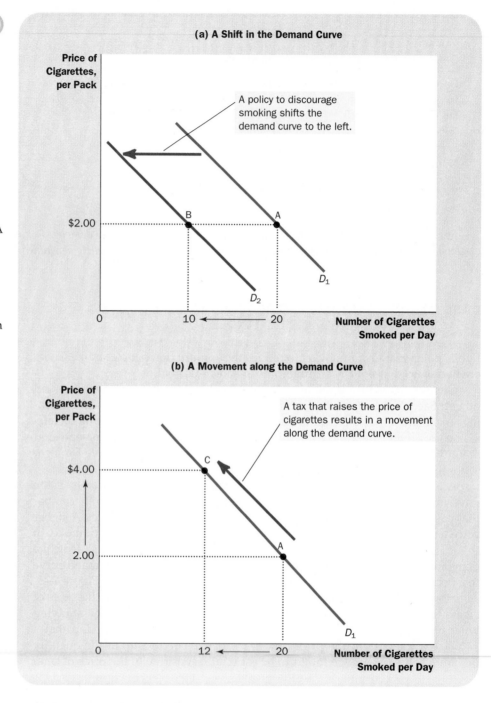

(a) A Shift in the Demand Curve

Price of Cigarettes, per Pack

A policy to discourage smoking shifts the demand curve to the left.

$2.00 ··· B ········· A

D_1

D_2

0   10 ←— 20   Number of Cigarettes Smoked per Day

(b) A Movement along the Demand Curve

Price of Cigarettes, per Pack

A tax that raises the price of cigarettes results in a movement along the demand curve.

$4.00 ··· C

2.00 ····················· A

D_1

0   12 ←— 20   Number of Cigarettes Smoked per Day

QUICK QUIZ: List the determinants of the quantity of pizza you demand. ◆ Make up an example of a demand schedule for pizza, and graph the implied demand curve. ◆ Give an example of something that would shift this demand curve. ◆ Would a change in the price of pizza shift this demand curve?

SUPPLY

We now turn to the other side of the market and examine the behaviour of sellers. The **quantity supplied** of any good or service is the amount that sellers are willing to sell. Once again, to focus our thinking, let's consider the market for ice cream and look at the factors that determine the quantity supplied.

quantity supplied
the amount of a good that sellers are willing to sell

WHAT DETERMINES THE QUANTITY AN INDIVIDUAL SUPPLIES?

Imagine that you are running Student Sweets, a company that produces and sells ice cream. What determines the quantity of ice cream you are willing to produce and offer for sale? Here are some possible answers.

Price   The price of ice cream is one determinant of the quantity supplied. When the price of ice cream is high, selling ice cream is profitable, and so the quantity supplied is large. As a seller of ice cream, you work long hours, buy many ice-cream machines, and hire many workers. By contrast, when the price of ice cream is low, your business is less profitable, and so you will produce less ice cream. At an even lower price, you may choose to go out of business altogether, and your quantity supplied falls to zero.

Because the quantity supplied rises as the price rises and falls as the price falls, we say that the quantity supplied is *positively related* to the price of the good. This relationship between price and quantity supplied is called the **law of supply:** Other things equal, when the price of a good rises, the quantity supplied of the good also rises.

law of supply
the claim that, other things equal, the quantity supplied of a good rises when the price of the good rises

Input Prices   To produce its output of ice cream, Student Sweets uses various inputs: cream, sugar, flavouring, ice-cream machines, the buildings in which the ice cream is made, and the labour of workers to mix the ingredients and operate the machines. When the price of one or more of these inputs rises, producing ice cream is less profitable, and your firm supplies less ice cream. If input prices rise substantially, you might shut down your firm and supply no ice cream at all. Thus, the supply of a good is negatively related to the price of the inputs used to make the good.

Technology   The technology for turning the inputs into ice cream is yet another determinant of supply. The invention of the mechanized ice-cream machine, for example, reduced the amount of labour necessary to make ice cream. By reducing firms' costs, the advance in technology raised the supply of ice cream.

Expectations   The amount of ice cream you supply today may depend on your expectations of the future. For example, if you expect the price of ice cream to rise in the future, you will put some of your current production into storage and supply less to the market today.

THE SUPPLY SCHEDULE AND THE SUPPLY CURVE

supply schedule

a table that shows the relationship between the price of a good and the quantity supplied

supply curve

a graph of the relationship between the price of a good and the quantity supplied

Consider how the quantity supplied varies with the price, holding input prices, technology, and expectations constant. Table 4-4 shows the quantity supplied by Ben, an ice-cream seller, at various prices of ice cream. At a price below $1.00, Ben does not supply any ice cream at all. As the price rises, he supplies a greater and greater quantity. This table is called the **supply schedule.**

Figure 4-5 graphs the relationship between the quantity of ice cream supplied and the price. The curve relating price and quantity supplied is called the **supply curve.** The supply curve slopes upward because, *ceteris paribus,* a higher price means a greater quantity supplied. A supply curve may be curved, or it may be a straight line, as in this simple example.

Table 4-4

BEN'S SUPPLY SCHEDULE.   The supply schedule shows the quantity supplied at each price.

PRICE OF ICE-CREAM CONE	QUANTITY OF CONES SUPPLIED
$0.00	0
0.50	0
1.00	1
1.50	2
2.00	3
2.50	4
3.00	5

Figure 4-5

BEN'S SUPPLY CURVE.   This supply curve, which graphs the supply schedule in Table 4-4, shows how the quantity supplied of the good changes as its price varies. Because a higher price increases the quantity supplied, the supply curve slopes upward.

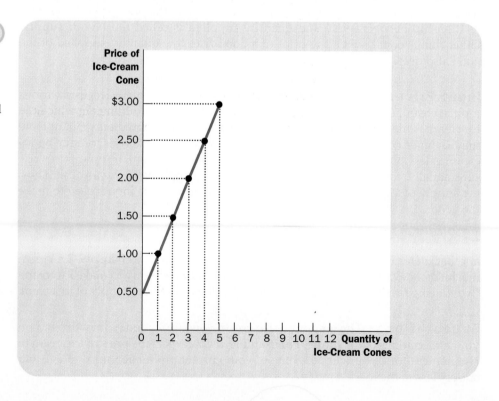

MARKET SUPPLY VERSUS INDIVIDUAL SUPPLY

Just as market demand is the sum of the demands of all buyers, market supply is the sum of the supplies of all sellers. Table 4-5 shows the supply schedules for two ice-cream producers—Ben and Jerry. At any price, Ben's supply schedule tells us the quantity of ice cream Ben supplies, and Jerry's supply schedule tells us the quantity of ice cream Jerry supplies. The market supply is the sum of the two individual supplies.

Market supply depends on all those factors that influence the supply of individual sellers, such as the prices of inputs used to produce the good, the available technology, and expectations. In addition, the supply in a market depends on the number of sellers. (If Ben or Jerry were to retire from the ice-cream business, the supply in the market would fall.) The supply schedules in Table 4-5 show what happens to quantity supplied as the price varies while all the other variables that determine quantity supplied are held constant.

Figure 4-6 shows the supply curves that correspond to the supply schedules in Table 4-5. As with demand curves, we sum the individual supply curves *horizontally* to obtain the market supply curve. That is, to find the total quantity supplied at any price, we add the individual quantities found on the horizontal axis of the individual supply curves. The market supply curve shows how the total quantity supplied varies as the price of the good varies.

SHIFTS IN THE SUPPLY CURVE

Suppose that the price of sugar falls. How does this change affect the supply of ice cream? Because sugar is an input into producing ice cream, the fall in the price of sugar makes selling ice cream more profitable. This raises the supply of ice cream: At any given price, sellers are now willing to produce a larger quantity. Thus, the supply curve for ice cream shifts to the right.

Whenever there is a change in any determinant of supply other than the good's price, the supply curve shifts. As Figure 4-7 shows, any change that raises quantity supplied at every price shifts the supply curve to the right. Similarly, any change that reduces the quantity supplied at every price shifts the supply curve to the left.

Table 4-5

PRICE OF ICE-CREAM CONE	BEN	JERRY	MARKET
$0.00	0 +	0 =	0
0.50	0	0	0
1.00	1	0	1
1.50	2	2	4
2.00	3	4	7
2.50	4	6	10
3.00	5	8	13

INDIVIDUAL AND MARKET SUPPLY SCHEDULES.   The quantity supplied in a market is the sum of the quantities supplied by all the sellers.

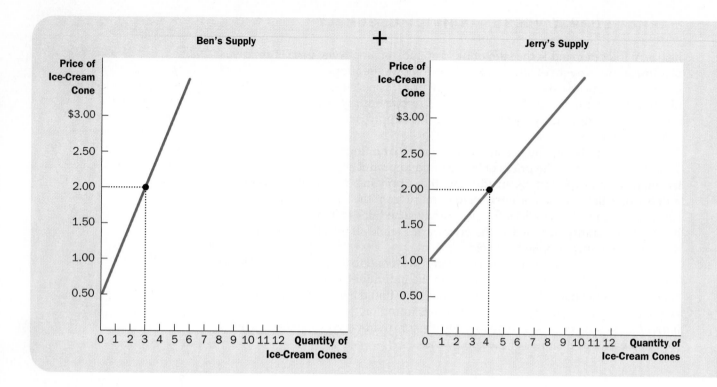

Figure 4-7

SHIFTS IN THE SUPPLY CURVE. Any change that raises the quantity that sellers wish to produce at a given price shifts the supply curve to the right. Any change that lowers the quantity that sellers wish to produce at a given price shifts the supply curve to the left.

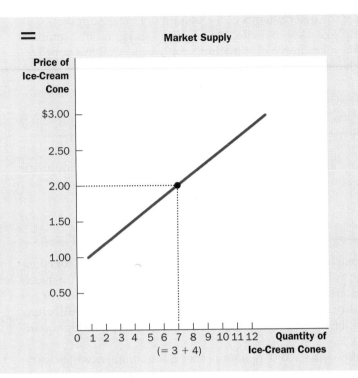

Market Supply

Figure 4-6

MARKET SUPPLY AS THE SUM OF INDIVIDUAL SUPPLIES. The market supply curve is found by adding horizontally the individual supply curves. At a price of $2, Ben supplies 3 ice-cream cones and Jerry supplies 4 ice-cream cones. The quantity supplied in the market at this price is 7 cones.

Table 4-6

THE DETERMINANTS OF QUANTITY SUPPLIED.   This table lists the variables that can influence the quantity supplied in a market. Notice the special role that price plays: A change in the price represents a movement along the supply curve, whereas a change in one of the other variables shifts the supply curve.

VARIABLES THAT AFFECT QUANTITY SUPPLIED	A CHANGE IN THIS VARIABLE . . .
Price	Represents a movement along the supply curve
Input prices	Shifts the supply curve
Technology	Shifts the supply curve
Expectations	Shifts the supply curve
Number of sellers	Shifts the supply curve

Table 4-6 lists the variables that determine the quantity supplied in a market and how a change in the variable affects the supply curve. Once again, price plays a special role in the table. Because price is on the vertical axis when we graph a supply curve, a change in price does not shift the curve but represents a movement along it. By contrast, when there is a change in input prices, technology, expectations, or the number of sellers, the quantity supplied at each price changes; this is represented by a shift in the supply curve.

In summary, *the supply curve shows what happens to the quantity supplied of a good when its price varies, holding constant all other determinants of quantity supplied. When one of these other determinants changes, the supply curve shifts.*

QUICK QUIZ: List the determinants of the quantity of pizza supplied. ◆ Make up an example of a supply schedule for pizza, and graph the implied supply curve. ◆ Give an example of something that would shift this supply curve. ◆ Would a change in the price of pizza shift this supply curve?

SUPPLY AND DEMAND TOGETHER

Having analyzed supply and demand separately, we now combine them to see how they determine the quantity of a good sold in a market and its price.

equilibrium

a situation in which supply and demand have been brought into balance

equilibrium price

the price that balances supply and demand

equilibrium quantity

the quantity supplied and the quantity demanded when the price has adjusted to balance supply and demand

EQUILIBRIUM

Figure 4-8 shows the market supply curve and market demand curve together. Notice that there is one point at which the supply and demand curves intersect; this point is called the market's **equilibrium.** The price at which these two curves cross is called the **equilibrium price,** and the quantity is called the **equilibrium quantity.** Here the equilibrium price is $2.00 per cone, and the equilibrium quantity is 7 ice-cream cones.

The dictionary defines the word *equilibrium* as a situation in which various forces are in balance—and this also describes a market's equilibrium. *At the*

Figure 4-8

THE EQUILIBRIUM OF SUPPLY AND DEMAND.   The equilibrium is found where the supply and demand curves intersect. At the equilibrium price, the quantity supplied equals the quantity demanded. Here the equilibrium price is $2: At this price, 7 ice-cream cones are supplied, and 7 ice-cream cones are demanded.

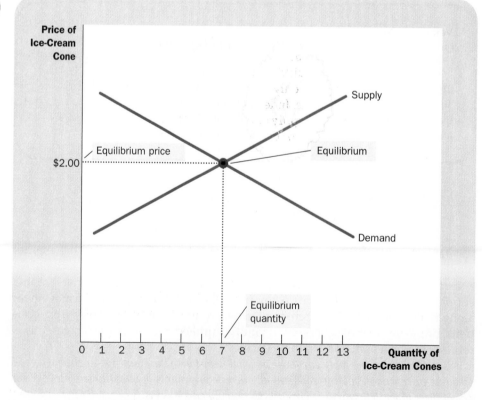

equilibrium price, the quantity of the good that buyers are willing to buy exactly balances the quantity that sellers are willing to sell. The equilibrium price is sometimes called the *market-clearing price* because, at this price, everyone in the market has been satisfied: Buyers have bought all they want to buy, and sellers have sold all they want to sell.

The actions of buyers and sellers naturally move markets toward the equilibrium of supply and demand. To see why, consider what happens when the market price is not equal to the equilibrium price.

Suppose first that the market price is above the equilibrium price, as in panel (a) of Figure 4-9. At a price of $2.50 per cone, the quantity of the good supplied (10 cones) exceeds the quantity demanded (4 cones). There is a **surplus** of the good: Suppliers are unable to sell all they want at the going price. When there is a surplus in the ice-cream market, for instance, sellers of ice cream find their freezers increasingly full of ice cream they would like to sell but cannot. They respond to the surplus by cutting their prices. Prices continue to fall until the market reaches the equilibrium.

Suppose now that the market price is below the equilibrium price, as in panel (b) of Figure 4-9. In this case, the price is $1.50 per cone, and the quantity of the good demanded exceeds the quantity supplied. There is a **shortage** of the good: Demanders are unable to buy all they want at the going price. When a shortage occurs in the ice-cream market, for instance, buyers have to wait in long lines for a chance to buy one of the few cones that are available. With too many buyers chasing too few goods, sellers can respond to the shortage by raising their prices without losing sales. As prices rise, the market once again moves toward the equilibrium.

Thus, the activities of the many buyers and sellers automatically push the market price toward the equilibrium price. Once the market reaches its equilibrium, all buyers and sellers are satisfied, and there is no upward or downward pressure on the price. How quickly equilibrium is reached varies from market to market, depending on how quickly prices adjust. In most free markets, however, surpluses and shortages are only temporary because prices eventually move toward their equilibrium levels. Indeed, this phenomenon is so pervasive that it is sometimes called the **law of supply and demand:** The price of any good adjusts to bring the supply and demand for that good into balance.

surplus
a situation in which quantity supplied is greater than quantity demanded

shortage
a situation in which quantity demanded is greater than quantity supplied

law of supply and demand
the claim that the price of any good adjusts to bring the supply and demand for that good into balance

THREE STEPS TO ANALYZING CHANGES IN EQUILIBRIUM

So far we have seen how supply and demand together determine a market's equilibrium, which in turn determines the price of the good and the amount of the good that buyers purchase and sellers produce. Of course, the equilibrium price and quantity depend on the position of the supply and demand curves. When some event shifts one of these curves, the equilibrium in the market changes. The analysis of such a change is called *comparative statics* because it involves comparing two static situations—an old and a new equilibrium.

When analyzing how some event affects a market, we proceed in three steps. First, we decide whether the event shifts the supply curve, the demand curve, or in some cases both curves. Second, we decide whether the curve shifts to the right or to the left. Third, we use the supply-and-demand diagram to examine how the

Figure 4-9

MARKETS NOT IN EQUILIBRIUM. In panel (a), there is a surplus. Because the market price of $2.50 is above the equilibrium price, the quantity supplied (10 cones) exceeds the quantity demanded (4 cones). Suppliers try to increase sales by cutting the price of a cone, and this moves the price toward its equilibrium level. In panel (b), there is a shortage. Because the market price of $1.50 is below the equilibrium price, the quantity demanded (10 cones) exceeds the quantity supplied (4 cones). With too many buyers chasing too few goods, suppliers can take advantage of the shortage by raising the price. Hence, in both cases, the price adjustment moves the market toward the equilibrium of supply and demand.

shift affects the equilibrium price and quantity. Table 4-7 summarizes these three steps. To see how this recipe is used, let's consider various events that might affect the market for ice cream.

Example: A Change in Demand   Suppose that one summer the weather is very hot. How does this event affect the market for ice cream? To answer this question, let's follow our three steps.

1. The hot weather affects the demand curve by changing people's taste for ice cream. That is, the weather changes the amount of ice cream that people want to buy at any given price. The supply curve is unchanged because the weather does not directly affect the firms that sell ice cream.

2. Because hot weather makes people want to eat more ice cream, the demand curve shifts to the right. Figure 4-10 shows this increase in demand as the shift in the demand curve from D_1 to D_2. This shift indicates that the quantity of ice cream demanded is higher at every price.

3. As Figure 4-10 shows, the increase in demand raises the equilibrium price from $2.00 to $2.50 and the equilibrium quantity from 7 to 10 cones. In other words, the hot weather increases the price of ice cream and the quantity of ice cream sold.

Shifts in Curves versus Movements along Curves   Notice that when hot weather drives up the price of ice cream, the quantity of ice cream that firms supply rises, even though the supply curve remains the same. In this case, economists say there has been an increase in "quantity supplied" but no change in "supply."

Table 4-7

A THREE-STEP PROGRAM FOR ANALYZING CHANGES IN EQUILIBRIUM

1. Decide whether the event shifts the supply curve or demand curve (or perhaps both).
2. Decide in which direction the curve shifts.
3. Use the supply-and-demand diagram to see how the shift changes the equilibrium.

Figure 4-10

HOW AN INCREASE IN DEMAND AFFECTS THE EQUILIBRIUM. An event that raises quantity demanded at any given price shifts the demand curve to the right. The equilibrium price and the equilibrium quantity both rise. Here, an abnormally hot summer causes buyers to demand more ice cream. The demand curve shifts from D_1 to D_2, which causes the equilibrium price to rise from $2.00 to $2.50 and the equilibrium quantity to rise from 7 to 10 cones.

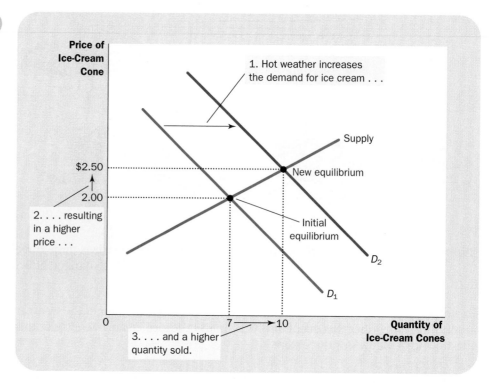

"Supply" refers to the position of the supply curve, whereas the "quantity supplied" refers to the amount suppliers wish to sell. In this example, supply does not change because the weather does not alter firms' desire to sell at any given price. Instead, the hot weather alters consumers' desire to buy at any given price and thereby shifts the demand curve. The increase in demand causes the equilibrium price to rise. When the price rises, the quantity supplied rises. This increase in quantity supplied is represented by the movement along the supply curve.

To summarize, a shift *in* the supply curve is called a "change in supply," and a shift *in* the demand curve is called a "change in demand." A movement *along* a fixed supply curve is called a "change in the quantity supplied," and a movement *along* a fixed demand curve is called a "change in the quantity demanded."

Example: A Change in Supply
Suppose that, during another summer, an earthquake destroys several ice-cream factories. How does this event affect the market for ice cream? Once again, to answer this question, we follow our three steps.

1. The earthquake affects the supply curve. By reducing the number of sellers, the earthquake changes the amount of ice cream that firms produce and sell at any given price. The demand curve is unchanged because the earthquake does not directly change the amount of ice cream households wish to buy.

2. The supply curve shifts to the left because, at every price, the total amount that firms are willing to sell is reduced. Figure 4-11 illustrates this decrease in supply as a shift in the supply curve from S_1 to S_2.

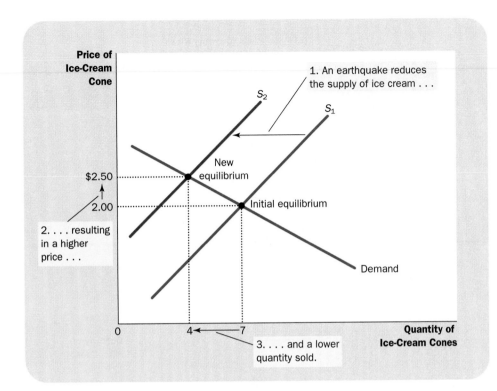

Figure 4-11

How a Decrease in Supply Affects the Equilibrium. An event that reduces quantity supplied at any given price shifts the supply curve to the left. The equilibrium price rises, and the equilibrium quantity falls. Here, an earthquake causes sellers to supply less ice cream. The supply curve shifts from S_1 to S_2, which causes the equilibrium price to rise from $2.00 to $2.50 and the equilibrium quantity to fall from 7 to 4 cones.

3. As Figure 4-11 shows, the shift in the supply curve raises the equilibrium price from $2.00 to $2.50 and lowers the equilibrium quantity from 7 to 4 cones. As a result of the earthquake, the price of ice cream rises, and the quantity of ice cream sold falls.

Example: A Change in Both Supply and Demand   Now suppose that the hot weather and the earthquake occur at the same time. To analyze this combination of events, we again follow our three steps.

1. We determine that both curves must shift. The hot weather affects the demand curve because it alters the amount of ice cream that households want to buy at any given price. At the same time, the earthquake alters the supply curve because it changes the amount of ice cream that firms want to sell at any given price.
2. The curves shift in the same directions that they did in our previous analysis: The demand curve shifts to the right, and the supply curve shifts to the left. Figure 4-12 illustrates these shifts.
3. As Figure 4-12 shows, two possible outcomes might result, depending on the relative size of the demand and supply shifts. In both cases, the equilibrium price rises. In panel (a), where demand increases substantially while supply falls just a little, the equilibrium quantity also rises. By contrast, in panel (b), where supply falls substantially while demand rises just a little, the equilibrium quantity falls. Thus, these events certainly raise the price of ice cream, but their impact on the amount of ice cream sold is ambiguous.

Figure 4-12

A SHIFT IN BOTH SUPPLY AND DEMAND.   Here we observe a simultaneous increase in demand and decrease in supply. Two outcomes are possible. In panel (a), the equilibrium price rises from P_1 to P_2, and the equilibrium quantity rises from Q_1 to Q_2. In panel (b), the equilibrium price again rises from P_1 to P_2, but the equilibrium quantity falls from Q_1 to Q_2.

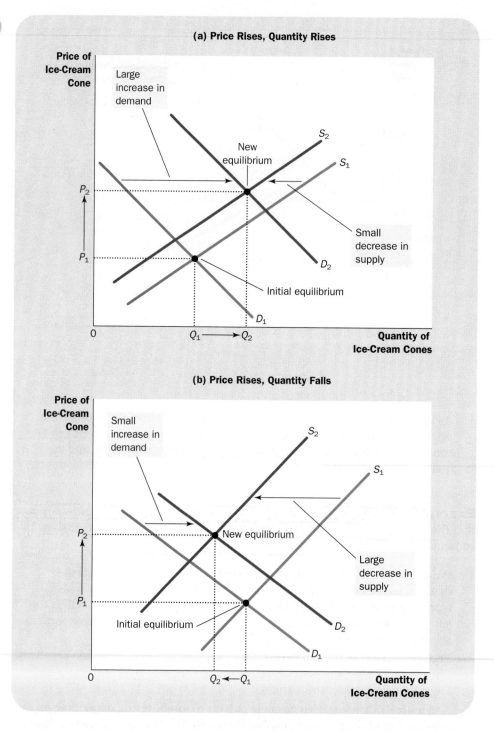

Summary   We have just seen three examples of how to use supply and demand curves to analyze a change in equilibrium. Whenever an event shifts the supply curve, the demand curve, or perhaps both curves, you can use these tools to predict

	NO CHANGE IN SUPPLY	AN INCREASE IN SUPPLY	A DECREASE IN SUPPLY
NO CHANGE IN DEMAND	P same Q same	P down Q up	P up Q down
AN INCREASE IN DEMAND	P up Q up	P ambiguous Q up	P up Q ambiguous
A DECREASE IN DEMAND	P down Q down	P down Q ambiguous	P ambiguous Q down

Table 4-8

WHAT HAPPENS TO PRICE AND QUANTITY WHEN SUPPLY OR DEMAND SHIFTS?

how the event will alter the amount sold in equilibrium and the price at which the good is sold. Table 4-8 shows the predicted outcome for any combination of shifts in the two curves. To make sure you understand how to use the tools of supply and demand, pick a few entries in this table and make sure you can explain to yourself why the table contains the prediction it does.

QUICK QUIZ: Analyze what happens to the market for pizza if the price of tomatoes rises. ◆ Analyze what happens to the market for pizza if the price of hamburgers falls.

CONCLUSION: HOW PRICES ALLOCATE RESOURCES

This chapter has analyzed supply and demand in a single market. Although our discussion has centred around the market for ice cream, the lessons learned here apply in most other markets as well. Whenever you go to a store to buy something, you are contributing to the demand for that item. Whenever you look for a job, you are contributing to the supply of labour services. Because supply and demand are such pervasive economic phenomena, the model of supply and demand is a powerful tool for analysis. We will be using this model repeatedly in the following chapters.

One of the *Ten Principles of Economics* discussed in Chapter 1 is that markets are usually a good way to organize economic activity. Although it is still too early to judge whether market outcomes are good or bad, in this chapter we have begun to see how markets work. In any economic system, scarce resources have to be allocated among competing uses. Market economies harness the forces of supply and demand to serve that end. Supply and demand together determine the prices of the economy's many different goods and services; prices in turn are the signals that guide the allocation of resources.

For example, consider the allocation of beachfront land. Because the amount of this land is limited, not everyone can enjoy the luxury of living by the beach. Who gets this resource? The answer is whoever is willing and able to pay the price.

THE FOLLOWING ARTICLE DESCRIBES DEVELopments in the cranberry market. As you read the article, try to identify shifts in the demand curve. Be careful to distinguish between shifts *in* the curves and movements *along* the curves.

Cranberry Farmers Not Giving Thanks

BY ROBERT MATAS

VANCOUVER—The incredible splendour of Mother Nature's bountiful harvest this Thanksgiving weekend is a bit too much for Canada's cranberry farmers.

Demand for the tart crusty berry has never been higher. Its popularity has soared since a medical study six years ago identified its role in preventing urinary-tract infections in older women.

However, cranberry production has also soared, pushing prices into the dirt. More farms, bigger farms, and better farming methods have produced too much.

This means cranberry farmers are having the worst year in memory.

This summer, for the first time, a production quota was imposed.

Cranberry farmers in B.C., who account for about 15 percent of the North American market, are counting on things to work out in three or four years.

But this Thanksgiving, they're tightening their belts.

"The farm is surviving, that's about all I can say," said Dick Middleton, a cranberry farmer in Pitt Meadows, B.C., about 60 kilometres east of Vancouver.

"I'm living off the expectation I'll be getting a decent price in a few years."

Mark Sweeney, a berry specialist with the B.C. Ministry of Agriculture, said Thanksgiving this year is "a very difficult time for the cranberry industry."

To climb out of this slump, Mr. Sweeney said the farmers will have to persuade people to eat more cranberries. "That's the key," he said.

The industry also needs to expand into new markets, such as Japan and Europe, he added.

Cranberries—which have high vitamin-C content—have been part of the North American diet for hundreds of years.

Indians mashed wild cranberries with deer meat to make pemmican. Cranberry juices were used as a healing agent, to draw poison from arrow wounds as well as to colour rugs, blankets, and clothing. Whalers and mariners ate cranberries to prevent scurvy.

The price of beachfront land adjusts until the quantity of land demanded exactly balances the quantity supplied. Thus, in market economies, prices are the mechanism for rationing scarce resources.

Similarly, prices determine who produces each good and how much is produced. For instance, consider farming. Because we need food to survive, it is crucial that some people work on farms. What determines who is a farmer and who is not? In a free society, there is no government planning agency making this decision and ensuring an adequate supply of food. Instead, the allocation of workers to farms is based on the job decisions of millions of workers. This decentralized system works well because these decisions depend on prices. The prices of food and the wages of farmworkers (the price of their labour) adjust to ensure that enough people choose to be farmers.

If a person had never seen a market economy in action, the whole idea might seem preposterous. Economies are large groups of people engaged in many interdependent activities. What prevents decentralized decision making from degenerating into chaos? What coordinates the actions of the millions of people with their varying abilities and desires? What ensures that what needs to get done does in fact get done? The answer, in a word, is *prices*. If market economies

WORKER WAIST DEEP IN FLOATING CRANBERRIES DURING THE HARVEST.

Nevertheless, cranberries remained mostly a holiday treat, at least until 1994 when Harvard University researchers discovered that women who drank 300 millilitres of cranberry juice every day significantly reduced their odds of getting a urinary-tract infection.

A Rutgers University study four years later pinpointed the compound in cranberries that prevents bacteria from adhering to cells of the urinary tract. Researchers at Israel's Tel Aviv University subsequently discovered the anti-adhesion compound in cranberries also prevents bacteria from forming in the mouth and minimizes the formation of dental plaque, the leading cause of gum disease.

Ever since, health conscious Canadians have gone cranberry crazy. In the past five years, demand has increased by about 25 percent a year, said Ralph May, a director of the B.C. Cranberry Growers Association.

Production increased even faster, partly because farmers were able to extract more berries per acre and partly because they put more acreage into growing berries.

Canada's cranberry crop is worth about $55-million at the farms gate. B.C. has some of the highest-yielding cranberry fields in North America and about 75 percent of the Canadian crop comes from B.C. About 20 percent grows in Quebec and the rest in New Brunswick and Ontario.

Almost all of the B.C. harvest is shipped to the United States for processing into juice and sauce; less than 5 percent of the crop is sold fresh. (By comparison, Quebec processes about 33 percent of its harvest in the province.)

However, across North America, almost five million barrels (each with about 440 000 cranberries), were in storage before farmers even began to harvest this year's crop.

Prices, about $50 (U.S.) per barrel in better times, hit bottom at about $10 a barrel. There are signs the market will soon bounce back, however, and the next crop could command more than $20, Mr. May said.

It's not too difficult to figure out the problem, he said. "There's too many cranberries around."

SOURCE: *The Globe and Mail*, October 7, 2000, p. A5.

are guided by an invisible hand, as Adam Smith famously suggested, then the price system is the baton that the invisible hand uses to conduct the economic orchestra.

"Two dollars."

"—and seventy-five cents."

Summary

- Economists use the model of supply and demand to analyze competitive markets. In a competitive market, there are many buyers and sellers, each of whom has little or no influence on the market price.

- The demand curve shows how the quantity of a good demanded depends on the price. According to the law of demand, as the price of a good falls, the quantity demanded rises. Therefore, the demand curve slopes downward.

- In addition to price, other determinants of the quantity demanded include income, tastes, expectations, and the prices of substitutes and complements. If one of these other determinants changes, the demand curve shifts.

- The supply curve shows how the quantity of a good supplied depends on the price. According to the law of supply, as the price of a good rises, the quantity supplied rises. Therefore, the supply curve slopes upward.

- In addition to price, other determinants of the quantity supplied include input prices, technology, and expectations. If one of these other determinants changes, the supply curve shifts.

- The intersection of the supply and demand curves determines the market equilibrium. At the equilibrium price, the quantity demanded equals the quantity supplied.

- The behaviour of buyers and sellers naturally drives markets toward their equilibrium. When the market price is above the equilibrium price, there is a surplus of the good, which causes the market price to fall. When the market price is below the equilibrium price, there is a shortage, which causes the market price to rise.

- To analyze how any event influences a market, we use the supply-and-demand diagram to examine how the event affects the equilibrium price and quantity. To do this we follow three steps. First, we decide whether the event shifts the supply curve or the demand curve (or both). Second, we decide in which direction the curve shifts. Third, we compare the new equilibrium with the old equilibrium.

- In market economies, prices are the signals that guide economic decisions and thereby allocate scarce resources. For every good in the economy, the price ensures that supply and demand are in balance. The equilibrium price then determines how much of the good buyers choose to purchase and how much sellers choose to produce.

Key Concepts

market, p. 66
competitive market, p. 66
quantity demanded, p. 67
law of demand, p. 68
normal good, p. 68
inferior good, p. 68
substitutes, p. 68

complements, p. 68
demand schedule, p. 69
demand curve, p. 70
ceteris paribus, p. 70
quantity supplied, p. 75
law of supply, p. 75
supply schedule, p. 76

supply curve, p. 76
equilibrium, p. 80
equilibrium price, p. 80
equilibrium quantity, p. 80
surplus, p. 81
shortage, p. 81
law of supply and demand, p. 81

Questions for Review

1. What is a competitive market? Briefly describe the types of markets other than perfectly competitive markets.

2. What determines the quantity of a good that buyers demand?

3. What are the demand schedule and the demand curve, and how are they related? Why does the demand curve slope downward?

4. Does a change in consumers' tastes lead to a movement along the demand curve or a shift in the demand curve? Does a change in price lead to a movement along the demand curve or a shift in the demand curve?

5. Popeye's income declines and, as a result, he buys more spinach. Is spinach an inferior or a normal good? What happens to Popeye's demand curve for spinach?

6. What determines the quantity of a good that sellers supply?

7. What are the supply schedule and the supply curve, and how are they related? Why does the supply curve slope upward?

8. Does a change in producers' technology lead to a movement along the supply curve or a shift in the supply curve? Does a change in price lead to a movement along the supply curve or a shift in the supply curve?

9. Define the equilibrium of a market. Describe the forces that move a market toward its equilibrium.

10. Beer and pizza are complements because they are often enjoyed together. When the price of beer rises, what happens to the supply, demand, quantity supplied, quantity demanded, and price in the market for pizza?

11. Describe the role of prices in market economies.

Problems and Applications

1. Explain each of the following statements using supply-and-demand diagrams:
   a. When a cold snap hits Florida, the price of orange juice rises in supermarkets throughout Canada.
   b. When the weather turns warm in Quebec every summer, the prices of hotel rooms in Caribbean resorts plummet.
   c. When a war breaks out in the Middle East, the price of gasoline rises, while the price of a used Cadillac falls.

2. "An increase in the demand for notebooks raises the quantity of notebooks demanded, but not the quantity supplied." Is this statement true or false? Explain. *False, an ↑ in D result in an ↑ in Qˢ.*

3. Consider the market for minivans. For each of the events listed here, identify which of the determinants of demand or supply are affected. Also indicate whether demand or supply is increased or decreased. Then show the effect on the price and quantity of minivans.
   a. People decide to have more children. *D ↑*
   b. A strike by steelworkers raises steel prices. *↓ S, input prices*
   c. Engineers develop new automated machinery for the production of minivans. *↑S, technology*
   d. The price of station wagons rises. *↑ D*
   e. A stock-market crash lowers people's wealth. *↓ D, ↓ income*

4. During the 1990s, technological advance reduced the cost of computer chips. How do you think this affected the market for computers? For computer software? For typewriters?

5. Using supply-and-demand diagrams, show the effect of the following events on the market for sweatshirts:
   a. A hurricane in South Carolina damages the cotton crop. *↓S ⇒ higher input costs*
   b. The price of leather jackets falls. *↓ D*
   c. All universities require morning calisthenics in appropriate attire. *D ↓*
   d. New knitting machines are invented. *↑S, technology*

6. Suppose that in the year 2005 the number of births is temporarily high. How does this baby boom affect the price of baby-sitting services in 2010 and 2020? (Hint: 5-year-olds need baby-sitters, whereas 15-year-olds can be baby-sitters.)

7. Ketchup is a complement (as well as a condiment) for hot dogs. If the price of hot dogs rises, what happens to the market for ketchup? For tomatoes? For tomato juice? For orange juice?

8. The case study presented in the chapter discussed cigarette taxes as a way to reduce smoking. Now think about the markets for other tobacco products such as cigars and chewing tobacco.
   a. Are these goods substitutes or complements for cigarettes?
   b. Using a supply-and-demand diagram, show what happens in the markets for cigars and chewing tobacco if the tax on cigarettes is increased.
   c. If policymakers wanted to reduce total tobacco consumption, what policies could they combine with the cigarette tax?

9. The market for pizza has the following demand and supply schedules:

PRICE	QUANTITY DEMANDED	QUANTITY SUPPLIED
$4	135	26
5	104	53
6	81	81
7	68	98
8	53	110
9	39	121

Graph the demand and supply curves. What is the equilibrium price and quantity in this market? If the actual price in this market were *above* the equilibrium price, what would drive the market toward the equilibrium? If the actual price in this market were *below* the equilibrium price, what would drive the market toward the equilibrium?

10. Because bagels and cream cheese are often eaten together, they are complements.

    a. We observe that both the equilibrium price of cream cheese and the equilibrium quantity of bagels have risen. What could be responsible for this pattern—a fall in the price of flour or a fall in the price of milk? Illustrate and explain your answer.

    b. Suppose instead that the equilibrium price of cream cheese has risen but the equilibrium quantity of bagels has fallen. What could be responsible for this pattern—a rise in the price of flour or a rise in the price of milk? Illustrate and explain your answer.

11. Suppose that the price of football tickets at your university is determined by market forces. Currently, the demand and supply schedules are as follows:

PRICE	QUANTITY DEMANDED	QUANTITY SUPPLIED
$ 4	10 000	8000
8	8 000	8000
12	6 000	8000
16	4 000	8000
20	2 000	8000

a. Draw the demand and supply curves. What is unusual about this supply curve? Why might this be true?

b. What are the equilibrium price and quantity of tickets?

c. Your university plans to increase total enrollment next year by 5000 students. The additional students will have the following demand schedule:

PRICE	QUANTITY DEMANDED
$ 4	4000
8	3000
12	2000
16	1000
20	0

Now add the old demand schedule and the demand schedule for the new students to calculate the new demand schedule for the entire university. What will be the new equilibrium price and quantity?

12. An article in *The New York Times* described a successful marketing campaign by the French champagne industry. The article noted that "many executives felt giddy about the stratospheric champagne prices. But they also feared that such sharp price increases would cause demand to decline, which would then cause prices to plunge." What mistake are the executives making in their analysis of the situation? Illustrate your answer with a graph.

5

ELASTICITY AND
ITS APPLICATION

**IN THIS CHAPTER
YOU WILL . . .**

*Learn the meaning
of the elasticity of
demand*

*Examine what
determines the
elasticity of demand*

*Learn the meaning
of the elasticity of
supply*

*Examine what
determines the
elasticity of supply*

*Apply the concept of
elasticity in three
very different
markets*

Imagine yourself as a Saskatchewan wheat farmer. Because you earn all your income from selling wheat, you devote much effort to making your land as productive as it can be. You monitor weather and soil conditions, check your fields for pests and disease, and study the latest advances in farm technology. You know that the more wheat you grow, the more you will have to sell after the harvest, and the higher will be your income and your standard of living.

One day the University of Saskatchewan announces a major discovery. Researchers in its agronomy department have devised a new hybrid of wheat that raises the amount farmers can produce from each hectare of land by 20 percent. How should you react to this news? Should you use the new hybrid? Does this discovery make you better off or worse off than you were before? In this chapter we will see that these questions can have surprising answers. The surprise will come from applying the most basic tools of economics—supply and demand—to the market for wheat.

The previous chapter introduced supply and demand. In any competitive market, such as the market for wheat, the upward-sloping supply curve represents the behaviour of sellers, and the downward-sloping demand curve represents the behaviour of buyers. The price of the good adjusts to bring the quantity supplied and quantity demanded of the good into balance. To apply this basic analysis to understand the impact of the agronomists' discovery, we must first develop one more tool: the concept of *elasticity*. Elasticity, a measure of how much buyers and sellers respond to changes in market conditions, allows us to analyze supply and demand with greater precision.

THE ELASTICITY OF DEMAND

When we discussed the determinants of demand in Chapter 4, we noted that buyers usually demand more of a good when its price is lower, when their incomes are higher, when the prices of substitutes for the good are higher, or when the prices of complements of the good are lower. Our discussion of demand was qualitative, not quantitative. That is, we discussed the direction in which the quantity demanded moves, but not the size of the change. To measure how much demand responds to changes in its determinants, economists use the concept of **elasticity.**

elasticity
a measure of the responsiveness of quantity demanded or quantity supplied to one of its determinants

THE PRICE ELASTICITY OF DEMAND AND ITS DETERMINANTS

price elasticity of demand
a measure of how much the quantity demanded of a good responds to a change in the price of that good, computed as the percentage change in quantity demanded divided by the percentage change in price

The law of demand states that a fall in the price of a good raises the quantity demanded. The **price elasticity of demand** measures how much the quantity demanded responds to a change in price. Demand for a good is said to be *elastic* if the quantity demanded responds substantially to changes in the price. Demand is said to be *inelastic* if the quantity demanded responds only slightly to changes in the price.

What determines whether the demand for a good is elastic or inelastic? Because the demand for any good depends on consumer preferences, the price elasticity of demand depends on the many economic, social, and psychological forces that shape individual desires. Based on experience, however, we can state some general rules about what determines the price elasticity of demand.

Necessities versus Luxuries Necessities tend to have inelastic demands, whereas luxuries have elastic demands. When the price of a visit to the dentist rises, people will not dramatically alter the number of times they go to the dentist, although they might go somewhat less often. By contrast, when the price of sailboats rises, the quantity of sailboats demanded falls substantially. The reason is that most people view dentist visits as a necessity and sailboats as a luxury. Of course, whether a good is a necessity or a luxury depends not on the intrinsic properties of the good but on the preferences of the buyer. For an avid sailor with little concern over his teeth, sailboats might be a necessity with inelastic demand and dentist visits a luxury with elastic demand.

Availability of Close Substitutes   Goods with close substitutes tend to have more elastic demand because it is easier for consumers to switch from that good to others. For example, butter and margarine are easily substitutable. A small increase in the price of butter, assuming the price of margarine is held fixed, causes the quantity of butter sold to fall by a large amount. By contrast, because eggs are a food without a close substitute, the demand for eggs is probably less elastic than the demand for butter.

Definition of the Market   The elasticity of demand in any market depends on how we draw the boundaries of the market. Narrowly defined markets tend to have more elastic demand than broadly defined markets, because it is easier to find close substitutes for narrowly defined goods. For example, food, a broad category, has a fairly inelastic demand because there are no good substitutes for food. Ice cream, a more narrow category, has a more elastic demand because it is easy to substitute other desserts for ice cream. Vanilla ice cream, a very narrow category, has a very elastic demand because other flavours of ice cream are almost perfect substitutes for vanilla.

Time Horizon   Goods tend to have more elastic demand over longer time horizons. When the price of gasoline rises, the quantity of gasoline demanded falls only slightly in the first few months. Over time, however, people buy more fuel-efficient cars, switch to public transportation, and move closer to where they work. Within several years, the quantity of gasoline demanded falls substantially.

COMPUTING THE PRICE ELASTICITY OF DEMAND

Now that we have discussed the price elasticity of demand in general terms, let's be more precise about how it is measured. Economists compute the price elasticity of demand as the percentage change in the quantity demanded divided by the percentage change in the price. That is,

$$\text{Price elasticity of demand} = \frac{\text{Percentage change in quantity demanded}}{\text{Percentage change in price}}.$$

For example, suppose that a 10-percent increase in the price of an ice-cream cone causes the amount of ice cream you buy to fall by 20 percent. We calculate your elasticity of demand as

$$\text{Price elasticity of demand} = \frac{20 \text{ percent}}{10 \text{ percent}} = 2.$$

In this example, the elasticity is 2, reflecting that the change in the quantity demanded is proportionately twice as large as the change in the price.

Because the quantity demanded of a good is negatively related to its price, the percentage change in quantity will always have the opposite sign as the percentage change in price. In this example, the percentage change in price is a *positive* 10 percent (reflecting an increase), and the percentage change in quantity demanded is a *negative* 20 percent (reflecting a decrease). For this reason, price elasticities of demand are sometimes reported as negative numbers. In this book we follow the common practice of dropping the minus sign and reporting all price elasticities as positive numbers. (Mathematicians call this the *absolute value*.) With this convention, a larger price elasticity implies a greater responsiveness of quantity demanded to price.

THE MIDPOINT METHOD: A BETTER WAY TO CALCULATE PERCENTAGE CHANGES AND ELASTICITIES

If you try calculating the price elasticity of demand between two points on a demand curve, you will quickly notice an annoying problem: The elasticity from point A to point B seems different from the elasticity from point B to point A. For example, consider these numbers:

Point A: Price = $4   Quantity = 120

Point B: Price = $6   Quantity = 80

Going from point A to point B, the price rises by 50 percent, and the quantity falls by 33 percent, indicating that the price elasticity of demand is 33/50, or 0.66. By contrast, going from point B to point A, the price falls by 33 percent, and the quantity rises by 50 percent, indicating that the price elasticity of demand is 50/33, or 1.5.

One way to avoid this problem is to use the *midpoint method* for calculating elasticities. Rather than computing a percentage change using the standard way (by dividing the change by the initial level), the midpoint method computes a percentage change by dividing the change by the midpoint of the initial and final levels. For instance, $5 is the midpoint of $4 and $6. Therefore, according to the midpoint method, a change from $4 to $6 is considered a 40 percent rise, because $(6 - 4)/5 \times 100 = 40$. Similarly, a change from $6 to $4 is considered a 40 percent fall.

Because the midpoint method gives the same answer regardless of the direction of change, it is often used when calculating the price elasticity of demand between two points. In our example, the midpoint between point A and point B is

Midpoint: Price = $5   Quantity = 100.

According to the midpoint method, when going from point A to point B, the price rises by 40 percent, and the quantity falls by 40 percent. Similarly, when going from point B to point A, the price falls by 40 percent, and the quantity rises by 40 percent. In both directions, the price elasticity of demand equals 1.

We can express the midpoint method with the following formula for the price elasticity of demand between two points, denoted (Q_1, P_1) and (Q_2, P_2):

$$\text{Price elasticity of demand} = \frac{(Q_2 - Q_1)/[(Q_2 + Q_1)/2]}{(P_2 - P_1)/[(P_2 + P_1)/2]}.$$

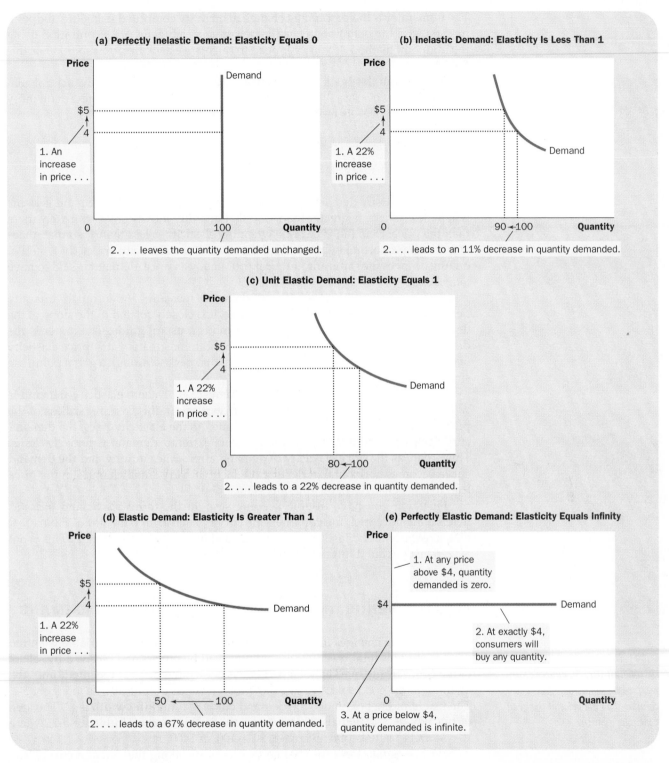

THE PRICE ELASTICITY OF DEMAND. The price elasticity of demand determines whether the demand curve is steep or flat. Note that all percentage changes are calculated using the midpoint method.

Figure 5-1

The numerator is the percentage change in quantity computed using the midpoint method, and the denominator is the percentage change in price computed using the midpoint method. If you ever need to calculate elasticities, you should use this formula.

Throughout this book, however, we only rarely need to perform such calculations. For our purposes, what elasticity represents—the responsiveness of quantity demanded to price—is more important than how it is calculated.

THE VARIETY OF DEMAND CURVES

Economists classify demand curves according to their elasticity. Demand is *elastic* when the elasticity is greater than 1, so that quantity moves proportionately more than the price. Demand is *inelastic* when the elasticity is less than 1, so that quantity moves proportionately less than the price. If the elasticity is exactly 1, so that quantity moves the same amount proportionately as price, demand is said to have *unit elasticity.*

Because the price elasticity of demand measures how much quantity demanded responds to changes in the price, it is closely related to the slope of the demand curve. The following rule of thumb is a useful guide: The flatter is the demand curve that passes through a given point, the greater is the price elasticity of demand. The steeper is the demand curve that passes through a given point, the smaller is the price elasticity of demand.

Figure 5-1 shows five cases. In the extreme case of a zero elasticity, demand is *perfectly inelastic,* and the demand curve is vertical. In this case, regardless of the price, the quantity demanded stays the same. As the elasticity rises, the demand curve gets flatter and flatter. At the opposite extreme, demand is *perfectly elastic.* This occurs as the price elasticity of demand approaches infinity and the demand curve becomes horizontal, reflecting the fact that very small changes in the price lead to huge changes in the quantity demanded.

Finally, if you have trouble keeping straight the terms *elastic* and *inelastic,* here's a memory trick for you: *I*nelastic curves, such as in panel (a) of Figure 5-1, look like the letter *I*. *E*lastic curves, as in panel (e), look like the letter *E*. This is not a deep insight, but it might help on your next exam.

TOTAL REVENUE AND THE PRICE ELASTICITY OF DEMAND

total revenue

the amount paid by buyers and received by sellers of a good, computed as the price of the good times the quantity sold

When studying changes in supply or demand in a market, one variable we often want to study is **total revenue,** the amount paid by buyers and received by sellers of the good. In any market, total revenue is $P \times Q$, the price of the good times the quantity of the good sold. We can show total revenue graphically, as in Figure 5-2. The height of the box under the demand curve is P, and the width is Q. The area of this box, $P \times Q$, equals the total revenue in this market. In Figure 5-2, where $P = \$4$ and $Q = 100$, total revenue is $\$4 \times 100$, or $\$400$.

How does total revenue change as one moves along the demand curve? The answer depends on the price elasticity of demand. If demand is inelastic, as in Figure 5-3, then an increase in the price causes an increase in total revenue. Here an increase in price from $\$1$ to $\$3$ causes the quantity demanded to fall only from 100

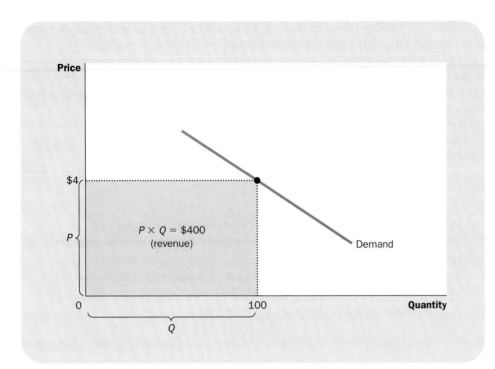

Figure 5-2

TOTAL REVENUE.   The total amount paid by buyers, and received as revenue by sellers, equals the area of the box under the demand curve, $P \times Q$. Here, at a price of \$4, the quantity demanded is 100, and total revenue is \$400.

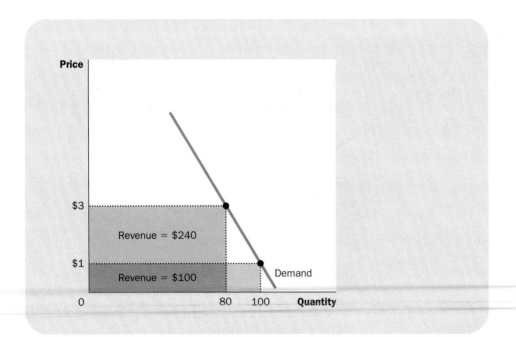

HOW TOTAL REVENUE CHANGES WHEN PRICE CHANGES: INELASTIC DEMAND.   With an inelastic demand curve, an increase in the price leads to a decrease in quantity demanded that is proportionately smaller. Therefore, total revenue (the product of price and quantity) increases. Here, an increase in the price from \$1 to \$3 causes the quantity demanded to fall from 100 to 80, and total revenue rises from \$100 to \$240.

Figure 5-3

to 80, and so total revenue rises from $100 to $240. An increase in price raises $P \times Q$ because the fall in Q is proportionately smaller than the rise in P.

We obtain the opposite result if demand is elastic: An increase in the price causes a decrease in total revenue. In Figure 5-4, for instance, when the price rises from $4 to $5, the quantity demanded falls from 50 to 20, and so total revenue falls from $200 to $100. Because demand is elastic, the reduction in the quantity demanded is so great that it more than offsets the increase in the price. That is, an increase in price reduces $P \times Q$ because the fall in Q is proportionately greater than the rise in P.

Although the examples in these two figures are extreme, they illustrate a general rule:

◆   When a demand curve is inelastic (a price elasticity less than 1), a price increase raises total revenue, and a price decrease reduces total revenue.

◆   When a demand curve is elastic (a price elasticity greater than 1), a price increase reduces total revenue, and a price decrease raises total revenue.

◆   In the special case of unit elastic demand (a price elasticity exactly equal to 1), a change in the price does not affect total revenue.

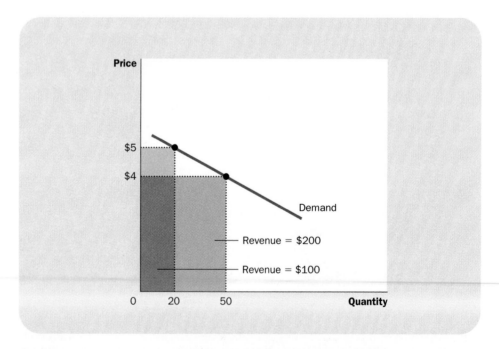

Figure 5-4

HOW TOTAL REVENUE CHANGES WHEN PRICE CHANGES: ELASTIC DEMAND.   With an elastic demand curve, an increase in the price leads to a decrease in quantity demanded that is proportionately larger. Therefore, total revenue (the product of price and quantity) decreases. Here, an increase in the price from $4 to $5 causes the quantity demanded to fall from 50 to 20, so total revenue falls from $200 to $100.

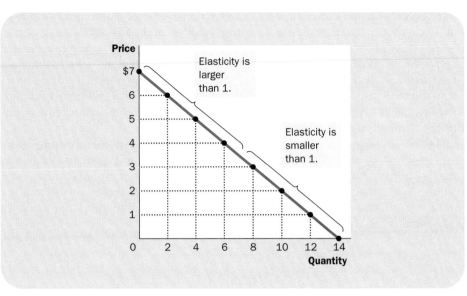

Figure 5-5

A LINEAR DEMAND CURVE.
The slope of a linear demand
curve is constant, but its elasticity
is not.

PRICE	QUANTITY	TOTAL REVENUE (PRICE × QUANTITY)	PERCENTAGE CHANGE IN PRICE	PERCENTAGE CHANGE IN QUANTITY	ELASTICITY	DESCRIPTION
$7	0	$ 0				
6	2	12	15	200	13.0	Elastic
5	4	20	18	67	3.7	Elastic
4	6	24	22	40	1.8	Elastic
3	8	24	29	29	1.0	Unit elastic
2	10	20	40	22	0.6	Inelastic
1	12	12	67	18	0.3	Inelastic
0	14	0	200	15	0.1	Inelastic

COMPUTING THE ELASTICITY OF A LINEAR DEMAND CURVE

Table 5-1

NOTE: Elasticity is calculated here using the midpoint method.

ELASTICITY AND TOTAL REVENUE ALONG A LINEAR DEMAND CURVE

Although some demand curves have an elasticity that is the same along the entire
curve, that is not always the case. An example of a demand curve along which
elasticity changes is a straight line, as shown in Figure 5-5. A linear demand curve
has a constant slope. Recall that slope is defined as "rise over run," which here is
the ratio of the change in price ("rise") to the change in quantity ("run"). This particular demand curve's slope is constant because each $1 increase in price causes
the same 2-unit decrease in the quantity demanded.

Even though the slope of a linear demand curve is constant, the elasticity is not. The reason is that the slope is the ratio of *changes* in the two variables, whereas the elasticity is the ratio of *percentage changes* in the two variables. You can see this most easily by looking at Table 5-1. This table shows the demand schedule for the linear demand curve in Figure 5-5 and calculates the price elasticity of demand using the midpoint method discussed earlier. At points with a low price and high quantity, the demand curve is inelastic. At points with a high price and low quantity, the demand curve is elastic.

Table 5-1 also presents total revenue at each point on the demand curve. These numbers illustrate the relationship between total revenue and elasticity. When the price is $1, for instance, demand is inelastic, and a price increase to $2 raises total revenue. When the price is $5, demand is elastic, and a price increase to $6 reduces total revenue. Between $3 and $4, demand is exactly unit elastic, and total revenue is the same at these two prices.

IF THE PRICE OF ADMISSION WERE HIGHER, HOW MUCH SHORTER WOULD THIS LINE BECOME?

CASE STUDY   PRICING ADMISSION TO A MUSEUM

You are curator of a major art museum. Your director of finance tells you that the museum is running short of funds and suggests that you consider changing the price of admission to increase total revenue. What do you do? Do you raise the price of admission, or do you lower it?

The answer depends on the elasticity of demand. If the demand for visits to the museum is inelastic, then an increase in the price of admission would increase total revenue. But if the demand is elastic, then an increase in price would cause the number of visitors to fall by so much that total revenue would decrease. In this case, you should cut the price. The number of visitors would rise by so much that total revenue would increase.

To estimate the price elasticity of demand, you would need to turn to your statisticians. They might use historical data to study how museum attendance varied from year to year as the admission price changed. Or they might use data on attendance at the various museums around the country to see how the admission price affects attendance. In studying either of these sets of data, the statisticians would need to take account of other factors that affect attendance—weather, population, size of collection, and so forth—to isolate the effect of price. In the end, such data analysis would provide an estimate of the price elasticity of demand, which you could use in deciding how to respond to your financial problem.

OTHER DEMAND ELASTICITIES

income elasticity of demand

a measure of how much the quantity demanded of a good responds to a change in consumers' income, computed as the percentage change in quantity demanded divided by the percentage change in income

In addition to the price elasticity of demand, economists also use other elasticities to describe the behaviour of buyers in a market.

The Income Elasticity of Demand   Economists use the **income elasticity of demand** to measure how the quantity demanded changes as consumer income changes. The income elasticity is the percentage change in quantity demanded divided by the percentage change in income. That is,

IN THE NEWS
On the Road with Elasticity

HOW SHOULD A FIRM THAT OPERATES A private toll road set a price for its service? As the following article makes clear, answering this question requires an understanding of the demand curve and its elasticity.

For Whom the Booth Tolls, Price Really Does Matter

BY STEVEN PEARLSTEIN

All businesses face a similar question: What price for their product will generate the maximum profit?

The answer is not always obvious: Raising the price of something often has the effect of reducing sales as price-sensitive consumers seek alternatives or simply do without. For every product, the extent of that sensitivity is different. The trick is to find the point for each where the ideal tradeoff between profit margin and sales volume is achieved.

Right now, the developers of a new private toll road between Leesburg and Washington-Dulles International Airport are trying to discern the magic point. The group originally projected that it could charge nearly $2 for the 14-mile one-way trip, while attracting 34 000 trips on an average day from overcrowded public roads such as nearby Route 7. But after spending $350 million to build their much heralded "Greenway," they discovered to their dismay that only about a third that number of commuters were willing to pay that much to shave 20 minutes off their daily commute. . . .

It was only when the company, in desperation, lowered the toll to $1 that it came even close to attracting the expected traffic flows.

Although the Greenway still is losing money, it is clearly better off at this new point on the demand curve than it was when it first opened. Average daily revenue today is $22 000, compared with $14 875 when the "special introductory" price was $1.75. And with traffic still light even at rush hour, it is possible that the owners may lower tolls even further in search of higher revenue.

After all, when the price was lowered by 45 percent last spring, it generated a 200 percent increase in volume three months later. If the same ratio applies again, lowering the toll another 25 percent would drive the daily volume up to 38 000 trips, and daily revenue up to nearly $29 000.

The problem, of course, is that the same ratio usually does not apply at every price point, which is why this pricing business is so tricky. . . .

Clifford Winston of the Brookings Institution and John Calfee of the American Enterprise Institute have considered the toll road's dilemma. . . .

Last year, the economists conducted an elaborate market test with 1170 people across the country who were each presented with a series of options in which they were, in effect, asked to make a personal tradeoff between less commuting time and higher tolls.

In the end, they concluded that the people who placed the highest value on reducing their commuting time already had done so by finding public transportation, living closer to their work, or selecting jobs that allowed them to commute at off-peak hours.

Conversely, those who commuted significant distances had a higher tolerance for traffic congestion and were willing to pay only 20 percent of their hourly pay to save an hour of their time.

Overall, the Winston/Calfee findings help explain why the Greenway's original toll and volume projections were too high: By their reckoning, only commuters who earned at least $30 an hour (about $60 000 a year) would be willing to pay $2 to save 20 minutes.

SOURCE: *The Washington Post*, October 24, 1996, p. E1.

$$\text{Income elasticity of demand} = \frac{\text{Percentage change in quantity demanded}}{\text{Percentage change in income}}.$$

As we discussed in Chapter 4, most goods are *normal goods:* Higher income raises quantity demanded. Because quantity demanded and income move in the same direction, normal goods have positive income elasticities. A few goods, such as bus rides, are *inferior goods:* Higher income lowers the quantity demanded. Because quantity demanded and income move in opposite directions, inferior goods have negative income elasticities.

Even among normal goods, income elasticities vary substantially in size. Necessities, such as food and clothing, tend to have small income elasticities because consumers, regardless of how low their incomes, choose to buy some of these goods. Luxuries, such as caviar and furs, tend to have large income elasticities because consumers feel that they can do without these goods altogether if their income is too low.

**cross-price elasticity
of demand**

*a measure of how much the quantity
demanded of one good responds to a
change in the price of another good,
computed as the percentage change
in quantity demanded of the first
good divided by the percentage
change in the price of the
second good*

The Cross-Price Elasticity of Demand Economists use the **cross-price elasticity of demand** to measure how the quantity demanded of one good changes as the price of another good changes. It is calculated as the percentage change in quantity demanded of good 1 divided by the percentage change in the price of good 2. That is,

$$\text{Cross-price elasticity of demand} = \frac{\text{Percentage change in quantity demanded of good 1}}{\text{Percentage change in the price of good 2}}.$$

Whether the cross-price elasticity is a positive or negative number depends on whether the two goods are substitutes or complements. As we discussed in Chapter 4, substitutes are goods that are typically used in place of one another, such as hamburgers and hot dogs. An increase in hot dog prices induces people to grill hamburgers instead. Because the price of hot dogs and the quantity of hamburgers demanded move in the same direction, the cross-price elasticity is positive. Conversely, complements are goods that are typically used together, such as computers and software. In this case, the cross-price elasticity is negative, indicating that an increase in the price of computers reduces the quantity of software demanded.

> **QUICK QUIZ:** Define the *price elasticity of demand.* ◆ Explain the relationship between total revenue and the price elasticity of demand.

THE ELASTICITY OF SUPPLY

When we discussed the determinants of supply in Chapter 4, we noted that sellers of a good increase the quantity supplied when the price of the good rises, when their input prices fall, or when their technology improves. To turn from qualitative to quantitative statements about supply, we once again use the concept of elasticity.

price elasticity of supply

*a measure of how much the quantity
supplied of a good responds to a
change in the price of that good,
computed as the percentage change
in quantity supplied divided by the
percentage change in price*

THE PRICE ELASTICITY OF SUPPLY
AND ITS DETERMINANTS

The law of supply states that higher prices raise the quantity supplied. The **price elasticity of supply** measures how much the quantity supplied responds to changes in the price. Supply of a good is said to be *elastic* if the quantity supplied responds substantially to changes in the price. Supply is said to be *inelastic* if the quantity supplied responds only slightly to changes in the price.

The price elasticity of supply depends on the flexibility of sellers to change the amount of the good they produce. For example, beachfront land has an inelastic supply because it is almost impossible to produce more of it. By contrast, manufactured goods, such as books, cars, and televisions, have elastic supplies because the firms that produce them can run their factories longer in response to a higher price.

In most markets, a key determinant of the price elasticity of supply is the time period being considered. Supply is usually more elastic in the long run than in the short run. Over short periods of time, firms cannot easily change the size of their factories to make more or less of a good. Thus, in the short run, the quantity supplied is not very responsive to the price. By contrast, over longer periods, firms can build new factories or close old ones. In addition, new firms can enter a market, and old firms can shut down. Thus, in the long run, the quantity supplied can respond substantially to the price.

COMPUTING THE PRICE ELASTICITY OF SUPPLY

Now that we have some idea about what the price elasticity of supply is, let's be more precise. Economists compute the price elasticity of supply as the percentage change in the quantity supplied divided by the percentage change in the price. That is,

$$\text{Price elasticity of supply} = \frac{\text{Percentage change in quantity supplied}}{\text{Percentage change in price}}.$$

For example, suppose that an increase in the price of milk from $1.90 to $2.10 a litre raises the amount that dairy farmers produce from 9000 to 11 000 L per month. Using the midpoint method, we calculate the percentage change in price as

$$\text{Percentage change in price} = (2.10 - 1.90)/2.00 \times 100 = 10 \text{ percent.}$$

Similarly, we calculate the percentage change in quantity supplied as

$$\text{Percentage change in quantity supplied} = (11\,000 - 9000)/10\,000 \times 100$$
$$= 20 \text{ percent.}$$

In this case, the price elasticity of supply is

$$\text{Price elasticity of supply} = \frac{20 \text{ percent}}{10 \text{ percent}} = 2.0.$$

In this example, the elasticity of 2 reflects the fact that the quantity supplied moves proportionately twice as much as the price.

THE VARIETY OF SUPPLY CURVES

Because the price elasticity of supply measures the responsiveness of quantity supplied to the price, it is reflected in the appearance of the supply curve. Figure 5-6

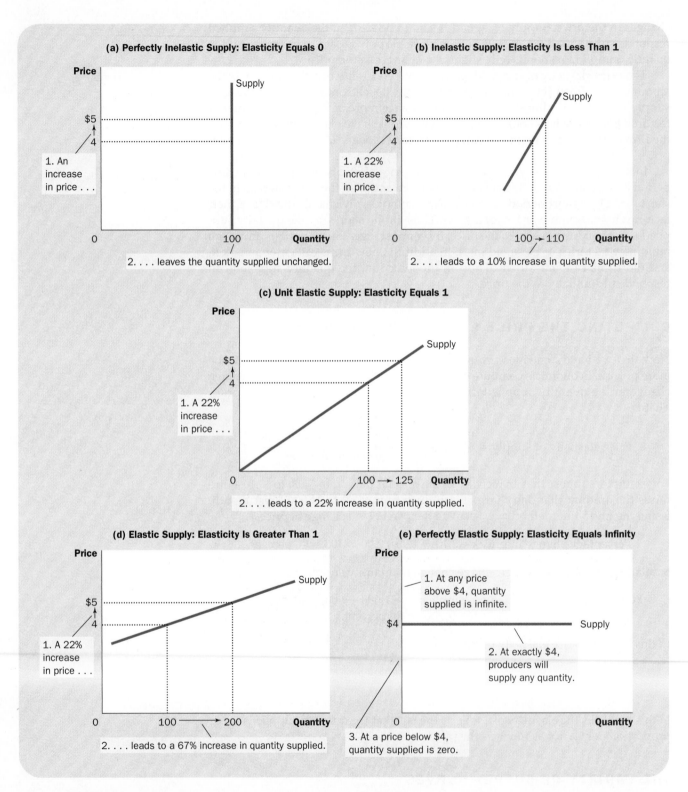

Figure 5-6

THE PRICE ELASTICITY OF SUPPLY.   The price elasticity of supply determines whether the supply curve is steep or flat. Note that all percentage changes are calculated using the midpoint method.

Figure 5-7

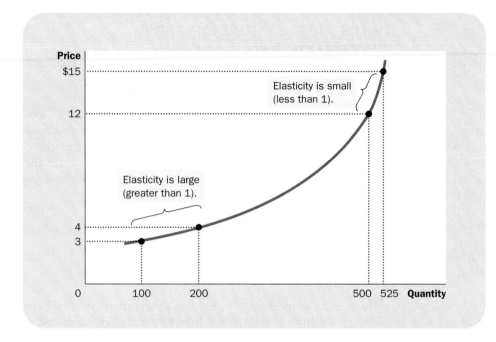

Price

$15 ···

12 ···

Elasticity is small
(less than 1).

Elasticity is large
(greater than 1).

4 ··

3 ········

0   100   200   500 525   **Quantity**

HOW THE PRICE ELASTICITY OF SUPPLY CAN VARY.   Because firms often have a maximum capacity for production, the elasticity of supply may be very high at low levels of quantity supplied and very low at high levels of quantity supplied. Here, an increase in price from $3 to $4 increases the quantity supplied from 100 to 200. Because the increase in quantity supplied of 67 percent is larger than the increase in price of 29 percent, the supply curve is elastic in this range. By contrast, when the price rises from $12 to $15, the quantity supplied rises only from 500 to 525. Because the increase in quantity supplied of 5 percent is smaller than the increase in price of 22 percent, the supply curve is inelastic in this range.

shows five cases. In the extreme case of a zero elasticity, supply is *perfectly inelastic,* and the supply curve is vertical. In this case, the quantity supplied is the same regardless of the price. As the elasticity rises, the supply curve gets flatter, which shows that the quantity supplied responds more to changes in the price. At the opposite extreme, supply is *perfectly elastic.* This occurs as the price elasticity of supply approaches infinity and the supply curve becomes horizontal, meaning that very small changes in the price lead to very large changes in the quantity supplied.

In some markets, the elasticity of supply is not constant but varies over the supply curve. Figure 5-7 shows a typical case for an industry in which firms have factories with a limited capacity for production. For low levels of quantity supplied, the elasticity of supply is high, indicating that firms respond substantially to changes in the price. In this region, firms have capacity for production that is not being used, such as plants and equipment sitting idle for all or part of the day. Small increases in price make it profitable for firms to begin using this idle capacity. As the quantity supplied rises, firms begin to reach capacity. Once capacity is fully used, increasing production further requires the construction of new plants. To induce firms to incur this extra expense, the price must rise substantially, so supply becomes less elastic.

Figure 5-7 presents a numerical example of this phenomenon. When the price rises from $3 to $4 (a 29 percent increase, according to the midpoint method), the quantity supplied rises from 100 to 200 (a 67 percent increase). Because quantity supplied moves proportionately more than the price, the supply curve has elasticity greater than 1. By contrast, when the price rises from $12 to $15 (a 22 percent increase), the quantity supplied rises from 500 to 525 (a 5 percent increase). In this case, quantity supplied moves proportionately less than the price, so the elasticity is less than 1.

QUICK QUIZ: Define the *price elasticity of supply.* ◆ Explain why the the price elasticity of supply might be different in the long run than in the short run.

> ## THREE APPLICATIONS OF SUPPLY, DEMAND, AND ELASTICITY

Can good news for farming be bad news for farmers? Why did the Organization of Petroleum Exporting Countries (OPEC) fail to keep the price of oil high? Does drug interdiction increase or decrease drug-related crime? At first, these questions might seem to have little in common. Yet all three questions are about markets, and all markets are subject to the forces of supply and demand. Here we apply the versatile tools of supply, demand, and elasticity to answer these seemingly complex questions.

CAN GOOD NEWS FOR FARMING BE BAD NEWS FOR FARMERS?

Let's now return to the question posed at the beginning of this chapter: What happens to wheat farmers and the market for wheat when university agronomists discover a new wheat hybrid that is more productive than existing varieties? Recall from Chapter 4 that we answer such questions in three steps. First, we examine whether the supply curve or demand curve shifts. Second, we consider in which direction the curve shifts. Third, we use the supply-and-demand diagram to see how the market equilibrium changes.

In this case, the discovery of the new hybrid affects the supply curve. Because the hybrid increases the amount of wheat that can be produced on each hectare of land, farmers are now willing to supply more wheat at any given price. In other words, the supply curve shifts to the right. The demand curve remains the same because consumers' desire to buy wheat products at any given price is not affected by the introduction of a new hybrid. Figure 5-8 shows an example of such a change. When the supply curve shifts from S_1 to S_2, the quantity of wheat sold increases from 100 to 110, and the price of wheat falls from $3 to $2.

But does this discovery make farmers better off? As a first cut to answering this question, consider what happens to the total revenue received by farmers. Farmers' total revenue is $P \times Q$, the price of the wheat times the quantity sold. The discovery affects farmers in two conflicting ways. The hybrid allows farmers to produce more wheat (Q rises), but now each bushel of wheat sells for less (P falls).

Whether total revenue rises or falls depends on the elasticity of demand. In practice, the demand for basic foodstuffs such as wheat is usually inelastic, because these items are relatively inexpensive and have few good substitutes. When the demand curve is inelastic, as it is in Figure 5-8, a decrease in price causes total revenue to fall. You can see this in the figure: The price of wheat falls substantially, whereas the quantity of wheat sold rises only slightly. Total revenue falls from $300 to $220. Thus, the discovery of the new hybrid lowers the total revenue that farmers receive for the sale of their crops.

If farmers are made worse off by the discovery of this new hybrid, why do they adopt it? The answer to this question goes to the heart of how competitive markets work. Because each farmer is a small part of the market for wheat, he or she takes the price of wheat as given. For any given price of wheat, it is better to

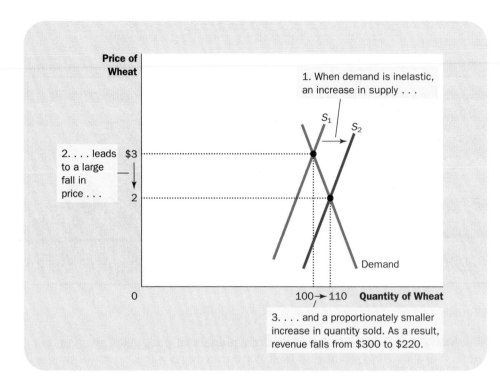

Price of Wheat

2. ... leads to a large fall in price ...

1. When demand is inelastic, an increase in supply ...

S_1

S_2

$3

2

Demand

0   100 → 110   **Quantity of Wheat**

3. . . . and a proportionately smaller increase in quantity sold. As a result, revenue falls from $300 to $220.

Figure 5-8

AN INCREASE IN SUPPLY IN THE MARKET FOR WHEAT.   When an advance in farm technology increases the supply of wheat from S_1 to S_2, the price of wheat falls. Because the demand for wheat is inelastic, the increase in the quantity sold from 100 to 110 is proportionately smaller than the decrease in the price from $3 to $2. As a result, farmers' total revenue falls from $300 ($3 × 100) to $220 ($2 × 110).

use the new hybrid in order to produce and sell more wheat. Yet when all farmers do this, the supply of wheat rises, the price falls, and farmers are worse off.

Although this example may at first seem only hypothetical, in fact it helps to explain a major change in the Canadian economy over the past century. Two hundred years ago, most Canadians lived on farms. Knowledge about farm methods was sufficiently primitive that most of us had to be farmers to produce enough food. Yet, over time, advances in farm technology increased the amount of food that each farmer could produce. This increase in food supply, together with inelastic food demand, caused farm revenues to fall, which in turn encouraged people to leave farming.

A few numbers show the magnitude of this historic change. Two hundred years ago, about 75 percent of the Canadian labour force worked in agriculture. These workers produced enough food to feed their own families and the families of the other 25 percent of the labour force. One hundred years ago, about 50 percent of the Canadian labour force worked on farms; thus, each agricultural worker produced enough to feed his or her own family and one other family. As recently as 50 years ago, about 25 percent of the Canadian labour force worked on farms. In 2001, however, only 3 percent of employed Canadians worked in agriculture, which means that each agricultural worker produced enough food to feed 33 workers and their families (and to export food as well). Since Canadians today eat at least as well as they did in the past, this decrease in the proportion of Canadians working in agriculture represents a tremendous increase in farm productivity.

This analysis of the market for farm products also helps to explain a seeming paradox of public policy: Certain farm programs try to help farmers by restricting the amount of milk and eggs that farmers are allowed to produce. For example, the

Milk Marketing Board sets a quota on the quantity of milk that Canadian dairy farmers are allowed to produce and sell. Any farmer who wants to produce and sell more milk must buy extra quota from another farmer, who in turn must reduce his or her own milk production by an equivalent amount. Why do these programs do this? Their purpose is to reduce the supply of milk and eggs and thereby raise prices. Because demand is inelastic, farmers as a group receive greater total revenue if they supply a smaller amount of milk and eggs to the market. No single farmer would choose to restrict supply on his or her own, since each takes the market price as given. But if all farmers do so together, each of them can be better off.

When analyzing the effects of farm technology or farm policy, it is important to keep in mind that what is good for farmers is not necessarily good for society as a whole. Improvement in farm technology can be bad for farmers, who become increasingly unnecessary, but it is surely good for consumers, who pay less for food. Similarly, a policy aimed at reducing the supply of farm products may raise the incomes of farmers, but it does so at the expense of consumers.

WHY DID OPEC FAIL TO KEEP THE PRICE OF OIL HIGH?

Many of the most disruptive events for the world's economies over the past several decades have originated in the world market for oil. In the 1970s members of the Organization of Petroleum Exporting Countries (OPEC) decided to raise the world price of oil in order to increase their incomes. These countries accomplished this goal by jointly reducing the amount of oil they supplied. From 1973 to 1974, the price of oil (adjusted for overall inflation) rose more than 50 percent. Then, a few years later, OPEC did the same thing again. The price of oil rose 14 percent in 1979, followed by 34 percent in 1980, and another 34 percent in 1981.

Yet OPEC found it difficult to maintain a high price. From 1982 to 1985, the price of oil steadily declined by about 10 percent per year. Dissatisfaction and dis-

(a) The Oil Market in the Short Run

Price of Oil

1. In the short run, when supply and demand are inelastic, a shift in supply . . .

S_2

S_1

P_2

2. . . . leads to a large increase in price.

P_1

Demand

0   Quantity of Oil

(b) The Oil Market in the Long Run

Price of Oil

1. In the long run, when supply and demand are elastic, a shift in supply . . .

S_2

S_1

2. . . . leads to a small increase in price.

P_2

P_1

Demand

0   Quantity of Oil

A REDUCTION IN SUPPLY IN THE WORLD MARKET FOR OIL.   When the supply of oil falls, the response depends on the time horizon. In the short run, supply and demand are relatively inelastic, as in panel (a). Thus, when the supply curve shifts from S_1 to S_2, the price rises substantially. By contrast, in the long run, supply and demand are relatively elastic, as in panel (b). In this case, the same size shift in the supply curve (S_1 to S_2) causes a smaller increase in the price.

Figure 5-9

array soon prevailed among the OPEC countries. In 1986 cooperation among OPEC members completely broke down, and the price of oil plunged 45 percent. In 1990 the price of oil (adjusted for overall inflation) was back to where it began in 1970, and it has stayed at that low level throughout most of the 1990s.

This episode shows how supply and demand can behave differently in the short run and in the long run. In the short run, both the supply and the demand for oil are relatively inelastic. Supply is inelastic because the quantity of known oil reserves and the capacity for oil extraction cannot be changed quickly. Demand is inelastic because buying habits do not respond immediately to changes in price. Many drivers with old gas-guzzling cars, for instance, will just pay the higher price. Thus, as panel (a) of Figure 5-9 shows, the short-run supply and demand curves are steep. When the supply of oil shifts from S_1 to S_2, the price increase from P_1 to P_2 is large.

The situation is very different in the long run. Over long periods of time, producers of oil outside of OPEC respond to high prices by increasing oil exploration and by building new extraction capacity. Consumers respond with greater conservation, for instance by replacing old inefficient cars with newer efficient ones. Thus, as panel (b) of Figure 5-9 shows, the long-run supply and demand curves are more elastic. In the long run, the shift in the supply curve from S_1 to S_2 causes a much smaller increase in the price.

This analysis shows why OPEC succeeded in maintaining a high price of oil only in the short run. When OPEC countries agreed to reduce their production of oil, they shifted the supply curve to the left. Even though each OPEC member sold less oil, the price rose by so much in the short run that OPEC incomes rose. By contrast, in the long run when supply and demand are more elastic, the same reduction in supply, measured by the horizontal shift in the supply curve, caused a smaller increase in the price. Thus, OPEC's coordinated reduction in supply proved less profitable in the long run.

OPEC still exists today, and it has from time to time succeeded at reducing supply and raising prices. But the price of oil (adjusted for overall inflation) has never returned to the peak reached in 1981. The cartel now seems to understand that raising prices is easier in the short run than in the long run.

DOES DRUG INTERDICTION INCREASE OR DECREASE DRUG-RELATED CRIME?

A persistent problem facing our society is the use of illegal drugs, such as heroin, cocaine, and crack. Drug use has several adverse effects. One is that drug dependency can ruin the lives of drug users and their families. Another is that drug addicts often turn to robbery and other violent crimes to obtain the money needed to support their habit. To discourage the use of illegal drugs, the Canadian government devotes millions of dollars each year to reduce the flow of drugs into the country. Let's use the tools of supply and demand to examine this policy of drug interdiction.

Suppose the government increases the number of police and customs officers devoted to the war on drugs. What happens in the market for illegal drugs? As usual, we answer this question in three steps. First, we consider whether the supply curve or demand curve shifts. Second, we consider the direction of the shift. Third, we see how the shift affects the equilibrium price and quantity.

Although the purpose of drug interdiction is to reduce drug use, its direct impact is on the sellers of drugs rather than the buyers. When the government stops some drugs from entering the country and arrests more smugglers, it raises the cost of selling drugs and, therefore, reduces the quantity of drugs supplied at any given price. The demand for drugs—the amount buyers want at any given price—is not changed. As panel (a) of Figure 5-10 shows, interdiction shifts the supply curve to the left from S_1 to S_2 and leaves the demand curve the same. The equilibrium price of drugs rises from P_1 to P_2, and the equilibrium quantity falls from Q_1 to Q_2. The fall in the equilibrium quantity shows that drug interdiction does reduce drug use.

But what about the amount of drug-related crime? To answer this question, consider the total amount that drug users pay for the drugs they buy. Because few drug addicts are likely to break their destructive habits in response to a higher price, it is likely that the demand for drugs is inelastic, as it is drawn in the figure. If demand is inelastic, then an increase in price raises total revenue in the drug market. That is, because drug interdiction raises the price of drugs proportionately more than it reduces drug use, it raises the total amount of money that drug users pay for drugs. Addicts who already had to steal to support their habit would have an even greater need for quick cash. Thus, drug interdiction could increase drug-related crime.

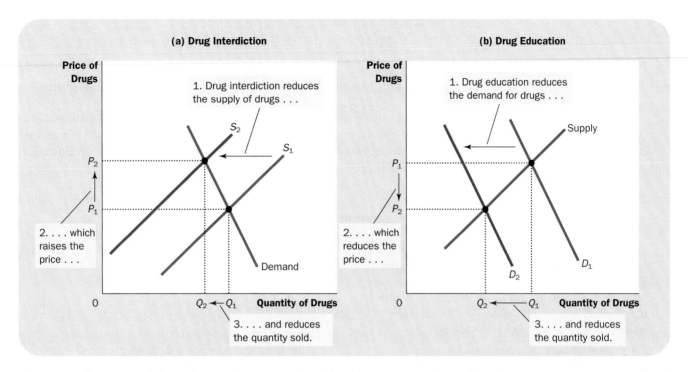

(a) Drug Interdiction

Price of Drugs

1. Drug interdiction reduces the supply of drugs . . .

S_2

S_1

P_2

P_1

2. . . . which raises the price . . .

Demand

0   Q_2 ← Q_1 **Quantity of Drugs**

3. . . . and reduces the quantity sold.

(b) Drug Education

Price of Drugs

1. Drug education reduces the demand for drugs . . .

Supply

P_1

P_2

2. . . . which reduces the price . . .

D_2

D_1

0   Q_2 ← Q_1 **Quantity of Drugs**

3. . . . and reduces the quantity sold.

POLICIES TO REDUCE THE USE OF ILLEGAL DRUGS.   Drug interdiction reduces the supply of drugs from S_1 to S_2, as in panel (a). If the demand for drugs is inelastic, then the total amount paid by drug users rises, even as the amount of drug use falls. By contrast, drug education reduces the demand for drugs from D_1 to D_2, as in panel (b). Because both price and quantity fall, the amount paid by drug users falls.

Figure 5-10

Because of this adverse effect of drug interdiction, some analysts argue for alternative approaches to the drug problem. Rather than trying to reduce the supply of drugs, policymakers might try to reduce the demand by pursuing a policy of drug education. Successful drug education has the effects shown in panel (b) of Figure 5-10. The demand curve shifts to the left from D_1 to D_2. As a result, the equilibrium quantity falls from Q_1 to Q_2, and the equilibrium price falls from P_1 to P_2. Total revenue, which is price times quantity, also falls. Thus, in contrast to drug interdiction, drug education can reduce both drug use and drug-related crime.

Advocates of drug interdiction might argue that the effects of this policy are different in the long run than in the short run, because the elasticity of demand may depend on the time horizon. The demand for drugs is probably inelastic over short periods of time because higher prices do not substantially affect drug use by established addicts. But demand may be more elastic over longer periods of time because higher prices would discourage experimentation with drugs among the young and, over time, lead to fewer drug addicts. In this case, drug interdiction would increase drug-related crime in the short run while decreasing it in the long run.

QUICK QUIZ: How might a drought that destroys half of all farm crops be good for farmers? If such a drought is good for farmers, why don't farmers destroy their own crops in the absence of a drought?

CONCLUSION

According to an old quip, even a parrot can become an economist simply by learning to say "supply and demand." These last two chapters should have convinced you that there is much truth in this statement. The tools of supply and demand allow you to analyze many of the most important events and policies that shape the economy. You are now well on your way to becoming an economist (or, at least, a well-educated parrot).

Summary

- The price elasticity of demand measures how much the quantity demanded responds to changes in the price. Demand tends to be more elastic if the good is a luxury rather than a necessity, if close substitutes are available, if the market is narrowly defined, or if buyers have substantial time to react to a price change.

- The price elasticity of demand is calculated as the percentage change in quantity demanded divided by the percentage change in price. If the elasticity is less than 1, so that quantity demanded moves proportionately less than the price, demand is said to be inelastic. If the elasticity is greater than 1, so that quantity demanded moves proportionately more than the price, demand is said to be elastic.

- Total revenue, the total amount paid for a good, equals the price of the good times the quantity sold. For inelastic demand curves, total revenue rises as price rises. For elastic demand curves, total revenue falls as price rises.

- The income elasticity of demand measures how much the quantity demanded responds to changes in

consumers' income. The cross-price elasticity of demand measures how much the quantity demanded of one good responds to the price of another good.

- The price elasticity of supply measures how much the quantity supplied responds to changes in the price. This elasticity often depends on the time horizon under consideration. In most markets, supply is more elastic in the long run than in the short run.

- The price elasticity of supply is calculated as the percentage change in quantity supplied divided by the percentage change in price. If the elasticity is less than 1, so that quantity supplied moves proportionately less than the price, supply is said to be inelastic. If the elasticity is greater than 1, so that quantity supplied moves proportionately more than the price, supply is said to be elastic.

- The tools of supply and demand can be applied in many different kinds of markets. This chapter uses them to analyze the market for wheat, the market for oil, and the market for illegal drugs.

Key Concepts

elasticity, p. 94
price elasticity of demand, p. 94

total revenue, p. 98
income elasticity of demand, p. 102

cross-price elasticity of demand, p. 104
price elasticity of supply, p. 104

Questions for Review

1. Define the price elasticity of demand and the income elasticity of demand.

2. List and explain some of the determinants of the price elasticity of demand.

3. If the elasticity is greater than 1, is demand elastic or inelastic? If the elasticity equals 0, is demand perfectly elastic or perfectly inelastic?

4. On a supply-and-demand diagram, show equilibrium price, equilibrium quantity, and the total revenue received by producers.

5. If demand is elastic, how will an increase in price change total revenue? Explain.

6. What do we call a good whose income elasticity is less than 0?

7. How is the price elasticity of supply calculated? Explain what this measures.

8. What is the price elasticity of supply of Picasso paintings?

9. Is the price elasticity of supply usually larger in the short run or in the long run? Why?

10. In the 1970s, OPEC caused a dramatic increase in the price of oil. What prevented it from maintaining this high price through the 1980s?

Problems and Applications

1. For each of the following pairs of goods, which good would you expect to have more elastic demand and why?
   a. required textbooks or mystery novels
   b. Beethoven recordings or classical music recordings in general
   c. heating oil during the next six months or heating oil during the next five years
   d. root beer or water

2. Suppose that business travellers and vacationers have the following demand for airline tickets from Toronto to Montreal:

PRICE	QUANTITY DEMANDED (BUSINESS TRAVELLERS)	QUANTITY DEMANDED (VACATIONERS)
$150	2100	1000
200	2000	800
250	1900	600
300	1800	400

   a. As the price of tickets rises from $200 to $250, what is the price elasticity of demand for (i) business travellers and (ii) vacationers? (Use the midpoint method in your calculations.)
   b. Why might vacationers have a different elasticity than business travellers?

3. Suppose that your demand schedule for compact discs is as follows:

PRICE	QUANTITY DEMANDED (INCOME = $10 000)	QUANTITY DEMANDED (INCOME = $12 000)
$ 8	40	50
10	32	45
12	24	30
14	16	20
16	8	12

   a. Use the midpoint method to calculate your price elasticity of demand as the price of compact discs increases from $8 to $10 if (i) your income is $10 000, and (ii) your income is $12 000.
   b. Calculate your income elasticity of demand as your income increases from $10 000 to $12 000 if (i) the price is $12, and (ii) the price is $16.

4. Emily has decided always to spend one-third of her income on clothing.
   a. What is her income elasticity of clothing demand?
   b. What is her price elasticity of clothing demand?
   c. If Emily's tastes change and she decides to spend only one-fourth of her income on clothing, how does her demand curve change? What are her income elasticity and price elasticity now?

5. *The Globe and Mail* (December 16, 1997) reported that milk consumption declined following price increases: "Since the early 1980s, the price of milk in Canada has increased 22 per cent. As prices rose, the demand for milk fell off. Total [consumption] of milk on a per capita basis dropped . . . to 2.62 hectolitres in 1995 from 2.92 hectolitres in 1986."
   a. Use these data to estimate the price elasticity of demand for milk.
   b. According to your estimate, what happens to milk producers' revenue when the price of milk rises?
   c. Why might your estimate of the elasticity be unreliable? (Hint: Notice that *The Globe and Mail* is careless about the distinction between demand and quantity demanded.)

6. Two drivers—Tom and Jerry—each drive up to a gas station. Before looking at the price, each places an order. Tom says, "I'd like 40 L of gas." Jerry says, "I'd like $10 worth of gas." What is each driver's price elasticity of demand?

7. Economists have observed that spending on restaurant meals declines more during economic downturns than does spending on food to be eaten at home. How might the concept of elasticity help to explain this phenomenon?

8. Consider public policy aimed at smoking.
    a. Studies indicate that the price elasticity of demand for cigarettes is about 0.4. If a pack of cigarettes currently costs $4 and the government wants to reduce smoking by 20 percent, by how much should it increase the price?
    b. If the government permanently increases the price of cigarettes, will the policy have a larger effect on smoking one year from now or five years from now?
    c. Studies also find that teenagers have a higher price elasticity than do adults. Why might this be true?

9. Would you expect the price elasticity of *demand* to be larger in the market for all ice cream or the market for vanilla ice cream? Would you expect the price elasticity of *supply* to be larger in the market for all ice cream or the market for vanilla ice cream? Be sure to explain your answers.

10. Pharmaceutical drugs have an inelastic demand, and computers have an elastic demand. Suppose that technological advance doubles the supply of both products (that is, the quantity supplied at each price is twice what it was).
    a. What happens to the equilibrium price and quantity in each market?
    b. Which product experiences a larger change in price?
    c. Which product experiences a larger change in quantity?
    d. What happens to total consumer spending on each product?

11. Beachfront resorts have an inelastic supply, and cars have an elastic supply. Suppose that a rise in population doubles the demand for both products (that is, the quantity demanded at each price is twice what it was).
    a. What happens to the equilibrium price and quantity in each market?
    b. Which product experiences a larger change in price?
    c. Which product experiences a larger change in quantity?
    d. What happens to total consumer spending on each product?

12. Several years ago, flooding along the Red River in Manitoba destroyed thousands of hectares of wheat.
    a. Farmers whose crops were destroyed by the floods were much worse off, but farmers whose crops were not destroyed benefited from the floods. Why?
    b. What information would you need about the market for wheat in order to assess whether farmers as a group were hurt or helped by the floods?

13. Explain why the following might be true: A drought around the world raises the total revenue that farmers receive from the sale of grain, but a drought only in Manitoba reduces the total revenue that Manitoba farmers receive.

14. Because better weather makes farmland more productive, farmland in regions with good weather conditions is more expensive than farmland in regions with bad weather conditions. Over time, however, as advances in technology have made all farmland more productive, the price of farmland (adjusted for overall inflation) has fallen. Use the concept of elasticity to explain why productivity and farmland prices are positively related across space but negatively related over time.

6

SUPPLY, DEMAND, AND GOVERNMENT POLICIES

Economists have two roles. As scientists, they develop and test theories to explain the world around them. As policy advisers, they use their theories to help change the world for the better. The focus of the preceding two chapters has been scientific. We have seen how supply and demand determine the price of a good and the quantity of the good sold. We have also seen how various events shift supply and demand and thereby change the equilibrium price and quantity.

This chapter offers our first look at policy. Here we analyze various types of government policy using only the tools of supply and demand. As you will see, the analysis yields some surprising insights. Policies often have effects that their architects did not intend or anticipate.

We begin by considering policies that directly control prices. For example, rent-control laws dictate a maximum rent that landlords may charge tenants. Minimum-wage laws dictate the lowest wage that firms may pay workers. Price controls are

Examine the effects of government policies that place a ceiling on prices

Examine the effects of government policies that put a floor under prices

Consider how a tax on a good affects the price of the good and the quantity sold

Learn that taxes levied on buyers and taxes levied on sellers are equivalent

See how the burden of a tax is split between buyers and sellers

usually enacted when policymakers believe that the market price of a good or service is unfair to buyers or sellers. Yet, as we will see, these policies can generate inequities of their own.

After our discussion of price controls, we next consider the impact of taxes. Policymakers use taxes both to influence market outcomes and to raise revenue for public purposes. Although the prevalence of taxes in our economy is obvious, their effects are not. For example, when the government levies a tax on the amount that firms pay their workers, do the firms or the workers bear the burden of the tax? The answer is not at all clear—until we apply the powerful tools of supply and demand.

CONTROLS ON PRICES

To see how price controls affect market outcomes, let's look once again at the market for ice cream. As we saw in Chapter 4, if ice cream is sold in a competitive market free of government regulation, the price of ice cream adjusts to balance supply and demand: At the equilibrium price, the quantity of ice cream that buyers want to buy exactly equals the quantity that sellers want to sell. To be concrete, suppose the equilibrium price is $3 per cone.

Not everyone may be happy with the outcome of this free-market process. Let's say the Canadian Association of Ice Cream Eaters complains that the $3 price is too high for everyone to enjoy a cone a day (their recommended diet). Meanwhile, the Canadian Organization of Ice Cream Makers complains that the $3 price—the result of "cutthroat competition"—is depressing the incomes of its members. Each of these groups lobbies the government to pass laws that alter the market outcome by directly controlling prices.

Of course, because buyers of any good always want a lower price while sellers want a higher price, the interests of the two groups conflict. If the Ice Cream Eaters are successful in their lobbying, the government imposes a legal maximum on the price at which ice cream can be sold. Because the price is not allowed to rise above this level, the legislated maximum is called a **price ceiling.** By contrast, if the Ice Cream Makers are successful, the government imposes a legal minimum on the price. Because the price cannot fall below this level, the legislated minimum is called a **price floor.** Let us consider the effects of these policies in turn.

price ceiling

a legal maximum on the price at which a good can be sold

price floor

a legal minimum on the price at which a good can be sold

HOW PRICE CEILINGS AFFECT MARKET OUTCOMES

When the government, moved by the complaints of the Ice Cream Eaters, imposes a price ceiling on the market for ice cream, two outcomes are possible. In panel (a) of Figure 6-1, the government imposes a price ceiling of $4 per cone. In this case, because the price that balances supply and demand ($3) is below the ceiling, the price ceiling is *not binding*. Market forces naturally move the economy to the equilibrium, and the price ceiling has no effect.

Panel (b) of Figure 6-1 shows the other, more interesting, possibility. In this case, the government imposes a price ceiling of $2 per cone. Because the equilibrium price of $3 is above the price ceiling, the ceiling is a *binding constraint* on the market.

A MARKET WITH A PRICE CEILING.   In panel (a), the government imposes a price ceiling of $4. Because the price ceiling is above the equilibrium price of $3, the price ceiling has no effect, and the market can reach the equilibrium of supply and demand. In this equilibrium, quantity supplied and quantity demanded both equal 100 cones. In panel (b), the government imposes a price ceiling of $2. Because the price ceiling is below the equilibrium price of $3, the market price equals $2. At this price, 125 cones are demanded and only 75 are supplied, so there is a shortage of 50 cones.

Figure 6-1

The forces of supply and demand tend to move the price toward the equilibrium price, but when the market price hits the ceiling, it can rise no further. Thus, the market price equals the price ceiling. At this price, the quantity of ice cream demanded (125 cones in the figure) exceeds the quantity supplied (75 cones). There is a shortage of ice cream, so some people who want to buy ice cream at the going price are unable to.

When a shortage of ice cream develops because of this price ceiling, some mechanism for rationing ice cream will naturally develop. The mechanism could be long lines: Buyers who are willing to arrive early and wait in line get a cone, while those unwilling to wait do not. Alternatively, sellers could ration ice cream according to their own personal biases, selling it only to friends, relatives, or members of their own racial or ethnic group. Notice that even though the price ceiling was motivated by a desire to help buyers of ice cream, not all buyers benefit from the policy. Some buyers do get to pay a lower price, although they may have to wait in line to do so, but other buyers cannot get any ice cream at all.

This example in the market for ice cream shows a general result: *When the government imposes a binding price ceiling on a competitive market, a shortage of the good arises, and sellers must ration the scarce goods among the large number of potential buyers.* The rationing mechanisms that develop under price ceilings are rarely desirable. Long lines are inefficient because they waste buyers' time. Discrimination according to seller bias is both inefficient (because the good does not go to the buyer who values it most highly) and potentially unfair. By contrast, the rationing mech-

WHO IS RESPONSIBLE FOR THIS—OPEC OR U.S. LAWMAKERS?

anism in a free, competitive market is both efficient and impersonal. When the market for ice cream reaches its equilibrium, anyone who wants to pay the market price can get a cone. Free markets ration goods with prices.

CASE STUDY   LINES AT THE GAS PUMP

As we discussed in the preceding chapter, in 1973 the Organization of Petroleum Exporting Countries (OPEC) raised the price of crude oil in world oil markets. Because crude oil is the major input used to make gasoline, the higher oil prices reduced the supply of gasoline. In Canada the price of gas increased, but there were very few shortages. In the United States it was very different. Long lines at gas stations became commonplace, and American motorists often had to wait for hours to buy only a few gallons of gas.

What was responsible for the long gas lines? Most people blame OPEC. Surely, if OPEC had not raised the price of crude oil, the shortage of gasoline would not have occurred. Yet economists blame government regulations that limited the price oil companies could charge for gasoline.

Figure 6-2 shows what happened. As shown in panel (a), before OPEC raised the price of crude oil, the equilibrium price of gasoline P_1 was below the

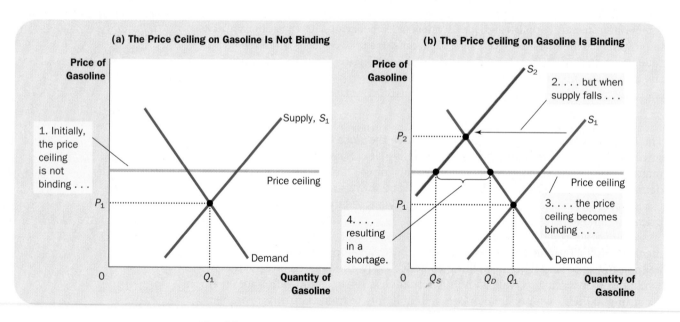

Figure 6-2

THE MARKET FOR GASOLINE WITH A PRICE CEILING.   Panel (a) shows the gasoline market when the price ceiling is not binding because the equilibrium price, P_1, is below the ceiling. Panel (b) shows the gasoline market after an increase in the price of crude oil (an input into making gasoline) shifts the supply curve to the left from S_1 to S_2. In an unregulated market, the price would have risen from P_1 to P_2. The price ceiling, however, prevents this from happening. At the binding price ceiling, consumers are willing to buy Q_D, but producers of gasoline are willing to sell only Q_S. The difference between quantity demanded and quantity supplied, $Q_D - Q_S$, measures the gasoline shortage.

IN THE NEWS

Does a Drought Need to Cause a Water Shortage?

DURING THE SUMMER OF 1999, THE EAST coast of the United States experienced unusually little rain and a shortage of water. The following article suggests a way that the shortage could have been averted.

Trickle-Down Economics

BY TERRY L. ANDERSON AND

CLAY J. LANDRY

Water shortages are being blamed on the drought in the East, but that's giving Mother Nature a bum rap. Certainly the drought is the immediate cause, but the real culprit is regulations that don't allow markets and prices to equalize demand and supply.

The similarity between water and gasoline is instructive. The energy crisis of the 1970s, too, was blamed on nature's niggardly supply of oil, but in fact it was the actions of the Organization of Petroleum Exporting Countries, combined with price controls, that were the main cause of the shortages. . . .

Once again, regulators are responding to shortages—in this case of water—with controls and regulations rather than allowing the market to work. Cities are restricting water usage; some have even gone so far as to prohibit restaurants from serving water except if the customer asks for a glass. But although cities initially saw declines in water use, some are starting to report increases in consumption. This has prompted some police departments to collect lists of residents suspected of wasting water.

There's a better answer than sending out the cops. Market forces could ensure plentiful water availability even in drought years. Contrary to popular belief, the supply of water is no more fixed than the supply of oil. Like all resources, water supplies change in response to economic growth and to the price. In developing countries, despite population growth, the percentage of people with access to safe drinking water has increased to 74 percent in 1994 from 44 percent in 1980. Rising incomes have given those countries the wherewithal to supply potable water.

Supplies also increase when current users have an incentive to conserve their surplus in the marketplace. California's drought-emergency water bank illustrates this. The bank allows farmers to lease water from other users during dry spells. In 1991, the first year the bank was tried, when the price was $125 per acre-foot (326 000 gallons), supply exceeded demand by two to one. That is, many more people wanted to sell their water than wanted to buy.

Data from every corner of the world show that when cities raise the price of water by 10 percent, water use goes down by as much as 12 percent. When the price of agricultural water goes up 10 percent, usage goes down by 20 percent. . . .

Unfortunately, Eastern water users do not pay realistic prices for water. According to the American Water Works Association, only 2 percent of municipal water suppliers adjust prices seasonally. . . .

Even more egregious, Eastern water laws bar people from buying and selling water. Just as tradable pollution permits established under the Clean Air Act have encouraged polluters to find efficient ways to reduce emissions, tradable water rights can encourage conservation and increase supplies. It is mainly a matter of following the lead of Western water courts that have quantified water rights and Western legislatures that have allowed trades.

By making water a commodity and unleashing market forces, policymakers can ensure plentiful water supplies for all. New policies won't make droughts disappear, but they will ease the pain they impose by priming the invisible pump of water markets.

SOURCE: *The Wall Street Journal*, August 23, 1999, p. A14.

price ceiling. The price regulation, therefore, had no effect. When the price of crude oil rose, however, the situation changed. The increase in the price of crude oil raised the cost of producing gasoline, and this reduced the supply of gasoline. As panel (b) shows, the supply curve shifted to the left from S_1 to S_2. In an unregulated market, this shift in supply would have raised the equilibrium price of gasoline from P_1 to P_2, and no shortage would have resulted. Instead, the price ceiling prevented the price from rising to the equilibrium level. At the price ceiling, producers were willing to sell Q_S, and consumers were willing to buy Q_D. Thus, the shift in supply caused a severe shortage at the regulated price.

Eventually, the laws regulating the price of gasoline were repealed. Lawmakers came to understand that they were partly responsible for the many hours Americans lost waiting in line to buy gasoline. Today, when the price of crude oil changes, the price of gasoline can adjust to bring supply and demand into equilibrium. In Canada there were no price controls on gasoline in 1973, and so no long gas lines either.

CASE STUDY   RENT CONTROL IN THE SHORT RUN AND THE LONG RUN

One common example of a price ceiling is rent control. In some provinces, the provincial government places a ceiling on rents that landlords may charge their tenants. The goal of this policy is to help the poor by making housing more affordable. Economists often criticize rent control, arguing that it is a highly inefficient way to help the poor raise their standard of living. One economist called rent control "the best way to destroy a city, other than bombing."

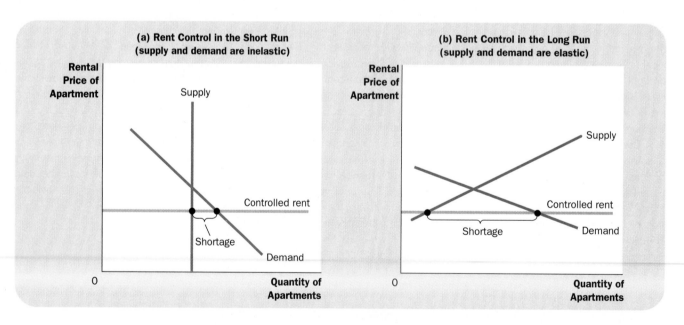

| Figure 6-3 | RENT CONTROL IN THE SHORT RUN AND IN THE LONG RUN. Panel (a) shows the short-run effects of rent control: Because the supply and demand for apartments are relatively inelastic, the price ceiling imposed by a rent-control law causes only a small shortage of housing. Panel (b) shows the long-run effects of rent control: Because the supply and demand for apartments are more elastic, rent control causes a large shortage. |

The adverse effects of rent control are less apparent to the general population because these effects occur over many years. In the short run, landlords have a fixed number of apartments to rent, and they cannot adjust this number quickly as market conditions change. Moreover, the number of people searching for housing in a city may not be highly responsive to rents in the short run because people take time to adjust their housing arrangements. Therefore, the short-run supply and demand for housing are relatively inelastic.

Panel (a) of Figure 6-3 shows the short-run effects of rent control on the housing market. As with any price ceiling, rent control causes a shortage. Yet because supply and demand are inelastic in the short run, the initial shortage caused by rent control is small. The primary effect in the short run is to reduce rents.

The long-run story is very different because the buyers and sellers of rental housing respond more to market conditions as time passes. On the supply side, landlords respond to low rents by not building new apartments and by failing to maintain existing ones. On the demand side, low rents encourage people to find their own apartments (rather than living with their parents or sharing apartments with roommates) and induce more people to move into a city. Therefore, both supply and demand are more elastic in the long run.

Panel (b) of Figure 6-3 illustrates the housing market in the long run. When rent control depresses rents below the equilibrium level, the quantity of apartments supplied falls substantially, and the quantity of apartments demanded rises substantially. The result is a large shortage of housing.

In provinces with rent control, landlords use various mechanisms to ration housing. Some landlords keep long waiting lists. Others give preference to tenants without children. Still others discriminate on the basis of race. Sometimes, apartments are allocated to those willing to offer under-the-table payments to building superintendents. In essence, these bribes bring the total price of an apartment (including the bribe) closer to the equilibrium price.

To understand fully the effects of rent control, we have to remember one of the *Ten Principles of Economics* from Chapter 1: People respond to incentives. In free markets, landlords try to keep their buildings clean and safe because desirable apartments command higher prices. By contrast, when rent control creates shortages and waiting lists, landlords lose their incentive to be responsive to tenants' concerns. Why should a landlord spend his money to maintain and improve his property when people are waiting to get in as it is? In the end, tenants get lower rents, but they also get lower-quality housing.

Policymakers often react to the effects of rent control by imposing additional regulations. For example, there are laws that make racial discrimination in housing illegal and require landlords to provide minimally adequate living conditions. These laws, however, are difficult and costly to enforce. By contrast, when rent control is eliminated and a market for housing is regulated by the forces of competition, such laws are less necessary. In a free market, the price of housing adjusts to eliminate the shortages that give rise to undesirable landlord behaviour.

HOW PRICE FLOORS AFFECT MARKET OUTCOMES

To examine the effects of another kind of government price control, let's return to the market for ice cream. Imagine now that the government is persuaded by the

IN THE NEWS

*Rent Control
in Canada*

THE FOLLOWING ARTICLE DESCRIBES THE politics and unintended consequences of rent controls.

Prisoners of Rent Control

BY DAVID GRATZER

Once upon a time, there was hope the Ontario Tories, with revolutionary vigour, would scrap Toronto's rent control regulations. Those days have long passed. In conversation with a government staffer, abolishing rent control was termed "neo-conservative excess."

Glen Murray has been accused of many things, but neo-conservatism is not one of them. Winnipeg's Mayor has never even belonged to a provincial Progressive Conservative party. Indeed, he was once a card-carrying New Democrat. In the mid-1990s, as a city councillor, he briefly flirted with running for the NDP. He chose to stay in municipal politics and, with a coalition of left-wing activists and unions, won the big job at City Hall in 1998.

But these days, you wouldn't know it. On the issue of rent control, Glen Murray sounds remarkably, well, free market. If the Ontario Tories deem this topic too controversial, Mr. Murray doesn't. Asked recently about Manitoba's decades-old policy, he was clear: Dump it. What would drive a bread-and-butter socialist such as Mr. Murray to dismiss the idea of rent control? Try nearly 30 years of failed public policy.

Historically, rent controls were widely used by governments across North America. New York introduced it as a temporary wartime measure during the Second World War. Many cities followed suit: Montreal, Washington, Toronto, Boston, and Los Angeles, among others. Faced with high inflation and ever-rising prices, the Manitoba government, like many jurisdictions both north and south of the border, embraced rent control in the early 1970s.

Why would a government want to dabble in the infinitely complicated world of rental pricing? The political rewards are clear: The tenants get guaranteed low rent at the expense of the landlords' profit potential. For politicians, it's a winning formula, given there will always be far more tenants than landlords.

But rent controls have an unintended consequence: They turn tenants into prisoners of their own apartments. Landlords, after all, have little capital (or incentive) to build new units. As a result, shortages of rental units develop. In the early 1990s, at the heyday of rent control in Toronto, a friend offered me advice about finding a place: Start by looking in the obituaries. As William Tucker notes in his book on the topic, in Europe, where rent control governs large sectors of the housing market, the result has been "labour immobility," where moving a factory across town can mean losing half the workforce.

In Winnipeg, the stagnation of rent control is obvious. It's been more than a decade since the last apartment rental building was built. Moreover, landlords are not in a rush to renovate their buildings. Winnipeg's apartments come complete with antique plumbing and electrical wiring. One way of measuring the quality of a rental unit is to look at its market value as a percentage of the replacement cost—in other words, the present sale price compared to the cost of building a new apartment. In 1976, the average unit replacement cost was 85 percent of the

market value. By 1993, it sunk to 43 percent. Winnipeg distinguishes itself as having the lowest property values of any major city in the country.

If rental units are not refurbished, their value stagnates and homeowners disproportionately pick up the slack in property taxes. In a Frontier Centre for Public Policy paper, the late Robert Hanson calculated that homeowners would save about $700 a year in property taxes if rent control had not been implemented—or about $13 000 in total.

This leaves Winnipeg homeowners with a big bill—and a decaying inner city. Victor Vrasnik, director of the Manitoba Taxpayers' Association, observes: "Plagued by depopulation and disregard, Winnipeg's inner city has become the preferred travel destination for vandals and pyromaniacs. Leave it to the rent control aficionados to blame the slum lords."

Faced with similar problems, many jurisdictions have reconsidered. During the '80s and '90s, 31 states prohibited this type of price-fixing by law or constitutional amendment. On this side of the border, one of the first major decisions of Roy Romanow's government was to end Saskatchewan's rent controls. And for those governments without the intestinal fortitude to fully scrap controls, there is a partial relaxation of the government regulation: allowing rents to rise when tenants move. This was the approach taken by the Mike Harris Tories in Ontario.

Will Winnipeg get Mr. Murray's wish? Right now, it appears unlikely. Despite pressure from the Mayor's office and growing property tax fatigue, the Manitoba government seems determined to stay the course, proving that just because the New Democrats are new to office doesn't mean they can't make old mistakes.

SOURCE: *National Post Online,* March 2, 2001. Available http://www: nationalpost.com, March 5, 2001.

A MARKET WITH A PRICE FLOOR.   In panel (a), the government imposes a price floor of $2. Because this is below the equilibrium price of $3, the price floor has no effect. The market price adjusts to balance supply and demand. At the equilibrium, quantity supplied and quantity demanded both equal 100 cones. In panel (b), the government imposes a price floor of $4, which is above the equilibrium price of $3. Therefore, the market price equals $4. Because 120 cones are supplied at this price and only 80 are demanded, there is a surplus of 40 cones.

Figure 6-4

pleas of the Canadian Organization of Ice-Cream Makers. In this case, the government might institute a price floor. Price floors, like price ceilings, are an attempt by the government to maintain prices at other than equilibrium levels. Whereas a price ceiling places a legal maximum on prices, a price floor places a legal minimum.

When the government imposes a price floor on the ice-cream market, two outcomes are possible. If the government imposes a price floor of $2 per cone when the equilibrium price is $3, we obtain the outcome in panel (a) of Figure 6-4. In this case, because the equilibrium price is above the floor, the price floor is not binding. Market forces naturally move the economy to the equilibrium, and the price floor has no effect.

Panel (b) of Figure 6-4 shows what happens when the government imposes a price floor of $4 per cone. In this case, because the equilibrium price of $3 is below the floor, the price floor is a binding constraint on the market. The forces of supply and demand tend to move the price toward the equilibrium price, but when the market price hits the floor, it can fall no further. The market price equals the price floor. At this floor, the quantity of ice cream supplied (120 cones) exceeds the quantity demanded (80 cones). Some people who want to sell ice cream at the going price are unable to. *Thus, a binding price floor causes a surplus.*

Just as price ceilings and shortages can lead to undesirable rationing mechanisms, so can price floors and surpluses. In the case of a price floor, some sellers are unable to sell all they want at the market price. The sellers who appeal to the personal biases of the buyers, perhaps due to racial or familial ties, are better able to sell their goods than those who do not. By contrast, in a free market, the price serves as the rationing mechanism, and sellers can sell all they want at the equilibrium price.

CASE STUDY   THE MINIMUM WAGE

An important example of a price floor is the minimum wage. Minimum-wage laws dictate the lowest price for labour that any employer may pay. Minimum-wage rates differ by province. In 2001, minimum wages ranged from a low of $5.50 per hour in Newfoundland to a high of $7.60 in British Columbia. Lower rates may apply for younger workers and for restaurant and bar staff (who can earn tips to supplement their wages).

To examine the effects of a minimum wage, we must consider the market for labour. Panel (a) of Figure 6-5 shows the labour market, which, like all markets, is subject to the forces of supply and demand. Workers determine the supply of labour, and firms determine the demand. If the government doesn't intervene, the wage normally adjusts to balance labour supply and labour demand.

Panel (b) of Figure 6-5 shows the labour market with a minimum wage. If the minimum wage is above the equilibrium level, as it is here, the quantity of labour supplied exceeds the quantity demanded. The result is unemployment. Thus, the minimum wage raises the incomes of those workers who have jobs, but it lowers the incomes of those workers who cannot find jobs.

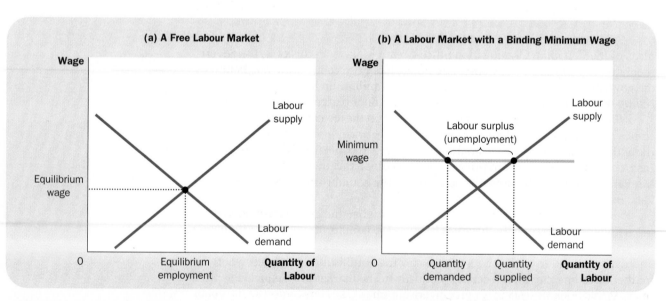

Figure 6-5

HOW THE MINIMUM WAGE AFFECTS THE LABOUR MARKET.   Panel (a) shows a labour market in which the wage adjusts to balance labour supply and labour demand. Panel (b) shows the impact of a binding minimum wage. Because the minimum wage is a price floor, it causes a surplus: The quantity of labour supplied exceeds the quantity demanded. The result is unemployment.

To fully understand the minimum wage, keep in mind that the economy contains not a single labour market, but many labour markets for different types of workers. The impact of the minimum wage depends on the skill and experience of the worker. Workers with high skills and much experience are not affected, because their equilibrium wages are well above the minimum. For these workers, the minimum wage is not binding.

The minimum wage has its greatest impact on the market for teenage labour. The equilibrium wages of teenagers are low because teenagers are among the least skilled and least experienced members of the labour force. In addition, teenagers are often willing to accept a lower wage in exchange for on-the-job training. (Some teenagers are willing to work as "interns" for no pay at all. Because internships pay nothing, however, the minimum wage does not apply to them. If it did, these jobs might not exist.) As a result, the minimum wage is more often binding for teenagers than for other members of the labour force.

Many economists have studied how minimum-wage laws affect the teenage labour market. These researchers compare the changes in the minimum wage over time with the changes in teenage employment. Although there is some debate about how much the minimum wage affects employment, the typical study finds that a 10 percent increase in the minimum wage depresses teenage employment between 1 and 3 percent. In interpreting this estimate, note that a 10 percent increase in the minimum wage does not raise the average wage of teenagers by 10 percent. A change in the law does not directly affect those teenagers who are already paid well above the minimum, and enforcement of minimum-wage laws is not perfect. Thus, the estimated drop in employment of 1 to 3 percent is significant.

In addition to altering the quantity of labour demanded, the minimum wage also alters the quantity supplied. Because the minimum wage raises the wage that teenagers can earn, it increases the number of teenagers who choose to look for jobs. Studies have found that a higher minimum wage influences which teenagers are employed. When the minimum wage rises, some teenagers who are still attending school choose to drop out and take jobs. These new dropouts displace other teenagers who had already dropped out of school and who now become unemployed.

The minimum wage is a frequent topic of political debate. Advocates of the minimum wage view the policy as one way to raise the income of the working poor. They correctly point out that workers who earn the minimum wage can afford only a meagre standard of living. For example, at a minimum wage of $6.00 per hour, two adults working 40 hours a week for every week of the year at minimum-wage jobs had a total annual income of only $24 960, which is less than half the average family income in Canada. Many advocates of the minimum wage admit that it has some adverse effects, including unemployment, but they believe that these effects are small and that, all things considered, a higher minimum wage makes the poor better off.

Opponents of the minimum wage contend that it is not the best way to combat poverty. They note that a high minimum wage causes unemployment, encourages teenagers to drop out of school, and prevents some unskilled workers from getting the on-the-job training they need. Moreover, opponents of the minimum wage point out that the minimum wage is a poorly targeted policy. Not all minimum-wage workers are heads of households trying to help their families escape poverty. In fact, fewer than a third of minimum-wage earners are in families with incomes below the poverty line. Many are teenagers from middle-class homes working at part-time jobs for extra spending money.

EVALUATING PRICE CONTROLS

One of the *Ten Principles of Economics* discussed in Chapter 1 is that markets are usually a good way to organize economic activity. This principle explains why economists usually oppose price ceilings and price floors. To economists, prices are not the outcome of some haphazard process. Prices, they contend, are the result of the millions of business and consumer decisions that lie behind the supply and demand curves. Prices have the crucial job of balancing supply and demand and, thereby, coordinating economic activity. When policymakers set prices by legal decree, they obscure the signals that normally guide the allocation of society's resources.

Another one of the *Ten Principles of Economics* is that governments can sometimes improve market outcomes. Indeed, policymakers are led to control prices because they view the market's outcome as unfair. Price controls are often aimed at helping the poor. For instance, rent-control laws try to make housing affordable for everyone, and minimum-wage laws try to help people escape poverty.

Yet price controls often hurt those they are trying to help. Rent control may keep rents low, but it also discourages landlords from maintaining their buildings and makes housing hard to find. Minimum-wage laws may raise the incomes of some workers, but they also cause other workers to be unemployed.

Helping those in need can be accomplished in ways other than controlling prices. For instance, the government can make housing more affordable by paying a fraction of the rent for poor families. Unlike rent control, such rent subsidies do not reduce the quantity of housing supplied and, therefore, do not lead to housing shortages. Similarly, wage subsidies raise the living standards of the working poor without discouraging firms from hiring them. An example of a wage subsidy is the *Youth Employment Program*, a government program that subsidizes the hiring of young workers.

Although these alternative policies are often better than price controls, they are not perfect. Rent and wage subsidies cost the government money and, therefore, require higher taxes. As we see in the next section, taxation has costs of its own.

QUICK QUIZ: Define *price ceiling* and *price floor,* and give an example of each. Which leads to a shortage? Which leads to a surplus? Why?

TAXES

All governments—from the federal government in Ottawa, to the local governments in small towns—use taxes to raise revenue for public projects, such as roads, schools, and national defence. Because taxes are such an important policy instrument, and because they affect our lives in many ways, the study of taxes is a topic to which we return several times throughout this book. In this section we begin our study of how taxes affect the economy.

To set the stage for our analysis, imagine that a local government decides to hold an annual ice-cream celebration—with a parade, fireworks, and speeches by town officials. To raise revenue to pay for the event, it decides to place a $0.50 tax on the sale of ice-cream cones. When the plan is announced, our two lobbying groups swing into action. The Canadian Organization of Ice-Cream Makers claims that its members are struggling to survive in a competitive market, and it argues that *buyers* of ice cream should have to pay the tax. The Canadian Association of

Ice-Cream Eaters claims that consumers of ice cream are having trouble making ends meet, and it argues that *sellers* of ice cream should pay the tax. The town mayor, hoping to reach a compromise, suggests that half the tax be paid by the buyers and half be paid by the sellers.

To analyze these proposals, we need to address a simple but subtle question: When the government levies a tax on a good, who bears the burden of the tax? The people buying the good? The people selling the good? Or, if buyers and sellers share the tax burden, what determines how the burden is divided? Can the government simply legislate the division of the burden, as the mayor is suggesting, or is the division determined by more fundamental forces in the economy? Economists use the term **tax incidence** to refer to these questions about the distribution of a tax burden. As we will see, we can learn some surprising lessons about tax incidence just by applying the tools of supply and demand.

tax incidence
the study of who bears the burden of taxation

HOW TAXES ON BUYERS AFFECT MARKET OUTCOMES

We first consider a tax levied on buyers of a good. Suppose, for instance, that our local government passes a law requiring buyers of ice-cream cones to send $0.50 to the government for each ice-cream cone they buy. How does this law affect the buyers and sellers of ice cream? To answer this question, we can follow the three steps in Chapter 4 for analyzing supply and demand: (1) We decide whether the law affects the supply curve or demand curve, (2) we decide which way the curve shifts, and (3) we examine how the shift affects the equilibrium.

The initial impact of the tax is on the demand for ice cream. The supply curve is not affected because, for any given price of ice cream, sellers have the same incentive to provide ice cream to the market. By contrast, buyers now have to pay a tax to the government (as well as the price to the sellers) whenever they buy ice cream. Thus, the tax shifts the demand curve for ice cream.

The direction of the shift is easy to determine. Because the tax on buyers makes buying ice cream less attractive, buyers demand a smaller quantity of ice cream at every price. As a result, the demand curve shifts to the left (or, equivalently, downward), as shown in Figure 6-6.

We can, in this case, be precise about how much the curve shifts. Because of the $0.50 tax levied on buyers, the effective price to buyers is now $0.50 higher than the market price. For example, if the market price of a cone happened to be $2.00, the effective price to buyers would be $2.50. Because buyers look at their total cost including the tax, they demand a quantity of ice cream as if the market price were $0.50 higher than it actually is. In other words, to induce buyers to demand any given quantity, the market price must now be $0.50 lower to make up for the effect of the tax. Thus, the tax shifts the demand curve *downward* from D_1 to D_2 by exactly the size of the tax ($0.50).

To see the effect of the tax, we compare the old equilibrium and the new equilibrium. You can see in the figure that the equilibrium price of ice cream falls from $3.00 to $2.80 and the equilibrium quantity falls from 100 to 90 cones. Because sellers sell less and buyers buy less in the new equilibrium, the tax on ice cream reduces the size of the ice-cream market.

Now let's return to the question of tax incidence: Who pays the tax? Although buyers send the entire tax to the government, buyers and sellers share the burden. Because the market price falls from $3.00 to $2.80 when the tax is introduced, sellers receive $0.20 less for each ice-cream cone than they did without the tax. Thus, the

Figure 6-6

A TAX ON BUYERS. When a tax of $0.50 is levied on buyers, the demand curve shifts down by $0.50 from D_1 to D_2. The equilibrium quantity falls from 100 to 90 cones. The price that sellers receive falls from $3.00 to $2.80. The price that buyers pay (including the tax) rises from $3.00 to $3.30. Even though the tax is levied on buyers, buyers and sellers share the burden of the tax.

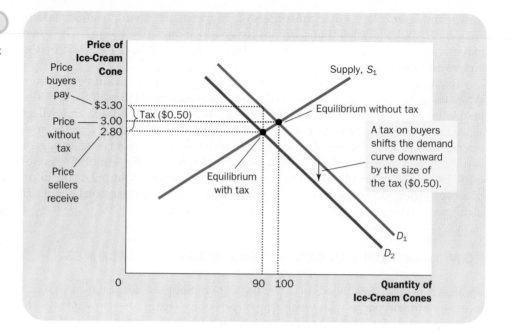

tax makes sellers worse off. Buyers pay sellers a lower price ($2.80), but the effective price including the tax rises from $3.00 before the tax to $3.30 with the tax ($2.80 + $0.50 = $3.30). Thus, the tax also makes buyers worse off.

To sum up, the analysis yields two general lessons:

◆ Taxes discourage market activity. When a good is taxed, the quantity of the good sold is smaller in the new equilibrium.

◆ Buyers and sellers share the burden of taxes. In the new equilibrium, buyers pay more for the good, and sellers receive less.

HOW TAXES ON SELLERS AFFECT MARKET OUTCOMES

Now consider a tax levied on sellers of a good. Suppose the local government passes a law requiring sellers of ice-cream cones to send $0.50 to the government for each cone they sell. What are the effects of this law?

In this case, the initial impact of the tax is on the supply of ice cream. Because the tax is not levied on buyers, the quantity of ice cream demanded at any given price is the same, so the demand curve does not change. By contrast, the tax on sellers raises the cost of selling ice cream, and leads sellers to supply a smaller quantity at every price. The supply curve shifts to the left (or, equivalently, upward).

Once again, we can be precise about the magnitude of the shift. For any market price of ice cream, the effective price to sellers—the amount they get to keep after paying the tax—is $0.50 lower. For example, if the market price of a cone happened to be $2.00, the effective price received by sellers would be $1.50. Whatever the market price, sellers will supply a quantity of ice cream as if the price were $0.50 lower than it is. Put differently, to induce sellers to supply any given

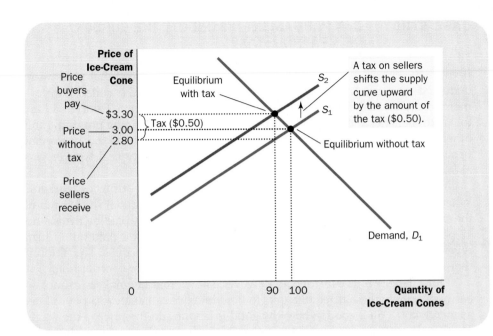

Figure 6-7

A TAX ON SELLERS.   When a tax of $0.50 is levied on sellers, the supply curve shifts up by $0.50 from S_1 to S_2. The equilibrium quantity falls from 100 to 90 cones. The price that buyers pay rises from $3.00 to $3.30. The price that sellers receive (after paying the tax) falls from $3.00 to $2.80. Even though the tax is levied on sellers, buyers and sellers share the burden of the tax.

quantity, the market price must now be $0.50 higher to compensate for the effect of the tax. Thus, as shown in Figure 6-7, the supply curve shifts *upward* from S_1 to S_2 by exactly the size of the tax ($0.50).

When the market moves from the old to the new equilibrium, the equilibrium price of ice cream rises from $3.00 to $3.30, and the equilibrium quantity falls from 100 to 90 cones. Once again, the tax reduces the size of the ice-cream market. And once again, buyers and sellers share the burden of the tax. Because the market price rises, buyers pay $0.30 more for each cone than they did before the tax was enacted. Sellers receive a higher price than they did without the tax, but the effective price (after paying the tax) falls from $3.00 to $2.80.

Comparing Figures 6-6 and 6-7 leads to a surprising conclusion: *Taxes on buyers and taxes on sellers are equivalent.* In both cases, the tax places a wedge between the price that buyers pay and the price that sellers receive. The wedge between the buyers' price and the sellers' price is the same, regardless of whether the tax is levied on buyers or sellers. In either case, the wedge shifts the relative position of the supply and demand curves. In the new equilibrium, buyers and sellers share the burden of the tax. The only difference between taxes on buyers and taxes on sellers is who sends the money to the government.

The equivalence of these two taxes is perhaps easier to understand if we imagine that the government collects the $0.50 ice-cream tax in a bowl on the counter of each ice-cream store. When the government levies the tax on buyers, the buyer is required to place $0.50 in the bowl every time a cone is bought. When the government levies the tax on sellers, the seller is required to place $0.50 in the bowl after the sale of each cone. Whether the $0.50 goes directly from the buyer's pocket into the bowl, or indirectly from the buyer's pocket into the seller's hand and then into the bowl, does not matter. Once the market reaches its new equilibrium, buyers and sellers share the burden, regardless of how the tax is levied.

CASE STUDY CAN PARLIAMENT DISTRIBUTE THE BURDEN OF A PAYROLL TAX?

If you have ever received a paycheque, you probably noticed that taxes were deducted from the amount you earned. One of these taxes is called Employment Insurance (EI). The federal government uses the revenue from the EI tax to pay for benefits to unemployed workers, as well as for training programs and other policies. EI is an example of a payroll tax, which is a tax on the wages that firms pay their workers. In 2001, the total EI tax for the typical worker was about 5 percent of earnings.

Who do you think bears the burden of this payroll tax—firms or workers? When Parliament passed this legislation, it attempted to mandate a division of the tax burden. According to the law, 58 percent of the tax is paid by firms, and 42 percent is paid by workers. That is, 58 percent of the tax is paid out of firm revenue, and 42 percent is deducted from workers' paycheques. The amount that shows up as a deduction on your pay stub is the worker contribution.

Our analysis of tax incidence, however, shows that lawmakers cannot so easily distribute the burden of a tax. To illustrate, we can analyze a payroll tax as merely a tax on a good, where the good is labour and the price is the wage. The key feature of the payroll tax is that it places a wedge between the wage that firms pay and the wage that workers receive. Figure 6-8 shows the outcome. When a payroll tax is enacted, the wage received by workers falls, and the wage paid by firms rises. In the end, workers and firms share the burden of the tax, much as the legislation requires. Yet this division of the tax burden between workers and firms has nothing to do with the legislated division: The division of the burden in Figure 6-8 is not necessarily 58–42, and the same outcome would prevail if the law levied the entire tax on workers or if it levied the entire tax on firms.

Figure 6-8

A PAYROLL TAX.   A payroll tax places a wedge between the wage that workers receive and the wage that firms pay. Comparing wages with and without the tax, you can see that workers and firms share the tax burden. This division of the tax burden between workers and firms does not depend on whether the government levies the tax on workers, levies the tax on firms, or divides the tax equally between the two groups.

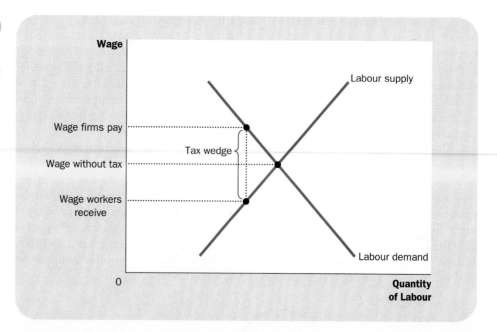

This example shows that the most basic lesson of tax incidence is often overlooked in public debate. Lawmakers can decide whether a tax comes from the buyer's pocket or from the seller's, but they cannot legislate the true burden of a tax. Rather, tax incidence depends on the forces of supply and demand.

ELASTICITY AND TAX INCIDENCE

When a good is taxed, buyers and sellers of the good share the burden of the tax. But how exactly is the tax burden divided? Only rarely will it be shared equally. To see how the burden is divided, consider the impact of taxation in the two markets in Figure 6-9. In both cases, the figure shows the initial demand curve, the initial

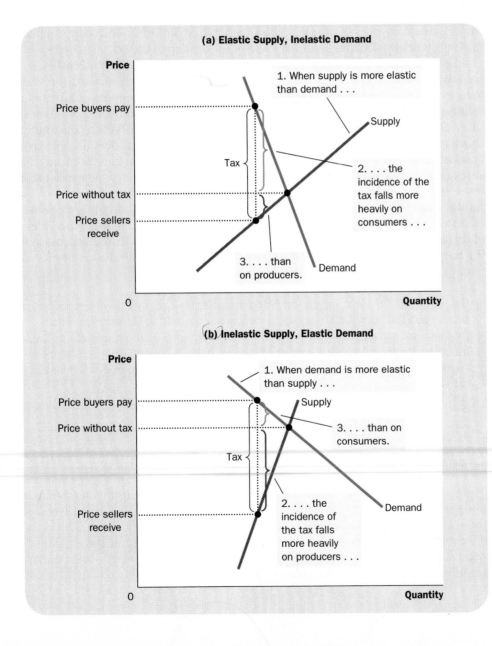

Figure 6-9

HOW THE BURDEN OF A TAX IS DIVIDED.   In panel (a), the supply curve is elastic, and the demand curve is inelastic. In this case, the price received by sellers falls only slightly, while the price paid by buyers rises substantially. Thus, buyers bear most of the burden of the tax. In panel (b), the supply curve is inelastic, and the demand curve is elastic. In this case, the price received by sellers falls substantially, while the price paid by buyers rises only slightly. Thus, sellers bear most of the burden of the tax.

(a) Elastic Supply, Inelastic Demand

1. When supply is more elastic than demand . . .

2. . . . the incidence of the tax falls more heavily on consumers . . .

3. . . . than on producers.

(b) Inelastic Supply, Elastic Demand

1. When demand is more elastic than supply . . .

3. . . . than on consumers.

2. . . . the incidence of the tax falls more heavily on producers . . .

supply curve, and a tax that drives a wedge between the amount paid by buyers and the amount received by sellers. (Not drawn in either panel of the figure is the new supply or demand curve. Which curve shifts depends on whether the tax is levied on buyers or sellers. As we have seen, this is irrelevant for the incidence of the tax.) The difference in the two panels is the relative elasticity of supply and demand.

Panel (a) of Figure 6-9 shows a tax in a market with very elastic supply and relatively inelastic demand. That is, sellers are very responsive to the price of the good, whereas buyers are not very responsive. When a tax is imposed on a market with these elasticities, the price received by sellers does not fall much, so sellers bear only a small burden. By contrast, the price paid by buyers rises substantially, indicating that buyers bear most of the burden of the tax.

Panel (b) of Figure 6-9 shows a tax in a market with relatively inelastic supply and very elastic demand. In this case, sellers are not very responsive to the price, while buyers are very responsive. The figure shows that when a tax is imposed, the price paid by buyers does not rise much, while the price received by sellers falls substantially. Thus, sellers bear most of the burden of the tax.

The two panels of Figure 6-9 show a general lesson about how the burden of a tax is divided: *A tax burden falls more heavily on the side of the market that is less elastic.* Why is this true? In essence, the elasticity measures the willingness of buyers or sellers to leave the market when conditions become unfavourable. A small elasticity of demand means that buyers do not have good alternatives to consuming this particular good. A small elasticity of supply means that sellers do not have good alternatives to producing this particular good. When the good is taxed, the side of the market with fewer good alternatives cannot easily leave the market and must, therefore, bear more of the burden of the tax.

We can apply this logic to the payroll tax, which was discussed in the previous case study. Most labour economists believe that the supply of labour is much less elastic than the demand. This means that workers, rather than firms, bear most of the burden of the payroll tax. In other words, the distribution of the tax burden is not at all close to the 58–42 split that lawmakers intended.

QUICK QUIZ: In a supply-and-demand diagram, show how a tax on car buyers of $1000 per car affects the quantity of cars sold and the price of cars. In another diagram, show how a tax on car sellers of $1000 per car affects the quantity of cars sold and the price of cars. In both of your diagrams, show the change in the price paid by car buyers and the change in the price received by car sellers.

CONCLUSION

The economy is governed by two kinds of laws: the laws of supply and demand and the laws enacted by governments. In this chapter we have begun to see how these laws interact. Price controls and taxes are common in various markets in the economy, and their effects are frequently debated in the press and among policy-makers. Even a little bit of economic knowledge can go a long way toward understanding and evaluating these policies.

In subsequent chapters we will analyze many government policies in greater detail. We will examine the effects of taxation more fully, and we will consider a broader range of policies than we considered here. Yet the basic lessons of this chapter will not change: When analyzing government policies, supply and demand are the first and most useful tools of analysis.

Summary

◆ A price ceiling is a legal maximum on the price of a good or service. An example is rent control. If the price ceiling is below the equilibrium price, the quantity demanded exceeds the quantity supplied. Because of the resulting shortage, sellers must in some way ration the good or service among buyers.

◆ A price floor is a legal minimum on the price of a good or service. An example is the minimum wage. If the price floor is above the equilibrium price, the quantity supplied exceeds the quantity demanded. Because of the resulting surplus, buyers' demands for the good or service must in some way be rationed among sellers.

◆ When the government levies a tax on a good, the equilibrium quantity of the good falls. That is, a tax on a market shrinks the size of the market.

◆ A tax on a good places a wedge between the price paid by buyers and the price received by sellers. When the market moves to the new equilibrium, buyers pay more for the good and sellers receive less for it. In this sense, buyers and sellers share the tax burden. The incidence of a tax does not depend on whether the tax is levied on buyers or sellers.

◆ The incidence of a tax depends on the price elasticities of supply and demand. The burden tends to fall on the side of the market that is less elastic because that side of the market can respond less easily to the tax by changing the quantity bought or sold.

Key Concepts

price ceiling, p. 118   price floor, p. 118   tax incidence, p. 129

Questions for Review

1. Give an example of a price ceiling and an example of a price floor.

2. Which causes a shortage of a good—a price ceiling or a price floor? Which causes a surplus?

3. What mechanisms allocate resources when the price of a good is not allowed to bring supply and demand into equilibrium?

4. Explain why economists usually oppose controls on prices.

5. What is the difference between a tax paid by buyers and a tax paid by sellers?

6. How does a tax on a good affect the price paid by buyers, the price received by sellers, and the quantity sold?

7. What determines how the burden of a tax is divided between buyers and sellers? Why?

Problems and Applications

1. Lovers of classical music persuade Parliament to impose a price ceiling of $40 per ticket. Does this policy get more or fewer people to attend classical music concerts?

2. The government has decided that the free-market price of cheese is too low.

   a. Suppose the government imposes a binding price floor in the cheese market. Use a supply-and-demand diagram to show the effect of this policy on the price of cheese and the quantity of cheese sold. Is there a shortage or surplus of cheese?

   b. Farmers complain that the price floor has reduced their total revenue. Is this possible? Explain.

   c. In response to farmers' complaints, the government agrees to purchase all of the surplus cheese at the price floor. Compared with the basic price floor, who benefits from this new policy? Who loses?

3. A recent study found that the demand and supply schedules for Frisbees are as follows:

PRICE PER FRISBEE	QUANTITY DEMANDED	QUANTITY SUPPLIED
$11	1 million	15 million
10	2	12
9	4	9
8	6	6
7	8	3
6	10	1

   a. What are the equilibrium price and quantity of Frisbees?

   b. Frisbee manufacturers persuade the government that Frisbee production improves scientists' understanding of aerodynamics and thus is important for national security. A concerned Parliament votes to impose a price floor $2 above the equilibrium price. What is the new market price? How many Frisbees are sold?

   c. Irate university students march on Ottawa and demand a reduction in the price of Frisbees. An even more concerned Parliament votes to repeal the price floor and impose a price ceiling $1 below the former price floor. What is the new market price? How many Frisbees are sold?

4. Suppose the provincial government requires beer drinkers to pay a $2 tax on each case of beer purchased.

   a. Draw a supply-and-demand diagram of the market for beer without the tax. Show the price paid by consumers, the price received by producers, and the quantity of beer sold. What is the difference between the price paid by consumers and the price received by producers?

   b. Now draw a supply-and-demand diagram for the beer market with the tax. Show the price paid by consumers, the price received by producers, and the quantity of beer sold. What is the difference between the price paid by consumers and the price received by producers? Has the quantity of beer sold increased or decreased?

5. An MP wants to raise tax revenue and make workers better off. A staff member proposes raising the payroll tax paid by firms and using part of the extra revenue to reduce the payroll tax paid by workers. Would this accomplish the MP's goal?

6. If the government places a $500 tax on luxury cars, will the price paid by consumers rise by more than $500, less than $500, or exactly $500? Explain.

7. Parliament decides that Canada should reduce air pollution by reducing its use of gasoline. It imposes a $0.10 tax on each litre of gasoline sold.

   a. Should Parliament impose this tax on producers or consumers? Explain carefully using a supply-and-demand diagram.

   b. If the demand for gasoline were more elastic, would this tax be more effective or less effective in reducing the quantity of gasoline consumed? Explain with both words and a diagram.

   c. Are consumers of gasoline helped or hurt by this tax? Why?

   d. Are workers in the oil industry helped or hurt by this tax? Why?

8. A case study in this chapter discusses the minimum-wage law.

   a. Suppose the minimum wage is above the equilibrium wage in the market for unskilled labour. Using a supply-and-demand diagram of the market for unskilled labour, show the market wage, the number of workers who are employed, and the number of workers who are unemployed. Also show the total wage payments to unskilled workers.

b. Now suppose the provincial government proposes an increase in the minimum wage. What effect would this increase have on employment? Does the change in employment depend on the elasticity of demand, the elasticity of supply, both elasticities, or neither?

c. What effect would this increase in the minimum wage have on unemployment? Does the change in unemployment depend on the elasticity of demand, the elasticity of supply, both elasticities, or neither?

d. If the demand for unskilled labour were inelastic, would the proposed increase in the minimum wage raise or lower total wage payments to unskilled workers? Would your answer change if the demand for unskilled labour were elastic?

9. Consider the following policies, each of which is aimed at reducing violent crime by reducing the use of guns. Illustrate each of these proposed policies in a supply-and-demand diagram of the gun market.

a. a tax on gun buyers

b. a tax on gun sellers

c. a price floor on guns

d. a tax on ammunition

10. The Canadian government administers two programs that affect the market for cigarettes. Media campaigns and labelling requirements are aimed at making the public aware of the dangers of cigarette smoking. At the same time, Agriculture Canada imposes production quotas on tobacco farmers, which raise the price of tobacco above the equilibrium price.

a. How do these two programs affect cigarette consumption? Use a graph of the cigarette market in your answer.

b. What is the combined effect of these two programs on the price of cigarettes?

c. Cigarettes are also heavily taxed. What effect does this tax have on cigarette consumption?

11. A subsidy is the opposite of a tax. With a $0.50 tax on the buyers of ice-cream cones, the government collects $0.50 for each cone purchased; with a $0.50 subsidy for the buyers of ice-cream cones, the government pays buyers $0.50 for each cone purchased.

a. Show the effect of a $0.50 per cone subsidy on the demand curve for ice-cream cones, the effective price paid by consumers, the effective price received by sellers, and the quantity of cones sold.

b. Do consumers gain or lose from this policy? Do producers gain or lose? Does the government gain or lose?

Three

SUPPLY AND DEMAND II: MARKETS AND WELFARE

7

CONSUMERS, PRODUCERS, AND THE EFFICIENCY OF MARKETS

When consumers go to grocery stores to buy their turkeys for Thanksgiving dinner, they may be disappointed that the price of turkey is as high as it is. At the same time, when farmers bring to market the turkeys they have raised, they wish the price of turkey were even higher. These views are not surprising: Buyers always want to pay less, and sellers always want to get paid more. But is there a "right price" for turkey from the standpoint of society as a whole?

In previous chapters we saw how, in market economies, the forces of supply and demand determine the prices of goods and services and the quantities sold. So far, however, we have described the way markets allocate scarce resources without directly addressing the question of whether these market allocations are desirable. In other words, our analysis has been *positive* (what is) rather than *normative* (what should be). We know that the price of turkey adjusts to ensure that the quantity of turkey supplied equals the quantity of turkey demanded. But, at this equilibrium, is the quantity of turkey produced and consumed too small, too large, or just right?

welfare economics

the study of how the allocation of resources affects economic well-being

In this chapter we take up the topic of **welfare economics,** the study of how the allocation of resources affects economic well-being. We begin by examining the benefits that buyers and sellers receive from taking part in a market. We then examine how society can make these benefits as large as possible. This analysis leads to a profound conclusion: The equilibrium of supply and demand in a market maximizes the total benefits received by buyers and sellers.

As you may recall from Chapter 1, one of the *Ten Principles of Economics* is that markets are usually a good way to organize economic activity. The study of welfare economics explains this principle more fully. It also answers our question about the right price of turkey: The price that balances the supply and demand for turkey is, in a particular sense, the best one because it maximizes the total welfare of turkey consumers and turkey producers.

CONSUMER SURPLUS

We begin our study of welfare economics by looking at the benefits buyers receive from participating in a market.

WILLINGNESS TO PAY

Imagine that you own a mint-condition recording of Elvis Presley's first album. Because you are not an Elvis Presley fan, you decide to sell it. One way to do so is to hold an auction.

Four Elvis fans show up for your auction: John, Paul, George, and Ringo. Each of them would like to own the album, but there is a limit to the amount that each is willing to pay for it. Table 7-1 shows the maximum price that each of the four possible buyers would pay. Each buyer's maximum is called his **willingness to pay,** and it measures how much that buyer values the good. Each buyer would be eager to buy the album at a price less than his willingness to pay, would refuse to

willingness to pay

the maximum amount that a buyer will pay for a good

Table 7-1

FOUR POSSIBLE BUYERS'
WILLINGNESS TO PAY

BUYER	WILLINGNESS TO PAY
John	$100
Paul	80
George	70
Ringo	50

buy the album at a price more than his willingness to pay, and would be indifferent about buying the album at a price exactly equal to his willingness to pay.

To sell your album, you begin the bidding at a low price, say $10. Because all four buyers are willing to pay much more, the price rises quickly. The bidding stops when John bids $80 (or slightly more). At this point, Paul, George, and Ringo have dropped out of the bidding, because they are unwilling to bid any more than $80. John pays you $80 and gets the album. Note that the album has gone to the buyer who values the album most highly.

What benefit does John receive from buying the Elvis Presley album? In a sense, John has found a real bargain: He is willing to pay $100 for the album but pays only $80 for it. We say that John receives *consumer surplus* of $20. **Consumer surplus** is the amount a buyer is willing to pay for a good minus the amount the buyer actually pays for it.

Consumer surplus measures the benefit to buyers of participating in a market. In this example, John receives a $20 benefit from participating in the auction because he pays only $80 for a good he values at $100. Paul, George, and Ringo get no consumer surplus from participating in the auction, because they left without the album and without paying anything.

Now consider a somewhat different example. Suppose that you had two identical Elvis Presley albums to sell. Again, you auction them off to the four possible buyers. To keep things simple, we assume that both albums are to be sold for the same price and that no buyer is interested in buying more than one album. Therefore, the price rises until two buyers are left.

In this case, the bidding stops when John and Paul bid $70 (or slightly higher). At this price, John and Paul are each happy to buy an album, and George and Ringo are not willing to bid any higher. John and Paul each receive consumer surplus equal to his willingness to pay minus the price. John's consumer surplus is $30, and Paul's is $10. John's consumer surplus is higher now than it was previously, because he gets the same album but pays less for it. The total consumer surplus in the market is $40.

consumer surplus
a buyer's willingness to pay minus the amount the buyer actually pays

USING THE DEMAND CURVE TO MEASURE CONSUMER SURPLUS

Consumer surplus is closely related to the demand curve for a product. To see how they are related, let's continue our example and consider the demand curve for this rare Elvis Presley album.

We begin by using the willingness to pay of the four possible buyers to find the demand schedule for the album. Table 7-2 shows the demand schedule that corresponds to Table 7-1. If the price is above $100, the quantity demanded in the market is 0, because no buyer is willing to pay that much. If the price is between $80 and $100, the quantity demanded is 1, because only John is willing to pay such a high price. If the price is between $70 and $80, the quantity demanded is 2, because both John and Paul are willing to pay the price. We can continue this analysis for other prices as well. In this way, the demand schedule is derived from the willingness to pay of the four possible buyers.

Figure 7-1 graphs the demand curve that corresponds to this demand schedule. Note the relationship between the height of the demand curve and the buyers' willingness to pay. At any quantity, the price given by the demand curve shows the

Table 7-2

THE DEMAND SCHEDULE FOR THE
BUYERS IN TABLE 7-1

PRICE	BUYERS	QUANTITY DEMANDED
More than $100	None	0
$80 to $100	John	1
$70 to $80	John, Paul	2
$50 to $70	John, Paul, George	3
$50 or less	John, Paul, George, Ringo	4

Figure 7-1

THE DEMAND CURVE.   This
figure graphs the demand curve
from the demand schedule in
Table 7-2. Note that the height of
the demand curve reflects buyers'
willingness to pay.

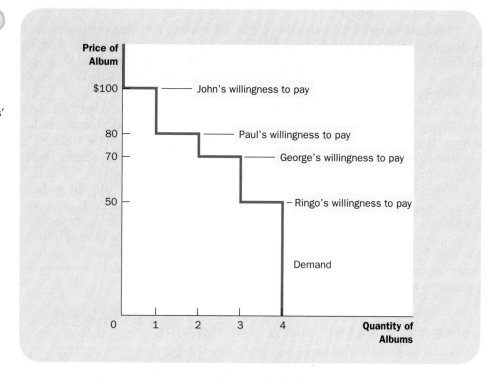

willingness to pay of the *marginal buyer,* the buyer who would leave the market first
if the price were any higher. At a quantity of 4 albums, for instance, the demand
curve has a height of $50, the price that Ringo (the marginal buyer) is willing to pay
for an album. At a quantity of 3 albums, the demand curve has a height of $70, the
price that George (who is now the marginal buyer) is willing to pay.

Because the demand curve reflects buyers' willingness to pay, we can also use
it to measure consumer surplus. Figure 7-2 uses the demand curve to compute
consumer surplus in our example. In panel (a), the price is $80 (or slightly above),
and the quantity demanded is 1. Note that the area above the price and below the
demand curve equals $20. This amount is exactly the consumer surplus we com-
puted earlier when only 1 album is sold.

Panel (b) of Figure 7-2 shows consumer surplus when the price is $70 (or
slightly above). In this case, the area above the price and below the demand curve

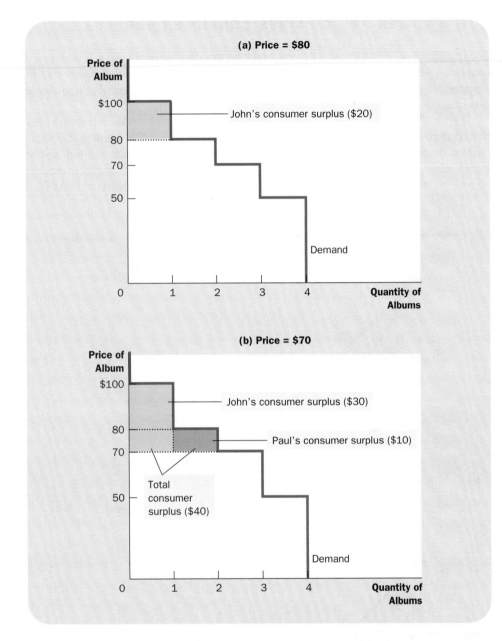

Figure 7-2

MEASURING CONSUMER SURPLUS WITH THE DEMAND CURVE.   In panel (a), the price of the good is $80, and the consumer surplus is $20. In panel (b), the price of the good is $70, and the consumer surplus is $40.

equals the total area of the two rectangles: John's consumer surplus at this price is $30 and Paul's is $10. This area equals a total of $40. Once again, this amount is the consumer surplus we computed earlier.

The lesson from this example holds for all demand curves: *The area below the demand curve and above the price measures the consumer surplus in a market.* The reason is that the height of the demand curve measures the value buyers place on the good, as measured by their willingness to pay for it. The difference between this willingness to pay and the market price is each buyer's consumer surplus. Thus, the total area below the demand curve and above the price is the sum of the consumer surplus of all buyers in the market for a good or service.

HOW A LOWER PRICE RAISES CONSUMER SURPLUS

Because buyers always want to pay less for the goods they buy, a lower price makes buyers of a good better off. But how much does buyers' well-being rise in response to a lower price? We can use the concept of consumer surplus to answer this question precisely.

Figure 7-3 shows a typical downward-sloping demand curve. Although this demand curve appears somewhat different in shape from the steplike demand curves in our previous two figures, the ideas we have just developed apply nonetheless: Consumer surplus is the area above the price and below the demand curve. In panel (a), consumer surplus at a price of P_1 is the area of triangle ABC.

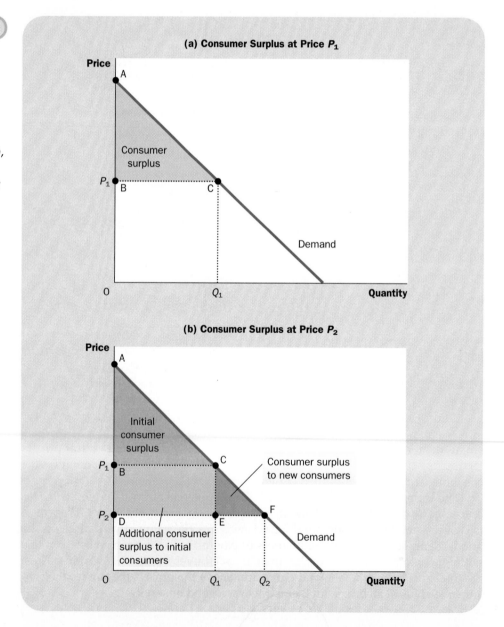

Figure 7-3

HOW THE PRICE AFFECTS CONSUMER SURPLUS.   In panel (a), the price is P_1, the quantity demanded is Q_1, and consumer surplus equals the area of the triangle ABC. When the price falls from P_1 to P_2, as in panel (b), the quantity demanded rises from Q_1 to Q_2, and the consumer surplus rises to the area of the triangle ADF. The increase in consumer surplus (area BCFD) occurs in part because existing consumers now pay less (area BCED) and in part because new consumers enter the market at the lower price (area CEF).

Now suppose that the price falls from P_1 to P_2, as shown in panel (b). The consumer surplus now equals area ADF. The increase in consumer surplus attributable to the lower price is the area BCFD.

This increase in consumer surplus is composed of two parts. First, those buyers who were already buying Q_1 of the good at the higher price P_1 are better off because they now pay less. The increase in consumer surplus of existing buyers is the reduction in the amount they pay; it equals the area of the rectangle BCED. Second, some new buyers enter the market because they are now willing to buy the good at the lower price. As a result, the quantity demanded in the market increases from Q_1 to Q_2. The consumer surplus these newcomers receive is the area of the triangle CEF.

WHAT DOES CONSUMER SURPLUS MEASURE?

Our goal in developing the concept of consumer surplus is to make normative judgements about the desirability of market outcomes. Now that you have seen what consumer surplus is, let's consider whether it is a good measure of economic well-being.

Imagine that you are a policymaker trying to design a good economic system. Would you care about the amount of consumer surplus? Consumer surplus, the amount that buyers are willing to pay for a good minus the amount they actually pay for it, measures the benefit that buyers receive from a good *as the buyers themselves perceive it*. Thus, consumer surplus is a good measure of economic well-being if policymakers want to respect the preferences of buyers.

In some circumstances, policymakers might choose not to care about consumer surplus because they do not respect the preferences that drive buyer behaviour. For example, drug addicts are willing to pay a high price for heroin. Yet we would not say that addicts get a large benefit from being able to buy heroin at a low price (even though addicts might say they do). From the standpoint of society, willingness to pay in this instance is not a good measure of the buyers' benefit, and consumer surplus is not a good measure of economic well-being, because addicts are not looking after their own best interests.

In most markets, however, consumer surplus does reflect economic well-being. Economists normally presume that buyers are rational when they make decisions and that their preferences should be respected. In this case, consumers are the best judges of how much benefit they receive from the goods they buy.

QUICK QUIZ: Draw a demand curve for turkey. In your diagram, show a price of turkey and the consumer surplus that results from that price. Explain in words what this consumer surplus measures.

PRODUCER SURPLUS

We now turn to the other side of the market and consider the benefits sellers receive from participating in a market. As you will see, our analysis of sellers' welfare is similar to our analysis of buyers' welfare.

COST AND THE WILLINGNESS TO SELL

Imagine now that you are a homeowner, and you need to get your house painted. You turn to four sellers of painting services: Mary, Frida, Georgia, and Grandma. Each painter is willing to do the work for you if the price is right. You decide to take bids from the four painters and auction off the job to the painter who will do the work for the lowest price.

cost

the value of everything a seller must give up to produce a good

Each painter is willing to take the job if the price she would receive exceeds her cost of doing the work. Here the term **cost** should be interpreted as the painters' opportunity cost: It includes the painters' out-of-pocket expenses (for paint, brushes, and so on) as well as the value that the painters place on their own time. Table 7-3 shows each painter's cost. Because a painter's cost is the lowest price she would accept for her work, cost is a measure of her willingness to sell her services. Each painter would be eager to sell her services at a price greater than her cost, would refuse to sell her services at a price less than her cost, and would be indifferent about selling her services at a price exactly equal to her cost.

When you take bids from the painters, the price might start off high, but it quickly falls as the painters compete for the job. Once Grandma has bid $600 (or slightly less), she is the sole remaining bidder. Grandma is happy to do the job for this price because her cost is only $500. Mary, Frida, and Georgia are unwilling to do the job for less than $600. Note that the job goes to the painter who can do the work at the lowest cost.

producer surplus

the amount a seller is paid for a good minus the seller's cost

What benefit does Grandma receive from getting the job? Because she is willing to do the work for $500 but gets $600 for doing it, we say that she receives *producer surplus* of $100. **Producer surplus** is the amount a seller is paid minus the cost of production. Producer surplus measures the benefit to sellers of participating in a market.

Now consider a somewhat different example. Suppose that you have two identical houses that need painting. Again, you auction off the jobs to the four painters. To keep things simple, let's assume that no painter is able to paint both houses and that you will pay the same amount to paint each house. Therefore, the price falls until two painters are left.

In this case, the bidding stops when Georgia and Grandma each offer to do the job for a price of $800 (or slightly less). At this price, Georgia and Grandma are willing to do the work, and Mary and Frida are not willing to bid a lower price. At a price of $800, Grandma receives producer surplus of $300, and Georgia receives producer surplus of $200. The total producer surplus in the market is $500.

Table 7-3

THE COSTS OF FOUR POSSIBLE SELLERS

SELLER	COST
Mary	$900
Frida	800
Georgia	600
Grandma	500

USING THE SUPPLY CURVE TO MEASURE PRODUCER SURPLUS

Just as consumer surplus is closely related to the demand curve, producer surplus is closely related to the supply curve. To see how, let's continue our example.

We begin by using the costs of the four painters to find the supply schedule for painting services. Table 7-4 shows the supply schedule that corresponds to the costs in Table 7-3. If the price is below $500, none of the four painters is willing to do the job, so the quantity supplied is zero. If the price is between $500 and $600, only Grandma is willing to do the job, so the quantity supplied is 1. If the price is between $600 and $800, Grandma and Georgia are willing to do the job, so the quantity supplied is 2, and so on. Thus, the supply schedule is derived from the costs of the four painters.

Figure 7-4 graphs the supply curve that corresponds to this supply schedule. Note that the height of the supply curve is related to the sellers' costs. At any quantity, the price given by the supply curve shows the cost of the *marginal seller,* the

PRICE	SELLERS	QUANTITY SUPPLIED
$900 or more	Mary, Frida, Georgia, Grandma	4
$800 to $900	Frida, Georgia, Grandma	3
$600 to $800	Georgia, Grandma	2
$500 to $600	Grandma	1
Less than $500	None	0

Table 7-4

THE SUPPLY SCHEDULE FOR THE SELLERS IN TABLE 7-3

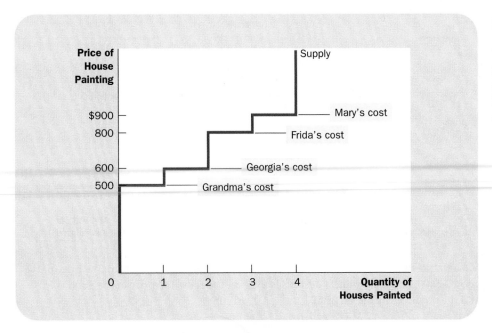

Figure 7-4

THE SUPPLY CURVE.   This figure graphs the supply curve from the supply schedule in Table 7-4. Note that the height of the supply curve reflects sellers' costs.

seller who would leave the market first if the price were any lower. At a quantity of 4 houses, for instance, the supply curve has a height of $900, the cost that Mary (the marginal seller) incurs to provide her painting services. At a quantity of 3 houses, the supply curve has a height of $800, the cost that Frida (who is now the marginal seller) incurs.

Because the supply curve reflects sellers' costs, we can use it to measure producer surplus. Figure 7-5 uses the supply curve to compute producer surplus in our example. In panel (a), we assume that the price is $600. In this case, the quantity supplied is 1. Note that the area below the price and above the supply curve equals $100. This amount is exactly the producer surplus we computed earlier for Grandma.

Panel (b) of Figure 7-5 shows producer surplus at a price of $800. In this case, the area below the price and above the supply curve equals the total area of the two rectangles. This area equals $500, the producer surplus we computed earlier for Georgia and Grandma when two houses needed painting.

The lesson from this example applies to all supply curves: *The area below the price and above the supply curve measures the producer surplus in a market.* The logic is straightforward: The height of the supply curve measures sellers' costs, and the difference between the price and the cost of production is each seller's producer surplus. Thus, the total area is the sum of the producer surplus of all sellers.

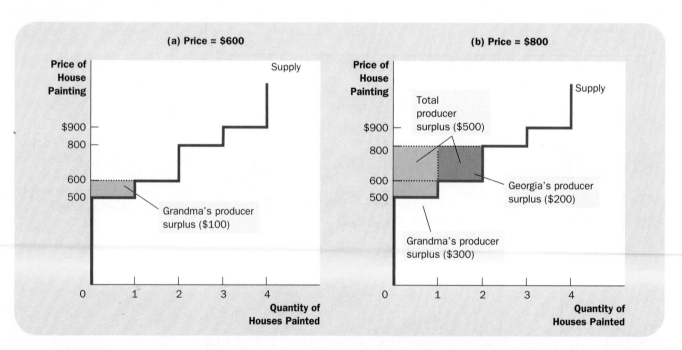

Figure 7-5   MEASURING PRODUCER SURPLUS WITH THE SUPPLY CURVE.   In panel (a), the price of the good is $600, and the producer surplus is $100. In panel (b), the price of the good is $800, and the producer surplus is $500.

HOW A HIGHER PRICE RAISES PRODUCER SURPLUS

You will not be surprised to hear that sellers always want to receive a higher price for the goods they sell. But how much does sellers' well-being rise in response to a higher price? The concept of producer surplus offers a precise answer to this question.

Figure 7-6 shows a typical upward-sloping supply curve. Even though this supply curve differs in shape from the steplike supply curves in the previous figure, we measure producer surplus in the same way: Producer surplus is the area below the price and above the supply curve. In panel (a), the price is P_1, and producer surplus is the area of triangle ABC.

Panel (b) shows what happens when the price rises from P_1 to P_2. Producer surplus now equals area ADF. This increase in producer surplus has two parts. First, those sellers who were already selling Q_1 of the good at the lower price P_1 are better off because they now get more for what they sell. The increase in producer surplus for existing sellers equals the area of the rectangle BCED. Second, some new sellers enter the market because they are now willing to produce the good at the higher price, resulting in an increase in the quantity supplied from Q_1 to Q_2. The producer surplus of these newcomers is the area of the triangle CEF.

HOW THE PRICE AFFECTS PRODUCER SURPLUS.   In panel (a), the price is P_1, the quantity demanded is Q_1, and producer surplus equals the area of the triangle ABC. When the price rises from P_1 to P_2, as in panel (b), the quantity supplied rises from Q_1 to Q_2, and the producer surplus rises to the area of the triangle ADF. The increase in producer surplus (area BCFD) occurs in part because existing producers now receive more (area BCED) and in part because new producers enter the market at the higher price (area CEF).

Figure 7-6

As this analysis shows, we use producer surplus to measure the well-being of sellers in much the same way we use consumer surplus to measure the well-being of buyers. Because these two measures of economic welfare are so similar, it is natural to use them together. And, indeed, that is exactly what we do in the next section.

> **QUICK QUIZ:**   Draw a supply curve for turkey. In your diagram, show a price of turkey and the producer surplus that results from that price. Explain in words what this producer surplus measures.

MARKET EFFICIENCY

Consumer surplus and producer surplus are the basic tools that economists use to study the welfare of buyers and sellers in a market. These tools can help us address a fundamental economic question: Is the allocation of resources determined by free markets in any way desirable?

THE BENEVOLENT SOCIAL PLANNER

To evaluate market outcomes, we introduce into our analysis a new, hypothetical character called the benevolent social planner. The benevolent social planner is an all-knowing, all-powerful, well-intentioned dictator. The planner wants to maximize the economic well-being of everyone in society. What do you suppose this planner should do? Should he just leave buyers and sellers at the equilibrium that they reach naturally on their own? Or can he increase economic well-being by altering the market outcome in some way?

To answer this question, the planner must first decide how to measure the economic well-being of a society. One possible measure is the sum of consumer and producer surplus, which we call *total surplus.* Consumer surplus is the benefit that buyers receive from participating in a market, and producer surplus is the benefit that sellers receive. It is therefore natural to use total surplus as a measure of society's economic well-being.

To better understand this measure of economic well-being, recall how we measure consumer and producer surplus. We define consumer surplus as

Consumer surplus = Value to buyers − Amount paid by buyers.

Similarly, we define producer surplus as

Producer surplus = Amount received by sellers − Cost to sellers.

When we add consumer and producer surplus together, we obtain

Total surplus = Value to buyers − Amount paid by buyers
+ Amount received by sellers − Cost to sellers.

The amount paid by buyers equals the amount received by sellers, so the middle two terms in this expression cancel each other. As a result, we can write total surplus as

$$\text{Total surplus} = \text{Value to buyers} - \text{Cost to sellers.}$$

Total surplus in a market is the total value to buyers of the goods, as measured by their willingness to pay, minus the total cost to sellers of providing those goods.

If an allocation of resources maximizes total surplus, we say that the allocation exhibits **efficiency.** If an allocation is not efficient, then some of the gains from trade among buyers and sellers are not being realized. For example, an allocation is inefficient if a good is not being produced by the sellers with lowest cost. In this case, moving production from a high-cost producer to a low-cost producer will lower the total cost to sellers and raise total surplus. Similarly, an allocation is inefficient if a good is not being consumed by the buyers who value it most highly. In this case, moving consumption of the good from a buyer with a low valuation to a buyer with a high valuation will raise total surplus.

efficiency
the property of a resource allocation of maximizing the total surplus received by all members of society

In addition to efficiency, the social planner might also care about **equity**—the fairness of the distribution of well-being among the various buyers and sellers. In essence, the gains from trade in a market are like a pie to be distributed among the market participants. The question of efficiency is whether the pie is as big as possible. The question of equity is whether the pie is divided fairly. Evaluating the equity of a market outcome is more difficult than evaluating the efficiency. Whereas efficiency is an objective goal that can be judged on strictly positive grounds, equity involves normative judgements that go beyond economics and enter into the realm of political philosophy.

equity
the fairness of the distribution of well-being among the members of society

In this chapter we concentrate on efficiency as the social planner's goal. Keep in mind, however, that real policymakers often care about equity as well. That is, they care about both the size of the economic pie and how the pie gets sliced and distributed among members of society.

EVALUATING THE MARKET EQUILIBRIUM

Figure 7-7 shows consumer and producer surplus when a market reaches the equilibrium of supply and demand. Recall that consumer surplus equals the area above the price and under the demand curve and producer surplus equals the area below the price and above the supply curve. Thus, the total area between the supply and demand curves up to the point of equilibrium represents the total surplus from this market.

Is this equilibrium allocation of resources efficient? Does it maximize total surplus? To answer these questions, keep in mind that when a market is in equilibrium, the price determines which buyers and sellers participate in the market. Those buyers who value the good more than the price (represented by the segment AE on the demand curve) choose to buy the good; those buyers who value it less than the price (represented by the segment EB) do not. Similarly, those sellers whose costs are less than the price (represented by the segment CE on the supply curve) choose to produce and sell the good; those sellers whose costs are greater than the price (represented by the segment ED) do not.

Figure 7-7

CONSUMER AND PRODUCER SURPLUS IN THE MARKET EQUILIBRIUM.   Total surplus—the sum of consumer and producer surplus—is the area between the supply and demand curves up to the equilibrium quantity.

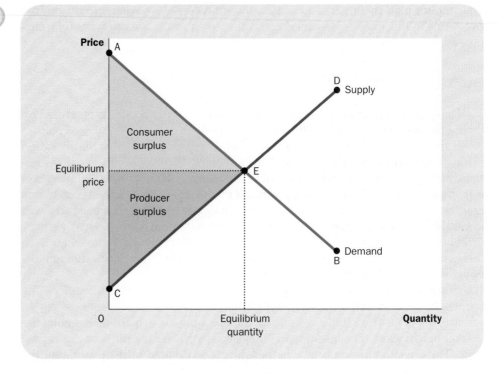

These observations lead to two insights about market outcomes:

1. Free markets allocate the supply of goods to the buyers who value them most highly, as measured by their willingness to pay.
2. Free markets allocate the demand for goods to the sellers who can produce them at least cost.

Thus, given the quantity produced and sold in a market equilibrium, the social planner cannot increase economic well-being by changing the allocation of consumption among buyers or the allocation of production among sellers.

But can the social planner raise total economic well-being by increasing or decreasing the quantity of the good? The answer is no, as stated in this third insight about market outcomes:

3. Free markets produce the quantity of goods that maximizes the sum of consumer and producer surplus.

To see why this is true, consider Figure 7-8. Recall that the demand curve reflects the value to buyers and that the supply curve reflects the cost to sellers. At quantities below the equilibrium level, the value to buyers exceeds the cost to sellers. In this region, increasing the quantity raises total surplus, and it continues to do so until the quantity reaches the equilibrium level. Beyond the equilibrium quantity, however, the value to buyers is less than the cost to sellers. Producing more than the equilibrium quantity would, therefore, lower total surplus.

These three insights about market outcomes tell us that the equilibrium of supply and demand maximizes the sum of consumer and producer surplus. In other

Figure 7-8

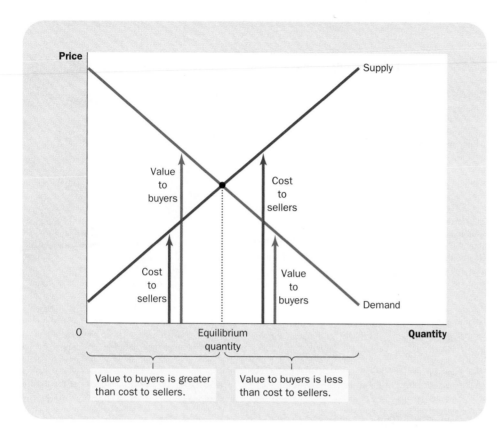

THE EFFICIENCY OF THE EQUILIBRIUM QUANTITY.   At quantities less than the equilibrium quantity, the value to buyers exceeds the cost to sellers. At quantities greater than the equilibrium quantity, the cost to sellers exceeds the value to buyers. Therefore, the market equilibrium maximizes the sum of producer and consumer surplus.

words, the equilibrium outcome is an efficient allocation of resources. The job of the benevolent social planner is, therefore, very easy: He can leave the market outcome just as he finds it. This policy of leaving well enough alone goes by the French expression *laissez-faire,* which literally translated means "allow them to do."

We can now better appreciate Adam Smith's invisible hand of the marketplace, which we first discussed in Chapter 1. The benevolent social planner doesn't need to alter the market outcome because the invisible hand has already guided buyers and sellers to an allocation of the economy's resources that maximizes total surplus. This conclusion explains why economists often advocate free markets as the best way to organize economic activity.

QUICK QUIZ: Draw the supply and demand for turkey. In the equilibrium, show producer and consumer surplus. Explain why producing more turkey would lower total surplus.

CONCLUSION: MARKET EFFICIENCY AND MARKET FAILURE

This chapter introduced the basic tools of welfare economics—consumer and producer surplus—and used them to evaluate the efficiency of free markets. We

IN THE NEWS

Ticket Scalping

IF AN ECONOMY IS TO ALLOCATE ITS SCARCE resources efficiently, goods must get to those consumers who value them most highly. Ticket scalping is one example of how markets reach efficient outcomes. Scalpers buy tickets to plays, concerts, and sports events and then sell the tickets at a price above their original cost. By charging the highest price the market will bear, scalpers help ensure that consumers with the greatest willingness to pay for the tickets actually do get them. In some places, however, there is debate over whether this market activity should be legal.

Tickets? Supply Meets Demand on Sidewalk

BY JOHN TIERNEY

Ticket scalping has been very good to Kevin Thomas, and he makes no apologies. He sees himself as a classic American entrepreneur: a high-school dropout from the Bronx who taught himself a trade, works seven nights a week, earns $40 000 a year, and at age 26 has $75 000 in savings, all by providing a public service outside New York's theatres and sports arenas.

He has just one complaint. "I've been busted about 30 times in the last year," he said one recent evening, just after making $280 at a Knicks game. "You learn to deal with it—I give the cops a fake name, and I pay the fines when I have to, but I don't think it's fair. I look at scalping like working as a stockbroker, buying low and selling high. If people are willing to pay me the money, what kind of problem is that?"

It is a significant problem to public officials in New York and New Jersey,

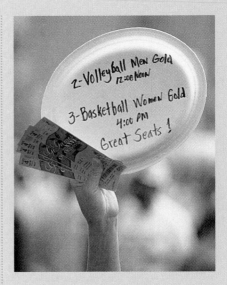

THE INVISIBLE HAND AT WORK

who are cracking down on street scalpers like Mr. Thomas and on licensed ticket brokers. Undercover officers are enforcing new restrictions on reselling tickets at marked-up prices, and the attorneys general of the two states are pressing well-publicized

showed that the forces of supply and demand allocate resources efficiently. That is, even though each buyer and seller in a market is concerned only about his or her own welfare, they are together led by an invisible hand to an equilibrium that maximizes the total benefits to buyers and sellers.

A word of warning is in order. To conclude that markets are efficient, we made several assumptions about how markets work. When these assumptions do not hold, our conclusion that the market equilibrium is efficient may no longer be true. As we close this chapter, let's consider briefly two of the most important of these assumptions.

First, our analysis assumed that markets are perfectly competitive. In the world, however, competition is sometimes far from perfect. In some markets, a single buyer or seller (or a small group of them) may be able to control market prices. This ability to influence prices is called *market power*. Market power can cause markets to be inefficient because it keeps the price and quantity away from the equilibrium of supply and demand.

Second, our analysis assumed that the outcome in a market matters only to the buyers and sellers in that market. Yet, in the world, the decisions of buyers and cases against more than a dozen ticket brokers.

But economists tend to see scalping from Mr. Thomas's perspective. To them, the governments' crusade makes about as much sense as the old campaigns by Communist authorities against "profiteering." Economists argue that the restrictions inconvenience the public, reduce the audience for cultural and sports events, waste the police's time, deprive New York City of tens of millions of dollars of tax revenue, and actually drive up the cost of many tickets.

"It is always good politics to pose as defender of the poor by declaring high prices illegal," says William J. Baumol, the director of the C.V. Starr Center for Applied Economics at New York University. "I expect politicians to try to solve the AIDS crisis by declaring AIDS illegal as well. That would be harmless, because nothing would happen, but when you outlaw high prices you create real problems."

Dr. Baumol was one of the economists who came up with the idea of selling same-day Broadway tickets for half price at the TKTS booth in Times Square, which theatre owners thought dangerously radical when the booth opened in 1973. But the owners have profited by finding a new clientele for tickets that would have gone unsold, an illustration of the free-market tenet that both buyers and sellers ultimately benefit when price is adjusted to meet demand.

Economists see another illustration of that lesson at the Museum of Modern Art, where people wait in line for up to two hours to buy tickets for the Matisse exhibit. But there is an alternative on the sidewalk: Scalpers who evade the police have been selling the $12.50 tickets to the show at prices ranging from $20 to $50.

"You don't have to put a very high value on your time to pay $10 or $15 to avoid standing in line for two hours for a Matisse ticket," said Richard H. Thaler, an economist at Cornell University. "Some people think it's fairer to make everyone stand in line, but that forces everyone to engage in a totally unpro-

ductive activity, and it discriminates in favour of people who have the most free time. Scalping gives other people a chance, too. I can see no justification for outlawing it." . . .

Politicians commonly argue that without anti-scalping laws, tickets would become unaffordable to most people, but California has no laws against scalping, and ticket prices there are not notoriously high. And as much as scalpers would like to inflate prices, only a limited number of people are willing to pay $100 for a ticket. . . .

Legalizing scalping, however, would not necessarily be good news for everyone. Mr. Thomas, for instance, fears that the extra competition might put him out of business. But after 16 years—he started at age 10 outside of Yankee Stadium—he is thinking it might be time for a change anyway.

SOURCE: *The New York Times*, December 26, 1992, p. A1.

sellers sometimes affect people who are not participants in the market at all. Pollution is the classic example of a market outcome that affects people not in the market. Such side effects, called *externalities*, cause welfare in a market to depend on more than just the value to the buyers and the cost to the sellers. Because buyers and sellers do not take these side effects into account when deciding how much to consume and produce, the equilibrium in a market can be inefficient from the standpoint of society as a whole.

Market power and externalities are examples of a general phenomenon called *market failure*—the inability of some unregulated markets to allocate resources efficiently. When markets fail, public policy can potentially remedy the problem and increase economic efficiency. Microeconomists devote much effort to studying when market failure is likely and what sorts of policies are best at correcting market failures. As you continue your study of economics, you will see that the tools of welfare economics developed here are readily adapted to that endeavour.

Despite the possibility of market failure, the invisible hand of the marketplace is extraordinarily important. In many markets, the assumptions we made in this chapter work well, and the conclusion of market efficiency applies directly. Moreover, our analysis of welfare economics and market efficiency can be used to shed light on the effects of various government policies. In the next two chapters we apply the tools we have just developed to study two important policy issues—the welfare effects of taxation and of international trade.

Summary

◆ Consumer surplus equals buyers' willingness to pay for a good minus the amount they actually pay for it, and it measures the benefit buyers get from participating in a market. Consumer surplus can be computed by finding the area below the demand curve and above the price.

◆ Producer surplus equals the amount sellers receive for their goods minus their costs of production, and it measures the benefit sellers get from participating in a market. Producer surplus can be computed by finding the area below the price and above the supply curve.

◆ An allocation of resources that maximizes the sum of consumer and producer surplus is said to be efficient.

Policymakers are often concerned with the efficiency, as well as the equity, of economic outcomes.

◆ The equilibrium of supply and demand maximizes the sum of consumer and producer surplus. That is, the invisible hand of the marketplace leads buyers and sellers to allocate resources efficiently.

◆ Markets do not allocate resources efficiently in the presence of market failures such as market power or externalities.

Key Concepts

welfare economics, p. 142
willingness to pay, p. 142
consumer surplus, p. 143

cost, p. 148
producer surplus, p. 148

efficiency, p. 153
equity, p. 153

Questions for Review

1. Explain how buyers' willingness to pay, consumer surplus, and the demand curve are related.

2. Explain how sellers' costs, producer surplus, and the supply curve are related.

3. In a supply-and-demand diagram, show producer and consumer surplus in the market equilibrium.

4. What is efficiency? Is it the only goal of economic policymakers?

5. What does the invisible hand do?

6. Name two types of market failure. Explain why each may cause market outcomes to be inefficient.

Problems and Applications

1. A drought in Nova Scotia reduces the apple harvest. What happens to consumer surplus in the market for apples? What happens to consumer surplus in the market for apple juice? Illustrate your answers with diagrams.

2. Suppose the demand for French bread rises. What happens to producer surplus in the market for French bread? What happens to producer surplus in the market for flour? Illustrate your answer with diagrams.

3. It is a hot day, and Bert is very thirsty. Here is the value he places on a bottle of water:

Value of first bottle	$7
Value of second bottle	5
Value of third bottle	3
Value of fourth bottle	1

   a. From this information, derive Bert's demand schedule. Graph his demand curve for bottled water.

   b. If the price of a bottle of water is $4, how many bottles does Bert buy? How much consumer surplus does Bert get from his purchases? Show Bert's consumer surplus in your graph.

   c. If the price falls to $2, how does quantity demanded change? How does Bert's consumer surplus change? Show these changes in your graph.

4. Ernie owns a water pump. Because pumping large amounts of water is harder than pumping small amounts, the cost of producing a bottle of water rises as he pumps more. Here is the cost he incurs to produce each bottle of water:

Cost of first bottle	$1
Cost of second bottle	3
Cost of third bottle	5
Cost of fourth bottle	7

   a. From this information, derive Ernie's supply schedule. Graph his supply curve for bottled water.

   b. If the price of a bottle of water is $4, how many bottles does Ernie produce and sell? How much producer surplus does Ernie get from these sales? Show Ernie's producer surplus in your graph.

   c. If the price rises to $6, how does quantity supplied change? How does Ernie's producer surplus change? Show these changes in your graph.

5. Consider a market in which Bert from Question 3 is the buyer and Ernie from Question 4 is the seller.

   a. Use Ernie's supply schedule and Bert's demand schedule to find the quantity supplied and quantity demanded at prices of $2, $4, and $6. Which of these prices brings supply and demand into equilibrium?

   b. What are consumer surplus, producer surplus, and total surplus in this equilibrium?

   c. If Ernie produced and Bert consumed one less bottle of water, what would happen to total surplus?

   d. If Ernie produced and Bert consumed one additional bottle of water, what would happen to total surplus?

6. The cost of producing stereo systems has fallen over the past several decades. Let's consider some implications of this fact.

   a. Use a supply-and-demand diagram to show the effect of falling production costs on the price and quantity of stereos sold.

   b. In your diagram, show what happens to consumer surplus and producer surplus.

   c. Suppose the supply of stereos is very elastic. Who benefits most from falling production costs—consumers or producers of stereos?

7. Four consumers are willing to pay the following amounts for haircuts:

   Jerry: $7   Oprah: $2   Sally Jessy: $8   Montel: $5

   Four haircutting businesses have the following costs:

   Firm A: $3   Firm B: $6   Firm C: $4   Firm D: $2

   Each firm has the capacity to produce only one haircut. For efficiency, how many haircuts should be given? Which businesses should cut hair, and which consumers should have their hair cut? How large is the maximum possible total surplus?

8. Suppose a technological advance reduces the cost of making computers.

   a. Use a supply-and-demand diagram to show what happens to price, quantity, consumer surplus, and producer surplus in the market for computers.

   b. Computers and adding machines are substitutes. Use a supply-and-demand diagram to show what happens to price, quantity, consumer surplus, and producer surplus in the market for adding machines. Should adding machine producers be happy or sad about the technological advance in computers?

   c. Computers and software are complements. Use a supply-and-demand diagram to show what happens to price, quantity, consumer surplus, and producer surplus in the market for software. Should software producers be happy or sad about the technological advance in computers?

   d. Does this analysis help explain why Bill Gates, a software producer, is one of the world's richest men? Explain.

9. Consider how health insurance affects the quantity of health care services performed. Suppose that the typical medical procedure has a cost of $100, yet a person with health insurance pays nothing when she chooses to have an additional procedure performed. Her provincial health insurance pays the full $100. (The province will recoup the $100 through higher taxes for everybody, but the share paid by this individual is small.)

   a. Draw the demand curve in the market for medical care. (In your diagram, the horizontal axis should represent the number of medical procedures.) Show the quantity of procedures demanded if each procedure has a price of $100.

   b. On your diagram, show the quantity of procedures demanded if consumers pay nothing per procedure. If the cost of each procedure to society is truly $100, and if individuals have health insurance as just described, will the number of procedures performed maximize total surplus? Explain.

   c. Economists often blame the health insurance system for excessive use of medical care. Given your analysis, why might the use of care be viewed as "excessive"?

   d. What sort of policies might prevent this excessive use?

10. Many parts of California experienced a severe drought in the late 1980s and early 1990s.

   a. Use a diagram of the water market to show the effects of the drought on the equilibrium price and quantity of water.

   b. Many communities did not allow the price of water to change, however. What is the effect of this policy on the water market? Show on your diagram any surplus or shortage that arises.

   c. A 1991 op-ed piece in *The Wall Street Journal* stated that "all Los Angeles residents are required to cut their water usage by 10 percent as of March 1 and another 5 percent starting May 1, based on their 1986 consumption levels." The author criticized this policy on both efficiency and equity grounds, saying, "not only does such a policy reward families who 'wasted' more water back in 1986, it does little to encourage consumers who could make more drastic reductions, [and] . . . punishes consumers who cannot so readily reduce their water use." In what way is the Los Angeles system for allocating water inefficient? In what way does the system seem unfair?

   d. Suppose instead that Los Angeles allowed the price of water to increase until the quantity demanded equalled the quantity supplied. Would the resulting allocation of water be more efficient? In your view, would it be more or less fair than the proportionate reductions in water use mentioned in the newspaper article? What could be done to make the market solution more fair?

8

APPLICATION: THE COSTS OF TAXATION

IN THIS CHAPTER YOU WILL . . .

Examine how taxes reduce consumer and producer surplus

Learn the meaning and causes of the deadweight loss of a tax

Consider why some taxes have larger deadweight losses than others

Examine how tax revenue and deadweight loss vary with the size of a tax

Taxes are often a source of heated political debate. In 1993, Jean Chrétien succeeded Kim Campbell as prime minister of Canada, in part because voters believed he would scrap the Goods and Services Tax (GST) introduced by Brian Mulroney's government. In the 2000 federal election, a key issue was the Canadian Alliance plan to cut federal income taxes. When oil and gasoline prices spiked in the summer of 2000, truckers and other motorists demanded a reduction in gasoline taxes. In 1995, Mike Harris replaced Bob Rae as premier of Ontario on a promise to cut provincial income taxes. Municipal elections are often fought on the issue of whether to raise property taxes or to cut local government services.

We began our study of taxes in Chapter 6. There we saw how a tax on a good affects its price and the quantity sold and how the forces of supply and demand divide the burden of a tax between buyers and sellers. In this chapter we extend

"You know, the idea of taxation *with* representation doesn't appeal to me very much, either."

this analysis and look at how taxes affect welfare, the economic well-being of participants in a market.

The effects of taxes on welfare might at first seem obvious. The government enacts taxes to raise revenue, and that revenue must come out of someone's pocket. As we saw in Chapter 6, both buyers and sellers are worse off when a good is taxed: A tax raises the price buyers pay and lowers the price sellers receive. Yet to understand fully how taxes affect economic well-being, we must compare the reduced welfare of buyers and sellers with the amount of revenue the government raises. The tools of consumer and producer surplus allow us to make this comparison. The analysis will show that the costs of taxes to buyers and sellers exceed the revenue raised by the government.

THE DEADWEIGHT LOSS OF TAXATION

We begin by recalling one of the surprising lessons from Chapter 6: It does not matter whether a tax on a good is levied on buyers or sellers of the good. When a tax is levied on buyers, the demand curve shifts downward by the size of the tax; when it is levied on sellers, the supply curve shifts upward by that amount. In either case, when the tax is enacted, the price paid by buyers rises, and the price received by sellers falls. In the end, buyers and sellers share the burden of the tax, regardless of how it is levied.

Figure 8-1 shows these effects. To simplify our discussion, this figure does not show a shift in either the supply or the demand curve, although one curve must shift. Which curve shifts depends on whether the tax is levied on sellers (the supply curve shifts) or buyers (the demand curve shifts). In this chapter, we can simplify the graphs by not bothering to show the shift. The key result for our pur-

Figure 8-1

THE EFFECTS OF A TAX.   A tax on a good places a wedge between the price that buyers pay and the price that sellers receive. The quantity of the good sold falls.

Figure 8-2

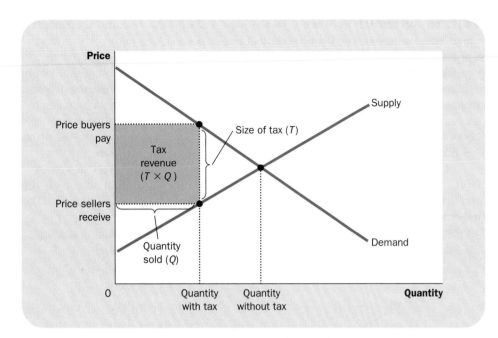

TAX REVENUE.   The tax revenue that the government collects equals $T \times Q$, the size of the tax T times the quantity sold Q. Thus, tax revenue equals the area of the rectangle between the supply and demand curves.

poses here is that the tax places a wedge between the price buyers pay and the price sellers receive. Because of this tax wedge, the quantity sold falls below the level that would be sold without a tax. In other words, a tax on a good causes the size of the market for the good to shrink. These results should be familiar from Chapter 6.

HOW A TAX AFFECTS MARKET PARTICIPANTS

Now let's use the tools of welfare economics to measure the gains and losses from a tax on a good. To do this, we must take into account how the tax affects buyers, sellers, and the government. The benefit received by buyers in a market is measured by consumer surplus—the amount buyers are willing to pay for the good minus the amount they actually pay for it. The benefit received by sellers in a market is measured by producer surplus—the amount sellers receive for the good minus their costs. These are precisely the measures of economic welfare we used in Chapter 7.

What about the third interested party, the government? If T is the size of the tax and Q is the quantity of the good sold, then the government gets total tax revenue of $T \times Q$. It can use this tax revenue to provide services—such as roads, police, and public education—or to help the needy. Therefore, to analyze how taxes affect economic well-being, we use tax revenue to measure the government's benefit from the tax. Keep in mind, however, that this benefit actually accrues not to government but to those on whom the revenue is spent.

Figure 8-2 shows that the government's tax revenue is represented by the rectangle between the supply and demand curves. The height of this rectangle is the size of the tax, T, and the width of the rectangle is the quantity of the good sold, Q. Because a rectangle's area is its height times its width, this rectangle's area is $T \times Q$, which equals the tax revenue.

Welfare without a Tax To see how a tax affects welfare, we begin by considering welfare before the government has imposed a tax. Figure 8-3 shows the supply-and-demand diagram and marks the key areas with the letters A through F.

Without a tax, the price and quantity are found at the intersection of the supply and demand curves. The price is P_1, and the quantity sold is Q_1. Because the demand curve reflects buyers' willingness to pay, consumer surplus is the area between the demand curve and the price, A + B + C. Similarly, because the supply curve reflects sellers' costs, producer surplus is the area between the supply curve and the price, D + E + F. In this case, because there is no tax, tax revenue equals zero.

Total surplus, the sum of consumer and producer surplus, equals the area A + B + C + D + E + F. In other words, as we saw in Chapter 7, total surplus is the area between the supply and demand curves up to the equilibrium quantity. The first column of Table 8-1 summarizes these conclusions.

Figure 8-3	

HOW A TAX AFFECTS WELFARE.
A tax on a good reduces
consumer surplus (by the area
B + C) and producer surplus (by
the area D + E). Because the fall
in producer and consumer
surplus exceeds tax revenue (area
B + D), the tax is said to impose a
deadweight loss (area C + E).

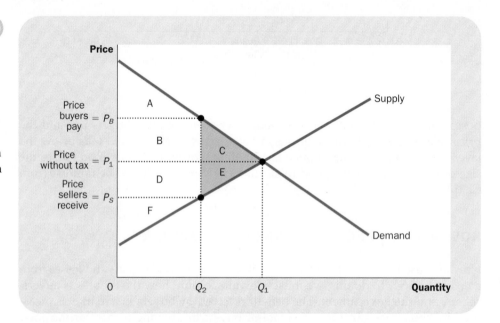

	WITHOUT TAX	WITH TAX	CHANGE
Consumer Surplus	A + B + C	A	−(B + C)
Producer Surplus	D + E + F	F	−(D + E)
Tax Revenue	None	B + D	+(B + D)
Total Surplus	A + B + C + D + E + F	A + B + D + F	−(C + E)

The area C + E shows the fall in total surplus and is the deadweight loss of the tax.

Table 8-1	

CHANGES IN WELFARE FROM A TAX. This table refers to the areas marked in Figure 8-3 to show how a tax affects the welfare of buyers and sellers in a market.

Welfare with a Tax   Now consider welfare after the tax is enacted. The price paid by buyers rises from P_1 to P_B, so consumer surplus now equals only area A (the area below the demand curve and above the buyer's price). The price received by sellers falls from P_1 to P_S, so producer surplus now equals only area F (the area above the supply curve and below the seller's price). The quantity sold falls from Q_1 to Q_2, and the government collects tax revenue equal to the area B + D.

To compute total surplus with the tax, we add consumer surplus, producer surplus, and tax revenue. Thus, we find that total surplus is area A + B + D + F. The second column of Table 8-1 provides a summary.

Changes in Welfare   We can now see the effects of the tax by comparing welfare before and after the tax is enacted. The third column in Table 8-1 shows the changes. The tax causes consumer surplus to fall by the area B + C and producer surplus to fall by the area D + E. Tax revenue rises by the area B + D. Not surprisingly, the tax makes buyers and sellers worse off and the government better off.

The change in total welfare includes the change in consumer surplus (which is negative), the change in producer surplus (which is also negative), and the change in tax revenue (which is positive). When we add these three pieces together, we find that total surplus in the market falls by the area C + E. *Thus, the losses to buyers and sellers from a tax exceed the revenue raised by the government.* The fall in total surplus that results when a tax (or some other policy) distorts a market outcome is called the **deadweight loss.** The area C + E measures the size of the deadweight loss.

deadweight loss
the fall in total surplus that results from a market distortion, such as a tax

To understand why taxes impose deadweight losses, recall one of the *Ten Principles of Economics* in Chapter 1: People respond to incentives. In Chapter 7 we saw that markets normally allocate scarce resources efficiently. That is, the equilibrium of supply and demand maximizes the total surplus of buyers and sellers in a market. When a tax raises the price to buyers and lowers the price to sellers, however, it gives buyers an incentive to consume less and sellers an incentive to produce less than they otherwise would. As buyers and sellers respond to these incentives, the size of the market shrinks below its optimum. Thus, because taxes distort incentives, they cause markets to allocate resources inefficiently.

DEADWEIGHT LOSSES AND THE GAINS FROM TRADE

To gain some intuition for why taxes result in deadweight losses, consider an example. Imagine that Raj cleans Amyra's house each week for $100. The opportunity cost of Raj's time is $80, and the value of a clean house to Amyra is $120. Thus, Raj and Amyra each receive a $20 benefit from their deal. The total surplus of $40 measures the gains from trade in this particular transaction.

Now suppose that the government levies a $50 tax on the providers of cleaning services. There is now no price that Amyra can pay Raj that will leave both of them better off after paying the tax. The most Amyra would be willing to pay is $120, but then Raj would be left with only $70 after paying the tax, which is less than his $80 opportunity cost. Conversely, for Raj to receive his opportunity cost of $80, Amyra would need to pay $130, which is above the $120 value she places on a clean house. As a result, Amyra and Raj cancel their arrangement. Raj goes without the income, and Amyra lives in a dirtier house.

The tax has made Raj and Amyra worse off by a total of $40, because they have lost this amount of surplus. At the same time, the government collects no revenue from Raj and Amyra because they decide to cancel their arrangement. The $40 is

Figure 8-4

THE DEADWEIGHT LOSS.   When the government imposes a tax on a good, the quantity sold falls from Q_1 to Q_2. As a result, some of the potential gains from trade among buyers and sellers do not get realized. These lost gains from trade create the deadweight loss.

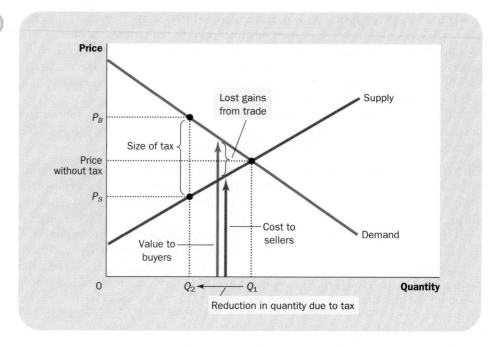

pure deadweight loss: It is a loss to buyers and sellers in a market not offset by an increase in government revenue. From this example, we can see the ultimate source of deadweight losses: *Taxes cause deadweight losses because they prevent buyers and sellers from realizing some of the gains from trade.*

The area of the triangle between the supply and demand curves (area C + E in Figure 8-3) measures these losses. This loss can be seen most easily in Figure 8-4 by recalling that the demand curve reflects the value of the good to consumers and that the supply curve reflects the costs of producers. When the tax raises the price to buyers to P_B and lowers the price to sellers to P_S, the marginal buyers and sellers leave the market, so the quantity sold falls from Q_1 to Q_2. Yet, as the figure shows, the value of the good to these buyers still exceeds the cost to these sellers. As in our example with Raj and Amyra, the gains from trade—the difference between buyers' value and sellers' cost—is less than the tax. Thus, these trades do not get made once the tax is imposed. The deadweight loss is the surplus lost because the tax discourages these mutually advantageous trades.

QUICK QUIZ: Draw the supply and demand curves for cookies. If the government imposes a tax on cookies, show what happens to the quantity sold, the price paid by buyers, and the price paid by sellers. In your diagram, show the deadweight loss from the tax. Explain the meaning of the deadweight loss.

THE DETERMINANTS OF THE DEADWEIGHT LOSS

What determines whether the deadweight loss from a tax is large or small? The answer is the price elasticities of supply and demand, which measure how much the quantity supplied and quantity demanded respond to changes in the price.

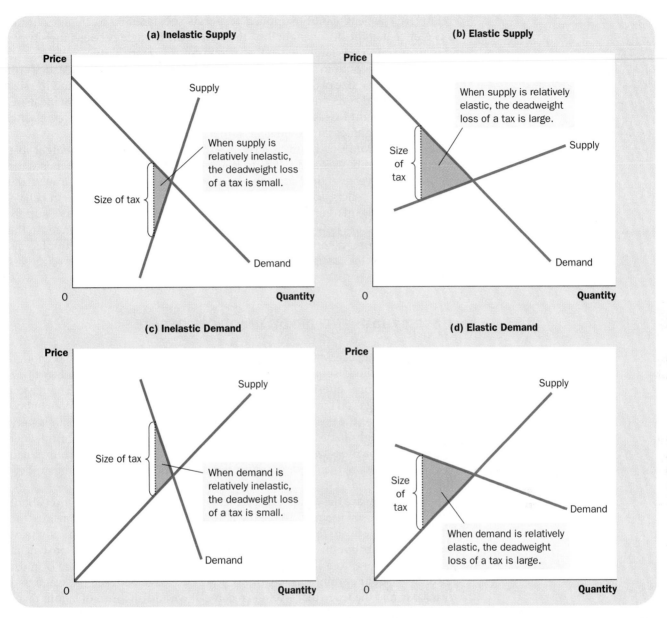

TAX DISTORTIONS AND ELASTICITIES. In panels (a) and (b), the demand curve and the size of the tax are the same, but the price elasticity of supply is different. Notice that the more elastic the supply curve, the larger the deadweight loss of the tax. In panels (c) and (d), the supply curve and the size of the tax are the same, but the price elasticity of demand is different. Notice that the more elastic the demand curve, the larger the deadweight loss of the tax.

Figure 8-5

Let's consider first how the elasticity of supply affects the size of the deadweight loss. In the top two panels of Figure 8-5, the demand curve and the size of the tax are the same. The only difference in these figures is the elasticity of the supply curve. In panel (a), the supply curve is relatively inelastic: Quantity supplied responds only slightly to changes in the price. In panel (b), the supply curve is relatively elastic: Quantity supplied responds substantially to changes in the price. Notice that the deadweight loss, the area of the triangle between the supply and demand curves, is larger when the supply curve is more elastic.

Similarly, the bottom two panels of Figure 8-5 show how the elasticity of demand affects the size of the deadweight loss. Here the supply curve and the size of the tax are held constant. In panel (c) the demand curve is relatively inelastic, and the deadweight loss is small. In panel (d) the demand curve is more elastic, and the deadweight loss from the tax is larger.

The lesson from this figure is easy to explain. A tax has a deadweight loss because it induces buyers and sellers to change their behaviour. The tax raises the price paid by buyers, so they consume less. At the same time, the tax lowers the price received by sellers, so they produce less. Because of these changes in behaviour, the size of the market shrinks below the optimum. The elasticities of supply and demand measure how much sellers and buyers respond to the changes in the price and, therefore, determine how much the tax distorts the market outcome. Hence, *the greater the elasticities of supply and demand, the greater the deadweight loss of a tax.*

CASE STUDY   THE DEADWEIGHT LOSS DEBATE

Supply, demand, elasticity, deadweight loss—all this economic theory is enough to make your head spin. But believe it or not, these ideas go to the heart of a profound political question: How big should the government be? The reason the debate hinges on these concepts is that the larger the deadweight loss of taxation, the larger the cost of any government program. If taxation entails very large deadweight losses, then these losses are a strong argument for a leaner government that does less and taxes less. By contrast, if taxes impose only small deadweight losses, then government programs are less costly than they otherwise might be.

So how big are the deadweight losses of taxation? This is a question about which economists disagree. To see the nature of the disagreement, consider the most important tax in the Canadian economy—the tax on labour. Employment Insurance contributions are a tax on labour. Both the federal and provincial income taxes are, to a large extent, labour taxes, because the source of most income is labour earnings. A labour tax places a wedge between the wage that firms pay and the wage that workers receive. If we add all forms of labour taxes together, the marginal tax rate on labour income—the tax on the last dollar of earnings—is over 50 percent for many workers.

Although the size of the labour tax is easy to determine, the deadweight loss of this tax is less straightforward. Economists disagree about whether this 50 percent labour tax has a small or a large deadweight loss. This disagreement arises because they hold different views about the elasticity of labour supply.

Economists who argue that labour taxes are not very distorting believe that labour supply is fairly inelastic. Most people, they claim, would work full-time regardless of the wage. If so, the labour supply curve is almost vertical, and a tax on labour has a small deadweight loss.

Economists who argue that labour taxes are highly distorting believe that labour supply is more elastic. They admit that some groups of workers may supply their labour inelastically but claim that many other groups respond more to incentives. Here are some examples:

"LET ME TELL YOU WHAT I THINK ABOUT THE ELASTICITY OF LABOUR SUPPLY."

◆   Many workers can adjust the number of hours they work—for instance, by working overtime, or by choosing jobs with longer or shorter hours. The higher the wage, the more hours they choose to work.

◆   Some families have second earners—often married women with children—with some discretion over whether to do unpaid work at home or paid work in the marketplace. When deciding whether to take a job, these second earners compare the benefits of being at home (including savings on the cost of child care) with the wages they could earn.

◆   Many elderly people can choose when to retire, and their decisions are partly based on the wage. Once they are retired, the wage determines their incentive to work part-time.

◆   Some people consider engaging in illegal economic activity, such as the drug trade, or working at jobs that pay "under the table" to evade taxes. Economists call this the *underground economy*. In deciding whether to work in the underground economy or at a legitimate job, these potential criminals compare what they can earn by breaking the law with the wage they can earn legally.

In each of these cases, the quantity of labour supplied responds to the wage (the price of labour). Thus, the decisions of these workers are distorted when their labour earnings are taxed. Labour taxes encourage workers to work fewer hours, second earners to stay at home, elderly people to retire early, and the unscrupulous to enter the underground economy.

These two views of labour taxation persist to this day. Indeed, whenever you see two political candidates debating whether the government should provide more services or reduce the tax burden, keep in mind that part of the disagreement may rest on different views about the elasticity of labour supply and the deadweight loss of taxation.

FYI

Henry George and the Land Tax

Is there an ideal tax? Henry George, the nineteenth-century American economist and social philosopher, thought so. In his 1879 book *Progress and Poverty*, George argued that the government should raise all its revenue from a tax on land. This "single tax" was, he claimed, both equitable and efficient. George's ideas won him a large political following, and in 1886 he lost a close race for mayor of New York City (although he finished well ahead of Republican candidate Theodore Roosevelt).

George's proposal to tax land was motivated largely by a concern over the distribution of economic well-being. He deplored the "shocking contrast between monstrous wealth and debasing want" and thought landowners benefited more than they should from the rapid growth in the overall economy.

George's arguments for the land tax can be understood using the tools of modern economics. Consider first supply and demand in the market for renting land. As immigration causes the population to rise and technological progress causes incomes to grow, the demand for land rises over time. Yet because the amount of land is fixed, the supply is perfectly inelastic. Rapid increases in demand together with inelastic supply lead to large increases in the equilibrium rents on land, so that economic growth makes rich landowners even richer.

Now consider the incidence of a tax on land. As we first saw in Chapter 6, the burden of a tax falls more heavily on the side of the market that is less elastic. A tax on land takes this principle to an extreme. Because the elasticity of supply is zero, the landowners bear the entire burden of the tax.

HENRY GEORGE

Consider next the question of efficiency. As we just discussed, the deadweight loss of a tax depends on the elasticities of supply and demand. Again, a tax on land is an extreme case. Because supply is perfectly inelastic, a tax on land does not alter the market allocation. There is no deadweight loss, and the government's tax revenue exactly equals the loss of the landowners.

Although taxing land may look attractive in theory, it is not as straightforward in practice as it may appear. For a tax on land not to distort economic incentives, it must be a tax on raw land. Yet the value of land often comes from improvements, such as clearing trees, providing sewers, and building roads. Unlike the supply of raw land, the supply of improvements has an elasticity greater than zero. If a land tax were imposed on improvements, it would distort incentives. Landowners would respond by devoting fewer resources to improving their land.

Today, few economists support George's proposal for a single tax on land. Not only is taxing improvements a potential problem, but the tax would not raise enough revenue to pay for the much larger government we have today. Yet many of George's arguments remain valid. As the eminent economist Milton Friedman observed a century after George's book was published: "In my opinion, the least bad tax is the property tax on the unimproved value of land, the Henry George argument of many, many years ago."

QUICK QUIZ: The demand for beer is more elastic than the demand for milk. Would a tax on beer or a tax on milk have a larger deadweight loss? Why?

DEADWEIGHT LOSS AND TAX REVENUE AS TAXES VARY

Taxes rarely stay the same for long periods of time. Policymakers in local, provincial, and federal governments are always considering raising one tax or lowering another. Here we consider what happens to the deadweight loss and tax revenue when the size of a tax changes.

Figure 8-6 shows the effects of a small, medium, and large tax, holding constant the market's supply and demand curves. The deadweight loss—the reduction in total surplus that results when the tax reduces the size of a market below the optimum—equals the area of the triangle between the supply and demand curves. For the small tax in panel (a), the area of the deadweight loss triangle is quite small. But as the size of the tax rises in panels (b) and (c), the deadweight loss grows larger and larger.

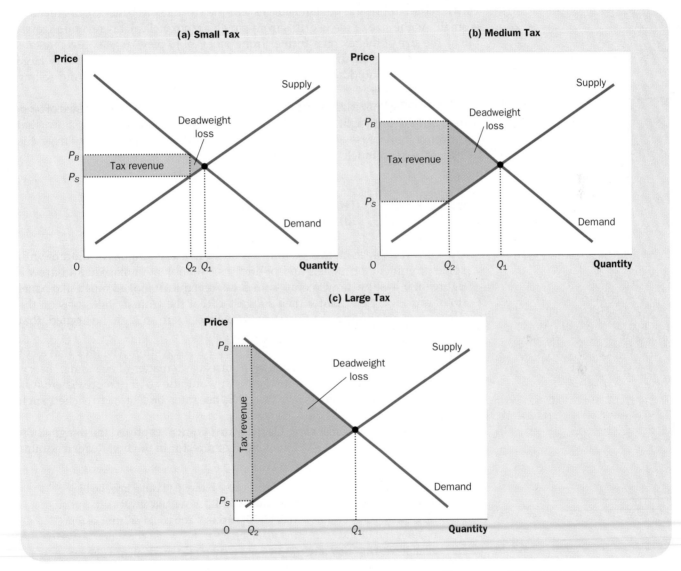

DEADWEIGHT LOSS AND TAX REVENUE FROM THREE TAXES OF DIFFERENT SIZE.   The deadweight loss is the reduction in total surplus due to the tax. Tax revenue is the amount of the tax times the amount of the good sold. In panel (a), a small tax has a small deadweight loss and raises a small amount of revenue. In panel (b), a somewhat larger tax has a larger deadweight loss and raises a larger amount of revenue. In panel (c), a very large tax has a very large deadweight loss, but because it has reduced the size of the market so much, the tax raises only a small amount of revenue.

Figure 8-6

Indeed, the deadweight loss of a tax rises even more rapidly than the size of the tax. The reason is that the deadweight loss is an area of a triangle, and an area of a triangle depends on the *square* of its size. If we double the size of a tax, for instance, the base and height of the triangle double, so the deadweight loss rises by a factor of 4. If we triple the size of a tax, the base and height triple, so the deadweight loss rises by a factor of 9.

The government's tax revenue is the size of the tax times the amount of the good sold. As Figure 8-6 shows, tax revenue equals the area of the rectangle between the supply and demand curves. For the small tax in panel (a), tax revenue is small. As the size of the tax rises from panel (a) to panel (b), tax revenue grows. But as the size of the tax rises further from panel (b) to panel (c), tax revenue falls because the higher tax drastically reduces the size of the market. For a very large tax, no revenue would be raised, because people would stop buying and selling the good altogether.

Figure 8-7 summarizes these results. In panel (a) we see that as the size of a tax increases, its deadweight loss quickly gets larger. By contrast, panel (b) shows that tax revenue first rises with the size of the tax; but then, as the tax gets larger, the market shrinks so much that tax revenue starts to fall.

CASE STUDY   THE LAFFER CURVE AND SUPPLY-SIDE ECONOMICS

One day in 1974, economist Arthur Laffer sat in a Washington restaurant with some prominent journalists and politicians. He took out a napkin and drew a figure on it to show how tax rates affect tax revenue. It looked much like panel (b) of our Figure 8-7. Laffer then suggested that the United States was on the downward-sloping side of this curve. Tax rates were so high, he argued, that reducing them would actually raise tax revenue.

Most economists were skeptical of Laffer's suggestion. The idea that a cut in tax rates could raise tax revenue was correct as a matter of economic theory, but there was more doubt about whether it would do so in practice. There was little evidence for Laffer's view that U.S. tax rates had in fact reached such extreme levels.

Nonetheless, the *Laffer curve* (as it became known) captured the imagination of Ronald Reagan. David Stockman, budget director in the first Reagan administration, offers the following story:

> [Reagan] had once been on the Laffer curve himself. "I came into the Big Money making pictures during World War II," he would always say. At that time the wartime income surtax hit 90 percent. "You could only make four pictures and then you were in the top bracket," he would continue. "So we all quit working after four pictures and went off to the country." High tax rates caused less work. Low tax rates caused more. His experience proved it.

When Reagan ran for president in 1980, he made cutting taxes part of his platform. Reagan argued that taxes were so high that they were discouraging hard work. He argued that lower taxes would give people the proper incentive to work, which would raise economic well-being and perhaps even tax revenue. Because the cut in tax rates was intended to encourage people to increase the quantity of labour they supplied, the views of Laffer and Reagan became known as *supply-side economics*.

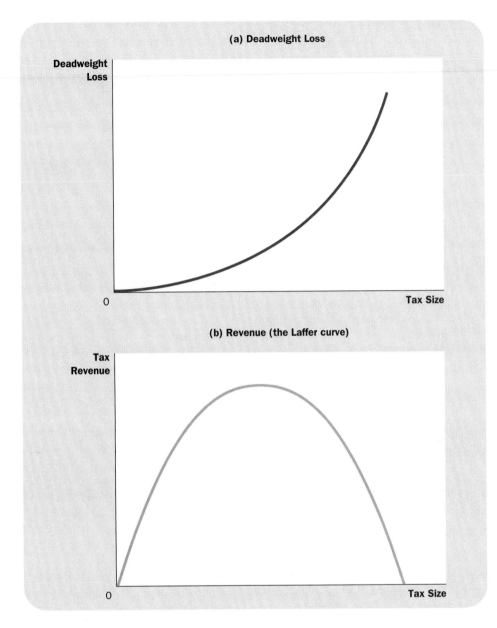

(a) Deadweight Loss

Deadweight Loss

0   Tax Size

(b) Revenue (the Laffer curve)

Tax Revenue

0   Tax Size

Figure 8-7

HOW DEADWEIGHT LOSS AND
TAX REVENUE VARY WITH THE
SIZE OF A TAX.   Panel (a) shows
that as the size of a tax grows
larger, the deadweight loss grows
larger. Panel (b) shows that tax
revenue first rises, then falls. This
relationship is sometimes called
the Laffer curve.

Subsequent history failed to confirm Laffer's conjecture that lower tax rates
would raise tax revenue. When Reagan cut taxes after he was elected, the result
was less tax revenue, not more. Revenue from personal income taxes (per
person, adjusted for inflation) fell by 9 percent from 1980 to 1984, even though
average income (per person, adjusted for inflation) grew by 4 percent over this
period. The tax cut, together with policymakers' unwillingness to restrain
spending, began a long period during which the government spent more than
it collected in taxes. Throughout Reagan's two terms in office, and for many
years thereafter, the government ran large budget deficits.

Yet Laffer's argument is not completely without merit. Although an overall
cut in tax rates normally reduces revenue, some taxpayers at some times may be

IN THE NEWS

Tax Evasion on the Rise

WHEN TAX RATES RISE, PEOPLE TRY TO AVOID taxes by buying and selling less of the taxed good, and this creates a Laffer curve. But when tax rates rise, people also have more incentive to try to evade taxes by not reporting their activities to the tax collector. (The difference between *tax avoidance* and *tax evasion* is that avoidance is legal, but evasion is illegal.) Just as tax avoidance can create a Laffer curve, so can tax evasion, as the following article reminds us.

High Taxes Lift Number of Would-Be Cheats

BY JONATHAN CHEVREAU

Canada's comparatively high tax rates have made us a nation of would-be tax cheats.

Two-thirds of Canadians would cheat on their taxes if they knew they could get away with it, according to a survey of 1000 adults being released today by Toronto-based CF Group Inc. The hated Goods and Services Tax continues to be the most likely to be evaded —37 percent of those polled would pay a contractor with cash to avoid the GST.

GST rage is not quite as intense as it was in the five years after its introduction in 1990. In 1995, the last time the survey was conducted, 47 percent said they would pay cash to avoid the GST. However, the number of taxpayers who would evade income taxes is on the rise, despite tax cuts from the federal government. About 17 percent would conveniently forget to report some income on their tax returns, up from 16 percent in 1995.

When Canadians travel, 22 percent would cheat customs authorities by not declaring goods bought abroad, down from 26 percent in 1995. About 14 percent would buy smuggled liquor or cigarettes, down from 17 percent in 1995. That likely reflects government cuts in cigarette taxes after smuggling became rampant in the mid-1990s.

If taxes were lower, fewer people would try to evade them, say 68 percent of those surveyed. That is about the same level as the 1995 survey and is consistent with the behavioural theory known as the Laffer curve:

The more taxes rise, the more people evade them, eventually reaching a point where extra taxes do not bring in any extra government revenue.

"There is still a sense the present tax system is unfair to Canadians," says David Stark, public affairs director of CF Group. "Half of Canadians believe they are not getting good value for their tax dollars and three-quarters think governments squander much of the money they get from taxes."

It is hardly surprising, then, that 19 percent believe "people who pay all the taxes they should are fools." That is up from 17 percent in 1995 and is most often stated by young people aged 18 to 24.

Still, only about a third (37 percent) believed tax evasion had increased over the past five years, down from 54 percent who believed that in 1995.

"There is a greater sense that the Canada Customs and Revenue Agency [formerly Revenue Canada] has stepped up its efforts to clamp down on tax evasion and the underground economy," Mr. Stark said.

That is reflected in a lower number of Canadians who believe there is little chance of being caught for tax evasion: 35 percent think so, compared with 41 percent in 1995.

Despite the number of taxpayers who say they would cheat in certain hypothetical situations, 67 percent nevertheless believe most people are honest and pay all the taxes they should. That is up from 59 percent in 1995.

The survey, which includes Canadians older than 18 from all provinces, was sponsored in 1995 by KPMG. The new survey was not commissioned by a corporate sponsor. It is considered accurate to within 3.2 percentage points 19 times out of 20.

SOURCE: *National Post Online,* May 3, 2001. Available http://www.nationalpost.com, May 3, 2001.

on the wrong side of the Laffer curve. In the 1980s, tax revenue collected from the richest Americans, who face the highest tax rates, did rise when their taxes were cut. The idea that cutting taxes can raise revenue may be correct if applied to those taxpayers facing the highest tax rates. In addition, Laffer's argument may be more plausible when applied to countries where tax rates are much higher than in the United States. In Sweden in the early 1980s, for instance, the typical worker faced a marginal tax rate of about 80 percent. Such a high tax rate provides a substantial disincentive to work. Studies have suggested that Sweden would indeed have raised more tax revenue if it had lowered its tax rates. And when the Republic of Ireland cut the tax rate on corporate profits in the 1990s, investment by foreign corporations increased so much that tax revenue increased.

In Canada, tax rates on labour income are higher than they are in the United States, but not as high as they are in Sweden. Canadian tax rates are probably not so high that cutting tax rates would raise tax revenues.

These ideas matter for many political debates. When cigarette taxes were cut to reduce smuggling, cigarette manufacturers argued that the tax revenue losses would be small because more cigarettes would be legally purchased. Antismoking groups argued that the revenue losses would be larger. Presumably, the antismoking groups believed that the demand for legally purchased cigarettes was less elastic, or that the supply of smuggled cigarettes was less elastic, than the manufacturers believed.

Provincial governments have much less ability to increase tax revenue by raising tax rates than does the federal government. A provincial government that raised income tax rates would find some of its residents migrating to other provinces in search of lower taxes. Because people can migrate more easily between provinces than they can migrate between countries, the supply of labour is more elastic in a single province than it is for Canada as a whole. The supply of labour would be even more elastic between different municipalities. Perhaps this explains why municipalities rely on property taxes rather than trying to tax labour income.

Policymakers disagree about whether to increase or decrease tax rates in part because they disagree about the size of the relevant elasticities. The more elastic that supply and demand are in any market, the more taxes in that market distort behaviour, and the more likely it is that a tax cut will raise tax revenue. There is no debate, however, about the general lesson: How much revenue the government gains or loses from a tax change cannot be computed just by looking at tax rates. It also depends on how the tax change affects people's behaviour.

QUICK QUIZ: If the government doubles the tax on gasoline, can you be sure that revenue from the gasoline tax will rise? Can you be sure that the deadweight loss from the gasoline tax will rise? Explain.

CONCLUSION

Taxes, Oliver Wendell Holmes once said, are the price we pay for a civilized society. Indeed, our society cannot exist without some form of taxes. We all expect the government to provide certain services, such as roads, parks, police, and national defence. These public services require tax revenue.

This chapter has shed some light on how high the price of civilized society can be. One of the *Ten Principles of Economics* discussed in Chapter 1 is that markets are usually a good way to organize economic activity. When the government imposes taxes on buyers or sellers of a good, however, society loses some of the benefits of market efficiency. Taxes are costly to market participants not only because taxes transfer resources from those participants to the government, but also because they alter incentives and distort market outcomes.

Summary

◆ A tax on a good reduces the welfare of buyers and sellers of the good, and the reduction in consumer and producer surplus usually exceeds the revenue raised by the government. The fall in total surplus—the sum of consumer surplus, producer surplus, and tax revenue—is called the deadweight loss of the tax.

◆ Taxes have deadweight losses because they cause buyers to consume less and sellers to produce less, and this change in behaviour shrinks the size of the market

below the level that maximizes total surplus. Because the elasticities of supply and demand measure how much market participants respond to market conditions, larger elasticities imply larger deadweight losses.

◆ As a tax grows larger, it distorts incentives more, and its deadweight loss grows larger. Tax revenue first rises with the size of a tax. Eventually, however, a larger tax reduces tax revenue because it reduces the size of the market.

Key Concepts

deadweight loss, p. 165

Questions for Review

1. What happens to consumer and producer surplus when the sale of a good is taxed? How does the change in consumer and producer surplus compare with the tax revenue? Explain.

2. Draw a supply-and-demand diagram with a tax on the sale of the good. Show the deadweight loss. Show the tax revenue.

3. How do the elasticities of supply and demand affect the deadweight loss of a tax? Why do they have this effect?

4. Why do experts disagree about whether labour taxes have small or large deadweight losses?

5. What happens to the deadweight loss and tax revenue when a tax is increased?

Problems and Applications

1. The market for pizza is characterized by a downward-sloping demand curve and an upward-sloping supply curve.
   a. Draw the competitive market equilibrium. Label the price, quantity, consumer surplus, and producer surplus. Is there any deadweight loss? Explain.

   b. Suppose that the government forces each pizzeria to pay a $1 tax on each pizza sold. Illustrate the effect of this tax on the pizza market, being sure to label the consumer surplus, producer surplus, government revenue, and deadweight loss. How does each area compare with the pre-tax case?

c. If the tax were removed, pizza eaters and sellers would be better off, but the government would lose tax revenue. Suppose that consumers and producers voluntarily transferred some of their gains to the government. Could all parties (including the government) be better off than they were with a tax? Explain using the labelled areas in your graph.

2. Evaluate the following two statements. Do you agree? Why or why not?
   a. "If the government taxes land, wealthy land-owners will pass the tax on to their poorer renters."
   b. "If the government taxes apartment buildings, wealthy landlords will pass the tax on to their poorer renters."

3. Evaluate the following two statements. Do you agree? Why or why not?
   a. "A tax that has no deadweight loss cannot raise any revenue for the government."
   b. "A tax that raises no revenue for the government cannot have any deadweight loss."

4. Consider the market for rubber bands.
   a. If this market has very elastic supply and very inelastic demand, how would the burden of a tax on rubber bands be shared between consumers and producers? Use the tools of consumer surplus and producer surplus in your answer.
   b. If this market has very inelastic supply and very elastic demand, how would the burden of a tax on rubber bands be shared between consumers and producers? Contrast your answer with your answer to part (a).

5. Suppose that the government imposes a tax on heating oil.
   a. Would the deadweight loss from this tax likely be greater in the first year after it is imposed or in the fifth year? Explain.
   b. Would the revenue collected from this tax likely be greater in the first year after it is imposed or in the fifth year? Explain.

6. After economics class one day, your friend suggests that taxing food would be a good way to raise revenue because the demand for food is quite inelastic. In what sense is taxing food a "good" way to raise revenue? In what sense is it not a "good" way to raise revenue?

7. U.S. Senator Daniel Patrick Moynihan once introduced a bill that would levy a 10 000 percent tax on certain hollow-tipped bullets.
   a. Do you expect that this tax would raise much revenue? Why or why not?
   b. Even if the tax would raise no revenue, what might be Senator Moynihan's reason for proposing it?

8. The government places a tax on the purchase of socks.
   a. Illustrate the effect of this tax on equilibrium price and quantity in the sock market. Identify the following areas both before and after the imposition of the tax: total spending by consumers, total revenue for producers, and government tax revenue.
   b. Does the price received by producers rise or fall? Can you tell whether total receipts for producers rise or fall? Explain.
   c. Does the price paid by consumers rise or fall? Can you tell whether total spending by consumers rises or falls? Explain carefully. (Hint: Think about elasticity.) If total consumer spending falls, does consumer surplus rise? Explain.

9. Suppose the government currently raises $100 million through a $0.01 tax on widgets, and another $100 million through a $0.10 tax on gadgets. If the government doubled the tax rate on widgets and eliminated the tax on gadgets, would it raise more money than today, less money, or the same amount of money? Explain.

10. Suppose the Canadian government decides that it needs to raise an additional $100 million in tax revenues. One Cabinet minister argues for a tax on all soft drinks. A second Cabinet minister argues for a tax on cola only, since this would give consumers a choice of paying the tax (by drinking cola) or avoiding it (by switching to another soft drink).
    a. Which market has the more elastic supply and demand curves: the market for cola, or the market for all soft drinks?
    b. To raise the same $100 million in revenue, which would require a higher rate: a tax on cola, or a tax on all soft drinks?
    c. Which would cause a larger deadweight loss: a tax on cola, or a tax on all soft drinks?
    d. Which would be the better tax? Explain.

11. Several years ago the British government imposed a "poll tax" that required each person to pay a flat

amount to the government independent of his or her income or wealth. What is the effect of such a tax on economic efficiency? What is the effect on economic equity? Do you think this was a popular tax?

12. This chapter analyzed the welfare effects of a tax on a good. Consider now the opposite policy. Suppose that the government subsidizes a good: For each unit of the good sold, the government pays $2 to the buyer. How does the subsidy affect consumer surplus, producer surplus, tax revenue, and total surplus? Does a subsidy lead to a deadweight loss? Explain.

13. (This problem uses some high-school algebra and is challenging.) Suppose that a market is described by the following supply and demand equations:

$$Q^S = 2P$$
$$Q^D = 300 - P$$

a.   Solve for the equilibrium price and the equilibrium quantity.

b.   Suppose that a tax of T is placed on buyers, so the new demand equation is

$$Q^D = 300 - (P + T).$$

Solve for the new equilibrium. What happens to the price received by sellers, the price paid by buyers, and the quantity sold?

c.   Tax revenue is $T \times Q$. Use your answer to part (b) to solve for tax revenue as a function of T. Graph this relationship for T between 0 and 300.

d.   The deadweight loss of a tax is the area of the triangle between the supply and demand curves. Recalling that the area of a triangle is $1/2 \times$ base $\times$ height, solve for deadweight loss as a function of T. Graph this relationship for T between 0 and 300. (Hint: Looking sideways, the base of the deadweight loss triangle is T, and the height is the difference between the quantity sold with the tax and the quantity sold without the tax.)

e.   The government now levies a tax on this good of $200 per unit. Is this a good policy? Why or why not? Can you propose a better policy?

9

APPLICATION:
INTERNATIONAL TRADE

**IN THIS CHAPTER
YOU WILL . . .**

*Consider what
determines whether
a country imports or
exports a good*

*Examine who wins
and who loses from
international trade*

*Learn that the gains
to winners from
international trade
exceed the losses
to losers*

*Analyze the welfare
effects of tariffs
and import quotas*

*Examine the
arguments people
use to advocate
trade restrictions*

If you check the labels on the clothes you are now wearing, you will probably find that some of your clothes were made in another country. A century ago the textiles and clothing industry was a major part of the Canadian economy, but that is no longer the case. Faced with foreign competitors that could produce quality goods at low cost, many Canadian firms found it increasingly difficult to produce and sell textiles and clothing at a profit. As a result, they laid off their workers and shut down their factories. Today, much of the textiles and clothing that Canadians consume are imported from abroad.

The story of the textiles industry raises important questions for economic policy: How does international trade affect economic well-being? Who gains and who loses from free trade among countries, and how do the gains compare with the losses?

Chapter 3 introduced the study of international trade by applying the principle of comparative advantage. According to this principle, all countries can benefit from trading with one another because trade allows each country to specialize in doing what it does best. But the analysis in Chapter 3 was incomplete. It did not explain how the international marketplace achieves these gains from trade or how the gains are distributed among various economic actors.

We now return to the study of international trade and take up these questions. Over the past several chapters, we have developed many tools for analyzing how markets work: supply, demand, equilibrium, consumer surplus, producer surplus, and so on. With these tools we can learn more about the effects of international trade on economic well-being.

THE DETERMINANTS OF TRADE

Consider the market for steel. The steel market is well suited to examining the gains and losses from international trade: Steel is made in many countries around the world, and there is much world trade in steel. Moreover, the steel market is one in which policymakers often consider (and sometimes implement) trade restrictions in order to protect domestic steel producers from foreign competitors. We examine here the steel market in the imaginary country of Isoland.

THE EQUILIBRIUM WITHOUT TRADE

As our story begins, the Isolandian steel market is isolated from the rest of the world. By government decree, no one in Isoland is allowed to import or export steel, and the penalty for violating the decree is so large that no one dares try.

Because there is no international trade, the market for steel in Isoland consists solely of Isolandian buyers and sellers. As Figure 9-1 shows, the domestic price adjusts to balance the quantity supplied by domestic sellers and the quantity demanded by domestic buyers. The figure shows the consumer and producer surplus in the equilibrium without trade. The sum of consumer and producer surplus measures the total benefits that buyers and sellers receive from the steel market.

Now suppose that, in an election upset, Isoland elects a new president. The president campaigned on a platform of "change" and promised the voters bold new ideas. Her first act is to assemble a team of economists to evaluate Isolandian trade policy. She asks them to report back on three questions:

◆ If the government allowed Isolandians to import and export steel, what would happen to the price of steel and the quantity of steel sold in the domestic steel market?

◆ Who would gain from free trade in steel and who would lose, and would the gains exceed the losses?

◆ Should a tariff (a tax on steel imports) or an import quota (a limit on steel imports) be part of the new trade policy?

Figure 9-1

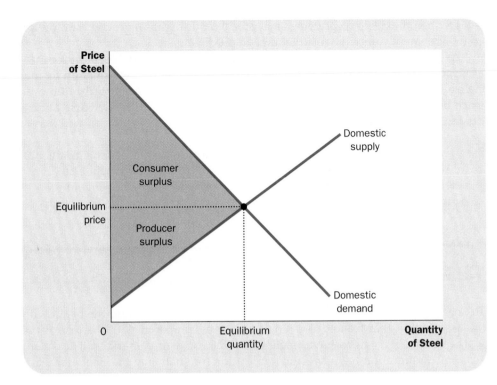

THE EQUILIBRIUM WITHOUT INTERNATIONAL TRADE.   When an economy cannot trade in world markets, the price adjusts to balance domestic supply and demand. This figure shows consumer and producer surplus in an equilibrium without international trade for the steel market in the imaginary country of Isoland.

After reviewing supply and demand in their favourite textbook (this one, of course), the Isolandian economics team begins its analysis.

THE WORLD PRICE AND COMPARATIVE ADVANTAGE

The first issue our economists take up is whether Isoland is likely to become a steel importer or a steel exporter. In other words, if free trade were allowed, would Isolandians end up buying or selling steel in world markets?

To answer this question, the economists compare the current Isolandian price of steel with the price of steel in other countries. We call the price prevailing in world markets the **world price.** If the world price of steel is higher than the domestic price, then Isoland would become an exporter of steel once trade is permitted. Isolandian steel producers would be eager to receive the higher prices available abroad and would start selling their steel to buyers in other countries. Conversely, if the world price of steel is lower than the domestic price, then Isoland would become an importer of steel. Because foreign sellers offer a better price, Isolandian steel consumers would quickly start buying steel from other countries.

In essence, comparing the world price and the domestic price before trade indicates whether Isoland has a comparative advantage in producing steel. The domestic price reflects the opportunity cost of steel: It tells us how much an Isolandian must give up to get one unit of steel. If the domestic price is low, the cost of producing steel in Isoland is low, suggesting that Isoland has a comparative advantage in producing steel relative to the rest of the world. If the domestic price

world price
the price of a good that prevails in the world market for that good

is high, then the cost of producing steel in Isoland is high, suggesting that foreign countries have a comparative advantage in producing steel.

As we saw in Chapter 3, trade among nations is ultimately based on comparative advantage. That is, trade is beneficial because it allows each nation to specialize in doing what it does best. By comparing the world price and the domestic price before trade, we can determine whether Isoland is better or worse at producing steel than the rest of the world.

> **QUICK QUIZ:**   The country Autarka does not allow international trade. In Autarka, you can buy a wool suit for 3 ounces of gold. Meanwhile, in neighbouring countries, you can buy the same suit for 2 ounces of gold. If Autarka were to allow free trade, would it import or export suits?

THE WINNERS AND LOSERS FROM TRADE

To analyze the welfare effects of free trade, the Isolandian economists begin with the assumption that Isoland is a small economy compared with the rest of the world so that its actions have negligible effect on world markets. The small-economy assumption has a specific implication for analyzing the steel market: If Isoland is a small economy, then the change in Isoland's trade policy will not affect the world price of steel. The Isolandians are said to be *price takers* in the world economy. That is, they take the world price of steel as given. They can sell steel at this price and be exporters or buy steel at this price and be importers.

The small-economy assumption is not necessary to analyze the gains and losses from international trade. But the Isolandian economists know from experience that this assumption greatly simplifies the analysis. They also know that the basic lessons do not change in the more complicated case of a large economy.

THE GAINS AND LOSSES OF AN EXPORTING COUNTRY

Figure 9-2 shows the Isolandian steel market when the domestic equilibrium price before trade is below the world price. Once free trade is allowed, the domestic price rises to equal the world price. No seller of steel would accept less than the world price, and no buyer would pay more than the world price.

With the domestic price now equal to the world price, the domestic quantity supplied differs from the domestic quantity demanded. The supply curve shows the quantity of steel supplied by Isolandian sellers. The demand curve shows the quantity of steel demanded by Isolandian buyers. Because the domestic quantity supplied is greater than the domestic quantity demanded, Isoland sells steel to other countries. Thus, Isoland becomes a steel exporter.

Although domestic quantity supplied and domestic quantity demanded differ, the steel market is still in equilibrium because there is now another participant in the market: the rest of the world. One can view the horizontal line at the world price as representing the demand for steel from the rest of the world. This demand curve is perfectly elastic because Isoland, as a small economy, can sell as much steel as it wants at the world price.

Figure 9-2

INTERNATIONAL TRADE IN AN EXPORTING COUNTRY.   Once trade is allowed, the domestic price rises to equal the world price. The supply curve shows the quantity of steel produced domestically, and the demand curve shows the quantity consumed domestically. Exports from Isoland equal the difference between the domestic quantity supplied and the domestic quantity demanded at the world price.

Now consider the gains and losses from opening up trade. Clearly, not everyone benefits. Trade forces the domestic price to rise to the world price. Domestic producers of steel are better off because they can now sell steel at a higher price, but domestic consumers of steel are worse off because they have to buy steel at a higher price.

To measure these gains and losses, we look at the changes in consumer and producer surplus, which are shown in Figure 9-3 and summarized in Table 9-1. Before trade is allowed, the price of steel adjusts to balance domestic supply and domestic demand. Consumer surplus, the area between the demand curve and the before-trade price, is area A + B. Producer surplus, the area between the supply curve and the before-trade price, is area C. Total surplus before trade, the sum of consumer and producer surplus, is area A + B + C.

After trade is allowed, the domestic price rises to the world price. Consumer surplus is area A (the area between the demand curve and the world price). Producer surplus is area B + C + D (the area between the supply curve and the world price). Thus, total surplus with trade is area A + B + C + D.

These welfare calculations show who wins and who loses from trade in an exporting country. Sellers benefit because producer surplus increases by area B + D. Buyers are worse off because consumer surplus decreases by area B. Because the gains of sellers exceed the losses of buyers by area D, total surplus in Isoland increases.

This analysis of an exporting country yields two conclusions:

◆   When a country allows trade and becomes an exporter of a good, domestic producers of the good are better off, and domestic consumers of the good are worse off.

Figure 9-3

How Free Trade Affects Welfare in an Exporting Country.   When the domestic price rises to equal the world price, sellers are better off (producer surplus rises from C to B + C + D), and buyers are worse off (consumer surplus falls from A + B to A). Total surplus rises by an amount equal to area D, indicating that trade raises the economic well-being of the country as a whole.

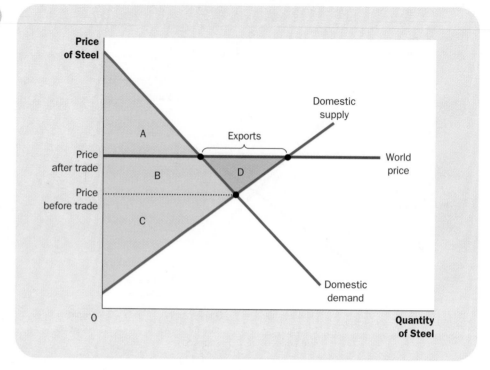

Table 9-1

Changes in Welfare from Free Trade: The Case of an Exporting Country.   The table examines changes in economic welfare resulting from opening up a market to international trade. Letters refer to the regions marked in Figure 9-3.

	BEFORE TRADE	**AFTER TRADE**	**CHANGE**
Consumer Surplus	A + B	A	−B
Producer Surplus	C	B + C + D	+(B + D)
Total Surplus	A + B + C	A + B + C + D	+D

Area D shows the increase in total surplus and represents the gains from trade.

◆   Trade raises the economic well-being of a nation in the sense that the gains of the winners exceed the losses of the losers.

THE GAINS AND LOSSES OF AN IMPORTING COUNTRY

Now suppose that the domestic price before trade is above the world price. Once again, after free trade is allowed, the domestic price must equal the world price. As Figure 9-4 shows, the domestic quantity supplied is less than the domestic quantity demanded. The difference between the domestic quantity demanded and the domestic quantity supplied is bought from other countries, and Isoland becomes a steel importer.

In this case, the horizontal line at the world price represents the supply of the rest of the world. This supply curve is perfectly elastic because Isoland is a small economy and, therefore, can buy as much steel as it wants at the world price.

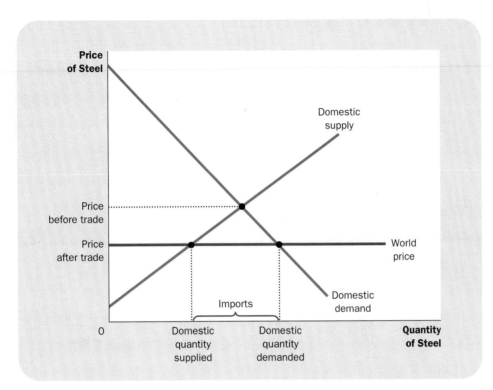

Figure 9-4

INTERNATIONAL TRADE IN AN IMPORTING COUNTRY.   Once trade is allowed, the domestic price falls to equal the world price. The supply curve shows the amount produced domestically, and the demand curve shows the amount consumed domestically. Imports equal the difference between the domestic quantity demanded and the domestic quantity supplied at the world price.

Now consider the gains and losses from trade. Once again, not everyone benefits. When trade forces the domestic price to fall, domestic consumers are better off (they can now buy steel at a lower price), and domestic producers are worse off (they now have to sell steel at a lower price). Changes in consumer and producer surplus measure the size of the gains and losses, as shown in Figure 9-5 and Table 9-2. Before trade, consumer surplus is area A, producer surplus is area B + C, and total surplus is area A + B + C. After trade is allowed, consumer surplus is area A + B + D, producer surplus is area C, and total surplus is area A + B + C + D.

These welfare calculations show who wins and who loses from trade in an importing country. Buyers benefit because consumer surplus increases by area B + D. Sellers are worse off because producer surplus falls by area B. The gains of buyers exceed the losses of sellers, and total surplus increases by area D.

This analysis of an importing country yields two conclusions parallel to those for an exporting country:

◆ When a country allows trade and becomes an importer of a good, domestic consumers of the good are better off, and domestic producers of the good are worse off.

◆ Trade raises the economic well-being of a nation in the sense that the gains of the winners exceed the losses of the losers.

Now that we have completed our analysis of trade, we can better understand one of the *Ten Principles of Economics* in Chapter 1: Trade can make everyone better off. If Isoland opens up its steel market to international trade, that change will create

Figure 9-5

HOW FREE TRADE AFFECTS WELFARE IN AN IMPORTING COUNTRY.   When the domestic price falls to equal the world price, buyers are better off (consumer surplus rises from A to A + B + D), and sellers are worse off (producer surplus falls from B + C to C). Total surplus rises by an amount equal to area D, indicating that trade raises the economic well-being of the country as a whole.

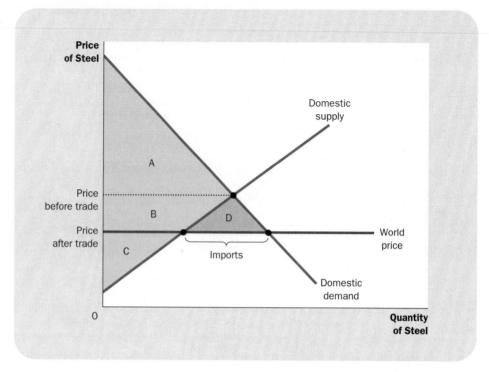

Table 9-2

CHANGES IN WELFARE FROM FREE TRADE: THE CASE OF AN IMPORTING COUNTRY.   The table examines changes in economic welfare resulting from opening up a market to international trade. Letters refer to the regions marked in Figure 9-5.

	BEFORE TRADE	AFTER TRADE	CHANGE
Consumer Surplus	A	A + B + D	+(B + D)
Producer Surplus	B + C	C	−B
Total Surplus	A + B + C	A + B + C + D	+D

Area D shows the increase in total surplus and represents the gains from trade.

winners and losers, regardless of whether Isoland ends up exporting or importing steel. In either case, however, the gains of the winners exceed the losses of the losers, so the winners could compensate the losers and still be better off. In this sense, trade *can* make everyone better off. But *will* trade make everyone better off? Probably not. In practice, compensation for the losers from international trade is rare. Without such compensation, opening up to international trade is a policy that expands the size of the economic pie, while perhaps leaving some participants in the economy with a smaller slice.

THE EFFECTS OF A TARIFF

tariff

a tax on goods produced abroad and sold domestically

The Isolandian economists next consider the effects of a **tariff**—a tax on imported goods. The economists quickly realize that a tariff on steel will have no effect if Isoland becomes a steel exporter. If no one in Isoland is interested in importing

IN THE NEWS

Bringing Free Trade to the Dairy Farm

ONE EXAMPLE OF A CANADIAN INDUSTRY that is currently protected from cheaper imports is the dairy industry. The Canadian Milk Marketing Board prevents imports of fresh milk, and also limits Canadian production by a system of quotas to keep prices high. The following article describes how Canadian milk producers see the prospect of free trade in milk and the elimination of the quota system.

Dairy Farmers Prepare for Loss of Milk Board

BY STUART LAIDLAW

Reg Gilmer came to the hills of Pennsylvania to plan a future he does not want.

The Ottawa dairy farmer fears for the survival of the milk marketing board and the protection it gives him from the big American farms and cheap imports.

"Supply management could be dead in 10 years," Gilmer says. "I don't like it, but I've got to face facts."

That's why he and about 90 other dairy farmers toured New York and Pennsylvania recently visiting farms with up to 2300 cows. The farms dwarfed the average Ontario operation, which has a mere 53 black-and-white Holsteins.

"We're all here to gather ideas," says Gilmer.

While consumers might like the idea of cheap imports, milk marketing board officials say there's no guarantee they would lead to cheaper milk at the grocery store. Consumer dairy prices in the United States are no lower than they are in Canada.

As well, imports could have a devastating impact on Canada's dairy sector, turning farmers into managers of hired help and forcing the government to spend millions buying out their production quotas.

While milk marketing board officials are quick to say they have no intention of giving away or letting the United States flood Canada with milk, Gilmer and other farmers on the tour are not so sure.

By American standards, Gilmer has a fairly modest farm—110 cows, and no deep desire to get any bigger.

But he figures he had better start growing so he can compete on the open market in case Ottawa buckles under pressure from the World Trade Organization. He plans to buy another 55 cows for a 50 percent boost in production.

Marketing boards control the flow of milk in Canada through production quotas. Farmers get a higher price for their milk than their American counterparts, but must buy quota to get into the system.

Quota sells for about $20 000 per cow. That gives the farmer the right to sell about 12 000 L of milk to the board each year, based on the average production of a cow.

Farmers like the system, but it is under threat because of complaints by the United States and New Zealand to the WTO that it restricts free trade. The two countries won their most recent complaint late last year when the WTO

decided that the higher domestic milk price is an export subsidy.

Some observers have said the decision could mark the beginning of the end of Canada's milk system. Cornell University professor Mark Stephenson says decades of guaranteed prices and set production limits have left Canadian farmers unable to compete on the open market.

"You guys are like Rip van Winkle up there. You've been asleep for 20 years," says Stephenson, an expert in world dairy markets.

Still, he says the government is doing the right thing to fight assaults on its milk system at every step, giving farmers more time to prepare.

"The transition will be very painful," Stephenson told the farm tour during one of its stops.

Gilmer and the other farmers on last week's tour hope to blunt some of that pain by expanding before the system they have come to rely on is yanked out from under them.

"If I grow now, maybe I can pay off some of the debt over the next 10 years," Gilmer says.

Getting there, however, could be tough. With quota selling at $20 000 a cow, Gilmer will have to spend $1.1 million to increase his herd by 55 cows. While their quota can make farmers millionaires on paper, its value is usually offset by the cost of borrowing to buy it, or other debt.

Worse, if the marketing board system does die, that quota will be worthless.

SOURCE: *The Toronto Star Online*, April 1, 2000. Available http://www.thestar.com.

steel, a tax on steel imports is irrelevant. The tariff matters only if Isoland becomes a steel importer. Concentrating their attention on this case, the economists compare welfare with and without the tariff.

Figure 9-6 shows the Isolandian market for steel. Under free trade, the domestic price equals the world price. A tariff raises the price of imported steel above the world price by the amount of the tariff. Domestic suppliers of steel, who compete with suppliers of imported steel, can now sell their steel for the world price plus the amount of the tariff. Thus, the price of steel—both imported and domestic—rises by the amount of the tariff and is, therefore, closer to the price that would prevail without trade.

Figure 9-6

THE EFFECTS OF A TARIFF. A tariff reduces the quantity of imports and moves a market closer to the equilibrium that would exist without trade. Total surplus falls by an amount equal to area D + F. These two triangles represent the deadweight loss from the tariff.

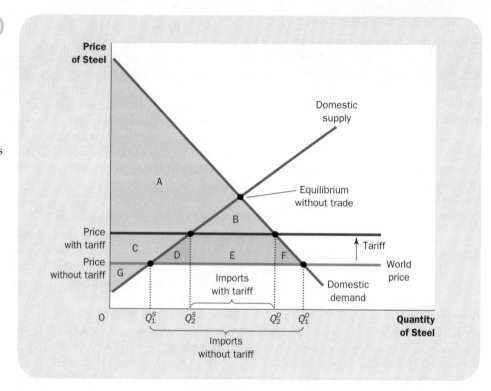

	BEFORE TARIFF	AFTER TARIFF	CHANGE
Consumer Surplus	A + B + C + D + E + F	A + B	−(C + D + E + F)
Producer Surplus	G	C + G	+C
Government Revenue	None	E	+E
Total Surplus	A + B + C + D + E + F + G	A + B + C + E + G	−(D + F)

Area D + F shows the fall in total surplus and represents the deadweight loss of the tariff.

Table 9-3

CHANGES IN WELFARE FROM A TARIFF. The table compares economic welfare when trade is unrestricted and when trade is restricted with a tariff. Letters refer to the regions marked in Figure 9-6.

The change in price affects the behaviour of domestic buyers and sellers. Because the tariff raises the price of steel, it reduces the domestic quantity demanded from Q_1^D to Q_2^D and raises the domestic quantity supplied from Q_1^S to Q_2^S. *Thus, the tariff reduces the quantity of imports and moves the domestic market closer to its equilibrium without trade.*

Now consider the gains and losses from the tariff. Because the tariff raises the domestic price, domestic sellers are better off, and domestic buyers are worse off. In addition, the government raises revenue. To measure these gains and losses, we look at the changes in consumer surplus, producer surplus, and government revenue. These changes are summarized in Table 9-3.

Before the tariff, the domestic price equals the world price. Consumer surplus, the area between the demand curve and the world price, is area A + B + C + D + E + F. Producer surplus, the area between the supply curve and the world price, is area G. Government revenue equals zero. Total surplus, the sum of consumer surplus, producer surplus, and government revenue, is area A + B + C + D + E + F + G.

Once the government imposes a tariff, the domestic price exceeds the world price by the amount of the tariff. Consumer surplus is now area A + B. Producer surplus is area C + G. Government revenue, which is the quantity of after-tariff imports times the size of the tariff, is area E. Thus, total surplus with the tariff is area A + B + C + E + G.

To determine the total welfare effects of the tariff, we add the change in consumer surplus (which is negative), the change in producer surplus (positive), and the change in government revenue (positive). We find that total surplus in the market decreases by area D + F. This fall in total surplus is called the *deadweight loss* of the tariff.

It is not surprising that a tariff causes a deadweight loss, because a tariff is a type of tax. Like any tax on the sale of a good, it distorts incentives and pushes the allocation of scarce resources away from the optimum. In this case, we can identify two effects. First, the tariff on steel raises the price of steel that domestic producers can charge above the world price and, as a result, encourages them to increase production of steel (from Q_1^S to Q_2^S). Second, the tariff raises the price that domestic steel buyers have to pay and, therefore, encourages them to reduce consumption of steel (from Q_1^D to Q_2^D). Area D represents the deadweight loss from the overproduction of steel, and area F represents the deadweight loss from the underconsumption. The total deadweight loss of the tariff is the sum of these two triangles.

THE EFFECTS OF AN IMPORT QUOTA

The Isolandian economists next consider the effects of an **import quota**—a limit on the quantity of imports. In particular, imagine that the Isolandian government distributes a limited number of import licences. Each licence gives the licence holder the right to import 1 tonne of steel into Isoland from abroad. The Isolandian economists want to compare welfare under a policy of free trade and welfare with the addition of this import quota.

Figure 9-7 shows how an import quota affects the Isolandian market for steel. Because the import quota prevents Isolandians from buying as much steel as they want from abroad, the supply of steel is no longer perfectly elastic at the world price. Instead, as long as the price of steel in Isoland is above the world price, the licence holders import as much as they are permitted, and the total supply of steel

import quota
a limit on the quantity of a good that can be produced abroad and sold domestically

Figure 9-7

THE EFFECTS OF AN IMPORT
QUOTA. An import quota, like
a tariff, reduces the quantity of
imports and moves a market
closer to the equilibrium that
would exist without trade. Total
surplus falls by an amount equal
to area D + F. These two triangles
represent the deadweight loss
from the quota. In addition, the
import quota transfers E' + E''
to whoever holds the import
licences.

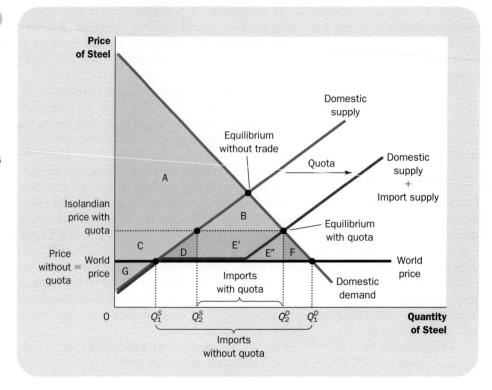

	BEFORE QUOTA	AFTER QUOTA	CHANGE
Consumer Surplus	A + B + C + D + E' + E'' + F	A + B	−(C + D + E' + E'' + F)
Producer Surplus	G	C + G	+C
Licence-Holder Surplus	None	E' + E''	+(E' + E'')
Total Surplus	A + B + C + D + E' + E'' + F + G	A + B + C + E' + E'' + G	−(D + F)

Area D + F shows the fall in total surplus and represents the deadweight loss of the quota.

Table 9-4

CHANGES IN WELFARE FROM AN IMPORT QUOTA. The table compares economic welfare
when trade is unrestricted and when trade is restricted with an import quota. Letters refer
to the regions marked in Figure 9-7.

in Isoland equals the domestic supply plus the quota amount. That is, the supply
curve above the world price is shifted to the right by exactly the amount of the
quota. (The supply curve below the world price does not shift because, in this case,
importing is not profitable for the licence holders.)

The price of steel in Isoland adjusts to balance supply (domestic plus
imported) and demand. As the figure shows, the quota causes the price of steel to
rise above the world price. The domestic quantity demanded falls from Q_1^D to Q_2^D,
and the domestic quantity supplied rises from Q_1^S to Q_2^S. Not surprisingly, the
import quota reduces steel imports.

Now consider the gains and losses from the quota. Because the quota raises the domestic price above the world price, domestic sellers are better off, and domestic buyers are worse off. In addition, the licence holders are better off because they make a profit from buying at the world price and selling at the higher domestic price. To measure these gains and losses, we look at the changes in consumer surplus, producer surplus, and licence-holder surplus, as shown in Table 9-4.

Before the government imposes the quota, the domestic price equals the world price. Consumer surplus, the area between the demand curve and the world price, is area A + B + C + D + E' + E'' + F. Producer surplus, the area between the supply curve and the world price, is area G. The surplus of licence holders equals zero because there are no licences. Total surplus—the sum of consumer, producer, and licence-holder surplus—is area A + B + C + D + E' + E'' + F + G.

After the government imposes the import quota and issues the licences, the domestic price exceeds the world price. Domestic consumers get surplus equal to area A + B, and domestic producers get surplus equal to area C + G. The licence holders make a profit on each unit imported equal to the difference between the Isolandian price of steel and the world price. Their surplus equals this price differential times the quantity of imports. Thus, it equals the area of the rectangle E' + E''. Total surplus with the quota is area A + B + C + E' + E'' + G.

To see how total welfare changes with the imposition of the quota, we add the change in consumer surplus (which is negative), the change in producer surplus (positive), and the change in licence-holder surplus (positive). We find that total surplus in the market decreases by area D + F. This area represents the deadweight loss of the import quota.

This analysis should seem somewhat familiar. Indeed, if you compare the analysis of import quotas in Figure 9-7 with the analysis of tariffs in Figure 9-6, you will see that they are essentially identical. *Both tariffs and import quotas raise the domestic price of the good, reduce the welfare of domestic consumers, increase the welfare of domestic producers, and cause deadweight losses.* There is only one difference between these two types of trade restriction: A tariff raises revenue for the government (area E in Figure 9-6), whereas an import quota creates surplus for licence holders (area E' + E'' in Figure 9-7).

Tariffs and import quotas can be made to look even more similar. Suppose that the government tries to capture the licence-holder surplus for itself by charging a fee for the licences. A licence to sell 1 tonne of steel is worth exactly the difference between the Isolandian price of steel and the world price, and the government can set the licence fee as high as this price differential. If the government does this, the licence fee for imports works exactly like a tariff: Consumer surplus, producer surplus, and government revenue are exactly the same under the two policies.

In practice, however, countries that restrict trade with import quotas rarely do so by selling the import licences. For example, the U.S. government has at times pressured Japan to "voluntarily" limit the sale of Japanese cars in the United States. In this case, the Japanese government allocates the import licences to Japanese firms, and the surplus from these licences (area E' + E'') accrues to those firms. This kind of import quota is, from the standpoint of U.S. welfare, strictly worse than a U.S. tariff on imported cars. Both a tariff and an import quota raise prices, restrict trade, and cause deadweight losses, but at least the tariff produces revenue for the U.S. government rather than for Japanese auto companies.

Although in our analysis so far import quotas and tariffs appear to cause similar deadweight losses, a quota can potentially cause an even larger deadweight loss, depending on the mechanism used to allocate the import licences. Suppose that when Isoland imposes a quota, everyone understands that the licences will go to those who spend the most resources lobbying the Isolandian government. In this case, there is an implicit licence fee—the cost of lobbying. The revenues from this fee, however, rather than being collected by the government, are spent on lobbying expenses. The deadweight losses from this type of quota include not only the losses from overproduction (area D) and underconsumption (area F) but also whatever part of the licence-holder surplus (area E'+E") is wasted on the cost of lobbying.

THE LESSONS FOR TRADE POLICY

The team of Isolandian economists can now write to the new president:

Dear Madam President,

You asked us three questions about opening up trade. After much hard work, we have the answers.

Question: If the government allowed Isolandians to import and export steel, what would happen to the price of steel and the quantity of steel sold in the domestic steel market?

Answer: Once trade is allowed, the Isolandian price of steel would be driven to equal the price prevailing around the world.

If the world price is now higher than the Isolandian price, our price would rise. The higher price would reduce the amount of steel Isolandians consume and raise the amount of steel that Isolandians produce. Isoland would, therefore, become a steel exporter. This occurs because, in this case, Isoland would have a comparative advantage in producing steel.

Conversely, if the world price is now lower than the Isolandian price, our price would fall. The lower price would raise the amount of steel that Isolandians consume and lower the amount of steel that Isolandians produce. Isoland would, therefore, become a steel importer. This occurs because, in this case, other countries would have a comparative advantage in producing steel.

Question: Who would gain from free trade in steel and who would lose, and would the gains exceed the losses?

Answer: The answer depends on whether the price rises or falls when trade is allowed. If the price rises, producers of steel gain, and consumers of steel lose. If the price falls, consumers gain, and producers lose. In both cases, the gains are larger than the losses. Thus, free trade raises the total welfare of Isolandians.

Question: Should a tariff or an import quota be part of the new trade policy?

Answer: A tariff, like most taxes, has deadweight losses: The revenue raised would be smaller than the losses to the buyers and sellers. In this case, the deadweight losses occur because the tariff would move the economy closer to our current no-trade equilibrium. An import quota works much like a tariff and would cause similar deadweight losses. The best policy, from the standpoint of economic efficiency, would be to allow trade without a tariff or an import quota.

We hope you find these answers helpful as you decide on your new policy.

Your faithful servants,
Isolandian economics team

QUICK QUIZ: Draw the supply and demand curve for wool suits in the country of Autarka. When trade is allowed, the price of a suit falls from 3 to 2 ounces of gold. In your diagram, what is the change in consumer surplus, the change in producer surplus, and the change in total surplus? How would a tariff on suit imports alter these effects?

THE ARGUMENTS FOR RESTRICTING TRADE

The letter from the economics team persuades the new president of Isoland to consider opening up trade in steel. She notes that the domestic price is now high compared with the world price. Free trade would, therefore, cause the price of steel to fall and hurt domestic steel producers. Before implementing the new policy, she asks Isolandian steel companies to comment on the economists' advice.

Not surprisingly, the steel companies are opposed to free trade in steel. They believe that the government should protect the domestic steel industry from foreign competition. Let's consider some of the arguments they might give to support their position and how the economics team would respond.

THE JOBS ARGUMENT

Opponents of free trade often argue that trade with other countries destroys domestic jobs. In our example, free trade in steel would cause the price of steel to fall, reducing the quantity of steel produced in Isoland and thus reducing employment in the Isolandian steel industry. Some Isolandian steelworkers would lose their jobs.

Yet free trade creates jobs at the same time that it destroys them. When Isolandians buy steel from other countries, those countries obtain the resources to buy other goods from Isoland. Isolandian workers would move from the steel industry to those industries in which Isoland has a comparative advantage. Although the transition may impose hardship on some workers in the short run, it allows Isolandians as a whole to enjoy a higher standard of living.

Opponents of trade are often skeptical that trade creates jobs. They might respond that *everything* can be produced more cheaply abroad. Under free trade, they might argue, Isolandians could not be profitably employed in any industry. As Chapter 3 explains, however, the gains from trade are based on comparative advantage, not absolute advantage. Even if one country is better than another country at producing everything, each country can still gain from trading with the

Berry's World

"You like protectionism as a 'working man.' How about as a consumer?"

FYI

Other Benefits of International Trade

Our conclusions so far have been based on the standard analysis of international trade. As we have seen, there are winners and losers when a nation opens itself up to trade, but the gains to the winners exceed the losses of the losers. Yet the case for free trade can be made even stronger. There are several other economic benefits of trade beyond those emphasized in the standard analysis.

Here, in a nutshell, are some of these other benefits:

◆ *Increased variety of goods:* Goods produced in different countries are not exactly the same. English beer, for instance, is not the same as Canadian beer. Free trade gives consumers in all countries greater variety from which to choose.

◆ *Lower costs through economies of scale:* Some goods can be produced at low cost only if they are produced in large quantities—a phenomenon called *economies of scale*. A firm in a small country cannot take full advan-

tage of economies of scale if it can sell only in a small domestic market. Free trade gives firms access to larger world markets and allows them to realize economies of scale more fully.

◆ *Increased competition:* A company shielded from foreign competitors is more likely to have market power, which in turn gives it the ability to raise prices above competitive levels. This is a type of market failure. Opening up trade fosters competition and gives the invisible hand a better chance to work its magic.

◆ *Enhanced flow of ideas:* The transfer of technological advances around the world is often thought to be linked to international trade in the goods that embody those advances. The best way for a poor, agricultural nation to learn about the computer revolution, for instance, is to buy some computers from abroad, rather than trying to make them domestically.

Thus, free international trade increases variety for consumers, allows firms to take advantage of economies of scale, makes markets more competitive, and facilitates the spread of technology. If the Isolandian economists thought these effects were important, their advice to their president would be even more forceful.

other. Workers in each country will eventually find jobs in the industry in which that country has a comparative advantage.

To see how this happens, suppose that Isolandian prices are higher than world prices for every good. Isolandians then import everything and export nothing, which is exactly what the opponents of free trade fear would happen. But then everybody wants to sell their Isolandian dollars to buy foreign currency to buy imported goods. As a result, the exchange rate of the Isolandian dollar falls, which in turn raises world prices as measured in Isolandian dollars. With higher world prices, some Isolandian industries become exporters, and hire the workers who lost their jobs in the other industries. Alternatively, if the exchange rate is held fixed, the unemployment caused by the flood of imports reduces wages and costs in Isoland. As a result, some Isolandian industries become competitive exporters and hire the unemployed workers. Thus, either the exchange rate or wages adjust to ensure that some Isolandian industries (those with a comparative advantage) are able to compete and export at world prices.

THE NATIONAL-SECURITY ARGUMENT

When an industry is threatened with competition from other countries, opponents of free trade often argue that the industry is vital for national security. In our example, Isolandian steel companies might point out that steel is used to make guns and tanks. Free trade would allow Isoland to become dependent on foreign countries to supply steel. If a war later broke out, Isoland might be unable to produce enough steel and weapons to defend itself.

Economists acknowledge that protecting key industries may be appropriate when there are legitimate concerns over national security. Yet they fear that this argument may be used too quickly by producers eager to gain at consumers' expense. Certainly, it is tempting for those in an industry to exaggerate their role in national defence in order to obtain protection from foreign competition.

THE INFANT-INDUSTRY ARGUMENT

New industries sometimes argue for temporary trade restrictions to help them get started. After a period of protection, the argument goes, these industries will mature and be able to compete with foreign competitors. Similarly, older industries sometimes argue that they need temporary protection to help them adjust to new conditions.

Economists are often skeptical about such claims. The primary reason is that the infant-industry argument is difficult to implement in practice. To apply protection successfully, the government would need to decide which industries will eventually be profitable and decide whether the benefits of establishing these industries exceed the costs to consumers of protection. Yet "picking winners" is extraordinarily difficult. It is made even more difficult by the political process, which often awards protection to those industries that are politically powerful. And once a powerful industry is protected from foreign competition, the "temporary" policy is hard to remove.

In addition, many economists are skeptical about the infant-industry argument even in principle. Suppose, for instance, that the Isolandian steel industry is young and unable to compete profitably against foreign rivals. Yet there is reason to believe that the industry can be profitable in the long run. In this case, the owners of the firms should be willing to incur temporary losses in order to obtain the eventual profits. Protection is not necessary for an industry to grow. Firms in various industries—such as many Internet firms today—incur temporary losses in the hope of growing and becoming profitable in the future. And many of them succeed, even without protection from foreign competition.

THE UNFAIR-COMPETITION ARGUMENT

A common argument is that free trade is desirable only if all countries play by the same rules. If firms in different countries are subject to different laws and regulations, then it is unfair (the argument goes) to expect the firms to compete in the international marketplace. For instance, suppose that the government of Neighbourland subsidizes its steel industry by giving steel companies large tax breaks. The Isolandian steel industry might argue that it should be protected from this foreign competition because Neighbourland is not competing fairly.

Would it, in fact, hurt Isoland to buy steel from another country at a subsidized price? Certainly, Isolandian steel producers would suffer, but Isolandian steel consumers would benefit from the low price. Moreover, the case for free trade is no different: The gains of the consumers from buying at the low price would exceed the losses of the producers. Neighbourland's subsidy to its steel industry may be a bad policy, but it is the taxpayers of Neighbourland who bear the burden. Isoland can benefit from the opportunity to buy steel at a subsidized price.

THE PROTECTION-AS-A-BARGAINING-CHIP ARGUMENT

Another argument for trade restrictions concerns the strategy of bargaining. Many policymakers claim to support free trade but, at the same time, argue that trade restrictions can be useful when we bargain with our trading partners. They claim that the threat of a trade restriction can help remove a trade restriction already imposed by a foreign government. For example, Isoland might threaten to impose a tariff on steel unless Neighbourland removes its tariff on wheat. If Neighbourland responds to this threat by removing its tariff, the result can be freer trade.

The problem with this bargaining strategy is that the threat may not work. If it doesn't work, the country has a difficult choice. It can carry out its threat and implement the trade restriction, which would reduce its own economic welfare. Or it can back down from its threat, which would cause it to lose prestige in international affairs. Faced with this choice, the country would probably wish that it had never made the threat in the first place.

CASE STUDY   TRADE AGREEMENTS

A country can take one of two approaches to achieving free trade. It can take a *unilateral* approach and remove its trade restrictions on its own. This is the approach that Great Britain took in the nineteenth century and that Chile and South Korea have taken in recent years. Alternatively, a country can take a *multilateral* approach and reduce its trade restrictions while other countries do the same. In other words, it can bargain with its trading partners in an attempt to reduce trade restrictions around the world.

One important example of the multilateral approach is the North American Free Trade Agreement (NAFTA), which in 1993 lowered trade barriers among Canada, the United States, and Mexico . Another is the General Agreement on Tariffs and Trade (GATT), which is a continuing series of negotiations among many of the world's countries with the goal of promoting free trade. Canada helped to found GATT after World War II in response to the high tariffs imposed during the Great Depression of the 1930s. Many economists believe that the high tariffs contributed to the economic hardship during that period. GATT has successfully reduced the average tariff among member countries from about 40 percent after World War II to about 5 percent today. The rules established under GATT are now enforced by an international institution called the World Trade Organization (WTO).

What are the pros and cons of the multilateral approach to free trade? One advantage is that the multilateral approach has the potential to result in freer trade than a unilateral approach because it can reduce trade restrictions abroad as well as at home. If international negotiations fail, however, the result could be more restricted trade than under a unilateral approach.

In addition, the multilateral approach may have a political advantage. In most markets, producers are fewer and better organized than consumers—and thus wield greater political influence. Reducing the Isolandian tariff on steel, for example, may be politically difficult if considered by itself. The steel companies

IN THE NEWS

A Chicken Invasion

WHEN DOMESTIC PRODUCERS COMPLAIN about competition from abroad, they often assert that consumers are not well served by imperfect foreign products. The following article documents how Russian producers of chicken reacted to competition from the United States.

U.S. Chicken in Every Pot? Nyet! Russians Cry Foul

BY MICHAEL R. GORDON

MOSCOW—A nasty little skirmish between Russia and the United States is brewing here over a threatened trade barrier.

But this fight is not about manufactured consumer goods or high technology, but about American chicken, which has flooded the Russian market.

To the frustration, and considerable anxiety, of American companies, the Russian government has threatened to ban further American poultry sales effective March 19. . . .

The ostensible reason for the Russian government's warning is health—a seemingly strange concern in a country with a generally lax record in observing safety standards, where virtually every able-bodied man and woman smokes.

Today, no less an authority than the Veterinary Department of the Russian Agriculture and Food Ministry said the ban was needed to protect consumers here against infected poultry until the United States improved its standards.

But the real agenda, American producers contend, is old-fashioned protectionism.

Agitated Russian producers, whose birds, Russian consumers say, are no match for their American competition in terms of quality and price, have repeatedly complained that the United States is trying to destroy the Russian poultry industry and capture its market. And now American companies fear the Russian producers are striking back. . . .

The first big invasion of frozen poultry [into Russia] came during the Bush administration. . . . The export proved to be very popular with Russian consumers, who dubbed them Bush legs.

After the demise of the Soviet Union, American poultry exports continued to soar. Russian poultry production, meanwhile, fell 40 percent, the result of rising grain prices and declining subsidies.

Astoundingly, a third of all American exports to Russia is poultry, American officials say. . . .

If the confrontation continues, the United States has a number of possible

A THREAT TO RUSSIA?

recourses, including arguing that the Russian action is inconsistent with Moscow's bid to join the World Trade Organization.

Some experts, however, believe there is an important countervailing force here that may lead to a softening of the Russian position: namely Russian consumers.

Russian consumers favour the American birds, which despite the dire warnings of the Russian government, have come to symbolize quality. And they vote, too.

SOURCE: *The New York Times*, February 24, 1996, pp. 33, 34.

would oppose free trade, and the users of steel who would benefit are so numerous that organizing their support would be difficult. Yet suppose that Neighbourland promises to reduce its tariff on wheat at the same time that Isoland reduces its tariff on steel. In this case, the Isolandian wheat farmers, who are also politically powerful, would back the agreement. Thus, the multilateral approach to free trade can sometimes win political support when a unilateral reduction cannot.

IN THE NEWS
The Case for Unilateral Disarmament in the Trade Wars

ECONOMIST JAGDISH BHAGWATI ARGUES that the United States should lower its trade barriers unilaterally.

Free Trade without Treaties

BY JAGDISH BHAGWATI

President Clinton and 17 Asian-Pacific leaders are meeting today in Vancouver. Rather than the convivial photo-op they'd planned, however, they must contend with worrisome trade news. A spate of Asian currency devaluations has raised the spectre of renewed protectionism around the world. South America's Mercosur trade bloc, led by Brazil, just raised its tariffs some 30 percent. And Congress turned its back on the president and refused to approve fast-track authority for him to negotiate further free-trade accords. [*Author's*

note: Fast-track authority would allow the president to negotiate trade deals that Congress would consider without the ability to attach amendments.]

In light of all this dismaying news, what are the prospects for free trade? Is the future bleak, or will the postwar trend of dramatic liberalization continue to accelerate despite these setbacks?

The immediate prospects for more U.S.-led multilateral trade accords do indeed look grim after the defeat of fast-track. But that doesn't mean that free trade itself is on the ropes. A large portion of the world's trade liberalization in the last quarter-century has been *unilateral.* Those countries that lower trade barriers of their own accord not only profit themselves, but also often induce the laggards to match their example. The most potent force for the worldwide freeing of trade, then, is unilateral U.S. action. If the United States continues to do away with tariffs and trade barriers, other countries will follow suit—fast-track or no fast-track.

To be sure, the General Agreement on Tariffs and Trade, the World Trade Organization, and other multilateral tariff reductions have greatly contributed to global wealth. The WTO has become the international institution for setting the

"rules" on public and private practices that affect competition among trading nations. Much still needs to be done in that mode, particularly on agriculture tariffs, which remain too high around the world. A future U.S. president, if not Mr. Clinton, will certainly need fast-track authority if another multilateral effort, such as the "millennium round" called for by Sir Leon Brittan of the European Union, is to pursue these goals.

But the good news is that even if organized labour, radical environmentalists, and others who fear the global economy continue to impede fast-track during Congress's next session, they cannot stop the historic freeing of trade that has been occurring unilaterally worldwide.

From the 1970s through the 1990s, Latin America witnessed dramatic lowering of trade barriers unilaterally by Chile, Bolivia, and Paraguay; and the entire continent has been moving steadily toward further trade liberalization. Mercosur's recent actions are a setback, but only a small one—so far.

Latin America's record has been bettered by unilateral liberalizers in Asia and the Pacific. New Zealand began dismantling its substantial trade protection apparatus in 1985. That effort was driven

QUICK QUIZ: The textile industry of Autarka advocates a ban on the import of wool suits. Describe five arguments its lobbyists might make. Give a response to each of these arguments.

CONCLUSION

Economists and the general public often disagree about free trade. In 1988, for example, Canada faced the question of whether to sign the Free Trade Agreement, which reduced trade restrictions between Canada and the United States. Opinion by the reformist views of then–Prime Minister David Lange, who declared, "In the course of about three years we changed from being a country run like a Polish shipyard into one that could be internationally competitive."

Since the 1980s, Hong Kong's and Singapore's enormous successes as free traders have served as potent examples of unilateral market opening, encouraging Indonesia, the Philippines, Thailand, South Korea, and Malaysia to follow suit. By 1991 even India, which has been astonishingly autarkic for more than four decades, had finally learned the virtue of free trade and had embarked on a massive lowering of its tariffs and nontariff barriers.

In Central and Eastern Europe, the collapse of communism led to a wholesale, unilateral, and nondiscriminatory removal of trade barriers as well. The French economist Patrick Messerlin has shown how this happened in three waves: Czechoslovakia, Poland, and Hungary liberalized right after the fall of the Berlin Wall; next came Bulgaria, Romania, and Slovenia; and finally, the Baltic countries began unilateral opening in 1991. . . .

U.S. leadership is crucial to maintaining the trend toward free trade. Such ultramodern industries as telecommunications and financial services gained their momentum largely from unilateral openness and deregulation in the United States. This in turn led to a softening of protectionist attitudes in the European Union and Japan.

These developed economies are now moving steadily in the direction of openness and competition—not because any officials in Washington threaten them with retribution, but because they've seen how U.S. companies become more competitive once regulation and other trade barriers have fallen. A Brussels bureaucrat can argue with a Washington bureaucrat, but he cannot argue with the markets. Faced with the prospect of being elbowed out of world markets by American firms, Japan and Europe have no option but to follow the U.S. example, belatedly but surely, in opening their own markets.

The biggest threat to free trade is not the loss of fast-track per se, but the signal it sends that Americans may not be interested in lowering their trade barriers any further. To counteract this attitude, President Clinton needs to mount the bully pulpit and explain the case for free trade—a case that Adam Smith first made more than 200 years ago, but that continues to come under attack.

The president, free from the burdens of constituency interests that cripple many in Congress, could argue, credibly and with much evidence, that free trade is in the interest of the whole world, but that, because the U.S. economy is the most competitive anywhere, we have the most to gain. The president could also point to plenty of evidence that debunks the claims of protectionists. The unions may argue that trade with poor countries depresses our workers' wages, for example, but in fact the best evidence shows that such trade has *helped* workers by moderating the fall in their wages from technological changes.

Assuming that the president can make the case for free trade at home, the prospects for free trade worldwide remain bright. The United States doesn't need to sign treaties to open markets or, heaven forbid, issue counterproductive threats to close our own markets if others are less open than we are. We simply need to offer an example of openness and deregulation to the rest of the world. Other countries will see our success, and seek to emulate it.

SOURCE: *The Wall Street Journal*, November 24, 1997, p. A22.

polls showed the general public in Canada to be about evenly split on the issue. Prime Minister Brian Mulroney campaigned for the Free Trade Agreement, and won re-election, but with a minority of the popular vote. Opponents viewed free trade as a threat to job security and the Canadian standard of living. By contrast, economists overwhelmingly supported the agreement. They viewed free trade as a way of allocating production efficiently and raising living standards in both countries.

Economists see the benefits of trade among countries the same way they see the benefits of trade among provinces, among cities, and among people. Individuals would have a much lower standard of living if they had to produce all their own food, clothing, and housing. So would a city. So would a province. The United States has always had unrestricted trade among the states, and the country as a whole has benefited from the specialization that trade allows in such a large market. With a few exceptions, Canada also has free trade among the provinces: Ontario builds cars, Alberta pumps oil, British Columbia saws lumber, and so on. The world could similarly benefit from free trade among countries.

To better understand economists' view of trade, let's continue our parable. Suppose that the country of Isoland ignores the advice of its economics team and decides not to allow free trade in steel. The country remains in the equilibrium without international trade.

Then, one day, some Isolandian inventor discovers a new way to make steel at very low cost. The process is quite mysterious, however, and the inventor insists on keeping it a secret. What is odd is that the inventor doesn't need any workers or iron ore to make steel. The only input he requires is wheat.

The inventor is hailed as a genius. Because steel is used in so many products, the invention lowers the cost of many goods and allows all Isolandians to enjoy a higher standard of living. Workers who had previously produced steel do suffer when their factories close, but eventually they find work in other industries. Some become farmers and grow the wheat that the inventor turns into steel. Others enter new industries that emerge as a result of higher Isolandian living standards. Everyone understands that the displacement of these workers is an inevitable part of progress.

After several years, a newspaper reporter decides to investigate this mysterious new steel process. She sneaks into the inventor's factory and learns that the inventor is a fraud. The inventor has not been making steel at all. Instead, he has been smuggling wheat abroad in exchange for steel from other countries. The only thing that the inventor had discovered was the gains from international trade.

When the truth is revealed, the government shuts down the inventor's operation. The price of steel rises, and workers return to jobs in steel factories. Living standards in Isoland fall back to their former levels. The inventor is jailed and held up to public ridicule. After all, he was no inventor. He was just an economist.

Summary

◆ The effects of free trade can be determined by comparing the domestic price without trade with the world price. A low domestic price indicates that the country has a comparative advantage in producing the good and that the country will become an exporter. A high domestic price indicates that the rest of the world has a comparative advantage in producing the good and that the country will become an importer.

◆ When a country allows trade and becomes an exporter of a good, producers of the good are better off, and consumers of the good are worse off. When a country allows trade and becomes an importer of a good, consumers are better off, and producers are worse off. In both cases, the gains from trade exceed the losses.

◆ A tariff—a tax on imports—moves a market closer to the equilibrium that would exist without trade and,

therefore, reduces the gains from trade. Although domestic producers are better off and the government raises revenue, the losses to consumers exceed these gains.

◆ An import quota has effects that are similar to those of a tariff. Under a quota, however, the holders of the import licences receive the revenue that the government would collect with a tariff.

◆ There are various arguments for restricting trade: protecting jobs, defending national security, helping infant industries, preventing unfair competition, and responding to foreign trade restrictions. Although some of these arguments have some merit in some cases, economists believe that free trade is usually the better policy.

Key Concepts

world price, p. 181   tariff, p. 186   import quota, p. 189

Questions for Review

1. What does the domestic price that prevails without international trade tell us about a nation's comparative advantage?

2. When does a country become an exporter of a good? An importer?

3. Draw the supply-and-demand diagram for an importing country. What is consumer surplus and producer surplus before trade is allowed? What is consumer surplus and producer surplus with free trade? What is the change in total surplus?

4. Describe what a tariff is, and describe its economic effects.

5. What is an import quota? Compare its economic effects with those of a tariff.

6. List five arguments often given to support trade restrictions. How do economists respond to these arguments?

7. What is the difference between the unilateral and multilateral approaches to achieving free trade? Give an example of each.

Problems and Applications

1. Canada represents a small part of the world apple market.
   a. Draw a diagram depicting the equilibrium in the Canadian apple market without international trade. Identify the equilibrium price, equilibrium quantity, consumer surplus, and producer surplus.
   b. Suppose that the world apple price is below the Canadian price before trade, and that the Canadian apple market is now opened to trade. Identify the new equilibrium price, quantity consumed, quantity produced domestically, and quantity imported. Also show the change in the surplus of domestic consumers and producers. Has domestic total surplus increased or decreased?

2. The world price of wine is below the price that would prevail in Canada in the absence of trade.
   a. Assuming that Canadian imports of wine are a small part of total world wine production, draw a graph for the Canadian market for wine under free trade. Identify consumer surplus, producer surplus, and total surplus in an appropriate table.
   b. Now suppose that an unusual shift of the Gulf Stream leads to an unseasonably cold summer in Europe, destroying much of the grape harvest there. What effect does this shock have on the world price of wine? Using your graph and table

from part (a), show the effect on consumer surplus, producer surplus, and total surplus in Canada. Who are the winners and losers? Is Canada as a whole better or worse off?

3. The world price of cotton is below the no-trade price in Country A and above the no-trade price in Country B. Using supply-and-demand diagrams and welfare tables such as those in the chapter, show the gains from trade in each country. Compare your results for the two countries.

4. Suppose that Parliament imposes a tariff on imported clothes to protect the Canadian clothing industry from foreign competition. Assuming that Canada is a price taker in the world clothing market, show on a diagram the change in the quantity of imports, the loss to Canadian consumers, the gain to Canadian manufacturers, government revenue, and the deadweight loss associated with the tariff. The loss to consumers can be divided into three pieces: a transfer to domestic producers, a transfer to the government, and a deadweight loss. Use your diagram to identify these three pieces.

5. Most Canadian dairy farmers oppose free trade, and most Canadian lumber producers support it. For simplicity, assume that Canada is a small country in the markets for both milk and lumber, and that without free

trade, Canada would not trade these goods internationally. (Both of these assumptions are false, but they do not affect the qualitative responses to the following questions.)

a. Based on who opposes and who supports free trade, do you think the world milk price is above or below the Canadian no-trade milk price? Do you think the world lumber price is above or below the Canadian no-trade lumber price? Now analyze the welfare consequences of free trade for both markets.

b. Considering both markets together, would free trade make Canadian producers as a group better off or worse off? Would it make Canadian consumers as a group better off or worse off? Does it make Canada as a whole better off or worse off?

6. Imagine that winemakers in British Columbia petitioned the provincial government to tax wines imported from Ontario. They argue that this tax would both raise tax revenue for the provincial government and raise employment in the British Columbian wine industry. Do you agree with these claims? Is it a good policy?

7. U.S. Senator Ernest Hollings once wrote that "consumers *do not* benefit from lower-priced imports. Glance through some mail-order catalogs and you'll see that consumers pay exactly the same price for clothing whether it is U.S.-made or imported." Comment.

8. Write a brief essay advocating or criticizing each of the following policy positions:

a. The government should not allow imports if foreign firms are selling below their costs of production (a phenomenon called "dumping").

b. The government should temporarily stop the import of goods for which the domestic industry is new and struggling to survive.

c. The government should not allow imports from countries with weaker environmental regulations than ours.

9. Suppose that a technological advance in Japan lowers the world price of televisions.

a. Assume that Canada is an importer of televisions and there are no trade restrictions. How does the technological advance affect the welfare of Canadian consumers and Canadian producers? What happens to total surplus in Canada?

b. Now suppose Canada has a quota on television imports. How does the Japanese technological advance affect the welfare of Canadian consumers, Canadian producers, and the holders of import licences?

10. When the government of Tradeland decides to impose an import quota on foreign cars, three proposals are suggested: (1) Sell the import licences in an auction, (2) distribute the licences randomly in a lottery, and (3) let people wait in line and distribute the licences on a first-come, first-served basis. Compare the effects of these policies. Which policy do you think has the largest deadweight losses? Which policy has the smallest deadweight losses? Why? (Hint: The government's other ways of raising tax revenue all cause deadweight losses themselves.)

11. Canada and other rich countries are participants in the Multi-Fibre Arrangement (MFA), which restricts imports of clothing from developing countries in order to protect the clothing industries of participating countries from competition from low-wage countries.

a. Illustrate the effect of import quotas on the Canadian market for clothes. Label the relevant prices and quantities under free trade and under the quota.

b. Analyze the effect of the quota using the tools of welfare analysis.

c. Critics of the MFA say that it has deprived numerous developing countries of export markets for their clothing industries. Illustrate the effect of the MFA quotas on the market for clothes in developing countries. Label the relevant prices and quantities under free trade and under the quota.

d. Analyze the effect of the quota on developing countries using the tools of welfare analysis.

e. Our usual welfare analysis includes only the gains and losses of Canadian producers and consumers. What role do you think the gains and losses to people in other countries should play in our economic policymaking?

12. (This question is challenging.) Consider a small country that exports steel. Suppose that a "pro-trade" government decides to subsidize the export of steel by paying a certain amount for each tonne sold abroad. How does this export subsidy affect the domestic price of steel, the quantity of steel produced, the quantity of steel consumed, and the quantity of steel exported? How does it affect consumer surplus, producer surplus, government revenue, and total surplus? (Hint: The analysis of an export subsidy is similar to the analysis of a tariff.)

Four

THE DATA OF
MACROECONOMICS

10

MEASURING A NATION'S INCOME

When you finish school and start looking for a full-time job, your experience will, to a large extent, be shaped by prevailing economic conditions. In some years, firms throughout the economy are expanding their production of goods and services, employment is rising, and jobs are easy to find. In other years, firms are cutting back on production, employment is declining, and finding a good job takes a long time. Not surprisingly, any university graduate would rather enter the labour force in a year of economic expansion than in a year of economic contraction.

Because the condition of the overall economy profoundly affects all of us, changes in economic conditions are widely reported by the media. Indeed, it is hard to pick up a newspaper without seeing some newly reported statistic about the economy. The statistic might measure the total income of everyone in the economy (GDP), the rate at which average prices are rising (inflation), the percentage of the labour force that is out of work (unemployment), total spending at stores (retail sales), or the imbalance of trade between Canada and the rest of the world (the trade deficit). All of these statistics are *macroeconomic*. Rather than telling us about a particular household or firm, they tell us something about the entire economy.

As you may recall from Chapter 2, economics is divided into two branches: microeconomics and macroeconomics. **Microeconomics** is the study of how individual households and firms make decisions and how they interact with one another in markets. **Macroeconomics** is the study of the economy as a whole. The goal of macroeconomics is to explain the economic changes that affect many households, firms, and markets at once. Macroeconomists address diverse questions: Why is average income high in some countries but low in others? Why do prices rise rapidly in some periods of time but they are more stable in other periods? Why do production and employment expand in some years and contract in others? What, if anything, can the government do to promote rapid growth in incomes, low inflation, and stable employment? These questions are all macroeconomic in nature because they concern the workings of the entire economy.

Because the economy as a whole is just a collection of many households and many firms interacting in many markets, microeconomics and macroeconomics are closely linked. The basic tools of supply and demand, for instance, are as central to macroeconomic analysis as they are to microeconomic analysis. Yet studying the economy in its entirety raises some new and intriguing challenges.

In this chapter and the next one, we discuss some of the data that economists and policymakers use to monitor the performance of the overall economy. These data reflect the economic changes that macroeconomists try to explain. This chapter considers *gross domestic product*, or simply GDP, which measures the total income of a nation. Although it is not a perfect measure, GDP is the most closely watched economic statistic because it is thought to be the best single measure of a society's economic well-being.

microeconomics

the study of how households and firms make decisions and how they interact in markets

macroeconomics

the study of economy-wide phenomena, including inflation, unemployment, and economic growth

THE ECONOMY'S INCOME AND EXPENDITURE

If you were to judge how a person is doing economically, you might first look at his or her income. A person with a high income can more easily afford life's necessities and luxuries. It is no surprise that people with higher incomes enjoy higher standards of living—better housing, better food, fancier cars, more opulent vacations, and so on.

The same logic applies to a nation's overall economy. When judging whether the economy is doing well or poorly, it is natural to look first at the total income that everyone in the economy is earning. That is the task of gross domestic product (GDP).

GDP measures two things at once: the total income of everyone in the economy and the total expenditure on the economy's output of goods and services. The reason that GDP can perform the trick of measuring both total income and total expenditure is that these two things are really the same. *For an economy as a whole, income must equal expenditure.*

Why is this true? The reason that an economy's income is the same as its expenditure is simply that every transaction has two parties: a buyer and a seller. Every dollar of spending by some buyer is a dollar of income for some seller. Suppose, for

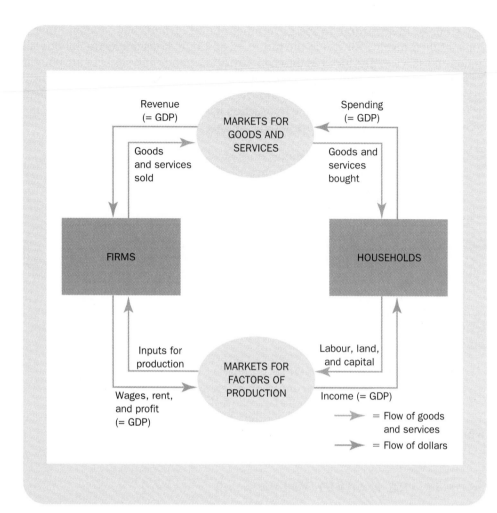

Figure 10-1

THE CIRCULAR-FLOW DIAGRAM. Households buy goods and services from firms, and firms use their revenue from sales to pay wages to workers, rent to landowners, and profit to firm owners. GDP equals the total amount spent by households in the market for goods and services. It also equals the total wages, rent, and profit paid by firms in the markets for the factors of production.

instance, that Karen pays Doug $100 to mow her lawn. In this case, Doug is a seller of a service, and Karen is a buyer. Doug earns $100, and Karen spends $100. Thus, the transaction contributes equally to the economy's income and to its expenditure. GDP, whether measured as total income or total expenditure, rises by $100.

Another way to see the equality of income and expenditure is with the circular-flow diagram in Figure 10-1. (You may recall this circular-flow diagram from Chapter 2.) This diagram describes all the transactions between households and firms in a simple economy. In this economy, households buy goods and services from firms; these expenditures flow through the markets for goods and services. The firms in turn use the money they receive from sales to pay workers' wages, landowners' rent, and firm owners' profit; this income flows through the markets for the factors of production. In this economy, money continuously flows from households to firms and then back to households.

We can compute GDP for this economy in one of two ways: by adding up the total expenditure by households or by adding up the total income (wages, rent, and profit) paid by firms. Because all expenditure in the economy ends up as someone's income, GDP is the same regardless of how we compute it.

The actual economy is, of course, more complicated than the one illustrated in Figure 10-1. In particular, households do not spend all of their income. Households pay some of their income to the government in taxes, and they save and invest some of their income for use in the future. In addition, households do not buy all goods and services produced in the economy. Some goods and services are bought by governments, and some are bought by firms that plan to use them in the future to produce their own output. Yet, regardless of whether a household, government, or firm buys a good or service, the transaction has a buyer and seller. Thus, for the economy as a whole, expenditure and income are always the same.

▎ **QUICK QUIZ:** What two things does gross domestic product measure? How can it measure two things at once?

> ## THE MEASUREMENT OF GROSS DOMESTIC PRODUCT

Now that we have discussed the meaning of gross domestic product in general terms, let's be more precise about how this statistic is measured. Here is a definition of GDP:

gross domestic product (GDP)

the market value of all final goods and services produced within a country in a given period of time

◆ **Gross domestic product (GDP)** is the market value of all final goods and services produced within a country in a given period of time.

This definition might seem simple enough. But, in fact, many subtle issues arise when computing an economy's GDP. Let's therefore consider each phrase in this definition with some care.

"GDP IS THE MARKET VALUE . . ."

You have probably heard the adage, "You can't compare apples and oranges." Yet GDP does exactly that. GDP adds together many different kinds of products into a single measure of the value of economic activity. To do this, it uses market prices. Because market prices measure the amount people are willing to pay for different goods, they reflect the value of those goods. If the price of an apple is twice the price of an orange, then an apple contributes twice as much to GDP as does an orange.

"OF ALL . . ."

GDP tries to be comprehensive. It includes all items produced in the economy and sold legally in markets. GDP measures the market value of not just apples and oranges, but also pears and grapefruit, books and movies, haircuts and health care, and on and on.

GDP also includes the market value of the housing services provided by the economy's stock of housing. For rental housing, this value is easy to calculate—the rent equals both the tenant's expenditure and the landlord's income. Yet many people own their home and, therefore, do not pay rent. The government includes this owner-occupied housing in GDP by estimating its rental value. That is, GDP is based on the assumption that owners, in effect, pay rent to themselves, so the rent is included both in expenditure and in their income.

However, GDP excludes some products because measuring them is so difficult. GDP excludes items produced and sold illicitly, such as illegal drugs. It also excludes most items that are produced and consumed at home and, therefore, never enter the marketplace. Vegetables you buy at the grocery store are part of GDP; vegetables you grow in your garden are not.

These exclusions from GDP can at times lead to paradoxical results. For example, when Karen pays Doug to mow her lawn, that transaction is part of GDP. If Karen were to marry Doug, the situation would change. Even though Doug may continue to mow Karen's lawn, the value of the mowing is now left out of GDP because Doug's service is no longer sold in a market. Thus, when Karen and Doug marry, GDP falls.

"FINAL . . ."

When E.B. Eddy makes paper, which Carlton Cards then uses to make a greeting card, the paper is called an *intermediate good,* and the card is called a *final good.* GDP includes only the value of final goods. The reason is that the value of intermediate goods is already included in the prices of the final goods. Adding the market value of the paper to the market value of the card would be double counting. That is, it would (incorrectly) count the paper twice.

An important exception to this principle arises when an intermediate good is produced and, rather than being used, is added to a firm's inventory of goods to be used or sold at a later date. In this case, the intermediate good is taken to be "final" for the moment, and its value as inventory investment is added to GDP. When the inventory of the intermediate good is later used or sold, the firm's inventory investment is negative, and GDP for the later period is reduced accordingly.

"GOODS AND SERVICES . . ."

GDP includes both tangible goods (food, clothing, cars) and intangible services (haircuts, housecleaning, dentist visits). When you buy a CD by your favourite band, you are buying a good, and the purchase price is part of GDP. When you pay to hear a concert by the same band, you are buying a service, and the ticket price is also part of GDP.

"PRODUCED . . ."

GDP includes goods and services currently produced. It does not include transactions involving items produced in the past. When General Motors produces and sells a new car, the value of the car is included in GDP. When one person sells a used car to another person, the value of the used car is not included in GDP.

"WITHIN A COUNTRY . . ."

GDP measures the value of production within the geographic confines of a country. When a U.S. citizen works temporarily in Canada, his production is part of Canadian GDP. When a Canadian citizen owns a factory in Haiti, the production at her factory is not part of Canadian GDP. (It is part of Haiti's GDP.) Thus, items

FYI

Other Measures of Income

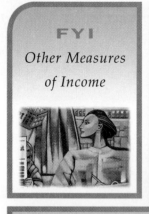

When Statistics Canada computes the nation's GDP every three months, it also computes various other measures of income to get a more complete picture of what's happening in the economy. These other measures differ from GDP by excluding or including certain categories of income. What follows is a brief description of five of these income measures, ordered from largest to smallest.

◆ *Gross national product (GNP)* is the total income earned by a nation's permanent residents (called *nationals*). It differs from GDP by including income that our citizens earn abroad and excluding income that foreigners earn here. For example, when a U.S. citizen works temporarily in Canada, his production is part of Canadian GDP, but it is not part of Canadian GNP. (It is part of U.S. GNP.) For most countries, including Canada, domestic residents are responsible for most domestic production, so GDP and GNP are quite close.

◆ *Net national product (NNP)* is the total income of a nation's residents (GNP) minus losses from depreciation. *Depreciation* is the wear and tear on the economy's stock of equipment and structures, such as trucks rusting and light bulbs burning out. In the national income accounts prepared by Statistics Canada, depreciation is called the "capital consumption allowance."

◆ *National income* is the total income earned by a nation's residents in the production of goods and serv-

ices. It differs from net national product by excluding indirect business taxes (such as sales taxes) and including business subsidies. NNP and national income also differ because of a "statistical discrepancy" that arises from problems in data collection.

◆ *Personal income* is the income that households and noncorporate businesses receive. Unlike national income, it excludes *retained earnings,* which is income that corporations have earned but have not paid out to their owners. It also subtracts corporate income taxes and contributions for social insurance (mostly Employment Insurance taxes). In addition, personal income includes the interest income that households receive from their holdings of government debt and the income that households receive from government transfer programs, such as welfare, Canada Pension Plan, and EI benefits.

◆ *Disposable personal income* is the income that households and noncorporate businesses have left after satisfying all of their obligations to the government. It equals personal income minus personal taxes and certain nontax payments (such as traffic tickets).

Although the various measures of income differ in detail, they almost always tell the same story about economic conditions. When GDP is growing rapidly, these other measures of income are usually growing rapidly. And when GDP is falling, these other measures are usually falling as well. For monitoring fluctuations in the overall economy, it does not matter much which measure of income we use.

are included in a nation's GDP if they are produced domestically, regardless of the nationality of the producer.

"... IN A GIVEN PERIOD OF TIME."

GDP measures the value of production that takes place within a specific interval of time. Usually that interval is a year or a quarter (three months). GDP measures the economy's flow of income and expenditure during that interval.

When the government reports the GDP for a quarter, it usually presents GDP "at an annual rate." This means that the figure reported for quarterly GDP is the amount of income and expenditure during the quarter multiplied by four. The government uses this convention so that quarterly and annual figures on GDP can be compared more easily.

In addition, when the government reports quarterly GDP, it presents the data after they have been modified by a statistical procedure called *seasonal adjustment.*

The unadjusted data show clearly that the economy produces more goods and services during some times of year than during others. (As you might guess, December's Christmas shopping season is a high point.) When monitoring the condition of the economy, economists and policymakers often want to look beyond these regular seasonal changes. Therefore, government statisticians adjust the quarterly data to take out the seasonal cycle. The GDP data reported in the news are always seasonally adjusted.

Now let's repeat the definition of GDP:

◆   Gross domestic product (GDP) is the market value of all final goods and services produced within a country in a given period of time.

It should be apparent that GDP is a sophisticated measure of the value of economic activity. In advanced courses in macroeconomics, you will learn more of the subtleties that arise in its calculation. But even now you can see that each phrase in this definition is packed with meaning.

QUICK QUIZ: Which contributes more to GDP—the production of a kilogram of hamburger or the production of a kilogram of caviar? Why?

THE COMPONENTS OF GDP

Spending in the economy takes many forms. At any moment, the Farag family may be having lunch at Burger King; General Motors may be building a car factory; the Navy may be repairing a submarine; and British Airways may be buying an airplane from Bombardier. GDP includes all of these various forms of spending on domestically produced goods and services.

To understand how the economy is using its scarce resources, economists are often interested in studying the composition of GDP among various types of spending. To do this, GDP (which we denote as Y) is divided into four components: consumption (C), investment (I), government purchases (G), and net exports (NX):

$$Y = C + I + G + NX.$$

This equation is an *identity*—an equation that must be true by the way the variables in the equation are defined. In this case, because each dollar of expenditure included in GDP is placed into one of the four components of GDP, the total of the four components must be equal to GDP.

We have just seen an example of each component. **Consumption** is spending by households on goods and services, such as the Farags' lunch at Burger King. **Investment** is spending on capital equipment, inventories, and structures, such as the General Motors factory. Investment also includes expenditure on new housing. (By convention, expenditure on new housing is the one form of household spending categorized as investment rather than consumption.) **Government purchases** include spending on goods and services by local, provincial, and federal governments, such as the Navy's repairing a submarine. **Net exports** equal the spending on domestically produced goods by foreigners (exports) minus the domestic spending on foreign goods (imports). A domestic firm's sale to a buyer in another country, such as the Bombardier sale to British Airways, increases net exports.

consumption 5%
spending by households on goods and services, with the exception of purchases of new housing

investment 17%
spending on capital equipment, inventories, and structures, including household purchases of new housing

government purchases 2%
spending on goods and services by local, provincial, and federal governments

net exports 5%
spending on domestically produced goods by foreigners (exports) minus spending on foreign goods by domestic residents (imports)

Table 10-1

GDP AND ITS COMPONENTS. This table shows total GDP for the Canadian economy in the fourth quarter of 2000 (at an annual rate) and the breakdown of GDP among its four components. When reading the table, recall the identity $Y = C + I + G + NX$.

	TOTAL (IN BILLIONS)	PER PERSON	PERCENTAGE OF TOTAL
Gross domestic product, Y	$1 058	$33 129	100%
Consumption, C	$604	$19 484	57%
Investment, I	$182	$5 871	17%
Government purchases, G	$216	$6 968	21%
Net exports, NX	$56	$1 806	5%
(exports	($491	($15 838	(46%
minus imports)	– $435)	– $14 032)	– 41%)

SOURCE: Statistics Canada.

The "net" in "net exports" refers to the fact that imports are subtracted from exports. This subtraction is made because imports of goods and services are included in other components of GDP. For example, suppose that a household buys a $30 000 car from Volkswagen, the German carmaker. That transaction increases consumption by $30 000 because car purchases are part of consumer spending. It also reduces net exports by $30 000 because the car is an import. In other words, net exports include goods and services produced abroad (with a minus sign) because these goods and services are included in consumption, investment, and government purchases (with a plus sign). Thus, when a domestic household, firm, or government buys a good or service from abroad, the purchase reduces net exports—but because it also raises consumption, investment, or government purchases, it does not affect GDP.

The meaning of "government purchases" also requires a bit of clarification. When the government pays the salary of an Army general, that salary is part of government purchases. But what happens when the government pays a Canada Pension Plan benefit to an elderly person? Such government spending is called a *transfer payment* because it is not made in exchange for a currently produced good or service. From a macroeconomic standpoint, transfer payments are like a tax rebate. Like taxes, transfer payments alter household income, but they do not reflect the economy's production. Because GDP is intended to measure income from (and expenditure on) the production of goods and services, transfer payments are not counted as part of government purchases.

Table 10-1 shows the composition of Canadian GDP in the fourth quarter of 2000. The annual GDP of Canada was about $1058 billion. If we divide this number by the 2000 Canadian population of about 31 million, we find that GDP per person—the amount of expenditure for the average Canadian—was about $34 129 per year. Consumption made up about 57 percent of GDP, or about $19 484 per person. Investment was about $5871 per person. Government purchases were about $6968 per person. Exports were about $15 838 per person and imports about $14 032 per person, so net exports—exports minus imports—were about $1806 per person. Net exports are usually positive for Canada but are negative for some countries that import more than they export.

■ **QUICK QUIZ:** List the four components of expenditure. Which is the largest?

| | PRICES AND QUANTITIES | | | |
YEAR	PRICE OF HOT DOGS	QUANTITY OF HOT DOGS	PRICE OF HAMBURGERS	QUANTITY OF HAMBURGERS
2001	$1	100	$2	50
2002	2	150	3	100
2003	3	200	4	150

YEAR	CALCULATING NOMINAL GDP
2001	($1 per hot dog × 100 hot dogs) + ($2 per hamburger × 50 hamburgers) = $200
2002	($2 per hot dog × 150 hot dogs) + ($3 per hamburger × 100 hamburgers) = $600
2003	($3 per hot dog × 200 hot dogs) + ($4 per hamburger × 150 hamburgers) = $1200

YEAR	CALCULATING REAL GDP (BASE YEAR 2001)
2001	($1 per hot dog × 100 hot dogs) + ($2 per hamburger × 50 hamburgers) = $200
2002	($1 per hot dog × 150 hot dogs) + ($2 per hamburger × 100 hamburgers) = $350
2003	($1 per hot dog × 200 hot dogs) + ($2 per hamburger × 150 hamburgers) = $500

YEAR	CALCULATING THE GDP DEFLATOR
2001	($200/$200) × 100 = 100
2002	($600/$350) × 100 = 171
2003	($1200/$500) × 100 = 240

REAL AND NOMINAL GDP.   This table shows how to calculate real GDP, nominal GDP, and the GDP deflator for a hypothetical economy that produces only hot dogs and hamburgers.

Table 10-2

REAL VERSUS NOMINAL GDP

As we have seen, GDP measures the total spending on goods and services in all markets in the economy. If total spending rises from one year to the next, one of two things must be true: (1) the economy is producing a larger output of goods and services, or (2) goods and services are being sold at higher prices. When studying changes in the economy over time, economists want to separate these two effects. In particular, they want a measure of the total quantity of goods and services the economy is producing that is not affected by changes in the prices of those goods and services.

To do this, economists use a measure called *real GDP*. Real GDP answers a hypothetical question: What would be the value of the goods and services produced this year if we valued these goods and services at the prices that prevailed in some specific year in the past? By evaluating current production using prices that are fixed at past levels, real GDP shows how the economy's overall production of goods and services changes over time.

To see more precisely how real GDP is constructed, let's consider an example.

A NUMERICAL EXAMPLE

Table 10-2 shows some data for an economy that produces only two goods—hot dogs and hamburgers. The table shows the quantities of the two goods produced and their prices in the years 2001, 2002, and 2003.

To compute total spending in this economy, we would multiply the quantities of hot dogs and hamburgers by their prices. In the year 2001, 100 hot dogs are sold at a price of $1 per hot dog, so expenditure on hot dogs equals $100. In the same year, 50 hamburgers are sold for $2 per hamburger, so expenditure on hamburgers also equals $100. Total expenditure in the economy—the sum of expenditure on hot dogs and expenditure on hamburgers—is $200. This amount, the production of goods and services valued at current prices, is called **nominal GDP.**

nominal GDP

the production of goods and services valued at current prices

The table shows the calculation of nominal GDP for these three years. Total spending rises from $200 in 2001 to $600 in 2002 and then to $1200 in 2003. Part of this rise is attributable to the increase in the quantities of hot dogs and hamburgers, and part is attributable to the increase in the prices of hot dogs and hamburgers.

To obtain a measure of the amount produced that is not affected by changes in prices, we use **real GDP,** which is the production of goods and services valued at constant prices. We calculate real GDP by first choosing one year as a *base year.* We then use the prices of hot dogs and hamburgers in the base year to compute the value of goods and services in all of the years. In other words, the prices in the base year provide the basis for comparing quantities in different years.

real GDP

the production of goods and services valued at constant prices

Suppose that we choose 2001 to be the base year in our example. We can then use the prices of hot dogs and hamburgers in 2001 to compute the value of goods and services produced in 2001, 2002, and 2003. Table 10-2 shows these calculations. To compute real GDP for 2001, we use the prices of hot dogs and hamburgers in 2001 (the base year) and the quantities of hot dogs and hamburgers produced in 2001. (Thus, for the base year, real GDP always equals nominal GDP.) To compute real GDP for 2002, we use the prices of hot dogs and hamburgers in 2001 (the base year) and the quantities of hot dogs and hamburgers produced in 2002. Similarly, to compute real GDP for 2003, we use the prices in 2001 and the quantities in 2003. When we find that real GDP has risen from $200 in 2001 to $350 in 2002 and then to $500 in 2003, we know that the increase is attributable to an increase in the quantities produced, because the prices are being held fixed at base-year levels.

To sum up: *Nominal GDP uses current prices to place a value on the economy's production of goods and services. Real GDP uses constant base-year prices to place a value on the economy's production of goods and services.* Because real GDP is not affected by changes in prices, changes in real GDP reflect only changes in the amounts being produced. Thus, real GDP is a measure of the economy's production of goods and services.

Our goal in computing GDP is to gauge how well the overall economy is performing. Because real GDP measures the economy's production of goods and services, it reflects the economy's ability to satisfy people's needs and desires. Thus, real GDP is a better gauge of economic well-being than is nominal GDP. When economists talk about the economy's GDP, they usually mean real GDP rather than nominal GDP. And when they talk about growth in the economy, they measure that growth as the percentage change in real GDP from one period to another.

THE GDP DEFLATOR

As we have just seen, nominal GDP reflects both the prices of goods and services and the quantities of goods and services the economy is producing. By contrast, by holding prices constant at base-year levels, real GDP reflects only the quantities produced. From these two statistics, we can compute a third, called the *GDP deflator*, which reflects the prices of goods and services but not the quantities produced.

The **GDP deflator** is calculated as follows:

$$\text{GDP deflator} = \frac{\text{Nominal GDP}}{\text{Real GDP}} \times 100.$$

GDP deflator
a measure of the price level calculated as the ratio of nominal GDP to real GDP times 100

Because nominal GDP and real GDP must be the same in the base year, the GDP deflator for the base year always equals 100. The GDP deflator for subsequent years measures the rise in nominal GDP from the base year that cannot be attributable to a rise in real GDP.

The GDP deflator measures the current level of prices relative to the level of prices in the base year. To see why this is true, consider a couple of simple examples. First, imagine that the quantities produced in the economy rise over time but prices remain the same. In this case, both nominal and real GDP rise together, so the GDP deflator is constant. Now suppose, instead, that prices rise over time but the quantities produced stay the same. In this second case, nominal GDP rises but real GDP remains the same, so the GDP deflator rises as well. Notice that, in both cases, the GDP deflator reflects what's happening to prices, not quantities.

Let's now return to our numerical example in Table 10-2. The GDP deflator is computed at the bottom of the table. For year 2001, nominal GDP is $200, and real GDP is $200, so the GDP deflator is 100. For the year 2002, nominal GDP is $600, and real GDP is $350, so the GDP deflator is 171. Because the GDP deflator rose in year 2002 from 100 to 171, we can say that the price level increased by 71 percent.

The GDP deflator is one measure that economists use to monitor the average level of prices in the economy. We examine another—the consumer price index—in the next chapter, where we also describe the differences between the two measures.

CASE STUDY   REAL GDP OVER RECENT HISTORY

Now that we know how real GDP is defined and measured, let's look at what this macroeconomic variable tells us about the recent history of Canada. Figure 10-2 shows quarterly data on real GDP for the Canadian economy since 1970.

The most obvious feature of these data is that real GDP grows over time. The real GDP of the Canadian economy in 2000 was more than twice its 1970 level. Put differently, the output of goods and services produced in Canada has grown on average about 3 percent per year since 1970. This continued growth in real GDP enables the typical Canadian to enjoy greater economic prosperity than his or her parents and grandparents did.

A second feature of the GDP data is that growth is not steady. The upward climb of real GDP is occasionally interrupted by periods during which GDP

Figure 10-2

REAL GDP IN CANADA.   This figure shows quarterly data on real GDP for the Canadian economy since 1970. Recessions—periods of falling real GDP—are marked with the shaded vertical bars.

SOURCE: Statistics Canada, CANSIM II Matrix, Table 38-0002.

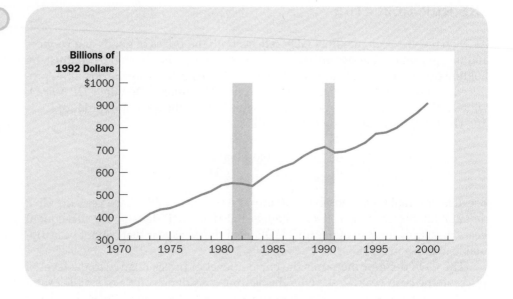

declines, called *recessions*. Figure 10-2 marks recessions with shaded vertical bars. (There is no ironclad rule for when the official business cycle dating committee will declare that a recession has occurred, but a good rule of thumb is two consecutive quarters of falling real GDP.) Recessions are associated not only with lower incomes but also with other forms of economic distress: rising unemployment, falling profits, increased bankruptcies, and so on.

Much of macroeconomics is aimed at explaining the long-run growth and short-run fluctuations in real GDP. As we will see in the coming chapters, we need different models for these two purposes. Because the short-run fluctuations represent deviations from the long-run trend, we first examine the behaviour of the economy in the long run. In particular, Chapters 12 through 18 examine how key macroeconomic variables, including real GDP, are determined in the long run. We then build on this analysis to explain short-run fluctuations in Chapters 19 through 21.

QUICK QUIZ: Define real and nominal GDP. Which is a better measure of economic well-being? Why?

GDP AND ECONOMIC WELL-BEING

Earlier in this chapter, GDP was called the best single measure of the economic well-being of a society. Now that we know what GDP is, we can evaluate this claim.

As we have seen, GDP measures both the economy's total income and the economy's total expenditure on goods and services. Thus, GDP per person tells us the income and expenditure of the average person in the economy. Because most people would prefer to receive higher income and enjoy higher expenditure, GDP per person seems a natural measure of the economic well-being of the average individual.

IN THE NEWS
GDP and Economic Well-Being

EVEN THOUGH GDP AND ECONOMIC WELL-being are different concepts, this textbook argues that they are usually closely related in practice. For an opposing view, read this article.

Think-Tank Asks Canadians What "Quality of Life" Means to Them

BY KATHRYN MAY

A survey by the Canadian Policy Research Network suggests that economic growth and prosperity don't even register with Canadians as factors they value when assessing the quality of their lives.

Rather, a booming economy is considered the means to achieve what Canadians really want or value. The four top priorities ranked by the people surveyed were health care, education, the environment, and social programs, followed by more general values such as civic involvement, civil rights, democracy, and freedom.

"Canadians don't value a well-performing economy in and of itself," said CPRN's Karen Jackson. "We value it because of its impact, such as providing a living wage. People want to earn enough to pay their bills and provide for their families."

The CPRN survey, funded by the federal and provincial governments, is the first step in putting together a set of quality-of-life indicators that will be the first national tracking tool of what really matters to Canadians.

Quality of life is a campaign constant trotted out by politicians at all levels of government, but there is no accepted way to measure and track it.

Until now, quality of life has been assessed by economic indicators such as growth in GDP, the consumer price index, unemployment rates, or productivity. Jackson said these indicators show economic activity, but don't reveal how wealth is distributed or who's benefiting.

In other words, the traditional economic indicators don't show anything about air quality, personal health, the availability of affordable housing, the safety of streets and neighbourhoods, and whether kids are getting good educations.

Prime Minister Jean Chrétien often refers to the United Nations' human development index, which ranks Canada as the best country in the world in which to live.

The index, which measures how 174 countries stack up against one another for overall quality of life, only takes into account life expectancy, education levels, and per capita GDP in its measure.

The CPRN survey, based on in-depth interviews with 350 Canadians, is a critical first step in its project to develop a measure that will reflect what Canadians want or value as essential to a high quality of life. The next stage is for the not-for-profit research institute to team up with Statistics Canada to

develop an experimental set of indicators for testing.

The survey was conducted in October in three-hour sessions with Canadians randomly selected from five key groups—youth, rural, urban, the "influencers" (including corporate and political decision makers), and the "hard-to-reach" (including low-income earners, homeless people, and the disabled).

The groups, regardless of income or region, showed a striking similarity in their responses. All cited their quality-of-life priorities as primary and secondary education, access to health care, public safety and security, clean air and water, job security, a living wage, social programs, a better balance between work and home, civic participation, and children's programs.

Economic growth was picked as a priority by the rural, influencer, and hard-to-reach groups. All groups, however, picked the need for a "living wage," which allows them to pay their bills and support their families.

Quality of life, however, doesn't necessarily take precedence over economic factors. Many argue that the "brain drain" resulted when the employment and income gap grew so wide between Canada and the United States that many gave up quality of life and moved for economic reasons.

SOURCE: *The Edmonton Journal*, December 28, 2000, p. A3.

Yet some people dispute the validity of GDP as a measure of well-being. When Senator Robert Kennedy was running for president of the United States in 1968, he gave a moving critique of such economic measures:

GDP REFLECTS THE FACTORY'S PRODUCTION, BUT NOT THE HARM THAT IT INFLICTS ON THE ENVIRONMENT.

[Gross domestic product] does not allow for the health of our children, the quality of their education, or the joy of their play. It does not include the beauty of our poetry or the strength of our marriages, the intelligence of our public debate or the integrity of our public officials. It measures neither our courage, nor our wisdom, nor our devotion to our country. It measures everything, in short, except that which makes life worthwhile, and it can tell us everything about America except why we are proud that we are Americans.

Much of what Robert Kennedy said is correct. Why then do we care about GDP?

The answer is that a large GDP does in fact help us to lead a good life. GDP does not measure the health of our children, but nations with larger GDP can afford better health care for their children. GDP does not measure the quality of their education, but nations with larger GDP can afford better educational systems. GDP does not measure the beauty of our poetry, but nations with larger GDP can afford to teach more of their citizens to read and to enjoy poetry. GDP does not take account of our intelligence, integrity, courage, wisdom, or devotion to country, but all of these laudable attributes are easier to foster when people are less concerned about being able to afford the material necessities of life. In short, GDP does not directly measure those things that make life worthwhile, but it does measure our ability to obtain the inputs into a worthwhile life.

GDP is not, however, a perfect measure of well-being. Some things that contribute to a good life are left out of GDP. One is leisure. Suppose, for instance, that everyone in the economy suddenly started working every day of the week, rather than enjoying leisure on weekends. More goods and services would be produced, and GDP would rise. Yet, despite the increase in GDP, we should not conclude that everyone would be better off. The loss from reduced leisure would offset the gain from producing and consuming a greater quantity of goods and services.

Because GDP uses market prices to value goods and services, it excludes the value of almost all activity that takes place outside of markets. In particular, GDP omits the value of goods and services produced at home. When a chef prepares a delicious meal and sells it at his restaurant, the value of that meal is part of GDP. But if the chef prepares the same meal for his spouse, the value he has added to the raw ingredients is left out of GDP. Similarly, child care provided in daycare centres is part of GDP, whereas child care by parents at home is not. Volunteer work also contributes to the well-being of those in society, but GDP does not reflect these contributions.

Another thing that GDP excludes is the quality of the environment. Imagine that the government eliminated all environmental regulations. Firms could then produce goods and services without considering the pollution they create, and GDP might rise. Yet well-being would most likely fall. The deterioration in the quality of air and water would more than offset the gains from greater production.

GDP also says nothing about the distribution of income. A society in which 100 people have annual incomes of $50 000 has GDP of $5 million and, not surprisingly, GDP per person of $50 000. So does a society in which 10 people earn $500 000 and 90 suffer with nothing at all. Few people would look at those two situations and call them equivalent. GDP per person tells us what happens to the average person, but behind the average lies a large variety of personal experiences.

In the end, we can conclude that GDP is a good measure of economic well-being for most—but not all—purposes. It is important to keep in mind what GDP includes and what it leaves out.

CASE STUDY   INTERNATIONAL DIFFERENCES IN GDP AND THE QUALITY OF LIFE

One way to gauge the usefulness of GDP as a measure of economic well-being is to examine international data. Rich and poor countries have vastly different levels of GDP per person. If a large GDP leads to a higher standard of living, then we should observe GDP to be strongly correlated with measures of the quality of life. And, in fact, we do.

Table 10-3 shows thirteen of the world's most populous countries ranked in order of GDP per person. The table also shows life expectancy (the expected life span at birth) and literacy (the percentage of the adult population that can read). These data show a clear pattern. In rich countries, such as Canada, the United States, Japan, and Germany, people can expect to live into their late seventies, and almost all of the population can read. In poor countries, such as Nigeria, Bangladesh, and Pakistan, people typically live only until their fifties or early sixties, and only about half of the population is literate.

Although data on other aspects of the quality of life are less complete, they tell a similar story. Countries with low GDP per person tend to have more infants with low birth weight, higher rates of infant mortality, higher rates of maternal mortality, higher rates of child malnutrition, and less common access to safe drinking water. In countries with low GDP per person, fewer school-age children are actually in school, and those who are in school must learn with fewer teachers per student. These countries also tend to have fewer televisions, fewer telephones, fewer paved roads, and fewer households with electricity. International data leave no doubt that a nation's GDP is closely associated with its citizens' standard of living.

QUICK QUIZ: Why should policymakers care about GDP?

Table 10-3

COUNTRY	REAL GDP PER PERSON, 1998 (U.S. DOLLARS)	LIFE EXPECTANCY	ADULT LITERACY
United States	$29 605	77 years	99%
Canada	23 582	79	99
Japan	23 257	80	99
Germany	22 169	77	99
Mexico	7 704	72	91
Brazil	6 625	67	84
Russia	6 460	67	99
China	3 105	70	83
Indonesia	2 651	66	86
India	2 077	63	56
Pakistan	1 715	64	44
Bangladesh	1 361	59	40
Nigeria	795	50	61

GDP, LIFE EXPECTANCY, AND LITERACY.   The table shows GDP per person and two measures of the quality of life for thirteen major countries.

SOURCE: United Nations Development Programme, *Human Development Report 2000* (New York: United Nations), pp. 157–60. Available http://www.undp.org/hdr2000/home.html, August 14, 2001.

IN THE NEWS

Hidden GDP

MEASURING A NATION'S GROSS DOMESTIC product is never easy, but it becomes especially difficult when people have every incentive to hide their economic activities from the eyes of government.

The Russian Economy: Notes from Underground

BY MICHAEL R. GORDON

If you want to know what is happening in the Russian economy, it helps to think about bread. Government statistics show that people are eating more bread and bakeries are selling less. Or consider vodka. Distillers are able to produce far more vodka than is officially being sold. But given the well-deserved Russian fondness for vodka there is every reason to think the distilleries are operating at full capacity.

The Russian government's top number crunchers say the contradictions are easy to explain: high taxes, government red tape, and the simple desire to sock away some extra cash have driven much of Russia's economic activity underground.

For the last six years, the Russian economy has been going down, down, down. But as President Boris N. Yeltsin tries to deliver the growth he has promised, economists are taking a closer look at the murky but vibrant shadow economy. It includes everything from small businesses that never report their sales to huge companies that understate their production to avoid taxes.

Government experts insist that if the shadow economy is taken into account, the overall economy is finally starting to grow. In turn, Mr. Yeltsin's critics complain that the new calculations are more propaganda than economics. . . .

There is no question that measuring economic activity in a former communist country on the road to capitalism is a frustratingly elusive task.

"There is a serious problem with post-socialist statistics," said Yegor T. Gaidar, the former prime minister and pro-reform director of the Institute of Economic Problems of the Transitional Period.

"Seven years ago to report an increase in the amount of production was to become a Hero of Socialist Labor," he said. "Now it is to get additional visits from the tax collector."

SOURCE: *The New York Times*, Week in Review, May 18, 1997, p. 4.

CONCLUSION

This chapter has discussed how economists measure the total income of a nation. Measurement is, of course, only a starting point. Much of macroeconomics is aimed at revealing the long-run and short-run determinants of a nation's gross domestic product. Why, for example, is GDP higher in Canada and Japan than in India and Nigeria? What can the governments of the poorest countries do to promote more rapid growth in GDP? Why does GDP in Canada rise rapidly in some years and fall in others? What can Canadian policymakers do to reduce the severity of these fluctuations in GDP? These are the questions we will take up shortly.

At this point, it is important to acknowledge the importance of just measuring GDP. We all get some sense of how the economy is doing as we go about our lives. But the economists who study changes in the economy and the policymakers who formulate economic policies need more than this vague sense—they need concrete data on which to base their judgements. Quantifying the behaviour of the economy with statistics such as GDP is, therefore, the first step to developing a science of macroeconomics.

Summary

◆ Because every transaction has a buyer and a seller, the total expenditure in the economy must equal the total income in the economy.

◆ Gross domestic product (GDP) measures an economy's total expenditure on newly produced goods and services and the total income earned from the production of these goods and services. More precisely, GDP is the market value of all final goods and services produced within a country in a given period of time.

◆ GDP is divided among four components of expenditure: consumption, investment, government purchases, and net exports. Consumption includes spending on goods and services by households, with the exception of purchases of new housing. Investment includes spending on new equipment and structures, including households' purchases of new housing. Government purchases include spending on goods and services by local, provincial, and federal governments. Net exports equal the value of goods and services produced domestically and sold abroad (exports) minus the value of goods and services produced abroad and sold domestically (imports).

◆ Nominal GDP uses current prices to value the economy's production of goods and services. Real GDP uses constant base-year prices to value the economy's production of goods and services. The GDP deflator—calculated from the ratio of nominal to real GDP—measures the level of prices in the economy.

◆ GDP is a good measure of economic well-being because people prefer higher to lower incomes. But it is not a perfect measure of well-being. For example, GDP excludes the value of leisure and the value of a clean environment.

Key Concepts

microeconomics, p. 206
macroeconomics, p. 206
gross domestic product (GDP), p. 208
consumption, p. 211

investment, p. 211
government purchases, p. 211
net exports, p. 211
nominal GDP, p. 214

real GDP, p. 214
GDP deflator, p. 215

Questions for Review

1. Explain why an economy's income must equal its expenditure.

2. Which contributes more to GDP—the production of an economy car or the production of a luxury car? Why?

3. A farmer sells wheat to a baker for $2. The baker uses the wheat to make bread, which is sold for $3. What is the total contribution of these transactions to GDP?

4. Many years ago Peggy paid $500 to put together a record collection. Today she sold her albums at a garage sale for $100. How does this sale affect current GDP?

5. List the four components of GDP. Give an example of each.

6. Why do economists use real GDP rather than nominal GDP to gauge economic well-being?

7. In the year 2001, the economy produces 100 loaves of bread that sell for $2 each. In the year 2002, the economy produces 200 loaves of bread that sell for $3 each. Calculate nominal GDP, real GDP, and the GDP deflator for each year. (Use 2001 as the base year.) By what percentage does each of these three statistics rise from one year to the next?

8. Why is it desirable for a country to have a large GDP? Give an example of something that would raise GDP and yet be undesirable.

Problems and Applications

1. What components of GDP (if any) would each of the following transactions affect? Explain.
   a. A family buys a new refrigerator.
   b. Aunt Margit buys a new house.
   c. Ford sells a Thunderbird from its inventory.
   d. You buy a pizza.
   e. Quebec repaves Highway 50.
   f. Your parents buy a bottle of French wine.
   g. Honda expands its factory in Alliston, Ontario.

2. The "government purchases" component of GDP does not include spending on transfer payments such as Employment Insurance. Thinking about the definition of GDP, explain why transfer payments are excluded.

3. Why do you think households' purchases of new housing are included in the investment component of GDP rather than the consumption component? Can you think of a reason why households' purchases of new cars should also be included in investment rather than in consumption? To what other consumption goods might this logic apply?

4. As the chapter states, GDP does not include the value of used goods that are resold. Why would including such transactions make GDP a less informative measure of economic well-being?

5. Below are some data from the land of milk and honey.

YEAR	PRICE OF MILK	QUANTITY OF MILK	PRICE OF HONEY	QUANTITY OF HONEY
2001	$1	100 L	$2	50 L
2002	$1	200	$2	100
2003	$2	200	$4	100

a. Compute nominal GDP, real GDP, and the GDP deflator for each year, using 2001 as the base year.
b. Compute the percentage change in nominal GDP, real GDP, and the GDP deflator in 2002 and 2003 from the preceding year. For each year, identify the variable that does not change. Explain in words why your answer makes sense.
c. Did economic well-being rise more in 2002 or 2003? Explain.

6. Consider the following data on Canadian GDP:

YEAR	NOMINAL GDP (IN BILLIONS)	GDP DEFLATOR (BASE YEAR 1992)
1996	$833	106.7
1997	878	107.7

a. What was the growth rate of nominal GDP between 1996 and 1997? (Note: The growth rate is the percentage change from one period to the next.)
b. What was the growth rate of the GDP deflator between 1996 and 1997?
c. What was real GDP in 1996 measured in 1992 prices?
d. What was real GDP in 1997 measured in 1992 prices?
e. What was the growth rate of real GDP between 1996 and 1997?

f. Was the growth rate of nominal GDP higher or lower than the growth rate of real GDP? Explain.

7. If prices rise, people's income from selling goods increases. The growth of real GDP ignores this gain, however. Why, then, do economists prefer real GDP as a measure of economic well-being?

8. Revised estimates of Canadian GDP are usually released by Statistics Canada near the end of each month. Go to a library and find a newspaper article that reports on the most recent release. Discuss the recent changes in real and nominal GDP and in the components of GDP. (Alternatively, you can get the data at http://www.statcan.ca, the Web site of Statistics Canada.)

9. One day Boutros the Barber, Inc., collects $400 for haircuts. Over this day, his equipment depreciates in value by $50. Of the remaining $350, Boutros sends $30 to the government in sales taxes, takes home $220 in wages, and retains $100 in his business to add new equipment in the future. From the $220 that Boutros takes home, he pays $70 in income taxes. Based on this information, compute Boutros' contribution to the following measures of income:
    a. gross domestic product
    b. net national product
    c. national income
    d. personal income
    e. disposable personal income

10. Goods and services that are not sold in markets, such as food produced and consumed at home, are generally not included in GDP. Can you think of how this might cause the numbers in the second column of Table 10-3 to be misleading in a comparison of the economic well-being of Canada and India? Explain.

11. Until the 1980s, the Canadian government emphasized GNP rather than GDP as a measure of economic well-being. Which measure should the government prefer if it cares about the total income of Canadians? Which measure should it prefer if it cares about the total amount of economic activity occurring in Canada?

12. The participation of women in the Canadian labour force has risen dramatically since 1970.
    a. How do you think this rise affected GDP?
    b. Now imagine a measure of well-being that includes time spent working in the home and taking leisure. How would the change in this measure of well-being compare with the change in GDP?
    c. Can you think of other aspects of well-being that are associated with the rise in women's labour-force participation? Would it be practical to construct a measure of well-being that includes these aspects?

11

MEASURING THE
COST OF LIVING

In 1957 the price of gasoline was 43 cents a gallon, or 9.5 cents a litre. In 2000 the average price was around 70 cents a litre. Why does gas now cost more than seven times as much as it did 43 years ago? Do we blame OPEC, the Organization of Petroleum Exporting Countries, for using its monopoly power to force up the price of crude oil? Are the big oil companies that buy the crude oil and sell gas at the pumps increasing their markup? Or is the rise in the price of gas the inevitable result of rising demand from more people driving more cars facing a diminishing supply of a nonrenewable natural resource?

At first sight, the increase in the price of gas might make you think that gas is a more scarce and valuable commodity today than it was 43 years ago. But, as everyone knows, the prices of nearly all goods and services have also increased, and so have people's incomes. So it is not clear whether gas is more or less affordable than it was 43 years ago. Has the value of gas increased, or has the value of money fallen?

In the preceding chapter we looked at how economists use gross domestic product (GDP) to measure the quantity of goods and services that the economy is producing. This chapter examines how economists measure the overall cost of living. To compare prices and incomes of 43 years ago with prices and incomes today, we need to find some way of turning dollar figures into meaningful measures of purchasing power. That is exactly the job of a statistic called the *consumer price index*. After seeing how the consumer price index is calculated, we discuss how we can use this index to compare dollar figures from different points in time.

The consumer price index is used to monitor changes in the cost of living over time. When the consumer price index rises, the typical family has to spend more to maintain the same standard of living. Economists use the term *inflation* to describe a situation in which the economy's overall price level is rising. The *inflation rate* is the percentage change in the price level from the previous period. As we will see in the coming chapters, inflation is a closely watched aspect of macroeconomic performance and is a key variable guiding macroeconomic policy. This chapter provides the background for that analysis by showing how economists measure the inflation rate using the consumer price index.

THE CONSUMER PRICE INDEX

consumer price index (CPI)

a measure of the overall cost of the goods and services bought by a typical consumer

The **consumer price index (CPI)** is a measure of the overall cost of the goods and services bought by a typical consumer. Each month Statistics Canada computes and reports the consumer price index. In this section we discuss how the consumer price index is calculated and what problems arise in its measurement. We also consider how this index compares with the GDP deflator, another measure of the overall level of prices, which we examined in the preceding chapter.

HOW THE CONSUMER PRICE INDEX IS CALCULATED

When Statistics Canada calculates the consumer price index and the inflation rate, it uses data on the prices of over 600 separate goods and services. To see exactly how these statistics are constructed, let's consider a simple economy in which consumers buy only two goods—hot dogs and hamburgers. Table 11-1 shows the five steps that the Statistics Canada follows.

1. *Fix the Basket.* The first step in computing the consumer price index is to determine which prices are most important to the typical consumer. If the typical consumer buys more hot dogs than hamburgers, then the price of hot dogs is more important than the price of hamburgers and, therefore, should be given greater weight in measuring the cost of living. Statistics Canada sets these weights by surveying consumers and finding the basket of goods and services that the typical consumer buys. In the example in the table, the typical consumer buys a basket of four hot dogs and two hamburgers.

Table 11-1

CALCULATING THE CONSUMER PRICE INDEX AND THE INFLATION RATE: AN EXAMPLE. This table shows how to calculate the consumer price index and the inflation rate for a hypothetical economy in which consumers buy only hot dogs and hamburgers.

STEP 1: SURVEY CONSUMERS TO DETERMINE A FIXED BASKET OF GOODS

4 hot dogs, 2 hamburgers

STEP 2: FIND THE PRICE OF EACH GOOD IN EACH YEAR

YEAR	PRICE OF HOT DOGS	PRICE OF HAMBURGERS
2001	$1	$2
2002	2	3
2003	3	4

STEP 3: COMPUTE THE COST OF THE BASKET OF GOODS IN EACH YEAR

2001   ($1 per hot dog × 4 hot dogs) + ($2 per hamburger × 2 hamburgers) = $8
2002   ($2 per hot dog × 4 hot dogs) + ($3 per hamburger × 2 hamburgers) = $14
2003   ($3 per hot dog × 4 hot dogs) + ($4 per hamburger × 2 hamburgers) = $20

STEP 4: CHOOSE ONE YEAR AS A BASE YEAR (2001) AND COMPUTE THE CONSUMER PRICE INDEX IN EACH YEAR

2001	($8/$8) × 100 = 100
2002	($14/$8) × 100 = 175
2003	($20/$8) × 100 = 250

STEP 5: USE THE CONSUMER PRICE INDEX TO COMPUTE THE INFLATION RATE FROM PREVIOUS YEAR

2002	(175 − 100)/100 × 100 = 75%
2003	(250 − 175)/175 × 100 = 43%

2. *Find the Prices.* The second step in computing the consumer price index is to find the prices of each of the goods and services in the basket for each point in time. The table shows the prices of hot dogs and hamburgers for three different years.

3. *Compute the Basket's Cost.* The third step is to use the data on prices to calculate the cost of the basket of goods and services at different times. The table shows this calculation for each of the three years. Notice that only the prices in this calculation change. By keeping the basket of goods the same (four hot dogs and two hamburgers), we are isolating the effects of price changes from the effect of any quantity changes that might be occurring at the same time.

4. *Choose a Base Year and Compute the Index.* The fourth step is to designate one year as the base year, which is the benchmark against which other years are compared. To calculate the index, the price of the basket of goods and services in each year is divided by the price of the basket in the base year,

What Is in the CPI's Basket?

When constructing the consumer price index, Statistics Canada tries to include all of the goods and services that the typical consumer buys. It also tries to weight these goods and services according to how much consumers buy of each item.

Figure 11-1 shows the breakdown of consumer spending into the major categories of goods and services. The numbers show the percentage of expenditure on that category of goods and services for the average consumer in 1992, when the CPI basket was last updated. The largest category is shelter, which makes up 27.9 percent of the typical consumer's budget. This category includes the cost of renting an apartment or making mortgage payments on a house (which means that a rise in interest rates can directly affect the CPI). The next-largest category at 18.3 percent is transportation, which includes spending on cars, gasoline, airfares, buses, and so on. The next category, at 18.0 percent, is food, including both food eaten at home and in restaurants. The next category is recreation, education, and reading, which includes your university tuition fees and the price of this book. This category makes up 10.4 percent of the typical consumer's budget but probably makes up a much larger percentage of your budget. Unless you happen to buy exactly the same goods and services that the typical consumer bought in 1992, changes in the CPI can never perfectly measure changes in your personal cost of living.

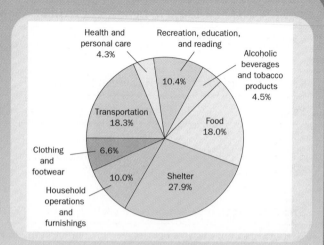

Figure 11-1

THE BASKET OF GOODS AND SERVICES. This figure shows how the typical Canadian consumer in 1992 divided his or her spending among various goods and services. These percentages are the weights that Statistics Canada uses to compute the CPI.

SOURCE: Statistics Canada, *Your Guide to the Consumer Price Index*, 1996, Catalogue No. 62-557XPB, Figure A, p. 6.

and this ratio is then multiplied by 100. The resulting number is the consumer price index.

In the example in the table, the year 2001 is the base year. In this year, the basket of hot dogs and hamburgers costs $8. Therefore, the price of the basket in all years is divided by $8 and multiplied by 100. The consumer price index is 100 in 2001. (The index is always 100 in the base year.) The consumer price index is 175 in 2002. This means that the price of the basket in 2002 is 175 percent of its price in the base year. Put differently, a basket of goods that costs $100 in the base year costs $175 in 2002. Similarly, the consumer price index is 250 in 2003, indicating that the price level in 2003 is 250 percent of the price level in the base year.

5. *Compute the Inflation Rate.* The fifth and final step is to use the consumer price index to calculate the **inflation rate,** which is the percentage change in the price index from the preceding period. That is, the inflation rate between two consecutive years is computed as follows:

inflation rate

the percentage change in the price index from the preceding period

$$\text{Inflation rate in year 2} = \frac{\text{CPI in year 2} - \text{CPI in year 1}}{\text{CPI in year 1}} \times 100.$$

In our example, the inflation rate is 75 percent in 2002 and 43 percent in 2003.

Although this example simplifies the real world by including only two goods, it shows how Statistics Canada computes the consumer price index and the inflation rate. Statistics Canada collects and processes data on the prices of hundreds of goods and services every month and, by following the five steps above, determines how quickly the cost of living for the typical consumer is rising. When Statistics Canada makes its monthly announcement of the consumer price index, you can usually hear about it on the evening television news or see it in the next day's newspaper.

In addition to the consumer price index for the overall economy, Statistics Canada calculates several other price indexes. It reports the index for each province and for sixteen cities across Canada and for some narrow categories of goods and services (such as food, clothing, and shelter). It also calculates the **industrial product price index**, which measures the cost of a basket of goods and services bought by firms rather than consumers. Because firms eventually pass on their costs to consumers in the form of higher consumer prices, changes in the industrial product price index can be useful in predicting changes in the consumer price index.

industrial product price index

a measure of the cost of a basket of goods and services bought by firms

PROBLEMS IN MEASURING THE COST OF LIVING

The goal of the consumer price index is to measure changes in the cost of living. In other words, the consumer price index tries to gauge how much incomes must rise in order to maintain a constant standard of living. The consumer price index, however, is not a perfect measure of the cost of living. Three problems with the index are widely acknowledged but difficult to solve.

The first problem is called *substitution bias*. When prices change from one year to the next, they do not all change proportionately: Some prices rise by more than others. Consumers respond to these differing price changes by buying less of the goods whose prices have risen by large amounts and by buying more of the goods whose prices have risen less or perhaps have even fallen. That is, consumers substitute toward goods that have become relatively less expensive. Yet the consumer price index is computed assuming a fixed basket of goods. By not taking into account the possibility of consumer substitution, the index overstates the increase in the cost of living from one year to the next.

Let's consider a simple example. Imagine that in the base year, apples are cheaper than pears, so consumers buy more apples than pears. When Statistics Canada constructs the basket of goods, it will include more apples than pears. Suppose that next year pears are cheaper than apples. Consumers will naturally respond to the price changes by buying more pears and fewer apples. Yet, when computing the consumer price index, Statistics Canada uses a fixed basket, which in essence assumes that consumers continue to buy the now expensive apples in the same quantities as before. For this reason, the index will measure a much larger increase in the cost of living than consumers actually experience.

IN THE NEWS

Are Oil Prices Too High?

MANY PEOPLE THINK OIL PRICES ARE TOO high, but not the author of this editorial. Notice how his argument is based on adjusting oil prices for inflation.

Crude Arguments

The price of oil is hovering at U.S. $35 a barrel, which sounds high. Yesterday, Ali Rodriguez, the Venezuelan president of the Organization of Petroleum Exporting Countries, warned that "the world is facing a possible energy crisis." This is not true. Adjusted for inflation, oil costs less than half what it did in 1981.

Things have changed since OPEC held the world economy hostage in 1973. Massive new oilfields have been developed and new technologies make it easier to find more reserves. Financial hedging insulates modern energy companies against price and foreign exchange volatility, reducing the risk to investors. Most important, the U.S.—the biggest energy consumer in the world—has largely abandoned the 1970s economics of rationing and price control, which prolonged and exaggerated OPEC's stranglehold. So the world is better prepared than ever to deal with a price blip.

Even if Mr. Rodriguez's U.S. $40 a barrel prediction came true, it would not be an unmitigated disaster. Hundreds of thousands of Canadians are employed in the energy sector, and millions more have a financial stake in the industry through Canada's resource-heavy stock markets, which are booming. Even Newfoundland, a "have-not" province, is sharing the wealth. Provincial royalties from offshore oil production there are expected to jump 25 percent this year, to $45 million. And oil and gas taxes feed $20 billion into government coffers.

Despite this, many politicians and pundits are eyeing the oil patch jealously. Federal Liberals have tried to discredit Alberta's tax cuts as the product of being "awash" in oil money. (Alberta was posting surpluses and cutting taxes even when oil dipped below U.S. $10 a barrel, two years ago.) And last weekend, three Toronto daily newspapers railed against the cost of oil, including one that referred to Alberta's royalties as an "oily Niagara."

Rising prices are no reason to interfere with the free market—not for Alberta-produced oil, nor for gas-guzzling automobiles made in Ontario and Quebec, which are also at record prices. Faced with high prices, customers will conserve or switch to other energy sources, voluntarily rolling back demand. That is how it has always worked—the median price of oil, in today's dollars, has remained at U.S. $15, since 1969. The most appropriate target of consumer anger is not the producer price, but the taxes that account for the bulk of the retail price.

SOURCE: *National Post*, September 12, 2000, p. A19.

THE INTRODUCTION OF NEW PRODUCTS BIASES THE CPI.

The second problem with the consumer price index is the *introduction of new goods*. When a new good is introduced, consumers have more variety from which to choose. Greater variety, in turn, makes each dollar more valuable, so consumers need fewer dollars to maintain any given standard of living. Yet because the consumer price index is based on a fixed basket of goods and services, it does not reflect this change in the purchasing power of the dollar.

Again, let's consider an example. When VCRs were introduced, consumers were able to watch their favourite movies at home. Compared with going to a movie theatre, the convenience is greater and the cost is less. A perfect cost-of-living index would reflect the introduction of the VCR with a decrease in the cost of living. The consumer price index, however, did not decrease in response to the introduction of the VCR. Eventually, Statistics Canada did revise the basket of goods to include VCRs, and subsequently the index reflected changes in VCR prices. But the reduction in the cost of living associated with the initial introduction of the VCR never showed up in the index.

The third problem with the consumer price index is *unmeasured quality change.* If the quality of a good deteriorates from one year to the next, the value of a dollar falls, even if the price of the good stays the same. Similarly, if the quality rises from one year to the next, the value of a dollar rises. Statistics Canada does its best to account for quality change. When the quality of a good in the basket changes—for example, when a car model has more horsepower or gets better gas mileage from one year to the next—Statistics Canada adjusts the price of the good to account for the quality change. It is, in essence, trying to compute the price of a basket of goods of constant quality. Despite these efforts, changes in quality remain a problem because quality is so hard to measure.

There is still much debate among economists about how severe these measurement problems are and what should be done about them. The issue is important because many government programs use the consumer price index to adjust for changes in the overall level of prices. Canada Pension Plan recipients, for instance, get annual increases in benefits that are tied to the consumer price index. Some economists have suggested modifying these programs to correct for the measurement problems. For example, most studies conclude that the consumer price index overstates inflation by about half a percentage point per year. In response to these findings, Parliament could change the Canada Pension Plan so that benefits increased every year by the measured inflation rate minus half a percentage point. Such a change would provide a crude way of offsetting the measurement problems and, at the same time, reduce government spending by millions of dollars each year.

THE GDP DEFLATOR VERSUS THE CONSUMER PRICE INDEX

In the preceding chapter, we examined another measure of the overall level of prices in the economy—the GDP deflator. The GDP deflator is the ratio of nominal GDP to real GDP. Because nominal GDP is current output valued at current prices and real GDP is current output valued at base-year prices, the GDP deflator reflects the current level of prices relative to the level of prices in the base year.

Economists and policymakers monitor both the GDP deflator and the consumer price index to gauge how quickly prices are rising. Usually, these two statistics tell a similar story. Yet two important differences can cause them to diverge.

The first difference is that the GDP deflator reflects the prices of all goods and services *produced domestically,* whereas the consumer price index reflects the prices of all goods and services *bought by consumers.* For example, suppose that the price of an airplane produced by Bombardier and sold to the Air Force rises. Even though the plane is part of GDP, it is not part of the basket of goods and services bought by a typical consumer. Thus, the price increase shows up in the GDP deflator but not in the consumer price index.

As another example, suppose that Volkswagen raises the price of its cars. Because Volkswagens are made in Germany, the car is not part of Canadian GDP. But Canadian consumers buy VWs, so the car is part of the typical consumer's basket of goods. Hence, a price increase in an imported consumption good, such as a VW, shows up in the consumer price index but not in the GDP deflator.

The second and more subtle difference between the GDP deflator and the consumer price index concerns how various prices are weighted to yield a single number for the overall level of prices. The consumer price index compares the price of a *fixed* basket of goods and services with the price of the basket in the base year. Only occasionally does Statistics Canada change the basket of goods. By contrast, the GDP deflator compares the price of *currently produced* goods and services with the price of the same goods and services in the base year. Thus, the group of goods and services used to compute the GDP deflator changes automatically over time. This difference is not important when all prices are changing proportionately. But if the prices of different goods and services are changing by varying amounts, the way we weight the various prices matters for the overall inflation rate.

Figure 11-2 shows the inflation rate as measured by both the GDP deflator and the consumer price index for each year since 1965. You can see that sometimes the two measures diverge. When they do diverge, it is possible to go behind these numbers and explain the divergence with the two differences we have discussed. The figure shows, however, that divergence between these two measures is the exception rather than the rule. In the 1970s, both the GDP deflator and the consumer price index show high rates of inflation. From the mid-1980s on, both measures show low rates of inflation.

▌**QUICK QUIZ:**   Explain briefly what the consumer price index is trying to measure and how it is constructed.

Figure 11-2

TWO MEASURES OF INFLATION. This figure shows the inflation rate—the percentage change in the level of prices—as measured by the GDP deflator and the consumer price index using annual data since 1965. Notice that the two measures of inflation generally move together.

SOURCE: Statistics Canada, "Gross Domestic Product (GDP) Indexes, Annual," CANSIM Matrix 2, Table 380-0018.

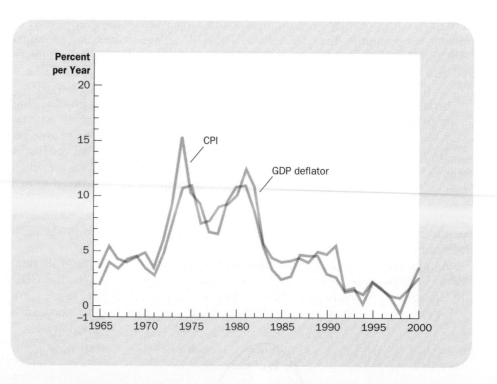

CORRECTING ECONOMIC VARIABLES FOR THE EFFECTS OF INFLATION

The purpose of measuring the overall level of prices in the economy is to permit comparison between dollar figures from different points in time. Now that we know how price indexes are calculated, let's see how we might use such an index to compare a dollar figure from the past with a dollar figure in the present.

DOLLAR FIGURES FROM DIFFERENT TIMES

We return to the issue of the price of gasoline. Was the 1957 price of 9.5 cents a litre high or low compared with today's price of gas?

To answer this question, we need to know the level of prices in 1957 and the level of prices today. How much of the rise in the price of gas is simply a reflection of the general rise in prices? In other words, how much of the rise in the price of gas is due to the fall in the value of money? To compare the 1957 price of gas with today's price of gas, we need to inflate the price of 9.5 cents a litre to turn 1957 dollars into today's dollars. A price index shows us the size of this inflation correction.

Statistics Canada gives a CPI of 17.6 for 1957 and 113.5 for the year 2000. (The base year is 1992.) Thus, the overall level of prices has risen by a factor of 6.45 (which equals 113.5/17.6). We can use these numbers to measure the 1957 price of gas in year 2000 dollars.

1957 gas price in 2000 dollars = 1957 gas price × (CPI in 2000/CPI in 1957)
= 9.5 cents × (113.5/17.6)
= 61.3 cents

The 1957 price of gas is equivalent to a price of 61.3 cents a litre today. This is only a little lower than today's actual price of gas. So, adjusting for inflation, the price of gas is only a little bit higher today than it was 43 years ago! The price of gas has increased by nearly the same percentage as the average increase in the price of goods and services. A litre of gas is not much more valuable than it used to be. Instead, it is money that is a lot less valuable than it used to be.

CASE STUDY   MR. INDEX GOES TO HOLLYWOOD

What was the most popular movie of all time? The answer might surprise you.

Movie popularity is usually gauged by box office receipts. By that measure, *Titanic* is the No. 1 movie of all time, followed by *Star Wars, Star Wars: The Phantom Menace,* and *E.T.* But this ranking ignores an obvious but important fact: Prices, including the price of movie tickets, have been rising over time. When we correct box office receipts for the effects of inflation, the story is very different.

Table 11-2 shows the top ten movies of all time ranked by inflation-adjusted box office receipts. The No. 1 movie is *Gone with the Wind*, which was released in 1939 and is well ahead of *Titanic*. In the 1930s, before everyone had televisions in their homes, millions more people went to the cinema each week compared with today. But the movies from that era rarely show up in popularity rankings because tickets prices cost only a quarter. Scarlett and Rhett fare a lot better once we correct for the effects of inflation.

THE WALL STREET JOURNAL

AUDIO - VIDEO

"The price may seem a little high, but you have to remember that's in today's dollars."

"FRANKLY, MY DEAR, I DON'T CARE MUCH FOR THE EFFECTS OF INFLATION."

Table 11-2		

THE MOST POPULAR MOVIES OF
ALL TIME, INFLATION ADJUSTED

FILM	YEAR OF RELEASE	TOTAL U.S. DOMESTIC GROSS (IN MILLIONS OF 2001 U.S. DOLLARS)
1. *Gone with the Wind*	1939	$1002
2. *Star Wars*	1977	866
3. *The Sound of Music*	1965	695
4. *E.T.*	1982	654
5. *Titanic*	1997	640
6. *The Ten Commandments*	1956	639
7. *Jaws*	1975	625
8. *Doctor Zhivago*	1965	591
9. *The Jungle Book*	1967	529
10. *Snow White and the Seven Dwarfs*	1937	519

SOURCE: The Movie Times. Available http://www.the-movie-times.com.

INDEXATION

As we have just seen, price indexes are used to correct for the effects of inflation when comparing dollar figures from different times. This type of correction shows up in many places in the economy. When some dollar amount is automatically corrected for inflation by law or contract, the amount is said to be **indexed** for inflation.

For example, many long-term contracts between firms and unions include partial or complete indexation of the wage to the consumer price index. Such a provision is called a *cost-of-living allowance,* or COLA. A COLA automatically raises the wage when the consumer price index rises.

Indexation is also a feature of many laws. Canada Pension Plan and Old Age Security benefits, for example, are adjusted every year to compensate elderly people for increases in prices. The brackets of the federal income tax—the income levels at which the tax rates change—are also indexed for inflation. There are, however, many ways in which the tax system is not indexed for inflation, even when perhaps it should be. We discuss these issues more fully when we discuss the costs of inflation later in this book.

indexation

the automatic correction of a dollar amount for the effects of inflation by law or contract

REAL AND NOMINAL INTEREST RATES

Correcting economic variables for the effects of inflation is particularly important, and somewhat tricky, when we look at data on interest rates. When you deposit your savings in a bank account, you will earn interest on your deposit. Conversely, when you borrow to pay your tuition, you will pay interest on your student loan. Interest represents a payment in the future for a transfer of money in the past. As a result, interest rates always involve comparing amounts of money at different points in time. To fully understand interest rates, we need to know how to correct for the effects of inflation.

Let's consider an example. Suppose that Sally Saver deposits $1000 in a bank account that pays an annual interest rate of 10 percent. After a year passes, Sally has accumulated $100 in interest. Sally then withdraws her $1100. Is Sally $100 richer than she was when she made the deposit a year earlier?

The answer depends on what we mean by "richer." Sally does have $100 more than she had before. In other words, the number of dollars has risen by 10 percent. But if prices have risen at the same time, each dollar now buys less than it did a year ago. Thus, her purchasing power has not risen by 10 percent. If the inflation rate is 4 percent, then the amount of goods she can buy has increased by only 6 percent. And if the inflation rate is 15 percent, then the price of goods has increased proportionately more than the number of dollars in her account. In that case, Sally's purchasing power has actually fallen by 5 percent.

The interest rate that the bank pays is called the **nominal interest rate,** and the interest rate corrected for inflation is called the **real interest rate.** We can write the relationship among the nominal interest rate, the real interest rate, and inflation as follows:

nominal interest rate
the interest rate as usually reported without a correction for the effects of inflation

$$\text{Real interest rate} = \text{Nominal interest rate} - \text{Inflation rate.}$$

real interest rate
the interest rate corrected for the effects of inflation

The real interest rate is the difference between the nominal interest rate and the rate of inflation. The nominal interest rate tells you how fast the number of dollars in your bank account rises over time. The real interest rate tells you how fast the purchasing power of your bank account rises over time.

Figure 11-3 shows real and nominal interest rates since 1965. The nominal interest rate is the interest rate on three-month corporate bonds. The real interest rate is computed by subtracting inflation—the percentage change in the consumer price index—from this nominal interest rate.

You can see that real and nominal interest rates do not always move together. For example, in the late 1970s, nominal interest rates were high. But because inflation was very high, real interest rates were low. Indeed, in some years, real interest

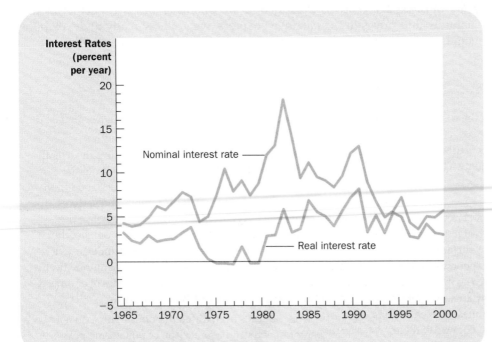

Figure 11-3

REAL AND NOMINAL INTEREST RATES.   This figure shows nominal and real interest rates using annual data since 1965. The nominal interest rate is the rate on a three-month corporate bond. The real interest rate is the nominal interest rate minus the inflation rate as measured by the consumer price index. Notice that nominal and real interest rates often do not move together.

SOURCE: Statistics Canada, "Financial Market Statistics," CANSIM Matrix 2, Table 176-0043.

rates were negative, because inflation eroded people's savings more quickly than nominal interest payments increased them. By contrast, in the late 1990s, nominal interest rates were low. But because inflation was also low, real interest rates were relatively high. In the coming chapters, when we study the causes and effects of changes in interest rates, it will be important for us to keep in mind the distinction between real and nominal interest rates.

QUICK QUIZ: Henry Ford paid his workers $5 a day in 1914. If the U.S. consumer price index was 10 in 1914 and 166 in 1999, how much was the Ford paycheque worth in 1999 dollars?

CONCLUSION

"A nickel ain't worth a dime anymore," baseball player Yogi Berra once quipped. Indeed, throughout recent history, the real values behind the nickel, the dime, and the dollar have not been stable. Persistent increases in the overall level of prices have been the norm. Such inflation reduces the purchasing power of each unit of money over time. When comparing dollar figures from different times, it is important to keep in mind that a dollar today is not the same as a dollar twenty years ago or, most likely, twenty years from now.

This chapter has discussed how economists measure the overall level of prices in the economy and how they use price indexes to correct economic variables for the effects of inflation. This analysis is only a starting point. We have not yet examined the causes and effects of inflation or how inflation interacts with other economic variables. To do that, we need to go beyond issues of measurement. Indeed, that is our next task. Having explained how economists measure macroeconomic quantities and prices in the past two chapters, we are now ready to develop the models that explain long-run and short-run movements in these variables.

Summary

- The consumer price index shows the cost of a basket of goods and services relative to the cost of the same basket in the base year. The index is used to measure the overall level of prices in the economy. The percentage change in the consumer price index measures the inflation rate.

- The consumer price index is an imperfect measure of the cost of living for three reasons. First, it does not take into account consumers' ability to substitute toward goods that become relatively cheaper over time. Second, it does not take into account increases in the purchasing power of the dollar due to the introduction of new goods. Third, it is distorted by unmeasured changes in the quality of goods and services. Because of these

measurement problems, the CPI overstates annual inflation by about half a percentage point.

- Although the GDP deflator also measures the overall level of prices in the economy, it differs from the consumer price index because it includes goods and services produced rather than goods and services consumed. As a result, imported goods affect the consumer price index but not the GDP deflator. In addition, whereas the consumer price index uses a fixed basket of goods, the GDP deflator automatically changes the group of goods and services over time as the composition of GDP changes.

- Dollar figures from different points in time do not represent a valid comparison of purchasing power. To compare a dollar figure from the past with a dollar figure today, the older figure should be inflated using a price index.

◆ Various laws and private contracts use price indexes to correct for the effects of inflation. The tax laws, however, are only partially indexed for inflation.

◆ A correction for inflation is especially important when looking at data on interest rates. The nominal interest

rate is the interest rate usually reported; it is the rate at which the number of dollars in a savings account increases over time. By contrast, the real interest rate takes into account changes in the value of the dollar over time. The real interest rate equals the nominal interest rate minus the rate of inflation.

Key Concepts

consumer price index (CPI), p. 224
inflation rate, p. 226

industrial product price index, p. 227
indexation, p. 232

nominal interest rate, p. 233
real interest rate, p. 233

Questions for Review

1. Which do you think has a greater effect on the consumer price index: a 10 percent increase in the price of chicken or a 10 percent increase in the price of caviar? Why?

2. Describe the three problems that make the consumer price index an imperfect measure of the cost of living.

3. If the price of military aircraft rises, is the consumer price index or the GDP deflator affected more? Why?

4. Over a long period of time, the price of a candy bar rose from $0.10 to $0.60. Over the same period, the consumer price index rose from 150 to 300. Adjusted for overall inflation, how much did the price of the candy bar change?

5. Explain the meaning of *nominal interest rate* and *real interest rate*. How are they related?

Problems and Applications

1. Suppose that people consume only three goods, as shown in this table.

	TENNIS BALLS	TENNIS RACQUETS	GATORADE
2001 price	$2	$40	$1
2001 quantity	100	10	200
2002 price	$2	$60	$2
2002 quantity	100	10	200

a. What is the percentage change in the price of each of the three goods? What is the percentage change in the overall price level?

b. Do tennis racquets become more or less expensive relative to Gatorade? Does the well-being of some

people change relative to the well-being of others? Explain.

2. Suppose that the residents of Vegopia spend all of their income on cauliflower, broccoli, and carrots. In 2001 they buy 100 heads of cauliflower for $200, 50 bunches of broccoli for $75, and 500 carrots for $50. In 2002 they buy 75 heads of cauliflower for $225, 80 bunches of broccoli for $120, and 500 carrots for $100. If the base year is 2001, what is the CPI in both years? What is the inflation rate in 2002?

3. From 1948 to 1998 the consumer price index in Canada rose 682 percent. Use this fact to adjust each of the following 1948 prices for the effects of inflation. Which items cost less in 1998 than in 1948 after adjusting for inflation? Which items cost more?

ITEM	1948 PRICE	1998 PRICE
The Globe and Mail	$0.05	$0.57
Bus fare for Ottawa–Toronto return	$10.65	$104.86
1 kg onions	$0.22	$1.52
1 kg peanut butter	$0.77	$5.99
1 kg pork shoulder	$0.86	$2.18

4. Beginning in 1994, environmental regulations in the United States have required that gasoline contain a new additive to reduce air pollution. This requirement raised the cost of gasoline. The U.S. Bureau of Labor Statistics (BLS) decided that this increase in cost represented an improvement in quality.
    a. Given this decision, did the increased cost of gasoline raise the CPI?
    b. What is the argument in favour of the BLS's decision? What is the argument for a different decision?

5. Which of the problems in the construction of the CPI might be illustrated by each of the following situations? Explain.
    a. the invention of the Sony Walkman
    b. the introduction of air bags in cars
    c. increased personal computer purchases in response to a decline in their price
    d. more scoops of raisins in each package of Raisin Bran
    e. greater use of fuel-efficient cars after gasoline prices increase

6. *The Ottawa Citizen* cost $0.10 in 1970 and $0.50 in 1990. The average wage in manufacturing was $3.01 per hour in 1970 and $14.19 in 1990.
    a. By what percentage did the price of the newspaper rise?
    b. By what percentage did the wage rise?
    c. In each year, how many minutes did a worker have to work to earn enough to buy a newspaper?
    d. Did workers' purchasing power in terms of newspapers rise or fall?

7. The chapter explains that Canada Pension Plan benefits are increased each year in proportion to the increase in the CPI, even though most economists believe that the CPI overstates actual inflation.
    a. If the elderly consume the same market basket as other people, does the Canada Pension Plan provide the elderly with an improvement in their standard of living each year? Explain.
    b. Suppose elderly people consume more prescription drugs than younger people, and drug prices have risen faster than overall inflation. What would you do to determine whether elderly people are actually better off from year to year?

8. How do you think the basket of goods and services you buy differs from the basket bought by the typical Canadian household? Do you think you face a higher or lower inflation rate than is indicated by the CPI? Why?

9. Income tax brackets were not indexed until 2000. When inflation pushed up people's nominal incomes during the 1990s, what do you think happened to real tax revenue? (Hint: This phenomenon was known as "bracket creep.")

10. When deciding how much of their income to save for retirement, should workers consider the real or the nominal interest rate that their savings will earn? Explain.

11. Suppose that a borrower and a lender agree on the nominal interest rate to be paid on a loan. Then inflation turns out to be higher than they both expected.
    a. Is the real interest rate on this loan higher or lower than expected?
    b. Does the lender gain or lose from this unexpectedly high inflation? Does the borrower gain or lose?
    c. Inflation during the 1970s was much higher than most people had expected when the decade began. How did this affect homeowners who obtained fixed-rate mortgages during the 1960s? How did it affect the banks that lent the money?

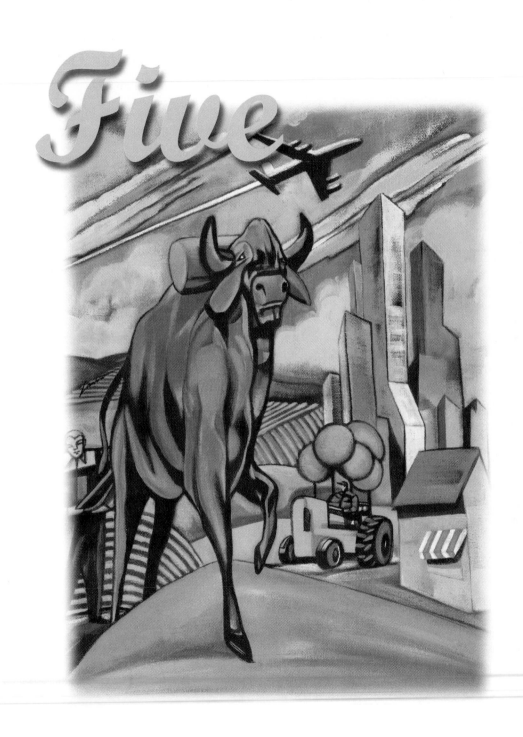

Five

THE REAL ECONOMY IN THE LONG RUN

12

PRODUCTION AND GROWTH

**IN THIS CHAPTER
YOU WILL . . .**

*See how economic
growth differs
around the world*

*Consider why
productivity is the
key determinant
of a country's
standard of living*

*Analyze the factors
that determine
a country's
productivity*

*Examine how a
country's policies
influence its
productivity growth*

When you travel around the world, you see tremendous variation in the standard of living. The average person in a rich country, such as Canada, the United States, or Germany, has an income more than ten times as high as the average person in a poor country, such as India, Indonesia, or Nigeria. These large differences in income are reflected in large differences in the quality of life. Richer countries have more automobiles, more telephones, more televisions, better nutrition, safer housing, better health care, and longer life expectancy.

Even within a country, there are large changes in the standard of living over time. In Canada over the past century, average income as measured by real GDP per person has grown by about 2 percent per year. Although 2 percent might seem small, this rate of growth implies that average income doubles every 35 years. Because of this growth, average income today is about eight times as high as average income a century ago. As a result, the typical Canadian enjoys much greater economic prosperity than did his or her parents, grandparents, and great-grandparents.

Growth rates vary substantially from country to country. In some East Asian countries, such as Singapore, South Korea, and Taiwan, average income has risen about 7 percent per year in recent decades. At this rate, average income doubles every ten years. These countries have, in the length of one generation, gone from being among the poorest in the world to being among the richest. By contrast, in some African countries, such as Chad, Ethiopia, and Nigeria, average income has been stagnant for many years.

What explains these diverse experiences? How can the rich countries be sure to maintain their high standard of living? What policies should the poor countries pursue to promote more rapid growth in order to join the developed world? These are among the most important questions in macroeconomics. As economist Robert Lucas put it, "The consequences for human welfare in questions like these are simply staggering: Once one starts to think about them, it is hard to think about anything else."

In the previous two chapters we discussed how economists measure macroeconomic quantities and prices. In this chapter we start studying the forces that determine these variables. As we have seen, an economy's gross domestic product (GDP) measures both the total income earned in the economy and the total expenditure on the economy's output of goods and services. The level of real GDP is a good gauge of economic prosperity, and the growth of real GDP is a good gauge of economic progress. Here we focus on the long-run determinants of the level and growth of real GDP. Later in this book we study the short-run fluctuations of real GDP around its long-run trend.

We proceed here in three steps. First, we examine international data on real GDP per person. These data will give you some sense of how much the level and growth of living standards vary around the world. Second, we examine the role of *productivity*—the amount of goods and services produced for each hour of a worker's time. In particular, we see that a nation's standard of living is determined by the productivity of its workers, and we consider the factors that determine a nation's productivity. Third, we consider the link between productivity and the economic policies that a nation pursues.

ECONOMIC GROWTH AROUND THE WORLD

As a starting point for our study of long-run growth, let's look at the experiences of some of the world's economies. Table 12-1 shows data on real GDP per person for thirteen countries. For each country, the data cover about a century of history. The first and second columns of the table present the countries and time periods. (The time periods differ somewhat from country to country because of differences in data availability.) The third and fourth columns show estimates of real GDP per person about a century ago and for a recent year.

The data on real GDP per person show that living standards vary widely from country to country. Income per person in Canada, for instance, is about six times that in China and about eleven times that in India. The poorest countries have average levels of income that have not been seen in Canada for many decades. The

COUNTRY	PERIOD	REAL GDP PER PERSON AT BEGINNING OF PERIOD[a]	REAL GDP PER PERSON AT END OF PERIOD[a]	GROWTH RATE PER YEAR
Japan	1890–1997	$1 656	$32 392	2.82%
Brazil	1900–1997	857	8 638	2.41
Mexico	1900–1997	1 276	11 240	2.27
Germany	1870–1997	2 406	29 485	1.99
Canada	1870–1997	2 616	30 261	1.95
China	1900–1997	789	4 942	1.91
Argentina	1900–1997	2 525	13 774	1.76
United States	1870–1997	4 413	39 784	1.75
Indonesia	1900–1997	980	4 776	1.65
India	1900–1997	743	2 699	1.34
United Kingdom	1870–1997	5 296	28 406	1.33
Pakistan	1900–1997	813	2 201	1.03
Bangladesh	1900–1997	685	1 454	0.78

[a]Real GDP is measured in 1997 Canadian dollars.

SOURCES: Robert J. Barro and Xavier Sala-i-Martin, *Economic Growth* (New York: McGraw-Hill, 1995), Tables 10.2 and 10.3; World Bank, *World Development Report 1998/99: Knowledge for Development* (New York: World Bank and Oxford University Press, 1999), Table 1; and author's calculations.

THE VARIETY OF GROWTH EXPERIENCES

Table 12-1

typical citizen of India in 1997 had about as much real income as the typical Canadian in 1870. The typical person in Bangladesh in 1997 had about one-half the real income of a typical Canadian a century ago.

The last column of the table shows each country's growth rate. The growth rate measures how rapidly real GDP per person grew in the typical year. In Canada, for example, real GDP per person was $2616 in 1870 and $30 261 in 1997. The growth rate was 1.95 percent per year. This means that if real GDP per person, beginning at $2616, were to increase by 1.95 percent for each of 127 years, it would end up at $30 261. Of course, real GDP per person did not actually rise exactly 1.95 percent every year: Some years it rose by more and other years by less. The growth rate of 1.95 percent per year ignores short-run fluctuations around the long-run trend and represents an average rate of growth for real GDP per person over many years.

The countries in Table 12-1 are ordered by their growth rate from the most to the least rapid. Japan tops the list, with a growth rate of 2.82 percent per year. A hundred years ago, Japan was not a rich country. Japan's average income was only somewhat higher than Mexico's, and it was well behind Argentina's. To put the issue another way, Japan's income in 1890 was less than India's income in 1997. But because of its spectacular growth, Japan is now an economic superpower, with average income slightly higher than Canada and only slightly behind that of the United States. At the bottom of the list of countries is Bangladesh, which has experienced growth of only 0.78 percent per year over the past century. As a result, the typical resident of Bangladesh continues to live in abject poverty.

Because of differences in growth rates, the ranking of countries by income changes substantially over time. As we have seen, Japan is a country that has risen

FYI

The Magic of Compounding and the Rule of 70

It may be tempting to dismiss differences in growth rates as insignificant. If one country's economy grows at 1 percent while another grows at 3 percent, so what? What difference can 2 percent make?

The answer is: a big difference. Even growth rates that seem small when written in percentage terms seem large after they are compounded for many years. *Compounding* refers to the accumulation of a growth rate over a period of time.

Consider an example. Suppose that two college graduates—Ari and Elaine—both take their first jobs at the age of 22 earning $30 000 a year. Ari lives in an economy where all incomes grow at 1 percent per year, while Elaine lives in one where incomes grow at 3 percent per year. Straightforward calculations show what happens. Forty years later, when both are 62 years old, Ari earns $45 000 a year, while Elaine earns $98 000. Because of that difference of two percentage points in the growth rate, Elaine's salary is more than twice Ari's.

An old rule of thumb, called the *rule of 70*, is helpful in understanding growth rates and the effects of compounding. According to the rule of 70, if some variable grows at a rate of *x* percent per year, then that variable doubles in approximately 70/*x* years. In Ari's economy, incomes grow at 1 percent per year, so it takes about 70 years for incomes to double. In Elaine's economy, incomes grow at 3 percent per year, so it takes about 70/3, or 23, years for incomes to double.

The rule of 70 applies not only to a growing economy but also to a growing savings account. Here is an example: In 1791, Ben Franklin died and left $5000 to be invested for a period of 200 years to benefit medical students and scientific research. If this money had earned 7 percent per year (which would, in fact, have been very possible to do), the investment would have doubled in value every ten years. Over 200 years, it would have doubled 20 times. At the end of 200 years of compounding, the investment would have been worth $2^{20} \times \$5000$, which is about $5 billion. (In fact, Franklin's $5000 grew to only $2 million over 200 years because some of the money was spent along the way.)

As these examples show, growth rates compounded over many years can lead to some spectacular results. That is probably why Albert Einstein once called compounding "the greatest mathematical discovery of all time."

relative to others. One country that has fallen behind is the United Kingdom. In 1870, the United Kingdom was the richest country in the world, with average income about twice that of Canada and about 20 percent higher than that of the United States. Today, average income in the United Kingdom is below average income in its two former colonies.

These data show that the world's richest countries have no guarantee that they will stay the richest and that the world's poorest countries are not doomed forever to remain in poverty. But what explains these changes over time? Why do some countries zoom ahead while others lag behind? These are precisely the questions that we take up next.

QUICK QUIZ: What is the approximate growth rate of real GDP per person in Canada? Name a country that has had faster growth and a country that has had slower growth.

PRODUCTIVITY: ITS ROLE AND DETERMINANTS

Explaining the large variation in living standards around the world is, in one sense, very easy. As we will see, the explanation can be summarized in a single word—*productivity*. But, in another sense, the international variation is deeply puzzling. To explain why incomes are so much higher in some countries than in others, we must look at the many factors that determine a nation's productivity.

WHY PRODUCTIVITY IS SO IMPORTANT

Let's begin our study of productivity and economic growth by developing a simple model based loosely on Daniel Defoe's famous novel *Robinson Crusoe.* Robinson Crusoe, as you may recall, is a sailor stranded on a desert island. Because Crusoe lives alone, he catches his own fish, grows his own vegetables, and makes his own clothes. We can think of Crusoe's activities—his production and consumption of fish, vegetables, and clothing—as being a simple economy. By examining Crusoe's economy, we can learn some lessons that also apply to more complex and realistic economies.

What determines Crusoe's standard of living? The answer is obvious. If Crusoe is good at catching fish, growing vegetables, and making clothes, he lives well. If he is bad at doing these things, he lives poorly. Because Crusoe gets to consume only what he produces, his living standard is tied to his productive ability.

The term **productivity** refers to the quantity of goods and services that a worker can produce for each hour of work. In the case of Crusoe's economy, it is easy to see that productivity is the key determinant of living standards and that growth in productivity is the key determinant of growth in living standards. The more fish Crusoe can catch per hour, the more he eats at dinner. If Crusoe finds a better place to catch fish, his productivity rises. This increase in productivity makes Crusoe better off: He could eat the extra fish, or he could spend less time fishing and devote more time to making other goods he enjoys.

productivity
the amount of goods and services produced from each hour of a worker's time

The key role of productivity in determining living standards is as true for nations as it is for stranded sailors. Recall that an economy's gross domestic product (GDP) measures two things at once: the total income earned by everyone in the economy and the total expenditure on the economy's output of goods and services. The reason GDP can measure these two things simultaneously is that, for the economy as a whole, they must be equal. Put simply, an economy's income is the economy's output.

Like Crusoe, a nation can enjoy a high standard of living only if it can produce a large quantity of goods and services. Canadians live better than Nigerians because Canadian workers are more productive than Nigerian workers. The Japanese have enjoyed more rapid growth in living standards than Argentineans because Japanese workers have experienced more rapidly growing productivity. Indeed, one of the *Ten Principles of Economics* in Chapter 1 is that a country's standard of living depends on its ability to produce goods and services.

Hence, to understand the large differences in living standards we observe across countries or over time, we must focus on the production of goods and services. But seeing the link between living standards and productivity is only the first step. It leads naturally to the next question: Why are some economies so much better at producing goods and services than others?

HOW PRODUCTIVITY IS DETERMINED

Although productivity is uniquely important in determining Robinson Crusoe's standard of living, many factors determine Crusoe's productivity. Crusoe will be better at catching fish, for instance, if he has more fishing poles, if he has been trained in the best fishing techniques, if his island has a plentiful fish supply, and if he invents a better fishing lure. Each of these determinants of Crusoe's productivity—which we can call *physical capital, human capital, natural resources,* and *technological knowledge*—has a counterpart in more complex and realistic economies. Let's consider each of these factors in turn.

physical capital

the stock of equipment and structures that are used to produce goods and services

Physical Capital   Workers are more productive if they have tools with which to work. The stock of equipment and structures that are used to produce goods and services is called **physical capital,** or just *capital.* For example, when woodworkers make furniture, they use saws, lathes, and drill presses. More tools allow work to be done more quickly and more accurately. That is, a worker with only basic hand tools can make less furniture each week than a worker with sophisticated and specialized woodworking equipment.

As you may recall from Chapter 2, the inputs used to produce goods and services—labour, capital, and so on—are called the *factors of production.* An important feature of capital is that it is a *produced* factor of production. That is, capital is an input into the production process that in the past was an output from the production process. The woodworker uses a lathe to make the leg of a table. Earlier the lathe itself was the output of a firm that manufactures lathes. The lathe manufacturer in turn used other equipment to make its product. Thus, capital is a factor of production used to produce all kinds of goods and services, including more capital.

human capital

the knowledge and skills that workers acquire through education, training, and experience

Human Capital   A second determinant of productivity is human capital. **Human capital** is the economist's term for the knowledge and skills that workers acquire through education, training, and experience. Human capital includes the skills accumulated in early childhood programs, elementary school, high school, college or university, and on-the-job training for adults in the labour force.

Although education, training, and experience are less tangible than lathes, bulldozers, and buildings, human capital is like physical capital in many ways. Like physical capital, human capital raises a nation's ability to produce goods and services. Also like physical capital, human capital is a produced factor of production. Producing human capital requires inputs in the form of teachers, libraries, and student time. Indeed, students can be viewed as "workers" who have the important job of producing the human capital that will be used in future production.

natural resources

the inputs into the production of goods and services that are provided by nature, such as land, rivers, and mineral deposits

Natural Resources   A third determinant of productivity is **natural resources.** Natural resources are inputs into production that are provided by nature, such as land, rivers, and mineral deposits. Natural resources take two forms: renewable and nonrenewable. A forest is an example of a renewable resource. When one tree is cut down, a seedling can be planted in its place to be harvested in the future. Oil is an example of a nonrenewable resource. Because oil is produced by nature over many thousands of years, there is only a limited supply. Once the supply of oil is depleted, it is impossible to create more.

Differences in natural resources are responsible for some of the differences in standards of living around the world. The historical success of Canada was driven in part by the large supply of land well suited for agriculture and by an abundance of mineral resources. Today, some countries in the Middle East, such as Kuwait and Saudi Arabia, are rich simply because they happen to be on top of some of the largest pools of oil in the world.

Although natural resources can be important, they are not necessary for an economy to be highly productive in producing goods and services. Japan, for instance, is one of the richest countries in the world, despite having few natural resources. International trade makes Japan's success possible. Japan imports many of the natural resources it needs, such as oil, and exports its manufactured goods to economies rich in natural resources.

Technological Knowledge   A fourth determinant of productivity is **technological knowledge**—the understanding of the best ways to produce goods and services. A hundred years ago, most Canadians worked on farms, because farm technology required a high input of labour in order to feed the entire population. Today, thanks to advances in the technology of farming, a small fraction of the population can produce enough food to feed the entire country. This technological change made labour available to produce other goods and services.

Technological knowledge takes many forms. Some technology is common knowledge—after it is used by one person, everyone becomes aware of it. For example, once Henry Ford successfully introduced production in assembly lines, other carmakers quickly followed suit. Other technology is proprietary—it is known only by the company that discovers it. Only the Coca-Cola Company, for instance, knows the secret recipe for making its famous soft drink. Still other technology is proprietary for a short time. When a pharmaceutical company discovers a new drug, the patent system gives that company a temporary right to be the

technological knowledge
society's understanding of the best ways to produce goods and services

---

FYI

The Production Function

Economists often use a *production function* to describe the relationship between the quantity of inputs used in production and the quantity of output from production. For example, suppose Y denotes the quantity of output, L the quantity of labour, K the quantity of physical capital, H the quantity of human capital, and N the quantity of natural resources. Then we might write

$$Y = A \, F(L, K, H, N),$$

where $F(\ )$ is a function that shows how the inputs are combined to produce output. A is a variable that reflects the available production technology. As technology improves, A rises, so the economy produces more output from any given combination of inputs.

Many production functions have a property called *constant returns to scale*. If a production function has constant returns to scale, then a doubling of all the inputs causes the amount of output to double as well. Mathematically, we write that a production function has constant returns to scale if, for any positive number x,

$$xY = A \, F(xL, xK, xH, xN).$$

A doubling of all inputs is represented in this equation by $x = 2$. The right-hand side shows the inputs doubling, and the left-hand side shows output doubling.

Production functions with constant returns to scale have an interesting implication. To see what it is, set $x = 1/L$. Then the equation above becomes

$$Y/L = A \, F(1, K/L, H/L, N/L).$$

Notice that Y/L is output per worker, which is a measure of productivity. This equation says that productivity depends on physical capital per worker (K/L), human capital per worker (H/L), and natural resources per worker (N/L). Productivity also depends on the state of technology, as reflected by the variable A. Thus, this equation provides a mathematical summary of the four determinants of productivity we have just discussed.

exclusive manufacturer of this particular drug. When the patent expires, however, other companies are allowed to make the drug. All of these forms of technological knowledge are important for the economy's production of goods and services.

It is worthwhile to distinguish between technological knowledge and human capital. Although they are closely related, there is an important difference. Technological knowledge refers to society's understanding of how the world works. Human capital refers to the resources expended transmitting this understanding to the labour force. To use a relevant metaphor, knowledge is the quality of society's textbooks, whereas human capital is the amount of time that the population has devoted to reading them. Workers' productivity depends on both the quality of textbooks they have available and the amount of time they have spent studying them.

CASE STUDY ARE NATURAL RESOURCES A LIMIT TO GROWTH?

The world's population is far larger today than it was a century ago, and many people are enjoying a much higher standard of living. A perennial debate concerns whether this growth in population and living standards can continue in the future.

Many commentators have argued that natural resources provide a limit to how much the world's economies can grow. At first, this argument might seem hard to ignore. If the world has only a fixed supply of nonrenewable natural resources, how can population, production, and living standards continue to grow over time? Eventually, won't supplies of oil and minerals start to run out? When these shortages start to occur, won't they stop economic growth and, perhaps, even force living standards to fall?

Despite the apparent appeal of such arguments, most economists are less concerned about such limits to growth than one might guess. They argue that technological progress often yields ways to avoid these limits. If we compare the economy today to the economy of the past, we see various ways in which the use of natural resources has improved. Modern cars have better gas mileage. New houses have better insulation and require less energy to heat and cool them. More efficient oil rigs waste less oil in the process of extraction. Recycling allows some nonrenewable resources to be reused. The development of alternative fuels, such as ethanol instead of gasoline, allows us to substitute renewable for nonrenewable resources.

Fifty years ago, some conservationists were concerned about the excessive use of tin and copper. At the time, these were crucial commodities: Tin was used to make many food containers, and copper was used to make telephone wire. Some people advocated mandatory recycling and rationing of tin and copper so that supplies would be available for future generations. Today, however, plastic has replaced tin as a material for making many food containers, and phone calls often travel over fibre-optic cables, which are made from sand. Technological progress has made once crucial natural resources less necessary.

But are all of these efforts enough to permit continued economic growth? One way to answer this question is to look at the prices of natural resources. In a market economy, scarcity is reflected in market prices. If the world were running out of natural resources, then the prices of those resources would be rising

TECHNOLOGICAL PROGRESS LEADS TO
NEW PRODUCTS, SUCH AS THIS HYBRID
ELECTRIC/GAS-POWERED CAR, THAT
REDUCE OUR DEPENDENCE ON
NONRENEWABLE RESOURCES.

over time. But, in fact, the opposite is more nearly true. The prices of most natural resources (adjusted for overall inflation) are stable or falling. It appears that
our ability to conserve these resources is growing more rapidly than their supplies are dwindling. Market prices give no reason to believe that natural
resources are a limit to economic growth.

QUICK QUIZ: List and describe four determinants of a country's
productivity.

ECONOMIC GROWTH AND PUBLIC POLICY

So far, we have determined that a society's standard of living depends on its ability
to produce goods and services and that its productivity depends on physical capital, human capital, natural resources, and technological knowledge. Let's now
turn to the question faced by policymakers around the world: What can government policy do to raise productivity and living standards?

THE IMPORTANCE OF SAVING AND INVESTMENT

Because capital is a produced factor of production, a society can change the
amount of capital it has. If today the economy produces a large quantity of new
capital goods, then tomorrow it will have a larger stock of capital and be able to
produce more of all types of goods and services. Thus, one way to raise future productivity is to invest more current resources in the production of capital.

One of the *Ten Principles of Economics* presented in Chapter 1 is that people face
tradeoffs. This principle is especially important when considering the accumulation of capital. Because resources are scarce, devoting more resources to producing
capital requires devoting fewer resources to producing goods and services for current consumption. That is, for society to invest more in capital, it must consume
less and save more of its current income. The growth that arises from capital accumulation is not a free lunch: It requires that society sacrifice consumption of goods
and services in the present in order to enjoy higher consumption in the future.

The next chapter examines in more detail how the economy's financial markets coordinate saving and investment. It also examines how government policies influence the amount of saving and investment that takes place. At this point it is important to note that encouraging saving and investment is one way that a government can encourage growth and, in the long run, raise the economy's standard of living.

To see the importance of investment for economic growth, consider Figure 12-1, which displays data on fifteen countries. Panel (a) shows each country's growth rate over a 31-year period. The countries are ordered by their growth rates, from most to least rapid. Panel (b) shows the percentage of GDP that each country devotes to investment. The correlation between growth and investment, although not perfect, is strong. Countries that devote a large share of GDP to investment, such as Singapore and Japan, tend to have high growth rates. Countries that devote a small share of GDP to investment, such as Bangladesh and Rwanda, tend to have low growth rates. Studies that examine a more comprehensive list of countries confirm this strong correlation between investment and growth.

There is, however, a problem in interpreting these data. As the appendix to Chapter 2 discussed, a correlation between two variables does not establish which variable is the cause and which is the effect. It is possible that high investment causes high growth, but it is also possible that high growth causes high

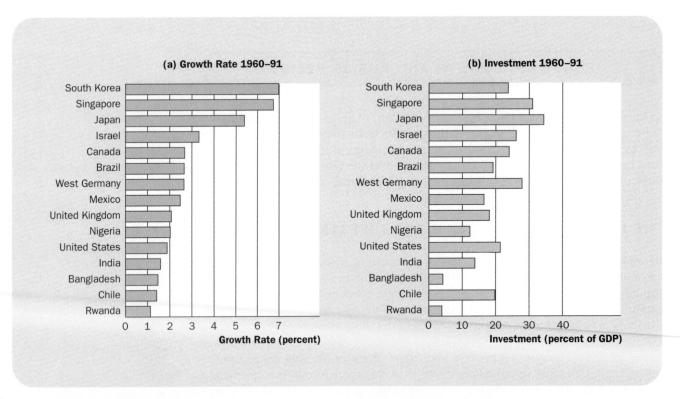

Figure 12-1

GROWTH AND INVESTMENT.   Panel (a) shows the growth rate of GDP per person for fifteen countries over the period from 1960 to 1991. Panel (b) shows the percentage of GDP that each country devoted to investment over this period. The figure shows that investment and growth are positively correlated.

investment. (Or, perhaps, high growth and high investment are both caused by a third variable that has been omitted from the analysis.) The data by themselves cannot tell us the direction of causation. Nonetheless, because capital accumulation affects productivity so clearly and directly, many economists interpret these data as showing that high investment leads to more rapid economic growth.

DIMINISHING RETURNS AND THE CATCH-UP EFFECT

Suppose that a government, convinced by the evidence in Figure 12-1, pursues policies that raise the nation's saving rate—the percentage of GDP devoted to saving rather than consumption. What happens? With the nation saving more, fewer resources are needed to make consumption goods, and more resources are available to make capital goods. As a result, the capital stock increases, leading to rising productivity and more rapid growth in GDP. But how long does this higher rate of growth last? Assuming that the saving rate remains at its new higher level, does the growth rate of GDP stay high indefinitely or only for a period of time?

The traditional view of the production process is that capital is subject to **diminishing returns:** As the stock of capital rises, the extra output produced from an additional unit of capital falls. In other words, when workers already have a large quantity of capital to use in producing goods and services, giving them an additional unit of capital increases their productivity only slightly. Because of diminishing returns, an increase in the saving rate leads to higher growth only for a while. As the higher saving rate allows more capital to be accumulated, the benefits from additional capital become smaller over time, and so growth slows down. *In the long run, the higher saving rate leads to a higher level of productivity and income, but not to higher growth in these variables.* Reaching this long run, however, can take quite a while. According to studies of international data on economic growth, increasing the saving rate can lead to substantially higher growth for a period of several decades.

diminishing returns
the property whereby the benefit from an extra unit of an input declines as the quantity of the input increases

The diminishing returns to capital have another important implication: Other things equal, it is easier for a country to grow fast if it starts out relatively poor. This effect of initial conditions on subsequent growth is sometimes called the **catch-up effect.** In poor countries, workers lack even the most rudimentary tools and, as a result, have low productivity. Small amounts of capital investment would substantially raise these workers' productivity. By contrast, workers in rich countries have large amounts of capital with which to work, and this partly explains their high productivity. Yet with the amount of capital per worker already so high, additional capital investment has a relatively small effect on productivity. Studies of international data on economic growth confirm this catch-up effect: Controlling for other variables, such as the percentage of GDP devoted to investment, poor countries do tend to grow faster than rich countries.

catch-up effect
the property whereby countries that start off poor tend to grow more rapidly than countries that start off rich

This catch-up effect can help explain some of the puzzling results in Figure 12-1. Over this 31-year period, Canada and South Korea devoted a similar share of GDP to investment. Yet Canada experienced only mediocre growth of about 2.5 percent, while Korea experienced spectacular growth of 7.0 percent. The explanation is the catch-up effect. In 1960, Korea had GDP per person less than one-tenth the Canadian level, in part because previous investment had been so low. With a small initial capital stock, the benefits to capital accumulation were much greater in Korea, and this gave Korea a higher subsequent growth rate.

This catch-up effect shows up in other aspects of life. When a school gives an end-of-year award to the "Most Improved" student, that student is usually one who began the year with relatively poor performance. Students who began the year not studying find improvement easier than students who always worked hard. Note that it is good to be "Most Improved," given the starting point, but it is even better to be "Best Student." Similarly, economic growth over the last several decades has been much more rapid in South Korea than in Canada, but GDP per person is still higher in Canada.

INVESTMENT FROM ABROAD

So far we have discussed how policies aimed at increasing a country's saving rate can increase investment and, thereby, long-term economic growth. Yet saving by domestic residents is not the only way for a country to invest in new capital. The other way is investment by foreigners.

Investment from abroad takes several forms. Nortel might build a plant to assemble telecommunications equipment in Mexico. A capital investment that is owned and operated by a foreign entity is called *foreign direct investment*. Alternatively, a Canadian might buy stock in a Mexican corporation (that is, buy a share in the ownership of the corporation); the Mexican corporation can use the proceeds from the stock sale to build a new factory. An investment that is financed with foreign money but operated by domestic residents is called *foreign portfolio investment*. In both cases, Canadians provide the resources necessary to increase the stock of capital in Mexico. That is, Canadian saving is being used to finance Mexican investment.

When foreigners invest in a country, they do so because they expect to earn a return on their investment. Nortel's assembly plant increases the Mexican capital stock and, therefore, increases Mexican productivity and Mexican GDP. Yet Nortel takes some of this additional income back to Canada in the form of profit. Similarly, when a Canadian investor buys Mexican stock, the investor has a right to a portion of the profit that the Mexican corporation earns.

Investment from abroad, therefore, does not have the same effect on all measures of economic prosperity. Recall that gross domestic product (GDP) is the income earned within a country by both residents and nonresidents, whereas gross national product (GNP) is the income earned by residents of a country both at home and abroad. When Nortel opens its assembly plant in Mexico, some of the income the factory generates accrues to people who do not live in Mexico. As a result, foreign investment in Mexico raises the income of Mexicans (measured by GNP) by less than it raises the production in Mexico (measured by GDP).

Nonetheless, investment from abroad is one way for a country to grow. Even though some of the benefits from this investment flow back to the foreign owners, this investment does increase the economy's stock of capital, leading to higher productivity and higher wages. Moreover, investment from abroad is one way for poor countries to learn the state-of-the-art technologies developed and used in richer countries. For these reasons, many economists who advise governments in less developed economies advocate policies that encourage investment from abroad. Often this means removing restrictions that governments have imposed on foreign ownership of domestic capital.

An organization that tries to encourage the flow of investment to poor countries is the World Bank. This international organization obtains funds from the world's advanced countries, such as Canada, and uses these resources to make loans to less developed countries so that they can invest in roads, sewer systems, schools, and other types of capital. It also offers the countries advice about how the funds might best be used. The World Bank, together with its sister organization, the International Monetary Fund, was set up after World War II. One lesson from the war was that economic distress often leads to political turmoil, international tensions, and military conflict. Thus, every country has an interest in promoting economic prosperity around the world. The World Bank and the International Monetary Fund are aimed at achieving that common goal.

EDUCATION

Education—investment in human capital—is at least as important as investment in physical capital for a country's long-run economic success. In Canada, each year of schooling raises a person's wage on average by about 10 percent. In less developed countries, where human capital is especially scarce, the gap between the wages of educated and uneducated workers is even larger. Thus, one way in which government policy can enhance the standard of living is to provide good schools and to encourage the population to take advantage of them.

Investment in human capital, like investment in physical capital, has an opportunity cost. When students are in school, they forgo the wages they could have earned. In less developed countries, children often drop out of school at an early age, even though the benefit of additional schooling is very high, simply because their labour is needed to help support the family.

Some economists have argued that human capital is particularly important for economic growth because human capital conveys positive externalities. An *externality* is the effect of one person's actions on the well-being of a bystander. An educated person, for instance, might generate new ideas about how best to produce goods and services. If these ideas enter society's pool of knowledge so everyone can use them, then the ideas are an external benefit of education. In this case, the return to schooling for society is even greater than the return for the individual. This argument would justify the large subsidies to human-capital investment that we observe in the form of public education.

One problem facing some poor countries is the *brain drain*—the emigration of many of the most highly educated workers to rich countries, where these workers can enjoy a higher standard of living. If human capital does have positive externalities, then this brain drain makes those people left behind poorer than they otherwise would be. This problem offers policymakers a dilemma. On the one hand, Canada and other rich countries have the best systems of higher education, and it would seem natural for poor countries to send their best students abroad to earn higher degrees. On the other hand, those students who have spent time abroad may choose not to return home, and this brain drain will reduce the poor nation's stock of human capital even further.

PROPERTY RIGHTS AND POLITICAL STABILITY

Another way in which policymakers can foster economic growth is by protecting property rights and promoting political stability. As we first noted when we discussed economic interdependence in Chapter 3, production in market

IN THE NEWS

Democracy and Economic Growth

HOW IMPORTANT IS DEMOCRACY FOR economic growth? In a number of his well-known works, the late economist Mancur Olson suggested that the nature of political power, and how different kinds of power promote different kinds of economic behaviour, plays a key role in determining why some countries are very rich while others are very poor. Here Olson's idea that democracy is a key ingredient in the mix of conditions that are required for sustained economic growth is described.

Out of Anarchy

Just before Mancur Olson died in 1998, he finished work on a new book, *Power*

and Prosperity: Outgrowing Communist and Capitalist Dictatorships.

As in his other well-known works, *The Logic of Collective Action* and *The Rise and Decline of Nations*, Olson grapples with a huge and, for most economists, intimidating question—why do some economies prosper while others fail? The book begins with Olson's memorable metaphor of rulers and robbers.

Through history, Olson observes, it has been better to live under political tyranny than to be subject to the depredations of roving bands of warrior-thieves. Indeed, advancing from the second to the first generally marks the start of civilization.

But this is a puzzle. Assuming that tyrants and thieves are alike, in that they are out for whatever they can extract from their subjects, why should one kind of predation be better than the other? The answer, Olson explains, is that the tyrant has a stake, an "encompassing interest," in the domain he is exploiting: if it prospers, he can extract more for himself in taxes and other ways. A roving bandit merely destroys and moves on. A stationary bandit keeps taxes low in the

short term in order to spur growth and gather more revenue later; in fact he goes further, and provides growth-promoting public goods, the better to improve his take.

Autocracy, then, is usually much better for the victims than anarchy. What about democracy? Suppose, just suppose, that democratic governments rule solely in the interests of the majority that keeps them in power; suppose, in other words, that they would exploit the minority with no more qualms than the tyrant has in exploiting all his subjects. Democracy would still have a great advantage over tyranny in purely economic terms. Even in a predatory democracy, the government has a greater encompassing interest than a tyranny.

Why? Because the majority in whose interests the government is ruling must pay a share of the taxes that finance redistribution in its direction; because the majority benefits directly from rising incomes (not merely indirectly, through redistribution of wealth); and because the majority likewise gains directly from new public goods.

The incentives that guide a tyrant to moderate his exactions therefore

economies arises from the interactions of millions of individuals and firms. When you buy a car, for instance, you are buying the output of a car dealer, a car manufacturer, a steel company, an iron ore mining company, and so on. This division of production among many firms allows the economy's factors of production to be used as effectively as possible. To achieve this outcome, the economy has to coordinate transactions among these firms, as well as between firms and consumers. Market economies achieve this coordination through market prices. That is, market prices are the instrument with which the invisible hand of the marketplace brings supply and demand into balance.

An important prerequisite for the price system to work is an economy-wide respect for *property rights*. Property rights refer to the ability of people to exercise authority over the resources they own. A mining company will not make the effort to mine iron ore if it expects the ore to be stolen. The company mines the ore only if it is confident that it will benefit from the ore's subsequent sale. For this reason, courts serve an important role in a market economy: They enforce property rights. Through the criminal justice system, the courts discourage direct theft. In addition, work far more powerfully in a democracy. The bigger the majority in whose interests the government is ruling, the larger the encompassing interest. Constitutions with checks and balances requiring supermajorities for certain actions may create what Olson calls "superencompassing" interests, leading as you might expect to even smaller growth-retarding exactions on the minority and greater attention to the supply of growth-promoting public goods. And this beneficial outcome follows, remember, on the extreme assumption that voters act not out of concern for the greater good, but out of pure self-interest.

This argument demolishes at a stroke the notion that democracy is a luxury only rich countries can afford. Historically, Olson argues, the dispersal of political power and the emergence of representative government have often been the trigger for faster economic growth. It is perfectly true that prosperity has been conducive to democracy, but the converse, improbable as it seems to many, is at least as true. The book explores at some length the implications of this claim for the transition economies of Eastern Europe and, especially, for the former Soviet Union.

In *Power and Prosperity* Olson also has much to say about markets—and again what he says is puzzling at first sight. Markets are pervasive in even the poorest countries, he points out. Excessive government intervention in those markets is no doubt damaging. Governments in rich countries also intervene a lot, and very often as clumsily. Misguided intervention cannot do enough harm to explain the chasm that separates Mozambique, say, from Sweden.

The crucial difference lies not in markets that exist, but in markets that are entirely missing. Markets in the poorest countries generally conduct "self-enforcing transactions," with goods exchanged on the spot for money or other goods. Transactions involving distance or, especially, time are not self-enforcing: a promise to pay next week for goods received this week is a risky contract for the seller. If such contracts cannot be made with confidence, the corresponding market may not exist at all. A feature the poorest countries have in common is that contract rights and property rights are badly defined or weakly enforced. Such rights, necessary for advanced markets, which in turn are necessary for rapid growth, are themselves a kind of public good. Again, therefore, Olson sees the failure to provide these rights as springing from the ruler's lack of a sufficiently encompassing interest. Again, the absence of democracy, serving to narrow the ruler's interest, is at the root of the country's economic failure.

SOURCE: Adapted from *The Economist*, February 19, 2000, p. 74.

through the civil justice system, the courts ensure that buyers and sellers live up to their contracts.

Although those of us in developed countries tend to take property rights for granted, those living in less developed countries understand that lack of property rights can be a major problem. In many countries, the system of justice does not work well. Contracts are hard to enforce, and fraud often goes unpunished. In more extreme cases, the government not only fails to enforce property rights but actually infringes upon them. To do business in some countries, firms are expected to bribe powerful government officials. Such corruption impedes the coordinating power of markets. It also discourages domestic saving and investment from abroad.

One threat to property rights is political instability. When revolutions and coups are common, there is doubt about whether property rights will be respected in the future. If a revolutionary government might confiscate the capital of some businesses, as was often true after communist revolutions, domestic residents have less incentive to save, invest, and start new businesses. At the same time, foreigners have less incentive to invest in the country. Even the threat of revolution can act to depress a nation's standard of living.

Thus, economic prosperity depends in part on political prosperity. A country with an efficient court system, honest government officials, and a stable constitution will enjoy a higher economic standard of living than a country with a poor court system, corrupt officials, and frequent revolutions and coups.

FREE TRADE

Some of the world's poorest countries have tried to achieve more rapid economic growth by pursuing *inward-oriented policies*. These policies are aimed at raising productivity and living standards within the country by avoiding interaction with the rest of the world. As we discussed in Chapter 9, domestic firms sometimes claim they need protection from foreign competition in order to compete and grow. This infant-industry argument, together with a general distrust of foreigners, has at times led policymakers in less developed countries to impose tariffs and other trade restrictions.

Most economists today believe that poor countries are better off pursuing *outward-oriented policies* that integrate these countries into the world economy. Chapters 3 and 9 showed how international trade can improve the economic well-being of a country's citizens. Trade is, in some ways, a type of technology. When a country exports wheat and imports steel, the country benefits in the same way as if it had invented a technology for turning wheat into steel. A country that eliminates trade restrictions will, therefore, experience the same kind of economic growth that would occur after a major technological advance.

The adverse impact of inward orientation becomes clear when one considers the small size of many less developed economies. The total GDP of Argentina, for instance, is about that of Toronto. Imagine what would happen if the Toronto City Council were to prohibit city residents from trading with people living outside the city limits. Without being able to take advantage of the gains from trade, Toronto would need to produce all the goods it consumes. It would also have to produce all of its own capital goods, rather than importing state-of-the-art equipment from other cities. Living standards in Toronto would fall immediately, and the problem would likely only get worse over time. This is precisely what happened when Argentina pursued inward-oriented policies throughout much of the twentieth century. By contrast, countries pursuing outward-oriented policies, such as South Korea, Singapore, and Taiwan, have enjoyed high rates of economic growth.

The amount that a nation trades with others is determined not only by government policy but also by geography. Countries with good natural seaports find trade easier than countries without this resource. It is not a coincidence that many of the world's major cities, such as New York, San Francisco, and Hong Kong, are located next to oceans. Similarly, because landlocked countries find international trade more difficult, they tend to have lower levels of income than countries with easy access to the world's waterways.

THE CONTROL OF POPULATION GROWTH

A country's productivity and living standard are determined in part by its population growth. Obviously, population is a key determinant of a country's labour

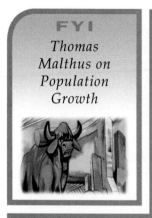

FYI

Thomas Malthus on Population Growth

You may have heard economics called "the dismal science." The field was pinned with this label many years ago because of a theory proposed by Thomas Robert Malthus (1766–1834), an English minister and early economic thinker. In a famous book called *An Essay on the Principle of Population as It Affects the Future Improvement of Society,* Malthus offered what may be history's most chilling forecast. Malthus argued that an ever-increasing population would continually strain society's ability to provide for itself. As a result, humanity was doomed to forever live in poverty.

Malthus's logic was very simple. He began by noting that "food is necessary to the existence of man" and that "the passion between the sexes is necessary and will remain nearly in its present state." He concluded that "the power of population is infinitely greater than the power in the earth to produce subsistence for man." According to Malthus, the only check on population growth was "misery and vice." Attempts by charities or governments to alleviate poverty were counterproductive, he argued, because they merely allowed the poor to have more children, placing even greater strains on society's productive capabilities.

Fortunately, Malthus's dire forecast was far off the mark. Although the world population has increased about sixfold over the past two centuries, living standards around the world are on average much higher. As a result of economic growth, chronic hunger and malnutrition are less common now than they were in Malthus's day. Famines occur from time to time, but they are more often the result of an unequal income distribution or political instability than an inadequate production of food.

Where did Malthus go wrong? He failed to appreciate that growth in humanity's ingenuity would exceed growth in population. New ideas about how to produce and even the kinds of goods to produce have led to greater prosperity than Malthus—or anyone else of his era—ever imagined. Pesticides, fertilizers, mechanized farm equipment, and new crop varieties have allowed each farmer to feed ever-greater numbers of people. The wealth-enhancing effects of technological progress have exceeded whatever wealth-diminishing effects might be attributed to population growth.

Indeed, some economists now go so far as to suggest that population growth may even have helped humanity achieve higher standards of living. If there are more people, then there are more scientists, inventors, and engineers to contribute to technological progress, which benefits everyone. Perhaps world population growth, rather than being a source of economic deprivation as Malthus predicted, has actually been an engine of technological progress and economic prosperity.

THOMAS MALTHUS

force. It is no surprise, therefore, that countries with large populations (such as the United States and Japan) tend to produce greater GDP than countries with small populations (such as Luxembourg and the Netherlands). But *total* GDP is not a good measure of economic well-being. For policymakers concerned about living standards, GDP *per person* is more important, for it tells us the quantity of goods and services available for the typical individual in the economy.

How does growth in the number of people affect the amount of GDP per person? Standard theories of economic growth predict that high population growth reduces GDP per person. The reason is that rapid growth in the number of workers forces the other factors of production to be spread more thinly. In particular, when population growth is rapid, equipping each worker with a large quantity of capital is more difficult. A smaller quantity of capital per worker leads to lower productivity and lower GDP per worker.

This problem is most apparent in the case of human capital. Countries with high population growth have large numbers of school-age children. This places a bigger burden on the educational system. It is not surprising, therefore, that educational attainment tends to be low in countries with high population growth.

The differences in population growth around the world are large. In developed countries, such as Canada, the United States, and Western Europe, the population has risen about 1 percent per year in recent decades, and it is expected to rise even more slowly in the future. By contrast, in many poor African countries, population growth is about 3 percent per year. At this rate, the population doubles every 23 years.

Reducing the rate of population growth is widely thought to be one way less developed countries can try to raise their standards of living. In some countries, this goal is accomplished directly with laws regulating the number of children families may have. China, for instance, allows only one child per family; couples who violate this rule are subject to substantial fines. In countries with greater freedom, the goal of reduced population growth is accomplished less directly by increasing awareness of birth control techniques.

The final way in which a country can influence population growth is to apply one of the *Ten Principles of Economics:* People respond to incentives. Bearing a child, like any decision, has an opportunity cost. When the opportunity cost rises, people will choose to have smaller families. In particular, women with the opportunity to receive good education and desirable employment tend to want fewer children than those with fewer opportunities outside the home. Hence, policies that foster equal treatment of women are one way for less developed economies to reduce the rate of population growth.

RESEARCH AND DEVELOPMENT

The primary reason that living standards are higher today than they were a century ago is that technological knowledge has advanced. The telephone, the transistor, the computer, and the internal combustion engine are among the thousands of innovations that have improved the ability to produce goods and services.

Although most technological advance comes from private research by firms and individual inventors, there is also a public interest in promoting these efforts. To a large extent, knowledge is a *public good:* Once one person discovers an idea, the idea enters society's pool of knowledge and other people can freely use it. Just as government has a role in providing a public good such as national defence, it also has a role in encouraging the research and development of new technologies.

The Canadian government has long played a role in creating and disseminating technological knowledge. Research at the Dominion Experimental Farms led to the introduction of the Marquis strain of wheat to Western Canada in 1911. Marquis matured earlier than other strains of wheat, making it feasible to cultivate much more of the Prairies than would otherwise have been possible. This research was therefore a significant contributor to Canada's early economic growth. More recently, the Canadian government has funded research that led to the development of the CANDU nuclear reactor. The government continues to encourage advances in knowledge with research grants from agencies such as the Natural Sciences and Engineering Research Council of Canada (NSERCC), the Medical Research Council (MRC), and the Social Sciences and Humanities Research Council of Canada (SSHRCC). The federal and provincial governments also encourage advances in knowledge by offering tax breaks to firms that engage in research and development.

Yet another way in which government policy encourages research is through the patent system. When a person or firm invents a new product, such as a new drug, the inventor can apply for a patent. If the product is deemed truly original, the government awards the patent, which gives the inventor the exclusive right to make the product for a specified number of years. In essence, the patent gives the inventor a property right over his or her invention, turning the new idea from a public good into a private good. By allowing inventors to profit from their inventions—even if only temporarily—the patent system enhances the incentive for individuals and firms to engage in research.

CASE STUDY   THE PRODUCTIVITY SLOWDOWN

From 1959 to 1973, productivity, as measured by output per hour worked in Canadian businesses, grew at a rate of 3.1 percent per year. From 1973 to 1998, productivity grew by only 1.0 percent per year. Not surprisingly, this slowdown in productivity growth has been reflected in reduced growth in real wages and family incomes. It is also reflected in a general sense of economic anxiety. Because it has accumulated over so many years, this fall in productivity growth of 2.1 percentage points has had a large effect on incomes. If this slowdown had not occurred, the income of the average Canadian would today be about 75 percent higher.

The slowdown in economic growth has been one of the most important problems facing economic policymakers. Economists are often asked what caused the slowdown and what can be done to reverse it. Unfortunately, despite much research on these questions, the answers remain elusive.

Two facts are well established. First, the slowdown in productivity growth is a worldwide phenomenon. Sometime in the mid-1970s, economic growth slowed not only in Canada but also in other industrial countries, including the United States, France, Germany, Italy, Japan, and the United Kingdom. Although some of these countries have had more rapid growth than Canada, all of them have had slow growth compared with their own past experience. To explain the slowdown in Canada's growth, therefore, it seems necessary to look beyond our borders.

Second, the slowdown cannot be traced to those factors of production that are most easily measured. Economists can measure directly the quantity of physical capital that workers have available. They can also measure human capital in the form of years of schooling. It appears that the slowdown in productivity is not primarily attributable to reduced growth in these inputs.

Technology appears to be one of the few remaining culprits. That is, having ruled out most other explanations, many economists attribute the slowdown in economic growth to a slowdown in the creation of new ideas about how to produce goods and services. Because the quantity of "ideas" is hard to measure, this explanation is difficult to confirm or refute.

In some ways, it is odd to say that the last 25 years have been a period of slow technological progress. This period has witnessed the spread of computers across the economy—a historic technological revolution that has affected almost every industry and almost every firm. Yet, for some reason, this change has not yet been reflected in more rapid economic growth. As economist Robert Solow put it, "You can see the computer age everywhere but in the productivity statistics."

What does the future of economic growth hold? An optimistic scenario is that the computer revolution will rejuvenate economic growth once these new machines are integrated into the economy and their potential is fully understood. Economic historians note that the discovery of electricity took many decades to have a large impact on productivity and living standards because people had to figure out the best ways to use the new resource. Perhaps the computer revolution will have a similar delayed effect. Some observers believe this may be starting to happen already, because productivity growth did pick up a bit in the late 1990s. It is still too early to say, however, whether this change will persist.

A more pessimistic scenario is that, after a period of rapid scientific and technological advance, we have entered a new phase of slower growth in

IN THE NEWS

A Solution to Africa's Problems

ECONOMIST JEFFREY SACHS HAS BEEN A prominent adviser to governments seeking to reform their economies and raise economic growth. He has also been a critic of the World Bank and the International Monetary Fund (IMF), the international policy organizations that dispense advice and money to struggling countries. Here Sachs discusses how the countries of Africa can escape their continuing poverty.

Growth in Africa: It Can Be Done

BY JEFFREY SACHS

In the old story, the peasant goes to the priest for advice on saving his dying chickens. The priest recommends prayer, but the chickens continue to die. The priest then recommends music for the chicken coop, but the deaths continue unabated. Pondering again, the priest recommends repainting the chicken coop in bright colours. Finally, all the chickens die. "What a shame," the priest tells the peasant. "I had so many more good ideas."

Since independence, African countries have looked to donor nations—often their former colonial rulers—and to the international finance institutions for guidance on growth. Indeed, since the onset of the African debt crises of the 1980s, the guidance has become a kind of economic receivership, with the policies of many African nations decided in a seemingly endless cycle of meetings with the IMF, the World Bank, donors, and creditors.

What a shame. So many good ideas, so few results. Output per head fell 0.7 percent between 1978 and 1987, and 0.6 percent during 1987–94. Some growth is estimated for 1995 but only at 0.6 percent—far below the faster-growing developing countries. . . .

The IMF and World Bank would be absolved of shared responsibility for slow growth if Africa were structurally incapable of growth rates seen in other parts of the world or if the continent's low growth were an impenetrable mystery. But Africa's growth rates are not huge mysteries. The evidence on cross-country growth suggests that Africa's chronically low growth can be explained by standard economic variables linked to identifiable (and remediable) policies. . . .

Studies of cross-country growth show that per capita growth is related to

- the initial income level of the country, with poorer countries tending to grow faster than richer countries;

- the extent of overall market orientation, including openness to trade, domestic market liberalization, private rather than state ownership, protection of private property rights, and low marginal tax rates;

- the national saving rate, which in turn is strongly affected by the government's own saving rate; and

- the geographic and resource structure of the economy. . . .

These four factors can account broadly for Africa's long-term growth predicament. While it should have grown faster than other developing areas because of relatively low income per head (and hence larger opportunity for "catch-up" growth), Africa grew more slowly. This was mainly because of much higher trade barriers; excessive tax knowledge, productivity, and incomes. Data from a longer span of history seem to support this conclusion. Figure 12-2 shows the average growth of real GDP per person in the developed world going back to 1870. The productivity slow-down is apparent in the last two entries: Around 1970, the growth rate slowed from 3.7 to 2.2 percent. But compared with earlier periods of history, the anomaly is not the slow growth of recent years but rather the rapid growth during the 1950s and 1960s. Perhaps the decades after World War II were a

rates; lower saving rates; and adverse structural conditions, including an unusually high incidence of inaccessibility to the sea (15 of 53 countries are land-locked). . . .

If the policies are largely to blame, why, then, were they adopted? The historical origins of Africa's antimarket orientation are not hard to discern. After almost a century of colonial depredations, African nations understandably if erroneously viewed open trade and foreign capital as a threat to national sovereignty. As in Sukarno's Indonesia, Nehru's India, and Peron's Argentina, "self-sufficiency" and "state leadership," including state ownership of much of industry, became the guideposts of the economy. As a result, most of Africa went into a largely self-imposed economic exile. . . .

Adam Smith in 1755 famously remarked that "little else is requisite to carry a state to the highest degrees of opulence from the lowest barbarism, but peace, easy taxes, and tolerable administration of justice." A growth agenda need not be long and complex. Take his points in turn.

Peace, of course, is not so easily guaranteed, but the conditions for peace on the continent are better than today's ghastly headlines would suggest. Several of the large-scale conflicts that have ravaged the continent are over or nearly so. . . . The ongoing disasters, such as in Liberia, Rwanda, and Somalia, would be better contained if the West were willing

to provide modest support to African-based peacekeeping efforts.

"Easy taxes" are well within the ambit of the IMF and World Bank. But here, the IMF stands guilty of neglect, if not malfeasance. African nations need simple, low taxes, with modest revenue targets as a share of GDP. Easy taxes are most essential in international trade, since successful growth will depend, more than anything else, on economic integration with the rest of the world. Africa's largely self-imposed exile from world markets can end quickly by cutting import tariffs and ending export taxes on agricultural exports. Corporate tax rates should be cut from rates of 40 percent and higher now prevalent in Africa, to rates between 20 percent and 30 percent, as in the outward-oriented East Asian economies. . . .

Adam Smith spoke of a "tolerable" administration of justice, not perfect justice. Market liberalization is the primary key to strengthening the rule of law. Free trade, currency convertibility, and automatic incorporation of business vastly reduce the scope for official corruption and allow the government to focus on the real public goods—internal public order, the judicial system, basic public health and education, and monetary stability. . . .

All of this is possible only if the government itself has held its own spending to the necessary minimum. The Asian economies show how to function with government spending of 20 percent of

GDP or less (China gets by with just 13 percent). Education can usefully absorb around 5 percent of GDP; health, another 3 percent; public administration, 2 percent; the army and police, 3 percent. Government investment spending can be held to 5 percent of GDP but only if the private sector is invited to provide infrastructure in telecommunications, port facilities, and power. . . .

This fiscal agenda excludes many popular areas for government spending. There is little room for transfers or social spending beyond education and health (though on my proposals, these would get a hefty 8 percent of GDP). Subsidies to publicly owned companies or marketing boards should be scrapped. Food and housing subsidies for urban workers cannot be financed. And, notably, interest payments on foreign debt are not budgeted for. This is because most bankrupt African states need a fresh start based on deep debt-reduction, which should be implemented in conjunction with far-reaching domestic reforms.

SOURCE: *The Economist*, June 29, 1996, pp. 19–21.

period of unusually rapid technological advance, and growth has slowed down simply because technological progress has returned to a more normal rate.

QUICK QUIZ: Describe three ways in which a government policymaker can try to raise the growth in living standards in a society. Are there any drawbacks to these policies?

Figure 12-2

THE GROWTH IN REAL GDP PER PERSON.   This figure shows the average growth rate of real GDP per person for sixteen advanced economies, including Canada, the major countries of Europe, the United States, Japan, and Australia. Notice that the growth rate rose substantially after 1950 and then fell after 1970.

SOURCE: Robert J. Barro and Xavier Sala-i-Martin, *Economic Growth* (New York: McGraw-Hill, 1995), p. 6.

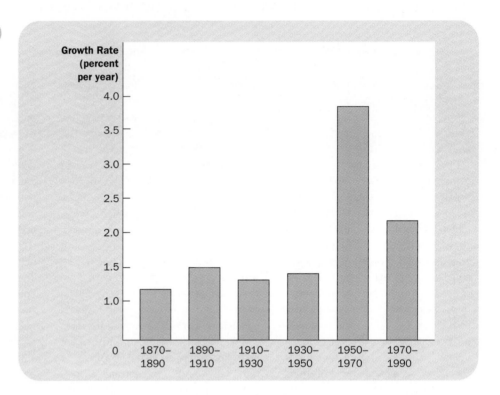

CONCLUSION: THE IMPORTANCE OF LONG-RUN GROWTH

In this chapter we have discussed what determines the standard of living in a nation and how policymakers can endeavour to raise the standard of living through policies that promote economic growth. Most of this chapter is summarized in one of the *Ten Principles of Economics:* A country's standard of living depends on its ability to produce goods and services. Policymakers who want to encourage growth in standards of living must aim to increase their nation's productive ability by encouraging rapid accumulation of the factors of production and ensuring that these factors are employed as effectively as possible.

Economists differ in their views of the role of government in promoting economic growth. At the very least, government can lend support to the invisible hand by maintaining property rights and political stability. More controversial is whether government should target and subsidize specific industries that might be especially important for technological progress. There is no doubt that these issues are among the most important in economics. The success of one generation's policymakers in learning and heeding the fundamental lessons about economic growth determines what kind of world the next generation will inherit.

Summary

- Economic prosperity, as measured by GDP per person, varies substantially around the world. The average income in the world's richest countries is more than ten times that in the world's poorest countries. Because growth rates of real GDP also vary substantially, the relative positions of countries can change dramatically over time.

- The standard of living in an economy depends on the economy's ability to produce goods and services. Productivity, in turn, depends on the amounts of physical capital, human capital, natural resources, and technological knowledge available to workers.

- Government policies can influence the economy's growth rate in many ways: encouraging saving and investment, encouraging investment from abroad,

fostering education, maintaining property rights and political stability, allowing free trade, controlling population growth, and promoting the research and development of new technologies.

- The accumulation of capital is subject to diminishing returns: The more capital an economy has, the less additional output the economy gets from an extra unit of capital. Because of diminishing returns, higher saving leads to higher growth for a period of time, but growth eventually slows down as the economy approaches a higher level of capital, productivity, and income. Also because of diminishing returns, the return to capital is especially high in poor countries. Other things equal, these countries can grow faster because of the catch-up effect.

Key Concepts

productivity, p. 243
physical capital, p. 244
human capital, p. 244

natural resources, p. 244
technological knowledge, p. 245
diminishing returns, p. 249

catch-up effect, p. 249

Questions for Review

1. What does the level of a nation's GDP measure? What does the growth rate of GDP measure? Would you rather live in a nation with a high level of GDP and a low growth rate, or in a nation with a low level of GDP and a high growth rate?

2. List and describe four determinants of productivity. P244

3. In what way is a university degree a form of capital?

4. Explain how higher saving leads to a higher standard of living. What might deter a policymaker from trying to raise the rate of saving?

5. Does a higher rate of saving lead to higher growth temporarily or indefinitely?

6. Why would removing a trade restriction, such as a tariff, lead to more rapid economic growth?

7. How does the rate of population growth influence the level of GDP per person?

8. Describe two ways in which the Canadian government tries to encourage advances in technological knowledge.

> ## Problems and Applications

1. Most countries, including Canada, import substantial amounts of goods and services from other countries. Yet the chapter says that a nation can enjoy a high standard of living only if it can produce a large quantity of goods and services itself. Can you reconcile these two facts?

2. List the capital inputs necessary to produce each of the following:
   a. cars
   b. high-school educations
   c. plane travel
   d. fruits and vegetables

3. Canadian income per person today is roughly nine times what it was a century ago. Many other countries have also experienced significant growth over that period. What are some specific ways in which your standard of living differs from that of your great-grandparents?

4. The chapter discusses how employment has declined relative to output in the farm sector. Can you think of another sector of the economy where the same phenomenon has occurred more recently? Would you consider the change in employment in this sector to represent a success or a failure from the standpoint of society as a whole?

5. Suppose that society decided to reduce consumption and increase investment.
   a. How would this change affect economic growth?
   b. What groups in society would benefit from this change? What groups might be hurt?

6. Societies choose what share of their resources to devote to consumption and what share to devote to investment. Some of these decisions involve private spending; others involve government spending.
   a. Describe some forms of private spending that represent consumption and some forms that represent investment.
   b. Describe some forms of government spending that represent consumption and some forms that represent investment.

7. What is the opportunity cost of investing in capital? Do you think a country can "over-invest" in capital? What is the opportunity cost of investing in human capital? Do you think a country can "over-invest" in human capital? Explain.

8. Suppose that an auto company owned entirely by German citizens opens a new factory in Quebec.
   a. What sort of foreign investment would this represent?
   b. What would be the effect of this investment on Canadian GDP? Would the effect on Canadian GNP be larger or smaller?

9. In the 1960s American investors made significant direct and portfolio investments in Canada. At the time, many Canadians were unhappy that this investment was occurring.
   a. In what way was it better for Canada to receive this American investment than not to receive it?
   b. In what way would it have been better still for Canadians to have done this investment?

10. In the countries of South Asia in 1992, only 56 young women were enrolled in secondary school for every 100 young men. Describe several ways in which greater educational opportunities for young women could lead to faster economic growth in these countries.

11. International data show a positive correlation between political stability and economic growth.
    a. Through what mechanism could political stability lead to strong economic growth?
    b. Through what mechanism could strong economic growth lead to political stability?

13

SAVING, INVESTMENT, AND THE FINANCIAL SYSTEM

IN THIS CHAPTER YOU WILL . . .

Learn about some of the important financial institutions in the Canadian economy

Consider how the financial system is related to key macroeconomic variables

Develop a model of the supply and demand for loanable funds in financial markets

Use the loanable-funds model to analyze various government policies

Consider how government budget deficits and surpluses affect the Canadian economy

Imagine that you have just graduated from university (with a degree in economics, of course) and you decide to start your own business—an economic forecasting firm. Before you make any money selling your forecasts, you have to incur substantial costs to set up your business. You have to buy computers with which to make your forecasts, as well as desks, chairs, and filing cabinets to furnish your new office. Each of these items is a type of capital that your firm will use to produce and sell its services.

How do you obtain the funds to invest in these capital goods? Perhaps you are able to pay for them out of your past savings. More likely, however, like most entrepreneurs, you do not have enough money of your own to finance the start of your business. As a result, you have to get the money you need from other sources.

There are various ways for you to finance these capital investments. You could borrow the money, perhaps from a bank or from a friend or relative. In this case, you would promise not only to return the money at a later date but also to pay interest for the use of the money. Alternatively, you could convince someone to provide the money you need for your business in exchange for a share of your future profits, whatever they might happen to be. In either case, your investment in computers and office equipment is being financed by someone else's saving.

financial system

the group of institutions in the economy that help to match one person's saving with another person's investment

The **financial system** consists of those institutions in the economy that help to match one person's saving with another person's investment. As we discussed in the previous chapter, saving and investment are key ingredients to long-run economic growth: When a country saves a large portion of its GDP, more resources are available for investment in capital, and higher capital raises a country's productivity and living standard. The previous chapter, however, did not explain how the economy coordinates saving and investment. At any time, some people want to save some of their income for the future, and others want to borrow in order to finance investments in new and growing businesses. What brings these two groups of people together? What ensures that the supply of funds from those who want to save balances the demand for funds from those who want to invest?

This chapter examines how the financial system works. First, we discuss the large variety of institutions that make up the financial system in our economy. Second, we discuss the relationship between the financial system and some key macroeconomic variables—notably saving and investment. Third, we develop a model of the supply and demand for funds in financial markets. In the model, the interest rate is the price that adjusts to balance supply and demand. The model shows how various government policies affect the interest rate and, thereby, society's allocation of scarce resources.

FINANCIAL INSTITUTIONS IN THE CANADIAN ECONOMY

At the broadest level, the financial system moves the economy's scarce resources from savers (people who spend less than they earn) to borrowers (people who spend more than they earn). Savers save for various reasons—to put a child through university in several years or to retire comfortably in several decades. Similarly, borrowers borrow for various reasons—to buy a house in which to live or to start a business with which to make a living. Savers supply their money to the financial system with the expectation that they will get it back with interest at a later date. Borrowers demand money from the financial system with the knowledge that they will be required to pay it back with interest at a later date.

The financial system is made up of various financial institutions that help coordinate savers and borrowers. As a prelude to analyzing the economic forces that drive the financial system, let's discuss the most important of these institutions. Financial institutions can be grouped into two categories—financial markets and financial intermediaries. We consider each category in turn.

FINANCIAL MARKETS

Financial markets are the institutions through which a person who wants to save can directly supply funds to a person who wants to borrow. The two most important financial markets in our economy are the bond market and the stock market.

financial markets
financial institutions through which savers can directly provide funds to borrowers

The Bond Market   When Intel, the giant maker of computer chips, wants to borrow to finance construction of a new factory, it can borrow directly from the public. It does this by selling bonds. A **bond** is a certificate of indebtedness that specifies the obligations of the borrower to the holder of the bond. Put simply, a bond is an IOU. It identifies the time at which the loan will be repaid, called the *date of maturity*, and the rate of interest that will be paid periodically until the loan matures. The buyer of a bond gives his or her money to Intel in exchange for this promise of interest and eventual repayment of the amount borrowed (called the *principal*). The buyer can hold the bond until maturity or can sell the bond at an earlier date to someone else.

bond
a certificate of indebtedness

There are literally millions of different bonds in the Canadian economy. When large corporations, the federal government, or provincial governments need to borrow to finance the purchase of a new factory, a new jet fighter, or a new school, they usually do so by issuing bonds. If you look at the business section of your local newspaper, you will find a listing of the prices and interest rates on some of the most important bond issues. Although these bonds differ in many ways, two characteristics of bonds are most important.

The first characteristic is a bond's *term*—the length of time until the bond matures. Some bonds have short terms, such as a few months, while others have terms as long as 30 years. (The British government has even issued a bond that never matures, called a *perpetuity*. This bond pays interest forever, but the principal is never repaid.) The interest rate on a bond depends, in part, on its term. Long-term bonds are riskier than short-term bonds because holders of long-term bonds have to wait longer for repayment of principal. If a holder of a long-term bond needs his or her money earlier than the distant date of maturity, he or she has no choice but to sell the bond to someone else, perhaps at a reduced price. To compensate for this risk, long-term bonds usually pay higher interest rates than short-term bonds.

The second important characteristic of a bond is its *credit risk*—the probability that the borrower will fail to pay some of the interest or principal. Such a failure to pay is called a *default*. Borrowers can (and sometimes do) default on their loans by declaring bankruptcy. When bond buyers perceive that the probability of default is high, they demand a higher interest rate to compensate them for this risk. Because the Canadian government is considered a safe credit risk, federal government bonds tend to pay low interest rates. Provincial governments also issue bonds, but because the provinces are considered to be a somewhat greater credit risk, they pay a higher rate of interest than federal government bonds. An interesting source of credit risk in Canada is the risk of Quebec separation. The financial community's concerns about possible separation affect the interest rate paid on all government bonds in Canada. The greatest impact, however, is on the interest rate paid on Quebec government bonds. Financially shaky corporations raise money by issuing *junk bonds*, which pay considerably higher interest rates than government bonds.

Buyers of bonds can judge credit risk by checking with various private agencies, such as Standard & Poor's, which rate the credit risk of different bonds.

stock

a claim to partial ownership in a firm

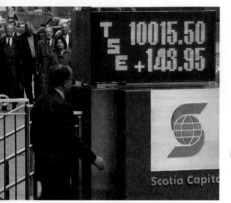

THE TORONTO STOCK EXCHANGE

The Stock Market Another way for Intel to raise funds to build a new semiconductor factory is to sell stock in the company. **Stock** represents ownership in a firm and is, therefore, a claim on the profits that the firm makes. For example, if Intel sells a total of 1 000 000 shares of stock, then each share represents ownership of 1/1 000 000 of the business.

The sale of stock to raise money is called *equity finance*, whereas the sale of bonds is called *debt finance*. Although corporations use both equity and debt finance to raise money for new investments, stocks and bonds are very different. The owner of shares of Intel stock is a part owner of Intel; the owner of an Intel bond is a creditor of the corporation. If Intel is very profitable, the stockholders enjoy the benefits of these profits, whereas the bondholders get only the interest on their bonds. And if Intel runs into financial difficulty, the bondholders are paid what they are due before stockholders receive anything at all. Compared with bonds, stocks offer the holder both a higher risk and a potentially higher return.

After a corporation issues stock by selling shares to the public, these shares trade among stockholders on organized stock exchanges. In these transactions, the corporation itself receives no money when its stock changes hands. The most important stock exchanges in the U.S. economy are the New York Stock Exchange and NASDAQ (National Association of Securities Dealers Automated Quotation system). In Canada, the Toronto Stock Exchange (TSE) is the most important. A more speculative stock exchange that raises money for junior companies is the Canadian Venture Exchange located in Calgary. Most of the world's countries have their own stock exchanges on which the shares of local companies trade.

The prices at which shares trade on stock exchanges are determined by the supply and demand for the stock in these companies. Because stock represents ownership in a corporation, the demand for a stock (and thus its price) reflects people's perception of the corporation's future profitability. When people become optimistic about a company's future, they raise their demand for its stock and thereby bid up the price of a share of stock. Conversely, when people come to expect a company to have little profit or even losses, the price of a share falls.

Various stock indexes are available to monitor the overall level of stock prices. A *stock index* is computed as an average of a group of stock prices. The most famous stock index is the Dow Jones Industrial Average, which has been computed regularly since 1896. It is now based on the prices of the stocks of 30 major U.S. companies, such as General Motors, General Electric, Microsoft, Coca-Cola, AT&T, and IBM. The best-known and most closely watched stock index in Canada is the TSE 300, which is based on the prices of 300 major firms listed on the TSE. Because stock prices reflect expected profitability, these stock indexes are watched closely as possible indicators of future economic conditions.

FINANCIAL INTERMEDIARIES

financial intermediaries

financial institutions through which savers can indirectly provide funds to borrowers

Financial intermediaries are financial institutions through which savers can indirectly provide funds to borrowers. The term *intermediary* reflects the role of these institutions in standing between savers and borrowers. Here we consider two of the most important financial intermediaries—banks and mutual funds.

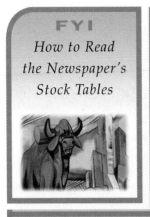

FYI

How to Read the Newspaper's Stock Tables

Most daily newspapers include stock tables, which contain information about recent trading in the stocks of several thousand companies. Here is the kind of information these tables usually provide:

◆ *Price.* The single most important piece of information about a stock is the price of a share. The newspaper usually presents several prices. The "last" or "closing" price is the price of the last transaction that occurred before the stock exchange closed the previous day. Many newspapers also give the "high" and "low" prices over the past day of trading and, sometimes, over the past year as well.

◆ *Volume.* Most newspapers present the number of shares sold during the past day of trading. This figure is called the *daily volume.*

◆ *Dividend.* Corporations pay out some of their profits to their stockholders; this amount is called the *dividend.* (Profits not paid out are called *retained earnings* and are used by the corporation for additional investment.) Newspapers often report the dividend paid over the previous year for each share of stock. They sometimes

report the *dividend yield,* which is the dividend expressed as a percentage of the stock's price.

◆ *Price–earnings ratio.* A corporation's earnings, or profit, are the amount of revenue it receives for the sale of its products minus its costs of production as measured by its accountants. Earnings per share are the company's total earnings divided by the number of shares of stock outstanding. Companies use some of their earnings to pay dividends to stockholders; the rest is kept in the firm to make new investments. The price–earnings ratio, often called the P/E, is the price of a corporation's stock divided by the amount the corporation earned per share over the past year. Historically, the typical price–earnings ratio is about 15. A higher P/E indicates that a corporation's stock is expensive relative to its recent earnings; this might indicate either that people expect earnings to rise in the future or that the stock is overvalued. Conversely, a lower P/E indicates that a corporation's stock is cheap relative to its recent earnings; this might indicate either that people expect earnings to fall or that the stock is undervalued.

Why does the newspaper report all these data every day? Many people who invest their savings in stock follow these numbers closely when deciding which stocks to buy and sell. By contrast, other stockholders follow a buy-and-hold strategy: They buy the stock of well-run companies, hold it for long periods of time, and do not respond to the daily fluctuations reported in the paper.

| 52 Weeks | | Stock | Sym | Div | Yld % | PE | Vol 100s | Hi | Lo | Close | Net Chg |
Hi	Lo										
6.35	3.60	PerkinPap	PKN	0.12	2.9	22.8	5	4.10	4.10	4.10	
18.75	0.87	PerleSys	PL				75	1.49	1.19	1.48	+ 0.28
38.60	19.00	PetroCan	PCA	0.40	1.1	17.4	6865	37.75	36.45	36.50	– 0.70
2.65	1.20	Petrobank	PBG			8.5	235	1.50	1.45	1.45	

Labels: Highest and lowest price of the stock over the past year — Name of company — Symbol for company's stock — Dividend amount — Dividend yield — Price–earnings ratio — Trading volume over the previous day — Highest and lowest price over the previous day — Last price at which the stock traded — Change in closing price from the day before

Banks

If the owner of a small grocery store wants to finance an expansion of his or her business, he or she probably takes a strategy quite different from Intel. Unlike Intel, a small grocer would find it difficult to raise funds in the bond and stock markets. Most buyers of stocks and bonds prefer to buy those issued by larger, more familiar companies. The small grocer, therefore, most likely finances the business expansion with a loan from a local bank.

Banks are the financial intermediaries with which people are most familiar. A primary job of banks is to take in deposits from people who want to save and use these deposits to make loans to people who want to borrow. Banks pay depositors interest on their deposits and charge borrowers slightly higher interest on their loans. The difference between these rates of interest covers the banks' costs and returns some profit to the owners of the banks.

Besides being financial intermediaries, banks play a second important role in the economy: They facilitate purchases of goods and services by allowing people to write cheques against their deposits. In other words, banks help create a special asset that people can use as a *medium of exchange.* A medium of exchange is an item that people can easily use to engage in transactions. A bank's role in providing a medium of exchange distinguishes it from many other financial institutions. Stocks and bonds, like bank deposits, are a possible *store of value* for the wealth that people have accumulated in past saving, but access to this wealth is not as easy, cheap, and immediate as just writing a cheque. For now, we ignore this second role of banks, but we will return to it when we discuss the monetary system in Chapter 15.

Mutual Funds   A financial intermediary of increasing importance in the Canadian economy is the mutual fund. A **mutual fund** is an institution that sells shares to the public and uses the proceeds to buy a selection, or *portfolio,* of various types of stocks, bonds, or both stocks and bonds. The shareholder of the mutual fund accepts all of the risk and return associated with the portfolio. If the value of the portfolio rises, the shareholder benefits; if the value of the portfolio falls, the shareholder suffers the loss.

The primary advantage of mutual funds is that they allow people with small amounts of money to diversify. Buyers of stocks and bonds are well advised to heed the adage "Don't put all your eggs in one basket." Because the value of any single stock or bond is tied to the fortunes of one company, holding a single kind of stock or bond is very risky. By contrast, people who hold a diverse portfolio of stocks and bonds face less risk because they have only a small stake in each company. Mutual funds make this diversification easy. With only a few hundred dollars, a person can buy shares in a mutual fund and, indirectly, become the part owner or creditor of hundreds of major companies. For this service, the company operating the mutual fund charges shareholders a fee, usually between 0.5 and 2.0 percent of assets each year.

mutual fund

an institution that sells shares to the public and uses the proceeds to buy a portfolio of stocks and bonds

ARLO AND JANIS by Jimmy Johnson

A second advantage claimed by mutual fund companies is that mutual funds give ordinary people access to the skills of professional money managers. The managers of most mutual funds pay close attention to the developments and prospects of the companies in which they buy stock. These managers buy the stock of those companies that they view as having a profitable future and sell the stock of companies with less promising prospects. This professional management, it is argued, should increase the return that mutual fund depositors earn on their savings.

Financial economists, however, are often skeptical of this second argument. With thousands of money managers paying close attention to each company's prospects, the price of a company's stock is usually a good reflection of the company's true value. As a result, it is hard to "beat the market" by buying good stocks and selling bad ones. In fact, mutual funds called *index funds*, which buy all the stocks in a given stock index, perform somewhat better on average than mutual funds that take advantage of active management by professional money managers. The explanation for the superior performance of index funds is that they keep costs low by buying and selling very rarely and by not having to pay the salaries of the professional money managers.

SUMMING UP

The Canadian economy contains a large variety of financial institutions. In addition to the bond market, the stock market, banks, and mutual funds, there are pension funds, credit unions, insurance companies, and even the local loan shark. These institutions differ in many ways. When analyzing the macroeconomic role of the financial system, however, it is more important to keep in mind the similarity of these institutions than the differences. These financial institutions all serve the same goal—directing the resources of savers into the hands of borrowers.

▌**QUICK QUIZ:**   What is stock? What is a bond? How are they different? How are they similar?

SAVING AND INVESTMENT IN THE NATIONAL INCOME ACCOUNTS

Events that occur within the financial system are central to understanding developments in the overall economy. As we have just seen, the institutions that make up this system—the bond market, the stock market, banks, and mutual funds—have the role of coordinating the economy's saving and investment. And as we saw in the previous chapter, saving and investment are important determinants of long-run growth in GDP and living standards. As a result, macroeconomists need to understand how financial markets work and how various events and policies affect them.

As a starting point for an analysis of financial markets, we discuss in this section the key macroeconomic variables that measure activity in these markets. Our

IN THE NEWS

The Stock Market Boom of the 1990s

NORTH AMERICAN STOCK MARKETS EXPERIenced a dramatic increase in stock prices during the 1990s. The following article tries to explain this remarkable boom. It suggests that people bid up stock prices because they came to view stocks as less risky than they previously thought. The increase in stock prices peaked in the fall of 2000 and was followed by a decline in values at the time of this writing (summer 2001). It is interesting to read this newspaper article in light of this recent experience.

Are Stocks Overvalued? Not a Chance

BY JAMES K. GLASSMAN
AND KEVIN A. HASSETT

The Dow Jones Industrial Average has returned more than 200 percent over the past five years, and the past three have set an all-time record. So it's hardly surprising that many observers worry the stock market is overvalued. One of the most popular measures of valuation, the ratio of a stock's price to its earnings per share, P/E, is close to an all-time high. The P/E of the average stock on the Dow is 22.5, meaning that it costs $22.50 to buy $1 in profits—or, conversely, that an investor's return (earnings divided by price) is just 4.4 percent, vs. 5.9 percent for long-term Treasury bonds.

Yet Warren Buffett, chairman of Berkshire Hathaway Corp. and the most successful large-scale investor of our time, told shareholders in a March 14 letter that "there is no reason to think of stocks as generally overvalued" as long as interest rates remain low and businesses continue to operate as profitably as they have in recent years. Investors were buoyed by this statement, even though Mr. Buffett provided no analysis to back up his assertion.

Mr. Buffett is right—and we have the numbers and the theory to back him up. Worries about overvaluation, we believe, are based on a serious and widespread misunderstanding of the returns and risks associated with equities. We are not so foolish as to predict the short-term course of stocks, but we are not reluctant to state that, based on modest assumptions about interest rates and profit levels, current P/E levels give us no great concern—nor would levels as much as twice as high.

The fact is that if you hold stocks instead of bonds the amount of money flowing into your pockets will be higher over time. Why? Both bonds and stocks provide their owners with a flow of cash over time. For bonds, the arithmetic is simple: If you buy a $10 000 bond paying 6 percent interest today, you'll receive $600 every year. For equities, the math is more complicated: Assume that a stock currently yields 2 percent, or $2 for each share priced at $100. Say you own 100 shares; total dividend payments are $200—much lower than for bonds.

But wait. There is a big difference. Profits grow over time. If that dividend should increase with profits, say at a rate of 5 percent annually, then, by the 30th year, your annual dividend payment will be over $800, or one-third more than the bond is yielding. The price of the stock almost certainly will have risen as well.

emphasis here is not on behaviour but on accounting. *Accounting* refers to how various numbers are defined and added up. A personal accountant might help an individual add up his or her income and expenses. A national income accountant does the same thing for the economy as a whole. The national income accounts include, in particular, GDP and the many related statistics.

The rules of national income accounting include several important identities. Recall that an *identity* is an equation that must be true because of the way the variables in the equation are defined. Identities are useful to keep in mind because they clarify how different variables are related to one another. Here we consider some accounting identities that shed light on the macroeconomic role of financial markets.

By this simple exercise, we can see that stocks—even with their profits growing at a moderate 5 percent—will return far more than bonds over long periods. Over the past 70 years, stocks have annually returned 4.8 percentage points more than long-term U.S. Treasury bonds and 6.8 points more than Treasury bills, according to Ibbotson Associates Inc., a Chicago research firm.

But isn't that extra reward—what economists call the "equity premium"—merely the bonus paid by the market to investors who accept higher risk, since returns for stocks are so much more uncertain than for bonds? To this question, we respond: What extra risk?

In his book *Stocks for the Long Run*, Jeremy J. Siegel of the University of Pennsylvania concludes: "It is widely known that stock returns, on average, exceed bonds in the long run. But it is little known that in the long run, the risks in stocks are less than those found in bonds or even bills!" Mr. Siegel looked at every twenty-year holding period from 1802 to 1992 and found that the worst real return for stocks was an annual average of 1.2 percent and the best was an annual average of 12.6 percent. For long-term bonds, the range was *minus* 3.1 percent to plus 8.8 percent; for T-bills, minus 3.0 percent to plus 8.3 percent.

Based on these findings, it would seem that there should be no need for an equity risk premium at all—and that the correct valuation for the stock market would be one that equalizes the present value of cash flow between stocks and bonds in the long run. Think of the market as offering you two assets, one that will pay you $1000 over the next 30 years in a steady stream and another that, just as surely, will pay you the $1000, but the cash flow will vary from year to year. Assuming you're investing for the long term, you will value them about the same. . . .

Allow us now to suggest a hypothesis about the huge returns posted by the stock market over the past few years: As mutual funds have advertised the reduction of risk acquired by taking the long view, the risk premium required by shareholders has gradually drifted down. Since Siegel's results suggest that the correct risk premium might be zero, this drift downward—and the corresponding trend toward higher stock prices—may not be over. . . . In the current environment, we are very comfortable both in holding stocks and in saying that pundits who claim the market is overvalued are foolish.

SOURCE: *The Wall Street Journal*, Monday, March 30, 1998, p. A18.

SOME IMPORTANT IDENTITIES

Recall that gross domestic product (GDP) is both total income in an economy and the total expenditure on the economy's output of goods and services. GDP (denoted as Y) is divided into four components of expenditure: consumption (C), investment (I), government purchases (G), and net exports (NX). We write

$$Y = C + I + G + NX.$$

This equation is an identity because every dollar of expenditure that shows up on the left-hand side also shows up in one of the four components on the right-hand side. Because of the way each of the variables is defined and measured, this equation must always hold.

In this chapter, we simplify our analysis by assuming that the economy we are examining is closed. A *closed economy* is one that does not interact with other economies. In particular, a closed economy does not engage in international trade in goods and services, nor does it engage in international borrowing and lending. Of course, actual economies are *open economies*—that is, they interact with other economies around the world. (We will examine the macroeconomics of open economies later in this book.) Nonetheless, assuming a closed economy is a useful simplification by which we can learn some lessons that apply to all economies. Moreover, this assumption applies perfectly to the world economy (inasmuch as interplanetary trade is not yet common).

Because a closed economy does not engage in international trade, imports and exports are exactly zero. Therefore, net exports (*NX*) are also zero. In this case, we can write

$$Y = C + I + G.$$

This equation states that GDP is the sum of consumption, investment, and government purchases. Each unit of output sold in a closed economy is consumed, invested, or bought by the government.

To see what this identity can tell us about financial markets, subtract C and G from both sides of this equation. We obtain

$$Y - C - G = I.$$

The left-hand side of this equation ($Y - C - G$) is the total income in the economy that remains after paying for consumption and government purchases. This amount is called **national saving,** or just **saving,** and is denoted S. Substituting S for $Y - C - G$, we can write the last equation as

$$S = I.$$

This equation states that saving equals investment.

To understand the meaning of national saving, it is helpful to manipulate the definition a bit more. Let T denote the amount that the government collects from households in taxes minus the amount it pays back to households in the form of transfer payments (such as Employment Insurance and welfare). We can then write national saving in either of two ways:

$$S = Y - C - G$$

or

$$S = (Y - T - C) + (T - G).$$

These equations are the same, because the two Ts in the second equation cancel each other, but each reveals a different way of thinking about national saving. In particular, the second equation separates national saving into two pieces: private saving ($Y - T - C$) and public saving ($T - G$).

Consider each of these two pieces. **Private saving** is the amount of income that households have left after paying their taxes and paying for their consumption. In particular, because households receive income of Y, pay taxes of T, and spend C on consumption, private saving is $Y - T - C$. **Public saving** is the amount of tax reve-

national saving (saving)
the total income in the economy that remains after paying for consumption and government purchases

private saving
the income that households have left after paying for taxes and consumption

public saving
the tax revenue that the government has left after paying for its spending

nue that the government has left after paying for its spending. The government receives T in tax revenue and spends G on goods and services. If T exceeds G, the government runs a **budget surplus** because it receives more money than it spends. This surplus of $T - G$ represents public saving. If the government spends more than it receives in tax revenue, then G is larger than T. In this case, the government runs a **budget deficit**, and public saving $T - G$ is a negative number.

budget surplus
an excess of tax revenue over government spending

budget deficit
a shortfall of tax revenue from government spending

Now consider how these accounting identities are related to financial markets. The equation $S = I$ reveals an important fact: *For the economy as a whole, saving must be equal to investment.* Yet this fact raises some important questions: What mechanisms lie behind this identity? What coordinates those people who are deciding how much to save and those people who are deciding how much to invest? The answer is the financial system. The bond market, the stock market, banks, mutual funds, and other financial markets and intermediaries stand between the two sides of the $S = I$ equation. They take in the nation's saving and direct it to the nation's investment.

THE MEANING OF SAVING AND INVESTMENT

The terms *saving* and *investment* can sometimes be confusing. Most people use these terms casually and sometimes interchangeably. By contrast, the macroeconomists who put together the national income accounts use these terms carefully and distinctly.

Consider an example. Suppose that Larry earns more than he spends and deposits his unspent income in a bank or uses it to buy a bond or some stock from a corporation. Because Larry's income exceeds his consumption, he adds to the nation's saving. Larry might think of himself as "investing" his money, but a macroeconomist would call Larry's act saving rather than investment.

In the language of macroeconomics, investment refers to the purchase of new capital, such as equipment or buildings. When Moe borrows from the bank to build himself a new house, he adds to the nation's investment. Similarly, when the Curly Corporation sells some stock and uses the proceeds to build a new factory, it also adds to the nation's investment.

Although the accounting identity $S = I$ shows that saving and investment are equal for the economy as a whole, this does not have to be true for every individual household or firm. Larry's saving can be greater than his investment, and he can deposit the excess in a bank. Moe's saving can be less than his investment, and he can borrow the shortfall from a bank. Banks and other financial institutions make these individual differences between saving and investment possible by allowing one person's saving to finance another person's investment.

QUICK QUIZ: Define *private saving, public saving, national saving,* and *investment.* How are they related?

THE MARKET FOR LOANABLE FUNDS

Having discussed some of the important financial institutions in our economy and the macroeconomic role of these institutions, we are ready to build a model of financial markets. Our purpose in building this model is to explain how financial markets coordinate the economy's saving and investment. The model also gives us a tool with which we can analyze various government policies that influence saving and investment.

To keep things simple, we assume that the economy has only one financial market, called the **market for loanable funds.** All savers go to this market to deposit their saving, and all borrowers go to this market to get their loans. Thus, the term *loanable funds* refers to all income that people have chosen to save and lend out rather than use for their own consumption. In the market for loanable funds, there is one interest rate, which is both the return to saving and the cost of borrowing.

The assumption of a single financial market, of course, is not literally true. As we have seen, the economy has many types of financial institutions. But, as we discussed in Chapter 2, the art in building an economic model is simplifying the world in order to explain it. For our purposes here, we can ignore the diversity of financial institutions and assume that the economy has a single financial market.

market for loanable funds

the market in which those who want to save supply funds and those who want to borrow to invest demand funds

SUPPLY AND DEMAND FOR LOANABLE FUNDS

The economy's market for loanable funds, like other markets in the economy, is governed by supply and demand. To understand how the market for loanable funds operates, therefore, we first look at the sources of supply and demand in that market.

"Whoops! There go those darned interest rates again!"

The supply of loanable funds comes from those people who have some extra income they want to save and lend out. This lending can occur directly, such as when a household buys a bond from a firm, or it can occur indirectly, such as when a household makes a deposit in a bank, which in turn uses the funds to make loans. In both cases, saving is the source of the supply of loanable funds.

The demand for loanable funds comes from households and firms that wish to borrow to make investments. This demand includes families taking out mortgages to buy homes. It also includes firms borrowing to buy new equipment or build factories. In both cases, investment is the source of the demand for loanable funds.

The interest rate is the price of a loan. It represents the amount that borrowers pay for loans and the amount that lenders receive on their saving. Because a high interest rate makes borrowing more expensive, the quantity of loanable funds demanded falls as the interest rate rises. Similarly, because a high interest rate makes saving more attractive, the quantity of loanable funds supplied rises as the interest rate rises. In other words, the demand curve for loanable funds slopes downward, and the supply curve for loanable funds slopes upward.

Figure 13-1 shows the interest rate that balances the supply and demand for loanable funds. In the equilibrium shown, the interest rate is 5 percent, and the quantity of loanable funds demanded and the quantity of loanable funds supplied both equal $120 billion. The adjustment of the interest rate to the equilibrium level occurs for the usual reasons. If the interest rate were lower than the equilibrium level, the quantity of loanable funds supplied would be less than the quantity of loanable funds demanded. The resulting shortage of loanable funds would encourage lenders to raise the interest rate they charge. Conversely, if the interest rate were higher than the equilibrium level, the quantity of loanable funds supplied would exceed the quantity of loanable funds demanded. As lenders competed for the scarce borrowers, interest rates would be driven down. In this way, the interest rate approaches the equilibrium level at which the supply and demand for loanable funds exactly balance.

Recall that economists distinguish between the real interest rate and the nominal interest rate. The nominal interest rate is the interest rate as usually reported—

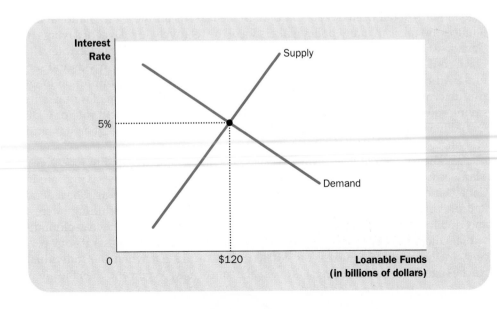

Figure 13-1

THE MARKET FOR LOANABLE FUNDS.   The interest rate in the economy adjusts to balance the supply and demand for loanable funds. The supply of loanable funds comes from national saving, including both private saving and public saving. The demand for loanable funds comes from firms and households that want to borrow for purposes of investment. Here the equilibrium interest rate is 5 percent, and $120 billion of loanable funds are supplied and demanded.

the monetary return to saving and cost of borrowing. The real interest rate is the nominal interest rate corrected for inflation; it equals the nominal interest rate minus the inflation rate. Because inflation erodes the value of money over time, the real interest rate more accurately reflects the real return to saving and cost of borrowing. Therefore, the supply and demand for loanable funds depend on the real (rather than nominal) interest rate, and the equilibrium in Figure 13-1 should be interpreted as determining the real interest rate in the economy. For the rest of this chapter, when you see the term *interest rate,* you should remember that we are talking about the real interest rate.

This model of the supply and demand for loanable funds shows that financial markets work much like other markets in the economy. In the market for milk, for instance, the price of milk adjusts so that the quantity of milk supplied balances the quantity of milk demanded. In this way, the invisible hand coordinates the behaviour of dairy farmers and the behaviour of milk drinkers. Once we realize that saving represents the supply of loanable funds and investment represents the demand, we can see how the invisible hand coordinates saving and investment. When the interest rate adjusts to balance supply and demand in the market for loanable funds, it coordinates the behaviour of people who want to save (the suppliers of loanable funds) and the behaviour of people who want to invest (the demanders of loanable funds).

We can now use this analysis of the market for loanable funds to examine various government policies that affect the economy's saving and investment. Because this model is just supply and demand in a particular market, we analyze any policy using the three steps discussed in Chapter 4. First, we decide whether the policy shifts the supply curve or the demand curve. Second, we determine the direction of the shift. Third, we use the supply-and-demand diagram to see how the equilibrium changes.

POLICY 1: TAXES AND SAVING

Canadian families save a smaller fraction of their incomes than their counterparts in many other countries, such as Japan and Germany, but they save slightly more than families in the United States. Although the reasons for these international differences are unclear, many policymakers view the relatively low level of savings in Canada as a major problem. One of the *Ten Principles of Economics* in Chapter 1 is that a country's standard of living depends on its ability to produce goods and services. And, as we discussed in the preceding chapter, saving is an important long-run determinant of a nation's productivity. If Canada could somehow raise its saving rate to the level that prevails in other countries, the growth rate of GDP would increase, and over time, Canadian citizens would enjoy a higher standard of living.

Another of the *Ten Principles of Economics* is that people respond to incentives. Many economists have used this principle to suggest that the low saving rate in Canada is at least partly attributable to tax laws that discourage saving. The federal and provincial governments collect revenue by taxing income, including interest and dividend income. To see the effects of this policy, consider a 25-year-old individual who saves $1000 and buys a 30-year bond that pays an interest rate of 9 percent. In the absence of taxes, the $1000 grows to $13 268 when the individual reaches age 55. Yet if that interest is taxed at a rate of, say, 33 percent, then the after-

FYI

Present Value

Imagine that someone offered to give you $100 today or $100 in ten years. Which would you choose? This is an easy question. Getting $100 today is clearly better, because you can always deposit the money in a bank, still have it in ten years, and earn interest along the way. The lesson: Money today is more valuable than the same amount of money in the future.

Now consider a harder question: Imagine that someone offered you $100 today or $200 in ten years. Which would you choose? To answer this question, you need some way to compare sums of money from different points in time. Economists do this with a concept called present value. The *present value* of any future sum of money is the amount today that would be needed, at current interest rates, to produce that future sum.

To learn how to use the concept of present value, let's work through a couple of simple problems:

Question: If you put $100 in a bank account today, how much will it be worth in *N* years? That is, what will be the future value of this $100?

Answer: Let's use *r* to denote the interest rate expressed in decimal form (so an interest rate of 5 percent means $r = 0.05$). If interest is paid each year, and if the interest paid remains in the bank account to earn more interest (a process called *compounding*), the $100 will become $(1 + r) \times \$100$ after one year, $(1 + r) \times (1 + r) \times \$100$ after two years, $(1 + r) \times (1 + r) \times (1 + r) \times \$100$ after three years, and so on. After *N* years, the $100 becomes $(1 + r)^N \times \$100$. For example, if we are investing at an interest rate of 5 percent for ten years, then the future value of the $100 will be $(1.05)^{10} \times \$100$, which is $163.

Question: Now suppose you are going to be paid $200 in *N* years. What is the present value of this future payment? That is, how much would you have to deposit in a bank right now to yield $200 in *N* years?

Answer: To answer this question, just turn the previous answer on its head. In the last question, we computed a future value from a present value by *multiplying* by the factor $(1 + r)^N$. To compute a present value from a future value, we *divide* by the factor $(1 + r)^N$. Thus, the present value of $200 in *N* years is $\$200/(1 + r)^N$. If that amount is deposited in a bank today, after *N* years it will become

$(1 + r)^N \times [\$200/(1 + r)^N]$, which is $200. For instance, if the interest rate is 5 percent, the present value of $200 in ten years is $\$200/(1.05)^{10}$, which is $123.

This illustrates the general formula: *If r is the interest rate, then an amount X to be received in N years has present value of* $X/(1 + r)^N$.

Let's now return to our earlier question: Should you choose $100 today or $200 in ten years? We can infer from our calculation of present value that if the interest rate is 5 percent, you should prefer the $200 in ten years. The future $200 has a present value of $123, which is greater than $100. You are, therefore, better off waiting for the future sum.

Notice that the answer to our question depends on the interest rate. If the interest rate were 8 percent, then the $200 in ten years would have a present value of $\$200/(1.08)^{10}$, which is only $93. In this case, you should take the $100 today. Why should the interest rate matter for your choice? The answer is that the higher the interest rate, the more you can earn by depositing your money at the bank, so the more attractive getting $100 today becomes.

The concept of present value is useful in many applications, including the decisions that companies face when evaluating investment projects. For instance, imagine that General Motors is thinking about building a new automobile factory. Suppose that the factory will cost $100 million today and will yield the company $200 million in ten years. Should General Motors undertake the project? You can see that this decision is exactly like the one we have been studying. To make its decision, the company will compare the present value of the $200 million return to the $100 million cost.

The company's decision, therefore, will depend on the interest rate. If the interest rate is 5 percent, then the present value of the $200 million return from the factory is $123 million, and the company will choose to pay the $100 million cost. By contrast, if the interest rate is 8 percent, then the present value of the return is only $93 million, and the company will decide to forgo the project. Thus, the concept of present value helps explain why investment—and thus the quantity of loanable funds demanded—declines when the interest rate rises.

Here is another application of present value: Suppose you win a million-dollar lottery, but the prize is going to be paid out as $20 000 a year for 50 years. How much is the prize really worth? After performing 50 calculations similar to those above (one calculation for each payment) and adding up the results, you would learn that the present value of this prize at a 7 percent interest rate is only $276 000.

tax interest rate is only 6 percent. In this case, the $1000 grows to only $5743 after 30 years. The tax on interest income substantially reduces the future payoff from current saving and, as a result, reduces the incentive for people to save.

In response to this problem, economists favour changes to the tax system that encourage greater saving. An important change to the Canadian tax system that most economists supported was the introduction of the federal Goods and Services Tax (GST) in 1991. The GST is a consumption tax. Under a consumption tax, income that is saved is not taxed, so the tax clearly encourages greater saving. The sales tax that provinces use to collect revenue is another example of a consumption tax. The only province not currently collecting a sales tax is Alberta but the evidence in favour of collecting more revenue from a sales tax and less from the income taxes as a way of encouraging greater savings is so strong that tax economists have recently urged the province to introduce such a tax. Another change to the tax system that would encourage saving is an increase in the amount that people can contribute to registered retirement savings plans (RRSPs). By buying an RRSP, people reduce the amount of their income that is subject to income tax. In this way, saving is encouraged. Let's consider the effect of such saving incentives on the market for loanable funds, as illustrated in Figure 13-2.

First, which curve would these tax changes affect? Because the tax changes would alter the incentive for households to save *at any given interest rate,* they would affect the quantity of loanable funds supplied at each interest rate. Thus, the supply of loanable funds would shift. The demand for loanable funds would remain the same, because the tax changes would not directly affect the amount that borrowers want to borrow at any given interest rate.

Second, which way would the supply curve shift? Because saving would be taxed less heavily than under current law, households would increase their saving by consuming a smaller fraction of their income. Households would use this addi-

---

Figure 13-2

AN INCREASE IN THE SUPPLY OF LOANABLE FUNDS.   A change in the tax laws to encourage Canadians to save more would shift the supply of loanable funds to the right from S_1 to S_2. As a result, the equilibrium interest rate would fall, and the lower interest rate would stimulate investment. Here the equilibrium interest rate falls from 5 percent to 4 percent, and the equilibrium quantity of loanable funds saved and invested rises from $120 billion to $160 billion.

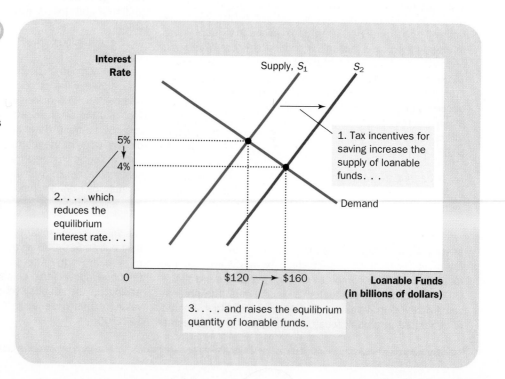

tional saving to increase their deposits in banks or to buy more bonds. The supply of loanable funds would increase, and the supply curve would shift to the right from S_1 to S_2, as shown in Figure 13-2.

Finally, we can compare the old and new equilibria. In the figure, the increased supply of loanable funds reduces the interest rate from 5 percent to 4 percent. The lower interest rate raises the quantity of loanable funds demanded from $120 billion to $160 billion. That is, the shift in the supply curve moves the market equilibrium along the demand curve. With a lower cost of borrowing, households and firms are motivated to borrow more to finance greater investment. Thus, *if a change in the tax laws encouraged greater saving, the result would be lower interest rates and greater investment.*

Although this analysis of the effects of increased saving is widely accepted among economists, there is less consensus about what kinds of tax changes should be enacted. Many economists endorse tax reform aimed at increasing saving in order to stimulate investment and growth. Yet others are skeptical that these tax changes would have much effect on national saving. These skeptics also doubt the equity of the proposed reforms. This argument would hold true, for example, with respect to increasing allowable RRSP contributions, because most RRSP contributions are made by those who are relatively wealthy. We examine this debate more fully in the final chapter of this book.

POLICY 2: TAXES AND INVESTMENT

Suppose that Parliament passed a law giving a tax reduction to any firm building a new factory. In essence, this is what Parliament does when it institutes an *investment*

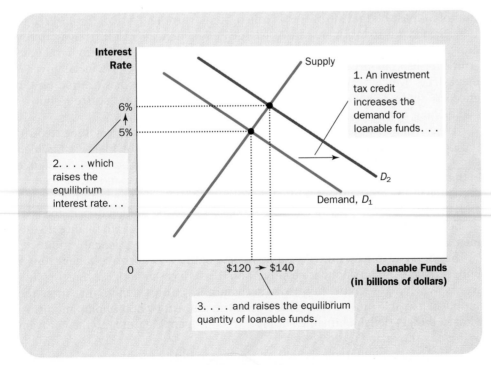

Figure 13-3

AN INCREASE IN THE DEMAND FOR LOANABLE FUNDS.   If the passage of an investment tax credit encouraged Canadian firms to invest more, the demand for loanable funds would increase. As a result, the equilibrium interest rate would rise, and the higher interest rate would stimulate saving. Here, when the demand curve shifts from D_1 to D_2, the equilibrium interest rate rises from 5 percent to 6 percent, and the equilibrium quantity of loanable funds saved and invested rises from $120 billion to $140 billion.

tax credit, which it does from time to time. Let's consider the effect of such a law on the market for loanable funds, as illustrated in Figure 13-3.

First, would the law affect supply or demand? Because the tax credit would reward firms that borrow and invest in new capital, it would alter investment at any given interest rate and, thereby, change the demand for loanable funds. By contrast, because the tax credit would not affect the amount that households save at any given interest rate, it would not affect the supply of loanable funds.

Second, which way would the demand curve shift? Because firms would have an incentive to increase investment at any interest rate, the quantity of loanable funds demanded would be higher at any given interest rate. Thus, the demand curve for loanable funds would move to the right, as shown by the shift from D_1 to D_2 in the figure.

Third, consider how the equilibrium would change. In Figure 13-3, the increased demand for loanable funds raises the interest rate from 5 percent to 6 percent, and the higher interest rate in turn increases the quantity of loanable funds supplied from $120 billion to $140 billion, as households respond by increasing the amount they save. This change in household behaviour is represented here as a movement along the supply curve. Thus, *if a change in the tax laws encouraged greater investment, the result would be higher interest rates and greater saving.*

POLICY 3: GOVERNMENT BUDGET DEFICITS AND SURPLUSES

One of the most pressing policy issues of the past 25 years in Canada has been the size of government budget deficits. When a government spends more than it receives in tax revenue, the shortfall is called the government's budget deficit. When a government spends less than it receives in tax revenue, the excess is called the government's budget surplus. The sum of all past budget deficits minus the sum of all past budget surpluses is called the government's debt. From 1975 to 1997, the federal government ran very large budget deficits, resulting in a rapidly growing federal government debt. During the same period, many provincial governments also ran large deficits, resulting in rapidly growing provincial government debts. Much public debate over the past twenty years has centred on the effects of these deficits both on the allocation of the economy's scarce resources and on long-term economic growth.

We can analyze the effects of a budget deficit by following our three steps in the market for loanable funds, which is illustrated in Figure 13-4. First, which curve shifts when the budget deficit rises? Recall that national saving—the source of the supply of loanable funds—is composed of private saving and public saving. A change in the government budget deficit represents a change in public saving and, thereby, in the supply of loanable funds. Because the budget deficit does not influence the amount that households and firms want to borrow to finance investment at any given interest rate, it does not alter the demand for loanable funds.

Second, which way does the supply curve shift? When a government runs a budget deficit, public saving is negative, and this reduces national saving. In other words, when a government borrows to finance its budget deficit, it reduces the supply of loanable funds available to finance investment by households and firms. Thus, a budget deficit shifts the supply curve for loanable funds to the left from S_1 to S_2, as shown in Figure 13-4.

Third, we can compare the old and new equilibria. In the figure, when the budget deficit reduces the supply of loanable funds, the interest rate rises from

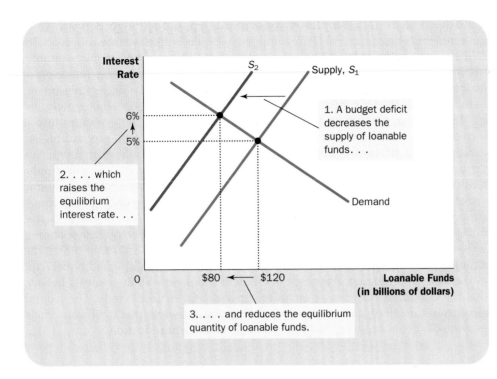

Figure 13-4

The Effect of a Government Budget Deficit.   When a government spends more than it receives in tax revenue, the resulting budget deficit lowers national saving. The supply of loanable funds decreases, and the equilibrium interest rate rises. Thus, when a government borrows to finance its budget deficit, it crowds out households and firms that otherwise would borrow to finance investment. Here, when the supply shifts from S_1 to S_2, the equilibrium interest rate rises from 5 percent to 6 percent, and the equilibrium quantity of loanable funds saved and invested falls from $120 billion to $80 billion.

5 percent to 6 percent. This higher interest rate then alters the behaviour of the households and firms that participate in the loan market. In particular, many demanders of loanable funds are discouraged by the higher interest rate. Fewer families buy new homes, and fewer firms choose to build new factories. The fall in investment because of government borrowing is called **crowding out** and is represented in the figure by the movement along the demand curve from a quantity of $120 billion in loanable funds to a quantity of $80 billion. That is, when the government borrows to finance its budget deficit, it crowds out private borrowers who are trying to finance investment.

Thus, the most basic lesson about budget deficits follows directly from their effects on the supply and demand for loanable funds: *When a government reduces national saving by running a budget deficit, the interest rate rises, and investment falls.* Because investment is important for long-run economic growth, government budget deficits reduce the economy's growth rate.

Long strings of government deficits such as those Canada experienced from 1975 to 1995 can push the economy into a **vicious circle** where deficits cause lower economic growth that in turn lead to lower tax revenue and higher spending on Employment Insurance and other income-support programs. Lower tax revenue and higher government spending lead to higher deficits and still slower economic growth. The only way to break out of this vicious circle is to raise tax rates and cut spending on government programs to eliminate the deficit and halt the circle of deficits, but this leads to slower economic growth and even higher deficits. Most analysts believe that the long string of deficits incurred by Canadian governments from 1975 to 1995 caused Canada to become trapped in such a vicious circle. The rapid run-up in tax rates and the large cuts to government spending on health care, defence, social services, and education during the late 1980s and early 1990s were the inevitable responses of highly indebted governments.

crowding out
a decrease in investment that results from government borrowing

vicious circle
cycle that results when deficits reduce the supply of loanable funds, increase interest rates, discourage investment, and result in slower economic growth; slower growth leads to lower tax revenue and higher spending on income-support programs, and the result can be still higher budget deficits

Government budget surpluses work just the opposite of budget deficits. When government collects more in tax revenue than it spends, its saves the difference by retiring some of the outstanding government debt. This budget surplus, or public saving, contributes to national saving. Thus, *a budget surplus increases the supply of loanable funds, reduces the interest rate, and stimulates investment.* Higher investment, in turn, means greater capital accumulation and more rapid economic growth.

Just as long strings of government deficits can push the economy into a vicious circle of higher deficits leading to slower growth leading to still higher deficits, so can strings of government budget surpluses push the economy into a **virtuous circle**. Here surpluses, by increasing the supply of loanable funds, reducing interest rates, and stimulating investment, encourage faster economic growth. Because this leads to higher tax revenues and lower spending on income-support programs, the government surplus grows over time. A virtuous circle produces very attractive choices: should government cut tax rates, increase spending on social programs, or pay down accumulated debt? By the end of the 1990s, the strong medicine required to break Canada out of the vicious circle had borne fruit in the form of large and growing government surpluses. Many analysts believe that the Canadian economy is about to experience a virtuous circle. The federal election in the fall of 2000 was fought over the very choices that a virtuous circle provides: tax cuts versus spending increases versus debt reduction.

virtuous circle

cycle that results when surpluses increase the supply of loanable funds, reduce interest rates, stimulate investment, and result in faster economic growth; faster growth leads to higher tax revenue and lower spending on income-support programs, and the result can be still higher budget surpluses

CASE STUDY   THE ACCUMULATION OF GOVERNMENT DEBT IN CANADA

Budget deficits have been a chronic problem in Canada only since the mid-1970s. From 1950 to 1974, the federal government ran budget surpluses as often as it ran budget deficits. These budget imbalances were generally small. In 1975, the federal government posted a large deficit and did so in every year until

"Our debt-reduction plan is simple, but it will require a great deal of money."

1997. In 1998, the federal government reported a budget surplus of $3.5 billion—the first time in 28 years that the federal government has actually paid down a portion of its debt.

Figure 13-5 shows the debt of the federal government and the combined debts of the ten provinces as a percentage of GDP. Throughout the 1950s and until 1975, the federal government's debt-to-GDP ratio declined. Although the federal government ran budget deficits during many of these years, the deficits were small enough that the government's debt grew less rapidly than the overall economy. Because GDP is a rough measure of the government's ability to raise tax revenue, a declining debt-to-GDP ratio indicates that the economy is, in some sense, living within its means. By contrast, in the years following 1975 when the federal government's budget deficit ballooned, the debt started rising more rapidly than the overall economy. As a result, the debt-to-GDP ratio quickly increased. On three occasions—1982, 1989, and 1996—the federal government managed to halt the rise in its debt-to-GDP ratio. The first two efforts only managed to halt the rise temporarily. On both occasions, an economic slowdown caused government spending to increase and tax revenues to fall so

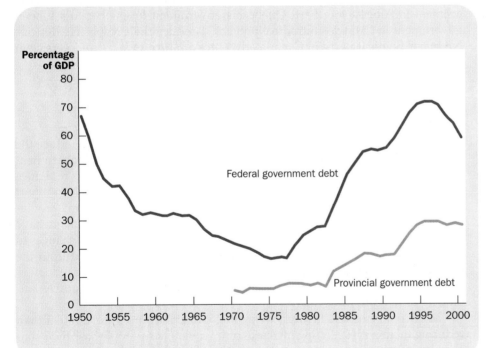

Figure 13-5

FEDERAL AND PROVINCIAL GOVERNMENT DEBT IN CANADA. The debt of the federal government and the combined debt of the ten provincial governments are expressed here as a percentage of GDP. Data on provincial government debt are available only from 1970. The federal government debt fell dramatically following World War II, but then started to increase quickly in 1975 when the government began to run large and persistent deficits. Since 1980 the provincial governments have also seen their debts quickly increase.

SOURCES: Authors' calculations, based on Statistics Canada information. Net debt is measured as the difference between financial assets and direct liabilities. Federal net debt is from CANSIM series D469420. Data on assets and liabilities of the provincial government sector are from CANSIM matrices 3202–3211. Calculation of Quebec's net debt requires an adjustment for the Quebec Pension Plan. The data for this adjustment are contained in CANSIM series D151784. Data on GDP is from CANSIM series D16439.

that debt began to accumulate again. The last effort, in 1996, proved more successful, and the federal government has actually managed to reduce its debt-to-GDP ratio from its high of 72 percent in 1996 to 59 percent in 2000.

Until 1982, the provincial governments together maintained a fairly constant level of debt relative to the economy. Although the provinces ran budget deficits, these were not large enough to cause the combined debt of the provinces to grow faster than the overall economy. As a result, the provincial debt-to-GDP ratio stayed at roughly 6 percent of GDP from 1970 to 1982. In 1982, a major recession caused the provinces to run larger deficits and caused the provincial debt-to-GDP ratio to begin to climb. By 1995, the ratio reached its maximum of 29 percent, where it has remained more or less constant.

As we saw in the previous chapter, national saving is a key ingredient in long-run economic growth. By using some of the private sector's saving to finance budget deficits, governments pull resources away from investment in new capital and, by doing so, depress the living standard of future generations. In recent years, all political parties in Canada have come to recognize this basic argument and now view persistent budget deficits as an important policy problem. As a result, Canadians have seen governments of all political stripes—from an NDP government in Saskatchewan to a Progressive Conservative government in Alberta to a Parti Québécois government in Quebec to a Liberal government in Ottawa—introduce policies to reduce their respective deficits. No major political party in Canada advocates a return to large and persistent government deficits.

CASE STUDY   THE DEBATE OVER BUDGET SURPLUSES

Since 1993, the federal government has taken forceful measures to reduce the size of its deficit. This effort has been so successful that the federal government now regularly reports budget surpluses and makes regular payments to reduce its outstanding debt. Some analysts expect the government to be able to report surpluses averaging $20 billion per year over the next few years. Many provincial governments have also been reducing their budget deficits, and many have reported budget surpluses for the past few years. As a result of these changes to government finances, public debate in Canada has recently shifted from the effects of large and growing budget deficits to the effects of deficit reduction and budget surpluses on the allocation of the economy's scarce resources and on long-term economic growth.

Many policymakers favour leaving the budget surpluses alone rather than reducing them with spending increases or tax cuts. These people base their conclusions on what was discussed above: Using the surplus to pay down government debt will stimulate private investment and economic growth.

Other policymakers take a different view. Some believe budget surpluses should be used to increase government spending on infrastructure, health care, and education. They base their conclusions on the belief that government investment in these areas receives a higher rate of return than what is received on private investment into new factories and housing. Other people want to see cuts, arguing that lower tax rates distort decision making less and lead to a more efficient allocation of resources. These analysts also caution that without tax cuts, governments will be tempted to spend the surplus on government projects of dubious value.

As this book was going to press, the debate over what to do with current and projected budget surpluses was still raging. All of the views discussed above are reasonable. The right policy depends on how much value you place on public versus private investment, how distortionary you view taxation, and how likely it is that the political process will avoid wasteful spending.

QUICK QUIZ: If more Canadians adopted a "live for today" approach to life, how would this affect saving, investment, and the interest rate?

FYI
Budget Rules

Recent efforts to reduce and even eliminate their budget deficits have caused many provincial governments to legislate *budget rules*. Budget rules are limits on the size of a government's deficit, the level of taxes it levies, its level of spending, the size of its outstanding debt, or any combination of these. The purpose of legislating budget rules is to reduce the possibility that the government will now, or in the future, allow its deficit and its accumulated debt to grow to an unmanageable size.

Many state governments in the United States use tax and expenditure limits and balanced budget rules to constrain state budget choices. In California, for example, per capita state tax revenue must be held constant. In Arizona, state taxes are limited to no more than 7 percent of personal income. Most states have long had budget rules that limit the ability of the state to run a budget deficit.

Many Canadian governments have recently introduced budget rules. New Brunswick was first off the mark with legislation introduced in 1993 that restricted the size of a budget deficit. In 1995, Alberta passed the Debt Retirement Act, which prohibited a budget deficit and established a schedule for the elimination of the province's net debt. Manitoba passed similar legislation in 1995, with the additional provision of financial penalties to be incurred by members of the provincial Cabinet should a deficit occur. Also in 1995, Saskatchewan passed its Balanced Budget Act, which required each newly elected government to publish a four-year fiscal plan; these plans cannot allow spending to exceed revenue. While the imposition of budget rules has been widespread among provincial governments, the federal government has been noticeably reticent about committing itself to any such rule.

One problem with a budget rule that is imposed on a government by legislation is that the rule can be repealed by the next government that is elected. This happened in British Columbia in 1992 when the newly elected government repealed legislation, passed in the previous year, that called for limits on spending growth. It is for this reason that economists prefer budget rules that are difficult to repeal. The government of Alberta has made one of its budget rules difficult to repeal by requiring a referendum to do so. According to the Alberta Taxpayers Protection Act, no Alberta government can introduce a provincial sales tax without first obtaining the approval of a majority of voters in a referendum.

The effectiveness of budget rules has been the subject of a number of recent studies by economists. In general, these studies find that budget rules limit the size of government deficits and cause unexpected deficits to be eliminated more quickly than they would otherwise. Budget rules also seem to increase the probability that a government will have a low debt-to-GDP ratio. Unfortunately, these favourable results come at a price: Budget rules limit the flexibility of governments to respond to changes in economic circumstances not foreseen by the designers of the budget rules. Suppose, for example, a new fuel technology makes Alberta's oil and gas reserves worthless and results in the government losing billions of dollars of energy royalties. With a rule prohibiting deficits, how could the government cope?

Studies of the effects of budget rules have been based on the experiences of U.S. state governments, but the spending responsibilities and revenue sources of Canadian provinces are substantially different from those of U.S. states. As a result, it is uncertain how effective budget rules will be at controlling provincial government budgets. Economists must wait a number of years to determine whether the existing budget rules do, in fact, achieve their goals. Economists will also need to assess whether the benefits of these rules outweigh their costs.

CONCLUSION

"Neither a borrower nor a lender be," Polonius advises his son in Shakespeare's *Hamlet*. If everyone followed this advice, this chapter would have been unnecessary.

Few economists would agree with Polonius. In our economy, people borrow and lend often, and usually for good reason. You may borrow one day to start your own business or to buy a home. And people may lend to you in the hope that the interest you pay will allow them to enjoy a more prosperous retirement. The financial system has the job of coordinating all of this borrowing and lending activity.

In many ways, financial markets are like other markets in the economy. The price of loanable funds—the interest rate—is governed by the forces of supply and demand, just as other prices in the economy are. And we can analyze shifts in supply or demand in financial markets as we do in other markets. One of the *Ten Principles of Economics* introduced in Chapter 1 is that markets are usually a good way to organize economic activity. This principle applies to financial markets as well. When financial markets bring the supply and demand for loanable funds into balance, they help allocate the economy's scarce resources to their most efficient use.

In one way, however, financial markets are special. Financial markets, unlike most other markets, serve the important role of linking the present and the future. Those who supply loanable funds—savers—do so because they want to convert some of their current income into future purchasing power. Those who demand loanable funds—borrowers—do so because they want to invest today in order to have additional capital in the future to produce goods and services. Thus, well-functioning financial markets are important not only for current generations but also for future generations who will inherit many of the resulting benefits.

Summary

◆ The Canadian financial system is made up of many types of financial institutions, such as the bond market, the stock market, banks, and mutual funds. All of these institutions act to direct the resources of households that want to save some of their income into the hands of households and firms that want to borrow.

◆ National income accounting identities reveal some important relationships among macroeconomic variables. In particular, for a closed economy, national saving must equal investment. Financial institutions are the mechanism through which the economy matches one person's saving with another person's investment.

◆ The interest rate is determined by the supply and demand for loanable funds. The supply of loanable funds comes from households that want to save some of their income and lend it out. The demand for loanable funds comes from households and firms that want to borrow for investment. To analyze how any policy or event affects the interest rate, one must consider how it affects the supply and demand for loanable funds.

◆ National saving equals private saving plus public saving. A government budget deficit represents negative public saving and, therefore, reduces national saving and the supply of loanable funds available to finance investment. When a government budget deficit crowds out investment, it reduces the growth of productivity and GDP.

Key Concepts

financial system, p. 264
financial markets, p. 265
bond, p. 265
stock, p. 266
financial intermediaries, p. 266

mutual fund, p. 268
national saving (saving), p. 272
private saving, p. 272
public saving, p. 272
budget surplus, p. 273

budget deficit, p. 273
market for loanable funds, p. 274
crowding out, p. 281
vicious circle, p. 281
virtuous circle, p. 282

Questions for Review

1. What is the role of the financial system? Name and describe two markets that are part of the financial system in our economy. Name and describe two financial intermediaries.

2. Why is it important for people who own stocks and bonds to diversify their holdings? What type of financial institution makes diversification easier?

3. What is national saving? What is private saving? What is public saving? How are these three variables related?

4. What is investment? How is it related to national saving?

5. Describe a change in the tax code that might increase private saving. If this policy were implemented, how would it affect the market for loanable funds?

6. What is a government budget deficit? How does it affect interest rates, investment, and economic growth?

Problems and Applications

1. For each of the following pairs, which bond would you expect to pay a higher interest rate? Explain.
   a. a bond of the Canadian government or a bond of an Eastern European government
   b. a bond that repays the principal in 2005 or a bond that repays the principal in 2025
   c. a bond from Coca-Cola or a bond from a software company you run in your garage
   d. a bond issued by the federal government or a bond issued by Prince Edward Island

2. Look up in a newspaper the stock of two companies you know something about (perhaps as a customer). What is the price–earnings ratio for each company? Why do you think they differ? If you were to buy one of these stocks, which would you choose? Why?

3. Theodore Roosevelt once said, "There is no moral difference between gambling at cards or in lotteries or on the race track and gambling in the stock market." What social purpose do you think is served by the existence of the stock market?

4. Use the Internet to look at the Web site for a mutual fund company, such as AGF Group of Funds (http://www.agf.com). Compare the return on an actively managed mutual fund with the return on an index fund. What explains the difference in these returns?

5. Declines in stock prices are sometimes viewed as harbingers of future declines in real GDP. Why do you suppose that might be true?

6. When the Russian government defaulted on its debt to foreigners in 1998, interest rates rose on bonds issued by many other developing countries. Why do you suppose this happened?

7. Many workers hold large amounts of stock issued by the firms at which they work. Why do you suppose companies encourage this behaviour? Why might a person *not* want to hold stock in the company where he or she works?

8. Your roommate says that she buys stock only in companies that everyone believes will experience big increases in profits in the future. How do you suppose the price–earnings ratio of these companies compares with the price–earnings ratio of other companies? What might be the disadvantage of buying stock in these companies?

9. Explain the difference between saving and investment as defined by a macroeconomist. Which of the following situations represent investment? Saving? Explain.
   a. Your family takes out a mortgage and buys a new house. *Investment , pay.*
   b. You use your $200 paycheque to buy stock in Bombardier. *Saving*
   c. Your roommate earns $100 and deposits it in her account at a bank. *Saving , she didn't buy any consumable goods.*
   d. You borrow $1000 from a bank to buy a car to use in your pizza delivery business. *Investment.*

10. Suppose GDP is $800 billion, taxes are $150 billion, private saving is $50 billion, and public saving is $20 billion. Assuming this economy is closed, calculate consumption, government purchases, national saving, and investment.

11. Suppose that Intel is considering building a new chip-making factory.
   a. Assuming that Intel needs to borrow money in the bond market, why would an increase in interest rates affect Intel's decision about whether to build the factory?
   b. If Intel has enough of its own funds to finance the new factory without borrowing, would an increase in interest rates still affect Intel's decision about whether to build the factory? Explain.

12. Suppose the government borrows $20 billion more next year than this year.
   a. Use a supply-and-demand diagram to analyze this policy. Does the interest rate rise or fall?
   b. What happens to investment? To private saving? To public saving? To national saving? Compare the size of the changes to the $20 billion of extra government borrowing.

   c. How does the elasticity of supply of loanable funds affect the size of these changes? (Hint: See Chapter 5 to review the definition of elasticity.)
   d. How does the elasticity of demand for loanable funds affect the size of these changes?
   e. Suppose households believe that greater government borrowing today implies higher taxes to pay off the government debt in the future. What does this belief do to private saving and the supply of loanable funds today? Does it increase or decrease the effects you discussed in parts (a) and (b)?

13. Over the past ten years, new computer technology has enabled firms to reduce substantially the amount of inventory they hold for each dollar of sales. Illustrate the effect of this change on the market for loanable funds. (Hint: Expenditure on inventory is a type of investment.) What do you think has been the effect on investment in factories and equipment?

14. "Some economists worry that the aging populations of industrial countries are going to start running down their savings just when the investment appetite of emerging economies is growing" (*The Economist*, May 6, 1995). Illustrate the effect of these phenomena on the world market for loanable funds.

15. This chapter explains that investment can be increased both by reducing taxes on private saving and by reducing the government budget deficit.
   a. Why is it difficult to implement both of these policies at the same time?
   b. What would you need to know about private saving in order to judge which of these two policies would be a more effective way to raise investment?

10. $Y = 800$, $T = 150$. $S = $ Private + Public
   $$= 50 + 20 = 70$$
   Private $Y - T - C$
   $$50 = 800 - 150 - C$$ Investment $= S$
   $$= 70$$
   $$C = 600$$
   Public $= T - G$
   $$20 = 150 - G$$
   $$G = 130$$

14

UNEMPLOYMENT AND ITS NATURAL RATE

Losing a job can be the most distressing economic event in a person's life. Most people rely on their labour earnings to maintain their standard of living, and many people get from their work not only income but also a sense of personal accomplishment. A job loss means a lower living standard in the present, anxiety about the future, and reduced self-esteem. It is not surprising, therefore, that politicians campaigning for office often speak about how their proposed policies will help create jobs.

In the preceding two chapters we have seen some of the forces that determine the level and growth of a country's standard of living. A country that saves and invests a high fraction of its income, for instance, enjoys more rapid growth in its capital stock and its GDP than a similar country that saves and invests less. An even more obvious determinant of a country's standard of living is the amount of unemployment it typically experiences. People who would like to work but cannot find a job are not contributing to the economy's production of goods and services. Although some degree of unemployment is inevitable in a complex economy with thousands of firms and millions of workers, the amount of unemployment varies substantially over time and across countries. When a country keeps its workers as fully employed as possible, it achieves a higher level of GDP than it would if it left many of its workers standing idle.

This chapter begins our study of unemployment. The problem of unemployment is usefully divided into two categories—the long-run problem and the short-run problem. The economy's *natural rate of unemployment* refers to the amount of unemployment that the economy normally experiences. *Cyclical unemployment* refers to the year-to-year fluctuations in unemployment around its natural rate, and it is closely associated with the short-run ups and downs of economic activity. Cyclical unemployment has its own explanation, which we defer until we study short-run economic fluctuations later in this book. In this chapter we discuss the determinants of an economy's natural rate of unemployment. As we will see, the designation *natural* does not imply that this rate of unemployment is desirable. Nor does it imply that it is constant over time or impervious to economic policy. It merely means that this unemployment does not go away on its own even in the long run.

We begin the chapter by looking at some of the relevant facts that describe unemployment. In particular, we examine three questions: How does the government measure the economy's rate of unemployment? What problems arise in interpreting the unemployment data? How long are unemployed people typically without work?

We then turn to the reasons why economies always experience some unemployment and the ways in which policymakers can help the unemployed. We discuss four explanations for the economy's natural rate of unemployment: job search, minimum-wage laws, unions, and efficiency wages. As we will see, long-run unemployment does not arise from a single problem that has a single solution. Instead, it reflects a variety of related problems. As a result, there is no easy way for policymakers to reduce the economy's natural rate of unemployment and, at the same time, to alleviate the hardships experienced by unemployed people.

IDENTIFYING UNEMPLOYMENT

We begin this chapter by examining more precisely what the term *unemployment* means. We consider how the government measures unemployment, what problems arise in interpreting the unemployment data, and how long the typical spell of unemployment lasts.

HOW IS UNEMPLOYMENT MEASURED?

Measuring unemployment is the job of Statistics Canada. Every month Statistics Canada produces data on unemployment and other aspects of the labour market, such as types of employment, length of the average workweek, and duration of unemployment. These data come from a regular survey of about 52 000 households called the Labour Force Survey.

Based on the answers to survey questions, Statistics Canada places each adult (aged 16 and older) in each surveyed household into one of three categories:

◆   employed
◆   unemployed
◆   not in the labour force

A person is considered employed if he or she spent most of the previous week working at a paid job. A person is unemployed if he or she is on temporary layoff, is looking for a job, or is waiting for the start date of a new job. A person who fits neither of the first two categories, such as a full-time student, homemaker, or retiree, is not in the labour force. Figure 14-1 shows this breakdown for 1999.

Once Statistics Canada has placed all the individuals covered by the survey in a category, it computes various statistics to summarize the state of the labour market. Statistics Canada defines the **labour force** as the sum of the employed and the unemployed:

labour force
the total number of workers, including both the employed and the unemployed

Labour force = Number employed + number of unemployed

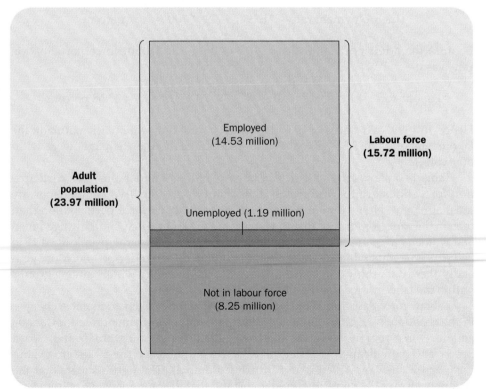

Figure 14-1

THE BREAKDOWN OF THE POPULATION IN 1999.   Statistics Canada divides the adult population into three categories: employed, unemployed, and not in the labour force.

SOURCE: Statistics Canada, CANSIM Matrix 3450.

Adult population (23.97 million)

Employed (14.53 million)

Labour force (15.72 million)

Unemployed (1.19 million)

Not in labour force (8.25 million)

unemployment rate
the percentage of the labour force that is unemployed

Statistics Canada defines the **unemployment rate** as the percentage of the labour force that is unemployed:

$$\text{Unemployment rate} = \frac{\text{Number of unemployed}}{\text{Labour force}} \times 100.$$

Statistics Canada computes unemployment rates for the entire adult population and for more narrow groups—young, old, men, women, and so on.

Statistics Canada uses the same survey to produce data on labour-force participation. The **labour-force participation rate** measures the percentage of the total adult population of Canada that is in the labour force:

labour-force participation rate
the percentage of the adult population that is in the labour force

$$\text{Labour-force participation rate} = \frac{\text{Labour force}}{\text{Adult population}} \times 100.$$

This statistic tells us the fraction of the population that has chosen to participate in the labour market. The labour-force participation rate, like the unemployment rate, is computed both for the entire adult population and for more narrow groups.

To see how these data are computed, consider the figures for 1999. In that year, 14.53 million people were employed, and 1.19 million people were unemployed. The labour force was

$$\text{Labour force} = 14.53 + 1.19 = 15.72 \text{ million.}$$

The unemployment rate was

$$\text{Unemployment rate} = (1.19/15.72) \times 100 = 7.57 \text{ percent.}$$

Because the adult population was 23.97 million, the labour-force participation rate was

$$\text{Labour-force participation rate} = (15.72/23.97) \times 100 = 65.58 \text{ percent.}$$

Hence, in 1999, two-thirds of Canada's adult population were participating in the labour market, and 7.57 percent of those labour-market participants were without work.

Table 14-1 shows the statistics on unemployment and labour-force participation for various groups within the Canadian population. Two comparisons are most apparent. First, women have lower rates of labour-force participation than men in the same age group. However, once in the labour force, similarly aged men and women have similar rates of unemployment. Second, young people aged 15 to 24 years have much higher rates of unemployment than older people. More generally, these data show that labour-market experiences vary widely among groups within the labour force.

Labour-force data also allow economists and policymakers to monitor changes in the economy over time. Figure 14-2 shows the unemployment rate for Canada and for three regions: Atlantic (Newfoundland, Prince Edward Island, Nova Scotia, and New Brunswick), Central (Ontario and Quebec), and Western (Manitoba, Saskatchewan, Alberta, and British Columbia). The figure shows that the economy always has some unemployment and that the amount changes from year to year. It also shows that both the unemployment rate and the amount by which

Table 14-1

DEMOGRAPHIC GROUP	UNEMPLOYMENT RATE	LABOUR-FORCE PARTICIPATION RATE
Both Sexes, 15 years and over	7.6%	65.6%
Males, 15–24 years	15.3	65.3
Males, 25–44 years	6.9	92.1
Males, 45-64 years	5.8	77.8
Females, 15-24 years	12.5	61.7
Females, 25-44 years	6.7	79.6
Females, 45-64 years	5.5	60.9

SOURCE: Statistics Canada, CANSIM Matrix 3450.

THE LABOUR-MARKET EXPERIENCES OF VARIOUS DEMOGRAPHIC GROUPS. This table shows the unemployment rate and the labour-force participation rate of various groups in the population for 1999.

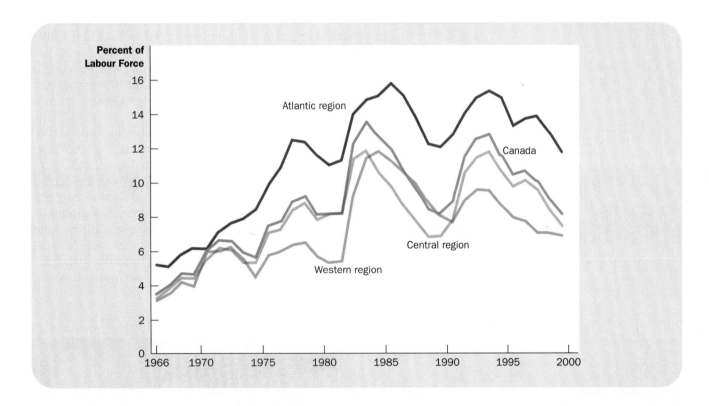

CANADIAN AND REGIONAL UNEMPLOYMENT RATES 1966–1999.

Figure 14-2

SOURCE: Statistics Canada and authors' calculation.

it changes from year to year vary widely for different regions of the country. The unemployment rate in the Atlantic region is consistently higher than in the rest of the country. Furthermore, the difference between the unemployment rate in the Atlantic region and that in the rest of the country, while quite small in 1970, has grown since then. The unemployment rate in the Western region has generally been lower than in the rest of the country. During the mid-to late 1980s, however, the Western region's unemployment rate was higher than the Canadian average.

This was mainly due to a fall in oil and natural gas prices—an event that harmed the economies in this region but benefited those in the rest of the country. Finally, the unemployment rate of the Central region closely follows the national unemployment rate. This is to be expected, since the Central region comprises more than 60 percent of the Canadian labour force.

CASE STUDY   **LABOUR-FORCE PARTICIPATION OF MEN AND WOMEN IN THE CANADIAN ECONOMY**

Women's role in Canadian society has changed dramatically over the past century. Social commentators have pointed to many causes for this change. In part, it is attributable to new technologies such as the washing machine, clothes dryer, refrigerator, freezer, and dishwasher, which have reduced the amount of time required to complete routine household tasks. In part, it is attributable to improved birth control, which has reduced the number of children born to the typical family. And, of course, this change in women's role is also partly attributable to changing political and social attitudes. Together these developments have had a profound impact on society in general and on the economy in particular.

Nowhere is that impact more obvious than in data on labour-force participation. Figure 14-3 shows the labour-force participation rates of men and women in Canada since 1951. Just after World War II, men and women had very different roles in society. Only 24 percent of women were working or looking for work, in contrast to 84 percent of men. Over the past several decades, the difference between the participation rates of men and women has gradually diminished as growing numbers of women have entered the labour force and some men have left it. Data for 1999 show that 59 percent of women were in the labour force, in contrast to 72 percent of men. As measured by labour-force participation, men and women are now playing a more equal role in the economy.

MORE WOMEN ARE WORKING NOW THAN EVER BEFORE.

The increase in women's labour-force participation is easy to understand, but the fall in men's may seem puzzling. There are several reasons for this decline. First, young men now stay in school longer than their fathers and grandfathers did. Second, older men now retire earlier and live longer. Third, with more women employed, more fathers now stay at home to raise their children. Full-time students, retirees, and stay-at-home fathers are all counted as out of the labour force.

DOES THE UNEMPLOYMENT RATE MEASURE WHAT WE WANT IT TO?

Measuring the amount of unemployment in the economy might seem straightforward. In fact, it is not. Whereas it is easy to distinguish between a person with a full-time job and a person who is not working at all, it is much harder to distinguish between a person who is unemployed and a person who is not in the labour force.

Movements into and out of the labour force are, in fact, very common. More than one-third of the unemployed are recent entrants into the labour force. These entrants include young workers looking for their first jobs, such as recent university and college graduates. They also include, in greater numbers, older workers who had previously left the labour force but have now returned to look for work. Moreover, not all unemployment ends with the job seeker finding a job. Almost half of all spells of unemployment end when the unemployed person leaves the labour force.

Because people move into and out of the labour force so often, statistics on unemployment are difficult to interpret. On the one hand, some of those who

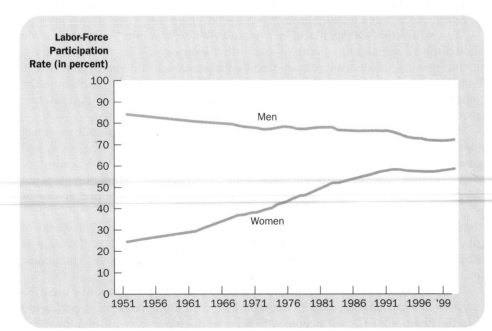

Figure 14-3

LABOUR-FORCE PARTICIPATION RATES FOR MEN AND WOMEN SINCE 1951.   This figure shows the percentage of adult men and women who are members of the labour force. It shows that over the past several decades, women have entered the labour force, and men have left it.

SOURCES: Data for 1966–99 are from Statistics Canada. Observations for 1951 and 1961 are from F.H. Leacy, ed., *Historical Statistics of Canada*, 2nd ed., (Ottawa: Statistics Canada, 1983). Values for 1952–60 and 1962–65 are linear interpolations among the 1951, 1961, and 1966 observations.

report being unemployed may not, in fact, be trying hard to find a job. They may be calling themselves unemployed because they want to qualify for Employment Insurance, a government program that financially assists unemployed people. It may be more realistic to view these individuals as out of the labour force or, in some cases, employed. On the other hand, some of those who report being out of the labour force may, in fact, want to work. These individuals may have tried to find a job but have given up after an unsuccessful search. Such individuals, called **discouraged workers,** do not show up in unemployment statistics, even though they are truly workers without jobs. According to most estimates, adding discouraged workers would increase the measured unemployment rate by about one-half of one percentage point.

discouraged workers
individuals who would like to work but have given up looking for a job

There is no easy way to fix the unemployment rate as reported by Statistics Canada to make it a more reliable indicator of conditions in the labour market. In the end, it is best to view the reported unemployment rate as a useful but imperfect measure of joblessness.

HOW LONG ARE UNEMPLOYED PEOPLE WITHOUT WORK?

In judging how serious the problem of unemployment is, one question to consider is whether unemployment is typically a short-term or long-term condition. If unemployment is short-term, one might conclude that it is not a big problem. Workers may require a few weeks between jobs to find the openings that best suit their tastes and skills. Yet if unemployment is long-term, one might conclude that it is a serious problem. Workers unemployed for many months are more likely to suffer economic and psychological hardship.

Because the duration of unemployment can affect our view about how big a problem unemployment is, economists have devoted much energy to studying data on the duration of unemployment spells. In this work, they have uncovered a result that is important, subtle, and seemingly contradictory: *Most spells of unemployment are short, and most unemployment observed at any given time is long-term.*

To see how this statement can be true, consider an example. Suppose that you visited the government's unemployment office every week for a year to survey unemployed people. Each week you find that there are four unemployed workers. Three of these workers are the same individuals for the whole year, while the fourth person changes every week. Based on this experience, would you say that unemployment is typically short-term or long-term?

Some simple calculations help answer this question. In this example, you meet a total of 55 unemployed people; 52 of them are unemployed for one week, and three are unemployed for the full year. This means that 52/55, or 95 percent, of unemployment spells end in one week. Thus, most spells of unemployment are short. Yet consider the total amount of unemployment. The three people unemployed for one year (52 weeks) make up a total of 156 weeks of unemployment. Together with the 52 people unemployed for one week, this makes 208 weeks of unemployment. In this example, 156/208, or 75 percent, of unemployment is attributable to those individuals who are unemployed for a full year. Thus, most unemployment observed at any given time is long-term.

This subtle conclusion implies that economists and policymakers must be careful when interpreting data on unemployment and when designing policies to help the unemployed. Most people who become unemployed will soon find jobs.

IN THE NEWS

Unemployment and the Participation Rate

IF THE UNEMPLOYMENT RATE FALLS, THAT'S good news, isn't it? It may or not be good news: It depends on whether the unemployment rate fell because employment increased or because people gave up looking for work. The following article discusses how employment and labour-force participation vary over the course of the business cycle and what this means for the unemployment rate.

Low Unemployment Has Hidden Cause

BY MARK MACKINNON

Falling unemployment is often cited by politicians as proof that their economic policies are working. And on the face of it, there is something to brag about.

The national unemployment rate—which measures the number of people looking for work as a percentage of the total labour force—has fallen from a high of 11.9 percent six years ago, at the height of the recession, to 8.1 percent last month, its lowest level since 1990. But there's a hitch: the labour force, as a percentage of the total working-age population, also has shrunk. This means the unemployment rate is being driven down, not only by the creation of new jobs, but also by people leaving the work force.

"The unemployment rate can be a very deceiving indicator," said Benjamin Tal, an economist with the Canadian Imperial Bank of Commerce. "Had the participation rate stayed at the 1989 level, the unemployment rate would have been about 3 percent higher during the past few years." In January 1990, just shy of 68 percent of Canadians were either working or looking for work. By the middle of the recession, 1992–93, that number—referred to by economists as the participation rate—had fallen below 66 percent.

And while the economy has since recovered and created more than a million new jobs over the past five years, the number of people looking for work hasn't bounced back. At the end of October, just over 65 percent of the potential labour force was working or looking for work. Many economists say this number reveals that there are hundreds of thousands of Canadians who have, for various reasons, given up looking for work. They argue that many of these people would work if they could, but were forced to the sidelines by the recession, and have never returned to the work force.

If 67.9 percent of Canadians 15 and over—the participation rate in January 1990—were looking for work today, there would be some 656 000 more people looking for the same number of jobs. This would make October's unemployment rate balloon to 11.7 percent.

Ontario and Quebec, Canada's two most populous provinces, have seen the biggest drops in participation in the work force. Adjusted to the 1990 participation rates, their unemployment rates—now 7.0 percent and 10.3 percent, respec-

tively—would rise to 12.3 percent and 14.2 percent. The decline in participation in the other eight provinces has been less dramatic. Nationally, the participation most of the 1970s and 1980s as more and more women entered the work force. But 90 percent of the recent decline has been the result of people in the under-25 and over-55 age groups leaving the work force.

Much of this can be attributed to structural factors—students spending more time in school and people retiring earlier.

Neither of those phenomena are necessarily a sign of a weak economy. But they can be considered as signs of weakness when students stay in school because they believe there are no jobs, and when older workers are forced out of the work force by corporate restructuring. Then there are the so-called "discouraged" unemployed, those who simply give up looking for a job because they think they're not going to find one.

Pierre Fortin, economics professor at the Université du Québec à Montréal, said that even when structural factors are accounted for, Canada's low participation rate demonstrates that the country hasn't entirely recovered from the last recession.

"The truth is that the participation rate reacts to the business cycle—if there is a drop in the amount of jobs available, there will be a drop in the participation rate."

SOURCE: *The Globe and Mail*, November 16, 1998, p. B1.

In 1996, for example, 28 percent of unemployed people in Canada were unemployed for just four weeks or less, while 25 percent were unemployed for between five and thirteen weeks. In that year, then, most of the unemployed were without work for a relatively short period of time. Most of the economy's unemployment problem in that year was attributable to the 47 percent of unemployed people who were jobless for fourteen weeks or more.

WHY ARE THERE ALWAYS SOME UNEMPLOYED PEOPLE?

We have discussed how the government measures the amount of unemployment, the problems that arise in interpreting unemployment statistics, and the findings of labour economists on the duration of unemployment. You should now have a good idea about what unemployment is.

This discussion, however, has not explained why economies experience unemployment. In most markets in the economy, prices adjust to bring quantity supplied and quantity demanded into balance. In an ideal labour market, wages would adjust to balance the quantity of labour supplied and the quantity of labour demanded. This adjustment of wages would ensure that all workers are always fully employed.

natural rate of unemployment

the rate of unemployment to which the economy tends to return in the long run

Of course, reality does not resemble this ideal. There are always some workers without jobs, even when the overall economy is doing well. Figure 14-4 shows Canada's observed unemployment rate and an estimate of Canada's natural unemployment rate. The **natural unemployment rate** is what economists judge to be the rate of unemployment to which the economy tends to return in the long run. The exact value of the natural unemployment rate is unknown, but most economists estimate the rate in Canada to be currently 6 to 8 percent. Economists form estimates of the natural unemployment rate based on those variables they believe are the underlying determinants of the natural rate of unemployment. We will discuss these underlying determinants in the remainder of this chapter.

The values of the natural unemployment rate shown in Figure 14-4 represent the authors' opinions. Because the natural unemployment rate is only an estimate, there may be some dispute about the level of the rate at any particular time. However, the movements shown in the figure represent a fairly widespread view among economists about what has happened to Canada's natural unemployment rate since 1966. During the 1970s and 1980s, the natural unemployment rate roughly doubled from about 4 percent to over 8 percent, and began falling in the mid-1990s. By 2000, the prevailing opinion was that the natural rate was very close to being equal to the observed unemployment rate.

cyclical unemployment

the deviation of unemployment from its natural rate

Figure 14-4 also shows that the observed unemployment rate fluctuates around the natural rate. The observed unemployment rate differs from the natural rate due to the existence of **cyclical unemployment.** Cyclical unemployment arises due to short-run economic fluctuations. Later in this book we discuss short-run economic fluctuations, including the year-to-year fluctuations in unemployment around its natural rate. In the rest of this chapter, however, we ignore the short-run fluctuations and examine why unemployment is a chronic problem for market economies. That is, we will examine the determinants of the natural unemployment rate.

To preview our conclusions, we will find that there are four ways to explain unemployment in the long run. The first explanation is that it takes time for workers to search for the jobs that are best suited for them. The unemployment

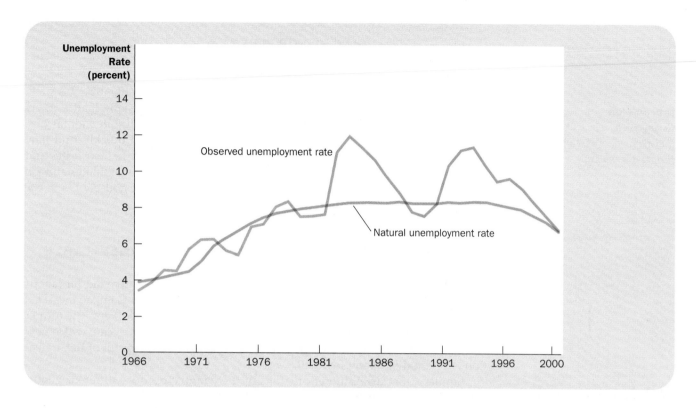

OBSERVED AND NATURAL UNEMPLOYMENT RATES, 1966–2000. Most economists judge that the natural unemployment rate increased during the 1970s but then stabilized at about 8 percent in the 1980s and 1990s. The difference between the observed unemployment rate and the natural unemployment rate is the cyclical unemployment rate.

Figure 14-4

SOURCES: Statistics Canada series D980745 and authors' assumptions.

that results from the process of matching workers and jobs is sometimes called **frictional unemployment,** and it is often thought to explain relatively short spells of unemployment.

The next three explanations for unemployment suggest that the number of jobs available in some labour markets may be insufficient to give a job to everyone who wants one. This occurs when the quantity of labour supplied exceeds the quantity demanded. Unemployment of this sort is sometimes called **structural unemployment,** and it is often thought to explain longer spells of unemployment. As we will see, this kind of unemployment results when wages are, for some reason, set above the level that brings supply and demand into equilibrium. We will examine three possible reasons for an above-equilibrium wage: minimum-wage laws, unions, and efficiency wages.

frictional unemployment
unemployment that results because it takes time for workers to search for the jobs that best suit their tastes and skills

structural unemployment
unemployment that results because the number of jobs available in some labour markets is insufficient to provide a job for everyone who wants one

QUICK QUIZ: How is the unemployment rate measured? ◆ How might the unemployment rate overstate the amount of joblessness? How might it understate it?

> # JOB SEARCH

job search

the process by which workers find appropriate jobs given their tastes and skills

One reason why economies always experience some unemployment is job search. **Job search** is the process of matching workers with appropriate jobs. If all workers and all jobs were the same, so that all workers were equally well suited for all jobs, job search would not be a problem. Laid-off workers would quickly find new jobs that were well suited for them. But, in fact, workers differ in their tastes and skills, jobs differ in their attributes, and information about job candidates and job vacancies is disseminated slowly among the many firms and households in the economy.

WHY SOME FRICTIONAL UNEMPLOYMENT IS INEVITABLE

Frictional unemployment is often the result of changes in the demand for labour among different firms. When consumers decide that they prefer Compaq over Dell computers, Compaq increases employment, and Dell lays off workers. The former Dell workers must now search for new jobs, and Compaq must decide which new workers to hire for the various jobs that have opened up. The result of this transition is a period of unemployment.

Similarly, because different regions of the country produce different goods, employment can rise in one region while it falls in another. Consider, for instance, what happens when the world price of oil falls. Oil-producing firms in Alberta respond to the lower price by cutting back on production and employment. At the same time, cheaper gasoline stimulates car sales, so automakers in Ontario raise production and employment. Changes in the composition of demand among industries or regions are called *sectoral shifts*. Because it takes time for workers to search for jobs in the new sectors, sectoral shifts temporarily cause unemployment.

Frictional unemployment is inevitable simply because the economy is always changing. Only 90 years ago, car manufacturing, petroleum, and aircraft manufacturing industries were very minor sources of employment in Canada. Today, these are three of the largest employers in the Canadian economy. At the same time, agriculture has fallen from being the largest single source of employment in Canada in 1911 to only a minor source of employment today. As this transition took place, jobs were created in some firms, and jobs were destroyed in others. The end result of this process has been higher productivity and higher living standards. But, along the way, workers in declining industries found themselves out of work and searching for new jobs.

Data show that, on average, Canadian companies that are expanding increase employment by roughly 10 percent each year. Companies that are contracting typically decrease employment by a somewhat smaller amount. The implication is that each year there is a very large transition of workers from contracting firms to expanding firms. This churning of the labour force is normal in a well-functioning and dynamic market economy, but it is inevitable that the labour market will have difficulty matching available jobs with available workers. The result is some amount of frictional unemployment. Recent estimates for Canada indicate that the mismatch between available jobs and people seeking employment explains why roughly one out of every eight unemployed workers is unemployed.

PUBLIC POLICY AND JOB SEARCH

Even if some frictional unemployment is inevitable, the precise amount is not. The faster information spreads about job openings and worker availability, the more rapidly the economy can match workers and firms. The Internet, for instance, may help facilitate job search and reduce frictional unemployment. In addition, public policy may play a role. If policy can reduce the time it takes unemployed workers to find new jobs, it can reduce the economy's natural rate of unemployment.

Government programs try to facilitate job search in various ways. One way is through government-run employment agencies, which give out information about job vacancies. Another way is through public training programs, which aim to ease the transition of workers from declining to growing industries and to help disadvantaged groups escape poverty. Government training programs in Canada are, for the most part, conducted through the federal government's Employment Insurance program. Recent reforms to this program have reallocated funds away from the payment of benefits to unemployed people and toward the funding of training programs.

Critics of these programs question whether the government should get involved with the process of job search. They argue that it is better to let the private market match workers and jobs. In fact, most job search in our economy takes place without intervention by the government. Newspaper ads, job newsletters, university placement offices, headhunters, and word of mouth all help spread information about job openings and job candidates. Similarly, much worker education is done privately, either through schools or through on-the-job training. These critics contend that the government is no better—and most likely worse—at disseminating the right information to the right workers and deciding what kinds of worker training would be most valuable. They claim that these decisions are best made privately by workers and employers.

Advocates of government programs designed to facilitate job search believe that the programs make the economy operate more efficiently by keeping the labour force more fully employed, and reduce the inequities inherent in a constantly changing market economy. These supporters also stress that in certain circumstances the private sector is incapable of helping those who lose their jobs. This is the case when job loss is the result of disasters, such as the collapse of the cod fishery in Newfoundland. It is argued that the virtual disappearance of an industry that is central to the economy of an entire region demands government involvement. In such cases, the solution is not simply for workers to find a similar job in the next company down the street, but rather to retrain for a new job in a new industry in a new area of the country. Government retraining and relocation programs may play a useful role in these cases, one the private sector may be incapable of playing.

EMPLOYMENT INSURANCE

In Canada, the federal government maintains a program of **Employment Insurance.** The program is intended to ease the burden of those who find themselves unemployed by temporarily providing them with income. Canada's EI program is expensive (in 2000, it cost almost $12 billion) and controversial. Many economists believe that, while EI eases the burden of being unemployed, it may also cause the

Employment Insurance
a government program that partially protects workers' incomes when they become unemployed

unemployment rate to be higher than it would be otherwise. Thus the program may increase the amount of frictional unemployment without intending to do so.

Since 1971, two considerations have determined when and for how long someone can collect EI benefits: the number of hours worked in the past year and the unemployment rate in the area of residence. More hours of work make a claimant eligible to collect EI benefits for a longer period of time. The higher the local unemployment rate, the longer a claimant can collect and the fewer hours the claimant must work in order to become eligible. The details of the program have changed a great deal since 1971, and revisions to the program occur frequently. As of early 2001, workers who live in a region where the unemployment rate exceeds 16 percent have to work only 420 hours (for example, 12 weeks of full-time, 35-hours-per-week employment) to become eligible for 32 weeks of benefits. Workers who live in a region where the unemployment rate is 6 percent or less have to work a minimum of 700 hours (for example, 20 weeks of full-time employment) to become eligible for benefits, and this minimum amount of work makes claimants eligible for just 14 weeks of insurance. In regions of the country with high unemployment rates, therefore, relatively few hours of work are needed to be eligible for EI, and EI benefits can be collected for a long time. In regions of the country with

---

IN THE NEWS

Provincial Natural Unemployment Rates

MANY OF THE FACTORS THAT AFFECT THE size of the natural unemployment rate differ in importance depending on the province in which one lives. As a result, we might expect that natural unemployment rates to differ across provinces. The following article presents estimates of provincial natural unemployment rates and relates these differences to how minimum wages, unionization, and the design of the Employment Insurance program differ across provinces.

Prairies Hit Full Employment: Study

BY BRUCE LITTLE

Canada's national unemployment rate is still stuck at more than 9 percent, but the three Prairie provinces have already arrived at what many economists regard as full employment, according to a new study by Nesbitt Burns Inc.

Sherry Cooper, Nesbitt's chief economist, said the jobless rate in Alberta, Saskatchewan, and Manitoba has fallen below what she called the natural unemployment rate and, as a result, widespread labour shortages and strong wage pressures have emerged.

Ms Cooper said the strong showing by the Prairie trio is evidence that governments in other parts of Canada should not try to cure their unemployment problems by increasing government spending.

"Manitoba, Alberta, and Saskatchewan were the first [provinces] to eliminate their fiscal deficits, launch debt repayment programs, and implement tax relief measures," she said in the report, jointly written with Nesbitt economist Alex Araujo. "Low unemployment rates have not been the result of government make-work projects—quite the contrary."

The economists said Canada's natural unemployment rate—which they defined as the lowest rate consistent with stable inflation—has fallen to about 7.5 percent in the 1990s from 8.5 in the 1980s, but added that there are huge variations across the country.

Using a technique developed by analysts at the U.S. Federal Reserve Board, they calculated that the natural jobless rate ranges from 5.5 percent in Ontario to 16.5 in Newfoundland.

Ontario, with an actual unemployment rate of 8.2 percent in the third quarter, is still a long way—2.7 percentage points—from the point at which the province would begin to generate inflation pressures.

low unemployment rates, many more hours of work are needed to be eligible for EI, and EI benefits can be collected for a much shorter time.

These features of the program suggest that while EI reduces the hardship of unemployment, it can also increase the amount of unemployment. The explanation is based on one of the *Ten Principles of Economics* in Chapter 1: People respond to incentives. Because EI benefits stop when a worker takes a new job, we might expect that the unemployed would devote less effort to job search and be more likely to turn down unattractive job offers. In addition, the design of the program provides an incentive for people to enter the labour force when they might not otherwise have done so. The reason is that the EI program increases the total income people receive by working: They not only earn a wage while working, but also become eligible to collect EI benefits should they leave the job.

Many studies by labour economists have examined the incentive effects of Employment Insurance. A federal government department, Human Resources Development Canada (HRDC), has released, and continues to release, studies that attempt to measure the impact of the EI program on the labour market, the distribution of income, and living standards in Canada. The results of the studies released so far confirm economists' expectations of the program's effects. In one

In the late 1980s, Ontario's booming—and eventually overheated economy—was blamed by many Westerners as a major cause of the Bank of Canada's decision to raise interest rates to levels that tipped the economy into recession. At the time, British Columbia and Alberta were still in the early stages of recovery from prolonged recessions.

Ms Cooper said the natural unemployment rate "is a true measure of the degree of structural unemployment in a particular region." High structural unemployment in some regions is caused by age demographics, education levels, worker mobility, and reliance on seasonal employment.

The study said Quebec and the four Atlantic provinces all have natural unemployment rates of more than 10 percent, partly because university graduates make up a smaller share of the region's work force than they do elsewhere. The Atlantic provinces also rely heavily on seasonal jobs and have relatively more young people (whose jobless rate is higher) than

other parts of Canada. Quebec's high rate also reflects "its relatively immobile labour force," which stays put "mainly because of language barriers."

Ontario's low rate is the result of a well-diversified economy, a highly educated labour force, and high-technology hotbeds of activity in Ottawa and southwestern Ontario.

In the Prairies, Alberta's tight job market has already "led to substantial upward pressure on wages and large net in-migration," the report said. In the past year, average wages have increased 5 percent in the three Prairie provinces, but only 3 percent in the rest of Canada. Because the three provinces account for only one-fifth of Canada's economy, however, there is "no risk of a nationwide wage runup."

British Columbia's 7.5 percent natural jobless rate is higher than neighbouring Alberta's 6 percent rate because of its "greater economic reliance on seasonal industry and relatively militant

unions" and because of government policies that are seen as "business-unfriendly," the report said.

At a news conference, Ms Cooper said B.C.'s minimum wage has increased 40 percent since the province's NDP government took power in 1991. When the latest rise takes effect next April, it will be $7.15 an hour, compared with $5.00 in Alberta. She noted that the unemployment rate among young people, many of whom work for minimum wages, is 16.5 percent in B.C. and 10.7 in Alberta.

Despite a high rate of unemployment in many parts of Canada, the study said, "insufficient job creation is not the coast-to-coast problem that many are led to believe. Skilled labour is in short supply in many sectors, most notably marketing, design, engineering, [computer] programming, and oil and gas technology."

Source: *The Globe and Mail*, November 15, 1997, p. B3.

study it was found that job duration is affected by the length of time required to become eligible to collect EI benefits. In particular, the study found that those who collect EI tend to quit their jobs much sooner than they would otherwise have done if not for the availability of EI. The same study found that employers also respond to incentives of the EI program. Employers initiate layoffs only after workers become eligible for EI benefits. This is presumably done as a benefit to workers who in return accept lower wages. Other studies have found that success at finding employment while collecting EI benefits is affected by the number of weeks of benefits remaining on the individual's claim: the likelihood of finding new employment increases as EI recipients near the end of their benefits. Finally, many studies have confirmed that joining the labour force is significantly influenced by the availability and generosity of EI benefits. These results all suggest that the design of the EI program influences behaviour in ways that increase the unemployment rate.

Even though Employment Insurance increases the unemployment rate, we should not necessarily conclude that the program is a bad one. EI does achieve its primary goal of reducing the income uncertainty faced by unemployed people. What's more, one of the HRDC studies found that Employment Insurance allows unemployed people to conduct a more thorough job search, resulting in a higher wage in their new job than would otherwise have been the case. On the basis of such results, some economists have argued that Employment Insurance improves the ability of the economy to match each worker with the most appropriate job.

As mentioned above, the design of Canada's EI program has changed considerably over time. Changes introduced in 1971 made it substantially easier to become eligible to collect EI benefits and to collect it for a long time. Most economists believe these changes were responsible for a large increase in Canada's natural unemployment rate. Since 1990, many changes introduced to the program have had the opposite effect. The conditions under which one is eligible to collect EI benefits, and the length of time one is able to collect them, are now more stringent than they were in 1971. Economists believe these changes have contributed to a fall in Canada's natural unemployment rate from a peak reached in the late 1980s.

The study of Employment Insurance shows that the unemployment rate is an imperfect measure of a nation's overall level of economic well-being. Most economists agree that eliminating Employment Insurance would reduce the amount of unemployment in the economy. Yet economists disagree on whether economic well-being would be enhanced or diminished by this change in policy.

QUICK QUIZ: How would an increase in the world price of oil affect the amount of frictional unemployment? Is this unemployment undesirable? What public policies might affect the amount of unemployment caused by this price change?

MINIMUM-WAGE LAWS

Having seen how frictional unemployment results from the process of matching workers and jobs, let's now examine how structural unemployment results when the number of jobs is insufficient for the number of workers.

To understand structural unemployment, we begin by reviewing how unemployment arises from minimum-wage laws—a topic we first analyzed in Chapter 6. Although minimum wages are not the predominant reason for unemployment in our economy, they have an important effect on certain groups with particularly high unemployment rates. Moreover, the analysis of minimum wages is a natural place to start because, as we will see, it can be used to understand some of the other reasons for structural unemployment.

Figure 14-5 reviews the basic economics of a minimum wage. When a minimum-wage law forces the wage to remain above the level that balances supply and demand, it raises the quantity of labour supplied and reduces the quantity of labour demanded compared with the equilibrium level. There is a surplus of labour. Because there are more workers willing to work than there are jobs, some workers are unemployed.

Because we discussed minimum-wage laws extensively in Chapter 6, we will not discuss them further here. It is, however, important to note why minimum-wage laws are not a predominant reason for unemployment: Most workers in the economy have wages well above the legal minimum. Minimum-wage laws are binding most often for the least skilled and least experienced members of the labour force, such as teenagers. It is only among these workers that minimum-wage laws explain the existence of unemployment.

Although Figure 14-5 is drawn to show the effects of a minimum-wage law, it also illustrates a more general lesson: *If the wage is kept above the equilibrium level for any reason, the result is unemployment.* Minimum-wage laws are just one reason why wages may be "too high." In the remaining two sections of this chapter, we consider two other reasons why wages may be kept above the equilibrium level—unions and efficiency wages. The basic economics of unemployment in these cases is the same as that shown in Figure 14-5, but these explanations of unemployment can apply to many more of the economy's workers.

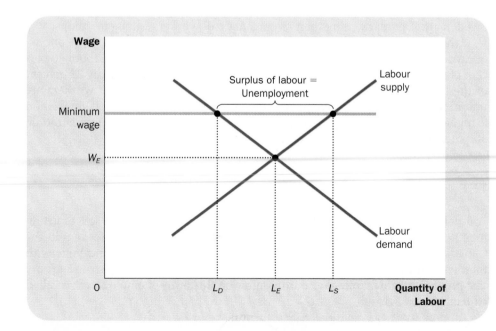

Figure 14-5

UNEMPLOYMENT FROM A WAGE ABOVE THE EQUILIBRIUM LEVEL.   In this labour market, the wage at which supply and demand balance is W_E. At this equilibrium wage, the quantity of labour supplied and the quantity of labour demanded both equal L_E. By contrast, if the wage is forced to remain above the equilibrium level, perhaps because of a minimum-wage law, the quantity of labour supplied rises to L_S, and the quantity of labour demanded falls to L_D. The resulting surplus of labour, L_S–L_D, represents unemployment.

At this point, however, we should stop and notice that the structural unemployment that arises from an above-equilibrium wage is, in an important sense, different from the frictional unemployment that arises from the process of job search. The need for job search is not due to the failure of wages to balance labour supply and labour demand. When job search is the explanation for unemployment, workers are *searching* for the jobs that best suit their tastes and skills. By contrast, when the wage is above the equilibrium level, the quantity of labour supplied exceeds the quantity of labour demanded, and workers are unemployed because they are *waiting* for jobs to open up.

QUICK QUIZ: Draw the supply curve and the demand curve for a labour market in which the wage is fixed above the equilibrium level. Show the quantity of labour supplied, the quantity demanded, and the amount of unemployment.

UNIONS AND COLLECTIVE BARGAINING

union

a worker association that bargains with employers over wages and working conditions

A **union** is a worker association that bargains with employers over wages and working conditions. About 30 percent of all Canadian workers now belong to unions. This level of labour-force unionization has remained more or less constant for the past twenty years. In the 1940s and 1950s, union membership as a fraction of the labour force was considerably smaller, at just 10 percent in 1941 and 20 percent in 1951. As union membership in Canada has grown, however, the opposite has occurred in the United States. Union membership in the United States peaked in the 1950s at about one-third of the labour force and has fallen ever since. Today, only about 16 percent of U.S. workers are union members. In contrast to North American rates, European union membership rates are quite high. For example, in Sweden and Denmark, more than 75 percent of all workers belong to unions.

Union membership as a fraction of the labour force varies by province and by occupation. Union membership is highest in Newfoundland, where about 40 percent of the labour force is unionized, and lowest in Alberta, where only 22 percent of the labour force is unionized. In the public sector 70 percent of workers are unionized, while in the private sector only 19 percent are unionized. Unionization is highest in industries within the public sector: education, public administration, and health care.

THE ECONOMICS OF UNIONS

collective bargaining

the process by which unions and firms agree on the terms of employment

A union is a type of cartel. Like any cartel, a union is a group of sellers acting together in the hope of exerting their joint market power. Most workers in the Canadian economy discuss their wages, benefits, and working conditions with their employers as individuals. By contrast, workers in a union do so as a group. The process by which unions and firms agree on the terms of employment is called **collective bargaining.**

When a union bargains with a firm, it asks for higher wages, better benefits, and better working conditions than the firm would offer in the absence of a union. If the union and the firm do not reach agreement, the union can organize a withdrawal of labour from the firm, called a **strike.** Because a strike reduces production, sales, and profit, a firm facing a strike threat is likely to agree to pay higher wages than it otherwise would. Economists who study the effects of unions typically find that union workers earn about 10 to 20 percent more than similar workers who do not belong to unions.

When a union raises the wage above the equilibrium level, it raises the quantity of labour supplied and reduces the quantity of labour demanded, resulting in unemployment. Those workers who remain employed are better off, but those who were previously employed and are now unemployed at the higher wage are worse off. Indeed, unions are often thought to cause conflict between different groups of workers—between the *insiders* who benefit from high union wages and the *outsiders* who do not get the union jobs.

The outsiders can respond to their status in one of two ways. Some of them remain unemployed and wait for the chance to become insiders and earn the high union wage. Others take jobs in firms that are not unionized. Thus, when unions raise wages in one part of the economy, the supply of labour increases in other parts of the economy. This increase in labour supply, in turn, reduces wages in industries that are not unionized. In other words, workers in unions reap the benefit of collective bargaining, while workers not in unions bear some of the cost.

The role of unions in the economy depends in part on the laws that govern union organization and collective bargaining. Normally, explicit agreements among members of a cartel are illegal. If firms that sell a common product were to agree to set a high price for that product, the agreement would be a "conspiracy to

strike

the organized withdrawal of labour from a firm by a union

"Gentlemen, nothing stands in the way of a final accord except that management wants profit maximization and the union wants more moola."

unduly limit competition." The government would prosecute these firms in civil and criminal court for violating Canada's competition laws. By contrast, unions are exempt from these laws. The policymakers who wrote the antitrust laws believed that workers needed greater market power as they bargained with employers. Indeed, various laws are designed to encourage the formation of unions. In particular, the National War Labour Order of 1944 provided private-sector employees with the right to union representation and collective bargaining. The Public Service Staff Relations Act of 1967 extended these rights to federal public-sector employees. Similar acts of provincial legislatures have extended these rights to provincial public-sector employees. Given these pieces of legislation, it is not surprising that 70 percent of public-sector employees are unionized. In the private sector, unions must approach workers in nonunionized companies and try to convince a majority of those workers of the benefits of union membership. While these membership drives are often unsuccessful, the very threat of such attempts at unionization likely have the effect of causing firms to increase wages and improve working conditions as a way of discouraging workers from joining the union.

ARE UNIONS GOOD OR BAD FOR THE ECONOMY?

Economists disagree about whether unions are good or bad for the economy as a whole. Let's consider both sides of the debate.

Critics of unions argue that unions are merely a type of cartel. When unions raise wages above the level that would prevail in competitive markets, they reduce the quantity of labour demanded, cause some workers to be unemployed, and reduce the wages in the rest of the economy. The resulting allocation of labour is, critics argue, both inefficient and inequitable. It is inefficient because high union wages reduce employment in unionized firms below the efficient, competitive level. It is inequitable because some workers benefit at the expense of other workers.

Advocates of unions contend that unions are a necessary antidote to the market power of the firms that hire workers. The extreme case of this market power is the "company town," where a single firm does most of the hiring in a geographic region. In a company town, if workers do not accept the wages and working conditions that the firm offers, they have little choice but to move or stop working. In the absence of a union, therefore, the firm could use its market power to pay lower wages and offer worse working conditions than would prevail if it had to compete with other firms for the same workers. In this case, a union may balance the firm's market power and protect the workers from being at the mercy of the firm owners.

Advocates of unions also claim that unions are important for helping firms respond efficiently to workers' concerns. Whenever a worker takes a job, the worker and the firm must agree on many attributes of the job in addition to the wage: hours of work, overtime, vacations, sick leave, health benefits, promotion schedules, job security, and so on. By representing workers' views on these issues, unions allow firms to provide the right mix of job attributes. Even if unions have the adverse effect of pushing wages above the equilibrium level and causing unemployment, they have the benefit of helping firms keep a happy and productive work force.

In the end, there is no consensus among economists about whether unions are good or bad for the economy. Like many institutions, their influence is probably beneficial in some circumstances and adverse in others.

QUICK QUIZ: How does a union in the auto industry affect wages and employment at General Motors and Ford? How does it affect wages and employment in other industries?

THE THEORY OF EFFICIENCY WAGES

A fourth reason why economies always experience some unemployment—in addition to job search, minimum-wage laws, and unions—is suggested by the theory of **efficiency wages.** According to this theory, firms operate more efficiently if wages are above the equilibrium level. Therefore, it may be profitable for firms to keep wages high even in the presence of a surplus of labour.

efficiency wages
above-equilibrium wages paid by firms in order to increase worker productivity

In some ways, the unemployment that arises from efficiency wages is similar to the unemployment that arises from minimum-wage laws and unions. In all three cases, unemployment is the result of wages above the level that balances the quantity of labour supplied and the quantity of labour demanded. Yet there is also an important difference. Minimum-wage laws and unions prevent firms from lowering wages in the presence of a surplus of workers. Efficiency-wage theory states that such a constraint on firms is unnecessary in many cases because firms may be better off keeping wages above the equilibrium level.

Why should firms want to keep wages high? In some ways, this decision seems odd, for wages are a large part of firms' costs. Normally, we expect profit-maximizing firms to want to keep costs—and therefore wages—as low as possible. The novel insight of efficiency-wage theory is that paying high wages might be profitable because they might raise the efficiency of a firm's workers.

There are several types of efficiency-wage theory. Each type suggests a different explanation for why firms may want to pay high wages. Let's now consider four of these types.

WORKER HEALTH

The first and simplest type of efficiency-wage theory emphasizes the link between wages and worker health. Better paid workers eat a more nutritious diet, and workers who eat a better diet are healthier and more productive. A firm may find it more profitable to pay high wages and have healthy, productive workers than to pay lower wages and have less healthy, less productive workers.

This type of efficiency-wage theory is not relevant for firms in rich countries such as Canada. In these countries, the equilibrium wages for most workers are well above the level needed for an adequate diet. Firms are not concerned that paying equilibrium wages would place their workers' health in jeopardy.

This type of efficiency-wage theory is more relevant for firms in less developed countries where inadequate nutrition is a more common problem. Unemployment is high in the cities of many poor African countries, for example. In these countries, firms may fear that cutting wages would, in fact, adversely influence their workers' health and productivity. In other words, concern over nutrition may explain why firms do not cut wages despite a surplus of labour.

WORKER TURNOVER

A second type of efficiency-wage theory emphasizes the link between wages and worker turnover. Workers quit jobs for many reasons—to take jobs in other firms, to move to other parts of the country, to leave the labour force, and so on. The frequency with which they quit depends on the entire set of incentives they face, including the benefits of leaving and the benefits of staying. The more a firm pays its workers, the less often its workers will choose to leave. Thus, a firm can reduce turnover among its workers by paying them a high wage.

Why do firms care about turnover? The reason is that it is costly for firms to hire and train new workers. Moreover, even after they are trained, newly hired workers are not as productive as experienced workers. Firms with higher turnover, therefore, will tend to have higher production costs. Firms may find it profitable to pay wages above the equilibrium level in order to reduce worker turnover.

WORKER EFFORT

A third type of efficiency-wage theory emphasizes the link between wages and worker effort. In many jobs, workers have some discretion over how hard to work. As a result, firms monitor the efforts of their workers, and workers caught shirking their responsibilities are fired. But not all shirkers are caught immediately because monitoring workers is costly and imperfect. A firm can respond to this problem by paying wages above the equilibrium level. High wages make workers more eager to keep their jobs and, thereby, give workers an incentive to put forward their best effort.

This particular type of efficiency-wage theory is similar to the old Marxist idea of the "reserve army of the unemployed." Marx thought that employers benefited from unemployment because the threat of unemployment helped to discipline those workers who had jobs. In the worker-effort variant of efficiency-wage theory, unemployment fills a similar role. If the wage were at the level that balanced supply and demand, workers would have less reason to work hard because if they were fired, they could quickly find new jobs at the same wage. Therefore, firms raise wages above the equilibrium level, causing unemployment and providing an incentive for workers not to shirk their responsibilities.

WORKER QUALITY

A fourth and final type of efficiency-wage theory emphasizes the link between wages and worker quality. When a firm hires new workers, it cannot perfectly

DILBERT® By Scott Adams

SOURCE: Copyright ©2001 United Feature Syndicate, Inc.

gauge the quality of the applicants. By paying a high wage, the firm attracts a better pool of workers to apply for its jobs.

To see how this might work, consider a simple example. Waterwell Company owns one well and needs one worker to pump water from the well. Two workers, Angelo and Ted, are interested in the job. Angelo, a proficient worker, is willing to work for $10 per hour. Below that wage, he would rather start his own lawn-mowing business. Ted, a complete incompetent, is willing to work for anything above $2 per hour. Below that wage, he would rather sit on the beach. Economists say that Angelo's *reservation wage*—the lowest wage he would accept—is $10, and Ted's reservation wage is $2.

What wage should the firm set? If the firm were interested in minimizing labour costs, it would set the wage at $2 per hour. At this wage, the quantity of workers supplied (one) would balance the quantity demanded. Ted would take the job, and Angelo would not apply for it. Yet suppose Waterwell knows that only one of these two applicants is competent, but it does not know whether it is Angelo or Ted. If the firm hires the incompetent worker, he will damage the well, causing the firm huge losses. In this case, the firm has a better strategy than paying the equilibrium wage of $2 and hiring Ted. It can offer $10 per hour, inducing both Angelo and Ted to apply for the job. By choosing randomly between these two applicants and turning the other away, the firm has a 50–50 chance of hiring the competent one. By contrast, if the firm offers any lower wage, it is sure to hire the incompetent worker.

This story illustrates a general phenomenon. When a firm faces a surplus of workers, it might seem profitable to reduce the wage it is offering. But by reducing the wage, the firm induces an adverse change in the mix of workers. In this case, at a wage of $10, Waterwell has two workers applying for one job. But if Waterwell responds to this labour surplus by reducing the wage, the competent worker (who has better alternative opportunities) will not apply. Thus, it is profitable for the firm to pay a wage above the level that balances supply and demand.

CASE STUDY   HENRY FORD AND THE VERY GENEROUS $5-A-DAY WAGE

Henry Ford was an industrial visionary. As founder of the Ford Motor Company, he was responsible for introducing modern techniques of production.

Rather than building cars with small teams of skilled artisans, Ford built cars on assembly lines in which unskilled workers were taught to perform the same simple tasks over and over again. The output of this assembly process was the Model T Ford, one of the most famous early cars.

In 1914, Ford introduced another innovation: the $5 workday. This might not seem like much today, but back then $5 was about twice the going wage. It was also far above the wage that balanced supply and demand. When the new $5-a-day wage was announced, long lines of job seekers formed outside the

FYI

The Economics of Asymmetric Information

In many situations in life, information is asymmetric: One person in a transaction knows more about what is going on than the other person. This possibility raises a variety of interesting problems for economic theory. Some of these problems were highlighted in our description of the theory of efficiency wages. These problems, however, go beyond the study of unemployment.

The worker-quality variant of efficiency-wage theory illustrates a general principle called *adverse selection*. Adverse selection arises when one person knows more about the attributes of a good than another, and as a result, the uninformed person runs the risk of being sold a good of low quality. In the case of worker quality, for instance, workers have better information about their own abilities than firms do. When a firm cuts the wage it pays, the selection of workers changes in a way that is adverse to the firm.

Adverse selection arises in many other circumstances. Here are two examples:

◆ Sellers of used cars know their vehicles' defects, whereas buyers often do not. Because owners of the worst cars are more likely to sell them than are owners of the best cars, buyers are correctly apprehensive about getting a "lemon." As a result, many people avoid buying cars in the used car market.

◆ Buyers of health insurance know more about their own health problems than do insurance companies. Because people with greater hidden health problems are more likely to buy health insurance than are other people, the price of health insurance reflects the costs of a sicker-than-average person. As a result, people with average health problems are discouraged from buying health insurance by the high price.

In each case, the market for the product—used cars or health insurance—does not work as well as it might because of the problem of adverse selection.

Similarly, the worker-effort variant of efficiency-wage theory illustrates a general phenomenon called *moral hazard*. Moral hazard arises when one person, called the *agent*, is performing some task on behalf of another person, called the *principal*. Because the principal cannot perfectly monitor the agent's behaviour, the agent tends to undertake less effort than the principal considers desirable. The term *moral hazard* refers to the risk of dishonest or otherwise inappropriate behaviour by the agent. In such a situation, the principal tries various ways to encourage the agent to act more responsibly.

In an employment relationship, the firm is the principal and the worker is the agent. The moral-hazard problem is the temptation of imperfectly monitored workers to shirk their responsibilities. According to the worker-effort variant of efficiency-wage theory, the principal can encourage the agent not to shirk by paying a wage above the equilibrium level because then the agent has more to lose if caught shirking. In this way, high wages reduce the problem of moral hazard.

Moral hazard arises in many other situations. Here are some examples:

◆ A homeowner with fire insurance buys too few fire extinguishers. The reason is that the homeowner bears the cost of the extinguisher while the insurance company receives much of the benefit.

◆ A baby sitter allows children to watch more television than the parents of the children prefer. The reason is that more educational activities require more energy from the baby sitter, even though they are beneficial for the children.

◆ A family lives near a river with a high risk of flooding. The reason it continues to live there is that the family enjoys the scenic views, and the government will bear part of the cost when it provides disaster relief after a flood.

Can you identify the principal and the agent in each of these three situations? How do you think the principal in each case might solve the problem of moral hazard?

Ford factories. The number of workers willing to work at this wage far exceeded the number of workers Ford needed.

Ford's high-wage policy had many of the effects predicted by efficiency-wage theory. Turnover fell, absenteeism fell, and productivity rose. Workers were so much more efficient that Ford's production costs were lower even though wages were higher. Thus, paying a wage above the equilibrium level was profitable for the firm. Henry Ford himself called the $5-a-day wage "one of the finest cost-cutting moves we ever made."

Historical accounts of this episode are also consistent with efficiency-wage theory. A historian of the early Ford Motor Company wrote, "Ford and his associates freely declared on many occasions that the high-wage policy turned out to be good business. By this they meant that it had improved the discipline of the workers, given them a more loyal interest in the institution, and raised their personal efficiency."

Why did it take Henry Ford to introduce this efficiency wage? Why were other firms not already taking advantage of this seemingly profitable business strategy? According to some analysts, Ford's decision was closely linked to his use of the assembly line. Workers organized in an assembly line are highly interdependent. If one worker is absent or works slowly, other workers are less able to complete their own tasks. Thus, while assembly lines made production more efficient, they also raised the importance of low worker turnover, high worker quality, and high worker effort. As a result, paying efficiency wages may have been a better strategy for the Ford Motor Company than for other businesses at the time.

WORKERS OUTSIDE AN EARLY FORD FACTORY

QUICK QUIZ: Give four explanations for why firms might find it profitable to pay wages above the level that balances quantity of labour supplied and quantity of labour demanded.

CONCLUSION

In this chapter we discussed the measurement of unemployment and the reasons why economies always experience some degree of unemployment. We have seen how job search, minimum-wage laws, unions, and efficiency wages can all help explain why some workers do not have jobs. Which of these four explanations for the natural rate of unemployment are the most important for the Canadian economy and other economies around the world? Unfortunately, there is no easy way to tell. Economists differ in which of these explanations of unemployment they consider most important.

The analysis of this chapter yields an important lesson: Although the economy will always have some unemployment, its natural rate is not immutable. Many events and policies can change the amount of unemployment the economy typically experiences. As the information revolution changes the process of job search, as governments adjust the minimum wage and alter the eligibility requirements for Employment Insurance, as workers form or quit unions, and as firms alter their reliance on efficiency wages, the natural rate of unemployment evolves. Unemployment is not a simple problem with a simple solution. But how we choose to organize our society can profoundly influence how prevalent a problem it is.

Summary

- The unemployment rate is the percentage of those who would like to work who do not have jobs. Statistics Canada calculates this statistic monthly based on a survey of thousands of households.

- The unemployment rate is an imperfect measure of joblessness. Some people who call themselves unemployed may actually not want to work, and some people who would like to work have left the labour force after an unsuccessful search.

- In the Canadian economy, most people who become unemployed find work within a short period of time. Nonetheless, most unemployment observed at any given time is attributable to those people who are unemployed for long periods of time.

- One reason for unemployment is the time it takes for workers to search for jobs that best suit their tastes and skills. Employment Insurance is a government policy that, while protecting workers' incomes, increases the amount of frictional unemployment.

- A second reason why our economy always has some unemployment is minimum-wage laws. By raising the wage of unskilled and inexperienced workers above the equilibrium level, minimum-wage laws raise the quantity of labour supplied and reduce the quantity demanded. The resulting surplus of labour represents unemployment.

- A third reason for unemployment is the market power of unions. When unions push the wages in unionized industries above the equilibrium level, they create a surplus of labour.

- A fourth reason for unemployment is suggested by the theory of efficiency wages. According to this theory, firms find it profitable to pay wages above the equilibrium level. High wages can improve worker health, lower worker turnover, increase worker effort, and raise worker quality.

Key Concepts

labour force, p. 291
unemployment rate, p. 292
labour-force participation rate, p. 292
discouraged workers, p. 296
natural rate of unemployment, p. 298

cyclical unemployment, p. 298
frictional unemployment, p. 299
structural unemployment, p. 299
job search, p. 300
Employment Insurance, p. 301

union, p. 306
collective bargaining, p. 306
strike, p. 307
efficiency wages, p. 309

Questions for Review

1. What are the three labour-market categories into which Statistics Canada divides everyone? How does it compute the labour force, the unemployment rate, and the labour-force participation rate?

2. Is unemployment typically short-term or long-term? Explain.

3. Why is frictional unemployment inevitable? How might the government reduce the amount of frictional unemployment?

4. Are minimum-wage laws a better explanation for structural unemployment among teenagers or among postsecondary graduates? Why?

5. How do unions affect the natural rate of unemployment?

6. What claims do advocates of unions make to argue that unions are good for the economy?

7. Explain four ways in which a firm might increase its profits by raising the wages it pays.

Problems and Applications

1. Statistics Canada announced that in December 2000, of all adult Canadians, 14 974 500 were employed, 1 015 300 were unemployed, and 8 459 400 were not in the labour force. How big was the labour force? What was the labour-force participation rate? What was the unemployment rate?

2. As shown in Figure 14-3, the overall labour-force participation rate of men declined between 1976 and 1997. This overall decline reflects different patterns for different age groups, however, as shown in the following table:

	ALL MEN	MEN 15–24	MEN 25–54	MEN 55 AND OVER
1976	78%	68%	95%	48%
1997	72	63	91	33

Which group experienced the largest decline? Given this information, what factor may have played an important role in the decline in overall male labour-force participation over this period?

3. The labour-force participation rate of women increased sharply between 1976 and 1997, as shown in Figure 14-3. As with men, however, there were different patterns for different age groups, as shown in this table:

	ALL WOMEN	WOMEN 15-24	WOMEN 25-54	WOMEN 55 AND OVER
1976	46%	58%	52%	18%
1997	57	59	76	17

Why do you think that younger women experienced a bigger increase in labour-force participation than older women?

4. Between December 1998 and December 1999, total Canadian employment increased by 427 400 workers, but the number of unemployed workers declined by only 182 600. How are these numbers consistent with each other? Why might one expect a reduction in the number of people counted as unemployed to be smaller than the increase in the number of people employed?

5. Are the following workers more likely to experience short-term or long-term unemployment? Explain.
    a. a construction worker laid off because of bad weather
    b. a manufacturing worker who loses her job at a plant in an isolated area
    c. a stagecoach-industry worker laid off because of competition from railroads
    d. a short-order cook who loses his job when a new restaurant opens across the street
    e. an expert welder with little formal education who loses her job when the company installs automatic welding machinery

6. Using a diagram of the labour market, show the effect of an increase in the minimum wage on the wage paid to workers, the number of workers supplied, the number of workers demanded, and the amount of unemployment.

7. Do you think that firms in small towns or cities have more market power in hiring? Do you think that firms generally have more market power in hiring today than 50 years ago, or less? How do you think this change over time has affected the role of unions in the economy? Explain.

8. Consider an economy with two labour markets, neither of which is unionized. Now suppose a union is established in one market.
    a. Show the effect of the union on the market in which it is formed. In what sense is the quantity of labour employed in this market an inefficient quantity?
    b. Show the effect of the union on the nonunionized market. What happens to the equilibrium wage in this market?

9. It can be shown that an industry's demand for labour will become more elastic when the demand for the industry's product becomes more elastic. Let's consider the implications of this fact for the Canadian automobile industry and the Canadian autoworkers' union (the CAW).
    a. What happened to the elasticity of demand for Canadian cars when the Japanese developed a strong auto industry? What happened to the elasticity of demand for Canadian autoworkers? Explain.
    b. As the chapter explains, a union generally faces a tradeoff in deciding how much to raise wages, because a bigger increase is better for workers who remain employed but also results in a greater reduction in employment. How did the rise in auto imports from Japan affect the wage–employment tradeoff faced by the CAW?
    c. Do you think the growth of the Japanese auto industry increased or decreased the gap between the competitive wage and the wage chosen by the CAW? Explain.

10. Some workers in the economy are paid a flat salary and some are paid by commission. Which compensation scheme would require more monitoring by supervisors? In which case do firms have an incentive to pay more than the equilibrium level (as in the worker-effort variant of efficiency-wage theory)? What factors do you think determine the type of compensation firms choose?

11. Each of the following situations involves moral hazard. In each case, identify the principal and the agent, and explain why there is asymmetric information. How does the action described reduce the problem of moral hazard?
    a. Landlords require tenants to pay security deposits.
    b. Firms compensate top executives with options to buy company stock at a given price in the future.
    c. Car insurance companies offer discounts to customers who install antitheft devices in their cars.

12. Suppose that the Live-Long-and-Prosper Health Insurance Company charges $5000 annually for a family insurance policy. The company's president suggests that the company raise the annual price to $6000 in order to increase its profits. If the firm followed this suggestion, what economic problem might arise? Would the firm's pool of customers tend to become more or less healthy on average? Would the company's profits necessarily increase?

13. (This problem is challenging.) Suppose that Parliament passes a law requiring employers to provide employees some benefit (such as dental care) that raises the cost of an employee by $4 per hour.
    a. What effect does this employer mandate have on the demand for labour? (In answering this and the following questions, be quantitative when you can.)
    b. If employees place a value on this benefit exactly equal to its cost, what effect does this employer mandate have on the supply of labour?
    c. If the wage is free to balance supply and demand, how does this law affect the wage and the level of employment? Are employers better or worse off? Are employees better or worse off?
    d. If a minimum-wage law prevents the wage from balancing supply and demand, how does the employer mandate affect the wage, the level of employment, and the level of unemployment? Are employers better or worse off? Are employees better or worse off?
    e. Now suppose that workers do not value the mandated benefit at all. How does this alternative assumption change your answers to parts (b), (c), and (d) above?

Six

MONEY AND PRICES IN THE LONG RUN

15

THE MONETARY SYSTEM

When you walk into a restaurant to buy a meal, you get something of value—a full stomach. To pay for this service, you might hand the restaurateur several worn-out pieces of coloured paper decorated with strange symbols, birds, government buildings, and portraits of the queen or a dead prime minister. Or you might hand over a single piece of paper or plastic with the name of a bank and your signature. Whether you pay by cash, cheque, or debit card, the restaurateur is happy to work hard to satisfy your gastronomical desires in exchange for these pieces of paper which, in and of themselves, are worthless.

To anyone who has lived in a modern economy, this social custom is not at all odd. Even though paper money has no intrinsic value, the restaurateur is confident that, in the future, some third person will accept it in exchange for something that the restaurateur does value. And that third person is confident that some fourth person will accept the money, with the knowledge that yet a fifth person will accept the money . . . and so on. To the restaurateur and to other people in our society, your cash or cheque represents a claim to goods and services in the future.

IN THIS CHAPTER
YOU WILL . . .

Consider the nature of money and its functions in the economy

Learn about the Bank of Canada

Examine how the banking system helps determine the supply of money

Examine the tools used by the Bank of Canada to alter the supply of money

The social custom of using money for transactions is extraordinarily useful in a large, complex society. Imagine, for a moment, that there was no item in the economy widely accepted in exchange for goods and services. People would have to rely on *barter*—the exchange of one good or service for another—to obtain the things they need. To get your restaurant meal, for instance, you would have to offer the restaurateur something of immediate value. You could offer to wash some dishes, wash his car, or give him your family's secret recipe for meat loaf. An economy that relies on barter will have trouble allocating its scarce resources efficiently. In such an economy, trade is said to require the *double coincidence of wants*—the unlikely occurrence that two people each have a good or service that the other wants.

The existence of money makes trade easier. The restaurateur does not care whether you can produce a valuable good or service for him. He is happy to accept your money, knowing that other people will do the same for him. Such a convention allows trade to be roundabout. The restaurateur accepts your money and uses it to pay his chef, the chef uses her paycheque to send her child to daycare, the daycare centre uses this tuition to pay a teacher; and the teacher hires you to mow his lawn. As money flows from person to person in the economy, it facilitates production and trade, thereby allowing each person to specialize in what he or she does best and raising everyone's standard of living.

In this chapter we begin to examine the role of money in the economy. We discuss what money is, the various forms that money takes, how the banking system helps create money, and how the government controls the quantity of money in circulation. Because money is so important in the economy, we devote much effort in the rest of this book to learning how changes in the quantity of money affect various economic variables, including inflation, interest rates, production, and employment. Consistent with our long-run focus in the previous three chapters, in the next chapter we will examine the long-run effects of changes in the quantity of money. The short-run effects of monetary changes are a more complex topic, which we will take up later in the book. This chapter provides the background for all of this further analysis.

THE MEANING OF MONEY

What is money? This might seem like an odd question. When you read that billionaire Bill Gates has a lot of money, you know what that means: He is so rich that he can buy almost anything he wants. In this sense, the term *money* is used to mean *wealth*.

money

the set of assets in the economy that people regularly use to buy goods and services from other people

Economists, however, use the word in a more specific sense: **Money** is the set of assets in the economy that people regularly use to buy goods and services from other people. The cash in your wallet is money because you can use it to buy a meal at a restaurant or a shirt at a clothing store. By contrast, if you happened to own most of Microsoft Corporation, as Bill Gates does, you would be wealthy, but this asset is not considered a form of money. You could not buy a meal or a shirt with this wealth without first obtaining some cash. According to the economist's definition, money includes only those few types of wealth that are regularly accepted by sellers in exchange for goods and services.

THE FUNCTIONS OF MONEY

Money has three functions in the economy: It is a *medium of exchange*, a *unit of account*, and a *store of value*. These three functions together distinguish money from other assets, such as stocks, bonds, real estate, art, and even hockey cards. Let's examine each of these functions of money in turn.

A **medium of exchange** is an item that buyers give to sellers when they purchase goods and services. When you buy a shirt at a clothing store, the store gives you the shirt, and you give the store your money. This transfer of money from buyer to seller allows the transaction to take place. When you walk into a store, you are confident that the store will accept your money for the items it is selling because money is the commonly accepted medium of exchange.

A **unit of account** is the yardstick people use to post prices and record debts. When you go shopping, you might observe that a shirt costs $20 and a hamburger costs $2. Even though it would be accurate to say that the price of a shirt is 10 hamburgers and the price of a hamburger is 1/10 of a shirt, prices are never quoted in this way. Similarly, if you take out a loan from a bank, the size of your future loan repayments will be measured in dollars, not in a quantity of goods and services. When we want to measure and record economic value, we use money as the unit of account.

A **store of value** is an item that people can use to transfer purchasing power from the present to the future. When a seller accepts money today in exchange for a good or service, that seller can hold the money and become a buyer of another good or service at another time. Of course, money is not the only store of value in the economy, for a person can also transfer purchasing power from the present to the future by holding other assets. The term *wealth* is used to refer to the total of all stores of value, including both money and nonmonetary assets.

Economists use the term **liquidity** to describe the ease with which an asset can be converted into the economy's medium of exchange. Because money is the economy's medium of exchange, it is the most liquid asset available. Other assets vary widely in their liquidity. Most stocks and bonds can be sold easily with small cost, so they are relatively liquid assets. By contrast, selling a house, a Rembrandt painting, or a 1976 Wayne Gretzky hockey card requires more time and effort, so these assets are less liquid.

When people decide in what form to hold their wealth, they have to balance the liquidity of each possible asset against the asset's usefulness as a store of value. Money is the most liquid asset, but it is far from perfect as a store of value. When prices rise, the value of money falls. In other words, when goods and services become more expensive, each dollar in your wallet can buy less. This link between the price level and the value of money will turn out to be important for understanding how money affects the economy.

medium of exchange
an item that buyers give to sellers when they want to purchase goods and services

unit of account
the yardstick people use to post prices and record debts

store of value
an item that people can use to transfer purchasing power from the present to the future

liquidity
the ease with which an asset can be converted into the economy's medium of exchange

THE KINDS OF MONEY

When money takes the form of a commodity with intrinsic value, it is called **commodity money.** The term *intrinsic value* means that the item would have value even if it were not used as money. One example of commodity money is gold. Gold has intrinsic value because it is used in industry and in the making of jewellery. Although today we no longer use gold as money, historically gold has been a common form of money because it is relatively easy to carry, measure, and verify

commodity money
money that takes the form of a commodity with intrinsic value

for impurities. When an economy uses gold as money (or uses paper money that is convertible into gold on demand), it is said to be operating under a *gold standard*.

IN THE NEWS

Money on the Island of Yap

THE ROLE OF SOCIAL CUSTOM IN THE MONetary system is most apparent in foreign cultures with customs very different from our own. The following article describes the money on the island of Yap. As you read the article, ask yourself whether Yap is using a type of commodity money, a type of fiat money, or something in between.

Fixed Assets, or Why a Loan in Yap Is Hard to Roll Over

BY ART PINE

YAP, MICRONESIA—On this tiny South Pacific island, life is easy and the currency is hard.

Elsewhere, the world's troubled monetary system creaks along; floating exchange rates wreak havoc on currency markets, and devaluations are commonplace. But on Yap the currency is as solid as a rock. In fact, it *is* rock. Limestone to be precise.

For nearly 2000 years the Yapese have used large stone wheels to pay for major purchases, such as land, canoes, and permissions to marry. Yap is a U.S. trust territory, and the dollar is used in grocery stores and gas stations. But reliance on stone money, like the island's

ancient caste system and the traditional dress of loincloths and grass skirts, continues.

Buying property with stones is "much easier than buying it with U.S. dollars," says John Chodad, who recently purchased a building lot with a 30-inch stone wheel. "We don't know the value of the U.S. dollar." . . .

Stone wheels don't make good pocket money, so for small transactions, Yapese use other forms of currency, such as beer. Beer is proffered as payment for all sorts of odd jobs, including construction. The 10 000 people on Yap consume 40 000 to 50 000 cases a year, mostly of Budweiser. . . .

The people of Yap have been using stone money ever since a Yapese warrior named Anagumang first brought the huge stones from limestone caverns on neighbouring Palau, some 1500 to 2000 years ago. Inspired by the moon, he fashioned the stone into large circles. The rest is history.

Yapese lean the stone wheels against their houses or prop up rows of them in village "banks." Most of the stones are 0.8 to 1.5 m in diameter, but some are as much as 3.7 m across. Each has a hole in the centre so it can be slipped onto the trunk of a fallen betel nut tree and carried. It takes twenty men to lift some stones.

By custom, the stones are worthless when broken. You never hear people on Yap musing about wanting a piece of the rock. Rather than risk a broken stone—or back—Yapese tend to leave the larger stones where they are and make a mental accounting that the ownership has been transferred—much

MONEY ON THE ISLAND OF YAP: NOT EXACTLY POCKET CHANGE

as gold bars used in international transactions change hands without leaving the vaults of the New York Federal Reserve Bank. . . .

There are some decided advantages to using massive stones for money. They are immune to blackmarket trading, for one thing, and they pose formidable obstacles to pickpockets. In addition, there aren't any sterile debates about how to stabilize the Yapese monetary system. With only 6600 stone wheels remaining on the island, the money supply stays put. . . .

Meanwhile, Yap's stone money may be about to take on international significance. Just yesterday, Washington received notice that Tosiho Nakayama, the president of Micronesia, plans to bring a stone disk when he visits the United States next month. It will be flown by Air Force jet.

Officials say Mr. Nakayama intends the stone as Micronesia's symbolic contribution toward reducing the U.S. budget deficit.

SOURCE: *The Wall Street Journal*, March 29, 1984, p. A1.

Another example of commodity money is cigarettes. In prisoner-of-war camps during World War II, prisoners traded goods and services with one another using cigarettes as the store of value, unit of account, and medium of exchange. Similarly, as the Soviet Union was breaking up in the late 1980s, cigarettes started replacing the ruble as the preferred currency in Moscow. In both cases, even non-smokers were happy to accept cigarettes in an exchange, knowing that they could use the cigarettes to buy other goods and services.

Money without intrinsic value is called **fiat money.** A *fiat* is simply an order or decree, and fiat money is established as money by government decree. For example, compare the paper dollars in your wallet (printed by the Canadian government) and the paper dollars from a game of Monopoly (printed by the Parker Brothers game company). Why can you use the first to pay your bill at a restaurant but not the second? The answer is that the Canadian government has decreed its dollars to be valid money. Each paper dollar in your wallet reads: "This note is legal tender."

Although the government is central to establishing and regulating a system of fiat money (by prosecuting counterfeiters, for example), other factors are also required for the success of such a monetary system. To a large extent, the acceptance of fiat money depends as much on expectations and social convention as on government decree. The Soviet government in the 1980s never abandoned the ruble as the official currency. Yet the people of Moscow preferred to accept cigarettes (or even American dollars) in exchange for goods and services because they were more confident that these alternative monies would be accepted by others in the future.

fiat money
money without intrinsic value that is used as money because of government decree

"Gee, these new twenties look just like Monopoly money."

MONEY IN THE CANADIAN ECONOMY

As we will see, the quantity of money circulating in the economy, called the *money stock,* has a powerful influence on many economic variables. But before we consider why that is true, we need to ask a preliminary question: What is the quantity of money? In particular, suppose you were given the task of measuring how much money there is in the Canadian economy. What would you include in your measure?

The most obvious asset to include is **currency**—the paper bills and coins in the hands of the public. Currency is clearly the most widely accepted medium of exchange in our economy. There is no doubt that it is part of the money stock.

Yet currency is not the only asset that you can use to buy goods and services. Many stores also accept debit cards or even personal cheques. Wealth held in your chequing account is almost as convenient for buying things as wealth held in your wallet. To measure the money stock, therefore, you might want to include **demand deposits**—balances in bank accounts that depositors can access on demand simply by writing a cheque or using a debit card.

Once you start to consider balances in chequing accounts as part of the money stock, you are led to consider the large variety of other accounts that people hold at banks and other financial institutions. Bank depositors can often write cheques against the balances in their savings accounts, but they can easily transfer funds from savings into chequing accounts. In addition, depositors in money market mutual funds can sometimes write cheques against their balances. Thus, these other accounts should plausibly be part of the Canadian money stock.

currency
the paper bills and coins in the hands of the public

demand deposits
balances in bank accounts that depositors can access on demand by writing a cheque or using a debit card

Table 15-1

TWO MEASURES OF THE MONEY STOCK FOR THE CANADIAN ECONOMY. The two most widely followed measures of the money stock are M1 and M2.

MEASURE	AMOUNT IN 2000	WHAT'S INCLUDED
M1	$106 billion	Currency Demand deposits
M2	$488 billion	Everything in M1 Savings deposits Personal term deposits

SOURCE: Bank of Canada.

In a complex economy such as ours, it is not easy to draw a line between assets that can be called "money" and assets that cannot. The coins in your pocket are clearly part of the money stock, and the CN Tower clearly is not, but there are many assets in between these extremes for which the choice is less clear. Therefore, various measures of the money stock are available for the Canadian economy. Table 15-1 shows the two most important, designated M1 and M2. Each of these measures uses a slightly different criterion for distinguishing monetary and non-monetary assets.

For our purposes in this book, we need not dwell on the differences between the various measures of money. The important point is that the money stock for the Canadian economy includes not just currency but also deposits in banks and other financial institutions that can be readily accessed and used to buy goods and services.

CASE STUDY   WHERE IS ALL THE CURRENCY?

One puzzle about the money stock of the Canadian economy concerns the amount of currency. In 2000 about $33 billion of currency was outstanding. To put this number in perspective, we can divide it by 25 million, the number of adults (age 15 and over) in Canada. This calculation implies that the average adult holds about $1300 of currency. Most people are surprised to learn that our economy has so much currency because they carry far less than this in their wallets.

Who is holding all of this currency? No one knows for sure. Some of the currency is held by banks and other firms, but a plausible explanation is that much of the currency is being held by tax evaders, drug dealers, and other criminals. For most people in the Canadian economy, currency is not a particularly good way to hold large amounts of wealth. Currency can be lost or stolen. Moreover, currency does not earn interest, unlike money in a bank account. Thus, most people hold only small amounts of currency. By contrast, criminals prefer not to hold their wealth in banks. A bank deposit would give police a paper trail with which to trace their illegal activities. For criminals, currency may be the best store of value available.

A similar calculation for the United States economy gives about $2500 in U.S. currency per adult, which is even more surprising. Perhaps there is more criminal activity in the United States than in Canada. But a second plausible

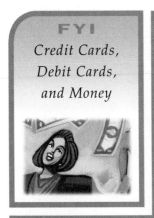

FYI

*Credit Cards,
Debit Cards,
and Money*

It might seem natural to include credit cards as part of the economy's stock of money. After all, people use credit cards to make many of their purchases. Aren't credit cards, therefore, a medium of exchange?

Although at first this argument may seem persuasive, credit cards are excluded from all measures of the quantity of money. The reason is that credit cards are not really a method of payment but a method of *deferring* payment. When you buy a meal with a credit card, the bank that issued the card pays the restaurant what it is due. At a later date, you will have to repay the bank (perhaps with interest). When the time comes to pay your credit card bill, you will probably do so by writing a cheque against your chequing account. The balance in this chequing account is part of the economy's stock of money.

Notice that credit cards are very different from debit cards, which automatically withdraw funds from a bank account to pay for items bought. Rather than allowing the user to postpone payment for a purchase, a debit card allows the user immediate access to deposits in a bank account. In this sense, a debit card is more similar to a cheque than to a credit card. The account balances that lie behind debit cards are included in measures of the quantity of money.

Even though credit cards are not considered a form of money, they are nonetheless important for analyzing the monetary system. People who have credit cards can pay many of their bills all at once at the end of the month, rather than sporadically as they make purchases. As a result, people who have credit cards probably hold less money on average than people who do not have credit cards. Thus, the introduction and increased popularity of credit cards may reduce the amount of money that people choose to hold.

IS THIS MONEY?

explanation is that much of the U.S. currency is held outside the United States. In countries without a stable monetary system, people often prefer U.S. dollars to domestic assets. It is, in fact, not unusual to see U.S. dollars being used around the world as a medium of exchange, unit of account, and store of value. The Canadian dollar, in contrast, is rarely used outside Canada.

■ **QUICK QUIZ:**   List and describe the three functions of money.

THE BANK OF CANADA

Whenever an economy relies on a system of fiat money, as the Canadian economy does, some organization must be responsible for controlling the stock of money. In Canada, that organization is the **Bank of Canada.** If you look at a Canadian bank note, you will see on it the words "Bank of Canada" and that it is signed by the governor and the deputy governor of the Bank. The Bank of Canada is an example of a **central bank**—an institution designed to control the quantity of money in the economy. Other major central banks around the world include the

Bank of Canada
the central bank of Canada

central bank
an institution designed to control the quantity of money in the economy

Bank of England, the Bank of Japan, the European Central Bank, and the Federal Reserve Board of the United States.

THE BANK OF CANADA ACT

Until the Great Depression of the 1930s, Canada had no central bank. Bank notes were issued by the Department of Finance and by the large commercial banks, like the Bank of Montreal. The monetary system was regulated by the Department of Finance acting together with the large commercial banks. The gold standard ensured that bank notes could normally be exchanged for a fixed quantity of gold. The economic problems of the Great Depression, and the need to control the quantity of fiat money when the gold standard collapsed, led the government to set up a royal commission to study the issues. The commission recommended that a central bank be established. As a result, in 1934 Parliament enacted the Bank of Canada Act, which laid down the responsibilities of the Bank of Canada. The Bank was established in 1935 and nationalized in 1938, so it is now owned by the Canadian government.

The Bank of Canada is managed by a board of directors composed of the governor, the senior deputy governor, and twelve directors, including the deputy minister of finance. The current governor of the Bank of Canada, David Dodge, was appointed in 2001. All members of the board of directors are appointed by the minister of finance, with seven-year terms for the governor and senior deputy governor and three-year terms for the other directors. The significance of this management structure is that ultimately the Bank of Canada is controlled by the Canadian government; the government not only appoints the board of directors but can, as a last resort, issue a written directive to the governor with which he or she must comply.

In practice, however, the Bank of Canada is largely independent of the Canadian government. Just as Supreme Court judges are appointed for life to insulate them from politics, the seven-year term of the governor of the Bank of Canada insulates him or her from short-term political pressures when he or she formulates monetary policy. And it is generally accepted that the governor would immediately resign if issued a written directive from the minister of finance. The threat of the turmoil in financial markets that would follow the governor's resignation means that the minister of finance rarely uses this weapon of last resort.

Commercial banks—like the Bank of Montreal, the Royal Bank, the Toronto-Dominion Bank, the Canadian Imperial Bank of Commerce, and the Bank of Nova Scotia—are owned by their individual shareholders. The primary responsibility of these commercial banks is to maximize the profits they earn on behalf of their shareholders. Central banks, like the Bank of Canada, are owned by the government and hand over any profits they earn to the government. Their primary responsibility, however, is not to maximize profits but to act in the national interest. The preamble to the Bank of Canada Act reads as follows:

> Whereas it is desirable to establish a central bank in Canada to regulate credit and currency in the best interests of the economic life of the nation, to control and protect the external value of the national monetary unit and to mitigate by its influence fluctuations in the general level of production, trade, prices and employment, so far as may be possible within the scope of monetary action, and generally to promote the economic and financial welfare of Canada. . . .

The Bank of Canada has four related jobs. The first is to issue currency. The Bank of Canada Act gives the Bank a monopoly over the right to issue notes for circulation in Canada. The second job is to act as banker to the commercial banks. Just as you may have a demand deposit at the Bank of Montreal, the Bank of Montreal (and the other large commercial banks) has a demand deposit at the Bank of Canada. These deposits at the Bank of Canada enable the commercial banks to make payments to one another. The Bank of Canada makes daily loans to banks when banks themselves need to borrow money to make payments to other banks. Also, when financially troubled banks find themselves short of cash, the Bank of Canada may occasionally act as a lender of last resort—a lender to those who cannot borrow anywhere else—in order to maintain stability in the overall banking system. The third job is to act as banker to the Canadian government. The government of Canada has a demand deposit at the Bank of Canada as well as demand deposits at the large commercial banks. The Bank manages the government's bank accounts, foreign exchange reserves, and national debt on behalf of the government.

The Bank of Canada's fourth and most important job is to control the quantity of money that is made available to the economy, called the **money supply**. Decisions by policy-makers concerning the money supply constitute **monetary policy**.

MONETARY POLICY

money supply
the quantity of money available in the economy

monetary policy
the setting of the money supply by policymakers in the central bank

The Bank of Canada has the power to increase or decrease the number of dollars in the economy. In simple metaphorical terms, you can imagine the Bank of Canada printing up $20 bills and dropping them around the country by helicopter. Similarly, you can imagine the Bank of Canada using a giant vacuum cleaner to suck $20 bills out of people's wallets. Although in practice the Bank of Canada's methods of controlling the money supply are more complex and subtle than this, the helicopter–vacuum metaphor is a good first approximation to the meaning of monetary policy. We discuss later how the Bank of Canada actually changes the money supply.

The Bank is an important institution because changes in the money supply can profoundly affect the economy. One of the *Ten Principles of Economics* in Chapter 1 is that prices rise when the government prints too much money. Another of the *Ten Principles of Economics* is that society faces a short-run tradeoff between inflation and unemployment. The power of the Bank of Canada rests on these principles. For reasons we discuss more fully in coming chapters, the Bank of Canada's policy decisions have an important influence on the economy's rate of inflation in the long run and the economy's employment and production in the short run. Indeed, the governor of the Bank of Canada might be called the second most powerful person in Canada.

To learn more about the Bank of Canada, check out its Web site at http://www.bankofcanada.ca.

QUICK QUIZ: What is the difference between a central bank like the Bank of Canada and a commercial bank like the Bank of Montreal?

COMMERCIAL BANKS AND THE MONEY SUPPLY

So far we have introduced the concept of "money" and discussed the role of the Bank of Canada. Although the Bank alone is responsible for Canadian monetary policy, it can control the supply of money only through its influence on the whole banking system. We now look at the role played by commercial banks (which include credit unions and trust companies) in the monetary system.

Recall that the amount of money you hold includes both currency (the bills in your wallet and coins in your pocket) and demand deposits (the balance in your chequing account). Because demand deposits are held in banks, the behaviour of banks can influence the quantity of demand deposits in the economy and, therefore, the money supply. This section examines how banks affect the money supply and how they complicate the Bank of Canada's job of controlling the money supply.

THE SIMPLE CASE OF 100-PERCENT-RESERVE BANKING

To see how banks influence the money supply, it is useful to imagine first a world without any banks at all. In this simple world, currency is the only form of money. To be concrete, let's suppose that the total quantity of currency is $100. The supply of money is, therefore, $100.

Now suppose that someone opens a bank, appropriately called First National Bank. First National Bank is only a depository institution—that is, it accepts deposits but does not make loans. The purpose of the bank is to give depositors a safe place to keep their money. Whenever a person deposits some money, the bank keeps the money in its vault until the depositor comes to withdraw it or writes a cheque against his or her balance. Deposits that banks have received but have not loaned out are called **reserves.** In this imaginary economy, all deposits are held as reserves, so this system is called *100-percent-reserve banking.*

We can express the financial position of First National Bank with a *T-account*, which is a simplified accounting statement that shows changes in a bank's assets and liabilities. Here is the T-account for First National Bank if the economy's entire $100 of money is deposited in the bank:

reserves

deposits that banks have received but have not loaned out

"I've heard a lot *about* money, and now I'd like to try some."

FIRST NATIONAL BANK

Assets		Liabilities	
Reserves	$100.00	Deposits	$100.00

On the left-hand side of the T-account are the bank's assets of $100 (the reserves it holds in its vaults). On the right-hand side of the T-account are the bank's liabilities of $100 (the amount it owes to its depositors). Notice that the assets and liabilities of First National Bank exactly balance.

Now consider the money supply in this imaginary economy. Before First National Bank opens, the money supply is the $100 of currency that people are holding. After the bank opens and people deposit their currency, the money supply is the $100 of demand deposits. (There is no longer any currency outstanding, because it is all in the bank vault.) Each deposit in the bank reduces currency and raises demand deposits by exactly the same amount, leaving the money supply unchanged. Thus, *if banks hold all deposits in reserve, banks do not influence the supply of money.*

MONEY CREATION WITH FRACTIONAL-RESERVE BANKING

Eventually, the bankers at First National Bank may start to reconsider their policy of 100-percent-reserve banking. Leaving all that money sitting idle in their vaults seems unnecessary. Why not use some of it to make loans? Families buying houses, firms building new factories, and students paying for university would all be happy to pay interest to borrow some of that money for a while. Of course, First National Bank has to keep some reserves so that currency is available if depositors want to make withdrawals. But if the flow of new deposits is roughly the same as the flow of withdrawals, First National needs to keep only a fraction of its deposits in reserve. Thus, First National adopts a system called **fractional-reserve banking.**

The fraction of total deposits that a bank holds as reserves is called the **reserve ratio.** This ratio is determined by a combination of government regulation and bank policy. Some central banks around the world place a minimum on the amount of reserves that banks hold, called a *reserve requirement.* The Bank of Canada used to do this, but has recently abandoned reserve requirements. But banks will hold reserves above any legal minimum, and will hold reserves even if they are not required to do so by law, so they can be more confident that they will not run short of cash. For our purpose here, we just take the reserve ratio as given and examine what fractional-reserve banking means for the money supply.

Let's suppose that First National has a reserve ratio of 10 percent. This means that it keeps 10 percent of its deposits in reserve and loans out the rest. Now let's look again at the bank's T-account:

fractional-reserve banking
a banking system in which banks hold only a fraction of deposits as reserves

reserve ratio
the fraction of deposits that banks hold as reserves

FIRST NATIONAL BANK

Assets		Liabilities	
Reserves	$10.00	Deposits	$100.00
Loans	90.00		

First National still has $100 in liabilities because making the loans did not alter the bank's obligation to its depositors. But now the bank has two kinds of assets: It has

$10 of reserves in its vault, and it has loans of $90. (These loans are liabilities of the people taking out the loans, but they are assets of the bank making the loans because the borrowers will later repay the bank.) In total, First National's assets still equal its liabilities.

Once again consider the supply of money in the economy. Before First National makes any loans, the money supply is the $100 of deposits in the bank. Yet when First National makes these loans, the money supply increases. The depositors still have demand deposits totalling $100, but now the borrowers hold $90 in currency. The money supply (which equals currency plus demand deposits) equals $190. Thus, *when banks hold only a fraction of deposits in reserve, banks create money.*

At first, this creation of money by fractional-reserve banking may seem too good to be true because it appears that the bank has created money out of thin air. To make this creation of money seem less miraculous, note that when First National Bank loans out some of its reserves and creates money, it does not create any wealth. Loans from First National give the borrowers some currency and thus the ability to buy goods and services. Yet the borrowers are also taking on debts, so the loans do not make them any richer. In other words, as a bank creates the asset of money, it also creates a corresponding liability for its borrowers. At the end of this process of money creation, the economy is more liquid in the sense that there is more of the medium of exchange, but the economy is no wealthier than before.

THE MONEY MULTIPLIER

The creation of money does not stop with First National Bank. Suppose the borrower from First National uses the $90 to buy something from someone who then deposits the currency in Second National Bank. Here is the T-account for Second National Bank:

SECOND NATIONAL BANK

ASSETS		LIABILITIES	
Reserves	$ 9.00	Deposits	$90.00
Loans	81.00		

After the deposit, this bank has liabilities of $90. If Second National also has a reserve ratio of 10 percent, it keeps assets of $9 in reserve and makes $81 in loans. In this way, Second National Bank creates an additional $81 of money. If this $81 is eventually deposited in Third National Bank, which also has a reserve ratio of 10 percent, this bank keeps $8.10 in reserve and makes $72.90 in loans. Here is the T-account for Third National Bank:

THIRD NATIONAL BANK

ASSETS		LIABILITIES	
Reserves	$ 8.10	Deposits	$81.00
Loans	72.90		

The process goes on and on. Each time that money is deposited and a bank loan is made, more money is created.

How much money is eventually created in this economy? Let's add it up:

Original deposit   = $ 100.00
First National lending   = $ 90.00 [= 0.9 × $100.00]
Second National lending   = $ 81.00 [= 0.9 × $90.00]
Third National lending   = $ 72.90 [= 0.9 × $81.00]
                 •   •
                 •   •
                 •   •
_____
Total money supply   = $1000.00

It turns out that even though this process of money creation can continue forever, it does not create an infinite amount of money. If you laboriously add the infinite sequence of numbers in the foregoing example, you find that the $100 of reserves generates $1000 of money. The amount of money the banking system generates with each dollar of reserves is called the **money multiplier**. In this imaginary economy, where the $100 of reserves generates $1000 of money, the money multiplier is 10.

What determines the size of the money multiplier? It turns out that the answer is simple: *The money multiplier is the reciprocal of the reserve ratio.* If R is the reserve ratio for all banks in the economy, then each dollar of reserves generates $1/R$ dollars of money. In our example, $R = 1/10$, so the money multiplier is 10.

money multiplier
the amount of money the banking system generates with each dollar of reserves

---

FYI

Zero Reserve Ratios

Over the years, Canadian banks have chosen to hold smaller and smaller ratios of reserves to deposits. The main reason for this decline is that Canadian banks are no longer legally required to hold reserves, and since they can quickly borrow currency from the Bank of Canada if they need it, they only hold enough currency for their customers' daily needs. Currently the reserve ratio is about 2 percent, which makes the money multiplier about 50! What would happen to the money supply if banks' reserve ratios became zero?

With a zero reserve ratio, all currency would be in people's wallets rather than in banks' reserves. For a given amount of currency, the size of the money supply depends on the *currency ratio*—the fraction of the total money supply that people want to hold in the form of currency. If the currency ratio is 100 percent, so that people want to hold all of their money in the form of currency, there will be no bank deposits at all and the money supply will equal the quantity of currency. If the currency ratio is 50 percent, so that people want to keep $1 in currency for every $1 they hold in bank deposits, the total money supply (currency plus deposits) in equilibrium will equal two times the quantity of currency. (If people held excess currency, they would deposit the excess currency in the banks, which would then expand loans, deposits, and the money supply until the equilibrium is reached.) If the currency ratio is 10 percent, so that people want to keep $1 in currency for every $9 they hold in bank deposits, the total money supply in equilibrium will equal ten times the quantity of currency.

In an economy where banks hold zero reserves against deposits, the money supply will be the reciprocal of the currency ratio times the quantity of currency. For example, if the currency ratio is 50 percent (equals 1/2), the money supply will be 2 times the quantity of currency in circulation.

In Canada's monetary system today, where banks' reserve ratios are very small, the reserve ratio is much less important than the currency ratio.

This reciprocal formula for the money multiplier makes sense. If a bank holds $1000 in deposits, then a reserve ratio of 1/10 (10 percent) means that the bank must hold $100 in reserves. The money multiplier just turns this idea around: If the banking system as a whole holds a total of $100 in reserves, it can have only $1000 in deposits. In other words, if R is the ratio of reserves to deposits at each bank (that is, the reserve ratio), then the ratio of deposits to reserves in the banking system (that is, the money multiplier) must be $1/R$.

This formula shows how the amount of money banks create depends on the reserve ratio. If the reserve ratio were only 1/20 (5 percent), then the banking system would have 20 times as much in deposits as in reserves, implying a money multiplier of 20. Each dollar of reserves would generate $20 of money. Similarly, if the reserve ratio were 1/5 (20 percent), deposits would be 5 times reserves, the money multiplier would be 5, and each dollar of reserves would generate $5 of money. *Thus, the higher the reserve ratio, the less of each deposit banks loan out, and the smaller the money multiplier.* In the special case of 100-percent-reserve banking, the reserve ratio is 1, the money multiplier is 1, and banks do not make loans or create money.

THE BANK OF CANADA'S TOOLS OF MONETARY CONTROL

As we have already discussed, the Bank of Canada is responsible for controlling the supply of money in the economy. Now that we understand how fractional-reserve banking works, we are in a better position to understand how the Bank of Canada can carry out this job. Because banks create money in a system of fractional-reserve banking, the Bank of Canada's control of the money supply is indirect. When the Bank decides to change the money supply, it must consider how its actions will work through the banking system.

Over its history, the Bank of Canada has used different methods of controlling the money supply. Different central banks around the world likewise use different tools of monetary control. Central banks have three main tools in their toolbox: open-market operations, reserve requirements, and the bank rate. The Bank of Canada currently uses open-market operations and the bank rate to control the money supply.

Open-Market Operations   Central banks can increase the supply of money in circulation by buying something. They can decrease the supply of money by selling something. It really doesn't matter what the Bank of Canada buys or sells. For example, if the Bank buys a new computer for its researchers with $1000 of newly printed currency, the firm that sold the computer to the Bank of Canada now holds an extra $1000 cash, so the money supply increases by $1000 immediately. If the Bank sells a used computer for $200 cash, the quantity of currency in circulation will immediately decrease by $200.

Now the Bank of Canada does not buy or sell a large quantity of computers, so any changes in the money supply from buying or selling computers are small enough to be ignored. But the Bank does buy and sell a large quantity of Canadian government bonds. It conducts **open-market operations** when it buys or sells government bonds from the public. To increase the money supply, the Bank can buy government bonds or Treasury bills (a Treasury bill is just a short-term government bond). The dollars the Bank of Canada pays for the bonds increase the number of

open-market operations
the purchase or sale of government bonds by the Bank of Canada

dollars in circulation. Some of these new dollars are held as currency, and some are deposited in banks. Each new dollar held as currency increases the money supply by exactly $1. Each new dollar deposited in a bank increases the money supply by a greater amount because it increases reserves and, thereby, the amount of money that a fractional-reserve banking system can create.

To reduce the money supply, the Bank of Canada can do just the opposite: It can sell government bonds to the public. The public pays for these bonds with its holdings of currency and bank deposits, directly reducing the amount of money in circulation. In addition, as people make withdrawals from banks, banks find themselves with a smaller quantity of reserves. In response, banks reduce their lending, and the process of money creation reverses itself.

The money supply increases whenever the Bank of Canada buys something; whether it is a computer or a government bond, the principle is the same. But Bank of Canada operations in the computer market are minuscule; Bank operations in the bond market are much bigger. Another important market in which the Bank of Canada buys and sells things is the foreign exchange market. Just as the Bank's purchases and sales of government bonds are called open-market operations, so its purchases and sales of foreign moneys are called **foreign exchange market operations.** If the Bank buys $100 million U.S. dollars in the foreign exchange market for $150 million Canadian, the Canadian money supply increases immediately by $150 million. If the Bank sells foreign currency from its foreign exchange reserves, it gets Canadian dollars in exchange. Those Canadian dollars are withdrawn from circulation, so the Canadian money supply is reduced.

foreign exchange market operations
the purchase or sale of foreign money by the Bank of Canada

Sometimes the Bank of Canada wants to sell foreign currency in the foreign exchange market to support the Canadian dollar's exchange rate, but it does not want the money supply to fall. To do this, the Bank uses the Canadian dollars it acquires in the foreign exchange market to buy government bonds, thus putting the Canadian dollars back into circulation. This process of offsetting a foreign exchange market operation with an open-market operation is called **sterilization.** Currently, the Bank of Canada routinely sterilizes foreign exchange market operations.

sterilization
the process of offsetting foreign exchange market operations with open-market operations, so that the effect on the money supply is cancelled out

When we discussed the role of the Bank of Canada in controlling the money supply, we introduced the helicopter–vacuum metaphor. Of course, the Bank does not literally hand out freshly printed money for free, nor does it literally vacuum money out of our wallets. But if the government of Canada borrows money by selling a government bond and gives that money away as transfer payments, and if the Bank of Canada buys that government bond in an open-market operation with newly printed money, the net result is that the public has more money and the same amount of bonds. This is exactly the same result as if the Bank of Canada had printed some money and loaned it to the government to drop out of a helicopter. And if the government of Canada increases taxes and uses the money to buy back a government bond and so reduce its debt, and if the Bank of Canada sells a government bond in an open-market operation, the net result is that the public has less money and the same amount of government bonds. This is exactly the same result as if the Bank of Canada had vacuumed money out of our wallets. The helicopter-vacuum metaphor is a lot more realistic than it first appeared!

Reserve Requirements Some central banks around the world (but not the Bank of Canada) also influence the money supply with **reserve requirements,** which are regulations on the minimum amount of reserves that banks must hold against deposits. Reserve requirements influence how much money the banking

reserve requirements
regulations on the minimum amount of reserves that banks must hold against deposits

system can create with each dollar of reserves. An increase in reserve requirements means that banks must hold more reserves and, therefore, can loan out less of each dollar that is deposited; as a result, reserve ratio goes up, money multiplier goes down, and the money supply decreases. Conversely, a decrease in reserve requirements lowers the reserve ratio, raises the money multiplier, and increases the money supply.

The Bank of Canada has rarely used changes in reserve requirements to control the money supply because frequent changes would disrupt the business of banking. Indeed, since 1994 the Bank has phased out reserve requirements altogether to give banks a level playing field with other financial institutions, which are not required to hold reserves. All that the Bank now requires is that banks that run out of reserves and are forced to borrow from the Bank of Canada to cover withdrawals pay a penalty to discourage them from doing so. With zero required reserves, Canadian banks choose a very low reserve ratio (currently around 2 percent), so the Canadian money multiplier is very large.

The Bank Rate   Central banks like the Bank of Canada act as bankers to the commercial banks. These banks hold demand deposits at the Bank of Canada, which are part of their reserves.

If Muriel, who has a chequing account at the Bank of Montreal, buys a car for $5000 from Julia, who has a chequing account at the Bank of Nova Scotia, the Bank of Montreal will deduct $5000 from Muriel's chequing account and pay $5000 to the Bank of Nova Scotia so that the Bank of Nova Scotia in turn can credit Julia's chequing account. Transfers between banks are done by the Bank of Canada. The Bank of Canada will deduct $5000 from the Bank of Montreal's demand deposit and add $5000 to the Bank of Nova Scotia's demand deposit. What happens if the Bank of Montreal doesn't have $5000 in its demand deposit at the Bank of Canada? The Bank of Montreal must then borrow from the Bank of Canada—in effect, it must get an overdraft. The rate of interest that central banks charge commercial banks for these loans is called the discount rate in some countries. In Canada it is called the **bank rate.**

bank rate
the interest rate the Bank of Canada charges on loans to the commercial banks

Since 1998 the Bank of Canada has allowed commercial banks to borrow freely at the bank rate and has paid commercial banks the bank rate, minus half a percent, on their deposits at the Bank of Canada. For example, if the bank rate is 5.0 percent, the Bank of Montreal must pay 5.0 percent interest if it needs to borrow from the Bank of Canada. And the Bank of Canada pays 4.5 percent interest if the Bank of Montreal has a positive balance in its demand deposit at the Bank of Canada. The "operating band" is then from 4.5 to 5.0 percent, which sets the pattern for all short-term interest rates in Canada. Commercial banks never need to pay more than the bank rate for short-term loans because they can always borrow from the Bank of Canada instead. Conversely, commercial banks never need to accept less than the bank rate, minus half a percent, when they make short-term loans because they can always lend to the Bank of Canada instead.

The Bank of Canada can alter the money supply by changing the bank rate. A higher bank rate discourages banks from borrowing reserves from the Bank. Thus, an increase in the bank rate reduces the quantity of reserves in the banking system, which in turn reduces the money supply. Conversely, a lower bank rate encourages bank borrowing from the Bank, increases the quantity of reserves, and increases the money supply.

The Bank of Canada currently uses open-market operations for long-run control of the money supply, and the bank rate for short-run control of the money supply. It lowers the bank rate whenever it wants the money supply to expand, and raises the bank rate whenever it wants the money supply to contract. Because the bank rate not only affects the money supply but also sets the pattern for all Canadian interest rates, changes in the bank rate are a closely watched indicator of the Bank of Canada's views about the sort of monetary policy the Canadian economy needs. Since November 2000, the Bank of Canada has fixed eight dates each year, roughly six weeks apart, on which to announce whether it will raise the bank rate, lower the bank rate, or leave the bank rate unchanged. It can also change the bank rate at any time if extraordinary action is needed.

PROBLEMS IN CONTROLLING THE MONEY SUPPLY

The Bank of Canada's tools—open-market operations and the bank rate—have powerful effects on the money supply. Yet the Bank's control of the money supply is not precise. The Bank must wrestle with two problems, each of which arises because much of the money supply is created by our system of fractional-reserve banking.

The first problem is that the Bank of Canada does not control the amount of money that households choose to hold as deposits in banks. The more money that households deposit, the more reserves banks have, and the more money the banking system can create. And the less money that households deposit, the less reserves banks have, and the less money the banking system can create. To see why this is a problem, suppose that one day people begin to lose confidence in the banking system and, therefore, decide to withdraw deposits and hold more currency. When this happens, the banking system loses reserves and creates less money. The money supply falls, even without any Bank of Canada action.

The second problem with monetary control is that the Bank of Canada does not control the amount that commercial bankers choose to lend. Once money is deposited in a bank, it creates more money only when the bank loans it out. Yet banks can choose simply to hold the money as extra reserves. Since 1994 the Bank of Canada has abandoned legal reserve requirements, so commercial banks can choose to hold any ratio of reserves to deposits they want. Even if there were a legal minimum reserve ratio, banks could choose to hold excess reserves above the required minimum. To see why excess reserves complicate control of the money supply, suppose that one day bankers become more cautious about economic conditions and decide to make fewer loans and hold greater reserves. When this happens, the banking system creates less money than it otherwise would. Because of the banks' decision, the money supply falls.

Hence, in a system of fractional-reserve banking, the amount of money in the economy depends in part on the behaviour of depositors and bankers. Because the Bank of Canada cannot control or perfectly predict this behaviour, it cannot perfectly control the money supply. But these problems need not be large. The Bank collects data on deposits every week, so it quickly becomes aware of any changes in the money supply caused by changes in depositor or banker behaviour. If the Bank discovers that the money supply is growing too fast, it can raise the bank rate to slow it down. If the Bank discovers that the money supply is growing too slowly or falling, it can lower the bank rate to increase the money supply. The Bank is like a driver of a car using the gas pedal to control the car's speed. Many things may cause the car to speed up or slow down, but by watching the speedometer and adjusting the gas pedal accordingly, the driver can keep the speed close to the level he or she chooses.

CASE STUDY   BANK RUNS AND THE MONEY SUPPLY

Although you have probably never witnessed a bank run in real life, you may have seen one depicted in movies such as *Mary Poppins* or *It's a Wonderful Life*. A bank run occurs when depositors suspect that a bank may go bankrupt and, "run" to the bank to withdraw their deposits.

Bank runs are a problem for banks under fractional-reserve banking. Because a bank holds only a fraction of its deposits in reserve, it cannot satisfy withdrawal requests from all depositors. Even if the bank is in fact solvent (meaning that its assets exceed its liabilities), it will not have enough cash on hand to allow all depositors immediate access to all of their money. When a run occurs, the bank is forced to close its doors until some bank loans are repaid or until some lender of last resort (such as the Bank of Canada) provides it with the currency it needs to satisfy depositors.

Bank runs complicate the control of the money supply. An important example of this problem occurred in the United States during the Great Depression in the early 1930s. After a wave of bank runs and bank closings, households and bankers became more cautious. Households withdrew their deposits from banks, preferring to hold their money in the form of currency. This decision reversed the process of money creation, as bankers responded to falling reserves by reducing bank loans. At the same time, bankers increased their reserve ratios so that they would have enough cash on hand to meet their depositors' demands in any future bank runs. The higher reserve ratio reduced the money multiplier, which also reduced the money supply. From 1929 to 1933,

A NOT-SO-WONDERFUL BANK RUN

the U.S. money supply fell by 28 percent, even without the Federal Reserve (the U.S. central bank) taking any deliberate contractionary action. Many economists point to this massive fall in the U.S. money supply to explain the high unemployment and falling prices that prevailed during this period. (In future chapters we examine the mechanisms by which changes in the money supply affect unemployment and prices.)

Canadian banks in the 1930s were larger, more diversified, and safer than American banks, so Canada did not experience the wave of bank runs and bank failures that happened in the United States. In Canada, banks' reserve ratios increased only slightly, and the decline in the Canadian money supply was much smaller. But the Great Depression was as bad in Canada as it was in the United States, perhaps because the Canadian economy was more dependent on international trade and exports of primary products, whose value dropped considerably during the Depression.

Today, bank runs are not a major problem for the banking system or the Bank of Canada. A few small banks did fail in the 1980s, but there were no major bank runs. The Office of the Superintendent of Financial Institutions monitors financial institutions in Canada to try to prevent bankruptcies. Also, the federal government now guarantees the safety of deposits up to $60 000 at Canadian banks through the Canada Deposit Insurance Corporation (CDIC). Small depositors do not run on their banks because they are confident that, even if their bank goes bankrupt, the CDIC will make good on the deposits. As a result, most people see bank runs only in the movies.

QUICK QUIZ: Describe how banks create money. ◆ If the Bank of Canada wanted to use all three of its policy tools to decrease the money supply, what would it do?

CONCLUSION

The monetary system plays an important role in our daily lives. Whenever we buy or sell anything, we are relying on the extraordinarily useful social convention called "money." Now that we know what money is and what determines its supply, we can discuss how changes in the quantity of money affect the economy. We begin to address that topic in the next chapter.

Summary

◆ The term *money* refers to assets that people regularly use to buy goods and services.

◆ Money serves three functions. As a medium of exchange, it provides the item used to make transactions. As a unit of account, it provides the way in which prices and other economic values are recorded. As a store of value, it provides a way of transferring purchasing power from the present to the future.

◆ Commodity money, such as gold, is money that has intrinsic value: It would be valued even if it were not used as money. Fiat money, such as paper dollars, is money without intrinsic value: It would be worthless if it were not used as money.

◆ In the Canadian economy, money takes the form of currency and various types of bank deposits, such as chequing accounts.

◆ The Bank of Canada, Canada's central bank, is responsible for controlling the supply of money in Canada. The governor and senior deputy governor of the Bank of Canada are appointed for seven-year terms, and the other directors are appointed for three-year terms. All of these appointments are made by the Canadian government, which owns the Bank of Canada.

◆ The Bank of Canada controls the supply of money primarily through changes in the bank rate. Lowering the bank rate increases the money supply, and raising the bank rate reduces the money supply. The Bank of Canada also controls the money supply through open-market operations. The purchase of government bonds increases the money supply, and the sale of government bonds reduces the money supply.

◆ When banks loan out some of their deposits, they increase the quantity of money in the economy. Because of this role of banks in determining the money supply, the Bank of Canada's control of the money supply is imperfect.

Key Concepts

money, p. 320
medium of exchange, p. 321
unit of account, p. 321
store of value, p. 321
liquidity, p. 321
commodity money, p. 321
fiat money, p. 323
currency, p. 323

demand deposits, p. 323
Bank of Canada, p. 325
central bank, p. 325
money supply, p. 327
monetary policy, p. 327
reserves, p. 328
fractional-reserve banking, p. 329
reserve ratio, p. 329

money multiplier, p. 331
open-market operations, p. 332
foreign exchange market operations, p. 333
sterilization, p. 333
reserve requirements, p. 333
bank rate, p. 334

Questions for Review

1. What distinguishes money from other assets in the economy?

2. What is commodity money? What is fiat money? Which kind do we use?

3. What are demand deposits, and why should they be included in the stock of money?

4. Who is responsible for setting monetary policy in Canada?

5. If the Bank of Canada wants to increase the money supply with open-market operations, what does it do?

6. Why don't banks hold 100 percent reserves? How is the amount of reserves banks hold related to the amount of money the banking system creates?

7. What is the bank rate? What happens to the money supply when the Bank of Canada raises the bank rate?

8. What are reserve requirements? What happens to the money supply when the Bank of Canada raises reserve requirements?

9. Why can't the Bank of Canada control the money supply perfectly?

Problems and Applications

1. Which of the following are money in the Canadian economy? Which are not? Explain your answers by discussing each of the three functions of money.
   a. a Canadian penny
   b. a Mexican peso
   c. a Picasso painting
   d. a plastic credit card

2. Every month *Yankee* magazine includes a "Swopper's [*sic*] Column" of offers to barter goods and services. Here is an example: "Will swop custom-designed wedding gown and up to 6 bridesmaids' gowns for 2 round-trip plane tickets and 3 nights' lodging in the countryside of England." Why would it be difficult to run our economy using a "Swopper's Column" instead

of money? In light of your answer, why might the *Yankee* "Swopper's Column" exist?

3.   What characteristics of an asset make it useful as a medium of exchange? As a store of value?

4.   Consider how the following situations would affect the economy's monetary system.

   a.   Suppose that the people on Yap discovered an easy way to make limestone wheels. How would this development affect the usefulness of stone wheels as money? Explain.

   b.   Suppose that someone in Canada discovered an easy way to counterfeit $100 bills. How would this development affect the Canadian monetary system? Explain.

5.   Your uncle repays a $100 loan from Tenth National Bank by writing a $100 cheque from his TNB chequing account. Use T-accounts to show the effect of this transaction on your uncle and on TNB. Has your uncle's wealth changed? Explain.

6.   Beleaguered Bank (BB) holds $250 million in deposits and maintains a reserve ratio of 10 percent.

   a.   Show a T-account for BB.

   b.   Now suppose that BB's largest depositor withdraws $10 million in cash from her account. If BB decides to restore its reserve ratio by reducing the amount of loans outstanding, show its new T-account.

   c.   Explain what effect BB's action will have on other banks.

   d.   Why might it be difficult for BB to take the action described in part (b)? Discuss another way for BB to return to its original reserve ratio.

7.   You take $100 you had kept under your pillow and deposit it in your bank account. If this $100 stays in the banking system as reserves and if banks hold reserves equal to 10 percent of deposits, by how much does the total amount of deposits in the banking system increase? By how much does the money supply increase?

8.   The Bank of Canada conducts a $10 million open-market purchase of government bonds. If the required reserve ratio is 10 percent, what is the largest possible increase in the money supply that could result? Explain. What is the smallest possible increase? Explain.

9.   Suppose that the T-account for First National Bank is as follows:

ASSETS		LIABILITIES	
Reserves	$100 000	Deposits	$500 000
Loans	400 000		

   a.   If the Bank of Canada requires banks to hold 5 percent of deposits as reserves, how much in excess reserves does First National now hold?

   b.   Assume that all other banks hold only the required amount of reserves. If First National decides to reduce its reserves to only the required amount, by how much would the economy's money supply increase?

10.   Suppose that the Bank of Canada sells £100 million from its foreign exchange reserves, and that the exchange rate is $2.40 Canadian per pound sterling.

   a.   Explain what happens to the Canadian money supply.

   b.   Now suppose that the Bank of Canada does not want the money supply to change. What would it need to do to sterilize its foreign exchange market operation?

11.   Assume that the reserve ratio is zero and that the currency ratio is 25 percent, so that people hold $1 in currency for every $3 they have in deposit accounts.

   a.   If the Bank of Canada buys $1 million of government bonds, what will be the effect on the amount of currency, the amount of deposits, and the total money supply?

   b.   If the Bank of Canada sells $1 million worth of foreign currency, what will be the effect on the amount of Canadian currency, the amount of deposits, and the total Canadian money supply?

12.   (This problem is challenging.) The economy of Elmendyn contains 2000 $1 bills.

   a.   If people hold all money as currency, what is the quantity of money?

   b.   If people hold all money as demand deposits and banks maintain 100 percent reserves, what is the quantity of money?

   c.   If people hold equal amounts of currency and demand deposits and banks maintain 100 percent reserves, what is the quantity of money?

   d.   If people hold all money as demand deposits and banks maintain a reserve ratio of 10 percent, what is the quantity of money?

   e.   If people hold equal amounts of currency and demand deposits and banks maintain a reserve ratio of 10 percent, what is the quantity of money?

16

MONEY GROWTH
AND INFLATION

Although today you need a dollar or two to buy yourself an ice-cream cone, life was very different 60 years ago, when a small scoop cost about three cents and a large scoop cost about a nickel.

You are probably not surprised at the increase in the price of ice cream. In our economy, most prices tend to rise over time. This increase in the overall level of prices is called *inflation*. Earlier in the book we examined how economists measure the inflation rate as the percentage change in the consumer price index, the GDP deflator, or some other index of the overall price level. These price indexes show that, over the past 60 years, prices have risen on average about 4 percent per year.

IN THIS CHAPTER YOU WILL . . .

See why inflation results from rapid growth in the money supply

Learn the meaning of the classical dichotomy and monetary neutrality

See why some countries print so much money that they experience hyperinflation

Examine how the nominal interest rate responds to the inflation rate

Consider the various costs that inflation imposes on society

Accumulated over so many years, a 4 percent annual inflation rate leads to 12-fold increase in the price level.

Inflation may seem natural and inevitable to a person who grew up in Canada during the second half of the twentieth century, but in fact it is not inevitable at all. There were long periods during which most prices fell—a phenomenon called *deflation*. The average level of prices in the Canadian economy was 37 percent lower in 1933 than in 1920, and this deflation was a major issue. Farmers, who had accumulated large debts, were suffering when the fall in crop prices reduced their incomes and thus their ability to pay off their debts. They advocated government policies to reverse the deflation.

Although inflation has been the norm in more recent history, there has been substantial variation in the rate at which prices rise. During the 1990s, prices rose at an average rate of about 2 percent per year. By contrast, in the 1970s, prices rose by 7 percent per year, which meant a doubling of the price level over the decade. The public often views such high rates of inflation as a major economic problem.

International data show an even broader range of inflation experiences. Germany after World War I experienced a spectacular example of inflation. The price of a newspaper rose from 0.3 marks in January 1921 to 70 000 000 marks less than two years later. Other prices rose by similar amounts. An extraordinarily high rate of inflation such as this is called *hyperinflation*. The German hyperinflation had such an adverse effect on the German economy that it is often viewed as one contributor to the rise of Nazism and, as a result, World War II. Over the past 50 years, with this episode still in mind, German policymakers have been extraordinarily averse to inflation, and Germany has had much lower inflation than Canada.

What determines whether an economy experiences inflation and, if so, how much? This chapter answers this question by developing the *quantity theory of money*. Chapter 1 summarized this theory as one of the *Ten Principles of Economics*: Prices rise when the government prints too much money. This insight has a long and venerable tradition among economists. The quantity theory was discussed by the famous eighteenth-century philosopher David Hume and has been advocated more recently by the prominent economist Milton Friedman. This theory of inflation can explain both moderate inflations, such as those we have experienced in Canada, and hyperinflations, such as those experienced in interwar Germany and, more recently, in some Latin American countries.

After developing a theory of inflation, we turn to a related question: Why is inflation a problem? At first glance, the answer to this question may seem obvious: Inflation is a problem because people don't like it. In the 1970s, when Canada experienced a relatively high rate of inflation, opinion polls placed inflation as the most important issue facing the nation.

But what, exactly, are the costs that inflation imposes on a society? The answer may surprise you. Identifying the various costs of inflation is not as straightforward as it first appears. As a result, although all economists decry hyperinflation, some economists argue that the costs of moderate inflation are not nearly as large as the general public believes.

THE CLASSICAL THEORY OF INFLATION

We begin our study of inflation by developing the quantity theory of money. This theory is often called "classical" because it was developed by some of the earliest thinkers about economic issues. Most economists today rely on this theory to explain the long-run determinants of the price level and the inflation rate.

THE LEVEL OF PRICES AND THE VALUE OF MONEY

Suppose we observe over some period of time the price of an ice-cream cone rising from a nickel to a dollar. What conclusion should we draw from the fact that people are willing to give up so much more money in exchange for a cone? It is possible that people have come to enjoy ice cream more (perhaps because some chemist has developed a miraculous new flavour). Yet that is probably not the case. It is more likely that people's enjoyment of ice cream has stayed roughly the same and that, over time, the money used to buy ice cream has become less valuable. Indeed, the first insight about inflation is that it is more about the value of money than about the value of goods.

"So what's it going to be? The same size as last year or the same price as last year?"

This insight helps point the way toward a theory of inflation. When the consumer price index and other measures of the price level rise, commentators are often tempted to look at the many individual prices that make up these price indexes: "The CPI rose by 3 percent last month, led by a 20 percent rise in the price of coffee and a 30 percent rise in the price of heating oil." Although this approach does contain some interesting information about what's happening in the economy, it also misses a key point: Inflation is an economy-wide phenomenon that concerns, first and foremost, the value of the economy's medium of exchange.

The economy's overall price level can be viewed in two ways. So far, we have viewed the price level as the price of a basket of goods and services. When the price level rises, people have to pay more for the goods and services they buy. Alternatively, we can view the price level as a measure of the value of money. A rise in the price level means a lower value of money because each dollar in your wallet now buys a smaller quantity of goods and services.

It may help to express these ideas mathematically. Suppose P is the price level as measured, for instance, by the consumer price index or the GDP deflator. Then P measures the number of dollars needed to buy a basket of goods and services. Now turn this idea around: The quantity of goods and services that can be bought with \$1 equals $1/P$. In other words, if P is the price of goods and services measured in terms of money, $1/P$ is the value of money measured in terms of goods and services. Thus, when the overall price level rises, the value of money falls.

MONEY SUPPLY, MONEY DEMAND, AND MONETARY EQUILIBRIUM

What determines the value of money? The answer to this question, like many in economics, is supply and demand. Just as the supply and demand for bananas determines the price of bananas, the supply and demand for money determines the value of money. Thus, our next step in developing the quantity theory of money is to consider the determinants of money supply and money demand.

First consider money supply. In the preceding chapter we discussed how the Bank of Canada, together with the banking system, determines the supply of money. When the Bank of Canada sells bonds in open-market operations, it receives dollars in exchange and contracts the money supply. When the Bank of Canada buys government bonds, it pays out dollars and expands the money supply. In addition, if any of these dollars are deposited in banks that then hold them as reserves, the money multiplier swings into action, and these open-market operations can have an even greater effect on the money supply. For our purposes in this chapter, we ignore the complications introduced by the banking system and simply take the quantity of money supplied as a policy variable that the Bank of Canada controls directly and completely.

Now consider money demand. There are many factors that determine the quantity of money people demand, just as there are many determinants of the quantity demanded of other goods and services. How much money people choose to hold in their wallets, for instance, depends on how much they rely on credit cards and on whether an automatic teller machine is easy to find. And, as we will emphasize in Chapter 20, the quantity of money demanded depends on the interest rate that a person could earn by using the money to buy an interest-bearing bond rather than leaving it in a wallet or low-interest chequing account.

Although many variables affect the demand for money, one variable stands out in importance: the average level of prices in the economy. People hold money

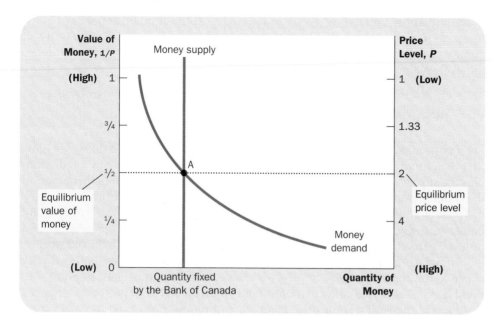

Figure 16-1

How the Supply and Demand for Money Determine the Equilibrium Price Level. The horizontal axis shows the quantity of money. The left vertical axis shows the value of money, and the right vertical axis shows the price level. The supply curve for money is vertical because the quantity of money supplied is fixed by the Bank of Canada. The demand curve for money is downward sloping because people want to hold a larger quantity of money when each dollar buys less. At the equilibrium, point A, the value of money (on the left axis) and the price level (on the right axis) have adjusted to bring the quantity of money supplied and the quantity of money demanded into balance.

because it is the medium of exchange. Unlike other assets, such as bonds or stocks, people can use money to buy the goods and services on their shopping lists. How much money they choose to hold for this purpose depends on the prices of those goods and services. The higher prices are, the more money the typical transaction requires, and the more money people will choose to hold in their wallets and chequing accounts. That is, a higher price level (a lower value of money) increases the quantity of money demanded.

What ensures that the quantity of money the Bank of Canada supplies balances the quantity of money people demand? The answer, it turns out, depends on the time horizon being considered. Later in this book we will examine the short-run answer, and we will see that interest rates play a key role. In the long run, however, the answer is different and much simpler. *In the long run, the overall level of prices adjusts to the level at which the demand for money equals the supply.* If the price level is above the equilibrium level, people will want to hold more money than the Bank of Canada has created, so the price level must fall to balance supply and demand. If the price level is below the equilibrium level, people will want to hold less money than the Bank of Canada has created, and the price level must rise to balance supply and demand. At the equilibrium price level, the quantity of money that people want to hold exactly balances the quantity of money supplied by the Bank of Canada.

Figure 16-1 illustrates these ideas. The horizontal axis of this graph shows the quantity of money. The left-hand vertical axis shows the value of money, $1/P$, and the right-hand vertical axis shows the price level, P. Notice that the price-level axis on the right is inverted: A low price level is shown near the top of this axis, and a high price level is shown near the bottom. This inverted axis illustrates that when the value of money is high (as shown near the top of the left axis), the price level is low (as shown near the top of the right axis).

The two curves in this figure are the supply and demand curves for money. The supply curve is vertical because the Bank of Canada has fixed the quantity of money available. The demand curve for money is downward sloping, indicating that when the value of money is low (and the price level is high), people demand a larger quantity of it to buy goods and services. At the equilibrium, shown in the figure as point A, the quantity of money demanded balances the quantity of money supplied. This equilibrium of money supply and money demand determines the value of money and the price level.

THE EFFECTS OF A MONETARY INJECTION

Let's now consider the effects of a change in monetary policy. To do so, imagine that the economy is in equilibrium and then, suddenly, the Bank of Canada doubles the supply of money by printing some dollar bills and dropping them around the country from helicopters. (Or, less dramatically and more realistically, the Bank of Canada could inject money into the economy by buying some government bonds from the public in open-market operations.) What happens after such a monetary injection? How does the new equilibrium compare with the old one?

Figure 16-2 shows what happens. The monetary injection shifts the supply curve to the right from MS_1 to MS_2, and the equilibrium moves from point A to point B. As a result, the value of money (shown on the left axis) decreases from 1/2 to 1/4, and the equilibrium price level (shown on the right axis) increases from 2 to 4. In other words, when an increase in the money supply makes dollars more plentiful, the result is an increase in the price level that makes each dollar less valuable.

This explanation of how the price level is determined and why it might change over time is called the **quantity theory of money.** According to the quantity theory, the quantity of money available in the economy determines the value of money, and growth in the quantity of money is the primary cause of inflation. As economist Milton Friedman once put it, "Inflation is always and everywhere a monetary phenomenon."

quantity theory of money

a theory asserting that the quantity of money available determines the price level and that the growth rate in the quantity of money available determines the inflation rate

---

Figure 16-2

AN INCREASE IN THE MONEY SUPPLY. When the Bank of Canada increases the supply of money, the money supply curve shifts from MS_1 to MS_2. The value of money (on the left axis) and the price level (on the right axis) adjust to bring supply and demand back into balance. The equilibrium moves from point A to point B. Thus, when an increase in the money supply makes dollars more plentiful, the price level increases, making each dollar less valuable.

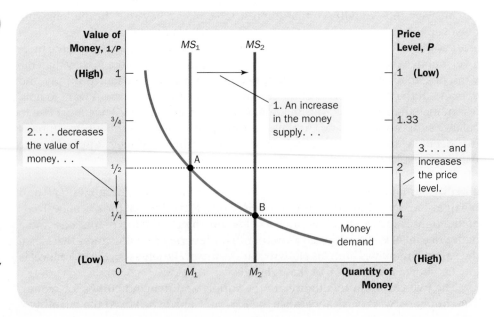

A BRIEF LOOK AT THE ADJUSTMENT PROCESS

So far we have compared the old equilibrium and the new equilibrium after an injection of money. How does the economy get from the old to the new equilibrium? A complete answer to this question requires an understanding of short-run fluctuations in the economy, which we examine later in this book. Yet, even now, it is instructive to consider briefly the adjustment process that occurs after a change in money supply.

The immediate effect of a monetary injection is to create an excess supply of money. Before the injection, the economy was in equilibrium (point A in Figure 16-2). At the prevailing price level, people had exactly as much money as they wanted. But after the helicopters drop the new money and people pick it up off the streets, people have more dollars in their wallets than they want. At the prevailing price level, the quantity of money supplied now exceeds the quantity demanded.

People try to get rid of this excess supply of money in various ways. They might buy goods and services with their excess holdings of money. Or they might use this excess money to make loans to others by buying bonds or by depositing the money in a bank savings account. These loans allow other people to buy goods and services. In either case, the injection of money increases the demand for goods and services.

The economy's ability to supply goods and services, however, has not changed. As we saw in Chapter 12, the economy's production is determined by the available labour, physical capital, human capital, natural resources, and technological knowledge. None of these is altered by the injection of money.

Thus, the greater demand for goods and services causes the prices of goods and services to increase. The increase in the price level, in turn, increases the quantity of money demanded because people are using more dollars for every transaction. Eventually, the economy reaches a new equilibrium (point B in Figure 16-2) at which the quantity of money demanded again equals the quantity of money supplied. In this way, the overall price level for goods and services adjusts to bring money supply and money demand into balance.

THE CLASSICAL DICHOTOMY AND MONETARY NEUTRALITY

We have seen how changes in the money supply lead to changes in the average level of prices of goods and services. How do these monetary changes affect other important macroeconomic variables, such as production, employment, real wages, and real interest rates? This question has long intrigued economists. Indeed, the great philosopher David Hume wrote about it in the eighteenth century. The answer we give today owes much to Hume's analysis.

Hume and his contemporaries suggested that all economic variables should be divided into two groups. The first group consists of **nominal variables**—variables measured in monetary units. The second group consists of **real variables**—variables measured in physical units. For example, the income of corn farmers is a nominal variable because it is measured in dollars, whereas the quantity of corn they produce is a real variable because it is measured in tonnes. Similarly, nominal GDP is a nominal variable because it measures the dollar value of the economy's output of goods and services, while real GDP is a real variable because it measures the total quantity of goods and services produced. This separation of variables into

nominal variables
variables measured in monetary units

real variables
variables measured in physical units

classical dichotomy
the theoretical separation of nominal and real variables

these groups is now called the **classical dichotomy.** (A *dichotomy* is a division into two groups, and *classical* refers to the earlier economic thinkers.)

Application of the classical dichotomy is somewhat tricky when we turn to prices. Prices in the economy are normally quoted in terms of money and, therefore, are nominal variables. For instance, when we say that the price of corn is $200 a tonne or that the price of wheat is $100 a tonne, both prices are nominal variables. But what about a *relative* price—the price of one thing compared with another? In our example, we could say that the price of a tonne of corn is two tonnes of wheat. Notice that this relative price is no longer measured in terms of money. When comparing the prices of any two goods, the dollar signs cancel, and the resulting number is measured in physical units. The lesson is that dollar prices are nominal variables, whereas relative prices are real variables.

This lesson has several important applications. For instance, the real wage (the dollar wage adjusted for inflation) is a real variable because it measures the rate at which the economy exchanges goods and services for each unit of labour. Similarly, the real interest rate (the nominal interest rate adjusted for inflation) is a real variable because it measures the rate at which the economy exchanges goods and services produced today for goods and services produced in the future.

Why bother separating variables into these two groups? Hume suggested that the classical dichotomy is useful in analyzing the economy because different forces influence real and nominal variables. In particular, he argued, nominal variables are heavily influenced by developments in the economy's monetary system, whereas the monetary system is largely irrelevant for understanding the determinants of important real variables.

Notice that Hume's idea was implicit in our earlier discussions of the real economy in the long run. In previous chapters, we examined how real GDP, saving, investment, real interest rates, and unemployment are determined without any mention of the existence of money. As explained in that analysis, the economy's production of goods and services depends on productivity and factor supplies, the real interest rate adjusts to balance the supply and demand for loanable funds, the real wage adjusts to balance the supply and demand for labour, and unemployment results when the real wage is for some reason kept above its equilibrium level. These important conclusions have nothing to do with the quantity of money supplied.

Changes in the supply of money, according to Hume, affect nominal variables but not real variables. When the central bank doubles the money supply, the price level doubles, the dollar wage doubles, and all other dollar values double. Real variables, such as production, employment, real wages, and real interest rates, are unchanged. This irrelevance of monetary changes for real variables is called **monetary neutrality.**

monetary neutrality
the proposition that changes in the money supply do not affect real variables

An analogy sheds light on the meaning of monetary neutrality. Recall that, as the unit of account, money is the yardstick we use to measure economic transactions. When a central bank doubles the money supply, all prices double, and the value of the unit of account falls by half. A similar change would occur if the government were to reduce the length of the yard from 36 to 18 inches: As a result of the new unit of measurement, all *measured* distances (nominal variables) would double, but the *actual* distances (real variables) would remain the same. The dollar, like the yard, is merely a unit of measurement, so a change in its value should not have important real effects.

Is this conclusion of monetary neutrality a realistic description of the world in which we live? The answer is: not completely. A change in the length of the yard from 36 to 18 inches would not matter much in the long run, but in the short run it would certainly lead to confusion and various mistakes. Similarly, most economists today believe that over short periods of time—within the span of a year or two—there is reason to think that monetary changes do have important effects on real variables. Hume himself also doubted that monetary neutrality would apply in the short run. (We will turn to the study of short-run non-neutrality in Chapters 19 to 21, and this topic will shed light on the reasons why the Bank of Canada changes the supply of money over time.)

Most economists today accept Hume's conclusion as a description of the economy in the long run. Over the course of a decade, for instance, monetary changes have important effects on nominal variables (such as the price level) but only negligible effects on real variables (such as real GDP). When studying long-run changes in the economy, the neutrality of money offers a good description of how the world works.

VELOCITY AND THE QUANTITY EQUATION

We can obtain another perspective on the quantity theory of money by considering the following question: How many times per year is the typical dollar bill used to pay for a newly produced good or service? The answer to this question is given by a variable called the **velocity of money**. In physics, the term *velocity* refers to the speed at which an object travels. In economics, the velocity of money refers to the speed at which the typical dollar bill travels around the economy from wallet to wallet.

velocity of money
the rate at which money changes hands

To calculate the velocity of money, we divide the nominal value of output (nominal GDP) by the quantity of money. If P is the price level (the GDP deflator), Y the quantity of output (real GDP), and M the quantity of money, then velocity is

$$V = (P \times Y)/M.$$

To see why this makes sense, imagine a simple economy that produces only pizza. Suppose that the economy produces 100 pizzas in a year, that a pizza sells for $10, and that the quantity of money in the economy is $50. Then the velocity of money is

$$V = (\$10 \times 100)/\$50$$
$$= 20.$$

In this economy, people spend a total of $1000 per year on pizza. For this $1000 of spending to take place with only $50 of money, each dollar bill must change hands on average twenty times per year.

With slight algebraic rearrangement, this equation can be rewritten as

$$M \times V = P \times Y.$$

quantity equation
the equation $M \times V = P \times Y$, which relates the quantity of money, the velocity of money, and the dollar value of the economy's output of goods and services

This equation states that the quantity of money (M) times the velocity of money (V) equals the price of output (P) times the amount of output (Y). It is called the **quantity equation** because it relates the quantity of money (M) to the nominal value of output ($P \times Y$). The quantity equation shows that an increase in the quantity of

Figure 16-3

NOMINAL GDP, THE QUANTITY OF MONEY, AND THE VELOCITY OF MONEY.   This figure shows the nominal value of output as measured by nominal GDP, the quantity of money as measured by M2, and the velocity of money as measured by their ratio. For comparability, all three series have been scaled to equal 100 in 1961. Notice that nominal GDP and the quantity of money have grown dramatically over this period, while velocity has been relatively stable.

SOURCES: Statistics Canada, "Gross Domestic Product, Expenditure-Based," CANSIM Ii Matrix, Table 38-0017, and "Currency Outside Banks and Chartered Bank Deposits," CANSIM II Matrix, Table 176-0020; velocity of money based on calculations by authors as nominal GDP divided by quantity of money.

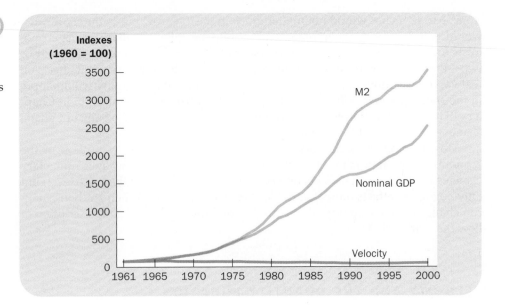

money in an economy must be reflected in one of the other three variables: The price level must rise, the quantity of output must rise, or the velocity of money must fall.

In many cases, it turns out that the velocity of money is relatively stable. For example, Figure 16-3 shows nominal GDP, the quantity of money (as measured by M2), and the velocity of money for the Canadian economy since 1961. Although the velocity of money is not exactly constant, it has not changed dramatically. By contrast, the money supply and nominal GDP during this period have increased more than 25 times. Thus, for some purposes, the assumption of constant velocity may be a good approximation.

We now have all of the elements necessary to explain the equilibrium price level and inflation rate. Here they are:

1. The velocity of money is relatively stable over time.
2. Because velocity is stable, when the Bank of Canada changes the quantity of money (M), it causes proportionate changes in the nominal value of output ($P \times Y$).
3. The economy's output of goods and services (Y) is primarily determined by factor supplies (labour, physical capital, human capital, and natural resources) and the available production technology. In particular, because money is neutral, money does not affect output.
4. With output (Y) determined by factor supplies and technology, when the Bank of Canada alters the money supply (M) and induces proportional changes in the nominal value of output ($P \times Y$), these changes are reflected in changes in the price level (P).
5. Therefore, when the Bank of Canada increases the money supply rapidly, the result is a high rate of inflation.

These five steps are the essence of the quantity theory of money.

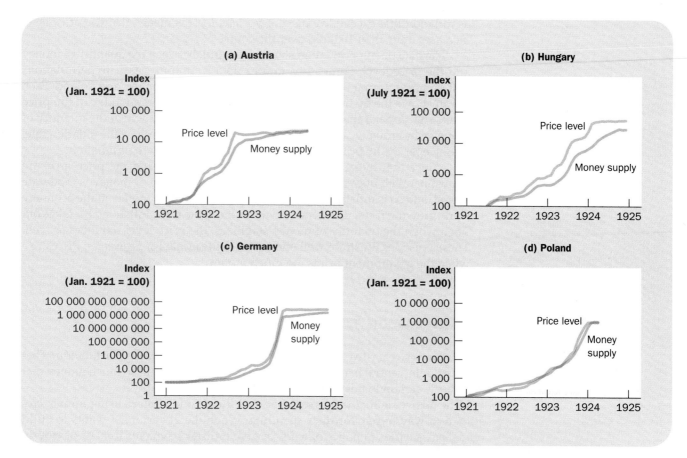

MONEY AND PRICES DURING FOUR HYPERINFLATIONS.   This figure shows the quantity of money and the price level during four hyperinflations. (Note that these variables are graphed on *logarithmic* scales. This means that equal vertical distances on the graph represent equal *percentage* changes in the variable.) In each case, the quantity of money and the price level move closely together. The strong association between these two variables is consistent with the quantity theory of money, which states that growth in the money supply is the primary cause of inflation.

Figure 16-4

SOURCE: Adapted from Thomas J. Sargent, "The End of Four Big Inflations," in Robert Hall, ed., *Inflation* (Chicago: University of Chicago Press, 1983), pp. 41–93.

**CASE STUDY   MONEY AND PRICES DURING
FOUR HYPERINFLATIONS**

Although earthquakes can wreak havoc on a society, they have the beneficial byproduct of providing much useful data for seismologists. These data can shed light on alternative theories and, thereby, help society predict and deal with future threats. Similarly, hyperinflations offer monetary economists a natural experiment they can use to study the effects of money on the economy.

Hyperinflations are interesting in part because the changes in the money supply and price level are so large. Indeed, hyperinflation is generally defined as inflation that exceeds 50 percent *per month*. This means that the price level increases more than 100-fold over the course of a year.

The data on hyperinflation show a clear link between the quantity of money and the price level. Figure 16-4 graphs data from four classic hyperinflations that occurred during the 1920s in Austria, Hungary, Germany, and Poland. Each graph shows the quantity of money in the economy and an index of the price level. The slope of the money line represents the rate at which the quantity of money was growing, and the slope of the price line represents the inflation rate. The steeper the lines, the higher the rates of money growth or inflation.

Notice that in each graph the quantity of money and the price level are almost parallel. In each instance, growth in the quantity of money is moderate at first, and so is inflation. But over time, the quantity of money in the economy starts growing faster and faster. At about the same time, inflation also takes off. Then when the quantity of money stabilizes, the price level stabilizes as well. These episodes illustrate well one of the *Ten Principles of Economics:* Prices rise when the government prints too much money.

THE INFLATION TAX

If inflation is so easy to explain, why do countries experience hyperinflation? That is, why do the central banks of these countries choose to print so much money that its value is certain to fall rapidly over time?

The answer is that the governments of these countries are using money creation as a way to pay for their spending. When the government wants to build roads, pay salaries to police officers, or give transfer payments to poor or elderly people, it first has to raise the necessary funds. Normally, the government does this by levying taxes, such as income and sales taxes, and by borrowing from the public by selling government bonds. Yet the government can also pay for spending by simply printing the money it needs.

inflation tax

the revenue the government raises by creating money

When the government raises revenue by printing money, it is said to levy an **inflation tax.** The inflation tax is not exactly like other taxes, however, because no one receives a bill from the government for this tax. Instead, the inflation tax is more subtle. When the government prints money, the price level rises, and the dollars in your wallet are less valuable. Thus, *the inflation tax is like a tax on everyone who holds money.*

The importance of the inflation tax varies from country to country and over time. In Canada in recent years, the inflation tax has been a trivial source of revenue: It has accounted for less than 3 percent of government revenue. During the 1770s, however, the Continental Congress of the fledgling United States relied heavily on the inflation tax to pay for military spending. Because the new government had a limited ability to raise funds through regular taxes or borrowing, printing dollars was the easiest way to pay the American soldiers. As the quantity theory predicts, the result was a high rate of inflation: Prices measured in terms of the continental dollar rose more than 100-fold over a few years.

Almost all hyperinflations follow the same pattern as the hyperinflation during the American Revolution. The government has high spending, inadequate tax revenue, and limited ability to borrow. As a result, it turns to the printing press to pay for its spending. The massive increases in the quantity of money lead to

IN THE NEWS

Russia Turns to the Inflation Tax

WHENEVER GOVERNMENTS FIND THEM-selves short of cash, they are tempted to solve the problem simply by printing some more. In 1998, Russian policy-makers found this temptation hard to resist, and the inflation rate rose to more than 100 percent per year.

Russia's New Leaders Plan to Pay Debts by Printing Money

BY MICHAEL WINES

MOSCOW—Russia's new communist-influenced government indicated today that it plans to satisfy old debts and bail out old friends by printing new rubles, a decision that drew a swift and strong re-action from President Boris N. Yeltsin's old capitalist allies.

The deputy head of the central bank said today that the bank intends to bail out many of the nation's bankrupt finan-cial institutions by buying back their multibillion-ruble portfolios of govern-ment bonds and Treasury bills. The gov-ernment temporarily froze $40 billion worth of notes when the fiscal crisis erupted last month because it lacked the money to pay investors who hold them.

Asked by the Reuters news service how the near-broke government would find the money to pay off the banks, the deputy, Andrei Kozlov, replied, "Emissions, of course, emissions." "Emissions" is a euphemism for printing money.

Hours later in Washington, Deputy Treasury Secretary Lawrence H. Sum-mers told a House subcommittee that Russia was heading toward a return of the four-digit inflation rates that sav-aged consumers and almost toppled Mr. Yeltsin's government in 1993.

Russia's new leaders cannot repeal "basic economic laws," he said.

SOURCE: *The New York Times*, September 18, 1998, p. A3.

massive inflation. The inflation ends when the government institutes fiscal reforms—such as cuts in government spending—that eliminate the need for the inflation tax.

THE FISHER EFFECT

According to the principle of monetary neutrality, an increase in the rate of money growth raises the rate of inflation but does not affect any real variable. An impor-tant application of this principle concerns the effect of money on interest rates. Interest rates are important variables for macroeconomists to understand because they link the economy of the present and the economy of the future through their effects on saving and investment.

To understand the relationship among money, inflation, and interest rates, recall from Chapter 11 the distinction between the nominal interest rate and the real interest rate. The *nominal interest rate* is the interest rate you hear about at your bank. If you have a savings account, for instance, the nominal interest rate tells you how fast the number of dollars in your account will rise over time. The *real interest rate* corrects the nominal interest rate for the effect of inflation to tell you how fast the purchasing power of your savings account will rise over time. The real interest rate is the nominal interest rate minus the inflation rate:

$$\text{Real interest rate} = \text{Nominal interest rate} - \text{Inflation rate.}$$

For example, if the bank posts a nominal interest rate of 7 percent per year and the inflation rate is 3 percent per year, then the real value of the deposits grows by 4 percent per year.

We can rewrite this equation to show that the nominal interest rate is the sum of the real interest rate and the inflation rate:

$$\text{Nominal interest rate} = \text{Real interest rate} + \text{Inflation rate.}$$

This way of looking at the nominal interest rate is useful because different economic forces determine each of the two terms on the right-hand side of this equation. As we discussed in Chapter 13, the supply and demand for loanable funds determine the real interest rate. And, according to the quantity theory of money, growth in the money supply determines the inflation rate.

Let's now consider how the growth in the money supply affects interest rates. In the long run over which money is neutral, a change in money growth should not affect the real interest rate. The real interest rate is, after all, a real variable. For the real interest rate not to be affected, the nominal interest rate must adjust one-for-one to changes in the inflation rate. Thus, *when the Bank of Canada increases the rate of money growth, the result is both a higher inflation rate and a higher nominal interest rate.* This adjustment of the nominal interest rate to the inflation rate is called the **Fisher effect,** after economist Irving Fisher (1867–1947), who first studied it.

The Fisher effect is, in fact, crucial for understanding changes over time in the nominal interest rate. Figure 16-5 shows the nominal interest rate and the inflation rate in the Canadian economy since 1961. The close association between these two variables is clear. The nominal interest rate rose from the early 1960s through the

Fisher effect

the one-for-one adjustment of the nominal interest rate to the inflation rate

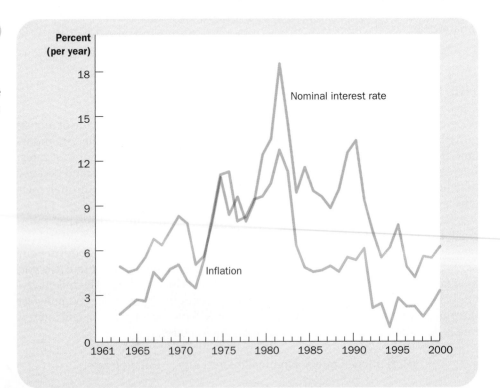

Figure 16-5

THE NOMINAL INTEREST RATE AND THE INFLATION RATE. This figure uses annual data since 1961 to show the nominal interest rate on three-month Treasury bills and the inflation rate as measured by the consumer price index. The close association between these two variables is evidence for the Fisher effect: When the inflation rate rises, so does the nominal interest rate.

SOURCE: Statistics Canada, "Financial Market Statistics," CANSIM II Matrix, Table 176-0043.

1970s because inflation was also rising during this time. Similarly, the nominal interest rate fell from the early 1980s through the 1990s because the Bank of Canada got inflation under control.

> **QUICK QUIZ:**   The government of a country increases the growth rate of the money supply from 5 percent per year to 50 percent per year. What happens to prices? What happens to nominal interest rates? Why might the government be doing this?

THE COSTS OF INFLATION

In the late 1970s, when the Canadian inflation rate reached about 10 percent per year, inflation dominated debates over economic policy. And even though inflation was low during the 1990s, inflation remained a closely watched macroeconomic variable. Inflation is closely watched and widely discussed because it is thought to be a serious economic problem. But is that true? And if so, why?

A FALL IN PURCHASING POWER? THE INFLATION FALLACY

If you ask the typical person why inflation is bad, he or she will tell you that the answer is obvious: Inflation robs people of the purchasing power of their hard-earned dollars. When prices rise, each dollar of income buys fewer goods and services. Thus, it might seem that inflation directly lowers living standards.

Yet further thought reveals a fallacy in this answer. When prices rise, buyers of goods and services pay more for what they buy. At the same time, however, sellers of goods and services get more for what they sell. Because most people earn their incomes by selling their services, such as their labour, inflation in incomes goes hand in hand with inflation in prices. Thus, *inflation does not in itself reduce people's real purchasing power.*

People believe the inflation fallacy because they do not appreciate the principle of monetary neutrality. Workers who receive an annual raise of 10 percent tend to view that raise as a reward for their own talent and effort. When an inflation rate of 6 percent reduces the real value of that raise to only 4 percent, the workers might feel that they have been cheated of what is rightfully their due. In fact, as we discussed in Chapter 12, real incomes are determined by real variables, such as physical capital, human capital, natural resources, and the available production technology. Nominal incomes are determined by those factors and the overall price level. If the Bank of Canada were to lower the inflation rate from 6 percent to zero, the workers' annual raise would fall from 10 percent to 4 percent. They might feel less robbed by inflation, but their real income would not rise more quickly.

If nominal incomes tend to keep pace with rising prices, why is inflation a problem? It turns out that there is no single answer to this question. Instead, economists have identified several costs of inflation. Each of these costs shows some way in which persistent growth in the money supply does, in fact, have some effect on real variables.

SHOELEATHER COSTS

As we have discussed, inflation is like a tax on the holders of money. The tax itself is not a cost to society: It is only a transfer of resources from households to the government. Yet, as we first saw in Chapter 8, most taxes give people an incentive to alter their behaviour to avoid paying the tax, and this distortion of incentives causes deadweight losses for society as a whole. Like other taxes, the inflation tax also causes deadweight losses because people waste scarce resources trying to avoid it.

How can a person avoid paying the inflation tax? Because inflation erodes the real value of the money in your wallet, you can avoid the inflation tax by holding less money. One way to do this is to go to the bank more often. For example, rather than withdrawing $200 every four weeks, you might withdraw $50 once a week. By making more frequent trips to the bank, you can keep more of your wealth in your interest-bearing savings account and less in your wallet, where inflation erodes its value.

shoeleather costs
the resources wasted when inflation encourages people to reduce their money holdings

The cost of reducing your money holdings is called the **shoeleather cost** of inflation because making more frequent trips to the bank causes your shoes to wear out more quickly. Of course, this term is not to be taken literally: The actual cost of reducing your money holdings is not the wear and tear on your shoes but the time and convenience you must sacrifice to keep less money on hand than you would if there were no inflation.

The shoeleather costs of inflation may seem trivial. And, in fact, they are in the Canadian economy, which has had only moderate inflation in recent years. But this cost is magnified in countries experiencing hyperinflation. Here is a description of one person's experience in Bolivia during its hyperinflation (as reported in the August 13, 1985, issue of *The Wall Street Journal*, p. 1):

> When Edgar Miranda gets his monthly teacher's pay of 25 million pesos, he hasn't a moment to lose. Every hour, pesos drop in value. So, while his wife rushes to market to lay in a month's supply of rice and noodles, he is off with the rest of the pesos to change them into black-market dollars.
>
> Mr. Miranda is practising the First Rule of Survival amid the most out-of-control inflation in the world today. Bolivia is a case study of how runaway inflation undermines a society. Price increases are so huge that the figures build up almost beyond comprehension. In one six-month period, for example, prices soared at an annual rate of 38 000 percent. By official count, however, last year's inflation reached 2000 percent, and this year's is expected to hit 8000 percent—though other estimates range many times higher. In any event, Bolivia's rate dwarfs Israel's 370 percent and Argentina's 1100 percent—two other cases of severe inflation.
>
> It is easier to comprehend what happens to the 38-year-old Mr. Miranda's pay if he doesn't quickly change it into [U.S.] dollars. The day he was paid 25 million pesos, a dollar cost 500 000 pesos. So he received $50. Just days later, with the rate at 900 000 pesos, he would have received $27.

As this story shows, the shoeleather costs of inflation can be substantial. With the high inflation rate, Mr. Miranda does not have the luxury of holding the local

IN THE NEWS

The Hyperinflation in Serbia

WHENEVER GOVERNMENTS TURN TO THE printing press to finance substantial amounts of spending, the result is hyperinflation. As residents of Serbia learned in the early 1990s, life under such circumstances is far from easy.

Special, Today Only: 6 Million Dinars for a Snickers Bar

BY ROGER THUROW

BELGRADE, YUGOSLAVIA—At the Luna boutique, a Snickers bar costs 6 million dinars. Or at least it does until manager Tihomir Nikolic reads the overnight fax from his boss.

"Raise prices 99 percent," the document tersely orders. It would be an even 100 percent except that the computers at the boutique, which would be considered a dime store in other parts of the world, can't handle three-digit changes.

So for the second time in three days, Mr. Nikolic sets about raising prices. He jams a mop across the door frame to keep customers from getting away with a bargain. The computer spits out the new prices on perforated paper. The manager and two assistants rip the paper into tags and tape them to the shelves. They used to put the prices directly on the goods, but there were so many stickers it was getting difficult to read the labels.

After four hours, the mop is removed from the door. The customers wander in, rub their eyes, and squint at the tags, counting the zeros. Mr. Nikolic himself squints as the computer prints another price, this one for a video recorder.

"Is that billions?" he asks himself. It is: 20 391 560 223 dinars, to be precise. He points to his T-shirt, which is emblazoned with the words "Far Out," the name of a fruit juice he once sold. He suggests it is an ideal motto for Serbia's bizarre economic situation. "It fits the craziness," he says.

How else would you describe it? Since the international community imposed economic sanctions, the inflation rate has been at least 10 percent *daily*. This translates to an annual rate in the quadrillions—so high as to be meaningless. In Serbia, one U.S. dollar will get you 10 million dinars at the Hyatt hotel, 12 million from the shady money changers on Republic Square, and 17 million from a bank run by Belgrade's underworld. Serbs complain that the dinar is as worthless as toilet paper. But for the moment, at least, there is plenty of toilet paper to go around.

The government mint, hidden in the park behind the Belgrade racetrack, is said to be churning out dinars 24 hours a day, furiously trying to keep up with the inflation that is fuelled, in turn, by its own nonstop printing. The government, which believes in throwing around money to damp dissent, needs dinars to pay workers for not working at closed factories and offices. It needs them to buy the harvest from the farmers. It needs them to finance its smuggling forays and other ways to evade the sanctions, bringing in everything from oil to Mr. Nikolic's Snickers bars. It also needs them to supply brother Serbs fighting in Bosnia-Herzegovina and Croatia.

The money changers, whose fingertips detect the slightest change in paper quality, insist that the mint is even contracting out to private printers to meet demand.

"We're experts. They can't fool us," says one of the changers as he hands over 800 million worth of 5-million-dinar bills. "These," he notes confidently, "are fresh from the mint." He says he got them from a private bank, which got them from the central bank, which got them from the mint—an unholy circuit linking the black market with the Finance Ministry. "It's collective lunacy," the money changer says, laughing wickedly.

SOURCE: *The Wall Street Journal*, August 4, 1993, p. A1.

money as a store of value. Instead, he is forced to convert his pesos quickly into goods or into U.S. dollars, which offer a more stable store of value. The time and effort that Mr. Miranda expends to reduce his money holdings are a waste of resources. If the monetary authority pursued a low-inflation policy, Mr. Miranda would be happy to hold pesos, and he could put his time and effort to more productive use. In fact, shortly after this article was written, the Bolivian inflation rate was reduced substantially with more restrictive monetary policy.

MENU COSTS

Most firms do not change the prices of their products every day. Instead, firms often announce prices and leave them unchanged for weeks, months, or even years. One survey found that the typical U.S. firm changes its prices about once a year.

menu costs
the costs of changing prices

Firms change prices infrequently because there are costs of changing prices. Costs of price adjustment are called **menu costs,** a term derived from a restaurant's cost of printing a new menu. Menu costs include the cost of deciding on new prices, the cost of printing new price lists and catalogues, the cost of sending these new price lists and catalogues to dealers and customers, the cost of advertising the new prices, and even the cost of dealing with customer annoyance over price changes.

Inflation increases the menu costs that firms must bear. In the current Canadian economy, with its low inflation rate, annual price adjustment is an appropriate business strategy for many firms. But when high inflation makes firms' costs rise rapidly, annual price adjustment is impractical. During hyperinflations, for example, firms must change their prices daily or even more often just to keep up with all the other prices in the economy.

RELATIVE-PRICE VARIABILITY AND THE MISALLOCATION OF RESOURCES

Suppose that the Eatabit Eatery prints a new menu with new prices every January and then leaves its prices unchanged for the rest of the year. If there is no inflation, Eatabit's relative prices—the prices of its meals compared with other prices in the economy—would be constant over the course of the year. By contrast, if the inflation rate is 12 percent per year, Eatabit's relative prices will automatically fall by 1 percent each month. The restaurant's relative prices (that is, its prices compared with others in the economy) will be high in the early months of the year, just after it has printed a new menu, and low in the later months. And the higher the inflation rate, the greater is this automatic variability. Thus, because prices change only once in a while, inflation causes relative prices to vary more than they otherwise would.

Why does this matter? The reason is that market economies rely on relative prices to allocate scarce resources. Consumers decide what to buy by comparing the quality and prices of various goods and services. Through these decisions, they determine how the scarce factors of production are allocated among industries and firms. When inflation distorts relative prices, consumer decisions are distorted, and markets are less able to allocate resources to their best use.

INFLATION-INDUCED TAX DISTORTIONS

Almost all taxes distort incentives, cause people to alter their behaviour, and lead to a less efficient allocation of the economy's resources. Many taxes, however, become even more problematic in the presence of inflation. The reason is that lawmakers often fail to take inflation into account when writing the tax laws.

Economists who have studied the tax code conclude that inflation tends to raise the tax burden on income earned from savings.

One example of how inflation discourages saving is the tax treatment of *capital gains*—the profits made by selling an asset for more than its purchase price. Suppose that in 1980 you used some of your savings to buy stock in the Bank of Nova Scotia for $10 and that in 2000 you sold the stock for $50. According to the tax law, you have earned a capital gain of $40, which you must include in your income when computing how much income tax you owe. But suppose the overall price level doubled from 1980 to 2000. In this case, the $10 you invested in 1980 is equivalent (in terms of purchasing power) to $20 in 2000. When you sell your stock for $50, you have a real gain (an increase in purchasing power) of only $30. The tax code, however, does not take account of inflation and assesses you a tax on a gain of $40. Thus, inflation exaggerates the size of capital gains and inadvertently increases the tax burden on this type of income.

Another example is the tax treatment of interest income. The income tax treats the *nominal* interest earned on savings as income, even though part of the nominal interest rate merely compensates for inflation. To see the effects of this policy, consider the numerical example in Table 16-1. The table compares two economies, both of which tax interest income at a rate of 25 percent. In Economy 1, inflation is zero, and the nominal and real interest rates are both 4 percent. In this case, the 25 percent tax on interest income reduces the real interest rate from 4 percent to 3 percent. In Economy 2, the real interest rate is again 4 percent, but the inflation rate is 8 percent. As a result of the Fisher effect, the nominal interest rate is 12 percent. Because the income tax treats this entire 12 percent interest as income, the government takes 25 percent of it, leaving an after-tax nominal interest rate of only 9 percent and an after-tax real interest rate of only 1 percent. In this case, the 25 percent tax on interest income reduces the real interest rate from 4 percent to 1 percent. Because the after-tax real interest rate provides the incentive to save, saving is much less attractive in the economy with inflation (Economy 2) than in the economy with stable prices (Economy 1).

	ECONOMY 1 (PRICE STABILITY)	ECONOMY 2 (INFLATION)
Real interest rate	4%	4%
Inflation rate	0	8
Nominal interest rate (real interest rate + inflation rate)	4	12
Reduced interest due to 25 percent tax (0.25 × nominal interest rate)	1	3
After-tax nominal interest rate (0.75 × nominal interest rate)	3	9
After-tax real interest rate (after-tax nominal interest rate − inflation rate)	3	1

Table 16-1

HOW INFLATION RAISES THE TAX BURDEN ON SAVING. In the presence of zero inflation, a 25 percent tax on interest income reduces the real interest rate from 4 percent to 3 percent. In the presence of 8 percent inflation, the same tax reduces the real interest rate from 4 percent to 1 percent.

The taxes on nominal capital gains and on nominal interest income are two examples of how the tax code interacts with inflation. There are many others. Because of these inflation-induced tax changes, higher inflation tends to discourage people from saving. Recall that the economy's saving provides the resources for investment, which in turn is a key ingredient to long-run economic growth. Thus, when inflation raises the tax burden on saving, it tends to depress the economy's long-run growth rate. There is, however, no consensus among economists about the size of this effect.

One solution to this problem, other than eliminating inflation, is to index the tax system. That is, the tax laws could be rewritten to take account of the effects of inflation. In the case of capital gains, for example, the tax code could adjust the purchase price using a price index and assess the tax only on the real gain. In the case of interest income, the government could tax only real interest income by excluding that portion of the interest income that merely compensates for inflation. To some extent, the tax laws have moved in the direction of indexation. For example, the income levels at which income tax rates change are adjusted automatically each year based on changes in the consumer price index. Yet many other aspects of the tax laws—such as the tax treatment of capital gains and interest income—are not indexed.

In an ideal world, the tax laws would be written so that inflation would not alter anyone's real tax liability. In the world in which we live, however, tax laws are far from perfect. More complete indexation would probably be desirable, but it would further complicate a tax code that many people already consider too complex.

CONFUSION AND INCONVENIENCE

Imagine that we took a poll and asked people the following question: "This year the yard is 36 inches. How long do you think it should be next year?" Assuming we could get people to take us seriously, they would tell us that the yard should stay the same length—36 inches. Anything else would just complicate life needlessly.

What does this finding have to do with inflation? Recall that money, as the economy's unit of account, is what we use to quote prices and record debts. In other words, money is the yardstick with which we measure economic transactions. The job of the Bank of Canada is a bit like the job of Measurement Canada (a division of Industry Canada)—to ensure the reliability of a commonly used unit of measurement. When the Bank of Canada increases the money supply and creates inflation, it erodes the real value of the unit of account.

It is difficult to judge the costs of the confusion and inconvenience that arise from inflation. Earlier we discussed how the tax code incorrectly measures real incomes in the presence of inflation. Similarly, accountants incorrectly measure firms' earnings when prices are rising over time. Because inflation causes dollars at different times to have different real values, computing a firm's profit—the difference between its revenue and costs—is more complicated in an economy with inflation. Therefore, to some extent, inflation makes investors less able to sort out successful from unsuccessful firms, which in turn impedes financial markets in their role of allocating the economy's saving to alternative types of investment.

A SPECIAL COST OF UNEXPECTED INFLATION: ARBITRARY REDISTRIBUTIONS OF WEALTH

So far, the costs of inflation we have discussed occur even if inflation is steady and predictable. Inflation has an additional cost, however, when it comes as a surprise. Unexpected inflation redistributes wealth among the population in a way that has nothing to do with either merit or need. These redistributions occur because many loans in the economy are specified in terms of the unit of account—money.

Consider an example. Suppose that Sam Student takes out a $20 000 loan at a 7 percent interest rate from Bigbank to attend college. In ten years, the loan will come due. After his debt has compounded for ten years at 7 percent, Sam will owe Bigbank $40 000. The real value of this debt will depend on inflation over the decade. If Sam is lucky, the economy will have a hyperinflation. In this case, wages and prices will rise so high that Sam will be able to pay the $40 000 debt out of pocket change. By contrast, if the economy goes through a major deflation, then wages and prices will fall, and Sam will find the $40 000 debt a greater burden than he anticipated.

This example shows that unexpected changes in prices redistribute wealth among debtors and creditors. A hyperinflation enriches Sam at the expense of Bigbank because it diminishes the real value of the debt; Sam can repay the loan in less valuable dollars than he anticipated. Deflation enriches Bigbank at Sam's expense because it increases the real value of the debt; in this case, Sam has to repay the loan in more valuable dollars than he anticipated. If inflation were predictable, then Bigbank and Sam could take inflation into account when setting the nominal interest rate. (Recall the Fisher effect.) But if inflation is hard to predict, it imposes risk on Sam and Bigbank that both would prefer to avoid.

This cost of unexpected inflation is important to consider together with another fact: Inflation is especially volatile and uncertain when the average rate of inflation is high. This is seen most simply by examining the experience of different countries. Countries with low average inflation, such as Germany in the late twentieth century, tend to have stable inflation. Countries with high average inflation, such as many countries in Latin America, tend also to have unstable inflation. There are no known examples of economies with high, stable inflation. This relationship between the level and volatility of inflation points to another cost of inflation: If a country pursues a high-inflation monetary policy, it will have to bear not only the costs of high expected inflation but also the arbitrary redistributions of wealth associated with unexpected inflation.

CASE STUDY   *THE WIZARD OF OZ* AND THE FREE-SILVER DEBATE

You have probably seen the movie *The Wizard of Oz*, based on a children's book written in 1900. The movie and book tell the story of a young girl, Dorothy, who finds herself lost in a strange land far from home. You probably did not know, however, that the story is actually an allegory about U.S. monetary policy in the late nineteenth century.

From 1880 to 1896, the price level in the U.S. economy fell by 23 percent. Because this event was unanticipated, it led to a major redistribution of wealth. Most farmers in the western part of the country were debtors. Their creditors were the bankers in the east. When the price level fell, it caused the real value of these debts to rise, which enriched the banks at the expense of the farmers.

According to populist politicians of the time, the solution to the farmers' problem was the free coinage of silver. During this period, the United States was operating with a gold standard. The quantity of gold determined the money supply and, thereby, the price level. The free-silver advocates wanted silver, as well as gold, to be used as money. If adopted, this proposal would have increased the money supply, pushed up the price level, and reduced the real burden of the farmers' debts.

The debate over silver was heated, and it was central to the politics of the 1890s. A common election slogan of the populists was "We Are Mortgaged. All but Our Votes." One prominent advocate of free silver was William Jennings Bryan, the Democratic nominee for president in 1896. He is remembered in part for a speech at the Democratic party's nominating convention in which he said, "You shall not press down upon the brow of labor this crown of thorns. You shall not crucify mankind upon a cross of gold." Rarely since then have politicians waxed so poetic about alternative approaches to monetary policy. Nonetheless, Bryan lost the election to Republican William McKinley, and the United States remained on the gold standard.

L. Frank Baum, the author of the book *The Wonderful Wizard of Oz,* was a midwestern journalist. When he sat down to write a story for children, he made the characters represent protagonists in the major political battle of his time. Although modern commentators on the story differ somewhat in the interpretation they assign to each character, there is no doubt that the story highlights the debate over monetary policy. Here is how economic historian Hugh Rockoff, writing in the August 1990 issue of the *Journal of Political Economy,* interprets the story:

DOROTHY:	Traditional American values
TOTO:	Prohibitionist party, also called the Teetotalers
SCARECROW:	Farmers
TIN WOODSMAN:	Industrial workers
COWARDLY LION:	William Jennings Bryan
MUNCHKINS:	Citizens of the east
WICKED WITCH OF THE EAST:	Grover Cleveland
WICKED WITCH OF THE WEST:	William McKinley
WIZARD:	Marcus Alonzo Hanna, chairman of the Republican party
OZ:	Abbreviation for ounce of gold
YELLOW BRICK ROAD:	Gold standard

In the end of Baum's story, Dorothy does find her way home, but not just by following the yellow brick road. After a long and perilous journey, she learns that the wizard is incapable of helping her or her friends. Instead, Dorothy finally discovers the magical power of her *silver* slippers. (When the book was made

AN EARLY DEBATE OVER
MONETARY POLICY

into a movie in 1939, Dorothy's slippers were changed from silver to ruby. Apparently, the Hollywood filmmakers were not aware that they were telling a story about nineteenth-century monetary policy.)

Although the populists lost the debate over the free coinage of silver, they did eventually get the monetary expansion and inflation that they wanted. In 1898 prospectors discovered gold near the Klondike River in the Yukon. Increased supplies of gold also arrived from the mines of South Africa. As a result, the money supply and the price level started to rise in the United States and other countries operating on the gold standard. Within fifteen years, prices in the United States were back to the levels that had prevailed in the 1880s, and farmers were better able to handle their debts.

■ **QUICK QUIZ:**   List and describe six costs of inflation.

CONCLUSION

This chapter discussed the causes and costs of inflation. The primary cause of inflation is simply growth in the quantity of money. When the central bank creates money in large quantities, the value of money falls quickly. To maintain stable prices, the central bank must maintain strict control over the money supply.

The costs of inflation are more subtle. They include shoeleather costs, menu costs, increased variability of relative prices, unintended changes in tax liabilities, confusion and inconvenience, and arbitrary redistributions of wealth. Are these costs, in total, large or small? All economists agree that they become huge during hyperinflation. But their size for moderate inflation—when prices rise by less than 10 percent per year—is more open to debate.

Although this chapter presented many of the most important lessons about inflation, the discussion is incomplete. When the Bank of Canada reduces the rate of money growth, prices rise less rapidly, as the quantity theory suggests. Yet as the economy makes the transition to this lower inflation rate, the change in monetary policy will have disruptive effects on production and employment. That is, even though monetary policy is neutral in the long run, it has profound effects on

AS WE HAVE SEEN, UNEXPECTED CHANGES in the price level redistribute wealth among debtors and creditors. This would no longer be true if debt contracts were written in real, rather than nominal, terms. In 1997 the U.S. Treasury started issuing bonds with a return indexed to the price level. In the following article, written a few months before the policy was implemented, two prominent economists discuss the merits of this policy.

Inflation Fighters for the Long Term

BY JOHN Y. CAMPBELL
AND ROBERT J. SHILLER

Treasury Secretary Robert Rubin announced on Thursday that the government plans to issue inflation-indexed bonds—that is, bonds whose interest and principal payments are adjusted upward for inflation, guaranteeing their real purchasing power in the future.

This is a historic moment. Economists have been advocating such bonds for many long and frustrating years. Index bonds were first called for in 1822 by the economist Joseph Lowe. In the 1870s, they were championed by the British economist William Stanley Jevons. In the early part of this century, the legendary Irving Fisher made a career of advocating them.

In recent decades, economists of every political stripe—from Milton Friedman to James Tobin, Alan Blinder to Alan Greenspan—have supported them. Yet, because there was little public clamour for such an investment, the government never issued indexed bonds.

Let's hope this lack of interest does not continue now that they will become available. The success of the indexed bonds depends on whether the public understands them—and buys them. Until now, inflation has made government bonds a risky investment. In 1966, when the inflation rate was only 3 percent, if someone had bought a 30-year government bond yielding 5 percent, he would have expected that by now his investment would be worth 180 percent of its original value. However, after years of higher-than-expected inflation, the investment is worth only 85 percent of its original value.

Because inflation has been modest in recent years, many people today are not worried about how it will affect their savings. This complacency is dangerous: Even a low rate of inflation can seriously erode savings over long periods of time.

Imagine that you retire today with a pension invested in Treasury bonds that pay a fixed $10 000 each year,

real variables in the short run. Later in this book we will examine the reasons for short-run monetary non-neutrality in order to enhance our understanding of the causes and costs of inflation.

Summary

♦ The overall level of prices in an economy adjusts to bring money supply and money demand into balance. When the central bank increases the supply of money, it causes the price level to rise. Persistent growth in the quantity of money supplied leads to continuing inflation.

♦ The principle of monetary neutrality asserts that changes in the quantity of money influence nominal variables but not real variables. Most economists believe that monetary neutrality approximately describes the behaviour of the economy in the long run.

regardless of inflation. If there is no inflation, in twenty years the pension will have the same purchasing power that it does today. But if there is an inflation rate of only 3 percent per year, in twenty years your pension will be worth only $5540 in today's dollars. Five percent inflation over twenty years will cut your purchasing power to $3770, and 10 percent will reduce it to a pitiful $1390. Which of these scenarios is likely? No one knows. Inflation ultimately depends on the people who are elected and appointed as guardians of our money supply.

At a time when Americans are living longer and planning for several decades of retirement, the insidious effects of inflation should be of serious concern. For this reason alone, the creation of inflation-indexed bonds, with their guarantee of a safe return over long periods of time, is a welcome development.

No other investment offers this kind of safety. Conventional government bonds make payments that are fixed in dollar terms; but investors should be concerned about purchasing power, not about the number of dollars they receive. Money market funds make dollar payments that increase with inflation to some degree, since short-term interest rates tend to rise with inflation. But many other factors also influence interest rates, so the real income from a money market fund is not secure.

The stock market offers a high rate of return on average, but it can fall as well as rise. Investors should remember the bear market of the 1970s as well as the bull market of the 1980s and 1990s.

Inflation-indexed government bonds have been issued in Britain for fifteen years, in Canada for five years, and in many other countries, including Australia, New Zealand, and Sweden. In Britain, which has the world's largest indexed-bond market, the bonds have offered a yield 3 to 4 percent higher than the rate of inflation. In the United States, a safe long-term return of this sort should make indexed bonds an important part of retirement savings.

We expect that financial institutions will take advantage of the new inflation-indexed bonds and offer innovative new products. Indexed-bond funds will probably appear first, but indexed annuities and even indexed mortgages—monthly payments would be adjusted for inflation—should also become available. [*Author's note:* Since this article was written, some of these indexed products have been introduced, but their use is not yet widespread.]

Although the Clinton administration may not get much credit for it today, the decision to issue inflation-indexed bonds is an accomplishment that historians decades hence will single out for special recognition.

Source: *The New York Times*, May 18, 1996, p. 19.

♦ A government can pay for some of its spending simply by printing money. When countries rely heavily on this "inflation tax," the result is hyperinflation.

♦ One application of the principle of monetary neutrality is the Fisher effect. According to the Fisher effect, when the inflation rate rises, the nominal interest rate rises by the same amount, so that the real interest rate remains the same.

♦ Many people think that inflation makes them poorer because it raises the cost of what they buy. This view is a fallacy, however, because inflation also raises nominal incomes.

♦ Economists have identified six costs of inflation: shoeleather costs associated with reduced money holdings, menu costs associated with more frequent adjustment of prices, increased variability of relative prices, unintended changes in tax liabilities due to nonindexation of the tax code, confusion and inconvenience resulting from a changing unit of account, and arbitrary redistributions of wealth between debtors and creditors. Many of these costs are large during hyperinflation, but the size of these costs for moderate inflation is less clear.

Key Concepts

quantity theory of money, p. 346
nominal variables, p. 347
real variables, p. 347
classical dichotomy, p. 348

monetary neutrality, p. 348
velocity of money, p. 349
quantity equation, p. 349
inflation tax, p. 352

Fisher effect, p. 354
shoeleather costs, p. 356
menu costs, p. 358

Questions for Review

1. Explain how an increase in the price level affects the real value of money.

2. According to the quantity theory of money, what is the effect of an increase in the quantity of money?

3. Explain the difference between nominal and real variables, and give two examples of each. According to the principle of monetary neutrality, which variables are affected by changes in the quantity of money?

4. In what sense is inflation like a tax? How does thinking about inflation as a tax help explain hyperinflation?

5. According to the Fisher effect, how does an increase in the inflation rate affect the real interest rate and the nominal interest rate?

6. What are the costs of inflation? Which of these costs do you think are most important for the Canadian economy?

7. If inflation is less than expected, who benefits—debtors or creditors? Explain.

Problems and Applications

1. Suppose that this year's money supply is $50 billion, nominal GDP is $1 trillion, and real GDP is $500 billion.
    a. What is the price level? What is the velocity of money?
    b. Suppose that velocity is constant and the economy's output of goods and services rises by 5 percent each year. What will happen to nominal GDP and the price level next year if the Bank of Canada keeps the money supply constant?
    c. What money supply should the Bank of Canada set next year if it wants to keep the price level stable?
    d. What money supply should the Bank of Canada set next year if it wants inflation of 10 percent?

2. Suppose that changes in bank regulations expand the availability of credit cards, so that people need to hold less cash.
    a. How does this event affect the demand for money?
    b. If the Bank of Canada does not respond to this event, what will happen to the price level?
    c. If the Bank of Canada wants to keep the price level stable, what should it do?

3. It is often suggested that the Bank of Canada try to achieve zero inflation. If we assume that velocity is constant, does this zero-inflation goal require that the rate of money growth equal zero? If yes, explain why. If no, explain what the rate of money growth should equal.

4. The economist John Maynard Keynes wrote: "Lenin is said to have declared that the best way to destroy the capitalist system was to debauch the currency. By a continuing process of inflation, governments can confiscate, secretly and unobserved, an important part of the wealth of their citizens." Justify Lenin's assertion.

5. Suppose that a country's inflation rate increases sharply. What happens to the inflation tax on the holders of money? Why is wealth that is held in savings accounts *not* subject to a change in the inflation tax? Can you think of any way in which holders of savings accounts are hurt by the increase in the inflation rate?

6. Hyperinflations are extremely rare in countries whose central banks are independent of the rest of the government. Why might this be so?

7. Let's consider the effects of inflation in an economy composed only of two people: Nik, a bean farmer, and Rita, a rice farmer. Nik and Rita both always consume equal amounts of rice and beans. In 2000, the price of beans was $1, and the price of rice was $3.
   a. Suppose that in 2001 the price of beans was $2 and the price of rice was $6. What was inflation? Was Nik better off, worse off, or unaffected by the changes in prices? What about Rita?
   b. Now suppose that in 2001 the price of beans was $2 and the price of rice was $4. What was inflation? Was Nik better off, worse off, or unaffected by the changes in prices? What about Rita?
   c. Finally, suppose that in 2001 the price of beans was $2 and the price of rice was $1.50. What was inflation? Was Nik better off, worse off, or unaffected by the changes in prices? What about Rita?
   d. What matters more to Nik and Rita—the overall inflation rate or the relative price of rice and beans?

8. If the tax rate is 40 percent, compute the before-tax real interest rate and the after-tax real interest rate in each of the following cases:
   a. The nominal interest rate is 10 percent and the inflation rate is 5 percent.
   b. The nominal interest rate is 6 percent and the inflation rate is 2 percent.
   c. The nominal interest rate is 4 percent and the inflation rate is 1 percent.

9. What are your shoeleather costs of going to the bank? How might you measure these costs in dollars? How do you think the shoeleather costs of your university president differ from your own?

10. Recall that money serves three functions in the economy. What are those functions? How does inflation affect the ability of money to serve each of these functions?

11. Suppose that people expect inflation to equal 3 percent, but in fact prices rise by 5 percent. Describe how this unexpectedly high inflation rate would help or hurt the following:
   a. the government
   b. a homeowner with a fixed-rate mortgage
   c. a union worker in the second year of a labour contract
   d. a university that has invested some of its endowment in government bonds

12. Explain one harm associated with unexpected inflation that is *not* associated with expected inflation. Then explain one harm associated with both expected and unexpected inflation.

13. Explain whether the following statements are true, false, or uncertain:
   a. "Inflation hurts borrowers and helps lenders because borrowers must pay a higher rate of interest."
   b. "If prices change in a way that leaves the overall price level unchanged, then no one is made better or worse off."
   c. "Inflation does not reduce the purchasing power of most workers."

Seven

THE
MACROECONOMICS OF
OPEN ECONOMIES

17

**IN THIS CHAPTER
YOU WILL . . .**

*Learn how net exports
measure the
international flow of
goods and services*

*Learn how net foreign
investment measures
the international
flow of capital*

*Consider why net
exports must always
equal net foreign
investment*

*See how saving,
domestic investment,
and net foreign
investment are
related*

*Learn the meaning of
the nominal exchange
rate and the real
exchange rate*

*Examine purchasing-
power parity as a
theory of how
exchange rates are
determined*

*Learn that Canada is
a small open economy
and the implications
of perfect capital
mobility*

OPEN-ECONOMY
MACROECONOMICS:
BASIC CONCEPTS

When you decide to buy a car, you may compare the latest models offered by Ford
and Toyota. When you take your next vacation, you may consider spending it on a
ski hill in British Columbia or a beach in Mexico. When you start saving for your
retirement, you may choose between a mutual fund that buys stock in Canadian
companies and one that buys stock in foreign companies. In all of these cases, you are
participating not just in the Canadian economy but in economies around the world.

There are clear benefits to being open to international trade: Trade allows
people to produce what they produce best and to consume the great variety of
goods and services produced around the world. Indeed, one of the *Ten Principles of
Economics* highlighted in Chapter 1 is that trade can make everyone better off.
Chapters 3 and 9 examined the gains from trade more fully. We learned that international trade can raise living standards in all countries by allowing each country

to specialize in producing those goods and services in which it has a comparative advantage.

So far our development of macroeconomics has largely ignored the economy's interaction with other economies around the world. For most questions in macroeconomics, international issues are peripheral. For instance, when we discussed the natural rate of unemployment in Chapter 14 and the causes of inflation in Chapter 16, the effects of international trade could safely be ignored. Indeed, to keep their analysis simple, macroeconomists often assume a **closed economy**—an economy that does not interact with other economies.

closed economy

an economy that does not interact with other economies in the world

open economy

an economy that interacts freely with other economies around the world

Yet some new macroeconomic issues arise in an **open economy**—an economy that interacts freely with other economies around the world. This chapter and the next one, therefore, provide an introduction to open-economy macroeconomics. We begin in this chapter by discussing the key macroeconomic variables that describe an open economy's interactions in world markets. You may have noticed mention of these variables—exports, imports, the trade balance, and exchange rates—when reading the newspaper or watching the nightly news. Our first job is to understand what these data mean. In the next chapter we develop a model to explain how these variables are determined and how they are affected by various government policies.

THE INTERNATIONAL FLOWS OF GOODS AND CAPITAL

An open economy interacts with other economies in two ways: It buys and sells goods and services in world product markets, and it buys and sells capital assets in world financial markets. Here we discuss these two activities and the close relationship between them.

exports

goods and services that are produced domestically and sold abroad

imports

goods and services that are produced abroad and sold domestically

net exports

the value of a nation's exports minus the value of its imports, also called the trade balance

trade balance

the value of a nation's exports minus the value of its imports, also called net exports

trade surplus

an excess of exports over imports

THE FLOW OF GOODS: EXPORTS, IMPORTS, AND NET EXPORTS

As we first noted in Chapter 3, **exports** are domestically produced goods and services that are sold abroad, and **imports** are foreign-produced goods and services that are sold domestically. When Bombardier, the Canadian aircraft manufacturer, builds a plane and sells it to Air France, the sale is an export for Canada and an import for France. When Volvo, the Swedish car manufacturer, makes a car and sells it to a Canadian resident, the sale is an import for Canada and an export for Sweden.

The **net exports** of any country are the value of its exports minus the value of its imports. The Bombardier sale raises Canada's net exports, and the Volvo sale reduces Canada's net exports. Because net exports tell us whether a country is, in total, a seller or a buyer in world markets for goods and services, net exports are also called the **trade balance.** If net exports are positive, exports are greater than imports, indicating that the country sells more goods and services abroad than it buys from other countries. In this case, the country is said to run a **trade surplus.**

"But we're not just talking about buying a car—we're talking about confronting this country's trade deficit with Japan."

If net exports are negative, exports are less than imports, indicating that the country sells fewer goods and services abroad than it buys from other countries. In this case, the country is said to run a **trade deficit.** If net exports are zero, exports and imports are exactly equal, and the country is said to have **balanced trade.**

In the next chapter we develop a theory that explains an economy's trade balance, but even at this early stage it is easy to think of many factors that might influence a country's exports, imports, and net exports. Those factors include the following:

◆ the tastes of consumers for domestic and foreign goods

◆ the prices of goods at home and abroad

◆ the exchange rates at which people can use domestic currency to buy foreign currencies

◆ the incomes of consumers at home and abroad

◆ the cost of transporting goods from country to country

◆ the policies of the government toward international trade

As these variables change over time, so does the amount of international trade.

trade deficit
an excess of imports over exports

balanced trade
a situation in which exports equal imports

CASE STUDY   THE INCREASING OPENNESS OF THE CANADIAN ECONOMY

Perhaps the most dramatic change in the Canadian economy over the past four decades has been the increasing importance of international trade and finance. This change is illustrated in Figure 17-1, which shows the total value of goods and services exported to other countries and imported from other countries expressed as a percentage of gross domestic product. In the 1960s, exports of goods and services averaged less than 20 percent of GDP. Today they are more than twice that level and still rising. Imports of goods and services have risen by a similar amount.

Figure 17-1 also shows the value of Canadian exports to and imports from the United States as a percentage of gross domestic product. Clearly, Canada's trade with the United States is the largest part of Canada's total trade. What's more, fluctuations in Canada's total exports and imports over time are mainly due to fluctuations in Canadian exports to and imports from the United States.

This increase in international trade is partly due to improvements in transportation. In 1960 the average merchant ship carried less than 10 000 tonnes of cargo; today, many ships carry more than 100 000 tonnes. The long-distance jet was introduced in 1958, and the wide-body jet in 1967, making air transport far cheaper. Because of these developments, goods that once had to be produced locally can now be traded around the world. Cut flowers, for instance, are now grown in Israel and flown to Canada to be sold. Fresh fruits and vegetables that can grow only in summer can now be consumed in winter as well, because they can be shipped to Canada from countries in the Southern Hemisphere.

The increase in international trade has also been influenced by advances in telecommunications, which have allowed businesses to reach overseas customers more easily. For example, the first transatlantic telephone cable was not laid until 1956. As recently as 1966, the technology allowed only 138 simultaneous conversations between North America and Europe. Today, communications satellites permit more than 1 million conversations to occur at the same time.

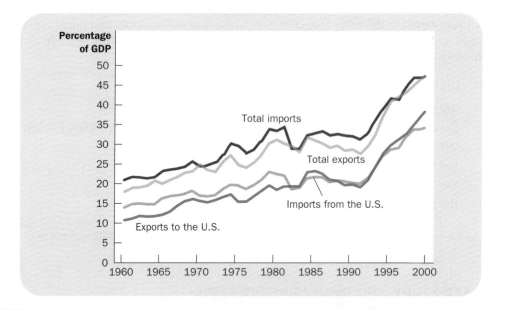

Figure 17-1

THE INTERNATIONALIZATION OF THE CANADIAN ECONOMY.   This figure shows the value of Canada's exports and imports as a fraction of GDP since 1960. It shows the value of exports and imports to the whole world and the value of exports and imports to the United States. The substantial increase over time shows the increasing importance of international trade, particularly trade with the United States. The dramatic increase in trade since the signing of the Free Trade Agreement in 1989 is especially noteworthy.

SOURCE: Statistics Canada Matrices 2360 and 2361. The values of exports and imports are defined as including transfer and investment income receipts and payments, respectively.

Technological progress has also fostered international trade by changing the kinds of goods that economies produce. When bulky raw materials (such as steel) and perishable goods (such as foodstuffs) were a large part of the world's output, transporting goods was often costly and sometimes impossible. By contrast, goods produced with modern technology are often light and easy to transport. Consumer electronics, for instance, have low weight for every dollar of value, which makes them easy to produce in one country and sell in another. An even more extreme example is the film industry. Once a studio in Hollywood makes a movie, it can send copies of the film around the world at almost zero cost. And, indeed, movies are a major export of the United States.

The government's trade policies have also been a factor in increasing international trade. For example, the Canada–U.S. Auto Pact, signed in 1966, made it possible for automobile manufacturers to move auto parts and finished automobiles across the Canada–U.S. border without having to pay import duties. The Auto Pact is largely responsible for the establishment in Canada of a large automobile manufacturing industry. In 1989 Canada signed the Canada–U.S. Free Trade Agreement, which called for the gradual elimination of tariffs on a much larger scale. This agreement was followed in 1993 by the North American Free Trade Agreement (NAFTA) among Canada, the United States, and Mexico. The effect of these free trade agreements on Canadian exports and imports is clear from Figure 17-1. Since 1989, Canada's exports and imports have dramatically increased. Virtually all of the increases in exports and imports have been due to increased trade with the United States. As we discussed in Chapters 3 and 9, economists have long believed that free trade between countries is mutually beneficial. Over time, policymakers around the world have come to accept this conclusion. International agreements, such as NAFTA and the World Trade Organization (WTO), have gradually lowered trade barriers, such as tariffs and import quotas. The pattern of increasing trade illustrated in Figure 17-1 is a phenomenon that most economists and policymakers endorse and encourage.

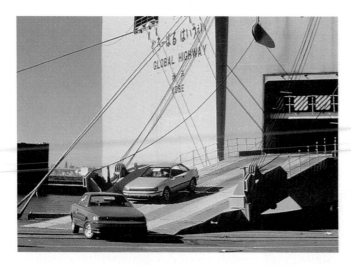

INTERNATIONAL TRADE IS INCREASINGLY IMPORTANT FOR THE CANADIAN ECONOMY.

THE FLOW OF CAPITAL: NET FOREIGN INVESTMENT

So far we have been discussing how residents of an open economy participate in world markets for goods and services. In addition, residents of an open economy participate in world financial markets. A Canadian resident with $20 000 could use that money to buy a car from Toyota, but he or she could instead use that money to buy stock in the Toyota corporation. The first transaction would represent a flow of goods, whereas the second would represent a flow of capital.

net foreign investment

the purchase of foreign assets by domestic residents minus the purchase of domestic assets by foreigners

The term **net foreign investment** refers to the purchase of foreign assets by domestic residents minus the purchase of domestic assets by foreigners. When a Canadian resident buys stock in Telmex, the Mexican phone company, the purchase raises Canada's net foreign investment. When a Japanese resident buys a bond issued by the Canadian government, the purchase reduces Canada's net foreign investment.

Recall that foreign investment takes two forms. If Tim Hortons opens up a fast food outlet in Russia, that is an example of *foreign direct investment.* Alternatively, if a Canadian buys stock in a Russian corporation, that is an example of *foreign portfolio investment.* In the first case, the Canadian owner is actively managing the investment, whereas in the second case the Canadian owner has a more passive role. In both cases, Canadian residents are buying assets located in another country, so both purchases increase Canadian net foreign investment.

We develop a theory to explain net foreign investment in the next chapter. Here, let's consider briefly some of the more important variables that influence net foreign investment:

- the real interest rates being paid on foreign assets
- the real interest rates being paid on domestic assets
- the perceived economic and political risks of holding assets abroad
- the government policies that affect foreign ownership of domestic assets

For example, consider Canadian investors deciding whether to buy Mexican government bonds or Canadian government bonds. (Recall that a bond is, in effect, an IOU of the issuer.) To make this decision, Canadian investors compare the real interest rates offered on the two bonds. The higher a bond's real interest rate, the more attractive it is. While making this comparison, however, Canadian investors must also take into account the risk that one of these governments might *default* on its debt (that is, not pay interest or principal when it is due), as well as any restrictions that the Mexican government has imposed, or might impose in the future, on foreign investors in Mexico.

THE EQUALITY OF NET EXPORTS AND NET FOREIGN INVESTMENT

We have seen that an open economy interacts with the rest of the world in two ways: in world markets for goods and services and in world financial markets. Net exports and net foreign investment each measure a type of imbalance in these markets. Net exports measure an imbalance between a country's exports and its imports. Net foreign investment measures an imbalance between the amount of

IN THE NEWS

It's the 21st Century—Do You Know Where Your Capital Is?

WHEN YOU HEAR ABOUT A FACTORY BEING built in Asia or Latin America, have you ever wondered who is financing that project? The answer might surprise you.

The World's New Financier Is You

BY EDWARD WYATT

Investors flocked to Eastern Europe after the Berlin Wall fell in 1989, eager to scoop up bargains in what they were sure would be a quick economic revival. A year later, the technology boom drew their money to the Far East. Then Latin America heated up—that is, until the Mexican peso went bust, which sent investors scurrying back to the Pacific Rim. Russia got sexy as an investment early [in 1997], and more recently South America has had allure.

Billions of dollars are sloshing back and forth over the globe with seemingly little rhyme or reason, chasing investments in once-obscure markets from Santiago to Kuala Lumpur. But there is at least some method to the madness—despite occasional debacles like the recent Bre-X gold mining fraud, in which mutual fund managers poured scads of money into what amounted to little more than holes in the ground in Borneo.

To begin with, foreign stock and bond markets are growing much faster than those in America, providing much higher returns to investors. In 1970, foreign markets accounted for only a third of the value of the world's stock and bond markets, with the United States alone accounting for the other two-thirds. But by last year, they had grown to nearly 60 percent of the total.

Stock markets in newly emerging economies like those of Turkey, Argentina, and South Africa now account for 14 percent of the world's total stock market value, up from 4 percent ten years ago.

Investors have flocked to them as global economic trends have shifted since the end of the Cold War. Centralized, state-planned economies have been scuttled for ones favouring private ownership of industry. With the transformation, the resulting vibrant new economies no longer need to rely on international development agencies or giant New York banks for foreign investment, as they did in the 1970s and 1980s; instead, much of their seed capital since 1990 has come from a surprising source: millions of average Americans who invest in mutual funds.

"This is a trend that has been led by America, which pushed the international lending agencies to encourage the development of private enterprise, to open up these markets and get the hands of government out of industrial ownership," said J. Mark Mobius, who oversees several Templeton mutual funds that invest in emerging markets. "That led to the development of capital markets—bond markets and stock markets—in many of these countries, and now to people like me trying to invest all the money that is flowing into our mutual funds." . . .

And these days, when the finance minister of a developing country wants to encourage foreigners to invest in his country, he is less likely to court the World Bank or the Agency for International Development than someone like Mr. Mobius.

SOURCE: *The New York Times*, May 25, 1997, Week in Review, p. 3.

foreign assets bought by domestic residents and the amount of domestic assets bought by foreigners.

An important but subtle fact of accounting states that, for an economy as a whole, these two imbalances must offset each other. That is, net foreign investment (*NFI*) always equals net exports (*NX*):

$$NFI = NX.$$

This equation holds because every transaction that affects one side of this equation must also affect the other side by exactly the same amount. This equation is an *identity*—an equation that must hold because of the way the variables in the equation are defined and measured.

IN THE NEWS
Flows between the Developing South and the Industrial North

WILL THE WORLD'S DEVELOPING COUN-
tries, such as those in Latin America,
flood the world's industrial countries
with cheap exports while refusing to
import goods from the industrial countries? Will the developing countries use
the world's saving to finance investment and growth, leaving the industrial countries with insufficient funds
for their own capital accumulation?
Some people fear that both of these outcomes might occur. But an accounting
identity, and economist Paul Krugman,
tell us not to worry.

Fantasy Economics

BY PAUL KRUGMAN

Reports by international organizations
are usually greeted with well-deserved
yawns. Occasionally, however, such a
report is a leading indicator of a sea
change in opinion.

A few weeks ago, the World Economic Forum—which every year draws
an unmatched assemblage of the world's
political and business elite to its conference in Davos, Switzerland—released
its annual report on international competitiveness. The report made headlines
because it demoted Japan and declared
America the world's most competitive
economy.

The revealing part of the report,
however, is not its more or less meaningless competitiveness rankings but its
introduction, which offers what seems to
be a very clear vision of the global economic future.

That vision, shared by many powerful people, is compelling and alarming.
It is also nonsense. And the fact that this
nonsense is being taken seriously by
many people who believe themselves to
be sophisticated about economics is
itself an ominous portent for the world
economy.

The report finds that the spread
of modern technology to newly industrializing nations is deindustrializing
high-wage nations: Capital is flowing to
the Third World and low-cost producers in these countries are flooding
world markets with cheap manufactured
goods.

The report predicts that these
trends will accelerate, that service jobs
will soon begin to follow the lost jobs in
manufacturing and that the future of the
high-wage nations offers a bleak choice
between declining wages and rising
unemployment.

This vision resonates with many
people. Yet as a description of what has

To see why this accounting identity is true, consider an example. Suppose that
Bombardier, the Canadian aircraft maker, sells some planes to a Japanese airline.
In this sale, a Canadian company gives planes to a Japanese company, and a
Japanese company gives yen to a Canadian company. Notice that two things have
occurred simultaneously. Canada has sold to a foreigner some of its output (the
planes), and this sale increases Canada's net exports. In addition, Canada has
acquired some foreign assets (the yen), and this acquisition increases Canada's net
foreign investment.

Although Bombardier most likely will not hold on to the yen it has acquired in
this sale, any subsequent transaction will preserve the equality of net exports and
net foreign investment. For example, Bombardier may exchange its yen for dollars
with a Canadian mutual fund that wants the yen to buy stock in Sony Corporation, the Japanese maker of consumer electronics. In this case, Bombardier's net
export of planes equals the mutual fund's net foreign investment in Sony stock.
Hence, *NX* and *NFI* rise by an equal amount.

Alternatively, Bombardier may exchange its yen for dollars with another
Canadian company that wants to buy computers from Toshiba, the Japanese computer maker. In this case, Canada's imports (of computers) exactly offset Canada's
exports (of planes). The sales by Bombardier and Toshiba together affect neither

actually happened in recent years, it is almost completely untrue.

Rapidly growing Third World economies have indeed increased their exports of manufactured goods. But today these exports absorb only about 1 percent of First World income. Moreover, Third World nations have also increased their imports.

Overall, the effect of Third World growth on the number of industrial jobs in Western nations has been minimal: Growing exports to the newly industrializing countries have created about as many jobs as growing imports have displaced.

What about capital flows? The numbers sound impressive. Last year, $24 billion flowed to Mexico, $11 billion to China. The total movement of capital from advanced to developing nations was about $60 billion. But though this sounds like a lot, it is pocket change in a world economy that invests more than $4 trillion a year.

In other words, if the vision of a Western economy battered by low-wage competition is meant to describe today's world, it is a fantasy with hardly any basis in reality.

Even if the vision does not describe the present, might it describe the future? Well, growing exports of manufactured goods from South to North will lead to a net loss of northern industrial jobs only if they are not matched by growth in exports from North to South.

The authors of the report evidently envision a future of large-scale Third World trade surpluses. But it is an unavoidable fact of accounting that a country that runs a trade surplus must also be a net investor in other countries. So large-scale deindustrialization can take place only if low-wage nations are major exporters of capital to high-wage nations. This seems unlikely. In any case, it contradicts the rest of the story, which predicts huge capital flows into low-wage nations.

Thus, the vision offered by the world competitiveness report conflicts not only with the facts but with itself. Yet it is a vision that a growing number of the world's most influential men and women seem to share. That is a dangerous trend.

Not everyone who worries about low-wage competition is a protectionist. Indeed, the authors of the world competitiveness report would surely claim to be champions of free trade. Nonetheless, the fact that such ideas have become respectable . . . suggests that the intellectual consensus that has kept world trade relatively free, and that has allowed hundreds of millions of people in the Third World to get their first taste of prosperity, may be unravelling.

SOURCE: *The New York Times*, September 26, 1994, p. A17.

Canada's net exports nor Canada's net foreign investment. That is, *NX* and *NFI* are the same as they were before these transactions took place.

The equality of net exports and net foreign investment follows from the fact that every international transaction is an exchange. When a seller country transfers a good or service to a buyer country, the buyer country gives up some asset to pay for this good or service. The value of that asset equals the value of the good or service sold. When we add everything up, the net value of goods and services sold by a country (*NX*) must equal the net value of assets acquired (*NFI*). The international flow of goods and services and the international flow of capital are two sides of the same coin.

SAVING, INVESTMENT, AND THEIR RELATIONSHIP TO THE INTERNATIONAL FLOWS

A nation's saving and investment are, as we have seen in Chapters 12 and 13, crucial to its long-run economic growth. Let's therefore consider how these variables are related to the international flows of goods and capital, as measured by net exports and net foreign investment. We can do this most easily with the help of some simple mathematics.

As you may recall, the term *net exports* first appeared earlier in the book when we discussed the components of gross domestic product. The economy's gross domestic product (Y) is divided among four components: consumption (C), investment (I), government purchases (G), and net exports (NX). We write this as

$$Y = C + I + G + NX.$$

Total expenditure on the economy's output of goods and services is the sum of expenditure on consumption, investment, government purchases, and net exports. Because each dollar of expenditure is placed into one of these four components, this equation is an accounting identity: It must be true because of the way the variables are defined and measured.

Recall that national saving is the income of the nation that is left after paying for current consumption and government purchases. National saving (S) equals $Y - C - G$. If we rearrange the above equation to reflect this fact, we get

$$Y - C - G = I + NX$$
$$S = I + NX.$$

Because net exports (NX) also equal net foreign investment (NFI), we can write this equation as

$$S \quad = \quad I \quad + \quad NFI$$

$$\text{Saving} = \frac{\text{Domestic}}{\text{investment}} + \frac{\text{Net foreign}}{\text{investment}}.$$

This equation shows that a nation's saving must equal its domestic investment plus its net foreign investment. In other words, when Canadian citizens save a dollar of their income for the future, that dollar can be used to finance accumulation of domestic capital or it can be used to finance the purchase of capital abroad.

This equation should look somewhat familiar. Earlier in the book, when we analyzed the role of the financial system, we considered this identity for the special case of a closed economy. In a closed economy, net foreign investment is zero ($NFI = 0$), so saving equals investment ($S = I$). By contrast, an open economy has two uses for its saving: domestic investment and net foreign investment.

As before, we can view the financial system as standing between the two sides of this identity. For example, suppose the Cho family decides to save some of its income for retirement. This decision contributes to national saving, the left-hand side of our equation. If the Chos deposit their saving in a mutual fund, the mutual fund may use some of the deposit to buy stock issued by Stelco, which uses the proceeds to build a new steel plant in Ontario. In addition, the mutual fund may use some of the Chos' deposit to buy stock issued by Toyota, which uses the proceeds to build a factory in Osaka. These transactions show up on the right-hand side of the equation. From the standpoint of Canadian accounting, the Stelco expenditure on a new steel plant is domestic investment, and the purchase of Toyota stock by a Canadian resident is net foreign investment. Thus, all saving in the Canadian economy shows up as investment in the Canadian economy or as Canadian net foreign investment.

CASE STUDY   SAVING, INVESTMENT, AND NET FOREIGN INVESTMENT OF CANADA

Canada is a net debtor in world financial markets. This means that foreigners own more Canadian assets than Canadians own of foreign assets. In the 1960s and 1970s, a good deal of concern was expressed about the extent of foreign investment in Canada. At the time, many people advocated restrictions on foreign ownership of Canadian assets. Was this a sensible policy to recommend? Is the fact that Canada is a net debtor a legitimate source of concern?

To answer these questions, let's see what these macroeconomic accounting identities tell us about the Canadian economy. Panel (a) of Figure 17-2 shows national saving and domestic investment as a percentage of GDP since 1961. Panel (b) shows net foreign investment as a percentage of GDP. Notice that, as the identities require, net foreign investment always equals national saving minus domestic investment.

Panel (b) shows that Canada typically experiences negative net foreign investment (NFI). That is, it is typically true that each year foreigners purchase more Canadian assets than Canadians purchase foreign assets. This net purchase of Canadian assets by foreigners has allowed domestic investment in Canada to exceed Canada's national saving by an average of 2.3 percent of GDP over the period 1961 to 1999. Because net exports must equal net foreign investment, net exports in Canada have also typically been negative over this period, something we saw from Figure 17-1.

In 1999 both net exports and net foreign investment were quite small as a fraction of GDP. For this reason, national saving and domestic investment were almost equal in that year. From Figure 17-2, we can see that this is a dramatic change from the experience in Canada over the period 1982 to 1993. During those years national saving fell, primarily as a result of large deficits run by the provincial and federal governments. Although domestic investment fell as well, it did so by much less than national saving. The growing gap between national saving and domestic investment was made up by a large increase in the purchase of Canadian assets by foreigners. In other words, the large fall in net foreign investment enabled domestic investment to remain much higher than would otherwise have been possible given the fall in national saving. Since 1993 national saving has been increasing, largely as a result of the efforts by provincial and federal governments to reduce their deficits and to begin to post surpluses.

Are trade deficits and their counterpart, negative amounts of net foreign investment, problems for the Canadian economy? Most economists argue that they are not a problem in themselves but perhaps are a symptom of a problem—reduced national saving. Reduced national saving is potentially a problem because it means that the nation is putting away less to provide for its future. However, there is no reason to become concerned if the result is a trade deficit. As our accounting identities teach us, a fall in national saving must result in either a larger trade deficit or a fall in domestic investment. If national saving falls without inducing a trade deficit, domestic investment in Canada must fall instead. This fall in investment, in turn, would adversely affect growth in the capital stock, labour productivity, and real wages. If national saving falls and the trade deficit increases as well, then the savings of foreigners are being used to finance Canadian investment. In other words, given the fact that Canadians are not saving much, it is better to have foreigners invest in the Canadian economy than no one at all. Had it not been for a willingness on the part of foreigners to put their savings into Canada, the fall in national saving brought about by large government deficits in the 1980s would have resulted in a much larger reduction in domestic investment than otherwise.

QUICK QUIZ: Define *net exports* and *net foreign investment*. Explain how they are related.

Figure 17-2

NATIONAL SAVING, DOMESTIC INVESTMENT, AND NET FOREIGN INVESTMENT. Panel (a) shows national saving and domestic investment as a percentage of GDP. Panel (b) shows net foreign investment as a percentage of GDP. In all but three years from 1961 to 1999, net foreign investment has been negative. This indicates that foreigners typically purchase more Canadian assets than Canadians purchase foreign assets. This imbalance has enabled domestic investment to exceed national saving, as illustrated in panel (a).

SOURCE: Statistics Canada Matrices 0743 and 6521 and authors' calculations.

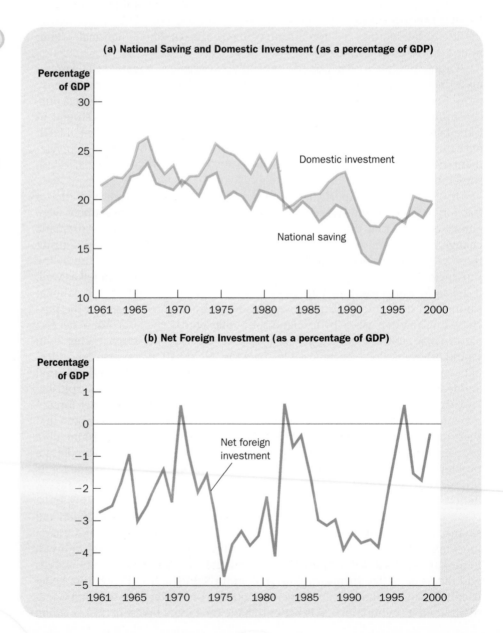

(a) National Saving and Domestic Investment (as a percentage of GDP)

(b) Net Foreign Investment (as a percentage of GDP)

THE PRICES FOR INTERNATIONAL TRANSACTIONS: REAL AND NOMINAL EXCHANGE RATES

So far we have discussed measures of the flow of goods and services and the flow of capital across a nation's border. In addition to these quantity variables, macroeconomists also study variables that measure the prices at which these international transactions take place. Just as the price in any market serves the important role of coordinating buyers and sellers in that market, international prices help coordinate the decisions of consumers and producers as they interact in world markets. Here we discuss the two most important international prices—the nominal and real exchange rates.

NOMINAL EXCHANGE RATES

The **nominal exchange rate** is the rate at which a person can trade the currency of one country for the currency of another. For example, if you go to a bank, you might see a posted exchange rate of 80 yen per dollar. If you give the bank one Canadian dollar, it will give you 80 Japanese yen; and if you give the bank 80 Japanese yen, it will give you one Canadian dollar. (In actuality, the bank will post slightly different prices for buying and selling yen. The difference gives the bank some profit for offering this service. For our purposes here, we can ignore these differences.)

An exchange rate can always be expressed in two ways. If the exchange rate is 80 yen per dollar, it is also 1/80 (= 0.0125) dollar per yen. Throughout this book, we always express the nominal exchange rate as units of foreign currency per Canadian dollar, such as 80 yen per dollar.

If the exchange rate changes so that a dollar buys more foreign currency, that change is called an **appreciation** of the dollar. If the exchange rate changes so that a dollar buys less foreign currency, that change is called a **depreciation** of the dollar. For example, when the exchange rate rises from 80 to 90 yen per dollar, the dollar is said to appreciate. At the same time, because a Japanese yen now buys less of the Canadian currency, the yen is said to depreciate. When the exchange rate falls from 80 to 70 yen per dollar, the dollar is said to depreciate, and the yen is said to appreciate.

At times you may have heard the media report that the dollar is either "strong" or "weak." These descriptions usually refer to recent changes in the nominal exchange rate. When a currency appreciates, it is said to *strengthen* because it can then buy more foreign currency. Similarly, when a currency depreciates, it is said to *weaken*.

For any country, there are many nominal exchange rates. The Canadian dollar can be used to buy Japanese yen, British pounds, French francs, U.S. dollars, Mexican pesos, and so on. When economists study changes in the exchange rate, they often use indexes that average these many exchange rates. Just as the consumer price index turns the many prices in the economy into a single measure of the price level, an exchange rate index turns these many exchange rates into a single measure of the international value of the currency. So when economists talk about the dollar appreciating or depreciating, they often are referring to an exchange rate index that takes into account many individual exchange rates.

nominal exchange rate
the rate at which a person can trade the currency of one country for the currency of another

appreciation
an increase in the value of a currency as measured by the amount of foreign currency it can buy

depreciation
a decrease in the value of a currency as measured by the amount of foreign currency it can buy

REAL EXCHANGE RATES

The **real exchange rate** is the rate at which a person can trade the goods and services of one country for the goods and services of another. For example, suppose that you go shopping and find that a case of German beer is twice as expensive as a case of Canadian beer. We would then say that the real exchange rate is 1/2 case of German beer per case of Canadian beer. Notice that, like the nominal exchange rate, we express the real exchange rate as units of the foreign item per unit of the domestic item. But in this instance the item is a good rather than a currency.

Real and nominal exchange rates are closely related. To see how, consider an example. Suppose that a bushel of Canadian wheat sells for $200, and a bushel of French wheat sells for 1600 francs. What is the real exchange rate between Canadian and French wheat? To answer this question, we must first use the nominal exchange rate to convert the prices into a common currency. If the nominal exchange rate is 4 francs per dollar, then a price for Canadian wheat of $200 per bushel is equivalent to 800 francs per bushel. Canadian wheat is half as expensive as French wheat. The real exchange rate is 1/2 bushel of French wheat per bushel of Canadian wheat.

We can summarize this calculation for the real exchange rate with the following formula:

$$\text{Real exchange rate} = \frac{\text{Nominal exchange rate} \times \text{Domestic price}}{\text{Foreign price}}.$$

Using the numbers in our example, the formula applies as follows:

$$\text{Real exchange rate} = \frac{(4 \text{ francs per dollar}) \times (\$200 \text{ per bushel of Canadian wheat})}{1600 \text{ francs per bushel of French wheat}}$$

$$= \frac{800 \text{ francs per bushel of Canadian wheat}}{1600 \text{ francs per bushel of French wheat}}$$

$$= 1/2 \text{ bushel of French wheat per tonne of Canadian wheat.}$$

Thus, the real exchange rate depends on the nominal exchange rate and on the prices of goods in the two countries measured in the local currencies.

Why does the real exchange rate matter? As you might guess, the real exchange rate is a key determinant of how much a country exports and imports. When Five Roses Inc. is deciding whether to buy Canadian wheat or French wheat to make flour, for example, it will ask which wheat is cheaper. The real exchange rate gives the answer. As another example, imagine that you are deciding whether to take a seaside vacation in Tofino, British Columbia, or in Cancun, Mexico. You might ask your travel agent the price of a hotel room in Tofino (measured in dollars), the price of a hotel room in Cancun (measured in pesos), and the exchange rate between pesos and dollars. If you decide where to vacation by comparing costs, you are basing your decision on the real exchange rate.

When studying an economy as a whole, macroeconomists focus on overall prices rather than the prices of individual items. That is, to measure the real exchange rate, they use price indexes, such as the consumer price index, which measure the price of a basket of goods and services. By using a price index for a Canadian basket (P), a price index for a foreign basket (P^*), and the nominal exchange rate between the Canadian dollar and foreign currencies (e), we can compute the overall real exchange rate between Canada and other countries as follows:

$$\text{Real exchange rate} = (e \times P)/P^*.$$

This real exchange rate measures the price of a basket of goods and services available domestically relative to a basket of goods and services available abroad.

As we examine more fully in the next chapter, a country's real exchange rate is a key determinant of its net exports of goods and services. A depreciation (fall) in the Canada's real exchange rate means that Canadian goods have become cheaper relative to foreign goods. This change encourages consumers both at home and abroad to buy more Canadian goods and fewer goods from other countries. As a result, Canadian exports rise, and Canadian imports fall, and both of these changes raise Canadian net exports. Conversely, an appreciation (rise) in Canada's real exchange rate means that Canadian goods have become more expensive compared with foreign goods, so Canada's net exports fall.

> **QUICK QUIZ:**   Define *nominal exchange rate* and *real exchange rate,* and explain how they are related. ◆ If the nominal exchange rate goes from 100 to 120 yen per dollar, has the dollar appreciated or depreciated?

A FIRST THEORY OF EXCHANGE-RATE DETERMINATION: PURCHASING-POWER PARITY

Exchange rates vary substantially over time. In 1970, a Canadian dollar could be used to buy 3.49 German marks or 600 Italian lira. In 2000, a Canadian dollar bought 1.43 German marks or 1413 Italian lira. In other words, over this period the value of the dollar fell compared with the mark and rose compared with the lira.

What explains these large and opposite changes? Economists have developed many models to explain how exchange rates are determined, each emphasizing just some of the many forces at work. Here we develop the simplest theory of exchange rates, called **purchasing-power parity.** This theory states that a unit of any given currency should be able to buy the same quantity of goods in all countries. Many economists believe that purchasing-power parity describes the forces that determine exchange rates in the long run. We now consider the logic on which this long-run theory of exchange rates is based, as well as the theory's implications and limitations.

purchasing-power parity
a theory of exchange rates whereby a unit of any given currency should be able to buy the same quantity of goods in all countries

THE BASIC LOGIC OF PURCHASING-POWER PARITY

The theory of purchasing-power parity is based on a principle called the *law of one price.* This law asserts that a good must sell for the same price in all locations. Otherwise, opportunities for profit would be left unexploited. For example, suppose that coffee beans sold for less in Vancouver than in Halifax. A person could buy coffee in Vancouver for, say, $4 a pound and then sell it in Halifax for $5 a pound,

FYI

The Value of the Canadian Dollar

When Canadians think about the value of the Canadian dollar, they typically compare it with the U.S. dollar. This is not surprising, given that when they leave Canada on holiday or on business, the vast majority of Canadians go to the United States. The value of the Canadian dollar relative to the U.S. dollar is therefore foremost in the minds of Canadians.

It is important to remember, however, that there is a nominal exchange rate between the Canadian dollar and the currency of every other country. What's more, Canada trades with many countries other than the United States. There are, then, many ways of defining the value of the Canadian dollar. We can compare it with the U.S. dollar, the British pound, or any other currency in the world.

The four graphs of Figure 17-3 show how the exchange rate has changed recently between the Canadian dollar and four currencies: the U.S. dollar, the British pound, the Japanese yen, and the Australian dollar. The graphs show that from January 1996 to January 2001, the Canadian dollar has fallen in value relative to the U.S. dollar while rising in value relative to the Australian dollar. The Canadian dollar first fell in value relative to the British pound, but over the past two years the Canadian dollar has increased in value. Conversely, the Canadian dollar first gained in value relative to the Japanese yen, but over the past two years it has fallen in value. This information is useful to Canadians wondering where to go on their next holiday. These graphs indicate that while a holiday in Florida has become more expensive since 1996, a trip to Australia would now be substantially cheaper than it was in the mid-1990s.

Figure 17-3

THE VALUE OF THE CANADIAN DOLLAR. The graphs show how the value of the Canadian dollar has changed relative to the values of other currencies from January 1996 to January 2001.

SOURCE: *Bank of Canada Review*, Table 11.

making a profit of $1 per pound from the difference in price. The process of taking advantage of differences in prices in different markets is called *arbitrage*. In our example, as people took advantage of this arbitrage opportunity, they would increase the demand for coffee in Vancouver and increase the supply in Halifax. The price of coffee would rise in Vancouver (in response to greater demand) and fall in Halifax (in response to greater supply). This process would continue until, eventually, the prices were the same in the two markets.

Now consider how the law of one price applies to the international marketplace. If a dollar (or any other currency) could buy more coffee in Canada than in Japan, international traders could profit by buying coffee in Canada and selling it in Japan. This export of coffee from Canada to Japan would drive up the Canadian price of coffee and drive down the Japanese price. Conversely, if a dollar could buy more coffee in Japan than in Canada, traders could buy coffee in Japan and sell it in Canada. This import of coffee into Canada from Japan would drive down the Canadian price of coffee and drive up the Japanese price. In the end, the law of one price tells us that a dollar must buy the same amount of coffee in all countries.

This logic leads us to the theory of purchasing-power parity. According to this theory, a currency must have the same purchasing power in all countries. That is, a Canadian dollar must buy the same quantity of goods in Canada and Japan, and a Japanese yen must buy the same quantity of goods in Japan and Canada. Indeed, the name of this theory describes it well. *Parity* means equality, and *purchasing power* refers to the value of money. *Purchasing-power parity* states that a unit of all currencies must have the same real value in every country.

IMPLICATIONS OF PURCHASING-POWER PARITY

What does the theory of purchasing-power parity say about exchange rates? It tells us that the nominal exchange rate between the currencies of two countries depends on the price levels in those countries. If a dollar buys the same quantity of goods in Canada (where prices are measured in dollars) as in Japan (where prices are measured in yen), then the number of yen per dollar must reflect the prices of goods in Canada and Japan. For example, if a pound of coffee costs 500 yen in Japan and $5 in Canada, then the nominal exchange rate must be 100 yen per dollar (500 yen/$5 = 100 yen per dollar). Otherwise, the purchasing power of the dollar would not be the same in the two countries.

To see more fully how this works, it is helpful to use just a bit of mathematics. Suppose that P is the price of a basket of goods in Canada (measured in dollars), P^* is the price of a basket of goods in Japan (measured in yen), and e is the nominal exchange rate (the number of yen a dollar can buy). Now consider the quantity of goods a dollar can buy at home and abroad. At home, the price level is P, so the purchasing power of $1 at home is $1/P$. Abroad, a dollar can be exchanged into e units of foreign currency, which in turn have purchasing power e/P^*. For the purchasing power of a dollar to be the same in the two countries, it must be the case that

$$1/P = e/P^*.$$

With rearrangement, this equation becomes

$$1 = eP/P^*.$$

Notice that the left-hand side of this equation is a constant, and the right-hand side is the real exchange rate. Thus, *if the purchasing power of the dollar is always the same at home and abroad, then the real exchange rate—the relative price of domestic and foreign goods—cannot change.*

To see the implication of this analysis for the nominal exchange rate, we can rearrange the last equation to solve for the nominal exchange rate:

$$e = P^*/P.$$

That is, the nominal exchange rate equals the ratio of the foreign price level (measured in units of the foreign currency) to the domestic price level (measured in units of the domestic currency). *According to the theory of purchasing-power parity, the nominal exchange rate between the currencies of two countries must reflect the different price levels in those countries.*

A key implication of this theory is that nominal exchange rates change when price levels change. As we saw in the preceding chapter, the price level in any country adjusts to bring the quantity of money supplied and the quantity of money demanded into balance. Because the nominal exchange rate depends on the price levels, it also depends on the money supply and money demand in each country. When a central bank in any country increases the money supply and causes the price level to rise, it also causes that country's currency to depreciate relative to other currencies in the world. In other words, *when the central bank prints large quantities of money, that money loses value both in terms of the goods and services it can buy and in terms of the amount of other currencies it can buy.*

We can now answer the question that began this section: Why has the Canadian dollar lost value compared with the German mark and gained value compared with the Italian lira? The answer is that Germany has pursued a less inflationary monetary policy than Canada, and Italy has pursued a more inflationary monetary policy. From 1970 to 1998, inflation in Canada was 5.4 percent per year. By contrast, inflation was 3.5 percent in Germany and 9.6 percent in Italy. As Canadian prices rose relative to German prices, the value of the dollar fell relative to the mark. Similarly, as Canadian prices fell relative to Italian prices, the value of the dollar rose relative to the lira.

CASE STUDY   THE NOMINAL EXCHANGE RATE DURING A HYPERINFLATION

Macroeconomists can only rarely conduct controlled experiments. Most often, they must glean what they can from the natural experiments that history gives them. One natural experiment is hyperinflation—the high inflation that arises when a government turns to the printing press to pay for large amounts of government spending. Because hyperinflations are so extreme, they illustrate some basic economic principles with clarity.

Consider the German hyperinflation of the early 1920s. Figure 17-4 shows the German money supply, the German price level, and the nominal exchange rate (measured as U.S. cents per German mark) for that period. Notice that these series move closely together. When the supply of money starts growing quickly, the price level also takes off, and the German mark depreciates. When the money supply stabilizes, so does the price level and the exchange rate.

The pattern shown in this figure appears during every hyperinflation. It leaves no doubt that there is a fundamental link among money, prices, and the nominal exchange rate. The quantity theory of money discussed in the previous chapter explains how the money supply affects the price level. The theory of purchasing-power parity discussed here explains how the price level affects the nominal exchange rate.

LIMITATIONS OF PURCHASING-POWER PARITY

Purchasing-power parity provides a simple model of how exchange rates are determined. For understanding many economic phenomena, the theory works well. In particular, it can explain many long-term trends, such as the depreciation of the Canadian dollar against the German mark and the appreciation of the Canadian dollar against the Italian lira. It can also explain the major changes in exchange rates that occur during hyperinflations.

Yet the theory of purchasing-power parity is not completely accurate. That is, exchange rates do not always move to ensure that a dollar has the same real value in all countries all the time. There are two reasons why the theory of purchasing-power parity does not always hold in practice.

The first reason is that many goods are not easily traded. Imagine, for instance, that haircuts are more expensive in Paris than in Montreal. International travellers

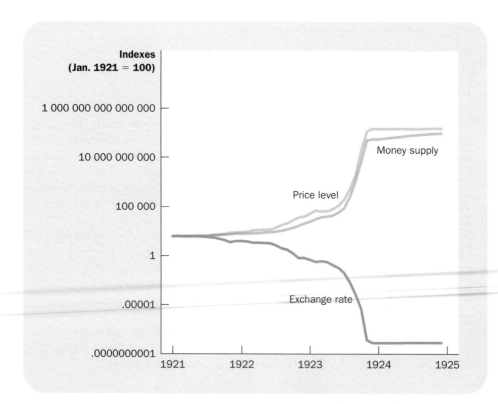

Figure 17-4

MONEY, PRICES, AND THE NOMINAL EXCHANGE RATE DURING THE GERMAN HYPERINFLATION. This figure shows the money supply, the price level, and the exchange rate (measured as U.S. cents per mark) for the German hyperinflation from January 1921 to December 1924. Notice how similarly these three variables move. When the quantity of money started growing quickly, the price level followed, and the mark depreciated relative to the dollar. When the German central bank stabilized the money supply, the price level and exchange rate stabilized as well.

SOURCE: Adapted from Thomas J. Sargent, "The End of Four Big Inflations," in Robert Hall, ed., *Inflation* (Chicago: University of Chicago Press, 1983), pp. 41–93.

might avoid getting their haircuts in Paris, and some haircutters might move from Montreal to Paris. Yet such arbitrage would probably be too limited to eliminate the differences in prices. Thus, the deviation from purchasing-power parity might persist, and a dollar (or franc) would continue to buy less of a haircut in Paris than in Montreal.

The second reason that purchasing-power parity does not always hold is that even tradable goods are not always perfect substitutes when they are produced in different countries. For example, some consumers prefer German beer, and others prefer Canadian beer. Moreover, consumer tastes for beer change over time. If German beer suddenly becomes more popular, the increase in demand will drive up the price of German beer. As a result, a dollar (or a mark) might then buy more beer in the Canada than in Germany. But despite this difference in prices in the two markets, there might be no opportunity for profitable arbitrage because consumers do not view the two beers as equivalent.

Thus, both because some goods are not tradable and because some tradable goods are not perfect substitutes with their foreign counterparts, purchasing-power parity is not a perfect theory of exchange-rate determination. For these reasons, real exchange rates fluctuate over time. Nonetheless, the theory of purchasing-power parity does provide a useful first step in understanding exchange rates. The basic logic is persuasive: As the real exchange rate drifts from the level predicted by purchasing-power parity, people have greater incentive to move goods across national borders. Even if the forces of purchasing-power parity do not completely fix the real exchange rate, they provide a reason to expect that changes in the real exchange rate are most often small or temporary. As a result, large and persistent movements in nominal exchange rates typically reflect changes in price levels at home and abroad.

In Canada the price of a Big Mac is $2.85; in Japan it is 294 yen.

CASE STUDY   THE HAMBURGER STANDARD

When economists apply the theory of purchasing-power parity to explain exchange rates, they need data on the prices of a basket of goods available in different countries. One analysis of this sort is conducted by *The Economist*, an international newsmagazine. The magazine occasionally collects data on a basket of goods consisting of "two all-beef patties, special sauce, lettuce, cheese, pickles, onions, on a sesame seed bun." It's called the "Big Mac" and is sold by McDonald's around the world.

Once we have the prices of Big Macs in two countries denominated in the local currencies, we can compute the exchange rate predicted by the theory of purchasing-power parity. The predicted exchange rate is the one that makes the cost of the Big Mac the same in the two countries. For instance, if the price of a Big Mac is $2 in the United States and 200 yen in Japan, purchasing-power parity would predict an exchange rate of 100 yen per dollar.

How well does purchasing-power parity work when applied using Big Mac prices? Here are some examples from an *Economist* article published on April 29, 2000, when the price of a Big Mac was $2.51 in the United States:

COUNTRY	PRICE OF A BIG MAC	PREDICTED EXCHANGE RATE	ACTUAL EXCHANGE RATE
Canada	2.85 $ Canadian	1.14 $C/$U.S.	1.47 $C/$U.S.
Italy	4500 lira	1793 lira/$U.S.	2088 lira/$U.S.
Japan	294 yen	117 yen/$U.S.	106 yen/$U.S.
Russia	39.5 rubles	15.7 rubles/$U.S.	28.5 rubles/$U.S.
Germany	4.99 marks	1.99 marks/$U.S.	2.11 marks/$U.S.
Brazil	2.95 reals	1.18 reals/$U.S.	1.79 reals/$U.S.
Britain	1.90 pounds	0.76 pound/$U.S.	0.63 pound/$U.S.

You can see that the predicted and actual exchange rates are not exactly the same. After all, international arbitrage in Big Macs is not easy. Yet the two exchange rates are usually in the same ballpark. Purchasing-power parity is not a precise theory of exchange rates, but it often provides a reasonable first approximation.

QUICK QUIZ: Over the past twenty years, Spain has had high inflation and Japan has had low inflation. What do you predict has happened to the number of Spanish pesetas a person can buy with a Japanese yen?

INTEREST RATE DETERMINATION IN A SMALL OPEN ECONOMY WITH PERFECT CAPITAL MOBILITY

When they want to predict whether Canadian interest rates will rise or fall, Canadian economists tend to pay a lot of attention to anticipated changes in U.S. interest rates. They do so because interest rates in Canada tend to increase when interest rates in the United States increase and fall when interest rates in the United States fall.

Why do interest rates in Canada and the United States tend to move up and down together? Recall that in Chapter 13 we examined the market for loanable funds. We used the market for loanable funds to explain the determination of the real interest rate. That discussion assumed a closed economy—one that does not trade goods and services with other economies. This assumption is not appropriate for describing the Canadian economy. As we saw earlier in this chapter, Canada is an open economy in which trade with other countries makes up a very large part of GDP. For this reason, economists prefer to use a model of the Canadian economy that takes into consideration these trade flows. The model most economists prefer to use is one that describes Canada as a *small open economy with perfect capital mobility*.

In this section, we take a first step toward modifying our description of the market for loanable funds in a small open economy with perfect capital mobility.

We will see that determining the real interest rate in such an economy is pretty straightforward. In the next chapter we will make use of this discussion to modify our discussion of the market for loanable funds in a way that is appropriate for a small open economy.

A SMALL OPEN ECONOMY

small open economy

an economy that trades goods and services with other economies and, by itself, has a negligible effect on world prices and interest rates

What do we mean when we say Canada is a **small open economy** with perfect capital mobility?

By "small" we mean an economy that is a small part of the world economy. In particular, we are describing an economy that, by itself, has only a negligible effect on the prices of goods and services and on interest rates in the rest of the world. Thus, for example, an increase in demand for computer chips by Canadians is unlikely to have an effect on the world price for computer chips. Canada's share of the total world demand for computer chips is too small for such a change to have anything but a negligible effect on the world price. Canadian financial markets are also "small" in this sense. An increase in the supply of Canadian bonds has a negligible effect on the total world supply of bonds. Changes in Canadian financial markets therefore have negligible effects on world interest rates.

PERFECT CAPITAL MOBILITY

perfect capital mobility

full access to world financial markets

By **perfect capital mobility** we mean that Canadians have full access to world financial markets and that people in the rest of the world have full access to the Canadian financial market.

The implication of perfect capital mobility for a small open economy like Canada's is that the real interest rate in Canada should equal the real interest rate prevailing in world financial markets. In simple mathematical terms, if r is the Canadian real interest rate and r^w is the world real interest rate, then

$$r = r^w.$$

Why should this be so? Some examples will illustrate. If $r^w = 8$ percent and $r = 5$ percent, this situation cannot persist. The reason is simple: With full access to world financial markets, Canadian savers would prefer to buy foreign assets that pay an interest rate of 8 percent than Canadian assets that pay an interest rate of just 5 percent. We would expect to see savers sell their Canadian assets and buy foreign assets instead. The sale of Canadian assets then forces Canadian borrowers to offer a more attractive interest rate. Indeed, we would expect them to offer an interest rate of 8 percent, the world interest rate. Similarly, if $r^w = 5$ percent and $r = 8$ percent, this situation cannot persist either. With full access to world financial markets, Canadian borrowers would prefer to borrow from foreigners at an interest rate of 5 percent than from Canadians at an interest rate of 8 percent. In order to find someone to whom to lend money, Canadian savers would have to offer to lend their savings at 5 percent, the world interest rate. As long as the Canadian and the foreign assets are close substitutes, the difference in interest rates provides an arbitrage opportunity for either borrowers or savers.

The logic by which the real interest rates in Canada should adjust to equal the real interest rate in the rest of the world should remind you of our discussion of the law of one price and purchasing-power parity. This is because the concepts are closely related. Just as we discussed earlier in the context of the prices of goods, people taking advantage of arbitrage opportunities will ensure that price differentials disappear. The only difference is that here the price we are talking about is the price of borrowing: the real interest rate. The theory that the real interest rate in Canada should equal that in the rest of the world is known as **interest rate parity**.

LIMITATIONS TO INTEREST RATE PARITY

Just as there are limitations to purchasing-power parity explaining how exchange rates are determined, there are also limitations to interest rate parity explaining how real interest rates are determined. The real interest rate in Canada is not always equal to the real interest rate in the rest of the world, for two key reasons.

The first reason is that financial assets carry with them the possibility of default. That is, while the seller of a financial asset promises to repay the buyer at some future date, the possibility always exists that the seller may not do so. If the seller does in fact renege on this agreement, the seller is said to be in default of the loan. Buyers of financial assets are therefore said to incur a *default risk*. Buyers of financial assets try to learn about relative levels of default risk in order to better evaluate the relative attractiveness of different financial assets. The higher the default risk, the higher the interest rate asset buyers (savers) demand from asset sellers (borrowers). If the seller of one financial asset is perceived to be more likely to default than the seller of another otherwise similar asset, the difference in the rate of interest paid on these assets may not necessarily represent an arbitrage opportunity. For this reason, interest rate differences may persist.

The second reason why interest rate parity does not always hold in practice is because financial assets offered for sale in different countries are not necessarily perfect substitutes for one another. For example, how governments tax the returns earned on financial assets differs across countries. While similar assets in two countries may pay the same rate of pre-tax return, different tax regimes in these two countries may result in different after-tax returns. Those seeking arbitrage opportunities look only at after-tax returns. Thus, while after-tax returns will be equalized internationally, differences in pre-tax rates of return will persist.

Because of the differences in default risk and in tax treatments, interest rate parity is not a perfect theory of real interest rate determination in a small open economy. For this reason, we do not expect real interest rates in Canada to exactly equal those in the rest of the world. Nonetheless, interest rate parity does offer a persuasive argument for believing that the difference in real interest rates in Canada versus the rest of the world will be relatively small, and that Canadian interest rates will fluctuate with those in the rest of the world.

The data bear this out. Over the fifteen year period 1986–2000, the real interest rates paid on long-term government debt in Canada and the United States have tended to move up and down together. The average real interest rate was 4.7 percent in Canada and 4.2 percent in the United States. The 0.5 percentage-point difference is a measure of how much more Canadian lenders must offer to compensate borrowers for higher default risk and higher tax rates in Canada. This difference has grown somewhat over time as Canadian tax rates have increased relative to those in the United States, and as frequent constitutional crises have raised concerns in the minds of lenders about the possibility of the Canadian government defaulting on its debt. If we interpret the U.S. interest rate as the "world"

interest rate parity
a theory of interest rate determination whereby the real interest rate on comparable financial assets should be the same in all economies with full access to world financial markets

interest rate, r^w, then these data provide support for our imposing the interest rate parity condition on our model. That will be our strategy when we turn to the macroeconomic theory of the open economy.

CONCLUSION

The purpose of this chapter has been to develop some basic concepts that macro-economists use to study open economies. You should now understand why a nation's net exports must equal its net foreign investment, and why national saving must equal domestic investment plus net foreign investment. You should also understand the meaning of the nominal and real exchange rates, as well as the implications and limitations of purchasing-power parity as a theory of how exchange rates are determined. Finally, you should understand why real interest rates in Canada tend to rise and fall with interest rates in the rest of the world.

The macroeconomic variables defined here offer a starting point for analyzing an open economy's interactions with the rest of the world. In the next chapter we develop a model that can explain what determines these variables. We can then discuss how various events and policies affect a country's trade balance and the rate at which nations make exchanges in world markets.

Summary

◆ Net exports are the value of domestic goods and services sold abroad minus the value of foreign goods and services sold domestically. Net foreign investment is the acquisition of foreign assets by domestic residents minus the acquisition of domestic assets by foreigners. Because every international transaction involves an exchange of an asset for a good or service, an economy's net foreign investment always equals its net exports.

◆ An economy's saving can be used either to finance investment at home or to buy assets abroad. Thus, national saving equals domestic investment plus net foreign investment.

◆ The nominal exchange rate is the relative price of the currency of two countries, and the real exchange rate is the relative price of the goods and services of two countries. When the nominal exchange rate changes so that each dollar buys more foreign currency, the dollar is said to *appreciate* or *strengthen*. When the nominal exchange rate changes so that each dollar buys less foreign currency, the dollar is said to *depreciate* or *weaken*.

◆ According to the theory of purchasing-power parity, a dollar (or a unit of any other currency) should be able to buy the same quantity of goods in all countries. This theory implies that the nominal exchange rate between the currencies of two countries should reflect the price levels in those countries. As a result, countries with relatively high inflation should have depreciating currencies, and countries with relatively low inflation should have appreciating currencies.

◆ Most economists prefer to use a model that describes Canada as a small open economy with perfect capital mobility. In such economies interest rate parity is expected to hold. Interest rate parity is a theory that predicts interest rates in Canada will equal those in the rest of the world. Due to differences in tax rates and concerns about default risk, interest rates in Canada are not expected to exactly equal those in the rest of the world, but we do expect Canadian interest rates to rise and fall with increases and decreases in world interest rates.

Key Concepts

closed economy, p. 372
open economy, p. 372
exports, p. 372
imports, p. 372
net exports, p. 372
trade balance, p. 372

trade surplus, p. 372
trade deficit, p. 373
balanced trade, p. 373
net foreign investment, p. 376
nominal exchange rate, p. 383
appreciation, p. 383

depreciation, p. 383
real exchange rate, p. 384
purchasing-power parity, p. 385
small open economy, p. 392
perfect capital mobility, p. 392
interest rate parity, p. 393

Questions for Review

1. Define net exports and net foreign investment. Explain how and why they are related.

2. Explain the relationship among saving, investment, and net foreign investment.

3. If a Japanese car costs 500 000 yen, a similar Canadian-produced car costs $10 000, and a dollar can buy 100 yen, what are the nominal and real exchange rates?

4. Describe the economic logic behind the theory of purchasing-power parity.

5. Describe the economic logic behind the theory of interest rate parity.

6. If the Bank of Canada started printing large quantities of Canadian dollars, what would happen to the number of Japanese yen a dollar could buy?

Problems and Applications

1. How would the following transactions affect Canada's exports, imports, and net exports?
   a. A Canadian art professor spends the summer touring museums in Europe.
   b. Students in Paris flock to see the latest Celine Dion concert.
   c. Your uncle buys a new Volvo.
   d. The student bookstore at Oxford University sells a pair of Bauer hockey skates.
   e. A Canadian citizen shops at a store in northern Vermont to avoid Canadian sales taxes.

2. International trade in each of the following products has increased over time. Suggest some reasons why this might be so.
   a. wheat
   b. banking services
   c. computer software
   d. cars

3. Describe the difference between foreign direct investment and foreign portfolio investment. Who is more likely to engage in foreign direct investment—a corporation or an individual investor? Who is more likely to engage in foreign portfolio investment?

4. How would the following transactions affect Canadian net foreign investment? Also, state whether each involves direct investment or portfolio investment.

   a. A Canadian cellular phone company establishes an office in the Czech Republic.
   b. Harrod's of London sells stock to the Ontario Teachers Pension Plan.
   c. Honda expands its factory in Alliston, Ontario.
   d. An Altamira mutual fund sells its Volkswagen stock to a French investor.

5. Holding national saving constant, does an increase in net foreign investment increase, decrease, or have no effect on a country's accumulation of domestic capital?

6. The business section of most major newspapers contains a table showing Canadian exchange rates. Find such a table and use it to answer the following questions:
   a. Does this table show nominal or real exchange rates? Explain.
   b. What are the exchange rates between Canada and the United States and between Canada and Japan? Calculate the exchange rate between the United States and Japan.
   c. If Canadian inflation exceeds Japanese inflation over the next year, would you expect the Canadian dollar to appreciate or depreciate relative to the Japanese yen?

7. Would each of the following groups be happy or unhappy if the Canadian dollar appreciated? Explain.

a.   Dutch pension funds holding Canadian government bonds

b.   Canadian manufacturing industries

c.   Australian tourists planning a trip to Canada

d.   a Canadian firm trying to purchase property overseas

8. What is happening to Canada's real exchange rate in each of the following situations? Explain.

a.   The Canadian nominal exchange rate is unchanged, but prices rise faster in Canada than abroad.

b.   The Canadian nominal exchange rate is unchanged, but prices rise faster abroad than in Canada.

c.   The Canadian nominal exchange rate declines, and prices are unchanged in Canada and abroad.

d.   The Canadian nominal exchange rate declines, and prices rise faster abroad than in Canada.

9. List three goods for which the law of one price is likely to hold, and three goods for which it is not. Justify your choices.

10. A can of pop costs $0.75 in Canada and 12 pesos in Mexico. What would the peso–dollar exchange rate be if purchasing-power parity holds? If a monetary expansion caused all prices in Mexico to double, so that pop rose to 24 pesos, what would happen to the peso–dollar exchange rate?

11. Assume that Canadian wheat sells for $100 per bushel, French wheat sells for 1600 francs per bushel, and the nominal exchange rate is 4 francs per dollar.

a.   Explain how you could make a profit from this situation. What would be your profit per bushel of wheat? If other people exploit the same opportunity, what would happen to the price of wheat in France and the price of wheat in Canada?

b.   Suppose that wheat is the only commodity in the world. What would happen to the real exchange rate between Canada and France?

12. A case study in the chapter analyzed purchasing-power parity for several countries using the price of a Big Mac. Here are data for a few more countries:

Country	Price of a Big Mac	Predicted ($U.S.) Exchange Rate	Actual ($U.S.) Exchange Rate
South Korea	3000 won	_____ won	1218 won
Spain	375 pesetas	_____ pesetas	155 pesetas
Mexico	19.9 pesos	_____ pesos	9.54 pesos
Netherlands	5.45 guilders	_____ guilders	2.05 guilders

a.   For each country, compute the predicted exchange rate of the local currency per U.S. dollar. (Recall that the U.S. price of a Big Mac is $2.43.) How well does the theory of purchasing-power parity explain exchange rates?

b.   According to purchasing-power parity, what is the predicted exchange rate between the South Korean won and Spanish peseta? What is the actual exchange rate?

c.   Which of these countries offers the cheapest Big Mac? Why do you think that might be the case?

18

A MACROECONOMIC THEORY
OF THE OPEN ECONOMY

IN THIS CHAPTER YOU WILL . . .

Build a model to explain an open economy's trade balance and exchange rate

Use the model to analyze the effects of government budget deficits

Use the model to analyze the macroeconomic effects of trade policies

Use the model to analyze political instability and capital flight

Issues related to international trade are of constant concern to Canadians. In part this is because many Canadians are employed in industries that depend on international trade, and because all Canadians consume goods and services that are available only because of trade. Trade issues are also of concern to Canadians because these issues are often the sources of conflict with our trading partners. For example, softwood lumber producers in the United States have claimed that Canadian softwood lumber producers receive an unfair competitive advantage due to the nature of certain government policies. These claims have led to conflict and spawned a prolonged process of negotiation to resolve the issue.

Canadians have also expressed concern about the purchase of Canadian assets by foreigners. As we have seen, Canada's net foreign investment (*NFI*) is generally negative, indicating that foreigners purchase more Canadian assets than Canadians purchase foreign assets. As a result, many firms that are located in Canada are owned by foreigners. In the past, this situation has prompted the government to introduce legislation designed to limit the extent of foreign ownership.

Imagine that you are the prime minister and people are demanding that you do something about the fact that Canada's net exports and net foreign investment are negative. What should you do? Should you try to limit imports of cars from Japan? Should you prevent Americans from buying Canadian oil and gas firms? Or should you try to influence net exports and net foreign investment in some other way?

To understand what factors determine a country's trade balance and how government policies can affect it, we need a macroeconomic theory of the open economy. The preceding chapter introduced some of the key macroeconomic variables that describe an economy's relationship with other economies—including net exports, net foreign investment, and the real and nominal exchange rates. This chapter develops a model that shows what forces determine these variables and how these variables are related to one another.

To develop this macroeconomic model of an open economy, we build on our previous analysis in three important ways. First, the model takes the economy's GDP as given. We assume that the economy's output of goods and services, as measured by real GDP, is determined by the supplies of the factors of production and by the available production technology that turns these inputs into output. Second, the model takes the economy's price level as given. We assume that the price level adjusts to bring the supply and demand for money into balance. Third, the model takes the real interest rate as given. The real interest rate is assumed to equal the world interest rate because of perfect capital mobility. In other words, this chapter takes as a starting point the lessons learned in previous chapters about the determination of the economy's output, interest rate, and price level.

The goal of the model in this chapter is to highlight those forces that determine the economy's trade balance and exchange rate. In one sense, the model is simple: It merely applies the tools of supply and demand to an open economy. Yet the model is also more complicated than others we have seen because it involves looking simultaneously at two related markets—the market for loanable funds and the market for foreign-currency exchange. After we develop this model of the open economy, we use it to examine how various events and policies affect the economy's trade balance and exchange rate.

SUPPLY AND DEMAND FOR LOANABLE FUNDS AND FOR FOREIGN-CURRENCY EXCHANGE

To understand the forces at work in an open economy, we focus on supply and demand in two markets. The first is the market for loanable funds, which coordinates the economy's saving and investment (including its net foreign investment). The second is the market for foreign-currency exchange, which coordinates people who want to exchange the domestic currency for the currency of other countries. In this section we discuss supply and demand in each of these markets. In the next section we put these markets together to explain the overall equilibrium for an open economy.

THE MARKET FOR LOANABLE FUNDS

When we first analyzed the role of the financial system in Chapter 13, we made the simplifying assumption that the financial system consists of only one market, the *market for loanable funds*. All savers go to this market to deposit their savings, and all borrowers go to this market to get their loans. In this market, there is one interest rate, which is both the return to saving and the cost of borrowing.

To understand the market for loanable funds in an open economy, the place to start is the identity discussed in the preceding chapter:

$$S \quad = \quad I \quad + \quad NFI$$

Saving = Domestic investment + Net foreign investment.

The amount that a nation saves does not have to equal the amount it spends to purchase domestic capital. Should the amount of national saving exceed the amount needed to finance the purchase of domestic capital, the amount left over can be used to finance the purchase of an asset abroad. In this case, net foreign investment (*NFI*) is a positive number. If national saving is insufficient to finance the purchase of domestic capital, the shortfall can be met by the savings of foreigners. In this case, *NFI* is a negative number. The equation identifies the three components of the market for loanable funds in an open economy. We have seen that, in Canada, net foreign investment is typically negative, indicating that foreigners are adding to the supply of loanable funds available in this country. Thus, in Canada the supply of loanable funds typically comes from national saving (*S*) and from net foreign investment (*NFI*). The demand for loanable funds comes from domestic investment (*I*).

As we learned in our earlier discussion of the market for loanable funds, the quantity of loanable funds supplied and the quantity of loanable funds demanded depend on the real interest rate. A higher real interest rate encourages people to save and, therefore, raises the quantity of loanable funds made available by national saving. A higher interest rate also makes borrowing to finance capital projects more costly; thus, it discourages investment and reduces the quantity of loanable funds demanded.

The next step in understanding the market for loanable funds in a small open economy is to recall our discussion from the preceding chapter on interest rate determination. We found that in a small open economy with perfect capital mobility, like Canada, if we ignore differences in tax treatments and default risk, the domestic interest rate will equal the world interest rate. The reason for this is simple. Suppose that the Canadian interest rate is 5 percent and the world interest rate is 8 percent. This situation cannot persist because with full access to world financial markets, Canadian savers would prefer to buy foreign assets that pay the higher interest rate. We would expect to see savers sell their holdings of Canadian assets and buy foreign assets instead. To halt the sale of Canadian assets, Canadian borrowers would have to offer to pay the more attractive world interest rate of 8 percent. Similarly, if the world interest rate is 5 percent and the Canadian interest rate is 8 percent, Canadian borrowers would prefer to borrow from foreigners. In order to find someone to whom to lend money, Canadian savers would have to offer to lend their savings at 5 percent, the world interest rate.

The market for loanable funds is represented on the familiar supply-and-demand diagram in Figure 18-1. As in our earlier analysis of the financial system, the demand curve slopes downward because a higher interest rate decreases the quantity of loanable funds demanded, and the supply curve slopes upward because a higher interest rate increases the quantity of loanable funds supplied. Unlike the situation in our previous discussion, however, in a small open economy with perfect capital mobility, the supply curve represents only part of the supply of loanable funds available. The supply curve shows the amount of national saving—the savings of Canadians—available at every real interest rate. It shows, then, that a higher interest rate increases the quantity of loanable funds made available by Canadians. If, we were discussing a closed economy, we would need to consider only the supply of loanable funds made available by the savings of Canadians. In that case we would conclude that the real rate of interest would be determined by the intersection of the demand and supply curves for loanable funds. In a small open economy with perfect capital mobility, however, the interest rate is equal to the world interest rate, and we need to also consider the role played by the savings of foreigners.

In panel (a) of Figure 18-1, the world interest rate is greater than the Canadian interest rate would be if this were a closed economy. Because there is perfect capital mobility, the Canadian interest rate is given by the world interest rate. At this interest rate, the demand for loanable funds in Canada (I) is $100 billion, and the supply of loanable funds that Canadians make available (S) is $150 billion. At this world interest rate, the supply of Canadians' savings is more than enough to satisfy the demand for loanable funds in Canada. The excess supply of loanable funds, $50 billion, is therefore available to purchase foreign assets. In this situation, net foreign investment (NFI) is $50 billion. Note that $S = I + NFI$, as required by our accounting identity.

In panel (b) of Figure 18-1, the world interest rate is shown as being less than the interest rate would be if this were a closed economy. At this world interest rate, the demand for loanable funds in Canada (I) is now $130 billion, and the supply of loanable funds that Canadians make available (S) is $90 billion. At this world interest rate, the supply of Canadians' savings is not enough to satisfy the demand for loanable funds in Canada. The excess demand for loanable funds, $40 billion, must therefore be satisfied by the savings of foreigners. In this situation, net foreign investment (NFI) takes on a negative value: –$40 billion. (Do not be confused by the negative number. We have defined net foreign investment as the amount of foreign assets that Canadians purchase minus the amount of Canadian assets that foreigners buy. A negative value simply indicates that there is a net purchase of Canadian assets by foreigners.) Note that, once again, $S = I + NFI$ as required by our accounting identity.

These two diagrams show that the market for loanable funds in a small open economy with perfect capital mobility is different from that in a closed economy. In particular, the interest rate is no longer determined by the demand and supply of loanable funds. Instead, the interest rate is equal to the world interest rate. As a result, the quantity of loanable funds made available by the savings of Canadians do not have to equal the quantity of loanable funds demanded for domestic investment. The difference between these two amounts is net foreign investment. Net foreign investment is determined by the difference between the supply of loanable funds due to national saving (S) and the demand for loanable funds (I) at the world interest rate. If we recall another identity from the preceding chapter,

$$NFI = NX$$
Net foreign investment = Net exports,

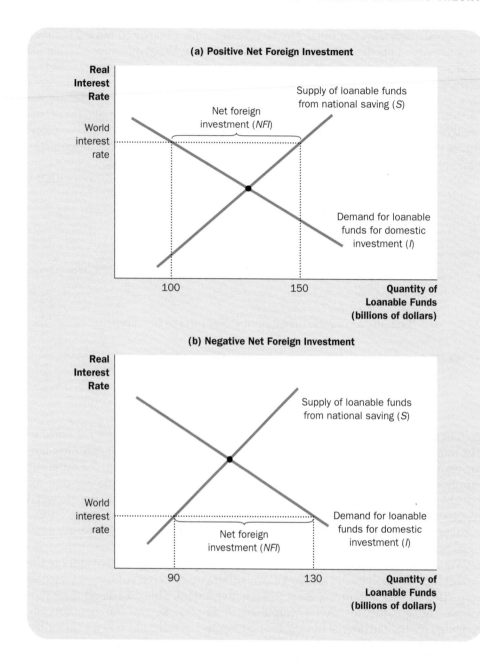

(a) Positive Net Foreign Investment

Real Interest Rate

World interest rate

Net foreign investment (*NFI*)

Supply of loanable funds from national saving (*S*)

Demand for loanable funds for domestic investment (*I*)

100   150

Quantity of Loanable Funds (billions of dollars)

(b) Negative Net Foreign Investment

Real Interest Rate

Supply of loanable funds from national saving (*S*)

World interest rate

Net foreign investment (*NFI*)

Demand for loanable funds for domestic investment (*I*)

90   130

Quantity of Loanable Funds (billions of dollars)

Figure 18-1

THE MARKET FOR LOANABLE FUNDS.   In a small open economy with perfect capital mobility, like Canada, the domestic real interest rate is equal to the world real interest rate. Domestic investment determines the demand for loanable funds. National saving determines the supply of loanable funds provided by Canadians. In panel (a), at the world interest rate domestic investment is $100 billion and Canadians save $150 billion. The difference between domestic investment and national saving, $50 billion, is net foreign investment. It measures the value of foreign assets purchased by Canadians. In panel (b), at the world interest rate domestic investment is $130 billion and Canadians save only $90 billion. The shortfall of national saving relative to domestic investment, $40 billion, is made up by the savings of foreigners. In this case, net foreign investment is negative, indicating that foreigners are purchasing more Canadian assets than Canadians are purchasing foreign assets.

we can also state this result as follows: Net exports are determined by the difference between the supply of loanable funds due to national saving (*S*) and the demand for loanable funds (*I*) at the world interest rate. These two statements are equivalent because net exports must equal net foreign investment.

THE MARKET FOR FOREIGN-CURRENCY EXCHANGE

The second market in our model of the open economy is the market for foreign-currency exchange. The market for foreign exchange exists because people want to trade goods, services, and financial assets with people in other countries, but they want to be paid for these things in their own currency. What this means is that for a Canadian to purchase a good, service, or financial asset from someone in another country, he or she must purchase the other country's currency as well. Similarly, for a foreigner to purchase a good, service, or financial asset from someone in Canada, he or she must purchase Canadian dollars. The need to make these currency exchanges means that there must exist a market where they can take place. This is the foreign-currency exchange market. In this section we will describe the market in which Canadian dollars are traded for foreign currencies.

To understand the market for foreign-currency exchange, we begin with the accounting identity we just discussed:

$$NFI = NX$$
Net foreign investment = Net exports.

If we combine this identity with the identity we discussed earlier,

$$S = I + NFI$$
Saving = Domestic investment + Net foreign investment,

we see that

$$S - I = NX$$
Saving – Domestic investment = Net exports.

Each of these statements is an identity and, as such, each describes a relationship that must be true. The last identity is useful for describing the market for foreign-currency exchange. This identity states that the imbalance between the domestic supply of loanable funds that is due to national saving (S) and the demand for loanable funds for domestic investment (I) must equal the imbalance between exports and imports (NX). This must be true because, as we have just seen, the imbalance between the domestic supply and demand for loanable funds must equal net foreign investment (NFI), which in turn must equal net exports.

We can view the two sides of this identity as representing the two sides of the market for foreign-currency exchange. The difference between national saving and domestic investment represents net foreign investment. This difference, then, represents the quantity of dollars supplied in the market for foreign-currency exchange for the purpose of buying foreign assets. For example, when a Canadian mutual fund wants to buy a Japanese government bond, it needs to exchange dollars for yen, so it *supplies* dollars in a market for foreign-currency exchange. Net exports represent the quantity of dollars demanded in that market for the purpose of buying Canadian net exports of goods and services. For example, when a Japanese airline wants to buy a plane made by Bombardier, it needs to exchange its yen for dollars, so it demands dollars in the market for foreign-currency exchange.

What price balances the supply and demand in the market for foreign-currency exchange? The answer is the real exchange rate. As we saw in the preceding chapter, the real exchange rate is the relative price of domestic and foreign goods and, therefore, is a key determinant of net exports. When Canada's real exchange rate appreciates, Canadian goods become more expensive relative to foreign goods, making Canadian goods less attractive to consumers both at home and

Figure 18-2

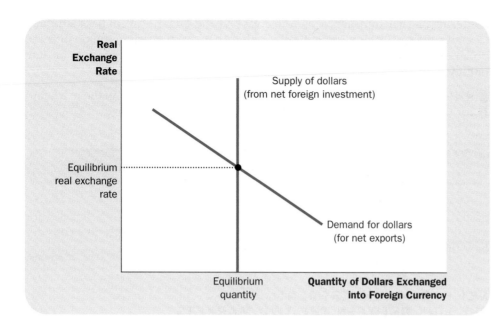

THE MARKET FOR FOREIGN-CURRENCY EXCHANGE.   The real exchange rate is determined by the supply and demand for foreign-currency exchange. The supply of dollars to be exchanged into foreign currency comes from net foreign investment. Net foreign investment, in turn, equals the difference between the demand for loanable funds (domestic investment) and the supply of loanable funds made available by the savings of Canadians. Because neither savings nor investment depends on the real exchange rate, the supply curve is vertical. The demand for dollars comes from net exports. Because a lower real exchange rate stimulates net exports (and thus increases the quantity of dollars demanded to pay for these net exports), the demand curve is downward sloping. At the equilibrium real exchange rate, the number of dollars people supply to buy foreign assets exactly balances the number of dollars people demand to buy net exports.

abroad. As a result, exports from Canada fall, and imports into Canada rise. For both reasons, net exports fall. Hence, an appreciation of the real exchange rate reduces the quantity of dollars demanded in the market for foreign-currency exchange.

Figure 18-2 shows supply and demand in the market for foreign-currency exchange. The demand curve slopes downward for the reason we just discussed: A higher real exchange rate makes Canadian goods more expensive and reduces the quantity of dollars demanded to buy those goods. The supply curve is vertical because the quantity of dollars supplied for net foreign investment does not depend on the real exchange rate. (As discussed earlier, net foreign investment depends on the real world interest rate. When discussing the market for foreign-currency exchange, we take the real world interest rate and net foreign investment as given.)

The real exchange rate adjusts to balance the supply and demand for dollars just as the price of any good adjusts to balance supply and demand for that good. If the real exchange rate were below the equilibrium level, the quantity of dollars supplied would be less than the quantity demanded. The resulting shortage of dollars would push the value of the dollar upward. Conversely, if the real exchange rate were above the equilibrium level, the quantity of dollars supplied would exceed the quantity demanded. The surplus of dollars would drive the value of the dollar downward. *At the equilibrium real exchange rate, the demand for dollars to buy net exports exactly balances the supply of dollars to be exchanged into foreign currency to buy assets abroad.*

At this point, it is worth noting that the division of transactions between "supply" and "demand" in this model is somewhat artificial. In our model, net exports are the source of the demand for dollars, and net foreign investment is the source of the supply. Thus, when a Canadian resident imports a car made in Japan, our model treats that transaction as a decrease in the quantity of dollars demanded (because net exports fall) rather than an increase in the quantity of dollars supplied. Similarly, when a Japanese citizen buys a Canadian government bond, our model treats that transaction as a decrease in the quantity of dollars supplied (because net foreign investment falls) rather than an increase in the quantity of dollars demanded. This use of language may seem somewhat unnatural at first, but it will prove useful when analyzing the effects of various policies.

▌**QUICK QUIZ:** Describe the sources of supply and demand in the market for loanable funds and the market for foreign-currency exchange.

EQUILIBRIUM IN THE OPEN ECONOMY

So far we have discussed supply and demand in two markets—the market for loanable funds and the market for foreign-currency exchange. Let's now consider how these markets are related to each other.

NET FOREIGN INVESTMENT: THE LINK BETWEEN THE TWO MARKETS

We begin by recapping what we've learned so far in this chapter. We have been discussing how the economy coordinates four important macroeconomic variables: national saving (S), domestic investment (I), net foreign investment (NFI), and net exports (NX). Keep in mind the following identities:

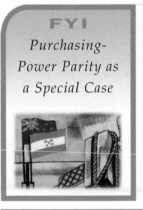

FYI

Purchasing-Power Parity as a Special Case

An alert reader of this book might ask: Why are we developing a theory of the exchange rate here? Didn't we already do that in the preceding chapter?

As you may recall, the preceding chapter developed a theory of the exchange rate called *purchasing-power parity.* This theory asserts that a dollar (or any other currency) must buy the same quantity of goods and services in every country. As a result, the real exchange rate is fixed, and all changes in the nominal exchange rate between two currencies reflect changes in the price levels in the two countries.

The model of the exchange rate developed here is related to the theory of purchasing-power parity. According to the theory of purchasing-power parity, international trade responds quickly to international price differences. If goods were cheaper in one country than in another, they would be exported from the first country and imported into the second until the price difference disappeared. In other words, the theory of purchasing-power parity assumes that net exports are highly responsive to small changes in the real exchange rate. If net exports were in fact so responsive, the demand curve in Figure 18-2 would be horizontal.

Thus, the theory of purchasing-power parity can be viewed as a special case of the model considered here. In that special case, the demand curve for foreign-currency exchange, rather than being downward sloping, is horizontal at the level of the real exchange rate that ensures parity of purchasing power at home and abroad. That special case is a good place to start when studying exchange rates, but it is far from the end of the story.

This chapter, therefore, concentrates on the more realistic case in which the demand curve for foreign-currency exchange is downward sloping. This allows for the possibility that the real exchange rate changes over time, as in fact it sometimes does in the real world.

$$S = I + NFI$$

and

$$NFI = NX.$$

In the market for loanable funds, national saving provides the domestic supply, demand comes from domestic investment, and net foreign investment is the difference between the two at the world interest rate. In the market for foreign-currency exchange, supply comes from net foreign investment, demand comes from net exports, and the real exchange rate balances supply and demand.

Net foreign investment is the variable that links these two markets. In the market for loanable funds, net foreign investment is the difference between domestic investment and national saving at the world interest rate. A change in domestic investment, national saving, or the world interest rate will cause net foreign investment to change. A change in net foreign investment means a Canadian is buying or selling foreign assets. Because a person who wants to buy an asset in another country must supply dollars in order to exchange them for the currency of that country, a change in net foreign investment affects the market for foreign-currency exchange.

The key determinant of net foreign investment, as we have discussed, is the world interest rate. When the world interest rate is higher than the interest rate that equates the demand for loanable funds in Canada to the supply of loanable funds coming from the savings of Canadians, as in panel (a) of Figure 18-1, net foreign investment is positive and is equal to the difference between national saving and the demand for loanable funds. When the world interest rate is lower than the interest rate that equates the demand for loanable funds in Canada to the supply of loanable funds coming from the savings of Canadians, as in panel (b) of Figure 18-1, net foreign investment is negative and is equal to the difference between national saving and the demand for loanable funds.

SIMULTANEOUS EQUILIBRIUM IN TWO MARKETS

We can now put all of the pieces of our model together in Figure 18-3. This figure shows how the market for loanable funds and the market for foreign-currency exchange jointly determine the important macroeconomic variables of an open economy.

Panel (a) of Figure 18-3 shows the market for loanable funds (taken from Figure 18-1). As before, national saving measures the supply of loanable funds made available by the savings of Canadians. Domestic investment is the source of the demand for loanable funds. The world interest rate determines the quantity of loanable funds demanded ($100 billion) and the quantity of loanable funds supplied by the savings of Canadians ($150 billion). The difference between these amounts, $50 billion, measures the amount of national saving available to purchase foreign assets. Because national saving is more than sufficient to provide loanable funds for domestic investment, the excess is used to buy foreign assets. This is net foreign investment.

Panel (b) of the figure shows the market for foreign-currency exchange (taken from Figure 18-2). Because national saving is more than enough to provide for domestic investment, Canadians are purchasing foreign assets. Since to do so they

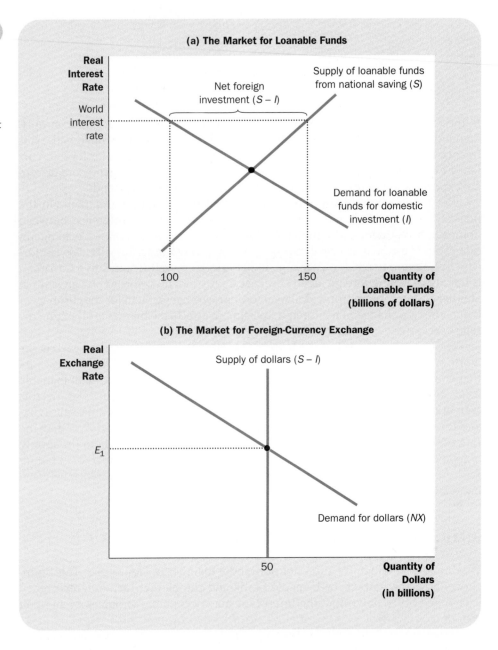

Figure 18-3

THE REAL EQUILIBRIUM IN A SMALL OPEN ECONOMY. In panel (a), the real interest rate is determined by the world real interest rate. At the world interest rate, national saving (S) exceeds the demand for loanable funds for domestic investment (I). The difference (S – I) measures net foreign investment. In panel (b), net foreign investment determines the supply of Canadian dollars offered for sale in the market for foreign-currency exchange. The demand for foreign-currency exchange is determined by Canada's net exports. The equilibrium real exchange rate (E_1) brings into balance the quantity of dollars supplied and the quantity of dollars demanded in the market for foreign-currency exchange.

must purchase foreign currency, they must sell Canadian dollars in the market for foreign exchange. For this reason, the quantity of net foreign investment from panel (a) determines the supply of dollars to be exchanged into foreign currencies. The real exchange rate does not affect net foreign investment, so the supply curve is vertical. The demand for dollars comes from net exports. Because a depreciation of the real exchange rate increases net exports, the demand curve for foreign-currency exchange slopes downward. The equilibrium real exchange rate (E_1) brings into balance the quantity of dollars supplied and the quantity of dollars demanded in the market for foreign-currency exchange.

The two markets shown in Figure 18-3 determine the real exchange rate, national saving, domestic investment, and the size of net foreign investment. National saving, domestic investment, and net foreign investment are determined in panel (a). National saving and domestic investment are determined by the world interest rate. Net foreign investment is the difference between these amounts. The real exchange rate determined in panel (b) is the price of domestic goods and services relative to foreign goods and services. In a moment, we will use this model to see how all of these variables change when some policy or event causes one of these curves to shift.

QUICK QUIZ: In the model of the open economy just developed, two markets determine one price and the value of three variables. What are the markets? What three variables are determined? What price is determined?

HOW POLICIES AND EVENTS AFFECT AN OPEN ECONOMY

Having developed a model to explain how key macroeconomic variables are determined in an open economy, we can now use the model to analyze how changes in

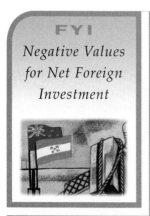

FYI

Negative Values for Net Foreign Investment

In this section we use our model to analyze how policy changes and economic events alter the economy's equilibrium. Throughout this section we will be considering a small open economy such as the one described in Figure 18-3, an economy in which net foreign investment is a positive amount. Earlier, we saw evidence that in Canada *NFI* is typically negative. How would our analyses in this section change for this case?

The answer is: very little. The difference is that now national saving is insufficient to provide for domestic investment, and Canada must rely on the savings of foreigners to make up the difference. This is net foreign investment again, but this time it is a negative number. Since *NFI* must equal net exports, it must be the case that net exports are negative too. What this means is that foreigners are seeking to buy Canadian assets and therefore want to purchase Canadian dollars in the foreign-currency exchange market. On the goods side, Canadians are buying more foreign goods than foreigners are buying Canadian goods. Thus, Canadians want to purchase foreign currencies and to do so they must sell Canadian dollars in the foreign-currency exchange market. Now the demand for dollars is coming from net foreign investment, while the supply is coming from net exports.

It is worth repeating what we noted earlier, that the division of transactions between "supply" and "demand" in the market for foreign-currency exchange is somewhat artificial. Whether net foreign investment is a source of supply to this market or a source of demand depends on whether it takes on a positive or a negative value. Similarly, whether the value of net exports is a source of supply or demand in this market depends on whether net exports are positive or negative. What is essential to understand is that the real exchange rate is determined by the supply and demand for foreign-currency exchange and that the supply and demand of foreign-currency exchange come from net foreign investment and net exports.

Fortunately, for our purposes in this section, whether net foreign investment and net exports are positive or negative is not relevant. All that matters is the *direction of change* in these values. For this reason, we rely on presentations that involve positive values of net foreign investment and net exports because this makes for an easier discussion. However, the results we derive in this section would be exactly the same whether we assumed positive or negative values of net foreign investment and net exports.

policy and other events alter the economy's equilibrium. As we proceed, keep in mind that our model is just supply and demand in two markets—the market for loanable funds and the market for foreign-currency exchange. When using the model to analyze any event, we can apply the three steps outlined in Chapter 4. First, we determine which of the supply and demand curves the event affects. Second, we determine which way the curves shift. Third, we use the supply-and-demand diagrams to examine how these shifts alter the economy's equilibrium.

INCREASE IN WORLD INTEREST RATES

We have seen that in a small open economy with perfect capital mobility, the real interest rate is equal to the world real interest rate. One implication of this fact is that events outside Canada that cause the world interest rate to change can have important effects on the Canadian economy. This explains why Canadian newspapers so often report changes to interest rates in the United States. Because the United States is the largest economy in the world, movements in U.S. interest rates are responsible in large part for movements in the world interest rate. Indeed, it is not unreasonable to treat the U.S. interest rate as the world interest rate. Changes in U.S. interest rates therefore have important implications for Canada.

Figure 18-4 shows the effect of an increase in the world interest rate on a small open economy with perfect capital mobility. In panel (a), which shows the market for loanable funds, no curves shift. Instead, the increase in the world interest rate causes a slide up the supply and demand curves for loanable funds. The quantity of loanable funds made available by the savings of Canadians rises. The quantity of loanable funds demanded for domestic investment falls. Both of these changes cause an increase in the amount by which the savings of Canadians exceed the demand for loanable funds in Canada. This excess is net foreign investment, and it measures the amount of Canadian saving that is available to purchase foreign assets.

In panel (b), the increase in net foreign investment shifts the curve that measures the supply of dollars to be exchanged in the market for foreign-currency exchange to the right, from $(S - I)_1$ to $(S - I)_2$. The increased supply of dollars causes the real exchange rate to depreciate from E_1 to E_2. That is, the dollar becomes less valuable relative to other currencies. This depreciation, in turn, makes Canadian goods less expensive compared with foreign goods. Because people both at home and abroad switch their purchases toward the less expensive Canadian goods, exports from Canada rise and imports into Canada fall. For both reasons, Canada's net exports rise. Hence, *in a small open economy with perfect capital mobility, an increase in the world interest rate crowds out domestic investment, causes the dollar to depreciate, and causes net exports to rise.*

This analysis indicates why it is not surprising to find Canadians closely watching movements in world interest rates. Such movements are of interest to exporters, importers, Canadian consumers, and Canadian firms. An increase in world interest rates, by causing the Canadian dollar to depreciate, benefits exporters by making goods priced in Canadian dollars cheaper to foreigners. At the same time, the depreciation of the dollar hurts Canadian importers by making goods priced in foreign currencies more expensive to Canadians. Given the large quantity of foreign goods they purchase, Canadian consumers are also hurt by increases in world interest rates. Finally, of course, those Canadian firms planning new investment projects must now pay a higher rate of interest on funds they borrow for that purpose.

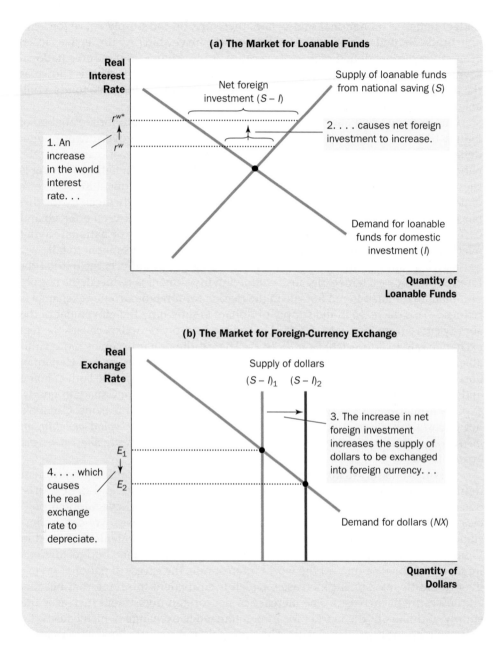

(a) The Market for Loanable Funds

Real Interest Rate

Net foreign investment ($S - I$)

Supply of loanable funds from national saving (S)

r^{w*}

r^w

2. . . . causes net foreign investment to increase.

1. An increase in the world interest rate. . .

Demand for loanable funds for domestic investment (I)

Quantity of Loanable Funds

(b) The Market for Foreign-Currency Exchange

Real Exchange Rate

Supply of dollars

$(S - I)_1$ $(S - I)_2$

E_1

3. The increase in net foreign investment increases the supply of dollars to be exchanged into foreign currency. . .

4. . . . which causes the real exchange rate to depreciate.

E_2

Demand for dollars (NX)

Quantity of Dollars

Figure 18-4

THE EFFECTS OF AN INCREASE IN THE WORLD INTEREST RATE. When the world interest rate increases, it increases the supply of loanable funds made available by Canadians and reduces the quantity of loanable funds demanded for domestic investment. For both of these reasons, net foreign investment increases. An increase in the supply of dollars in the market for foreign-currency exchange causes the Canadian dollar to depreciate. The depreciation of the dollar causes net exports to rise.

GOVERNMENT BUDGET DEFICITS AND SURPLUSES

When we first discussed the supply and demand for loanable funds earlier in the book, we examined the effects of government budget deficits, which occur when government spending exceeds government revenue. Because a government budget deficit represents *negative* public saving, it reduces national saving (the sum of public and private saving). Thus, a government budget deficit reduces the supply of loanable funds, drives up the interest rate, and crowds out investment.

Now let's consider the effects of a budget deficit in an open economy. First, which curve in our model shifts? As in a closed economy, the initial impact of the budget deficit is on national saving and, therefore, on the supply curve for loanable funds. Second, which way does this supply curve shift? Again, as in a closed economy, a budget deficit represents *negative* public saving, so it reduces national saving and shifts the supply curve for loanable funds to the left. This is shown as the shift to the left of the curve that measures the supply of loanable funds available from national saving in panel (a) of Figure 18-5.

Our third and final step is to compare the old and new equilibria. Panel (a) of Figure 18-5 shows the impact of an increase in a Canadian government budget deficit on the Canadian market for loanable funds. At the world interest rate, national saving is less now than it was before. This decrease in national saving is shown by the movement from point A to point B. As a result of this shift, the excess of national saving over domestic investment, which was initially given by the distance between points A and C, is now given by the distance between points B and C. The increase in the government deficit reduces the excess of national saving over domestic investment and therefore causes net foreign investment to fall.

Panel (b) shows how the increase in the budget deficit affects the market for foreign-currency exchange. Because net foreign investment is reduced, the supply of Canadian dollars offered for sale in the market for foreign-currency exchange is reduced. This decrease in the supply of dollars is shown by the movement of the supply curve from $(S - I)_1$ to $(S - I)_2$. The reduced supply of dollars causes the real exchange rate to appreciate from E_1 to E_2. That is, the dollar becomes more valuable relative to foreign currencies. This appreciation, in turn, makes Canadian goods more expensive compared with foreign goods. Because people both at home and abroad switch their purchases away from more expensive Canadian goods, exports from Canada fall and imports to Canada rise. For both reasons, Canada's net exports fall. Hence, *in a small open economy with perfect capital mobility, an increase in government budget deficits causes the dollar to appreciate and causes net exports to fall.*

This analysis shows how decisions made in the past that caused government deficits to increase have affected Canada's real exchange rate and net exports. Since the mid-1990s, more and more Canadian governments have adopted policies to eliminate deficits and even introduce budget surpluses. We can understand the implications of these policies by reversing the movements described in Figure 18-5 and discussed above. A decrease in government budget deficits increases national saving. At the world interest rate, the excess of national saving over domestic investment increases, which is equivalent to saying that net foreign investment increases. The increase in net foreign investment increases the supply of dollars in the market for foreign-currency exchange, which causes the real exchange rate to depreciate. This depreciation, in turn, makes Canadian goods less expensive compared with foreign goods. Because people both at home and abroad switch their purchases toward less expensive Canadian goods, exports from Canada rise and imports to Canada fall. For both reasons, Canada's net exports rise. Hence, *in a small open economy with perfect capital mobility, a decrease in government budget deficits causes the dollar to depreciate and causes net exports to rise.*

This analysis indicates why it is not surprising to find Canadians closely watching movements in government budget balances. The change in government policy from running large deficits over the period 1975 to 1995 to running large surpluses currently, has had a depressing influence on the value of the Canadian dollar. While benefiting Canadian exporters, the lower dollar has hurt importers and Canadian consumers of imported goods.

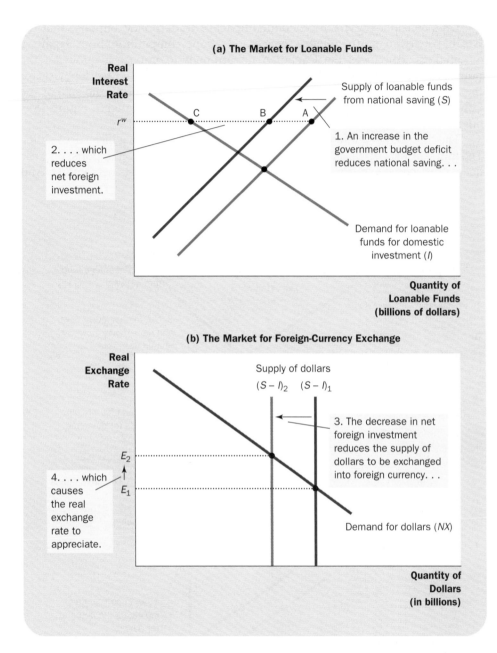

(a) The Market for Loanable Funds

Real Interest Rate

Supply of loanable funds from national saving (S)

r^w

C   B   A

1. An increase in the government budget deficit reduces national saving. . .

2. . . . which reduces net foreign investment.

Demand for loanable funds for domestic investment (I)

Quantity of Loanable Funds (billions of dollars)

(b) The Market for Foreign-Currency Exchange

Real Exchange Rate

Supply of dollars

$(S - I)_2$ $(S - I)_1$

3. The decrease in net foreign investment reduces the supply of dollars to be exchanged into foreign currency. . .

E_2

4. . . . which causes the real exchange rate to appreciate.

E_1

Demand for dollars (NX)

Quantity of Dollars (in billions)

Figure 18-5

THE EFFECTS OF AN INCREASE IN THE GOVERNMENT BUDGET DEFICIT.   An increase in the size of the government budget deficit reduces the supply of loanable funds available from national saving. As a result, the supply curve shifts to the left, as shown in panel (a). Net foreign investment therefore also decreases from the amount given by the distance between points A and C to the amount given by the distance between points B and C. In panel (b), the decrease in net foreign investment reduces the supply of dollars in the market for foreign exchange. This decrease in the supply of dollars causes the supply curve to shift to the left, from $(S - I)_1$ to $(S - I)_2$, and causes the real exchange rate to appreciate from E_1 to E_2. The appreciation of the exchange rate causes net exports to fall.

TRADE POLICY

A **trade policy** is a government policy that directly influences the quantity of goods and services that a country imports or exports. As we saw in Chapter 9, trade policy takes various forms. One common trade policy is a *tariff*, a tax on imported goods. Another is an *import quota*, a limit on the quantity of a good that can be produced abroad and sold domestically. Trade policies are common throughout the world, although sometimes they are disguised. For example, the Canadian and U.S. governments have often pressured Japanese automakers to reduce the number of cars they sell in North America. These so-called "voluntary export restrictions" are not really voluntary and, in essence, are a form of import quota.

trade policy
a government policy that directly influences the quantity of goods and services that a country imports or exports

Let's consider the macroeconomic impact of trade policy. Suppose that the North American auto industry, concerned about competition from Japanese automakers, convinces the Canadian government to impose a quota on the number of cars that can be imported from Japan. In making their case, lobbyists for the auto industry assert that the trade restriction would shrink the size of the Canadian trade deficit. Are they right? Our model, as illustrated in Figure 18-6, offers an answer.

The first step in analyzing the trade policy is to determine which curve shifts. The initial impact of the import restriction is, not surprisingly, on imports. Because net exports equal exports minus imports, the policy also affects net exports. And

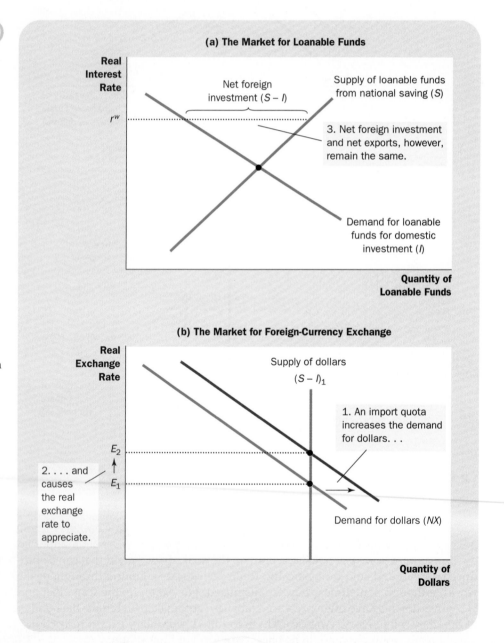

because net exports are the source of demand for dollars in the market for foreign-currency exchange, the policy affects the demand curve in this market.

The second step is to determine which way this demand curve shifts. Because the quota restricts the number of Japanese cars sold in Canada, it reduces imports at any given real exchange rate. Net exports, which equal exports minus imports, will therefore *rise* for any given real exchange rate. Because foreigners need dollars to buy Canada's net exports, there is an increased demand for dollars in the market for foreign-currency exchange. This increase in the demand for dollars is shown in panel (b) of Figure 18-6 as the shift to the right of the demand curve.

The third step is to compare the old and new equilibria. As we can see in panel (b), the increase in the demand for dollars causes the real exchange rate to appreciate from E_1 to E_2. Because nothing has happened in the market for loanable funds in panel (a), there is no change in net foreign investment. And because there is no change in net foreign investment, there can be no change in net exports, even though the import quota has reduced imports.

The reason that net exports can stay the same while imports fall is explained by the change in the real exchange rate: When the dollar appreciates in value in the market for foreign-currency exchange, domestic goods become more expensive relative to foreign goods. This appreciation encourages imports and discourages exports—and both of these changes work to offset the direct increase in net exports due to the import quota. In the end, an import quota reduces both imports and exports, but net exports (exports minus imports) are unchanged.

We have thus come to a surprising implication: *Trade policies do not affect the trade balance.* That is, policies that directly influence exports or imports do not alter net exports. This conclusion seems less surprising if one recalls the accounting identity:

$$NX = NFI = S - I.$$

Net exports equal net foreign investment, which equals national saving minus domestic investment. Trade policies do not alter the trade balance because they do not alter national saving or domestic investment. For given levels of national saving and domestic investment, the real exchange rate adjusts to keep the trade balance the same, regardless of the trade policies the government puts in place.

Although trade policies do not affect a country's overall trade balance, these policies do affect specific firms, industries, and countries. When the Canadian government imposes an import quota on Japanese cars, General Motors has less competition from abroad and will sell more cars. At the same time, because the dollar has appreciated in value, Bombardier, the Canadian aircraft maker, will find it harder to compete with Embraer, the Brazilian aircraft maker. Canadian exports of aircraft will fall, and Canadian imports of aircraft will rise. In this case, the import quota on Japanese cars will increase net exports of cars and decrease net exports of planes. In addition, it will increase net exports from Canada to Japan and decrease net exports from Canada to Brazil. The overall trade balance of the Canadian economy, however, stays the same.

The effects of trade policies are, therefore, more microeconomic than macroeconomic. Although advocates of trade policies sometimes claim (incorrectly) that these policies can alter a country's trade balance, they are usually more motivated by concerns about particular firms or industries. One should not be surprised, for instance, to hear an executive from General Motors advocating import quotas for

Japanese cars. Economists almost always oppose such trade policies. As we saw in Chapters 3 and 9, free trade allows economies to specialize in doing what they do best, making residents of all countries better off. Trade restrictions interfere with these gains from trade and, thus, reduce overall economic well-being.

POLITICAL INSTABILITY AND CAPITAL FLIGHT

capital flight

a large and sudden reduction in the demand for assets located in a country

In 1994 political instability in Mexico, including the assassination of a prominent political leader, made world financial markets nervous. People began to view Mexico as a much less stable country than they had previously thought. They decided to pull some of their assets out of Mexico in order to move these funds to the United States, and other "safe havens." Such a large and sudden movement of funds out of a country is called **capital flight.** To see the implications of capital flight for the Mexican economy, we again follow our three steps for analyzing a change in equilibrium, but this time we apply our model of the open economy from the perspective of Mexico rather than Canada.

Panel (a) of Figure 18-7 shows the market for loanable funds in Mexico before the flight of capital. At the world interest rate, r^w, the supply of loanable funds made available by the savings of Mexicans is greater than the demand for loanable funds for investment in Mexico. The difference is the amount of Mexican saving that is available to purchase foreign assets—in other words, Mexico's net foreign investment. Mexico's net foreign investment is shown in panel (a) by the distance between points A and B. The level of net foreign investment determines the supply of pesos in the market for foreign-currency exchange. This is shown in panel (b) by the curve $(S - I)_1$. The point at which the demand and supply of pesos are in equilibrium determines the real exchange rate, E_1.

Now consider which curves are affected, and which way the affected curves shift, if the world financial community suddenly loses confidence in the Mexican economy. As we have seen previously, if lenders lose confidence in the ability of a borrower to repay debts, they will demand that that borrower pay them a higher interest rate. Lenders, then, by receiving a higher interest rate, are compensated for the greater default risk that they incur. If the world financial community begins to question the ability of Mexico to repay its debts, lenders will only hold Mexican debt if they receive a higher interest rate than they can receive in other countries. In a small open economy like Mexico, this requires that Mexican borrowers offer to pay an interest rate greater than the world interest rate.

Let's define γ as the extra amount lenders need to receive from Mexican borrowers if they are to hold Mexican debt. This amount is commonly referred to as the *risk premium* that risky borrowers must pay. To prevent the sale of all Mexican assets, borrowers in Mexico must now pay the world interest rate, r^w, plus the risk premium, γ. To save the same quantity of loanable funds as before the confidence crisis, Mexican savers also demand that they receive $r^w + \gamma$. This response of Mexican savers is shown in panel (a) by a shift upward of the curve that represents the supply of loanable funds made available by Mexicans. The curve shifts up by the amount of the risk premium to indicate that Mexicans will choose to contribute the same quantity of their savings to the Mexican market for loanable funds only if they are compensated for the greater risk they incur by doing so. After all, Mexican savers could otherwise put their savings into Canada's, Japan's, or some other country's market for loanable funds. Paying the risk premium enables Mexican borrowers to halt the sale of Mexican assets, and receiving the risk premium

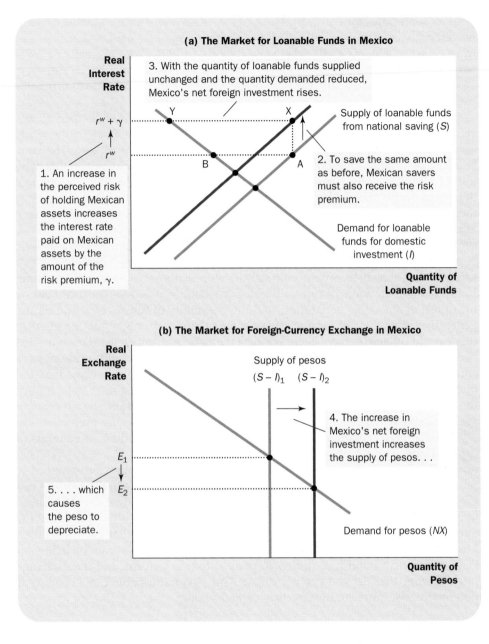

(a) The Market for Loanable Funds in Mexico

Real Interest Rate

3. With the quantity of loanable funds supplied unchanged and the quantity demanded reduced, Mexico's net foreign investment rises.

$r^w + \gamma$

r^w

Y   X

Supply of loanable funds from national saving (S)

B   A

2. To save the same amount as before, Mexican savers must also receive the risk premium.

1. An increase in the perceived risk of holding Mexican assets increases the interest rate paid on Mexican assets by the amount of the risk premium, γ.

Demand for loanable funds for domestic investment (I)

Quantity of Loanable Funds

(b) The Market for Foreign-Currency Exchange in Mexico

Real Exchange Rate

Supply of pesos

$(S - I)_1$ $(S - I)_2$

E_1

4. The increase in Mexico's net foreign investment increases the supply of pesos. . .

5. . . . which causes the peso to depreciate.

E_2

Demand for pesos (NX)

Quantity of Pesos

Figure 18-7

THE EFFECTS OF CAPITAL FLIGHT. If Mexico is judged to be a risky place to keep savings, savers in Mexico and elsewhere will demand that they receive a risk premium if they are to continue to hold Mexican assets. The response of Mexican savers is shown in panel (a) by the upward shift in the curve that represents the supply of loanable funds available from the savings of Mexicans. Because borrowers in Mexico must now pay a higher interest rate, $r^w + \gamma$, than they paid before the crisis of confidence, the quantity of loanable funds demanded for domestic investment falls. The increase in the interest rate paid by Mexican borrowers and the shift of the supply curve causes an increase in the net foreign investment of Mexico. Net foreign investment increases from an amount measured by the distance between points A and B to an amount measured by the distance between points X and Y. The increase in net foreign investment means that the supply of pesos in the market for foreign-currency exchange increases. This is shown in panel (b) by the shift to the right of the supply curve from $(S - I)_1$ to $(S - I)_2$. This increase in the supply of pesos causes the peso to depreciate from E_1 to E_2, so the peso becomes less valuable compared with other currencies.

causes Mexicans to save the same quantity of loanable funds as they did before the capital flight. Thus the capital flight stops.

However, as we can see from panel (a), the addition of the risk premium also reduces domestic investment. The net effect of these changes is that net foreign investment has increased by the time the sale of Mexican assets has been halted. In panel (a), Mexico's net foreign investment is now represented by the distance between points X and Y. In panel (b), the increase in net foreign investment increases the supply of pesos in the market for foreign-currency exchange from $(S - I)_1$ to $(S - I)_2$. That is, the rush to sell Mexican assets causes a large increase in the supply of pesos to be converted into dollars. This increase in supply causes the peso to depreciate from E_1 to E_2. Thus, *capital flight from Mexico increases Mexican interest rates and decreases the value of the Mexican peso in the market for foreign-currency exchange.* This is exactly what was observed in 1994. From November 1994 to March 1995, the interest rate on short-term Mexican government bonds rose from 14 percent to 70 percent, and the peso depreciated in value from 40 to 21 Canadian cents per peso.

The events that we have been describing in Mexico could happen to any economy in the world, and in fact they do from time to time. In 1997, the world learned that the banking systems of several Asian economies, including Thailand, South Korea, and Indonesia, were at or near the point of bankruptcy, and this news induced capital to flee from these nations. In 1998, the Russian government defaulted on its debt, inducing international investors to take whatever money they could and run. In each of these cases of capital flight, the results were much as our model predicts: rising interest rates and a falling currency.

Could the events that occurred in Mexico, Southeast Asia, and Russia ever happen in Canada? Although the Canadian economy has long been viewed as a safe place in which to invest, political developments in Canada have at times induced small amounts of capital flight. For example, past referendums held on the question of Quebec separation, and the possibility of future referendums, are generally acknowledged to have caused interest rates to be higher in Canada than they would otherwise have been. Because the issue of Quebec separation has led some international investors to wonder whether Canada will continue to exist as a country, Canadian borrowers have had to pay a risk premium to Canadian and international lenders. In addition to causing Canadian interest rates to be higher, the uncertainty about Canada's political future has caused domestic investment and the value of the Canadian dollar to be lower, as our model has predicted.

Even a large economy like the United States has suffered small amounts of capital flight. For example, the September 22, 1995, issue of *The New York Times* reported that on the previous day, "House Speaker Newt Gingrich threatened to send the United States into default on its debt for the first time in the nation's history, to force the Clinton administration to balance the budget on Republican terms" (p. A1). Even though most people believed such a default was unlikely, the effect of the announcement was, in a small way, similar to that experienced by Mexico in 1994. Over the course of that single day, the interest rate on a 30-year U.S. government bond rose from 6.46 percent to 6.55 percent, and the exchange rate fell from 102.7 to 99.0 yen per dollar. Thus, even the stable U.S. economy is potentially susceptible to the effects of capital flight.

QUICK QUIZ: Suppose that Canadians decided to spend a smaller fraction of their incomes. What would be the effect on saving, domestic investment, net foreign investment, the real exchange rate, and the trade balance?

CONCLUSION

International economics is a topic of increasing importance. More and more, Canadian citizens are buying goods produced abroad and producing goods to be sold overseas. Through mutual funds and other financial institutions, they borrow and lend in world financial markets. As a result, a full analysis of Canadian economy requires an understanding of how the Canadian economy interacts with other economies in the world. This chapter has provided a basic model for thinking about the macroeconomics of small open economies with perfect capital mobility.

It is worth noting, however, that the model that has been presented in this chapter is, well, a model. As such, it relies on a number of assumptions and simplifications. These assumptions and simplifications produce answers that need to be modified when these assumptions and simplifications are relaxed. There is nothing unusual about this. (Recall our discussion in Chapter 2 when we talked about the scientific method and the role of models.) The model presented in this chapter dispenses with various details that, for some purposes, are significant. More complex models of the sort you will see in future courses in macroeconomics will include, for example, the role of people's expectations with respect to the future and the longer-run implications of capital flows. More complex models may also allow for a relaxation of our assumption of perfectly mobile capital. Having said that, it is nonetheless true that the basic model presented in this chapter provides a very useful way of thinking about the macroeconomics of a small open economy.

Although the study of international economics is valuable, we should be careful not to exaggerate its importance. Policymakers and commentators are often quick to blame foreigners for problems facing the Canadian economy. By contrast, economists more often view these problems as homegrown. For example, politicians often discuss foreign competition as a threat to Canadian living standards. Economists are more likely to lament the low level of national saving. Low saving impedes growth in capital, productivity, and living standards, regardless of whether the economy is open or closed. Foreigners are a convenient target for politicians because blaming foreigners provides a way to avoid responsibility without insulting any domestic constituency. Whenever you hear popular discussions of international trade and finance, therefore, it is especially important to try to separate myth from reality. The tools you have learned in the past two chapters should help in that endeavour.

Summary

◆ Most economists prefer to use a model that describes Canada as a small open economy with perfect capital mobility. This means that borrowers must pay, and lenders demand that they receive, the world interest rate. In the analysis of the macroeconomics of such an economy, two markets are central—the market for loanable funds and the market for foreign-currency exchange. In the market for loanable funds, the world interest rate determines the quantity of loanable funds demanded for domestic investment and the quantity of loanable funds made available from national saving. The difference between the quantity of loanable funds demanded and the quantity of loanable funds supplied at the world interest rate is net foreign investment. In the market for foreign-currency exchange, the real exchange rate adjusts to balance the supply of dollars (from net foreign investment) and the demand for dollars (from net exports). Because net foreign investment is determined in the market for loanable funds and provides the supply of dollars for foreign-currency exchange, it is the variable that connects these two markets.

◆ An increase in a government budget deficit reduces the supply of loanable funds available from national saving. This reduces net foreign investment and in turn reduces the supply of dollars in the market for foreign-currency exchange. The fall in the supply of dollars causes the real exchange rate to appreciate and therefore causes net exports to fall. A decrease in a government deficit, or an increase in a government surplus, increases the supply of loanable funds and increases net foreign investment. The increase in the supply of dollars in the market for foreign-currency exchange causes the real exchange rate to depreciate and net exports to rise.

◆ Although restrictive trade policies, such as tariffs or quotas on imports, are sometimes advocated as a way to alter the trade balance, they do not necessarily have that effect. A trade restriction increases net exports for a given exchange rate and, therefore, increases the demand for dollars in the market for foreign-currency exchange. As a result, the dollar appreciates in value,

making domestic goods more expensive relative to foreign goods. This appreciation offsets the initial impact of the trade restriction on net exports.

◆ When investors change their attitudes about holding assets of a country, the ramifications for the country's economy can be profound. In particular, political instability can lead to capital flight, which tends to increase interest rates and cause the currency to depreciate.

Key Concepts

trade policy, p. 411

capital flight, p. 414

Questions for Review

1. Describe supply and demand in the market for loanable funds and the market for foreign-currency exchange. How are these markets linked?

2. How would a fall in U.S. interest rates affect Canadian investment, saving, and net foreign investment, and the Canadian real exchange rate?

3. Suppose that a textile workers' union encourages people to buy only Canadian-made clothes. What would this

policy do to the trade balance and the real exchange rate? What is the impact on the textile industry? What is the impact on the auto industry?

4. What is capital flight? When a country experiences capital flight, what is the effect on its interest rate and exchange rate?

Problems and Applications

1. Japan generally runs a significant trade surplus. Do you think this is most related to high foreign demand for Japanese goods, low Japanese demand for foreign goods, a high Japanese saving rate relative to Japanese investment, or structural barriers against imports into Japan? Explain your answer.

2. How would an increase in foreigners' incomes affect Canada's net exports curve? How would this affect the value of the dollar in the market for foreign-currency exchange?

3. Suppose that Parliament passes an investment tax credit, which subsidizes domestic investment. How does this policy affect national saving, domestic investment, net foreign investment, the exchange rate, and the trade balance?

4. Economists generally favour reductions in trade restrictions. Many policymakers, however, insist that any lowering of Canadian import restrictions must be accompanied by reductions in other countries' import quotas on Canadian exports. Only in this way, these policymakers believe, can Canadian exporters benefit from a lowering of Canadian import quotas. Explain how a reduction in import restrictions will benefit exporters even if other countries do not follow Canada's example and reduce their import quotas on Canadian exports.

5. In fiscal year 1996–97, the government of Ontario ran a budget deficit of $7.5 billion. At this size, the deficit was only slightly smaller than the federal government's budget deficit of $8.9 billion, and larger than the combined deficits of all of the other provinces. The

Ontario government plans to reduce its provincial budget deficit to zero by the year 2001. What effect will this reduction have on the economies of the other provinces?

6. Economists often lament the low level of national saving. Low saving impedes capital growth, productivity, and living standards. For this reason, economists tend to favour policies designed to increase saving. Suppose that all Canadians choose to increase their saving. What would be the effect of increased saving on the value of the dollar and on net exports?

7. Changes in government deficits are closely related to changes in net exports. In particular, increases in government deficits lead to reductions in net exports, while reductions in government deficits lead to increases in net exports. Use a two-panel diagram to explain this important relationship.

8. Suppose the French suddenly develop a strong taste for British Columbia wines. Answer the following questions in words and using a diagram:
   a. What happens to the demand for dollars in the market for foreign-currency exchange?
   b. What happens to the value of dollars in the market for foreign-currency exchange?
   c. What happens to the quantity of net exports?

9. A Member of Parliament renounces her past support for protectionism: "Canada's trade deficit must be reduced, but import quotas only annoy our trading partners. If we subsidize Canadian exports instead, we can reduce the deficit by increasing our competitiveness." Using a two-panel diagram, show the effect of an export subsidy on net exports and the real exchange rate. Do you agree with the MP?

10. Suppose that the federal government increases the tax on corporate profits. Such a tax has the effect of reducing domestic investment. What effect would this tax increase have on Canada's real exchange rate and net exports?

11. Suppose that the world interest rate rises.
    a. If the elasticity of national saving with respect to the world interest rate is very high, will this rise in the world interest rate have a large or small effect on Canada's net foreign investment?

    b. If the elasticity of Canada's exports with respect to the real exchange rate is very low, will this rise in the world interest rate have a large or small effect on Canada's real exchange rate?

12. Suppose that Europeans suddenly become very interested in investing in Canada.
    a. What happens to Canadian net foreign investment?
    b. What effect does this have on Canadian private saving and Canadian domestic investment?
    c. What is the long-run effect on the Canadian capital stock?

13. During the 1960s, there was a commonly held concern among Canadians that Americans were "buying Canada." This concern stemmed from the fact that Canada's net foreign investment during the 1960s was consistently negative. As a result, foreigners, particularly Americans, were buying more Canadian assets than Canadians were buying foreign assets. Because many of these assets were firms operating in Canada, Canadians were concerned that eventually all of Canada would be owned by Americans. In response to this concern, the federal government of the time passed legislation limiting the amount that foreigners could invest in certain sectors of the economy. How do you think this legislation affected investment in Canada? What do you think happened to Canada's real exchange rate and net exports as a result?

14. Figure 18-4 shows the effect of an increase in the world interest rate on a small open economy with perfect capital mobility. In the figure, we assumed that net foreign investment (NFI) was positive. For most of the past 30 years, however, Canada's NFI has been negative. Redraw the two panels of Figure 18-4, but this time assume that NFI is negative at the world interest rate. Now suppose that the world interest rate increases. What happens to national saving (S)? What happens to domestic investment (I)? What happens to NFI and the real exchange rate? Does the conclusion we reached in our discussion of Figure 18-4—that an increase in world interest rates causes the Canadian dollar to depreciate and net exports to increase—still hold?

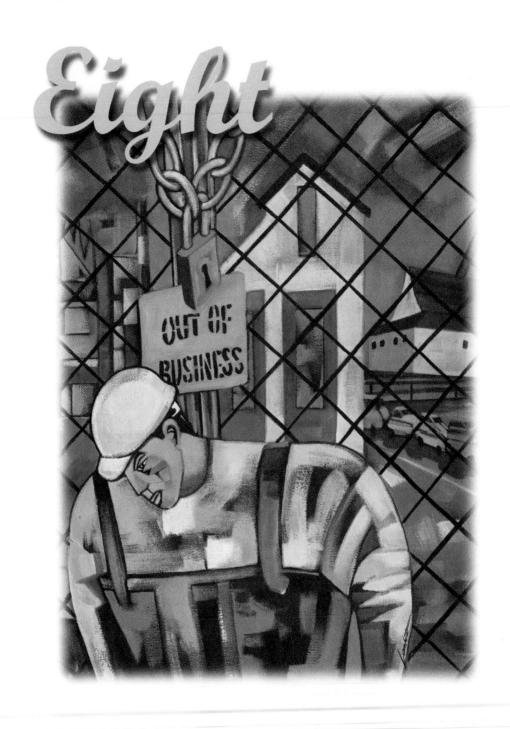

Eight

SHORT-RUN
ECONOMIC FLUCTUATIONS

19

AGGREGATE DEMAND
AND AGGREGATE SUPPLY

Economic activity fluctuates from year to year. In most years, the production of goods and services rises. Because of increases in the labour force, increases in the capital stock, and advances in technological knowledge, the economy can produce more and more over time. This growth allows everyone to enjoy a higher standard of living. On average over the past 100 years, the production of the Canadian economy as measured by real GDP has grown by about 4 percent per year.

In some years, however, this normal growth does not occur. Firms find themselves unable to sell all of the goods and services they have to offer, so they cut back on production. Workers are laid off, unemployment rises, and factories are left idle. With the economy producing fewer goods and services, real GDP and other measures of income fall. Such a period of falling incomes and rising

recession
a period of declining real incomes and rising unemployment

depression
a severe recession

unemployment is called a **recession** if it is relatively mild and a **depression** if it is more severe.

What causes short-run fluctuations in economic activity? What, if anything, can public policy do to prevent periods of falling incomes and rising unemployment? When recessions and depressions occur, can policymakers reduce their length and severity? If so, how? These are the questions that we take up in this and the next two chapters.

The variables that we study in the coming chapters are largely those we have already seen. They include GDP, unemployment, interest rates, exchange rates, and the price level. Also familiar are the policy instruments of government spending, taxes, and the money supply. What differs in the next few chapters is the time horizon of our analysis. Our focus in the previous seven chapters has been on the behaviour of the economy in the long run. Our focus now is on the economy's short-run fluctuations around its long-run trend.

Although there remains some debate among economists about how to analyze short-run fluctuations, most economists use the *model of aggregate demand and aggregate supply*. Learning how to use this model for analyzing the short-run effects of various events and policies is the primary task ahead. This chapter introduces the model's two key pieces—the aggregate-demand curve and the aggregate-supply curve. After getting a sense of the overall structure of the model in this chapter, we examine the pieces of the model in more detail in the next two chapters.

THREE KEY FACTS ABOUT ECONOMIC FLUCTUATIONS

Short-run fluctuations in economic activity occur in all countries and in all times throughout history. As a starting point for understanding these year-to-year fluctuations, let's discuss some of their most important properties.

FACT 1: ECONOMIC FLUCTUATIONS ARE IRREGULAR AND UNPREDICTABLE

Fluctuations in the economy are often called *the business cycle*. As this term suggests, economic fluctuations correspond to changes in business conditions. When real GDP grows rapidly, business is good. Firms find that customers are plentiful and profits are growing. On the other hand, when real GDP falls, businesses have trouble. In recessions, most firms experience declining sales and profits.

The term *business cycle* is somewhat misleading, however, because it seems to suggest that economic fluctuations follow a regular, predictable pattern. In fact, economic fluctuations are not at all regular, and they are almost impossible to predict with much accuracy. Panel (a) of Figure 19-1 shows the real GDP of the Canadian economy since 1966. The shaded areas represent times of recession. As the figure shows, recessions do not come at regular intervals. Sometimes recessions

Figure 19-1

Panel (a) Real GDP

(b) Investment Spending

(c) Unemployment Rate

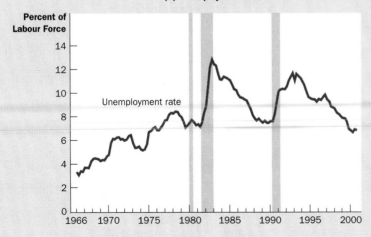

A LOOK AT SHORT-RUN
ECONOMIC FLUCTUATIONS.
This figure shows real GDP in
panel (a), investment spending
in panel (b), and unemployment
in panel (c) for the Canadian
economy using quarterly data
since 1966. Recessions, defined
here as two or more consecutive
quarters of negative real GDP
growth, are shown as the shaded
areas. Notice that real GDP and
investment spending decline
during recessions, while
unemployment rises.

SOURCE: Statistics Canada CANSIM
database, series D16339, D15612, D15247,
and D980745.

are close together, such as the recessions of 1980 and 1982. Sometimes the economy goes many years without a recession.

FACT 2: MOST MACROECONOMIC QUANTITIES FLUCTUATE TOGETHER

Real GDP is the variable that is most commonly used to monitor short-run changes in the economy because it is the most comprehensive measure of economic activity. Real GDP measures the value of all final goods and services produced within a given period of time. It also measures the total income (adjusted for inflation) of everyone in the economy.

It turns out, however, that for monitoring short-run fluctuations, it does not really matter which measure of economic activity one looks at. Most macroeconomic variables that measure some type of income, spending, or production fluctuate closely together. When real GDP falls in a recession, so do personal income, corporate profits, consumer spending, investment spending, industrial production, retail sales, home sales, auto sales, and so on. Because recessions are economy-wide phenomena, they show up in many sources of macroeconomic data.

Although many macroeconomic variables fluctuate together, they fluctuate by different amounts. In particular, as panel (b) of Figure 19-1 shows, investment spending varies greatly over the business cycle. Even though investment averages about one-fifth of GDP, declines in investment accounted for about 80 percent of the declines in GDP during Canada's last two recessions. In other words, when economic conditions deteriorate, much of the decline is attributable to reductions in spending on new factories, housing, and inventories.

"You're fired. Pass it on."

FACT 3: AS OUTPUT FALLS, UNEMPLOYMENT RISES

Changes in the economy's output of goods and services are strongly correlated with changes in the economy's utilization of its labour force. In other words, when real GDP declines, the rate of unemployment rises. This fact is hardly surprising: When firms choose to produce a smaller quantity of goods and services, they lay off workers, expanding the pool of unemployed people.

Panel (c) of Figure 19-1 shows the unemployment rate in the Canadian economy since 1966. Once again, recessions are shown as the shaded areas in the figure. The figure shows clearly the impact of recessions on unemployment. In each of the recessions, the unemployment rate rises substantially. When the recession ends and real GDP starts to expand, the unemployment rate gradually declines. The unemployment rate never approaches zero; instead, it fluctuates around its natural rate. As we discussed in Chapter 14, because the value of the natural rate is only an estimate, there may be some dispute about the level of the rate at any particular time. However, most economists believe that the natural unemployment rate in Canada increased during the 1970s, peaked at about 8 percent in the 1980s, and has fallen slowly since the mid-1990s to some value between 6 and 8 percent.

■ **QUICK QUIZ:**   List and discuss three key facts about economic fluctuations.

EXPLAINING SHORT-RUN ECONOMIC FLUCTUATIONS

Describing the regular patterns that economies experience as they fluctuate over time is easy. Explaining what causes these fluctuations is more difficult. Indeed, compared with the topics we have studied in previous chapters, the theory of economic fluctuations remains controversial. In this and the next two chapters, we develop the model that most economists use to explain short-run fluctuations in economic activity.

HOW THE SHORT RUN DIFFERS FROM THE LONG RUN

In previous chapters we developed theories to explain what determines most important macroeconomic variables in the long run. Chapter 12 explained the level and growth of productivity and real GDP. Chapter 13 explained how the real interest rate adjusts to balance saving and investment in a closed economy. Chapter 14 explained why there is always some unemployment in the economy. Chapters 15 and 16 explained the monetary system and how changes in the money supply affect the price level, the inflation rate, and the nominal interest rate. Chapters 17 and 18 extended this analysis to open economies in order to explain the trade balance and the exchange rate. There we learned that, as a result of perfect capital mobility, the real interest rate in Canada must increase and decrease with increases and decreases in the value of the world real interest rate.

All of this previous analysis was based on two related ideas—the classical dichotomy and monetary neutrality. Recall that the classical dichotomy is the separation of variables into real variables (those that measure quantities or relative prices) and nominal variables (those measured in terms of money). According to classical macroeconomic theory, changes in the money supply affect nominal variables but not real variables. As a result of this monetary neutrality, Chapters 12, 13, and 14 were able to examine the determinants of real variables (real GDP, the real interest rate, and unemployment) without introducing nominal variables (the money supply and the price level).

Do these assumptions of classical macroeconomic theory apply to the world in which we live? The answer to this question is of central importance to understanding how the economy works: *Most economists believe that classical theory describes the world in the long run but not in the short run*. Beyond a period of several years, changes in the money supply affect prices and other nominal variables but do not affect real GDP, unemployment, or other real variables. When studying year-to-year changes in the economy, however, the assumption of monetary neutrality is no longer appropriate. Most economists believe that, in the short run, real and nominal variables are highly intertwined. In particular, changes in the money supply can temporarily push output away from its long-run trend.

To understand the economy in the short run, therefore, we need a new model. To build this new model, we rely on many of the tools we have developed in previous chapters, but we have to abandon the classical dichotomy and the neutrality of money.

THE BASIC MODEL OF ECONOMIC FLUCTUATIONS

Our model of short-run economic fluctuations focuses on the behaviour of two variables. The first variable is the economy's output of goods and services, as measured by real GDP. The second variable is the overall price level, as measured by the CPI or the GDP deflator. Notice that output is a real variable, whereas the price level is a nominal variable. Hence, by focusing on the relationship between these two variables, we are highlighting the breakdown of the classical dichotomy.

We analyze fluctuations in the economy as a whole with the **model of aggregate demand and aggregate supply,** which is illustrated in Figure 19-2. On the vertical axis is the overall price level in the economy. On the horizontal axis is the overall quantity of goods and services. The **aggregate-demand curve** shows the quantity of goods and services that households, firms, and the government want to buy at each price level. The **aggregate-supply curve** shows the quantity of goods and services that firms produce and sell at each price level. According to this model, the price level and the quantity of output adjust to bring aggregate demand and aggregate supply into balance.

It may be tempting to view the model of aggregate demand and aggregate supply as nothing more than a large version of the model of market demand and market supply, which we introduced in Chapter 4. Yet in fact this model is quite different. When we consider demand and supply in a particular market—ice cream, for instance—the behaviour of buyers and sellers depends on the ability of resources to move from one market to another. When the price of ice cream rises, the quantity demanded falls because buyers will use their incomes to buy products other than ice cream. Similarly, a higher price of ice cream raises the quantity

model of aggregate demand and aggregate supply
the model that most economists use to explain short-run fluctuations in economic activity around its long-run trend

aggregate-demand curve
a curve that shows the quantity of goods and services that households, firms, and the government want to buy at each price level

aggregate-supply curve
a curve that shows the quantity of goods and services that firms choose to produce and sell at each price level

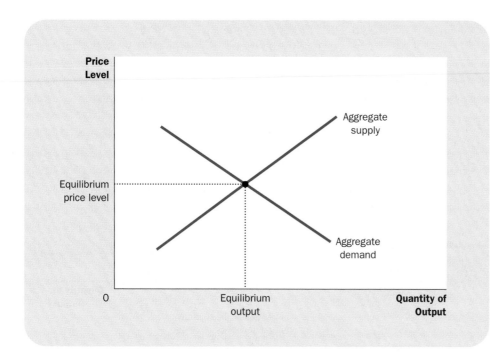

Figure 19-2

AGGREGATE DEMAND
AND AGGREGATE SUPPLY.
Economists use the model of
aggregate demand and aggregate
supply to analyze economic
fluctuations. On the vertical
axis is the overall level of prices.
On the horizontal axis is the
economy's total output of
goods and services. Output
and the price level adjust
to the point at which
the aggregate-supply
and aggregate-demand
curves intersect.

supplied because firms that produce ice cream can increase production by hiring workers away from other parts of the economy. This *microeconomic* substitution from one market to another is impossible when we are analyzing the economy as a whole. After all, the quantity that our model is trying to explain—real GDP—measures the total quantity produced in all of the economy's markets. To understand why the aggregate-demand curve is downward sloping and why the aggregate-supply curve is upward sloping, we need a *macroeconomic* theory. Developing such a theory is our next task.

QUICK QUIZ: How does the economy's behaviour in the short run differ from its behaviour in the long run? ◆ Draw the model of aggregate demand and aggregate supply. What variables are on the two axes?

THE AGGREGATE-DEMAND CURVE

The aggregate-demand curve tells us the quantity of all goods and services demanded in the economy at any given price level. As Figure 19-3 illustrates, the aggregate-demand curve is downward sloping. This means that, other things equal, a fall in the economy's overall level of prices (from, say, P_1 to P_2) tends to raise the quantity of goods and services demanded (from Y_1 to Y_2).

Figure 19-3

THE AGGREGATE-DEMAND CURVE.   A fall in the price level from P_1 to P_2 increases the quantity of goods and services demanded from Y_1 to Y_2. There are three reasons for this negative relationship. As the price level falls, real wealth rises, interest rates fall, and the exchange rate depreciates. These effects stimulate spending on consumption, investment, and net exports. Increased spending on these components of output means a larger quantity of goods and services demanded.

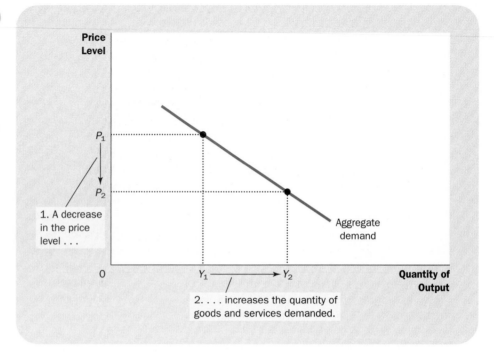

WHY THE AGGREGATE-DEMAND CURVE SLOPES DOWNWARD

Why does a fall in the price level raise the quantity of goods and services demanded? To answer this question, it is useful to recall that GDP (which we denote as Y) is the sum of consumption (C), investment (I), government purchases (G), and net exports (NX):

$$Y = C + I + G + NX.$$

Each of these four components contributes to the aggregate demand for goods and services. For now, we assume that government spending is fixed by policy. The other three components of spending—consumption, investment, and net exports—depend on economic conditions and, in particular, on the price level. To understand the downward slope of the aggregate-demand curve, therefore, we must examine how the price level affects the quantity of goods and services demanded for consumption, investment, and net exports.

The Price Level and Consumption: The Wealth Effect   Consider the money that you hold in your wallet and your bank account. The nominal value of this money is fixed, but its real value is not. When prices fall, these dollars are more valuable because they can be used to buy more goods and services. Thus, *a decrease in the price level makes consumers feel more wealthy, which in turn encourages them to spend more. The increase in consumer spending means a larger quantity of goods and services demanded.*

The Price Level and Investment: The Interest Rate Effect

As we discussed in Chapter 16, the price level is one determinant of the quantity of money demanded. The lower the price level, the less money households need to hold to buy the goods and services they want. When the price level falls, therefore, households try to reduce their holdings of money by lending some of it out. For instance, a household might use its excess money to buy interest-bearing bonds. Or it might deposit its excess money in an interest-bearing savings account, and the bank would use these funds to make more loans. In either case, as households try to convert some of their money into interest-bearing assets, they drive down interest rates. Lower interest rates, in turn, encourage borrowing by firms that want to invest in new plants and equipment and by households who want to invest in new housing. Thus, *a lower price level reduces the interest rate, encourages greater spending on investment goods, and thereby increases the quantity of goods and services demanded.*

The Price Level and Net Exports: The Real Exchange-Rate Effect

The real exchange rate measures the rate at which a person can trade Canadian-produced goods and services for the goods and services of other countries. For a given nominal exchange rate, a lower price level reduces the real exchange rate. This depreciation makes Canadian-produced goods and services cheaper relative to foreign-produced goods and services. As a result, Canadians and foreigners substitute away from foreign-produced goods and services in favour of Canadian-produced goods and services. Thus, *a fall in the Canadian price level causes the real exchange rate to depreciate, and this depreciation stimulates Canadian net exports and thereby increases the quantity of goods and services demanded.*

Summary

There are, therefore, three distinct but related reasons why a fall in the price level increases the quantity of goods and services demanded: (1) Consumers feel wealthier, which stimulates the demand for consumption goods; (2) interest rates fall, which stimulates the demand for investment goods; and (3) the exchange rate depreciates, which stimulates the demand for net exports. For all three reasons, the aggregate-demand curve slopes downward.

It is important to keep in mind that the aggregate-demand curve (like all demand curves) is drawn holding "other things equal." In particular, our three explanations of the downward-sloping aggregate-demand curve assume that the money supply is fixed. That is, we have been considering how a change in the price level affects the demand for goods and services, holding the amount of money in the economy constant. As we will see, a change in the quantity of money shifts the aggregate-demand curve. At this point, just keep in mind that the aggregate-demand curve is drawn for a given quantity of money.

WHY THE AGGREGATE-DEMAND CURVE MIGHT SHIFT

The downward slope of the aggregate-demand curve shows that a fall in the price level raises the overall quantity of goods and services demanded. Many other factors, however, affect the quantity of goods and services demanded at a given price level. When one of these other factors changes, the aggregate-demand curve shifts.

Let's consider some examples of events that shift aggregate demand. We can categorize them according to which component of spending is most directly affected.

Shifts Arising from Consumption

Suppose Canadians suddenly become more concerned about saving for retirement and, as a result, reduce their current consumption. This concern about retirement savings might arise because of a fall in stock prices that makes people feel less wealthy. Because the quantity of goods and services demanded at any price level is lower, the aggregate-demand curve shifts to the left. Conversely, imagine that a stock market boom makes people feel wealthier and less concerned about saving. The resulting increase in consumer spending means a greater quantity of goods and services demanded at any given price level, so the aggregate-demand curve shifts to the right.

Thus, any event that changes how much people want to consume at a given price level shifts the aggregate-demand curve. One policy variable that has this effect is the level of taxation. When the government cuts taxes, it encourages people to spend more, so the aggregate-demand curve shifts to the right. When the government raises taxes, people cut back on their spending, and the aggregate-demand curve shifts to the left.

Shifts Arising from Investment

Any event that changes how much firms want to invest at a given price level also shifts the aggregate-demand curve. For instance, imagine that the computer industry introduces a faster line of computers, and many firms decide to invest in new computer systems. Because the quantity of goods and services demanded at any price level is higher, the aggregate-demand curve shifts to the right. Conversely, if firms become pessimistic about future business conditions, they may cut back on investment spending, shifting the aggregate-demand curve to the left.

Tax policy can also influence aggregate demand through investment. As we saw in Chapter 13, an investment tax credit (a tax rebate tied to a firm's investment spending) increases the quantity of investment goods that firms demand at any given interest rate. It therefore shifts the aggregate-demand curve to the right. The repeal of an investment tax credit reduces investment and shifts the aggregate-demand curve to the left.

Another policy variable that can influence investment and aggregate demand is the money supply. As we discuss more fully in the next chapter, an increase in the money supply lowers the interest rate in the short run. This makes borrowing less costly, which stimulates investment spending and thereby shifts the aggregate-demand curve to the right. Conversely, a decrease in the money supply raises the interest rate, discourages investment spending, and thereby shifts the aggregate-demand curve to the left. Many economists believe that throughout Canada's history changes in monetary policy have been an important source of shifts in aggregate demand.

Shifts Arising from Government Purchases

The most direct way that policymakers shift the aggregate-demand curve is through government purchases. For example, suppose Parliament decides to reduce purchases of new ships for the armed forces. Because the quantity of goods and services demanded at any price level is lower, the aggregate-demand curve shifts to the left. Conversely, if provincial governments start building more highways, the result is a greater quantity of goods and services demanded at any price level, so the aggregate-demand curve shifts to the right.

Shifts Arising from Net Exports   Any event that changes net exports for a given price level also shifts aggregate demand. For instance, when the United States experiences a recession, it buys fewer goods from Canada. This reduces Canada's net exports and shifts the aggregate-demand curve for the Canadian economy to the left. When the United States recovers from its recession, it starts buying Canadian goods again, shifting the aggregate-demand curve to the right.

Net exports sometimes change because of movements in the exchange rate. Suppose, for instance, that international speculators bid up the value of the Canadian dollar in the market for foreign-currency exchange. This appreciation of the dollar would make Canadian goods more expensive compared with foreign goods, which would depress net exports and shift the aggregate-demand curve to the left. Conversely, a depreciation of the dollar stimulates net exports and shifts the aggregate-demand curve to the right.

Summary   In the next chapter we analyze the aggregate-demand curve in more detail. There we examine more precisely how the tools of monetary and fiscal policy can shift aggregate demand and whether policymakers should use these tools for that purpose. At this point, however, you should have some idea about why the aggregate-demand curve slopes downward and what kinds of

---

Table 19-1

THE AGGREGATE-DEMAND CURVE: SUMMARY

WHY DOES THE AGGREGATE-DEMAND CURVE SLOPE DOWNWARD?

1. *The Wealth Effect:* A lower price level increases real wealth, which encourages spending on consumption.
2. *The Interest Rate Effect:* A lower price level reduces the interest rate, which encourages spending on investment.
3. *The Real Exchange-Rate Effect:* A lower price level causes the real exchange rate to depreciate, which encourages spending on net exports.

WHY MIGHT THE AGGREGATE-DEMAND CURVE SHIFT?

1. *Shifts Arising from Consumption:* An event that makes consumers spend more at a given price level (a tax cut, a stock market boom) shifts the aggregate-demand curve to the right. An event that makes consumers spend less at a given price level (a tax hike, a stock market decline) shifts the aggregate-demand curve to the left.
2. *Shifts Arising from Investment:* An event that makes firms invest more at a given price level (optimism about the future, a fall in interest rates due to an increase in the money supply) shifts the aggregate-demand curve to the right. An event that makes firms invest less at a given price level (pessimism about the future, a rise in interest rates due to a decrease in the money supply) shifts the aggregate-demand curve to the left.
3. *Shifts Arising from Government Purchases:* An increase in government purchases of goods and services (greater spending on defence or highway construction) shifts the aggregate-demand curve to the right. A decrease in government purchases on goods and services (a cutback in defence or highway spending) shifts the aggregate-demand curve to the left.
4. *Shifts Arising from Net Exports:* An event that raises spending on net exports at a given price level (a boom experienced by a major trading partner, an exchange-rate depreciation) shifts the aggregate-demand curve to the right. An event that reduces spending on net exports at a given price level (a recession experienced by a major trading partner, an exchange-rate appreciation) shifts the aggregate-demand curve to the left.

events and policies can shift this curve. Table 19-1 summarizes what we have learned so far.

QUICK QUIZ: Explain the three reasons why the aggregate-demand curve slopes downward. ◆ Give an example of an event that would shift the aggregate-demand curve. In which way would this event shift the curve?

THE AGGREGATE-SUPPLY CURVE

The aggregate-supply curve tells us the total quantity of goods and services that firms produce and sell at any given price level. Unlike the aggregate-demand curve, which is always downward sloping, the aggregate-supply curve shows a relationship that depends crucially on the time horizon being examined. *In the long run, the aggregate-supply curve is vertical, whereas in the short run, the aggregate-supply curve is upward sloping.* To understand short-run economic fluctuations, and how the short-run behaviour of the economy deviates from its long-run behaviour, we need to examine both the long-run aggregate-supply curve and the short-run aggregate-supply curve.

WHY THE AGGREGATE-SUPPLY CURVE IS VERTICAL IN THE LONG RUN

What determines the quantity of goods and services supplied in the long run? We implicitly answered this question earlier in the book when we analyzed the process of economic growth. *In the long run, an economy's production of goods and services (its real GDP) depends on its supplies of labour, capital, and natural resources and on the available technology used to turn these factors of production into goods and services.* Because the price level does not affect these long-run determinants of real GDP, the long-run aggregate-supply curve is vertical, as in Figure 19-4. In other words, in the long run, the economy's labour, capital, natural resources, and technology determine the total quantity of goods and services supplied, and this quantity supplied is the same regardless of what the price level happens to be.

The vertical long-run aggregate-supply curve is, in essence, just an application of the classical dichotomy and monetary neutrality. As we have already discussed, classical macroeconomic theory is based on the assumption that real variables do not depend on nominal variables. The long-run aggregate-supply curve is consistent with this idea because it implies that the quantity of output (a real variable) does not depend on the level of prices (a nominal variable). As noted earlier, most economists believe that this principle works well when studying the economy over a period of many years, but not when studying year-to-year changes. Thus, the aggregate-supply curve is vertical only in the long run.

One might wonder why supply curves for specific goods and services can be upward sloping if the long-run aggregate-supply curve is vertical. The reason is that the supply of specific goods and services depends on *relative prices*—the prices of those goods and services compared with other prices in the economy. For example, when the price of ice cream rises, suppliers of ice cream increase their

Figure 19-4

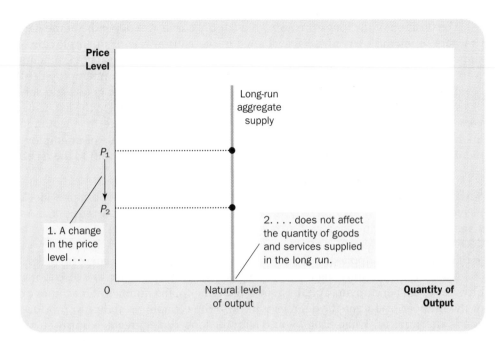

THE LONG-RUN AGGREGATE-SUPPLY CURVE.   In the long run, the quantity of output supplied depends on the economy's quantities of labour, capital, and natural resources and on the technology for turning these inputs into output. The quantity supplied does not depend on the overall price level. As a result, the long-run aggregate-supply curve is vertical at the natural level of output.

production, taking labour, milk, chocolate, and other inputs away from the production of other goods, such as frozen yogurt. By contrast, the economy's overall production of goods and services is limited by its labour, capital, natural resources, and technology. Thus, when all prices in the economy rise together, there is no change in the overall quantity of goods and services supplied.

WHY THE LONG-RUN AGGREGATE-SUPPLY CURVE MIGHT SHIFT

The position of the long-run aggregate-supply curve shows the quantity of goods and services predicted by classical macroeconomic theory. This level of production is sometimes called *potential output* or *full-employment output.* To be more accurate, we call it the *natural level of output* because it shows what the economy produces when the unemployment rate is at its natural, or normal, rate. The natural level of output is the level of production toward which the economy gravitates in the long run.

Any change in the economy that alters the natural level of output shifts the long-run aggregate-supply curve. Because output in the classical model depends on labour, capital, natural resources, and technological knowledge, we can categorize shifts in the long-run aggregate-supply curve as arising from these sources.

Shifts Arising from Labour   Imagine that an economy experiences an increase in immigration from abroad. Because there would be a greater number of workers, the quantity of goods and services supplied would increase. As a result, the long-run aggregate-supply curve would shift to the right. Conversely, if many workers left the economy to go abroad, the long-run aggregate-supply curve would shift to the left.

The position of the long-run aggregate-supply curve also depends on the natural rate of unemployment, so any change in the natural rate of unemployment shifts the long-run aggregate-supply curve. For example, if provincial governments were to raise the minimum wage substantially, the natural rate of unemployment would rise, and the economy would produce a smaller quantity of goods and services. As a result, the long-run aggregate-supply curve would shift to the left. Conversely, if a reform of the Employment Insurance system were to encourage unemployed workers to search harder for new jobs, the natural rate of unemployment would fall, and the long-run aggregate-supply curve would shift to the right.

Shifts Arising from Capital   An increase in the economy's capital stock increases productivity and, thereby, the quantity of goods and services supplied. As a result, the long-run aggregate-supply curve shifts to the right. Conversely, a decrease in the economy's capital stock decreases productivity and the quantity of goods and services supplied, shifting the long-run aggregate-supply curve to the left.

Notice that the same logic applies regardless of whether we are discussing physical capital or human capital. An increase either in the number of machines or in the number of university degrees will raise the economy's ability to produce goods and services. Thus, either would shift the long-run aggregate-supply curve to the right.

Shifts Arising from Natural Resources   An economy's production depends on its natural resources, including its land, minerals, and weather. A discovery of a new mineral deposit shifts the long-run aggregate-supply curve to the right. A change in weather patterns that makes farming more difficult shifts the long-run aggregate-supply curve to the left.

In many countries, important natural resources are imported from abroad. A change in the availability of these resources can also shift the aggregate-supply curve. As we discuss later in this chapter, events occurring in the world oil market have historically been an important source of shifts in aggregate supply.

Shifts Arising from Technological Knowledge   Perhaps the most important reason that the economy today produces more than it did a generation ago is that our technological knowledge has advanced. The invention of the computer, for instance, has allowed us to produce more goods and services from any given amounts of labour, capital, and natural resources. As a result, it has shifted the long-run aggregate-supply curve to the right.

Although not literally technological, many other events act like changes in technology. As Chapter 9 explains, opening up international trade has effects similar to inventing new production processes, so it also shifts the long-run aggregate-supply curve to the right. Conversely, if the government passed new regulations preventing firms from using some production methods, perhaps because they produced too much pollution, the result would be a leftward shift in the long-run aggregate-supply curve.

Summary   The long-run aggregate-supply curve reflects the classical model of the economy we developed in previous chapters. Any policy or event that raised real GDP in previous chapters can now be viewed as increasing the quantity of goods and services supplied and shifting the long-run aggregate-supply curve to the right. Any policy or event that lowered real GDP in previous chapters can now be viewed as decreasing the quantity of goods and services supplied and shifting the long-run aggregate-supply curve to the left.

A NEW WAY TO DEPICT LONG-RUN GROWTH AND INFLATION

Having introduced the economy's aggregate-demand curve and the long-run aggregate-supply curve, we now have a new way to describe the economy's long-run trends. Figure 19-5 illustrates the changes that occur in the economy from decade to decade. Notice that both curves are shifting. Although many forces govern the economy in the long run and can in principle cause such shifts, the two most important in practice are technology and monetary policy. Technological progress enhances the economy's ability to produce goods and services, and this continually shifts the long-run aggregate-supply curve to the right. At the same time, because the Bank of Canada increases the money supply over time, the aggregate-demand curve also shifts to the right. The figure illustrates the aggregate-demand curve shifting farther to the right than the aggregate-supply curve. The result is trend growth in output (as shown by increasing Y) and inflation (as shown by increasing P). If the Bank of Canada introduced smaller increases in the money supply, the shifts to the right in the aggregate-demand curve would also be smaller. The result would be lower inflation (as shown by smaller increases in P)

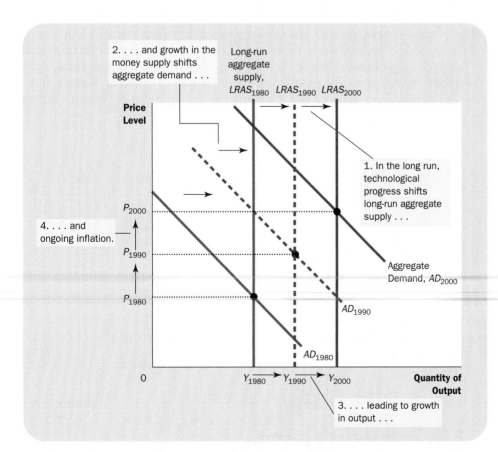

Figure 19-5

LONG-RUN GROWTH AND INFLATION IN THE MODEL OF AGGREGATE DEMAND AND AGGREGATE SUPPLY.   As the economy becomes better able to produce goods and services over time, primarily because of technological progress, the long-run aggregate-supply curve shifts to the right. At the same time, as the Bank of Canada increases the money supply, the aggregate-demand curve also shifts to the right. In this figure, output grows from Y_{1980} to Y_{1990} and then to Y_{2000}, and the price level rises from P_{1980} to P_{1990} and then to P_{2000}. Thus, the model of aggregate demand and aggregate supply offers a new way to describe the classical analysis of growth and inflation.

but no change in the trend growth in output. This is just another way of representing the classical analysis of growth and inflation we conducted in Chapters 12 and 16.

The purpose of developing the model of aggregate demand and aggregate supply, however, is not to dress our long-run conclusions in new clothing. Instead, it is to provide a framework for short-run analysis, as we will see in a moment. As we develop the short-run model, we keep the analysis simple by not showing the continuing growth and inflation depicted in Figure 19-5. But always remember that long-run trends provide the background for short-run fluctuations. *Short-run fluctuations in output and the price level should be viewed as deviations from the continuing long-run trends.*

WHY THE AGGREGATE-SUPPLY CURVE SLOPES UPWARD IN THE SHORT RUN

We now come to the key difference between the economy in the short run and in the long run: the behaviour of aggregate supply. As we have already discussed, the long-run aggregate-supply curve is vertical. By contrast, in the short run, the aggregate-supply curve is upward sloping, as shown in Figure 19-6. That is, over a period of a year or two, an increase in the overall level of prices in the economy tends to raise the quantity of goods and services supplied, and a decrease in the level of prices tends to reduce the quantity of goods and services supplied.

What causes this positive relationship between the price level and output? Macroeconomists have proposed three theories for the upward slope of the short-run aggregate-supply curve. In each theory, a specific market imperfection causes the supply side of the economy to behave differently in the short run than it does in the long run. Although each of the following theories will differ in detail, they share a common theme: The quantity of output supplied deviates from its long-run, or "natural," level when the price level deviates from the price level that

---

Figure 19-6

THE SHORT-RUN AGGREGATE-SUPPLY CURVE.   In the short run, a fall in the price level from P_1 to P_2 reduces the quantity of output supplied from Y_1 to Y_2. This positive relationship could be due to misperceptions, sticky wages, or sticky prices. Over time, perceptions, wages, and prices adjust, so this positive relationship is only temporary.

people expected. When the price level rises above the expected level, output rises above its natural level, and when the price level falls below the expected level, output falls below its natural level.

The Misperceptions Theory   One approach to the short-run aggregate-supply curve is the misperceptions theory. According to this theory, changes in the overall price level can temporarily mislead suppliers about what is happening in the individual markets in which they sell their output. As a result of these short-run misperceptions, suppliers respond to changes in the level of prices, and this response leads to an upward-sloping aggregate-supply curve.

To see how this might work, suppose the overall price level falls below the level that people expected. When suppliers see the prices of their products fall, they may mistakenly believe that their *relative* prices have fallen. For example, wheat farmers may notice a fall in the price of wheat before they notice a fall in the prices of the many items they buy as consumers. They may infer from this observation that the reward to producing wheat is temporarily low, and they may respond by reducing the quantity of wheat they supply. Similarly, workers may notice a fall in their nominal wages before they notice a fall in the prices of the goods they buy. They may infer that the reward to working is temporarily low and respond by reducing the quantity of labour they supply. In both cases, *a lower price level causes misperceptions about relative prices, and these misperceptions induce suppliers to respond to the lower price level by decreasing the quantity of goods and services supplied.*

The Sticky-Wage Theory   A second explanation of the upward slope of the short-run aggregate-supply curve is the sticky-wage theory. According to this theory, the short-run aggregate-supply curve slopes upward because nominal wages are slow to adjust, or are "sticky," in the short run. To some extent, the slow adjustment of nominal wages is attributable to long-term contracts between workers and firms that fix nominal wages, sometimes for as long as three years. In addition, this slow adjustment may be attributable to social norms and notions of fairness that influence wage setting and that change only slowly over time.

To see what sticky nominal wages mean for aggregate supply, imagine that a firm has agreed in advance to pay its workers a certain nominal wage based on what it expected the price level to be. If the price level P falls below the level that was expected and the nominal wage remains stuck at W, then the real wage W/P rises above the level the firm planned to pay. Because wages are a large part of a firm's production costs, a higher real wage means that the firm's real costs have risen. The firm responds to these higher costs by hiring less labour and producing a smaller quantity of goods and services. In other words, *because nominal wages do not adjust immediately to the price level, a lower price level makes employment and production less profitable, which induces firms to reduce the quantity of goods and services supplied.*

The Sticky-Price Theory   Recently, some economists have advocated a third approach to the short-run aggregate-supply curve, called the sticky-price theory. As we just discussed, the sticky-wage theory emphasizes that nominal wages adjust slowly over time. The sticky-price theory emphasizes that the prices of some goods and services also adjust sluggishly in response to changing economic conditions. This slow adjustment of prices occurs in part because there are costs to adjusting prices, called menu costs (explained in more detail in Chapter 16). These menu costs include the cost of printing and distributing catalogues and the time required to change price tags. As a result of these costs, prices as well as wages may be sticky in the short run.

To see the implications of sticky prices for aggregate supply, suppose that each firm in the economy announces its prices in advance based on the economic conditions it expects to prevail. Then, after prices are announced, the economy experiences an unexpected contraction in the money supply, which (as we have learned) will reduce the overall price level in the long run. Although some firms reduce their prices immediately in response to changing economic conditions, other firms may not want to incur additional menu costs and, therefore, may temporarily lag behind. Because these lagging firms have prices that are too high, their sales decline. Declining sales, in turn, cause these firms to cut back on production and employment. In other words, *because not all prices adjust instantly to changing conditions, an unexpected fall in the price level leaves some firms with higher-than-desired prices, and these higher-than-desired prices depress sales and induce firms to reduce the quantity of goods and services they produce.*

Summary   There are three alternative explanations for the upward slope of the short-run aggregate-supply curve: (1) misperceptions, (2) sticky wages, and (3) sticky prices. Economists debate the merits of these three theories. Most feel that there are elements of truth in all three. For our purposes in this book, the similarities of the theories are more important than the differences. All three theories suggest that output deviates from its natural level when the price level deviates from the price level that people expected. We can express this mathematically as follows:

$$\text{Quantity of output supplied} = \text{Natural level of output} + a\left(\text{Actual price level} - \text{Expected price level}\right)$$

where *a* is a number that determines how much output responds to unexpected changes in the price level.

Notice that each of the three theories of short-run aggregate supply emphasizes a problem that is likely to be only temporary. Whether the upward slope of the aggregate-supply curve is attributable to misperceptions, sticky wages, or sticky prices, these conditions will not persist forever. Eventually, as people adjust their expectations, misperceptions are corrected, nominal wages adjust, and prices become unstuck. In other words, the expected and actual price levels are equal in the long-run. In the long-run, then, our mathematical statement becomes

$$\text{Quantity of output supplied} = \text{Natural level of output,}$$

which indicates that the aggregate-supply curve is vertical rather than upward sloping. This is the mathematical description of the long-run aggregate-supply curve drawn in Figure 19-4.

WHY THE SHORT-RUN AGGREGATE-SUPPLY CURVE MIGHT SHIFT

The short-run aggregate-supply curve tells us the quantity of goods and services supplied in the short run for any given level of prices. We can think of this curve as similar to the long-run aggregate-supply curve but made upward sloping by the presence of misperceptions, sticky wages, and sticky prices. Thus, when thinking about what shifts the short-run aggregate-supply curve, we have to consider all of those variables that shift the long-run aggregate-supply curve plus a new variable—the expected price level—that influences misperceptions, sticky wages, and sticky prices.

Let's start with what we know about the long-run aggregate-supply curve. As we discussed earlier, shifts in the long-run aggregate-supply curve normally arise from changes in labour, capital, natural resources, or technological knowledge. These same variables shift the short-run aggregate-supply curve. For example, when an increase in the economy's capital stock increases productivity, both the long-run and short-run aggregate-supply curves shift to the right. When an increase in the minimum wage raises the natural rate of unemployment, both the long-run and short-run aggregate-supply curves shift to the left.

The important new variable that affects the position of the short-run aggregate-supply curve is people's expectation of the price level. As we have discussed, the quantity of goods and services supplied depends, in the short run, on misperceptions, sticky wages, and sticky prices. Yet perceptions, wages, and prices are set on the basis of expectations of the price level. So when expectations change, the short-run aggregate-supply curve shifts.

To make this idea more concrete, let's consider a specific theory of aggregate supply—the sticky-wage theory. According to this theory, when people expect the price level to be high, they tend to set wages high. High wages raise firms' costs and, for any given actual price level, reduce the quantity of goods and services that firms supply. Thus, when the expected price level rises, wages rise, costs rise, and firms choose to supply a smaller quantity of goods and services at any given actual price level. Thus, the short-run aggregate-supply curve shifts to the left. Conversely, when the expected price level falls, wages fall, costs fall, firms increase production, and the short-run aggregate-supply curve shifts to the right.

A similar logic applies in each theory of aggregate supply. The general lesson is the following: *An increase in the expected price level reduces the quantity of goods and services supplied and shifts the short-run aggregate-supply curve to the left. A decrease in the expected price level raises the quantity of goods and services supplied and shifts the short-run aggregate-supply curve to the right.* As we will see in the next section, this influence of expectations on the position of the short-run aggregate-supply curve plays a key role in reconciling the economy's behaviour in the short run with its behaviour in the long run. In the short run, expectations are fixed, and the economy finds itself at the intersection of the aggregate-demand curve and the short-run aggregate-supply curve. In the long run, expectations adjust, and the short-run aggregate-supply curve shifts. This shift ensures that the economy eventually finds itself at the intersection of the aggregate-demand curve and the long-run aggregate-supply curve.

You should now have some understanding about why the short-run aggregate-supply curve slopes upward and what events and policies can cause this curve to shift. Table 19-2 summarizes our discussion.

QUICK QUIZ: Explain why the long-run aggregate-supply curve is vertical. ◆ Explain three theories for why the short-run aggregate-supply curve is upward sloping.

Table 19-2

THE SHORT-RUN
AGGREGATE-SUPPLY
CURVE: SUMMARY

WHY DOES THE SHORT-RUN AGGREGATE-SUPPLY CURVE SLOPE UPWARD?

1. *The Misperceptions Theory:* An unexpectedly low price level leads some suppliers to think their relative prices have fallen, which induces a fall in production.
2. *The Sticky-Wage Theory:* An unexpectedly low price level raises the real wage, which causes firms to hire fewer workers and produce a smaller quantity of goods and services.
3. *The Sticky-Price Theory:* An unexpectedly low price level leaves some firms with higher-than-desired prices, which depresses their sales and leads them to cut back production.

WHY MIGHT THE SHORT-RUN AGGREGATE-SUPPLY CURVE SHIFT?

1. *Shifts Arising from Labour:* An increase in the quantity of labour available (perhaps due to a fall in the natural rate of unemployment) shifts the aggregate-supply curve to the right. A decrease in the quantity of labour available (perhaps due to a rise in the natural rate of unemployment) shifts the aggregate-supply curve to the left.
2. *Shifts Arising from Capital:* An increase in physical or human capital shifts the aggregate-supply curve to the right. A decrease in physical or human capital shifts the aggregate-supply curve to the left.
3. *Shifts Arising from Natural Resources:* An increase in the availability of natural resources shifts the aggregate-supply curve to the right. A decrease in the availability of natural resources shifts the aggregate-supply curve to the left.
4. *Shifts Arising from Technology:* An advance in technological knowledge shifts the aggregate-supply curve to the right. A decrease in the available technology (perhaps due to government regulation) shifts the aggregate-supply curve to the left.
5. *Shifts Arising from the Expected Price Level:* A decrease in the expected price level shifts the short-run aggregate-supply curve to the right. An increase in the expected price level shifts the short-run aggregate-supply curve to the left.

TWO CAUSES OF ECONOMIC FLUCTUATIONS

Now that we have introduced the model of aggregate demand and aggregate supply, we have the basic tools we need to analyze fluctuations in economic activity. In the next two chapters we will refine our understanding of how to use these tools. But even now we can use what we have learned about aggregate demand and aggregate supply to examine the two basic causes of short-run fluctuations.

Figure 19-7 shows an economy in long-run equilibrium. Equilibrium output and the price level are determined by the intersection of the aggregate-demand curve and the long-run aggregate-supply curve, shown as point A in the figure. At this point, output is at its natural level. The short-run aggregate-supply curve passes through this point as well, indicating that perceptions, wages, and prices

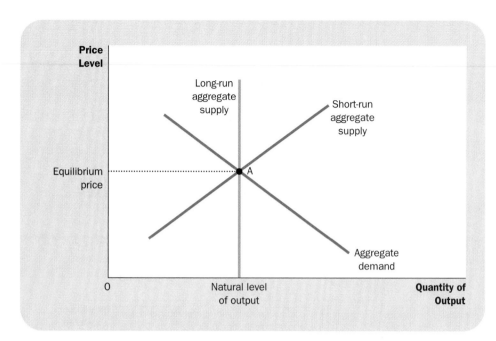

Figure 19-7

THE LONG-RUN EQUILIBRIUM. The long-run equilibrium of the economy is found where the aggregate-demand curve crosses the long-run aggregate-supply curve (point A). When the economy reaches this long-run equilibrium, perceptions, wages, and prices will have adjusted so that the short-run aggregate-supply curve crosses this point as well.

have fully adjusted to this long-run equilibrium. That is, when an economy is in its long-run equilibrium, perceptions, wages, and prices must have adjusted so that the intersection of aggregate demand with short-run aggregate supply is the same as the intersection of aggregate demand with long-run aggregate supply.

THE EFFECTS OF A SHIFT IN AGGREGATE DEMAND

Suppose that for some reason a wave of pessimism suddenly overtakes the economy. The cause might be a crash in the stock market or the outbreak of a war overseas. Because of this event, many people lose confidence in the future and alter their plans. Households may cut back on their spending and delay major purchases, firms may put off buying new equipment, or people may sell equities in order to hold more of their wealth in the form of money.

What is the impact of such a wave of pessimism on the economy? Such an event reduces the aggregate demand for goods and services. That is, for any given price level, households and firms now want to buy a smaller quantity of goods and services. As Figure 19-8 shows, the aggregate-demand curve shifts to the left from AD_1 to AD_2.

In this figure we can examine the effects of the fall in aggregate demand. In the short run, the economy moves along the initial short-run aggregate-supply curve AS_1, going from point A to point B. As the economy moves from point A to point B, output falls from Y_1 to Y_2, and the price level falls from P_1 to P_2. The falling level of output indicates that the economy is in a recession. Although not shown in the figure, firms respond to lower sales and production by reducing employment. Thus, the pessimism that caused the shift in aggregate demand is, to some extent, self-fulfilling: Pessimism about the future leads to falling incomes and rising unemployment.

Figure 19-8

A CONTRACTION IN AGGREGATE DEMAND.   A fall in aggregate demand, which might be due to a wave of pessimism in the economy, is represented with a leftward shift in the aggregate-demand curve from AD_1 to AD_2. The economy moves from point A to point B. Output falls from Y_1 to Y_2, and the price level falls from P_1 to P_2. Over time, as perceptions, wages, and prices adjust, the short-run aggregate-supply curve shifts to the right from AS_1 to AS_2, and the economy reaches point C, where the new aggregate-demand curve crosses the long-run aggregate-supply curve. The price level falls to P_3, and output returns to its natural level, Y_1.

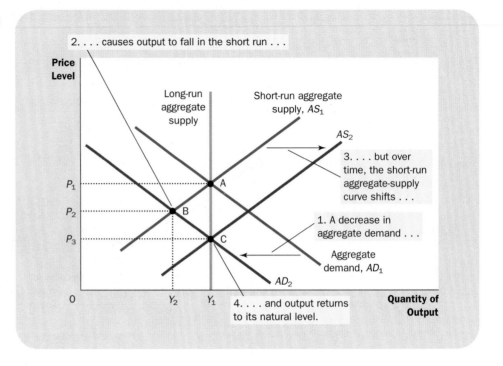

What should policymakers do when faced with such a recession? One possibility is to take action to increase aggregate demand. As we noted earlier, an increase in government spending or an increase in the money supply would increase the quantity of goods and services demanded at any price and, therefore, would shift the aggregate-demand curve to the right. If policymakers can act with sufficient speed and precision, they can offset the initial shift in aggregate demand, return the aggregate-demand curve back to AD_1, and bring the economy back to point A. (The next chapter discusses in more detail the ways in which monetary and fiscal policy influence aggregate demand, as well as some of the practical difficulties in using these policy instruments.)

Even without action by policymakers, the recession will remedy itself over a period of time. Because of the reduction in aggregate demand, the price level falls. Eventually, expectations catch up with this new reality, and the expected price level falls as well. Because the fall in the expected price level alters perceptions, wages, and prices, it shifts the short-run aggregate-supply curve to the right from AS_1 to AS_2 in Figure 19-8. This adjustment of expectations allows the economy over time to approach point C, where the new aggregate-demand curve (AD_2) crosses the long-run aggregate-supply curve.

In the new long-run equilibrium, point C, output is back to its natural level. Even though the wave of pessimism has reduced aggregate demand, the price level has fallen sufficiently (to P_3) to offset the shift in the aggregate-demand curve. Thus, in the long run, the shift in aggregate demand is reflected fully in the price level and not at all in the level of output. In other words, the long-run effect of a shift in aggregate demand is a nominal change (the price level is lower) but not a real change (output is the same).

To sum up, this story about shifts in aggregate demand has two important lessons:

◆ In the short run, shifts in aggregate demand cause fluctuations in the economy's output of goods and services.

◆ In the long run, shifts in aggregate demand affect the overall price level but do not affect output.

CASE STUDY BIG SHIFTS IN AGGREGATE DEMAND: TWO DEPRESSIONS AND WORLD WAR II

At the beginning of this chapter we established three key facts about economic fluctuations by looking at data since 1966. Let's now take a much longer look at Canadian economic history. Figure 19-9 shows data on real GDP per person going back to 1870. Most short-run economic fluctuations are hard to see in this figure; they are dwarfed by the fourteen-fold increase in GDP per person over the past 130 years. The figure also shows a trend line, which indicates how GDP per person would have grown over time had it increased by a steady 2.1 percent

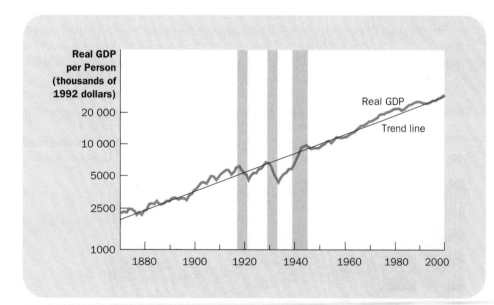

Figure 19-9

CANADIAN REAL GDP PER PERSON SINCE 1870. Over the course of Canadian economic history, three fluctuations stand out as being especially large. Between World War I and World War II, the economy suffered through the two worst depressions in Canadian history. During World War II the economy experienced rapid economic growth. These major fluctuations are usually explained as resulting from large shifts in aggregate demand.

NOTE: Real GDP is graphed here using a *proportional scale*. This means that equal distances on the vertical axis represent equal *percentage* changes. For example, the distance between 5000 and 10 000 (a 100 percent increase) is the same as the distance between 10 000 and 20 000 (a 100 percent increase). With such a scale, stable growth shows up as an upward sloping straight line. Thus the trend line shows the average rate of growth in real GDP per person since 1870: 2.1 percent per year.

SOURCES: Data for 1870–1925 from M.C. Urquhart, "New Estimates of Gross National Product, Canada, 1870–1926: Some Implications for Canadian Development" in S. Engerman and R. Gallman, eds., *Long-Term Factors in American Economic Growth* (Chicago: University of Chicago Press, 1986); data for 1926–1960 from F.H. Leacy, ed., *Historical Statistics of Canada*, 2nd ed. (Ottawa; Statistics Canada, 1983); data for 1961–2000 from Statistics Canada, CANSIM database, series D1, D23203, and D16439.

per year (the average rate of growth in real GDP per person since 1870). Clearly, the rate of growth in GDP has at times varied quite considerably from the average. Three episodes jump out as being particularly significant—the large drop in real GDP following World War I, another large drop in the early 1930s, and the rapid increase in real GDP in the 1940s. All three of these events are attributable to shifts in aggregate demand.

In what was up to then the most severe recession in Canada's history, real GDP per person fell by 27 percent between 1917 and 1921. The view of economic historians is that the 1917–21 depression was the result of two key events. One was the end of an investment and export boom. From 1900 to 1914, huge investments were made in settling Western Canada, mainly in the form of railway construction. This investment and the settlement that accompanied it, both of which were driven by a rapid increase in wheat prices, sparked a tremendous increase in Canadian exports. By 1914 this boom was ending, but by then a second source of increase in aggregate demand arose: World War I. The war brought with it a tremendous expansion of industry, which enabled growth in per capita GDP to continue. The end of the war, however, meant an end to war production. Now the industrial expansion of the war years was mirrored by industrial contraction following them. The end of the war and the end of the earlier investment and export boom resulted in a major contraction of aggregate demand and fall in GDP.

The economic calamity of the early 1930s is called the *Great Depression*, and as you can see from Figure 19-9 it is the largest economic downturn in Canadian history. Real GDP per person fell by 30 percent from 1929 to 1933, and unemployment rose from 4 percent to 25 percent. At the same time, the price level fell by 19 percent over these four years. Many other countries experienced similar declines in output and prices during this period.

Economic historians continue to debate the causes of the Great Depression in Canada, but most explanations centre on a large decline in aggregate demand. What caused this decline is still the subject of disagreement.

Many economists emphasize the decline in the money supply, which from 1929 to 1933 fell by 16 percent. As households' savings fell and bankers became

WARS: ONE WAY TO STIMULATE AGGREGATE DEMAND

more cautious and started holding greater reserves, the process of money creation under fractional-reserve banking went into reverse. Many economists suggest that the Great Depression was so severe because Canada did not have a central bank (the Bank of Canada was not created until 1935) that could have offset this fall in the money supply with expansionary open-market operations. Indeed, it was the economic problems of the Great Depression that led the government to establish the Bank of Canada.

Other economists emphasize that Canada's exposure to the U.S. economy because of the large amount of trade Canada has with the United States as an important cause of the Great Depression. Thus a fall in aggregate demand arising from a fall in net exports is also a likely contributor.

Finally, still other economists suggest the collapse of the stock market in 1929 as an explanation for the Great Depression. Stock prices fell by 90 percent during this period, depressing household wealth and thereby consumer spending. The collapse in stock prices may also have made it difficult for firms to finance new investment projects, leading to a fall in investment spending. Of course, all of these forces may have acted together to contract aggregate demand during the Great Depression.

The third significant episode identified in Figure 19-9—the economic boom of the 1940s—is easier to explain. The obvious cause of this boom was World War II. As Canada entered the war in 1939, the federal government had to devote more resources to the military. Government spending dramatically increased from 1939 to 1944. The huge expansion of aggregate demand increased real GDP per person by 60 percent over this period, and the unemployment rate fell from 15 percent to under 2 percent, the lowest in Canada's history.

THE EFFECTS OF A SHIFT IN AGGREGATE SUPPLY

Imagine once again an economy in its long-run equilibrium. Now suppose that suddenly some firms experience an increase in their costs of production. For example, bad weather might destroy some crops, driving up the cost of producing food products. Or a war in the Middle East might interrupt the shipping of crude oil, driving up the cost of producing oil products.

What is the macroeconomic impact of such an increase in production costs? For any given price level, firms now want to supply a smaller quantity of goods and services. Thus, as Figure 19-10 shows, the short-run aggregate-supply curve shifts to the left from AS_1 to AS_2. (Depending on the event, the long-run aggregate-supply curve might also shift. To keep things simple, however, we will assume that it does not.)

In this figure we can trace the effects of the leftward shift in aggregate supply. In the short run, the economy moves along the existing aggregate-demand curve, going from point A to point B. The output of the economy falls from Y_1 to Y_2, and the price level rises from P_1 to P_2. Because the economy is experiencing both *stagnation* (falling output) and *inflation* (rising prices), such an event is sometimes called **stagflation.**

What should policymakers do when faced with stagflation? As we will discuss more fully later in this book, there are no easy choices. One possibility is to do nothing. In this case, the output of goods and services remains depressed at Y_2 for

stagflation
a period of falling output and rising prices

Figure 19-10

AN ADVERSE SHIFT IN
AGGREGATE SUPPLY.   When
some event increases firms' costs,
the short-run aggregate-supply
curve shifts to the left from AS_1 to
AS_2. The economy moves from
point A to point B. The result is
stagflation: Output falls from Y_1
to Y_2, and the price level rises
from P_1 to P_2.

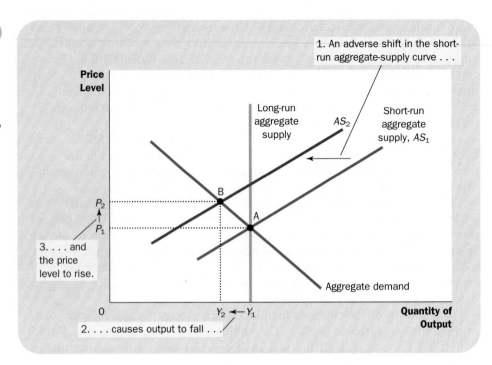

a while. Eventually, however, the recession will remedy itself as perceptions, wages, and prices adjust to the higher production costs. A period of low output and high unemployment, for instance, puts downward pressure on workers' wages. Lower wages, in turn, increase the quantity of output supplied. Over time, as the short-run aggregate-supply curve shifts back toward AS_1, the price level falls, and the quantity of output approaches its natural level. In the long run, the economy returns to point A, where the aggregate-demand curve crosses the long-run aggregate-supply curve. In this case, policymakers make the choice of maintaining a low price level at the cost of temporarily lower output and employment.

Alternatively, policymakers who control monetary and fiscal policy might attempt to offset some of the effects of the shift in the short-run aggregate-supply curve by shifting the aggregate-demand curve. This possibility is shown in Figure 19-11. In this case, changes in policy shift the aggregate-demand curve to the right from AD_1 to AD_2—exactly enough to prevent the shift in aggregate supply from affecting output. The economy moves directly from point A to point C. Output remains at its natural level, and the price level rises from P_1 to P_3. In this case, policymakers are said to *accommodate* the shift in aggregate supply because they allow the increase in costs to affect the level of prices permanently. Policymakers make the choice of maintaining a constant level of real output and employment at the cost of a permanently higher price level.

To sum up, this story about shifts in aggregate supply has two important implications:

◆ Shifts in aggregate supply can cause stagflation—a combination of recession (falling output) and inflation (rising prices).

◆ Policymakers who can influence aggregate demand cannot offset both of these adverse effects simultaneously.

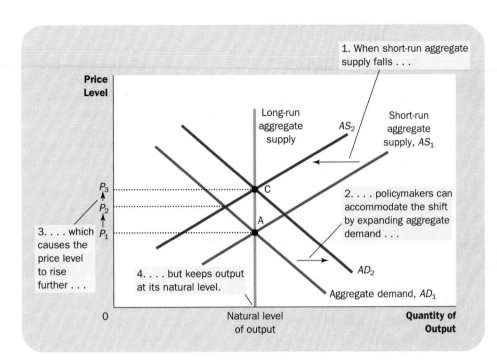

Figure 19-11

ACCOMMODATING AN ADVERSE SHIFT IN AGGREGATE SUPPLY. Faced with an adverse shift in aggregate supply from AS_1 to AS_2, policymakers who can influence aggregate demand might try to shift the aggregate-demand curve to the right from AD_1 to AD_2. The economy would move from point A to point C. This policy would prevent the supply shift from reducing output in the short run, but the price level would permanently rise from P_1 to P_3.

CASE STUDY   OIL AND THE ECONOMY

Some of the largest economic fluctuations in the Canadian economy since 1970 have originated in the oil fields of the Middle East. Crude oil is a key input into the production of many goods and services, and much of the world's oil comes from Saudi Arabia, Kuwait, and other Middle Eastern countries. When some event (usually political in origin) reduces the supply of crude oil flowing from this region, the price of oil rises around the world. Canadian firms that produce gasoline, tires, and many other products experience rising costs. The result is a leftward shift in the aggregate-supply curve, which in turn leads to stagflation. In major oil-producing provinces like Alberta and Saskatchewan, increases in oil prices also cause an increase in aggregate demand because provincial income and net exports rise. For Canada as a whole, however, the effect on aggregate supply is the dominant influence.

The first episode of this sort occurred in the mid-1970s. The countries with large oil reserves got together as members of OPEC, the Organization of Petroleum Exporting Countries. OPEC is a *cartel*—a group of sellers that attempts to thwart competition and reduce production in order to raise prices. And, indeed, oil prices rose substantially. From 1973 to 1975, the world price of oil almost tripled. Oil-importing countries around the world experienced simultaneous inflation and recession. In Canada, the inflation rate as measured by the GDP price deflator exceeded 14 percent in 1974. The unemployment rate rose from 5.5 percent in 1973 to 7.0 percent in 1975. Not surprisingly, the effects of the increase in oil prices differed considerably across oil-exporting and oil-importing provinces. For example, from 1973 to 1975, the unemployment rate in Alberta fell from 5.3 percent to 4.1 percent, while the unemployment rate in Ontario increased from 4.3 percent to 6.3 percent.

IN THE NEWS

How Oil Price Changes Affect Aggregate Supply

WE HAVE SEEN HOW CHANGES IN THE price of oil affect other prices and the level of output by affecting the position of the aggregate-supply curve. Large fluctuations in the price of oil can therefore have serious economic consequences. According to the following article, however, there are reasons to believe that oil price shocks have a smaller effect on the economy than they did in the past.

Oil's Pleasant Surprise

Could the bad old days of stagflation be about to return? Since OPEC agreed to supply cuts in March, the price of crude oil has jumped to almost $26 a barrel, up from less than $10 last December and its highest since the Gulf War in 1991. This near-tripling of oil prices evokes scary memories of the 1973 oil shock, when prices quadrupled, and 1979–80, when they also almost tripled. Both previous shocks resulted in double-digit inflation and global recession. So where are the headlines warning of gloom and doom this time?

Their absence is even more striking given that, at the start of the year, many commentators (including, rather prominently, this newspaper) expected prices to fall, not rise. OPEC's agreement to cut output has so far proved more durable than many predicted. The oil price was given another nudge up this week when Iraq suspended oil exports in a showdown with the UN over sanctions. Strengthening economic growth, at the same time as winter grips the Northern Hemisphere, could push the price higher still in the short term.

Yet there are good reasons to expect the economic consequences now to be less severe than in the 1970s. The sharp rise in oil prices follows an equally sharp collapse over the previous two years, when prices fell by more than half to their lowest level in real terms since before the 1973 shock. Even now, prices are not much higher than in early 1997.

Moreover, in most countries the cost of crude oil now accounts for a smaller share of the price of gasoline than it did in the 1970s. In Europe, taxes account for up to four-fifths of the retail price, so even quite big changes in the price of crude have a more muted effect on pump prices than in the past.

Rich economies are also less dependent on oil than they were, and so

Almost the same thing happened again a few years later. In the late 1970s, the OPEC countries again restricted the supply of oil to raise the price. From 1978 to 1981, the price of oil more than doubled. Once again, the costs to firms that used oil as an input in the production process increased as a result. This second shock to oil prices prompted the federal government to introduce the National Energy Program (NEP) in 1980. The NEP was intended to slow the growth in oil prices in Canada to below the rate of growth in world markets, and thereby minimize the stagflation effects of the most recent jump in oil prices. The NEP helped industries that used oil as an input, but it also harmed industries that produced oil. As a result, although this policy response to the OPEC price shock reduced the stagflation effects for Canada on average, it did so by favouring some industries over others and, in oil-producing provinces, caused a great deal of bitterness toward the federal government.

The world market for oil can also be a source of favourable shifts in aggregate supply. In 1986 squabbling broke out among members of OPEC. Member countries reneged on their agreements to restrict oil production. In the world market for crude oil, prices fell by about half. This fall in oil prices reduced costs to firms that used oil as an input in the production process. As a result, Canada's aggregate-supply curve shifted to the right and the Canadian economy experienced the opposite of stagflation: Output grew rapidly, and the Canadian unem-

CHANGES IN MIDDLE EASTERN OIL PRODUCTION ARE ONE SOURCE OF CANADIAN ECONOMIC FLUCTUATIONS.

less sensitive to swings in the oil price. Energy conservation, a shift to other fuels, and a decline in the importance of heavy, energy-intensive industries have reduced oil consumption. Software, consultancy, and mobile telephones use far less oil than steel or car production. For each dollar of GDP (in constant prices) rich economies now use nearly 5 percent less oil than in 1973. The OECD estimates in its latest *Economic Outlook* that, if oil prices averaged $22 a barrel for a full year, compared with $13 in 1998, this would increase the oil import bill in rich economies by only 0.25–0.5 percent of GDP. That is less than one-quarter of the income loss in 1974 or 1980. On the other hand, oil-importing emerging economies—to which heavy industry has shifted—have become more energy-intensive, and so could be more seriously squeezed. . . .

One more reason not to lose sleep over the surge in oil prices is that, unlike the rises in the 1970s, it has not occurred against the backdrop of general commodity-price inflation and global excess demand. A sizable chunk of the world is only just emerging from recession. *The Economist's* commodity price index is broadly unchanged from a year ago. In 1973 commodity prices jumped by 70 percent, and in 1979 by almost 30 percent.

Refining the Argument

Even if the impact will be more modest than in the past, dearer oil will still leave some mark. Inflation will be higher and output lower than they would be otherwise. The OECD's rule of thumb is that a $10 increase, if sustained for a year, would increase the inflation rate in rich economies by about half a percentage point and knock about a quarter-point off growth.

The impact of higher oil prices varies by country too. Perhaps the biggest risk is in America, where rising oil prices may push the inflation rate higher than is currently predicted. The slide in oil prices in recent years was one of the main factors that helped to hold down American inflation, so prolonging the country's long economic expansion. That positive factor is now going into reverse. Higher oil prices have already helped to lift America's inflation rate to 2.6 percent in October, up from 1.5 percent a year ago; the latest rise in oil prices could well push it above 3 percent. The core inflation rate remains relatively subdued, but headline inflation could still spill into wages and hence other prices. If it does, the [Federal Reserve] might be forced to raise interest rates by more than is now forecast. So OPEC could yet do more damage than most people expect.

SOURCE: *The Economist,* November 27, 1999, p. 16.

ployment rate fell from 10.5 percent in 1985 to 7.5 percent in 1989. Once again, however, the effects of the decrease in oil prices differed considerably across oil-exporting and oil-importing provinces. For example, from 1985 to 1987, the unemployment rate in Alberta remained constant at about 10.0 percent, while the unemployment rate in Ontario fell from 8.0 percent to 6.1 percent.

Clearly, the world market for crude oil is often very volatile. This volatility is in part a reflection of the inherent instability of cartels. Members of cartels have an incentive to undercut the agreed-upon price and, in doing so, increase their share of the market. Because all members of the cartel face this incentive, the price agreed on by the cartel occasionally collapses. The volatility of crude oil prices also reflects the political turmoil associated with the Middle East in recent years. Both of these influences were behind the collapse of world oil prices in early 1998. Between October 1997 and December 1998, the price of crude oil fell by 41 percent. Soon after this collapse in prices, however, OPEC met and decided to restrict output. The result was that from December 1998 to November 2000 the price of crude oil *increased* by 200 percent.

Fortunately, the Canadian economy is far less dependent on oil than it once was. For each dollar of real GDP produced, Canada uses only about half the amount of oil that it did before the first OPEC price shock in 1973. As a result, changes in the price of oil now have a smaller impact on Canada's aggregate-supply curve, and the macroeconomic impact of large changes in oil prices is less likely to resemble the stagflations of the 1970s.

QUICK QUIZ: Suppose that the election of a popular prime minister suddenly increases people's confidence in the future. Use the model of aggregate demand and aggregate supply to analyze the effect on the economy.

CONCLUSION

This chapter has achieved two goals. First, we have discussed some of the important facts about short-run fluctuations in economic activity. Second, we have introduced a basic model to explain those fluctuations, called the model of aggregate demand and aggregate supply. In the next two chapters we look at each piece of this model in more detail in order to understand more fully what causes fluctuations in the economy and how policymakers might respond to these fluctuations.

Now that we have a preliminary understanding of this model, it is worthwhile to step back from it and consider its history. How did this model of short-run fluctuations develop? The answer is that this model, to a large extent, is a byproduct of the Great Depression of the 1930s. Economists and policymakers at the time were puzzled about what had caused this calamity and were uncertain about how to deal with it.

In 1936, economist John Maynard Keynes published a book titled *The General Theory of Employment, Interest, and Money*, which attempted to explain short-run economic fluctuations in general and the Great Depression in particular. Keynes's primary message was that recessions and depressions can occur because of inadequate aggregate demand for goods and services. Keynes had long been a critic of classical economic theory—the theory we examined in Chapters 12 through 18—because it could explain only the long-run effects of policies. A few years before offering *The General Theory*, Keynes had written the following about classical economics:

> The long run is a misleading guide to current affairs. In the long run we are all dead. Economists set themselves too easy, too useless a task if in tempestuous seasons they can only tell us when the storm is long past, the ocean will be flat.

Keynes's message was aimed at policymakers as well as economists. As the world's economies suffered with high unemployment, Keynes advocated policies to increase aggregate demand, including government spending on public works. In the next chapter we examine in detail how policymakers can try to use the tools of monetary and fiscal policy to influence aggregate demand. The analysis in the next chapter, as well as in this one, owes much to the legacy of John Maynard Keynes.

Summary

- All societies experience short-run economic fluctuations around long-run trends. These fluctuations are irregular and largely unpredictable. When recessions do occur, real GDP and other measures of income, spending, and production fall, and unemployment rises.

- Economists analyze short-run economic fluctuations using the model of aggregate demand and aggregate supply. According to this model, the output of goods and services and the overall level of prices adjust to balance aggregate demand and aggregate supply.

- The aggregate-demand curve slopes downward for three reasons. First, a lower price level raises the real value of households' money holdings, which stimulates consumer spending. Second, a lower price level reduces the quantity of money households demand; as households try to convert money into interest-bearing assets, interest rates fall, which stimulates investment spending. Third, a lower price level reduces the real exchange rate. This depreciation makes Canadian-produced goods and services cheaper relative to foreign-produced goods and services, and in this way stimulates net exports.

- Any event or policy that raises consumption, investment, government purchases, or net exports at a given price level increases aggregate demand. Any event or policy that reduces consumption, investment, government purchases, or net exports at a given price level decreases aggregate demand.

- The long-run aggregate-supply curve is vertical. In the long run, the quantity of goods and services supplied depends on the economy's labour, capital, natural resources, and technology, but not on the overall level of prices.

- Three theories have been proposed to explain the upward slope of the short-run aggregate-supply curve.

- According to the misperceptions theory, an unexpected fall in the price level leads suppliers to mistakenly believe that their relative prices have fallen, which induces them to reduce production. According to the sticky-wage theory, an unexpected fall in the price level temporarily raises real wages, which induces firms to reduce employment and production. According to the sticky-price theory, an unexpected fall in the price level leaves some firms with prices that are temporarily too high, which reduces their sales and causes them to cut back production. All three theories imply that output deviates from its natural rate when the price level deviates from the price level that people expected.

- Events that alter the economy's ability to produce output, such as changes in labour, capital, natural resources, or technology, shift the short-run aggregate-supply curve (and may shift the long-run aggregate-supply curve as well). In addition, the position of the short-run aggregate-supply curve depends on the expected price level.

- One possible cause of economic fluctuations is a shift in aggregate demand. When the aggregate-demand curve shifts to the left, for instance, output and prices fall in the short run. Over time, as a change in the expected price level causes perceptions, wages, and prices to adjust, the short-run aggregate-supply curve shifts to the right, and the economy returns to its natural level of output at a new, lower price level.

- A second possible cause of economic fluctuations is a shift in aggregate supply. When the aggregate-supply curve shifts to the left, the short-run effect is falling output and rising prices—a combination called stagflation. Over time, as perceptions, wages, and prices adjust, the price level falls back to its original level, and output recovers.

Key Concepts

Questions for Review

1. Name two macroeconomic variables that decline when the economy goes into a recession. Name one macroeconomic variable that rises during a recession.

2. Draw a diagram with aggregate demand, short-run aggregate supply, and long-run aggregate supply. Be careful to label the axes correctly.

3. List and explain the three reasons why the aggregate-demand curve is downward sloping.

4. Explain why the long-run aggregate-supply curve is vertical.

5. List and explain the three theories for why the short-run aggregate-supply curve is upward sloping.

6. What might shift the aggregate-demand curve to the left? Use the model of aggregate demand and aggregate supply to trace through the effects of such a shift.

7. What might shift the aggregate-supply curve to the left? Use the model of aggregate demand and aggregate supply to trace through the effects of such a shift.

Problems and Applications

1. Why do you think that investment is more variable over the business cycle than consumer spending? Which category of consumer spending do you think would be most volatile: durable goods (such as furniture and car purchases), nondurable goods (such as food and clothing), or services (such as haircuts and medical care)? Why?

2. Suppose that the economy is undergoing a recession because of a fall in aggregate demand.
   a. Using an aggregate-demand/aggregate-supply diagram, depict the current state of the economy.
   b. What is happening to the unemployment rate?
   c. "Capacity utilization" is a measure of how intensively the capital stock is being used. In a recession, is capacity utilization above or below its long-run average? Explain.

3. Explain whether each of the following events will increase, decrease, or have no effect on long-run aggregate supply:
   a. Canada experiences a wave of immigration.
   b. Provincial governments raise the minimum wage to $10 per hour.
   c. Intel invents a new and more powerful computer chip.
   d. A severe ice storm damages factories along the east coast.

4. In Figure 19-8, how does the unemployment rate at points B and C compare with the unemployment rate at point A? Under the sticky-wage explanation of the short-run aggregate-supply curve, how does the real wage at points B and C compare with the real wage at point A?

5. Explain why the following statements are false:
   a. "The aggregate-demand curve slopes downward because it is the horizontal sum of the demand curves for individual goods."
   b. "The long-run aggregate-supply curve is vertical because economic forces do not affect long-run aggregate supply."
   c. "If firms adjusted their prices every day, then the short-run aggregate-supply curve would be horizontal."
   d. "Whenever the economy enters a recession, its long-run aggregate-supply curve shifts to the left."

6. For each of the three theories for the upward slope of the short-run aggregate-supply curve, carefully explain the following:
   a. how the economy recovers from a recession and returns to its long-run equilibrium without any policy intervention
   b. what determines the speed of that recovery

7. Suppose the Bank of Canada expands the money supply, but because the public expects this action, it simultaneously raises its expectation of the price level. What will happen to output and the price level in the short run? Compare this result with the outcome if the Bank of Canada expanded the money supply but the public didn't change its expectation of the price level.

8. Suppose that the economy is currently in a recession. If policymakers take no action, how will the economy evolve over time? Explain in words and using an aggregate-demand/aggregate-supply diagram.

9. Suppose workers and firms suddenly believe that inflation will be quite high over the coming year.

Suppose also that the economy begins in long-run equilibrium, and the aggregate-demand curve does not shift.

a. What happens to nominal wages? What happens to real wages?

b. Using an aggregate-demand/aggregate-supply diagram, show the effect of the change in expectations on both the short-run and long-run levels of prices and output.

c. Were the expectations of high inflation accurate? Explain.

10. Explain whether each of the following events shifts the short-run aggregate-supply curve, the aggregate-demand curve, both, or neither. For each event that does shift a curve, use a diagram to illustrate the effect on the economy.

a. Households decide to save a larger share of their income.

b. Okanagan peach orchards suffer a prolonged period of below-freezing temperatures.

c. Increased job opportunities overseas cause many people to leave the country.

11. For each of the following events, explain the short-run and long-run effects on output and the price level, assuming policymakers take no action:

a. The stock market declines sharply, reducing consumers' wealth.

b. The federal government increases spending on national defence.

c. A technological improvement raises productivity.

d. A recession overseas causes foreigners to buy fewer Canadian goods.

12. Suppose that firms become very optimistic about future business conditions and invest heavily in new capital equipment.

a. Use an aggregate-demand/aggregate-supply diagram to show the short-run effect of this optimism on the economy. Label the new levels of prices and real output. Explain in words why the aggregate quantity of output *supplied* changes.

b. Now use the diagram from part (a) to show the new long-run equilibrium of the economy. (For now, assume there is no change in the long-run aggregate-supply curve.) Explain in words why the aggregate quantity of output *demanded* changes between the short run and the long run.

c. How might the investment boom affect the long-run aggregate-supply curve? Explain.

20

THE INFLUENCE OF MONETARY AND FISCAL POLICY ON AGGREGATE DEMAND

IN THIS CHAPTER YOU WILL . . .

Learn the theory of liquidity preference as a short-run theory of the interest rate

Analyze how monetary policy affects interest rates and aggregate demand in open and closed economies

Analyze how fiscal policy affects interest rates and aggregate demand in open and closed economies

Discuss the debate over whether policymakers should try to stabilize the economy

Imagine that you are the governor of the Bank of Canada and therefore are in charge of setting monetary policy. You observe that the federal government has decided to cut government spending in order to eliminate its budget deficit. How should the Bank of Canada respond to this change in fiscal policy? Should it expand the money supply, contract the money supply, or leave the money supply the same?

To answer this question, you need to consider the impact of monetary and fiscal policy on the economy. In the preceding chapter we saw how to explain short-run economic fluctuations using the model of aggregate demand and aggregate supply. When the aggregate-demand curve or the aggregate-supply curve shifts, the result is fluctuations in the economy's overall output of goods and services and overall level of prices. As we noted in the previous chapter, monetary and fiscal policy can each influence aggregate demand. Thus, a change in one of these policies can lead to short-run fluctuations in output and prices. Policymakers will want to anticipate this effect and, perhaps, adjust the other policy in response.

In this chapter we examine in more detail how the government's tools of monetary and fiscal policy influence the position of the aggregate-demand curve. We have previously discussed the long-run effects of these policies. In Chapters 12 and 13 we saw how fiscal policy affects saving, investment, and long-run economic growth. In Chapters 15 and 16 we saw how the Bank of Canada controls the money supply and how the money supply affects the price level in the long run. In Chapters 17 and 18 we looked at macroeconomic relationships in open economies and saw how the real exchange rate, net exports, and net foreign investment are determined.

In this chapter we will also see how the tools of monetary and fiscal policy can shift the aggregate-demand curve and, in doing so, affect short-run economic fluctuations. We will also see that how policy tools affect the position of the aggregate-demand curve depends on the degree to which the economy is closed or open to trade in goods, services, and financial capital. In this chapter we begin our discussions of the influence of monetary and fiscal policy on aggregate demand by assuming a closed economy. This approach simplifies the analysis and puts us on the road to understanding what will happen in a small open economy. We will then show the implications for fiscal and monetary policy of Canada's being a small open economy.

As we have already learned, many factors influence aggregate demand besides monetary and fiscal policy. In particular, desired spending by households and firms determines the overall demand for goods and services. When desired spending changes, aggregate demand shifts. If policymakers do not respond, such shifts in aggregate demand cause short-run fluctuations in output and employment. As a result, monetary and fiscal policymakers sometimes use the policy levers at their disposal to try to offset these shifts in aggregate demand and thereby stabilize the economy. Here we discuss the theory behind these policy actions and some of the difficulties that arise in using this theory in practice.

HOW MONETARY POLICY INFLUENCES AGGREGATE DEMAND

The aggregate-demand curve shows the total quantity of goods and services demanded in the economy for any price level. As you may recall from the preceding chapter, the aggregate-demand curve slopes downward for three reasons:

◆ *The wealth effect:* A lower price level raises the real value of households' money holdings, and higher real wealth stimulates consumer spending.

◆ *The interest rate effect:* A lower price level lowers the interest rate as people try to lend out their excess money holdings, and the lower interest rate stimulates investment spending.

◆   *The real exchange-rate effect:* A lower price level reduces the real exchange rate. This depreciation makes Canadian-produced goods and services cheaper relative to foreign-produced goods and services. As a result, Canadian net exports rise.

These three effects should not be viewed as alternative theories. Instead, they occur simultaneously to increase the quantity of goods and services demanded when the price level falls and to decrease it when the price level rises.

Although all three effects work together in explaining the downward slope of the aggregate-demand curve, they are not of equal importance. Because money holdings are a small part of household wealth, the wealth effect is the least important of the three. In a closed economy, the real exchange-rate effect is nonexistent, leaving the interest rate effect as the most important reason for the downward slope of the aggregate-demand curve. Since it is our goal to begin our discussion of the influence of monetary and fiscal policy on aggregate demand by first assuming a closed economy, we examine the interest rate effect in more detail. When thinking about Canada, however, we need to keep in mind that exports and imports make up a large proportion of the Canadian economy and that over the past ten years their share of the economy has grown steadily. As a result, the real exchange-rate effect is an increasingly important explanation for why Canada's aggregate-demand curve slopes downward.

To begin developing an understanding of how policy influences aggregate demand, we examine the interest rate effect in more detail. This will involve discussing the **theory of liquidity preference.** After we develop this theory, we use it to understand the downward slope of the aggregate-demand curve and how monetary policy shifts this curve in a closed economy. We will then turn our attention to how monetary policy shifts the aggregate-demand curve in a small open economy.

theory of liquidity preference
Keynes's theory that the interest rate adjusts to bring money supply and money demand into balance

THE THEORY OF LIQUIDITY PREFERENCE

In his classic book, *The General Theory of Employment, Interest, and Money,* John Maynard Keynes proposed the theory of liquidity preference to explain what factors determine the economy's interest rate. The theory is, in essence, just an application of supply and demand. According to Keynes, the interest rate adjusts to balance the supply and demand for money.

You may recall from Chapter 11 that economists distinguish between two interest rates: The *nominal interest rate* is the interest rate as usually reported, and the *real interest rate* is the interest rate corrected for the effects of inflation. Which interest rate are we now trying to explain? The answer is both. In the analysis that follows, we hold constant the expected rate of inflation. (This assumption is reasonable for studying the economy in the short run, as we are now doing). Thus, when the nominal interest rate rises or falls, the real interest rate that people expect to earn rises or falls as well. For the rest of this chapter, when we refer to changes in the interest rate, you should envision the real and nominal interest rates moving in the same direction.

Let's now develop the theory of liquidity preference by considering the supply and demand for money and how each depends on the interest rate.

Money Supply   The first piece of the theory of liquidity preference is the supply of money. As we first discussed in Chapter 15, the money supply in the Canadian economy is controlled by the Bank of Canada. The Bank of Canada alters the money supply using two methods. The first is to change the quantity of reserves in the banking system through what is known as an open-market operation. One form that open-market operations take involves the Bank of Canada buying and selling federal government bonds in the bond market. When the Bank of Canada sells government bonds, the dollars it receives for the bonds are withdrawn from the banking system, and bank reserves fall. These changes in bank reserves, in turn, lead to changes in banks' ability to make loans and create money. A different form of open-market operation involves the Bank of Canada buying and selling foreign currencies in the market for foreign-currency exchange. These sales and purchases are referred to as foreign exchange market operations. As we discussed in Chapter 15, if the Bank of Canada buys U.S.$100 million in the market for foreign-currency exchange for CDN$150 million, the Canadian money supply increases immediately by $150 million. If the Bank of Canada sells foreign currency from its foreign exchange reserves, it gets Canadian dollars in exchange. Those Canadian dollars are withdrawn from circulation, so the Canadian money supply is reduced. The second method the Bank of Canada uses to alter the money supply is by changing the bank rate. The bank rate is the interest rate on the loans that the Bank of Canada makes to commercial banks. Commercial banks may borrow from the Bank of Canada if they find that their reserves are inadequate. By increasing the bank rate, the Bank of Canada makes such loans more expensive and thus discourages commercial banks from borrowing reserves. Therefore, an increase in the bank rate effectively reduces the quantity of reserves in the banking system, which in turn reduces the money supply. Similarly, a decrease in the bank rate makes it less expensive for banks to borrow from the Bank of Canada and thus effectively increases the quantity of reserves in the banking system, which in turn increases the money supply.

Open-market operations and changing the bank rate are the most important methods used by the Bank of Canada for changing the money supply. As we will see, the Bank of Canada's decision whether or not to buy and sell dollars in the market for foreign-currency exchange has important implications for the effect of monetary and fiscal policy on aggregate demand.

The relationship between money demand and money supply is shown in Figure 20-1, with the quantity of money on the horizontal axis and the interest rate on the vertical axis. We assume that the Bank of Canada controls the money supply directly. In particular, we assume that the supply of money is not affected at all by changes in the interest rate. For this reason, the money-supply curve is a vertical line.

Money Demand   The second piece of the theory of liquidity preference is the demand for money. As a starting point for understanding money demand, recall that any asset's *liquidity* refers to the ease with which that asset is converted into the economy's medium of exchange. Money is the economy's medium of exchange, so it is by definition the most liquid asset available. The liquidity of money explains the demand for it: People choose to hold money instead of other assets that offer higher rates of return because money can be used to buy goods and services.

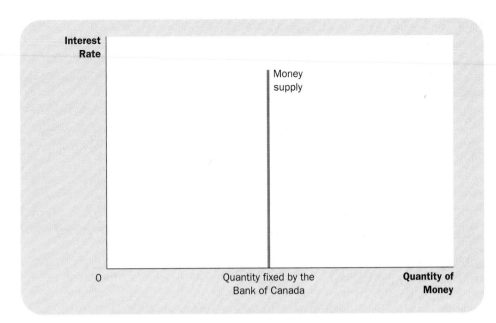

Figure 20-1

THE SUPPLY OF MONEY.   The supply of money in an economy is fixed by the central bank, which in Canada is the Bank of Canada. Because the quantity of money supplied does not depend on the interest rate, the supply curve is vertical.

Although there are many determinants of the quantity of money demanded, the theory of liquidity preference emphasizes that one of the most important is the interest rate. The reason is that the interest rate is the opportunity cost of holding money. That is, when you hold wealth as cash in your wallet instead of as an interest-bearing bond, you lose the interest you could have earned. An increase in the interest rate raises the cost of holding money and, as a result, reduces the quantity of money demanded. A decrease in the interest rate reduces the cost of holding money and raises the quantity demanded. Thus, as shown in Figure 20-2, the money-demand curve slopes downward.

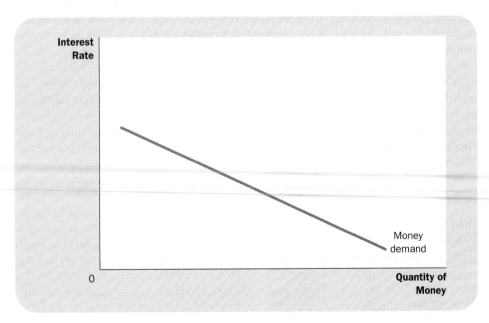

Figure 20-2

THE DEMAND FOR MONEY. Because the interest rate measures the opportunity cost of holding noninterest-bearing money instead of interest-bearing bonds, an increase in the interest rate reduces the quantity of money demanded. A downward sloping demand curve represents this negative relationship.

Figure 20-3

SHIFTS IN THE DEMAND FOR MONEY. People hold money in order to buy goods and services. If the dollar value of transactions increases because of an increase in either prices or GDP, then for any interest rate (r_1), people will hold more of their assets as money (increasing from (M_1^d to M_3^d). As a result, the money-demand curve shifts to the right. If the dollar value of transactions decreases because of a decrease in either price or GDP, then for any interest rate (r_1) people will hold less of their assets as money (decreasing from M_1^d to M_2^d). As a result, the money-demand curve shifts to the left.

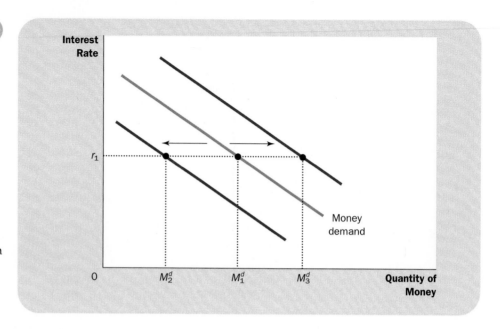

The other key determinant of the quantity of money demanded is the fact that money is used to buy goods and services. As a result, when either the quantity or the price of goods and services increases, people need to hold more of their assets in the form of money. The quantity of goods and services that people buy is simply equal to GDP. The price of goods and services in the economy is represented by a price index such as the consumer price index or the GDP deflator. The product of these two measures is the dollar value of all transactions in the economy. Figure 20-3 shows the influence on money demand of an increase in either the price level or the level of GDP. For a given interest rate, an increase in the dollar value of transactions causes the demand for money to increase. As a result, the money-demand curve shifts to the right. For a given interest rate, a decrease in the dollar value of transactions causes the demand for money to decrease. As a result, the money-demand curve shifts to the left.

Equilibrium in the Money Market According to the theory of liquidity preference, the interest rate adjusts to balance the supply and demand for money. There is one interest rate, called the *equilibrium interest rate,* at which the quantity of money demanded exactly balances the quantity of money supplied. If the interest rate is at any other level, people will try to adjust their portfolios of assets and, as a result, drive the interest rate toward the equilibrium.

For example, suppose that the interest rate is above the equilibrium level, such as r_1 in Figure 20-4. In this case, the quantity of money that people want to hold, M_1^d, is less than the quantity of money that the Bank of Canada has supplied. Those people who are holding the surplus of money will try to get rid of it by buying interest-bearing bonds or by depositing it in an interest-bearing bank account. Because bond issuers and banks prefer to pay lower interest rates, they respond to this surplus of money by lowering the interest rates they offer. As the interest rate falls, people become more willing to hold money until, at the equilibrium interest rate, people are happy to hold exactly the amount of money the Bank of Canada has supplied.

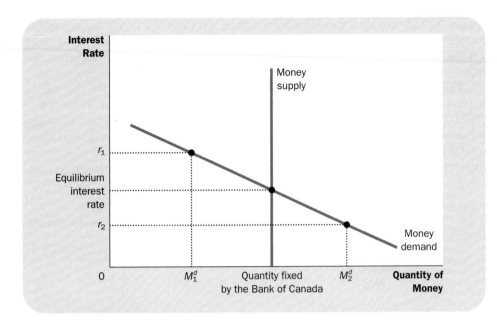

Figure 20-4

EQUILIBRIUM IN THE
MONEY MARKET.   According to
the theory of liquidity preference,
the interest rate adjusts to bring
the quantity of money supplied
and the quantity of money
demanded into balance. If the
interest rate is above the
equilibrium level (such as at r_1),
the quantity of money people
want to hold (M_1^d) is less than the
quantity the Bank of Canada has
created, and this surplus of
money puts downward pressure
on the interest rate. Conversely,
if the interest rate is below the
equilibrium level (such as at r_2),
the quantity of money people
want to hold (M_2^d) is greater than
the quantity the Bank of Canada
has created, and this shortage of
money puts upward pressure
on the interest rate. Thus, the
forces of supply and demand
in the market for money push
the interest rate toward the
equilibrium interest rate, at
which people are content
holding the quantity of
money the Bank of Canada has
created.

Conversely, at interest rates below the equilibrium level, such as r_2 in Figure 20-4, the quantity of money that people want to hold, M_2^d, is greater than the quantity of money that the Bank of Canada has supplied. As a result, people try to increase their holdings of money by reducing their holdings of bonds and other interest-bearing assets. As people cut back on their holdings of bonds, bond issuers find that they have to offer higher interest rates to attract buyers. Thus, the interest rate rises and approaches the equilibrium level.

THE DOWNWARD SLOPE OF
THE AGGREGATE-DEMAND CURVE

Having seen how the theory of liquidity preference explains the economy's equilibrium interest rate, we now consider its implications for the aggregate demand for goods and services. As a warm-up exercise, let's begin by using the theory to re-examine a topic we already understand—the interest rate effect and the downward slope of the aggregate-demand curve. In particular, suppose that the overall level of prices in the economy rises. What happens to the interest rate that balances the supply and demand for money, and how does that change affect the quantity of goods and services demanded?

As we have just discussed, the price level is one determinant of the quantity of money demanded. At higher prices, more money is exchanged every time a good or service is sold. As a result, people will choose to hold a larger quantity of money. That is, a higher price level increases the quantity of money demanded for any given interest rate. Thus, an increase in the price level from P_1 to P_2 shifts the money-demand curve to the right from MD_1 to MD_2, as shown in panel (a) of Figure 20-5.

Notice how this shift in money demand affects the equilibrium in the money market. For a fixed money supply, the interest rate must rise to balance money supply and money demand. The higher price level has increased the amount of money people want to hold and has shifted the money-demand curve to the right. Yet the quantity of money supplied is unchanged, so the interest rate must rise from r_1 to r_2 to discourage the additional demand.

This increase in the interest rate has ramifications not only for the money market but also for the quantity of goods and services demanded, as shown in panel (b). At a higher interest rate, the cost of borrowing and the return to saving are greater. Fewer households choose to borrow to buy a new house, and those who do buy smaller houses, so the demand for residential investment falls. Fewer firms choose to borrow to build new factories and buy new equipment, so busi-

Figure 20-5

THE MONEY MARKET AND THE SLOPE OF THE AGGREGATE-DEMAND CURVE. An increase in the price level from P_1 to P_2 shifts the money-demand curve to the right, as in panel (a). This increase in money demand causes the interest rate to rise from r_1 to r_2. Because the interest rate is the cost of borrowing, the increase in the interest rate reduces the quantity of goods and services demanded from Y_1 to Y_2. This negative relationship between the price level and quantity demanded is represented with a downward sloping aggregate-demand curve, as in panel (b).

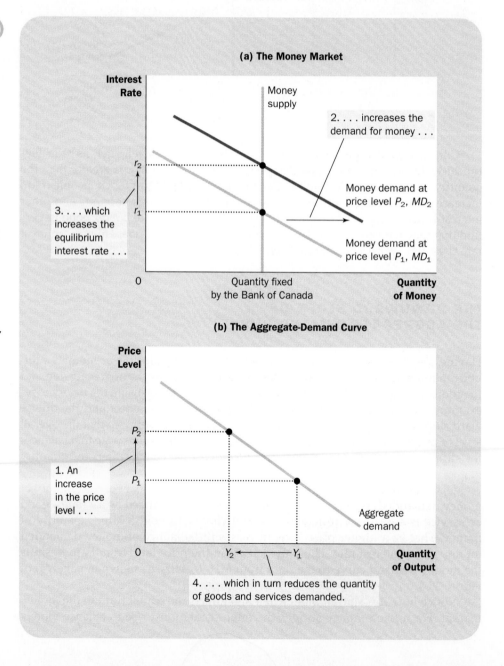

ness investment falls. Thus, when the price level rises from P_1 to P_2, increasing money demand from MD_1 to MD_2 and raising the interest rate from r_1 to r_2, the quantity of goods and services demanded falls from Y_1 to Y_2.

Hence, this analysis of the interest rate effect can be summarized in three steps: (1) A higher price level raises money demand, (2) higher money demand leads to a higher interest rate, and (3) a higher interest rate reduces the quantity of goods and services demanded.

Of course, the same logic works in reverse as well: A lower price level reduces money demand, which leads to a lower interest rate, and this in turn increases the quantity of goods and services demanded. The end result of this analysis is a negative relationship between the price level and the quantity of goods and services demanded, which is illustrated with a downward sloping aggregate-demand curve.

In an open economy, the other important influence is the real exchange-rate effect. An increase in the price level causes the real exchange rate to increase. Because this makes Canadian-produced goods more expensive relative to foreign-produced goods, both foreigners and Canadians substitute away from Canadian-produced goods. As a result, Canada's net exports fall. For this additional reason, then, in a small open economy an increase in the price level causes the quantity of Canadian-produced goods and services demanded to fall. Whether it is due primarily to the interest rate effect or to the real exchange-rate effect, the end result of this analysis is a negative relationship between the price level and the quantity of goods and services demanded. This relationship is illustrated with a downward sloping aggregate-demand curve.

CHANGES IN THE MONEY SUPPLY

So far we have used the theory of liquidity preference to explain more fully how the total quantity of goods and services demanded in the economy changes as the price level changes. That is, we have examined movements along the downward sloping aggregate-demand curve. The theory also sheds light, however, on some of the other events that alter the quantity of goods and services demanded. Whenever the quantity of goods and services demanded changes *for a given price level*, the aggregate-demand curve shifts. As we will see, how the economy responds to changes in the quantity of goods and services demanded depends on whether the economy is closed or open. It is worth repeating that our strategy will be to first show what happens in a closed economy. We will then turn to open-economy considerations. This is a useful way of proceeding because what happens in an open economy is essentially the same as what happens in a closed economy but with one or two additional considerations. Thus the closed-economy discussion is a helpful steppingstone to understanding what happens in an open economy like Canada.

One important variable that shifts the aggregate-demand curve is monetary policy. To see how monetary policy affects the economy in the short run, suppose that the Bank of Canada increases the money supply by buying government bonds in open-market operations. (Why the Bank of Canada might do this will become clear later after we understand the effects of such a move.) Let's consider how this monetary injection influences the equilibrium interest rate for a given price level. This will tell us what the injection does to the position of the aggregate-demand curve.

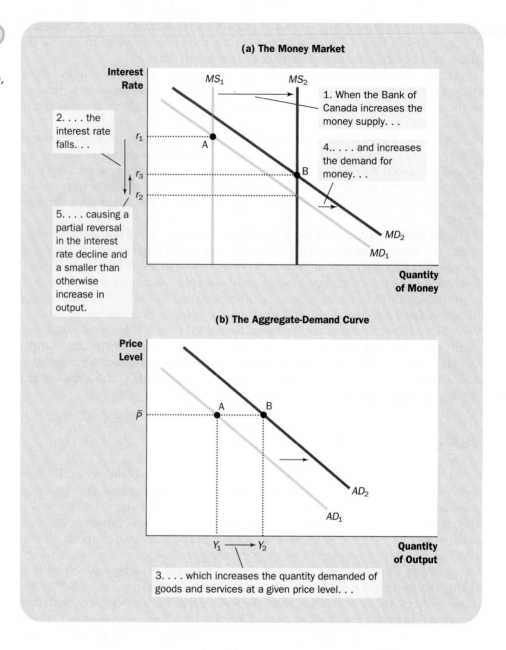

Figure 20-6

A MONETARY INJECTION IN A CLOSED ECONOMY.   In panel (a), an increase in the money supply from MS_1 to MS_2 reduces the equilibrium interest rate from r_1 to r_2. Because the interest rate is the cost of borrowing, the fall in the interest rate raises the quantity of goods and services demanded at a given price level. At the same time, the increase in output requires that people hold more money. This causes the demand for money to increase from MD_1 to MD_2 and causes a partial reversal in the interest rate, from r_2 to r_3. As a result, the increase in the quantity demanded of goods and services is smaller than it would otherwise have been. In the end, the aggregate-demand curve shifts to the right from AD_1 to AD_2, and we move from point A to point B in panels (a) and (b).

As panel (a) of Figure 20-6 shows, an increase in the money supply shifts the money-supply curve to the right from MS_1 to MS_2. Because the money-demand curve has not changed, the interest rate falls from r_1 to r_2 to balance money supply and money demand. That is, the interest rate must fall to induce people to hold the additional money the Bank of Canada has created.

Once again, the interest rate influences the quantity of goods and services demanded, as shown in panel (b) of Figure 20-6. The lower interest rate reduces the cost of borrowing and the return to saving. Households buy more and larger houses, stimulating the demand for residential investment. Firms spend more on new factories and new equipment, stimulating business investment. For all of these reasons, the quantity of goods and services demanded at the given price level, $\overline{P}$, rises. The increase in demand for goods and services increases the demand for money from MD_1 to MD_2, causing the interest rate to rise slightly from r_2 to r_3. This partial reversal in the fall in the interest rate reduces somewhat the stimulative effect on residential and firm investment. As a result, the shift in aggregate demand is smaller than it would otherwise have been. The net effect is an increase in the quantity of goods and services demanded at the given price level $\overline{P}$ from Y_1 to Y_2 and thus a shift to the right of the aggregate-demand curve from AD_1 to AD_2. Of course, there is nothing special about $\overline{P}$: The monetary injection raises the quantity of goods and services demanded at every price level. Thus, the entire aggregate-demand curve shifts to the right.

To sum up: *When the Bank of Canada increases the money supply, it lowers the interest rate and increases the quantity of goods and services demanded for any given price level, shifting the aggregate-demand curve to the right. Conversely, when the Bank of Canada contracts the money supply, it raises the interest rate and reduces the quantity of goods and services demanded for any given price level, shifting the aggregate-demand curve to the left.*

OPEN-ECONOMY CONSIDERATIONS

Our discussion of how monetary policy affects aggregate demand so far has ignored open-economy considerations. Earlier we discussed how Canada is described by macroeconomists as a small open economy with perfect capital mobility. We saw that one implication of this is that Canada's interest rate must move up and down with changes in the world interest rate. Canada's interest rate only differs from the world interest rate by an amount reflecting differences in the tax treatment of financial capital and differences in default risk in Canada versus the rest of the world. For simplicity, we will ignore these differences and thus assume that Canada's interest rate adjusts to equal the world interest rate. We turn now to the question of how a monetary injection affects the aggregate-demand curve in a small open economy. We will see that the story we have told so far, while correct for a closed economy, is incomplete for a small open economy like Canada.

Panel (a) of Figure 20-7 shows money-demand and money-supply curves intersecting at the world interest rate, r^w. Because eventually Canada's interest rate must equal the world interest rate, we begin our discussion of how monetary policy affects aggregate demand from this point. To obtain a true measure of the impact of monetary policy, we must show all of the adjustments in the economy that return Canada's interest rate to the world interest rate.

An increase in the money supply shifts the money-supply curve to the right, from MS_1 to MS_2. Because the money-demand curve has not changed, the interest rate falls below the world interest rate to r_2 in order to balance money supply and money demand. That is, the Canadian interest rate must fall to induce people to hold the additional money the Bank of Canada has created.

Once again, the interest rate influences the quantity of goods and services demanded, as shown in panel (b) of Figure 20-7. By lowering the cost of borrowing and the return to saving, the lower interest rate stimulates the demand for residential and business investment. Households save less and spend more on consumption goods. For all of these reasons, the quantity of goods and services demanded at the given price level, $\overline{P}$, rises. The increase in output increases the. demand for money from MD_1 to MD_2, causing the interest rate to rise slightly from r_2 to r_3. This partial reversal in the fall in the interest rate reduces somewhat the stimulative effect on residential and firm investment. As a result, the increase in demand for goods and services is smaller than it would otherwise have been. The net effect is a shift in the aggregate-demand curve from AD_1 to AD_2 and an increase in the quantity of goods and services demanded from Y_1 to Y_2

So far, all of this is exactly as it was previously. In a closed economy, the effect of a monetary injection would be summarized by the movement from point A to point B in panels (a) and (b) of Figure 20-7. In a small open economy like Canada, however, this cannot be the end of the story. We have left Canada's interest rate below the world interest rate. But, because of perfect capital mobility, Canada's interest rate must eventually adjust to equal the world interest rate. Something further must happen.

When Canada's interest rate falls below the world interest rate, Canadian and foreign savers find Canadian assets, which now pay interest rate r_3, less attractive than foreign assets that pay the world interest rate. As a result, Canadians and foreigners sell Canadian assets and buy foreign assets. Recall from our discussion in Chapter 18 that while people want to trade goods, services, and financial assets with people in other countries, they want to be paid for these things in their own currency. Thus the switch from Canadian assets to foreign assets requires a corresponding sale of Canadian dollars and purchase of foreign currencies. In the market for foreign-currency exchange, the supply of Canadian dollars therefore increases, causing the dollar to depreciate in value and the real exchange rate to fall. The fall in the real exchange rate makes Canadian-produced goods and services less expensive relative to foreign-produced goods and services. Consequently, Canada's net exports increase, which causes the quantity of Canadian-produced goods and services demanded at the given price level, $\overline{P}$, to increase still further. This is shown in panel (b) of Figure 20-7 by the shift of the aggregate-demand curve from AD_2 to AD_3. This additional increase in output increases the demand for money, which causes the interest rate to rise still further. This is shown in panel (a) of Figure 20-7 by the shift of the money-demand curve from MD_2 to MD_3. This shift must be such that Canada's interest rate is once again equal to the world interest rate. The end result of all of these adjustments is an increase in the demand for money to MD_3, a return of Canada's interest rate to the world interest rate, an increase in the quantity of goods and services demanded to Y_3, and a shift in the aggregate-demand curve to AD_3.

To sum up: *In a small open economy, a monetary injection by the Bank of Canada causes the dollar to depreciate in value. Because this depreciation of the dollar causes net exports to rise, there is an additional increase in demand for Canadian-produced goods and services that is not realized in a closed economy. In the end, a monetary injection in an open economy shifts the aggregate-demand curve farther to the right than it does in a closed economy.*

An important part of our explanation of how a monetary injection affects aggregate demand is our assumption that the Bank of Canada allows the exchange rate to change. That is, we have assumed that the Bank of Canada has chosen to allow the exchange rate to be flexible. As we explained in Chapter 15, the Bank of Canada can, if it wishes, buy and sell foreign currencies in what are known as foreign exchange market operations. Foreign exchange market operations are very similar to open-market operations in that they both involve the Bank of Canada

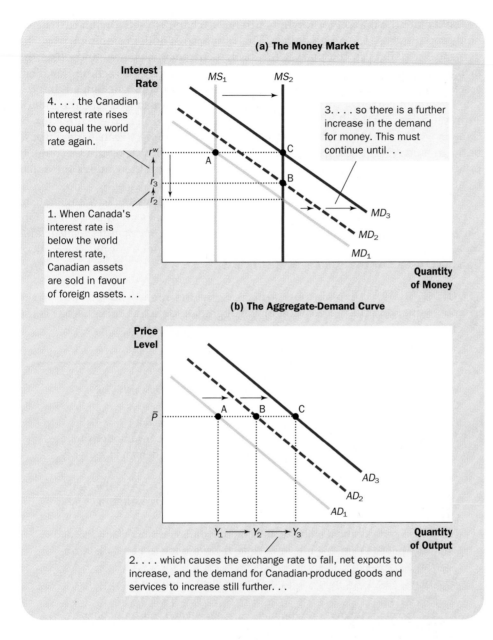

Figure 20-7

A MONETARY INJECTION IN AN OPEN ECONOMY.   In a closed economy, a monetary injection causes the interest rate to fall and output to increase. This is shown by the movements from point A to point B in panels (a) and (b). In a small open economy, the fact that the domestic interest rate, r_3, is less than the world interest rate, r^w, means that the rate must be further adjusted. Canadian and foreign savers find the Canadian interest rate less attractive than the world rate. As a result, they sell Canadian assets to buy foreign assets. This increases the supply of Canadian dollars in the market for foreign-currency exchange and causes the exchange rate to fall. Because the fall in the exchange rate increases net exports, the demand for Canadian-produced goods and services rises from AD_2 to AD_3 in panel (b). The expansion of output from Y_2 to Y_3 requires that people hold more money to make transactions. This is shown by the increase in the demand for money from MD_2 to MD_3 and the increase in the Canadian interest rate from r_3 to r^w in panel (a). In the end, the economy adjusts to point C in both panels. The interest rate returns to the world interest rate, and output increases by more than it would in a closed economy.

buying or selling something. When the Bank buys something, whether it is a government bond or foreign currency, it causes the money supply to increase. When the Bank sells something, whether it is a government bond or foreign currency, it causes the money supply to decrease. Now consider what would happen if the Bank of Canada wanted to expand the money supply while maintaining a constant value of the Canadian dollar.

By lowering the Canadian interest rate, a monetary injection causes Canadians and foreigners to sell Canadian assets in preference for foreign assets. This switch out of Canadian assets and into foreign assets increases the supply of Canadian dollars in the market for foreign-currency exchange, which causes the exchange rate to fall. If the Bank of Canada wanted to prevent this fall in the exchange rate, it would enter the market for foreign-currency exchange to sell foreign currency it holds and purchase Canadian dollars. This purchase of dollars would increase the demand for dollars in the market for foreign-currency exchange and offset the increased supply of dollars caused by Canadians and foreigners selling Canadian assets. In this way, the value of the Canadian dollars remains unchanged. But the sale of foreign currency by the Bank of Canada would also decrease the money supply. To prevent a fall in the value of the Canadian dollar, then, the Bank of Canada would need to contract the Canadian money supply. Because the purpose of the monetary injection was to expand the money supply, it would be counter-productive indeed for the Bank of Canada to try to prevent the value of the dollar from changing.

This explanation of why the Bank of Canada must allow the exchange rate to vary freely if it wants to change the money supply teaches an important lesson: *The Bank of Canada cannot simultaneously choose the size of the money supply and the value of the Canadian dollar.* By choosing to change the money supply, the Bank of Canada must allow the exchange rate to vary.

QUICK QUIZ: Explain how a decrease in the money supply affects the money market and the position of the aggregate-demand curve. What is the effect for a closed economy and for a small open economy?

Table 20-1

THE EFFECTS OF A MONETARY
INJECTION: SUMMARY

HOW DOES A MONETARY INJECTION SHIFT THE AGGREGATE-DEMAND CURVE IN A CLOSED ECONOMY?
1. An increase in money supply causes the interest rate to fall.
2. The fall in the interest rate stimulates investment and consumption of durable goods. The increase in spending increases the demand for money, causing a partial reversal of the fall in the interest rate.
3. The increase in spending shifts the aggregate-demand curve to the right.

HOW DOES A MONETARY INJECTION SHIFT THE AGGREGATE-DEMAND CURVE IN AN OPEN ECONOMY?
1. Due to perfect capital mobility, and ignoring differences in default risk and taxes, Canada's interest rate must equal the world interest rate. We begin with $r = r^w$.
2. An increase in the money supply causes Canada's interest rate to fall below r^w.
3. The fall in the interest rate stimulates investment and consumption of durable goods. The increase in spending increases the demand for money causing a partial reversal of the fall in the interest rate. Canada's interest rate remains below r^w.
4. With $r < r^w$, Canadian assets are sold in favour of buying foreign assets. The switch from Canadian to foreign assets requires that dollars be sold in the market for foreign-currency exchange. The real exchange rate falls.
5. The fall in the real exchange rate increases net exports, causing aggregate-demand curve to shift even farther to the right.
6. This additional stimulus to spending increases the demand for money until $r = r^w$.
7. It makes sense for the Bank of Canada to cause a monetary injection only if it allows the exchange rate to be flexible.

CASE STUDY   WHY CENTRAL BANKS WATCH THE STOCK MARKET (AND VICE VERSA)

"Irrational exuberance." That was how U.S. Federal Reserve (the U.S. central bank) Chairman Alan Greenspan once described the booming stock market of the late 1990s. He was right about the market being exuberant: Average stock prices in the United States increased about fourfold during the 1990s. While somewhat less exuberant, the average stock price in Canada nonetheless increased by two and a half times over this period. The dramatic fall in stock prices in early 2001 lends some credence to Mr. Greenspan's description of the market as "irrational."

Regardless of how they view booming (or crashing) stock markets, how should central banks respond to stock-market fluctuations? Central banks have no reason to care about stock prices in themselves, but they do have the job of monitoring and responding to developments in the overall economy, and the stock market is a piece of the puzzle. When the stock market booms, households become wealthier, and this increased wealth stimulates consumer spending. In addition, a rise in stock prices makes it more attractive for firms to sell new shares of stock, and this stimulates investment spending. For both reasons, a booming stock market expands the aggregate demand for goods and services.

As we discuss more fully later in the chapter, one of a central bank's goals is to stabilize aggregate demand, because greater stability in aggregate demand means greater stability in output and the price level. To do this, a central bank might respond to a stock-market boom by keeping the money supply lower and interest rates higher than it otherwise would. The contractionary effects of higher interest rates would offset the expansionary effects of higher stock prices. In fact, this analysis describes the behaviour of the U.S. Federal Reserve: Real interest rates in the United States were kept higher by historical standards during the "irrationally exuberant" U.S. stock-market boom of the 1990s.

The opposite occurs when the stock market falls. Spending on consumption and investment declines, depressing aggregate demand and pushing the economy toward recession. To stabilize aggregate demand, a central bank might increase the money supply and lower interest rates. Again, this analysis describes how the U.S. Federal Reserve responded when, on October 19, 1987, the U.S. stock market fell by 22.6 percent—its largest one-day drop in history. The Federal Reserve responded to the market crash by increasing the money supply and lowering interest rates. In part because of its quick action, the U.S. economy avoided a recession.

While central banks keep an eye on the stock market, stock-market participants also keep an eye on central banks. Because central banks can influence interest rates and economic activity, they can alter the value of stocks. For example, when the a central bank raises interest rates by reducing the money supply, it makes owning stocks less attractive for two reasons. First, a higher interest rate means that bonds, the alternative to stocks, are earning a higher return. Second, tightening monetary policy risks pushing the economy into a recession, which reduces profits. As a result, stock prices often fall when central banks raise interest rates.

IN THE NEWS
European Central Bankers Expand Aggregate Demand

NEWSPAPERS ARE FILLED WITH STORIES about monetary policymakers adjusting the money supply and interest rates in response to changing economic conditions. Here's an example.

European Banks, Acting in Unison, Cut Interest Rate: Eleven Nations Decide that Growth, Not Inflation, Is Top Concern

BY EDMUND L. ANDREWS
FRANKFURT, DEC. 3—In the most coordinated action yet toward European monetary union, eleven nations simultaneously cut their interest rates today to a nearly uniform level.

The move came a month before the nations adopt the euro as a single currency and marked a drastic shift in policy. As recently as two months ago, European central bankers had adamantly resisted demands from political leaders to lower rates because they were intent on establishing the credibility of the euro and the fledgling European Central Bank in world markets.

But today, citing signs that the global economic slowdown has begun to chill Europe, the central banks of the eleven euro-zone nations reduced their benchmark interest rates by at least three-tenths of a percent. The cuts are intended to help bolster the European economies by making it cheaper for businesses and consumers to borrow.

"We are deaf to political pressure, but we are not blind to facts and arguments," Hans Tietmeyer, the president of Germany's central bank, the Bundesbank, said. . . .

In announcing the decision, Mr. Tietmeyer said today that the central bankers had acted in response to mounting evidence that European growth rates would be significantly slower next year than they had predicted as recently as last summer.

SOURCE: *The New York Times,* December 4, 1998, p. A1.

HOW FISCAL POLICY INFLUENCES AGGREGATE DEMAND

The government can influence the behaviour of the economy not only with monetary policy but also with fiscal policy. Fiscal policy refers to the government's choices regarding the overall level of government purchases or taxes. Earlier in the book we examined how fiscal policy influences saving, investment, and growth in the long run. In the short run, however, the primary effect of fiscal policy is on the aggregate demand for goods and services.

CHANGES IN GOVERNMENT PURCHASES

When policymakers change the money supply or the level of taxes, they shift the aggregate-demand curve by influencing the spending decisions of firms or households. By contrast, when the government alters its own purchases of goods and services, it shifts the aggregate-demand curve directly.

Suppose, for example, that the federal government chooses to introduce a $5 billion job-creation program. The program will finance expenditures on new roads, sewers, and bridges. The program raises the demand for construction work and induces construction firms to hire more workers. The increase in demand for construction work is reflected in an increase in the aggregate demand for goods and services. As a result, the aggregate-demand curve shifts to the right.

By how much does this $5 billion government expenditure shift the aggregate-demand curve? At first, one might guess that the aggregate-demand curve shifts to the right by exactly $5 billion. It turns out, however, that this is not correct. Two macroeconomic effects that make the size of the shift in aggregate demand differ from the change in government purchases. The first—the multiplier effect—suggests that the shift in aggregate demand could be *larger* than $5 billion. The second—the crowding-out effect on investment—suggests that the shift in aggregate demand could be *smaller* than $5 billion. We now discuss each of these effects in turn.

THE MULTIPLIER EFFECT

When the government spends $5 billion on construction work, that expenditure has repercussions. The immediate impact of the higher demand from the government is to raise employment and profits of the construction firms involved. Then, as the workers see higher earnings and the firm owners see higher profits, they respond to this increase in income by raising their own spending on consumer goods. As a result, the government expenditure of $5 billion raises the demand for the products of many other firms in the economy. Because each dollar spent by the government can raise the aggregate demand for goods and services by more than a dollar, government purchases are said to have a **multiplier effect** on aggregate demand.

multiplier effect
the additional shifts in aggregate demand that result when expansionary fiscal policy increases income and thereby increases consumer spending

This multiplier effect continues even after this first round. When consumer spending rises, the firms that produce these consumer goods hire more people and experience higher profits. Higher earnings and profits stimulate consumer spending once again, and so on. Thus, there is positive feedback as higher demand leads to higher income, which in turn leads to even higher demand. Once all of these effects are added together, the total impact on the quantity of goods and services demanded can be much larger than the initial impulse from higher government spending.

Figure 20-8 illustrates the multiplier effect. The increase in government spending of $5 billion initially shifts the aggregate-demand curve to the right from AD_1 to AD_2 by exactly $5 billion. But when consumers respond by increasing their spending, the aggregate-demand curve shifts still further to AD_3.

This multiplier effect arising from the response of consumer spending can be strengthened by the response of investment to higher levels of demand. For instance, the construction firms might respond to the higher demand for roads and bridges by deciding to buy more paving equipment or build another cement plant. In this case, higher government demand spurs higher demand for investment goods. This positive feedback from demand to investment is sometimes called the *investment accelerator*.

A FORMULA FOR THE SPENDING MULTIPLIER

A little high-school algebra lets us derive a formula for the size of the multiplier effect that arises from consumer spending. An important number in this formula

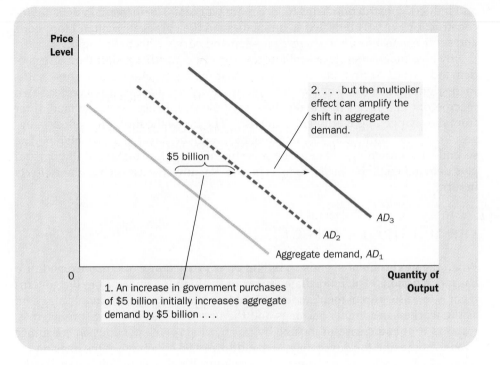

Figure 20-8

THE MULTIPLIER EFFECT.   An increase in government purchases of $5 billion can shift the aggregate-demand curve to the right by more than $5 billion. This multiplier effect arises because increases in aggregate income stimulate additional spending by consumers.

is the *marginal propensity to consume* (*MPC*)—the fraction of extra income that a household consumes rather than saves. For example, suppose that the marginal propensity to consume is 3/4. This means that for every extra dollar that a household earns, the household spends $0.75 (3/4 of the dollar) and saves $0.25. With an *MPC* of 3/4, when the workers and owners of the construction firms earn $5 billion from the government contract, they increase their consumer spending by 3/4 × $5 billion, or $3.75 billion.

To gauge the impact on aggregate demand of a change in government purchases, we follow the effects step-by-step. The process begins when the government spends $5 billion, which implies that national income (earnings and profits) also rises by this amount. This increase in income in turn raises consumer spending by *MPC* × $5 billion, which in turn raises the income for the workers and owners of the firms that produce the consumption goods. This second increase in income again raises consumer spending, this time by *MPC* × (*MPC* × $5 billion). These feedback effects go on and on.

To find the total impact on the demand for goods and services, we add up all of these effects:

Change in government purchases = $5 billion
First change in consumption   = *MPC* × $5 billion
Second change in consumption   = MPC^2 × $5 billion
Third change in consumption   = MPC^3 × $5 billion
•   •
•   •
•   •

Total change in demand =
(1 + *MPC* + MPC^2 + MPC^3 + . . .) × $5 billion.

Here, "..." represents an infinite number of similar terms. Thus, we can write the multiplier as follows:

$$\text{Multiplier} = 1 + MPC + MPC^2 + MPC^3 + \dots.$$

This multiplier tells us the demand for goods and services that each dollar of government purchases generates.

To simplify this equation for the multiplier, recall from math class that this expression is an infinite geometric series. For x between -1 and $+1$,

$$1 + x + x^2 + x^3 + \dots = 1/(1 - x).$$

In our case, $x = MPC$. Thus,

$$\text{Multiplier} = 1/(1 - MPC).$$

For example, if MPC is $3/4$, the multiplier is $1/(1 - 3/4)$, which is 4. In this case, the $5 billion of government spending generates $20 billion of demand for goods and services.

In an open economy, the formula for the multiplier looks a bit different. In an open economy, many of the goods and services people purchase are imported. Recognition of this requires that we be a bit more specific about how we define the multiplier. The government-spending multiplier tells us the demand for *Canadian-*produced goods and services that each additional dollar of government expenditures generates. Suppose that the fraction of extra income that a Canadian household spends on imported goods—what we call the *marginal propensity to import (MPI)*—is $1/4$. Now for every extra dollar that a household earns, the household saves $0.25 and spends $0.75, as before, but only $0.50 of that spending is on Canadian-produced goods while $0.25 is spent on imported goods. When the construction workers and firms earn $5 billion from the government contract, they increase their spending on all goods by $3/4 \times \$5$ billion, or $3.75 billion, but increase their spending on Canadian-produced goods by just $1/2 \times \$5$ billion, or $2.5 billion. Only this second, smaller, amount adds to the incomes of other Canadians. Because Canadians spend some of their additional income on imported goods and services, therefore, the feedback effects are smaller than in a closed economy.

The relevant formula for the government-purchases multiplier in an open economy is

$$\text{Multiplier} = 1/(1 - MPC + MPI).$$

Now, because $MPC = 3/4$ and $MPI = 1/4$, the multiplier is $1/(1 - 3/4 + 1/4)$, which is 2. In this case, the $5 billion of government spending generates $10 billion of demand for Canadian-produced goods and services. This compares with the $20 billion of demand for goods and services generated by the $5 billion of government spending in a closed economy. The government-purchases multiplier is clearly much smaller in an open economy than in a closed economy.

These formulas for the multiplier show an important conclusion: The size of the multiplier depends on the marginal propensity to consume and, in an open economy, the marginal propensity to import. A larger MPC means a larger multiplier.

To see why this is true, remember that the multiplier arises because higher income induces greater spending on consumption. The larger the *MPC*, the greater this induced effect on consumption and the larger the multiplier. In an open economy we also need to consider the marginal propensity to import. A larger *MPI* means a *smaller* multiplier. To see why this is true, remember that the *MPI* measures the amount of higher income that is spent on foreign-produced goods and services. The greater this amount, the smaller the amount by which spending on *Canadian-produced* goods and services increases for any increase in income. A larger *MPI*, then, means that every increase in income induces a smaller increase in spending on Canadian-produced goods and services.

An interesting implication of the role played by the marginal propensity to import in determining the size of the multiplier in Canada is the likelihood that the *MPI* has recently grown larger. We saw earlier how the signing of free trade agreements in 1989 and 1993 has resulted in a dramatic increase in the amount of trade Canada does with the rest of the world, and the United States in particular. As a result of this growth in trade, it seems likely that any change in income now results in a larger change in spending on imported goods than would have been the case only ten years ago. The *MPI*, then, has likely grown larger. If so, the multiplier in Canada has grown smaller over the past ten years.

OTHER APPLICATIONS OF THE MULTIPLIER EFFECT

Because of the multiplier effect, a dollar of government purchases can generate more than a dollar of aggregate demand. The logic of the multiplier effect, however, is not restricted to changes in government purchases. Instead, it applies to any event that alters spending on any component of GDP—consumption, investment, government purchases, or net exports.

For example, suppose that a recession in the United States reduces the demand for Canada's net exports by $10 billion. This reduced spending on Canadian-produced goods and services depresses Canada's national income, which reduces spending by Canadian consumers. If the marginal propensity to consume is 3/4, the marginal propensity to import is 1/4, and the multiplier is 2, then the $10 billion fall in net exports means a $20 billion contraction in aggregate demand.

As another example, suppose that a stock-market boom increases households' wealth and stimulates their spending on goods and services by $20 billion. This extra consumer spending increases national income, which in turn generates even more consumer spending. If the marginal propensity to consume is 3/4, the marginal propensity to import is 1/4, and the multiplier is 2, then the initial impulse of $20 billion in consumer spending translates into a $40 billion increase in aggregate demand.

The multiplier is an important concept in macroeconomics because it shows how the economy can amplify the impact of changes in spending. A small initial change in consumption, investment, government purchases, or net exports can end up having a large effect on aggregate demand and, therefore, the economy's production of goods and services. It is because of this amplified impact of initial changes in consumption, investment, government purchases, or net exports that policymakers must pay close attention to events such as the possibility of recession among our trading partners and the possibility of stock-market booms or crashes.

THE CROWDING-OUT EFFECT ON INVESTMENT

The multiplier effect seems to suggest that when the government spends $5 billion on construction work, the resulting expansion in aggregate demand is necessarily larger than $5 billion. Yet another effect is working in the opposite direction. While an increase in government purchases stimulates the aggregate demand for goods and services, it also causes the interest rate to rise, and a higher interest rate reduces investment spending and chokes off aggregate demand. The reduction in aggregate demand that results when a fiscal expansion raises the interest rate is called the **crowding-out effect on investment.**

To see why crowding out occurs, let's consider what happens in the money market when the government spends $5 billion on construction work. As we have discussed, this increase in demand raises the incomes of the workers and owners of construction firms (and, because of the multiplier effect, of other firms as well). As incomes rise, households plan to buy more goods and services and, as a result, choose to hold more of their wealth in liquid form. That is, the increase in income caused by the fiscal expansion raises the demand for money.

The effect of the increase in money demand is shown in panel (a) of Figure 20-9. Because the Bank of Canada has not changed the money supply, the vertical supply curve remains the same. When the higher level of income shifts the money-demand curve to the right from MD_1 to MD_2, the interest rate must rise from r_1 to r_2 to keep supply and demand in balance.

The increase in the interest rate, in turn, reduces the quantity of goods and services demanded. In particular, because borrowing is more expensive, the demand for residential and business investment goods declines. That is, as the increase in government purchases increases the demand for goods and services, it may also crowd out investment. This crowding-out effect partially offsets the impact of government purchases on aggregate demand, as illustrated in panel (b) of Figure 20-9. The initial impact of the increase in government purchases is to shift the aggregate-demand curve from AD_1 to AD_2, but once crowding out takes place, the aggregate-demand curve drops back to AD_3.

To sum up: *When the government increases its purchases by $5 billion, the aggregate demand for goods and services could rise by more or less than $5 billion, depending on whether the multiplier effect or the crowding-out effect on investment is larger.*

crowding-out effect on investment
the offset in aggregate demand that results when expansionary fiscal policy raises the interest rate and thereby reduces investment spending

OPEN-ECONOMY CONSIDERATIONS

Our discussion of how fiscal policy affects aggregate demand so far has ignored open-economy considerations. Just as we found when we considered the open-economy implications for monetary policy, we will see that the story we have told so far, while correct for a closed economy, is incomplete for a small open economy like Canada.

Panel (a) of Figure 20-10 shows money-demand and money-supply curves intersecting at the world interest rate, r^w. Just as we did before, we begin our discussion of how fiscal policy affects aggregate demand from this point. Because eventually Canada's interest rate must equal the world interest rate, we begin our discussion of how fiscal policy affects aggregate demand from this point. To obtain a true measure of the impact of fiscal policy, we must show all of the adjustments in the economy that return Canada's interest rate to the world interest rate.

Figure 20-9

THE CROWDING-OUT EFFECT ON INVESTMENT.   Panel (a) shows the money market. When the government increases its spending on goods and services, the resulting increase in income raises the demand for money from MD_1 to MD_2, and this causes the equilibrium interest rate to rise from r_1 to r_2. Panel (b) shows the effects on aggregate demand. The multiplier effect of the increase in government spending shifts the aggregate-demand curve from AD_1 to AD_2. Yet, because the interest rate is the cost of borrowing, the increase in the interest rate tends to reduce the quantity of goods and services demanded, particularly for investment goods. This crowding out of investment partially offsets the impact of the fiscal expansion on aggregate demand. In the end, the aggregate-demand curve shifts only to AD_3.

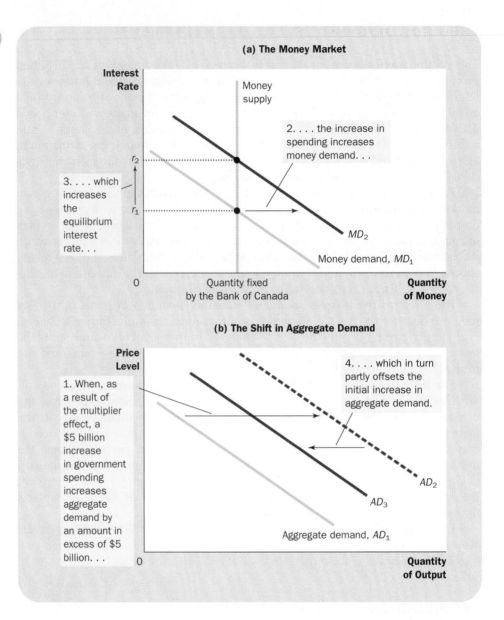

The \$5 billion job-creation program raises the incomes of those directly employed and increases the incomes of workers and owners of other firms. This is the multiplier effect, and it is represented by the shift of the aggregate-demand curve to the right from AD_1 to AD_2, as shown in panel (b) of Figure 20-10. The increase in demand for goods and services also increases the demand for money. In panel (a), this is shown by the shift of the demand for money curve from MD_1 to MD_2. Because the Bank of Canada has not changed the money-supply curve, the vertical money-supply curve remains the same. As a result, the interest rate must rise above the world interest rate, to r_2, in order to balance money supply and money demand.

Once again, the interest rate influences the quantity of goods and services demanded, as shown in panel (b). In particular, by increasing the cost of borrowing, the higher interest rate reduces the demand for residential and business

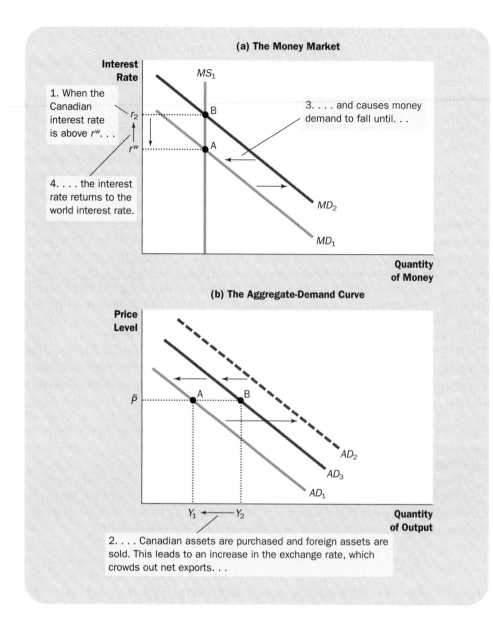

(a) The Money Market

1. When the Canadian interest rate is above r^w. . .

3. . . . and causes money demand to fall until. . .

4. . . . the interest rate returns to the world interest rate.

MS_1

r_2

B

A

r^w

MD_2

MD_1

Interest Rate

Quantity of Money

(b) The Aggregate-Demand Curve

Price Level

$\bar{P}$

A

B

AD_2

AD_3

AD_1

Y_1 Y_2

Quantity of Output

2. . . . Canadian assets are purchased and foreign assets are sold. This leads to an increase in the exchange rate, which crowds out net exports. . .

Figure 20-10

A FISCAL EXPANSION IN AN OPEN ECONOMY WITH A FLEXIBLE EXCHANGE RATE.   In a closed economy, an increase in government purchases causes the interest rate to rise and output to increase. This is shown by the movement from point A to point B in panels (a) and (b). In a small open economy, the fact that the domestic interest rate, r_2, is greater than the world interest rate, r^w, means there must be further adjustment. Canadian and foreign savers find the Canadian interest rate more attractive than the world rate. As a result, they buy Canadian assets and sell foreign assets. This decreases the supply of Canadian dollars in the market for foreign-currency exchange and causes the exchange rate to rise. Because this increase in the interest rate decreases net exports, the demand for Canadian-produced goods and services falls from AD_2 to AD_1 in panel (b). The contraction of output from Y_2 to Y_1 requires that people hold less money to make transactions. This is shown by the decrease in the demand for money from MD_2 to MD_1 and the decrease in the Canadian interest rate from r_2 to r^w in panel (a). In the end, the economy adjusts back to point A in both panels, the interest rate returns to the world interest rate, and there is no lasting effect on aggregate demand.

investment. As a result, the quantity of goods and services demanded at the given price level, $\bar{P}$, falls. This is the crowding-out effect on investment. It is shown in panel (b) by the shift of the aggregate-demand curve from AD_2 to AD_3.

So far, all of this is exactly as it was previously. In a closed economy, the effect of a fiscal expansion would be summarized by the movement from point A to point B in panels (a) and (b) of Figure 20-10. In a small open economy like Canada, however, this cannot be the end of the story. We have left Canada's interest rate above the world interest rate. But, because of perfect capital mobility, Canada's interest rate must eventually adjust to equal the world interest rate. Something else must happen.

Flexible Exchange Rate   We begin by assuming that the Bank of Canada has chosen to allow the exchange rate to be flexible. As we saw in our examination of the effects of a monetary injection, the assumption about whether or not the exchange rate is flexible will prove to be an important one.

When Canada's interest rate rises above the world interest rate, Canadian and foreign savers find Canadian assets, which now pay interest rate r_2, to be more attractive than foreign assets that pay the world interest rate, r^w. As a result, Canadians and foreigners sell foreign assets and buy Canadian assets. Recall, again, our discussion in Chapter 18 that while people want to trade goods, services, and financial assets with people in other countries, they want to be paid for these things in their own currency. Thus the switch from foreign assets to Canadian assets requires a corresponding purchase of Canadian dollars and sale of foreign currencies. In the market for foreign-currency exchange, the demand for Canadian dollars therefore increases, causing the dollar to appreciate in value and the real exchange rate to rise. The rise in the real exchange rate makes Canadian-produced goods and services more expensive relative to foreign-produced goods and services. Consequently, Canada's net exports decrease. The reduction in net exports that results when a fiscal expansion in a small open economy with a flexible exchange rate raises the real exchange rate is called the **crowding-out effect on net exports.** The decrease in net exports causes the quantity of Canadian-produced goods and services demanded at the given price level, $\overline{P}$, to decrease. This is shown in panel (b) by the shift of the aggregate-demand curve from AD_3 to AD_1. This fall in demand for Canadian-produced goods and services also decreases the demand for money. This is shown in panel (a) by the shift of the money-demand curve from MD_2 to MD_1. This shift must be large enough to cause Canada's interest rate to fall back to the world interest rate. The end result of all of these adjustments is a decrease in the demand for money back to MD_1, a return of Canada's interest rate to the world interest rate, and a decrease in the quantity demanded of Canadian-produced goods and services, represented by a shift in the aggregate-demand curve back to AD_1.

To sum up: *In a small open economy, an expansionary fiscal policy causes the dollar to appreciate. Because this appreciation of the dollar causes net exports to fall, there is an additional crowding-out effect that reduces the demand for Canadian-produced goods and services. In the end, fiscal policy has no lasting effect on aggregate demand.*

Fixed Exchange Rate

Now consider the effect on aggregate demand of a fiscal policy in an open economy when the Bank of Canada chooses to prevent changes in the value of the exchange rate. Recall that the Bank of Canada can influence the value of the exchange rate by buying and selling foreign currencies in what are known as foreign exchange market operations. When firms and households are selling Canadian dollars in the market for foreign-currency exchange (thereby increasing the supply of dollars in that market), the Bank of Canada can prevent the value of the exchange rate from falling by increasing the demand for Canadian dollars in that market. It does this by selling foreign currencies and purchasing Canadian dollars. Similarly, when firms and households are buying Canadian dollars in the market for foreign-currency exchange (thereby increasing the demand for dollars in that market), the Bank of Canada can prevent the value of the exchange rate from rising by increasing the supply of Canadian dollars in that market. It does this by buying foreign currencies and selling Canadian dollars.

Figure 20-11 shows how expansionary fiscal policy affects aggregate demand in this case. As always, we start with the Canadian interest rate equal to the world interest rate, r^w. In panel (a), the demand for money, MD_1, is equal to the supply of money, MS_1, at r^w. An increase in government expenditures increases the quantity

crowding-out effect on net exports

the offset in aggregate demand that results when expansionary fiscal policy in a small open economy with a flexible exchange rate raises the real exchange rate and thereby reduces net exports of goods and services demanded for given price level $\bar{P}$. As a result of the multi-plier effect, the quantity of goods and services demanded increases by more than the increase in government expenditures. This is shown in panel (b) by the shift in the aggregate-demand curve from AD_1 to AD_2. As before, the increase in demand for goods and services requires that people hold more of their wealth as money. This is represented in panel (a) by the shift of the money-demand curve from MD_1 to MD_2. The increase in the demand for money increases the Canadian interest rate to r_2. As we have seen, this increase in the interest rate crowds out business and residential investment and reduces the demand for goods and services. In panel (b), this crowding-out effect on investment is shown by the shift of the aggregate-demand curve from AD_2 to AD_3.

So far, we have described the adjustment from point A to point B in panels (a) and (b). This is how a closed economy would respond to a fiscal expansion. In an

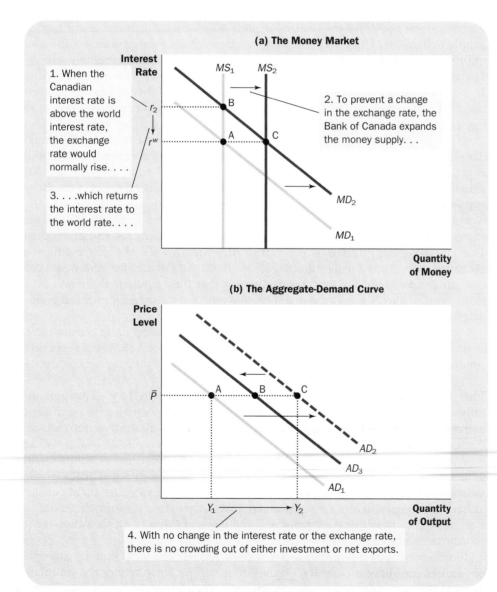

(a) The Money Market

1. When the Canadian interest rate is above the world interest rate, the exchange rate would normally rise. . . .

2. To prevent a change in the exchange rate, the Bank of Canada expands the money supply. . .

3. . . .which returns the interest rate to the world rate. . . .

(b) The Aggregate-Demand Curve

4. With no change in the interest rate or the exchange rate, there is no crowding out of either investment or net exports.

Figure 20-11

A FISCAL EXPANSION IN AN OPEN ECONOMY WITH A FIXED EXCHANGE RATE. In a closed economy, an increase in government purchases causes the interest rate to rise and output to increase. This is shown by the movements from point A to point B in panels (a) and (b). In an open economy, the fact that the Canadian interest rate is above the world interest rate would normally cause the dollar to appreciate, causing net exports to be crowded out. To prevent an increase in the value of the dollar, the Bank of Canada increases the money supply by selling dollars in the market for foreign-currency exchange. This increase in the money supply, shown by the shift of the money-supply curve from MS_1 to MS_2 in panel (a), also prevents the interest rate from changing. As a result, both forms of crowding out are avoided. In the end, the fiscal expansion has a large effect on aggregate demand, shown by the shift of AD_1 to AD_2 in panel (b) and the movement from point A to point C in both panels.

open economy, because Canada's interest rate is above the world interest rate, there is a tendency for the exchange rate to change. In particular, because Canada's interest rate is above the world interest rate, Canadian assets are preferred to foreign assets. The switch from foreign to Canadian assets requires a corresponding purchase of dollars in the market for foreign-currency exchange, and this causes the dollar to appreciate in value. We have seen that if the Bank of Canada allows the exchange rate to appreciate, net exports will fall and the economy will adjust back to point A in panels (a) and (b), so that the fiscal expansion has no lasting impact on aggregate demand. If the Bank of Canada chooses to fix the value of the exchange rate, it must increase the supply of dollars in the market for foreign-currency exchange. To do this, the Bank of Canada purchases foreign currency in exchange for dollars.

The actions taken by the Bank of Canada to fix the exchange rate also has an effect on the money supply. As we explained in Chapter 15, and reviewed earlier in this chapter, when the Bank of Canada buys something, it causes the money supply to increase. When the Bank of Canada sells something, it causes the money supply to decrease. Thus when the Bank of Canada buys foreign currency in order to prevent the value of the dollar from changing, it expands the money supply. This is shown in panel (a) by the shift of the money-supply curve from MS_1 to MS_2. The shift of the money-supply curve must be sufficient to lower Canada's interest rate back to the world interest rate. Only when Canada's interest rate is equal to the world interest rate is there no reason for the exchange rate to change.

The expansion of the money supply has two effects. First, it lowers the Canadian interest rate back to the world interest rate. This eliminates the crowding-out effect of government expenditures on business and residential investment. This crowding-out effect is what shifted AD_2 back to AD_3. The second effect of the monetary expansion is that, by lowering the Canadian interest rate to the level of the world interest rate, it removes the reason for the appreciation of the dollar. This eliminates the crowding-out effect of government expenditures on net exports. This crowding-out effect is what shifted AD_3 back to AD_1. By preventing the exchange rate from changing, the Bank of Canada therefore removes both crowding-out effects. The end result, then, is that the aggregate-demand curve shifts from AD_1 to AD_2 and the quantity demanded of Canadian-produced goods and services expands from Y_1 to Y_2.

To sum up: *If the Bank of Canada chooses to prevent any change in the exchange rate, expansionary fiscal policy will have no crowding-out effects and will therefore cause a very large increase in the demand for goods and services.*

The Coordination of Monetary and Fiscal Policy   The dramatically different effects of a fiscal expansion on aggregate demand under a fixed exchange rate and under a flexible exchange rate teaches us an important lesson: *For fiscal policy to have a lasting effect on the position of the aggregate-demand curve, the Bank of Canada must choose the appropriate exchange rate policy.* Interestingly, fiscal policy decisions are made by Parliament and by provincial legislatures, while monetary policy is determined by the Bank of Canada. Therefore, for fiscal policies to have a lasting influence on aggregate demand, these two sets of policymakers, elected politicians on the one hand and the Bank of Canada on the other, must coordinate their choices.

Such coordination has not always been observed. The most famous example of a lack of coordination was the Coyne Affair in 1961. In an attempt to stimulate

Table 20-2

THE EFFECTS OF FISCAL POLICY: SUMMARY

HOW DOES FISCAL POLICY SHIFT THE AGGREGATE-DEMAND CURVE IN A CLOSED ECONOMY?

1. An increase in government spending shifts the aggregate-demand curve to the right.
2. Increased spending increases money demand, and this increases the interest rate.
3. The rise in the interest rate crowds out investment and reduces somewhat the size of the shift in the aggregate-demand curve.

HOW DOES FISCAL POLICY SHIFT THE AGGREGATE-DEMAND CURVE IN AN OPEN ECONOMY WITH A FLEXIBLE EXCHANGE RATE?

1. Due to perfect capital mobility, and ignoring differences in default risk and taxes, Canada's interest rate must equal the world interest rate. We begin with $r = r^w$.
2. An increase in government spending shifts the aggregate-demand curve to the right.
3. Increased spending increases money demand, and this increases the interest rate.
4. The rise in the interest rate crowds out investment and reduces somewhat the size of the shift in the aggregate-demand curve. Now $r > r^w$.
5. Canadian assets now pay a higher interest rate than foreign assets. Increased demand for Canadian assets means an increased demand for dollars in the market for foreign-currency exchange. The dollar appreciates.
6. The appreciation of the dollar reduces net exports.
7. The fall in net exports means a fall in spending, a fall in money demand, and a fall in interest rates until $r = r^w$.
8. The increase in government spending has no lasting influence on the position of the aggregate-demand curve.

HOW DOES FISCAL POLICY SHIFT THE AGGREGATE-DEMAND CURVE IN AN OPEN ECONOMY WITH A FIXED EXCHANGE RATE?

1. Due to perfect capital mobility, and ignoring differences in default risk and taxes, Canada's interest rate must equal the world interest rate. We begin with $r = r^w$.
2. An increase in government spending shifts the aggregate-demand curve to the right.
3. Increased spending increases money demand, and this increases the interest rate.
4. The rise in the interest rate crowds out investment and reduces somewhat the size of the shift in the aggregate-demand curve. Now $r > r^w$.
5. Canadian assets now pay a higher interest rate than foreign assets. Increased demand for Canadian assets means an increased demand for dollars in the market for foreign-currency exchange. To fix the exchange rate, the Bank of Canada increases the supply of dollars traded in the market for foreign-currency exchange by purchasing foreign currency.
6. The purchase of foreign currency by the Bank of Canada causes the money supply to increase, and this causes the interest rate to fall until $r = r^w$.
7. The increase in the money supply shifts the aggregate-demand curve even farther to the right.

an economy mired in an economic slowdown, the federal government of the day introduced tax cuts and expenditure increases in the hope of shifting the aggregate-demand curve to the right. Unfortunately, the governor of the Bank of Canada, James Coyne, was determined to allow the exchange rate to be flexible. The result—predictable on the basis of our analysis—was a serious conflict between the federal government and the Bank of Canada. By maintaining a flexible exchange rate, Coyne was causing the federal government's expansionary fiscal policy to have no lasting influence on the position of the aggregate-demand curve. In the end, Coyne was forced to resign, and the Bank of Canada adopted a fixed exchange rate in order to enable the government's expansionary fiscal policy to shift the aggregate-demand curve. As Donald Fleming, the federal minister of finance in 1961, concluded, "This budget and Mr. Coyne were simply not compatible."

Currently, the Bank of Canada allows the exchange rate to vary. Indeed, the Canada–U.S. exchange rate garners considerable attention, and changes in its value often lead off news programs. On occasion, however, the Bank of Canada influences the value of the exchange rate by buying and selling dollars in the market for foreign-currency exchange. It does this to try to slow the rate of change in the exchange rate and thereby ensure that changes are not too abrupt. When considering what you think will be the outcome of fiscal policy choices of Canadian governments, therefore, you need to have a sense of how much the Bank of Canada will choose to try to influence the exchange rate. If the Bank of Canada is likely to allow the exchange rate to vary freely, then fiscal policy changes will have no lasting effect on the position of the aggregate-demand curve. If, however, you judge that the Bank of Canada will try to minimize changes in the exchange rate, fiscal policy changes will have a lasting influence on the position of the aggregate-demand curve.

CHANGES IN TAXES

The other important instrument of fiscal policy, besides the level of government purchases, is the level of taxation. When the government cuts personal income taxes, for instance, it increases households' take-home pay. Households will save some of this additional income, but they will also spend some of it on consumer goods. Because it increases consumer spending, the tax cut shifts the aggregate-demand curve to the right. Similarly, a tax increase depresses consumer spending and shifts the aggregate-demand curve to the left.

The size of the shift in aggregate demand resulting from a tax change is also affected by the multiplier and crowding-out effects. When the government cuts taxes and stimulates consumer spending, earnings and profits rise, which further stimulates consumer spending. This is the multiplier effect. At the same time, higher income leads to higher money demand, which tends to raise interest rates. Higher interest rates make borrowing more costly, which reduces investment spending. This is the crowding-out effect on investment. Depending on the size of the multiplier and crowding-out effects, the shift in aggregate demand could be larger or smaller than the tax change that causes it.

In a small open economy like Canada, whether the change in the position of the aggregate-demand curve that results from a change in taxes is a lasting one depends on the central bank's decision whether to allow the exchange rate to change. If the Bank of Canada chooses to allow the exchange rate to vary freely, tax

IN THE NEWS

Japan Tries a Fiscal Stimulus

IN THE 1990S, JAPAN EXPERIENCED A LONG and deep recession. As the decade was coming to a close, it looked like an end might be in sight, in part because the government was using fiscal policy to expand aggregate demand.

The Land of the Rising Outlook: Public Spending May Have Reversed Japan's Downturn

BY SHERYL WUDUNN

NAKANOJOMACHI, JAPAN—Bulldozers and tall cranes are popping up around the country like bamboo shoots after a spring rain, and this is raising hopes that Japan may finally be close to lifting itself out of recession.

No other country has ever poured as much money—more than $830 billion the last twelve months alone—into economic revival as has Japan, and much of that money is now sloshing around the country and creating a noticeable impact. Here in this village in central Japan, as in much of the country, construction crews are busy again, small companies are getting loans again, and some people are feeling a tad more confident.

Japanese leaders have traditionally funnelled money into brick-and-mortar projects to stimulate the economy, so the signs of life these days are interpreted by most experts as just a temporary comeback, not a self-sustaining recovery. There have been many false starts in the last eight years, but the economy has always sunk back, this time into the deepest recession since World War II.

To the pessimists Japan is like a vehicle being towed away along the road by all that deficit spending; they doubt its engine will start without an overhaul.

Whatever the reasons for the movement, whatever the concerns for the future, though, the passengers throughout Japan seem relieved that at least the vehicle may be going forward again.

SOURCE: *The New York Times*, March 11, 1999, p. C1.

---

changes will not have a lasting effect on the position of the aggregate-demand curve. For example, a tax cut, by pushing Canada's interest rate above the world interest rate, will cause the exchange rate to rise. Thus, the tax cut crowds out net exports just as an increase in government expenditures does. If, however, the Bank of Canada chooses to fix the value of the exchange rate, a tax cut has a large and lasting effect on the position of the aggregate-demand curve. This is so because the Bank of Canada, in order to fix the value of the exchange rate, must purchase dollars in the market for foreign-currency exchange, causing the money supply to increase. The increase in the money supply removes the crowding-out effects on investment and net exports that prevent fiscal policy from having a lasting influence on aggregate demand.

DEFICIT REDUCTION

In recent years, Canadian governments at both the federal and the provincial levels have taken steps to reduce or eliminate their budget deficits. Some governments have relied primarily on reductions in expenditures, others have relied primarily on tax increases, and others have relied on a combination of both approaches. Some analysts have suggested that efforts to reduce government deficits are hazardous to the health of the Canadian economy because they cause a reduction in aggregate demand. Our discussion of the effects of changes in government expenditures and taxes under fixed and flexible exchange rates sheds

FYI

How Fiscal Policy Might Affect Aggregate Supply

So far our discussion of fiscal policy has stressed how changes in government purchases and changes in taxes influence the quantity of goods and services demanded. Most economists believe that the short-run macroeconomic effects of fiscal policy work primarily through aggregate demand. Yet fiscal policy can potentially also influence the quantity of goods and services supplied.

For instance, consider the effects of tax changes on aggregate supply. One of the *Ten Principles of Economics* in Chapter 1 is that people respond to incentives. When government policymakers cut tax rates, workers get to keep more of each dollar they earn, so they have a greater incentive to work and produce goods and services. If they respond to this incentive, the quantity of goods and services supplied will be greater at each price level, and the long-run aggregate-supply curve will shift to the right. Some economists, called *supply-siders,* have argued that the influence of tax cuts on aggregate supply is very large. Indeed, as we discussed in Chapter 8, some supply-siders claim the

influence is so large that a cut in tax rates will actually increase tax revenue by increasing worker effort. Most economists, however, doubt that the supply-side effects of cuts to tax rates are as large as this.

The fact that tax cuts cause the aggregate-supply curve to shift to the right is important because it suggests that tax cuts have a permanent effect on output. As we saw in Chapter 19, any shift in the aggregate-demand curve has only a temporary effect on output. Over time, as perceptions, wages, and prices adjust, the short-run aggregate-supply curve shifts to where the aggregate-demand curve intersects the long-run aggregate-supply curve. Unless the long-run aggregate-supply curve shifts, the shift in the aggregate-demand curve will have only a temporary effect on output. If tax cuts cause a shift to the right in the long-run aggregate-supply curve, then this represents a permanent increase in the natural level of output.

While this sounds like an exciting policy prescription—keep cutting tax rates and cause more and more permanent increases in output—we must remember that we need taxes to finance useful government programs. There would be no national defence, no social programs, and no universal health care without taxes. A more sensible, though perhaps less exciting, policy prescription is to keep tax rates as low as possible given the need to finance desired government spending programs.

light on this claim. As long as the Bank of Canada chooses to allow the exchange rate to vary freely, there is no reason to expect that efforts at deficit reduction will have any lasting influence on the position of the aggregate-demand curve. Once again, we see the importance of a coordinated effort between Canadian governments and the Bank of Canada. Deficit reduction can have a minimal impact on the level of aggregate demand if the central bank adopts the appropriate exchange-rate policy.

QUICK QUIZ: Explain how a decrease in government expenditures affects the money market and the position of the aggregate-demand curve. What is the effect for a closed economy, for an open economy when the Bank of Canada allows the exchange rate to vary, and for an open economy when the Bank of Canada chooses to maintain a fixed value for the exchange rate?

USING POLICY TO STABILIZE THE ECONOMY

We have seen how monetary and fiscal policy can affect the economy's aggregate demand for goods and services. These theoretical insights raise some important policy questions: Should policymakers use these instruments to control aggregate demand and stabilize the economy? If so, when? If not, why not?

THE CASE FOR ACTIVE STABILIZATION POLICY

The Canadian economy is often subject to the effects of unexpected events. Conflicts in the Middle East, oil price fluctuations, exchange-rate fluctuations, and stock-market booms and busts can all have serious impacts on the Canadian economy. Events such as these have often been responsible for large changes in output, employment, and income. We have seen that fiscal and monetary policy can be used to influence the position of the aggregate-demand curve and thereby cause changes in output, employment, and income. If we put these ideas together, we seem to have a strong case in favour of using policy instruments to offset the negative consequences of unexpected events. Simply put, unexpected expansions and contractions in the economy impose costs on people and firms in the form of unemployment, inflation, and uncertainty. If monetary and fiscal policy can be used to stabilize the economy, then surely these tools should be used to offset the harmful effects of economic fluctuations. This is the case in favour of using monetary and fiscal policy to stabilize the economy.

As we discussed in the preceding chapter, John Maynard Keynes's *The General Theory of Employment, Interest, and Money* has been one of the most influential books ever written about economics. In it, Keynes emphasized the key role of aggregate demand in explaining short-run economic fluctuations. Keynes claimed that the government should actively stimulate aggregate demand when aggregate demand appeared insufficient to maintain production at its full-employment level. At the time Keynes wrote his book, the world's major economies were in the midst of the Great Depression. It is little wonder, then, that the Keynesian proposal to use policy instruments to lessen the severity of economic downturns proved popular. Keynes (and his many followers) was a strong advocate of using policy instruments to stabilize the economy.

THE CASE AGAINST ACTIVE STABILIZATION POLICY

Some economists argue that the government should avoid active use of monetary and fiscal policy to try to stabilize the economy. They claim that these policy instruments should be set to achieve long-run goals, such as rapid economic growth and low inflation, and that the economy should be left to deal with short-run fluctuations on its own. Although these economists may admit that monetary and fiscal policy can stabilize the economy in theory, they doubt whether it can do so in practice.

The primary argument against active monetary and fiscal policy is that these policies affect the economy with a substantial lag. As we have seen, monetary policy works by changing interest rates, which in turn influence investment spending. But many firms make investment plans far in advance. Thus, most economists believe that it takes at least six months for changes in monetary policy to have much effect on output and employment. Moreover, once these effects occur, they can last for several years. Critics of stabilization policy argue that because of this lag, the Bank of Canada should not try to fine-tune the economy. They claim that the Bank of Canada often reacts too late to changing economic conditions and, as a result, ends up being a cause of rather than a cure for economic fluctuations. These critics advocate a passive monetary policy, such as slow and steady growth in the money supply.

Fiscal policy also works with a lag, but unlike the lag in monetary policy, the lag in fiscal policy is largely attributable to the political process. In Canada, most changes in federal government spending and taxes must go through parliamentary committees in both the House of Commons and the Senate, and be passed by both legislative bodies. Completing this process can take months and, in some cases, years. By the time the change in fiscal policy is passed and ready to implement, the condition of the economy may well have changed.

These lags in monetary and fiscal policy are a problem in part because economic forecasting is so imprecise. If forecasters could accurately predict the condition of the economy a year in advance, then monetary and fiscal policymakers could look ahead when making policy decisions. In this case, policymakers could stabilize the economy despite the lags they face. In practice, however, major recessions and depressions arrive without much advance warning. The best policymakers can do at any time is to respond to economic changes as they occur.

AUTOMATIC STABILIZERS

automatic stabilizers
changes in fiscal policy that stimulate aggregate demand when the economy goes into a recession without policymakers having to take any deliberate action

All economists—both advocates and critics of stabilization policy—agree that the lags in implementation render policy less useful as a tool for short-run stabilization. The economy would be more stable, therefore, if policymakers could find a way to avoid some of these lags. In fact, they have. **Automatic stabilizers** are changes in fiscal policy that stimulate aggregate demand when the economy goes into a recession without policymakers having to take any deliberate action.

The most important automatic stabilizer is the tax system. When the economy goes into a recession, the amount of taxes collected by the government falls automatically because almost all taxes are closely tied to economic activity. The personal income tax depends on households' incomes, payroll taxes depend on workers' earnings, and the corporate income tax depends on firms' profits. Because incomes, earnings, and profits all fall in a recession, the government's tax revenue falls as well. This automatic tax cut stimulates aggregate demand and, thereby, reduces the magnitude of economic fluctuations.

Government spending also acts as an automatic stabilizer. In particular, when the economy goes into a recession and workers are laid off, more people apply for Employment Insurance benefits, welfare benefits, and other forms of income support. This automatic increase in government spending stimulates aggregate demand at exactly the time when aggregate demand is insufficient to maintain full employment. Indeed, when the unemployment insurance system was first enacted in the 1930s, economists who advocated this policy did so in part because of its power as an automatic stabilizer.

The automatic stabilizers in the Canadian economy are not sufficiently strong to prevent recessions completely. Nonetheless, without these automatic stabilizers, output and employment would probably be more volatile than they are. For this reason, many economists oppose legislation that would require the federal government always to run a balanced budget, as some politicians have proposed. When the economy goes into a recession, taxes fall, government spending rises, and the government's budget moves toward deficit. If the government faced a strict balanced-budget rule, it would be forced to look for ways to raise taxes or cut spending in a recession. In other words, a strict balanced-budget rule would eliminate the automatic stabilizers inherent in our current system of taxes and government spending.

A FLEXIBLE EXCHANGE RATE AS AN AUTOMATIC STABILIZER

In an open economy, policymakers can choose to make use of another type of automatic stabilizer: a flexible exchange rate. Suppose Canada's largest trading partner, the United States, slips into recession. As the incomes of American households and firms fall, they spend less and we can expect that they buy fewer Canadian-produced goods. Canada's net exports fall and the aggregate-demand curve shifts to the left. If the Bank of Canada has chosen to allow the exchange rate to be flexible, we would expect the following to occur: The fall in net exports causes the incomes of Canadians to fall, and this reduces the demand for money. This causes Canada's interest rate to fall below the world interest rate. Both Canadians and foreigners sell Canadian assets in favour of foreign assets that pay the higher world interest rate. The switch from Canadian to foreign assets requires a corresponding sale of dollars in the market for foreign-currency exchange. The increased supply of dollars in the market for foreign-currency exchange causes the exchange rate to depreciate, and this causes net exports to increase. Canada's aggregate-demand curve now shifts back to the right, increasing the incomes of Canadians and increasing the demand for money until Canada's interest rate is again equal to the world interest rate. The recession in the United States has no lasting effects on the position of Canada's aggregate-demand curve.

What we have just seen is how allowing the exchange rate to be flexible enables policymakers to insulate the Canadian economy from the effects of foreign recessions. Given Canada's dependence on foreign trade, and hence Canada's exposure to the effects of foreign recessions, this would seem to be an attractive policy choice. Indeed, most economists favour flexible exchange rates, partly for this reason. Unfortunately, as economists are fond of saying, there is no such thing as a free lunch. That is, the benefits of a flexible exchange rate do not come without costs. An important cost is the fact that a flexible exchange rate introduces uncertainty into the pricing decisions of exporting and importing firms. Unexpected changes in the exchange rate mean unexpected changes in the Canadian dollar prices of imported and exported goods. A firm hoping to produce goods for export might be discouraged from doing so if it cannot be sure of how many Canadian dollars it will end up receiving for goods it sells abroad. These sorts of costs are what is behind recent proposals from economists Richard Harris and Thomas Courchene that Canada form a monetary union with the United States. Essentially they argue that Canada should adopt the U.S. dollar as its currency and thereby avoid all uncertainty about the price importers will have to pay for U.S.-produced goods and the price exporters will receive for Canadian-produced goods sold in the United States. By eliminating this uncertainty, an important impediment to trade will be eliminated and the benefits of free trade will be maximized. At this point, the majority of economists judge that the benefit of using a flexible exchange rate as an automatic stabilizer exceeds the costs of the price uncertainty that a flexible exchange rate introduces. However, the debate continues.

❙ **QUICK QUIZ:**   How does a reduction in government spending affect the aggregate demand curve? How does your answer differ if we consider a closed economy versus an open economy?

FYI

Interest Rates in the Long Run and the Short Run

At this point, we should pause and reflect on a seemingly awkward embarrassment of riches. We appear to have many explanations of how the interest rate is determined. This embarrassment of riches is due to the fact that we have sought to explain the determination of the interest rate under a number of circumstances: in the short run and the long run, and in a closed economy and a small open economy. All of these explanations are correct, and each is useful for understanding the rest. It might be a good idea at this point to summarize their relation to one another.

It is important to remind ourselves of the differences between the long-run and short-run behaviour of the economy. Three macroeconomic variables are of central importance: the economy's output of goods and services, the interest rate, and the price level. According to the classical macroeconomic theory we developed in Chapters 12, 13, and 16, these variables are determined as follows:

1. *Output* is determined by the supplies of capital and labour and the available production technology for turning capital and labour into output. (We call this the natural level of output.) Changes in the price level have no influence on output.

2. In a closed economy, for any given level of output, the *interest rate* adjusts to balance the supply and demand for loanable funds. In a small open economy, the domestic interest rate is equal to the world interest rate. Net foreign investmet (*NFI*) balances the supply and demand for loanable funds.

3. The *price level* adjusts to balance the supply and demand for money. Changes in the supply of money lead to proportionate changes in the price level.

These are three of the essential propositions of classical economic theory. Most economists believe that these propositions do a good job of describing how the economy works *in the long run.*

Yet these propositions do not hold in the short run. As we discussed in the preceding chapter, many prices are slow to adjust to changes in the money supply; this is reflected in a short-run aggregate supply curve that is upward sloping rather than vertical. For issues concerning the short run, then, it is best to think about the economy as follows:

1. The *price level* is stuck at some level (based on previously formed expectations) and, in the short run, is relatively unresponsive to changing economic conditions.

2. In a closed economy, for any given price level, the *interest rate* adjusts to balance the supply and demand for money. The price level cannot adjust to balance the supply and demand for money as it does in the long run because of price stickiness. In a small open economy, the interest rate must adjust to equal the world interest rate. With a flexible exchange rate, this adjustment requires a change in the exchange rate. By affecting net exports, a change in the exchange rate affects output and thus the demand for money. In this case, then, the demand for money adjusts to balance the supply and demand for money at the world interest rate. With a fixed exchange rate, the adjustment of the domestic interest rate to the world interest rate requires the Bank of Canada to buy and sell foreign currencies, and this causes changes in the supply of money. In this case, then, the supply of money adjusts to balance the supply and demand for money at the world interest rate.

3. The level of *output* responds to net changes in the aggregate demand for goods and services that remain after the crowding-out effects induced by interest rate and exchange-rate changes are taken into account.

Thus, the different theories of the interest rate are useful for different purposes. When thinking about the long-run determinants of interest rates, it is best to keep in mind the loanable-funds theory. By contrast, when thinking about the short-run determinants of interest rates, it is best to keep in mind the liquidity-preference theory and, in a small open economy, the fact that the Canadian interest rate must equal the world interest rate.

A QUICK SUMMARY

We have accomplished a lot in this chapter. We have shown how fiscal and monetary policy can influence the position of the aggregate-demand curve in a closed economy and in a small open economy under both a fixed and a flexible exchange rate. Throughout this chapter we have made the assumption that the price level is relatively unresponsive to changing economic conditions. To emphasize the role of such price stickiness, we have assumed that the price level is fixed. This assumption characterizes the short run, the focus of this chapter. Figure 20-12 summarizes what we have discovered about how fiscal and monetary policy can be used to influence the position of the aggregate-demand curve in the short-run.

Panel (a) in Figure 20-12 shows how the aggregate-demand curve shifts in response to expansionary fiscal and monetary policies in a closed economy. Our starting position is at point A on aggregate-demand curve AD_1. The price level is fixed at value $\bar{P}$. An expansionary fiscal policy (either an increase in government spending or a cut in taxes) and an expansionary monetary policy (an increase in the supply of money) both shift the aggregate-demand curve to the right (to position AD_2). In a closed economy, then, fiscal and monetary policies have the same effect on the position of the aggregate-demand curve. As we discussed in this chapter, they differ with respect to how they affect the interest rate: An expansionary fiscal policy causes the interest rate to increase because it causes the demand for money to increase, an expansionary monetary policy causes the interest rate to decrease because it involves an increase in the supply of money.

Panel (b) in Figure 20-12 shows how the aggregate-demand curve shifts in response to an expansionary fiscal policy in a small open economy. Once again, our starting position is at point A on aggregate-demand curve AD_1, with the price level fixed at value $\bar{P}$. If this was a closed economy, an expansionary fiscal policy would shift the aggregate-demand curve to position AD_2, and we would move from point A to point B at the fixed price level $\bar{P}$. In an open economy, the influence of an expansionary fiscal policy on the position of the aggregate-demand curve depends on whether the exchange rate is fixed or flexible. Under a fixed exchange rate, the same expansionary fiscal policy that shifted AD_1 to AD_2 would shift AD_1 to AD_3, and we move from point A to point C. This occurs because the expansionary fiscal policy forces Canada's interest rate above the world interest rate and thus causes an increase in the demand for dollars traded in the market for foreign-currency exchange. To prevent the exchange rate from changing, the Bank of Canada must increase the supply of dollars in this market, something it accomplishes by buying foreign currencies. Because when the Bank of Canada buys something it causes the money supply to increase, this is what gives us the second shift in the aggregate-demand curve. Under a flexible exchange rate, the same expansionary fiscal policy that shifted AD_1 to AD_2 in a closed economy would have no lasting impact on the position of the aggregate-demand curve. The aggregate-demand curve would return to AD_1, and we would return to point A. This occurs because, while the expansionary fiscal policy once again forces Canada's interest rate above the world interest rate, this time the resulting increase in the demand for dollars traded in the market for foreign-currency exchange is not offset by the actions of the Bank of Canada. Instead, the Bank of Canada allows the exchange rate to appreciate, and this causes net exports to fall. The fall in net exports offsets the expansionary fiscal policy, with the net result that there is no lasting impact on the position of the aggregate-demand curve.

Panel (c) in Figure 20-12 shows how the aggregate-demand curve shifts in response to an expansionary monetary policy in a small open economy. Once again, our starting position is at point A on aggregate-demand curve AD_1, with the

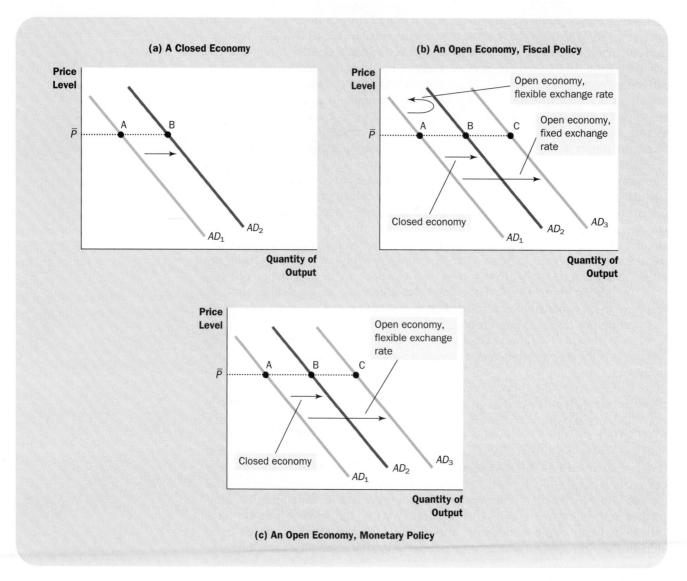

Figure 20-12

THE EFFECTS OF EXPANSIONARY MONETARY AND FISCAL POLICIES ON THE AGGREGATE-DEMAND CURVE. How fiscal and monetary policy affect the position of the aggregate-demand curve depends on whether the economy is closed or open. If the economy is open, the effect of fiscal and monetary policy depends on whether the Bank of Canada chooses to fix the value of the exchange rate or allow it to be flexible.

price level fixed at value $\bar{P}$. If this was a closed economy, an expansionary fiscal policy would shift the aggregate-demand curve to position AD_2, and we would move from point A to point B at the fixed price level $\bar{P}$. In an open economy, it makes sense for the Bank of Canada to pursue an expansionary monetary policy only if it allows the exchange rate to be flexible. Under a flexible exchange rate, the same expansionary monetary policy that shifted AD_1 to AD_2 would shift AD_1 to AD_3, and we would move from point A to point C. This occurs because the expansionary monetary policy forces Canada's interest rate below the world interest rate and thus causes an increase in the supply of dollars traded in the market for foreign-currency exchange. By causing the exchange rate to depreciate, the monetary expansion causes net exports to increase, and this is what gives us the second shift in the aggregate-demand curve.

Before leaving this quick summary, it is worthwhile to reiterate a point we have raised before: The predictions listed in this quick summary are based on an economic model characterized by a number of simplifications and assumptions. In macroeconomic courses you take in the future, some of these assumptions and simplifications will be relaxed. The result will be that some of the conclusions drawn from these models will need to modified and restated. As we discussed in Chapter 2, constructing models based on simplifying assumptions and then observing how predictions generated by the model change with these assumptions is a part of the scientific method. Having said that, it is nonetheless true that the basic models presented in this chapter provide a very useful way of thinking about the effects of fiscal and monetary policies on aggregate demand in open and closed economies.

CONCLUSION

Before policymakers make any change in policy, they need to consider all the effects of their decisions. Earlier in the book we examined classical models of the economy, which describe the long-run effects of monetary and fiscal policy. There we saw how fiscal policy influences saving, investment, the trade balance, and long-run growth, and how monetary policy influences the price level and the inflation rate.

In this chapter we examined the short-run effects of monetary and fiscal policy. We saw how these policy instruments can change the aggregate demand for goods and services and, thereby, alter the economy's production and employment in the short run. When Parliament reduces government spending in order to balance the budget, it needs to consider both the long-run effects on saving and growth and the short-run effects on aggregate demand and employment. When the Bank of Canada reduces the growth rate of the money supply, it must take into account the long-run effect on inflation as well as the short-run effect on production. In the next chapter we discuss the transition between the short run and the long run more fully, and we see that policymakers often face a tradeoff between long-run and short-run goals.

IN THE NEWS

The Independence of the Bank of Canada

CLOSELY RELATED TO THE QUESTION OF whether monetary and fiscal policy should be used to stabilize the economy is the question of who should set monetary and fiscal policy. In Canada, monetary policy is made by a central bank that operates free of most political pressures. Given the key role monetary policy plays in determining aggregate demand, it may seem unsatisfactory that in a democracy monetary policy decisions are not made by elected individuals. Most economists, however, favour this arrangement for reasons described in the following newspaper article.

An Independent Central Banker Serves Us Well

BY DAVID BOND

When the chair of the U.S. Federal Reserve characterized the bull market in stocks and bonds as exhibiting "irrational exuberance," prices plunged the following day, and there was fear of a crash such as occurred in October 1987. The markets came back, but that didn't deter the Republican leader in the U.S. Senate, Trent Lott, from musing that perhaps the central bank was just a tad too independent of political constraint. The implication was that Greenspan needed to be more careful.

Greenspan is a careful man. His comments were not some slip of the tongue. He chose his words because he knows that everything he says is scrutinized. The fact is, the stock and bond markets have been experiencing what one person refers to as "financial asset inflation," and Greenspan was simply trying to point out it will not continue forever.

Of course, with a vast pool of funds daily circling the globe in search of higher returns, even a modest shift in investment patterns can cause a price decline, such as hit the New York and other stock exchanges the day after his remarks. Markets are sensitive and fearful, and, given the high stakes involved, fund managers are a cautious lot. When someone of Greenspan's stature says something appears out of whack, the reaction is to get out before the rest of the world reacts. The herd instinct takes over and prices tumble.

Does this justify the remark that Greenspan is showing too much independence as a central banker? That question has plagued all central bankers since they began to function in the eighteenth century. The concept of an independent (from political interference) central banker is a practice born of necessity.

Ever wonder why there are those ridges on the side of the dime and quarter, or the curled surface on the penny, nickel, loonie, and new $2 coin?

Summary

◆ In developing a theory of short-run economic fluctuations, Keynes proposed the theory of liquidity preference to explain the determinants of the interest rate. According to this theory, the interest rate adjusts to balance the supply and demand for money.

◆ An increase in the price level raises money demand and increases the interest rate that brings the money market into equilibrium. Because the interest rate represents the cost of borrowing, a higher interest rate reduces investment and, thereby, the quantity of goods and services demanded. In a small open economy, an increase in the price level also increases the real

exchange rate. An increase in the real exchange rate makes Canadian-produced goods and services more expensive relative to foreign-produced goods and services. As a result, Canada's net exports fall, reducing the quantity demanded of Canadian goods and services. The downward sloping aggregate-demand curve expresses these negative relationships between the price level and the quantity demanded.

◆ Policymakers can influence aggregate demand with monetary policy. An increase in the money supply reduces the equilibrium interest rate for any given price level. Because a lower interest rate stimulates

That is a vestige of a bygone era when people, including monarchs, were given to "clipping" coins. Clipping occurred when coins were made of silver or gold and people made a practice of clipping a bit of the coin off before passing it on. Clip enough over time and you had a tidy amount of gold or silver to sell. The coin was but a ghost of its supposed weight after repeated clipping. Milled coins made clipping obvious.

What does that have to do with central bank independence? It's just a symbol. Keeping the central banker independent of political pressure is a method of ensuring the value of money is not debased by the modern-day equivalents of clipping, that is, resorting to the printing press to pay government bills.

The central banker has as a prime mandate the protection of the value of money, and that means controlling inflation, including inflation in financial assets. Take away that independence and you facilitate debasement of the monetary standard such as occurred in Serbia in the past three years, or in present-day Russia, or in earlier times Argentina and Chile.

What begins as a modest amount of inflation usually creeps upward as politicians become addicted to the ease with which they can spend ever more. If unchecked, it can yield hyperinflation of more than 1000 percent a day or even an hour. The result is the destruction of most savings, a rapid return to barter, and the eventual cessation of all economic activity.

Senator Lott wasn't advocating some move to inflation. He was exhibiting a casual attitude toward central banker independence and its essential role as part of the apparatus needed to effectively manage an economy.

In Canada, we have had our own measure of independent central bankers. James Coyne was fired in 1961 by the then-Conservative government over a fundamental policy disagreement. Subsequently each governor of the Bank of Canada has signed an accord with the government stating that the minister of finance can direct the bank to carry out a given policy, but that the governor can disagree and resign.

It is the thought of a governor resigning that causes governments to pause before insisting on policy. A resignation would destabilize money markets and probably hospitalize the dollar, which means the government gets its way, but at a price.

Independent central bankers may be irksome but they serve us well.

SOURCE: *Sun* (Vancouver), January 24, 1997, Final Edition, p. D2.

---

investment spending, the aggregate-demand curve shifts to the right. In a small open economy, the lower interest rate also means a fall in the exchange rate. Because a lower exchange rate increases the quantity demanded of Canadian-produced goods and services, a monetary injection in a small open economy shifts the aggregate-demand curve farther to the right than it does in a closed economy. Conversely, a decrease in the money supply raises the equilibrium interest rate for any given price level and shifts the aggregate-demand curve to the left. In a small open economy, the higher interest rate also means a rise in the exchange rate and, consequently, a fall in net exports. In a small open economy, then, a monetary contraction shifts the aggregate-demand curve farther to the left than it does in a closed economy.

◆ Policymakers can also influence aggregate demand with fiscal policy. An increase in government purchases or a cut in taxes shifts the aggregate-demand curve to the right. A decrease in government purchases or an increase in taxes shifts the aggregate-demand curve to the left.

◆ In a small open economy with perfect capital mobility, fiscal policy may or may not cause a lasting shift in the aggregate-demand curve. This depends on whether the Bank of Canada allows the exchange rate to vary freely. If the Bank of Canada allows the exchange rate to be flexible, fiscal policy has no lasting effect on the position of the aggregate-demand curve. This is so because the change in the exchange rate exerts an effect on net exports that is opposite to the fiscal policy in its influence on aggregate demand. If the Bank of Canada chooses to fix the value of the exchange rate, there is no such counteracting influence from net exports. In fact, by acting to fix the value of the exchange rate, the Bank of Canada causes the aggregate-demand curve to shift farther than it would in a closed economy. As a result, fiscal policy has a lasting effect on the position of the aggregate-demand curve.

◆ When the government alters spending or taxes, the resulting shift in aggregate demand can be larger or smaller than the fiscal change. The multiplier effect tends to amplify the effects of fiscal policy on aggregate demand. The crowding-out effect on investment tends to dampen the effects of fiscal policy on aggregate demand. The multiplier effect is much smaller in an open economy than in a closed economy.

◆ Because monetary and fiscal policy can influence aggregate demand, the government sometimes uses these policy instruments in an attempt to stabilize the economy. Economists disagree about how active the government should be in this effort. According to advocates of active stabilization policy, changes in unexpected economic conditions in Canada and abroad shift aggregate demand; if the government does not respond, the result is undesirable and unnecessary fluctuations in output and employment. According to critics of active stabilization policy, monetary and fiscal policy work with such long lags that attempts at stabilizing the economy often end up being destabilizing.

Key Concepts

theory of liquidity preference, p. 459

multiplier effect, p. 473
crowding-out effect on investment, p. 477

crowding-out effect on net exports, p. 480
automatic stabilizers, p. 488

Questions for Review

1. What is the theory of liquidity preference? How does it help explain the downward slope of the aggregate-demand curve?

2. Use the theory of liquidity preference to explain how a decrease in the money supply affects the aggregate-demand curve. Consider the effects in both a closed economy and a small open economy.   *graph*

3. The government spends $3 billion to buy police cars. Explain why aggregate demand might increase by more than $3 billion. Explain why aggregate demand might increase by less than $3 billion. Under what conditions might aggregate demand not change at all?

4. Suppose that survey measures of consumer confidence indicate a wave of pessimism is sweeping the country. If policymakers do nothing, what will happen to aggregate demand? What should the Bank of Canada do if it wants to stabilize aggregate demand? If the Bank of Canada does nothing, what might Parliament do to stabilize aggregate demand?

5. Give an example of a government policy that acts as an automatic stabilizer. Explain why this policy has this effect.

Problems and Applications

1. Explain how each of the following developments would affect the supply of money, the demand for money, and the interest rate. For each case, show what happens in a closed economy and in a small open economy. Illustrate your answers with diagrams.

a. The Bank of Canada's bond traders buy bonds in open-market operations.

b. An increase in credit card availability reduces the cash people hold.

c.   Households decide to hold more money to use for holiday shopping.

d.   A wave of optimism boosts business investment and expands aggregate demand.

e.   An increase in oil prices shifts the short-run aggregate-supply curve to the left.

2.   Suppose banks install automatic teller machines on every block and, by making cash readily available, reduce the amount of money people want to hold.

a.   Assume the Bank of Canada does not change the money supply. According to the theory of liquidity preference, what happens to the interest rate? What happens to aggregate demand? Assume a closed economy.

b.   If the Bank of Canada wants to stabilize aggregate demand, how should it respond?

3.   This chapter explains that expansionary monetary policy reduces the interest rate and thus stimulates demand for investment goods. Explain how such a policy also stimulates the demand for net exports.

4.   Suppose economists observe that in a closed economy an increase in government spending of $10 billion raises the total demand for goods and services by $30 billion.

a.   If these economists ignore the possibility of crowding out of investment, what would they estimate the marginal propensity to consume (*MPC*) to be?

b.   Now suppose the economists allow for crowding out. Would their new estimate of the *MPC* be larger or smaller than their initial one?

5.   Suppose the government of a closed economy reduces taxes by $20 billion, that there is no crowding out of investment, and that the marginal propensity to consume is 3/4.

a.   What is the initial effect of the tax reduction on aggregate demand?

b.   What additional effects follow this initial effect? What is the total effect of the tax cut on aggregate demand?

c.   How does the total effect of this $20 billion tax cut compare with the total effect of a $20 billion increase in government purchases? Why?

6.   Suppose government spending increases in a closed economy. Would the effect on aggregate demand be larger if the Bank of Canada took no action in response, or if the Bank were committed to maintaining a fixed interest rate? Explain.

7.   In which of the following circumstances is expansionary fiscal policy more likely to lead to a short-run increase in investment? Explain.

a.   when the investment accelerator is large, or when it is small?

b.   when the interest sensitivity of investment is large, or when it is small?

c.   when the marginal propensity to import is small, or when it is large?

8.   Suppose the Bank of Canada contracts the money supply in an effort to reduce aggregate demand by a particular amount, say $10 billion. Would the amount by which the Bank of Canada would need to reduce the supply of money to accomplish this goal if Canada was a closed economy be greater or smaller than the amount it would need to reduce the supply of money if Canada was an open economy with a flexible exchange rate?

9.   Suppose that the world interest rate rises. What happens to the position of the aggregate-demand curve in Canada? Assume that the Bank of Canada allows the exchange rate to be flexible. How does your answer change if you assume that the Bank of Canada maintains a fixed exchange rate? Illustrate your answer with diagrams.

10. Suppose that U.S. income rises. As a result, Canada's exports to the United States increase. What happens to the position of the aggregate-demand curve in Canada? Assume that the Bank of Canada allows the exchange rate to be flexible. How does your answer change if you assume that the Bank of Canada maintains a fixed exchange rate? Illustrate your answer with diagrams.

11. Suppose that the Bank of Canada decides to expand the money supply.

a.   Why would it be counterproductive for the Bank of Canada to fix the value of the exchange rate?

b.   What is the effect of this policy on the interest rate in the long run? How do you know?

12. For various reasons, fiscal policy changes automatically when output and employment fluctuate.

a.   Explain why tax revenue changes when the economy goes into a recession.

b.   Explain why government spending changes when the economy goes into a recession.

c.   If the government were to operate under a strict balanced-budget rule, what would it have to do in a recession? Would that make the recession more or less severe?

21

THE SHORT-RUN TRADEOFF
BETWEEN INFLATION
AND UNEMPLOYMENT

IN THIS CHAPTER
YOU WILL . . .

*Learn why
policymakers face a
short-run tradeoff
between inflation and
unemployment*

*Consider why
the inflation–
unemployment
tradeoff disappears
in the long run*

*See how supply
shocks can shift
the inflation–
unemployment
tradeoff*

*Consider the short-
run cost of reducing
the rate of inflation*

*See how
policymakers'
credibility might
affect the cost of
reducing inflation*

Two closely watched indicators of economic performance are inflation and unemployment. When Statistics Canada releases data on these variables each month, policymakers are eager to hear the news. Some commentators have added together the inflation rate and the unemployment rate to produce a *misery index,* which purports to measure the health of the economy.

How are these two measures of economic performance related to each other? Earlier in the book we discussed the long-run determinants of unemployment and the long-run determinants of inflation. We saw that the natural rate of unemployment depends on various features of the labour market, such as minimum-wage laws, the generosity of Employment Insurance, the market power of unions, the role of efficiency wages, and the effectiveness of job search. By contrast, the

499

inflation rate depends primarily on growth in the money supply, which a nation's central bank controls. In the long run, therefore, inflation and unemployment are largely unrelated problems.

In the short run, just the opposite is true. One of the *Ten Principles of Economics* discussed in Chapter 1 is that society faces a short-run tradeoff between inflation and unemployment. If monetary and fiscal policymakers expand aggregate demand and move the economy up along the short-run aggregate-supply curve, they can lower unemployment for a while, but only at the cost of higher inflation. If policymakers contract aggregate demand and move the economy down the short-run aggregate-supply curve, they can lower inflation, but only at the cost of temporarily higher unemployment.

In this chapter we examine this tradeoff more closely. The relationship between inflation and unemployment is a topic that has attracted the attention of some of the most important economists of the last half-century. The best way to understand this relationship is to see how thinking about it has evolved over time. As we will see, the history of thought regarding inflation and unemployment since the 1950s is inextricably connected to the history of the economies of North America and Western Europe. These two histories will show why the tradeoff between inflation and unemployment holds in the short run, why it does not hold in the long run, and what issues it raises for economic policymakers.

THE PHILLIPS CURVE

The short-run relationship between inflation and unemployment is often called the *Phillips curve*. We begin our story with the discovery of the Phillips curve.

ORIGINS OF THE PHILLIPS CURVE

The origins and early development of the Phillips curve had an international flavour. In 1958, New Zealand economist A.W. Phillips published an article in the British journal *Economica* that would make him famous. The article was titled "The Relationship between Unemployment and the Rate of Change of Money Wages in the United Kingdom, 1861–1957." In it, Phillips showed a negative correlation between the rate of unemployment and the rate of inflation. That is, he showed that years with low unemployment tend to have high inflation, and years with high unemployment tend to have low inflation. (Phillips examined inflation in nominal wages rather than inflation in prices, but for our purposes that distinction is not important. These two measures of inflation usually move together.) Phillips concluded that two important macroeconomic variables—inflation and unemployment—were linked in a way that economists had not previously appreciated. Two years later, Canadian economist Richard Lipsey confirmed and extended Phillips' observations. Lipsey used quantitative methods to derive a more accurate estimate of the change in inflation associated with particular rates of unemployment. In doing so, he introduced a methodology that economists would follow for many years to come.

Although the work of Phillips and Lipsey was based on data for the United Kingdom, researchers quickly confirmed their findings using data from many other countries. In the same year that Lipsey's article appeared, two American economists, Paul Samuelson and Robert Solow, entered the fray by testing the Phillips–Lipsey hypothesis using U.S. data. In their contribution, Samuelson and Solow reasoned that the negative correlation between inflation and unemployment that they found in U.S. data, and that others were finding in data from other countries, arose because low unemployment was associated with high aggregate demand and because high demand puts upward pressure on wages and prices throughout the economy. Samuelson and Solow dubbed the negative association between inflation and unemployment the **Phillips curve**. Figure 21-1 shows an example of a Phillips curve that reflects the hypothesis put forward by Samuelson and Solow.

Phillips curve
a curve that shows the short-run tradeoff between inflation and unemployment

Samuelson and Solow were interested in the Phillips curve because they believed that it held important lessons for policymakers. In particular, they suggested that the Phillips curve offers policymakers a menu of possible economic outcomes. By altering monetary and fiscal policy to influence aggregate demand, policymakers could choose any point on this curve. Point A offers high unemployment and low inflation. Point B offers low unemployment and high inflation. Policymakers might prefer both low inflation and low unemployment, but the historical data as summarized by the Phillips curve indicate that this combination is impossible. Thus, at this very early stage in the development of the Phillips curve, it seemed to economists that policymakers faced a permanent tradeoff between inflation and unemployment.

AGGREGATE DEMAND, AGGREGATE SUPPLY, AND THE PHILLIPS CURVE

The model of aggregate demand and aggregate supply provides an easy explanation for the menu of possible outcomes described by the Phillips curve. *The Phillips curve simply shows the combinations of inflation and unemployment that arise in the*

Figure 21-1

THE PHILLIPS CURVE.   The Phillips curve illustrates a negative association between the inflation rate and the unemployment rate. At point A, inflation is low and unemployment is high. At point B, inflation is high and unemployment is low.

short run as shifts in the aggregate-demand curve move the economy along the short-run aggregate-supply curve. As we saw in Chapter 19, an increase in the aggregate demand for goods and services leads, in the short run, to a larger output of goods and services and a higher price level. Larger output means greater employment and, thus, a lower rate of unemployment. In addition, whatever the previous year's price level happens to be, the higher the price level in the current year, the higher the rate of inflation. Thus, shifts in aggregate demand push inflation and unemployment in opposite directions in the short run—a relationship illustrated by the Phillips curve.

To see more fully how this works, let's consider an example. To keep the numbers simple, imagine that the price level (as measured, for instance, by the consumer price index) equals 100 in the year 2000. Figure 21-2 shows two possible outcomes that might occur in year 2001. Panel (a) shows the two outcomes using the model of aggregate demand and aggregate supply. Panel (b) illustrates the same two outcomes using the Phillips curve.

In panel (a) of the figure, we can see the implications for output and the price level in the year 2001. If the aggregate demand for goods and services is relatively low, the economy experiences outcome A. The economy produces output of 7500, and the price level is 102. By contrast, if aggregate demand is relatively high, the

Figure 21-2

How the Phillips Curve Is Related to the Model of Aggregate Demand and Aggregate Supply.   This figure assumes a price level of 100 for the year 2000 and charts possible outcomes for the year 2001. Panel (a) shows the model of aggregate demand and aggregate supply. If aggregate demand is low, the economy is at point A; output is low (7500), and the price level is low (102). If aggregate demand is high, the economy is at point B; output is high (8000), and the price level is high (106). Panel (b) shows the implications for the Phillips curve. Point A, which arises when aggregate demand is low, has high unemployment (7 percent) and low inflation (2 percent). Point B, which arises when aggregate demand is high, has low unemployment (4 percent) and high inflation (6 percent).

economy experiences outcome B. Output is 8000, and the price level is 106. Thus, higher aggregate demand moves the economy to an equilibrium with higher output and a higher price level.

In panel (b) of the figure, we can see what these two possible outcomes mean for unemployment and inflation. Because firms need more workers when they produce a greater output of goods and services, unemployment is lower in outcome B than in outcome A. In this example, when output rises from 7500 to 8000, unemployment falls from 7 percent to 4 percent. Moreover, because the price level is higher at outcome B than at outcome A, the inflation rate (the percentage change in the price level from the previous year) is also higher. In particular, since the price level was 100 in year 2000, outcome A has an inflation rate of 2 percent, and outcome B has an inflation rate of 6 percent. Thus, we can compare the two possible outcomes for the economy either in terms of output and the price level (using the model of aggregate demand and aggregate supply) or in terms of unemployment and inflation (using the Phillips curve).

As we saw in the preceding chapter, monetary and fiscal policy can shift the aggregate-demand curve. Therefore, monetary and fiscal policy can move the economy along the Phillips curve. Increases in the money supply, increases in government spending, or cuts in taxes expand aggregate demand and move the economy to a point on the Phillips curve with lower unemployment and higher inflation. Decreases in the money supply, cuts in government spending, or increases in taxes contract aggregate demand and move the economy to a point on the Phillips curve with lower inflation and higher unemployment. In this sense, the Phillips curve offers policymakers a menu of combinations of inflation and unemployment.

QUICK QUIZ: Draw the Phillips curve. Use the model of aggregate demand and aggregate supply to show how policy can move the economy from a point on this curve with high inflation to a point with low inflation.

SHIFTS IN THE PHILLIPS CURVE: THE ROLE OF EXPECTATIONS

The Phillips curve seems to offer policymakers a menu of possible inflation–unemployment outcomes. But does this menu remain stable over time? Is the Phillips curve a relationship on which policymakers can rely? These are the questions that economists took up in the late 1960s.

THE LONG-RUN PHILLIPS CURVE

In 1968, economist Milton Friedman published a paper in the *American Economic Review* based on an address he had recently given as president of the American Economic Association. The paper, titled "The Role of Monetary Policy," contained sections on "What Monetary Policy Can Do" and "What Monetary Policy Cannot Do." Friedman argued that one thing monetary policy cannot do, other than for only a short time, is pick a combination of inflation and unemployment on the

IN THE NEWS

The Effects of Low Unemployment

ACCORDING TO THE PHILLIPS CURVE, WHEN unemployment falls to low levels, wages and prices start to rise more quickly. The following article illustrates this link between labour-market conditions and inflation.

Power Returns to the Worker: Alberta's Surging Economy Is Putting Upward Pressure on Wages

BY TERRY MCCONNELL

Alberta's burgeoning economy is raising hopes within the province's labour movement that the gravy train is once again pulling into the station. There have already been two high-profile strikes in Alberta this year, one at Canada Safeway, the other at Cargill Foods in High River. Experts warn that labour disruptions will become more frequent as unions take advantage of the economic gains and demand higher wages.

"For anyone who works for a living, unionized or not, it's time to play catch-up," says Alberta Federation of Labour secretary-treasurer Les Steele. "With more hiring and fewer skilled workers available, the opportunity is there."

The job statistics would seem to bear him out. The overall unemployment rate in Alberta is down to a fifteen-year low of 5.6 percent. In Calgary, the rate is at 6.2 percent, while Edmonton is at 6.8 percent. Over 26 000 new jobs have been created in Edmonton in the past year, 5000 in Calgary. Inflation, at 2.4 percent, is only slightly higher than the national average, and that is due in part to rising housing prices in Calgary. Commercial rental space is shrinking and employment in business services is growing rapidly; Edmonton has seen a 35 percent increase in service-sector jobs in the past year. The weekend career sections in Calgary and Edmonton newspapers are well over twenty pages thick. The shortage of skilled labour has become so acute in some sectors that wage levels are beginning to rise dramatically. Entry-level receptionists in Calgary can now command salaries of up to $26 000, a 20 percent improvement over last year.

The demand is even greater for geologists, engineers, computer programmers, and various sorts of trades

Phillips curve. At about the same time, another economist, Edmund Phelps, also published a paper denying the existence of a long-run tradeoff between inflation and unemployment.

Friedman and Phelps based their conclusions on classical principles of macroeconomics, which we discussed in Chapters 12 through 18. Recall that classical theory points to growth in the money supply as the primary determinant of inflation. But classical theory also states that monetary growth does not have real effects—it merely alters all prices and nominal incomes proportionately. In particular, monetary growth does not influence those factors that determine the economy's unemployment rate, such as the market power of unions, the role of efficiency wages, or the process of job search. Friedman and Phelps concluded that there is no reason to think the rate of inflation would, *in the long run,* be related to the rate of unemployment.

Here, in his own words, is Friedman's view about what central banks can hope to accomplish in the long run:

> The monetary authority controls nominal quantities—directly, the quantity of its own liabilities [currency plus bank reserves]. In principle, it can use this control to peg a nominal quantity—an exchange rate, the price level, the nominal level of

people, especially carpenters and others related to the booming construction market. For the first time in more than a decade, workers have real bargaining power, and Mr. Steele figures they are due for it. In the past ten years, "the attitude was 'Be thankful you have a job,'" he observes. "That's not the attitude anymore. . . ."

The 1600 UFCW-backed workers at High River's Cargill Foods, Canada's largest beef-processing plant, went on strike July 10. They approved a 3 1/2 year deal last Friday that will see them paid higher wages and a $150 signing bonus. The demand for skilled labour is so high that during the strike, some workers were able to moonlight at other beef-processing plants to supplement their meagre strike pay. "People are less afraid of remaining unemployed," observes [labour historian Alvin] Finkel. "If workers are not afraid of the consequences of a strike, even of losing their jobs, then it will be difficult for compa-

nies to hold out against union demands." That makes Alberta fertile ground for the expansion of organized labour. . . .

Elsewhere in the province, a strike at the Marriott Corp.'s food services plant in Red Deer continues, while a strike or lockout looms at Edmonton's Maple Leaf Foods hog-processing plant. In the public sector, the province's teachers continue to ruminate about striking. School boards in Medicine Hat, Lethbridge, Elk Island, and the Catholic board in Calgary have all succumbed to teachers' demands for restoration of the 5 percent wage rollback imposed by the provincial government in 1993. . . .

Union officials believe the provincial economy can absorb rising labour costs without fuelling inflation or halting economic growth. "If unemployment was very low, 3 percent to 5 percent, then you might see some inflationary pressure," says Ian Thorn, national representative for the Communications, Energy and Paperworkers Union. "But we haven't got

that." Mr. Steele agrees. "I don't see inflation rampant like it was in the '70s and '80s," he says. "People learned their lesson from that."

All of which suggests labour demands will not prove excessive. "The inflation rate, the interest rate, the unemployment rate, have all been low in the U.S. and that didn't fuel major demands," says Mr. Thorn. "I don't think you will see a repeat of the '70s or '80s." Business leaders agree. Rising labour costs "are an indication of a healthier economy," says Edmonton Chamber of Commerce president Patrick Adams. He says the business community is not expecting a huge upward movement in prices as a result.

SOURCE: Excerpted from *Alberta Report*, Vol. 24, No. 35, August 11, 1997, pp. 18–19. Reprinted with permission.

national income, the quantity of money by one definition or another—or to peg the change in a nominal quantity—the rate of inflation or deflation, the rate of growth or decline in nominal national income, the rate of growth of the quantity of money. It cannot use its control over nominal quantities to peg a real quantity—the real rate of interest, the rate of unemployment, the level of real national income, the real quantity of money, the rate of growth of real national income, or the rate of growth of the real quantity of money.

These views have important implications for the Phillips curve. In particular, they imply that monetary policymakers face a long-run Phillips curve that is vertical, as in Figure 21-3. If the Bank of Canada increases the money supply slowly, the inflation rate is low, and the economy finds itself at point A. If the Bank of Canada increases the money supply quickly, the inflation rate is high, and the economy finds itself at point B. In either case, the unemployment rate tends toward its normal level, called the *natural rate of unemployment*. The vertical long-run Phillips curve illustrates the conclusion that unemployment does not depend on money growth and inflation in the long run.

The vertical long-run Phillips curve is, in essence, one expression of the classical idea of monetary neutrality. As you may recall, we expressed this idea in

Figure 21-3

THE LONG-RUN PHILLIPS CURVE. According to Friedman and Phelps, there is no tradeoff between inflation and unemployment in the long run. Growth in the money supply determines the inflation rate. Regardless of the inflation rate, the unemployment rate gravitates toward its natural rate. As a result, the long-run Phillips curve is vertical.

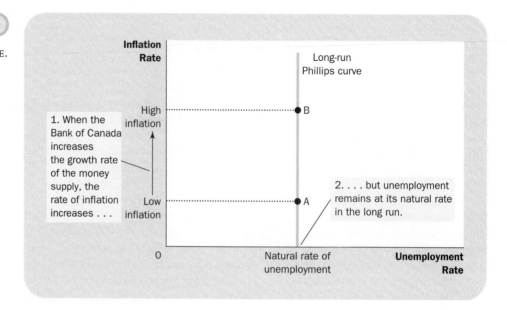

Chapter 19 with a vertical long-run aggregate-supply curve. Indeed, as Figure 21-4 illustrates, the vertical long-run Phillips curve and the vertical long-run aggregate-supply curve are two sides of the same coin. In panel (a) of this figure, an increase in the money supply shifts the aggregate-demand curve to the right from AD_1 to AD_2. As a result of this shift, the long-run equilibrium moves from point A to point B. The price level rises from P_1 to P_2, but because the aggregate-supply curve is vertical, output remains the same. In panel (b), more rapid growth in the money supply raises the inflation rate by moving the economy from point A to point B. But because the Phillips curve is vertical, the rate of unemployment is the same at these two points. Thus, the vertical long-run aggregate-supply curve and the vertical long-run Phillips curve both imply that monetary policy influences nominal variables (the price level and the inflation rate) but not real variables (output and unemployment). Regardless of the monetary policy pursued by the Bank of Canada, output and unemployment are, in the long run, at their natural rates.

What is so "natural" about the natural rate of unemployment? Friedman and Phelps used this adjective to describe the unemployment rate toward which the economy tends to gravitate in the long run. Yet the natural rate of unemployment is not necessarily the socially desirable rate of unemployment. Nor is the natural rate of unemployment constant over time. For example, suppose that a newly formed union uses its market power to raise the real wages of some workers above the equilibrium level. The result is a surplus of workers and, therefore, a higher natural rate of unemployment. This unemployment is "natural" not because it is good but because it is beyond the influence of monetary policy. More rapid money growth would not reduce the market power of the union or the level of unemployment; it would only lead to more inflation.

Although monetary policy cannot influence the natural rate of unemployment, other types of policy can. To reduce the natural rate of unemployment, policymakers should look to policies that improve the functioning of the labour market. Earlier in the book we discussed how various labour-market policies, such as minimum-wage laws, collective-bargaining laws, Employment Insurance, and job-training programs, affect the natural rate of unemployment. A policy change

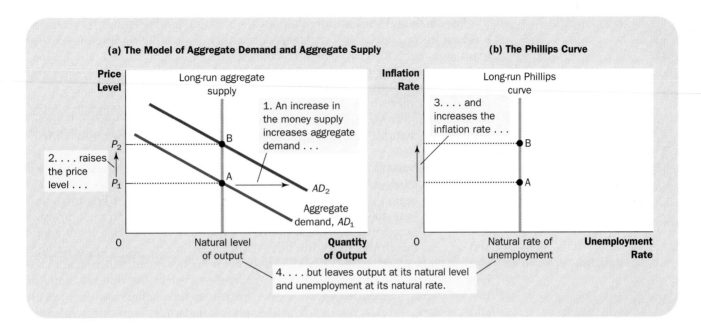

How the Long-Run Phillips Curve Is Related to the Model of Aggregate Demand and Aggregate Supply.   Panel (a) shows the model of aggregate demand and aggregate supply with a vertical aggregate-supply curve. When expansionary monetary policy shifts the aggregate-demand curve to the right from AD_1 to AD_2, the equilibrium moves from point A to point B. The price level rises from P_1 to P_2, while output remains the same. Panel (b) shows the long-run Phillips curve, which is vertical at the natural rate of unemployment. Expansionary monetary policy moves the economy from lower inflation (point A) to higher inflation (point B) without changing the rate of unemployment.

Figure 21-4

that reduced the natural rate of unemployment would shift the long-run Phillips curve to the left. In addition, because lower unemployment means more workers are producing goods and services, the quantity of goods and services supplied would be larger at any given price level, and the long-run aggregate-supply curve would shift to the right. The economy could then enjoy lower unemployment and higher output for any given rate of money growth and inflation.

EXPECTATIONS AND THE SHORT-RUN PHILLIPS CURVE

At first, the denial by Friedman and Phelps of a long-run tradeoff between inflation and unemployment might not seem persuasive. Their argument was based on an appeal to *theory*. By contrast, the negative correlation between inflation and unemployment uncovered by Phillips and Lipsey using UK data, and confirmed by economists using data from many countries, was based on *observation*, not theory. Why should anyone believe that policymakers faced a vertical Phillips curve when the world seemed to offer a downward-sloping one? Shouldn't the large number of observations of downward-sloping curves lead us to reject the classical conclusion of monetary neutrality?

Friedman and Phelps were well aware of these questions, and they offered a way to reconcile classical macroeconomic theory with the finding of a downward-sloping Phillips curve in data from the United Kingdom, the United States, and elswhere. They claimed that a negative relationship between inflation and unemployment holds in the short run but cannot be used by policymakers in the long run. In other words, policymakers can pursue expansionary monetary policy to achieve lower unemployment for a while, but eventually unemployment returns to its natural rate, and more expansionary monetary policy leads only to higher inflation.

Friedman and Phelps reasoned as we did in Chapter 19 when we explained the difference between the short-run and long-run aggregate-supply curves. (In fact, the discussion in that chapter drew heavily on the legacy of Friedman and Phelps.) As you may recall, the short-run aggregate-supply curve is upward sloping, indicating that an increase in the price level raises the quantity of goods and services that firms supply. By contrast, the long-run aggregate-supply curve is vertical, indicating that the price level does not influence quantity supplied in the long run. Chapter 19 presented three theories to explain the upward slope of the short-run aggregate-supply curve: misperceptions about relative prices, sticky wages, and sticky prices. Because perceptions, wages, and prices adjust to changing economic conditions over time, the positive relationship between the price level and quantity supplied applies in the short run but not in the long run. Friedman and Phelps applied this same logic to the Phillips curve. Just as the aggregate-supply curve slopes upward only in the short run, the tradeoff between inflation and unemployment holds only in the short run. And just as the long-run aggregate-supply curve is vertical, the long-run Phillips curve is also vertical.

To help explain the short-run and long-run relationship between inflation and unemployment, Friedman and Phelps introduced a new variable into the analysis: *expected inflation*. Expected inflation measures how much people expect the overall price level to change. As we discussed in Chapter 19, the expected price level affects the perceptions of relative prices that people form and the wages and prices that they set. As a result, expected inflation is one factor that determines the position of the short-run aggregate-supply curve. In the short run, the Bank of Canada can take expected inflation (and thus the short-run aggregate-supply curve) as already determined. When the money supply changes, the aggregate-demand curve shifts, and the economy moves along a given short-run aggregate-supply curve. In the short run, therefore, monetary changes lead to unexpected fluctuations in output, prices, unemployment, and inflation. In this way, Friedman and Phelps explained the downward-sloping Phillips curve that had been observed in the data from so many countries.

Yet the Bank of Canada's ability to create unexpected inflation by increasing the money supply exists only in the short run. In the long run, people come to expect whatever inflation rate the Bank chooses to produce. Because perceptions, wages, and prices will eventually adjust to the inflation rate, the long-run aggregate-supply curve is vertical. In this case, changes in aggregate demand, such as those due to changes in the money supply, do not affect the economy's output of goods and services. Thus, Friedman and Phelps concluded that unemployment returns to its natural rate in the long run.

The analysis of Friedman and Phelps can be summarized in the following equation (which is, in essence, another expression of the aggregate-supply equation we saw in Chapter 19):

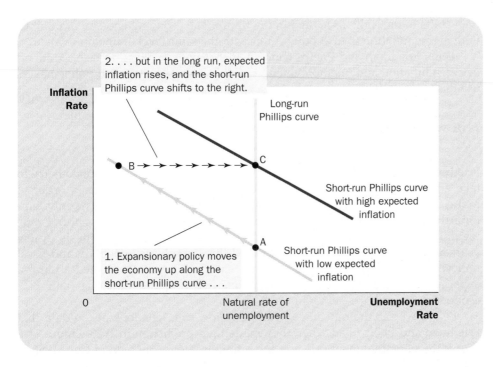

Figure 21-5

How Expected Inflation Shifts the Short-Run Phillips Curve.   The higher the expected rate of inflation, the higher the short-run tradeoff between inflation and unemployment. At point A, expected inflation and actual inflation are both low, and unemployment is at its natural rate. If the Bank of Canada pursues an expansionary monetary policy, the economy moves from point A to point B in the short run. At point B, expected inflation is still low, but actual inflation is high. Unemployment is below its natural rate. In the long run, expected inflation rises, and the economy moves to point C. At point C, expected inflation and actual inflation are both high, and unemployment is back to its natural rate.

$$\text{Unemployment rate} = \text{Natural rate of unemployment} - a\left(\text{Actual inflation} - \text{Expected inflation}\right).$$

This equation relates the unemployment rate to the natural rate of unemployment, actual inflation, and expected inflation. In the short run, expected inflation is given. As a result, higher actual inflation is associated with lower unemployment. (How much unemployment responds to unexpected inflation is determined by the size of a, a number that in turn depends on the slope of the short-run aggregate-supply curve.) In the long run, however, people come to expect whatever inflation the Bank of Canada produces. Thus, actual inflation equals expected inflation, and unemployment is at its natural rate.

This equation implies that there is no stable short-run Phillips curve. Each short-run Phillips curve reflects a particular expected rate of inflation. (To be precise, if you graph the equation, you'll find that the short-run Phillips curve intersects the long-run Phillips curve at the expected rate of inflation.) Whenever expected inflation changes, the short-run Phillips curve shifts.

According to Friedman and Phelps, it is dangerous to view the Phillips curve as a menu of options available to policymakers. To see why, imagine an economy at its natural rate of unemployment with low inflation and low expected inflation, shown in Figure 21-5 as point A. Now suppose that policymakers try to take advantage of the tradeoff between inflation and unemployment by using monetary or fiscal policy to expand aggregate demand. In the short run when expected inflation is given, the economy goes from point A to point B. Unemployment falls below its natural rate, and inflation rises above expected inflation. Over time, people get used to this higher inflation rate, and they raise their expectations of inflation. When expected inflation rises, firms and workers start taking higher inflation into account when setting wages and prices. The short-run Phillips curve then shifts to the right, as shown in the figure. The economy ends up at point C, with higher inflation than at point A but with the same level of unemployment.

Thus, Friedman and Phelps concluded that policymakers do face a tradeoff between inflation and unemployment, but only a temporary one. If policymakers use this tradeoff, they lose it.

THE NATURAL EXPERIMENT FOR THE NATURAL-RATE HYPOTHESIS

natural-rate hypothesis
the claim that unemployment eventually returns to its normal, or natural, rate, regardless of the rate of inflation

Friedman and Phelps had made a bold prediction in 1968: If policymakers try to take advantage of the Phillips curve by choosing higher inflation in order to reduce unemployment, they will succeed at reducing unemployment only temporarily. This view—that unemployment eventually returns to its natural rate, regardless of the rate of inflation—is called the **natural-rate hypothesis.** A few years after Friedman and Phelps proposed this hypothesis, monetary and fiscal policymakers in Canada and the United States inadvertently created a natural experiment to test it. Their laboratory consisted of the Canadian and U.S. economies.

Before we see the outcome of this test, however, let's look at the data that Friedman and Phelps had when they made their prediction in 1968. Figure 21-6 shows the unemployment rate and the inflation rate for the period from 1956 to 1968. These data trace out a Phillips curve. As inflation rose over these thirteen years, unemployment fell. The economic data from this era seemed to confirm the tradeoff between inflation and unemployment.

The apparent success of the Phillips curve in the 1950s and 1960s made the prediction of Friedman and Phelps all the more bold. In 1958 Phillips had sug-

Figure 21-6

THE PHILLIPS CURVE IN THE 1950S AND 1960S.   This figure uses annual data from 1956 to 1968 on the unemployment rate and on the inflation rate (as measured by the GDP deflator) to show the negative relationship between inflation and unemployment.

SOURCES: Data on the unemployment rate for the period 1966 to 1968 are from Statistics Canada, *Historical Labour Force Statistics*, Catalogue No. 71-201; data for 1956 to 1965 are from F.H. Leacy, ed., *Historical Statistics of Canada*, 2nd ed. (Ottawa: Statistics Canada, 1983), series D233; data on the GDP deflator are from Statistics Canada, *National Income and Expenditure Accounts*, Catalogue No. 13-001, and CANSIM.

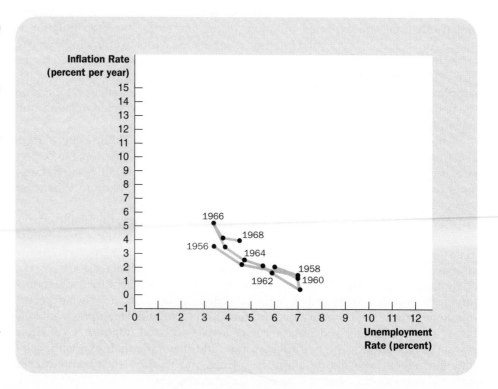

gested a negative association between inflation and unemployment. Another decade of data had confirmed the relationship for Canada, the United States, and many other countries. To some economists at the time, it seemed ridiculous to claim that the Phillips curve would break down once policymakers tried to use it.

But, in fact, that is exactly what happened. Beginning in the late 1960s, policies were enacted that expanded the aggregate demand for goods and services. In part, this expansion was due to fiscal policy: Federal and provincial government spending was increasing much faster than the economy. In part, it was due to monetary policy: Because the Bank of Canada was trying to hold down interest rates in the face of expansionary fiscal policy, during the period 1969 to 1973 the quantity of money (as measured by M1) was allowed to increase at twice the annual rate it did during the period 1956 to 1968. As a result, inflation stayed high (averaging 5.4 percent from 1969 to 1973, compared with 2.6 percent from 1956 to 1968). But, as Friedman and Phelps had predicted, unemployment did not stay low.

Figure 21-7 displays the history of inflation and unemployment from 1956 to 1973. It shows that the simple negative relationship between these two variables started to break down around 1970. In particular, as inflation remained high in the early 1970s, people's expectations of inflation caught up with reality, and the unemployment rate reverted to the 5 percent to 6 percent range that had prevailed in the early 1960s. Notice that the history illustrated in Figure 21-7 closely resembles the theory of a shifting short-run Phillips curve shown in Figure 21-5. By 1973, policymakers had learned that Friedman and Phelps were right: There is no tradeoff between inflation and unemployment in the long run.

QUICK QUIZ: Draw the short-run Phillips curve and the long-run Phillips curve. Explain why they are different.

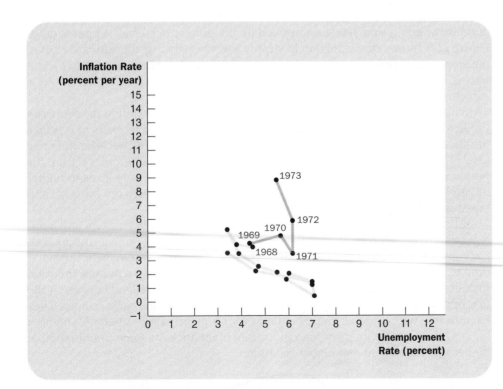

Figure 21-7

THE BREAKDOWN OF THE PHILLIPS CURVE.   This figure shows annual data from 1956 to 1973 on the unemployment rate and on the inflation rate (as measured by the GDP deflator). Notice that the Phillips curve of the 1960s breaks down in the early 1970s.

SOURCES: SEE FIGURE 21-6.

SHIFTS IN THE PHILLIPS CURVE:
THE ROLE OF SUPPLY SHOCKS

Friedman and Phelps had suggested in 1968 that changes in expected inflation shift the short-run Phillips curve, and the experience of the early 1970s convinced most economists that Friedman and Phelps were right. Within a few years, however, the economics profession would turn its attention to a different source of shifts in the short-run Phillips curve: shocks to aggregate supply.

This time, the shift in focus came not from two American economics professors but from events in the Middle East. The Organization of Petroleum Exporting Countries (OPEC) was founded in 1960, but it was ineffectual at influencing oil prices until the early 1970s. Following a military takeover of the Libyan government in 1969, and following the success that country had in imposing new agreements on oil companies concerning pricing following the takeover, OPEC members began to act together to push up oil prices. At first, these efforts met with limited success. However, in the midst of the 1973 Middle East war, a war that had already caused oil prices to rise, OPEC met again and began to effectively exert its market power as a cartel in the world oil market. The countries of OPEC, such as Saudi Arabia, Kuwait, and Iraq, restricted the amount of crude oil they pumped and sold on world markets. Within a few years, this reduction in supply caused the price of oil to almost double.

supply shock

an event that directly alters firms' costs and prices, shifting the economy's aggregate-supply curve and thus the Phillips curve

A large increase in the world price of oil is an example of a supply shock. A **supply shock** is an event that directly affects firms' costs of production and thus the prices they charge; it shifts the economy's aggregate-supply curve and, as a result, the Phillips curve. For example, when an oil price increase raises the cost of producing gasoline, heating oil, tires, and many other products, it reduces the quantity of goods and services supplied at any given price level. As panel (a) of Figure 21-8 shows, this reduction in supply is represented by the leftward shift in the aggregate-supply curve from AS_1 to AS_2. The price level rises from P_1 to P_2, and output falls from Y_1 to Y_2. The combination of rising prices and falling output is sometimes called *stagflation*.

This shift in aggregate supply is associated with a similar shift in the short-run Phillips curve, shown in panel (b). Because firms need fewer workers to produce the smaller output, employment falls and unemployment rises. Because the price level is higher, the inflation rate—the percentage change in the price level from the previous year—is also higher. Thus, the shift in aggregate supply leads to higher unemployment and higher inflation. The short-run tradeoff between inflation and unemployment shifts to the right from PC_1 to PC_2.

Confronted with an adverse shift in aggregate supply, policymakers face a difficult choice between fighting inflation and fighting unemployment. If they contract aggregate demand to fight inflation, they will raise unemployment further. If they expand aggregate demand to fight unemployment, they will raise inflation further. In other words, policymakers face a less favourable tradeoff between inflation and unemployment than they did before the shift in aggregate supply: They have to live with a higher rate of inflation for a given rate of unemployment, a higher rate of unemployment for a given rate of inflation, or some combination of higher unemployment and higher inflation.

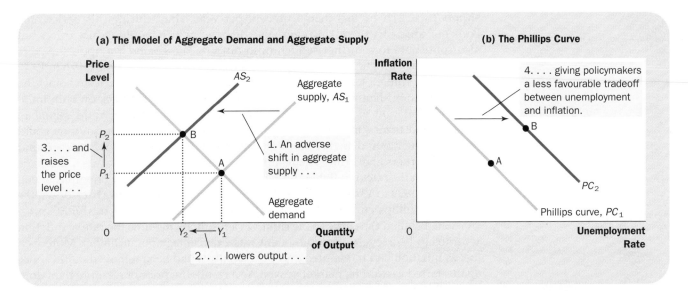

(a) The Model of Aggregate Demand and Aggregate Supply

(b) The Phillips Curve

Price Level

AS_2

Aggregate supply, AS_1

P_2 · · · · · · · · · · · · B

3. . . . and raises the price level . . .

P_1 · · · · · · · · · · · · A

1. An adverse shift in aggregate supply . . .

Aggregate demand

0   Y_2 ← Y_1 Quantity of Output

2. . . . lowers output . . .

Inflation Rate

4. . . . giving policymakers a less favourable tradeoff between unemployment and inflation.

B

A

PC_2

Phillips curve, PC_1

0   Unemployment Rate

AN ADVERSE SHOCK TO AGGREGATE SUPPLY.   Panel (a) shows the model of aggregate demand and aggregate supply. When the aggregate-supply curve shifts to the left from AS_1 to AS_2, the equilibrium moves from point A to point B. Output falls from Y_1 to Y_2, and the price level rises from P_1 to P_2. Panel (b) shows the short-run tradeoff between inflation and unemployment. The adverse shift in aggregate supply moves the economy from a point with lower unemployment and lower inflation (point A) to a point with higher unemployment and higher inflation (point B). The short-run Phillips curve shifts to the right from PC_1 to PC_2. Policymakers now face a worse tradeoff between inflation and unemployment.

Figure 21-8

An important question is whether this adverse shift in the Phillips curve is temporary or permanent. The answer depends on how people adjust their expectations of inflation. If people view the rise in inflation due to the supply shock as a temporary aberration, expected inflation does not change, and the Phillips curve will soon revert to its former position. But if people believe the shock will lead to a new era of higher inflation, then expected inflation rises, and the Phillips curve remains at its new, less desirable position.

Figure 21-9 shows inflation and unemployment in the Canadian economy during the 1970s. It shows that in the mid-1970s inflation increased dramatically as a result of the OPEC oil price shock. The increase in the price of oil meant that Canadian firms using oil as an input in their production processes would soon suffer dramatically higher costs. If nothing was done, the result would be both higher inflation and a higher unemployment rate: stagflation. Canadian policymakers were therefore faced with a difficult choice brought about by the threat of stagflation: Should they respond to the threat of stagflation by contracting aggregate demand to fight inflation but contribute to an increase in unemployment, or should they expand aggregate demand to fight unemployment but at the cost of increasing inflation and inflationary expectations even further?

Policymakers chose to attack the problem of stagflation in two ways. First, the Bank of Canada instituted a tight monetary policy. From 1974 to 1978, the money supply increased by less than 1 percent per year. Thus, during this period, the Bank of Canada was reducing aggregate demand, which would reduce prices but also contribute to a further reduction in output. The second way policymakers chose to attack inflation was to impose wage and price controls. From 1976 to 1978, federal government legislation limited increases in wages and prices to below the rate of inflation. These controls were designed to be a direct attack on both infla- tion and inflation expectations. The hope was that controls would signal to workers and firms that, because everyone was being made to do so, they could moderate their own demands for higher wages and prices without losing ground to other workers and firms. The result of this two-pronged attack was a dramatic reduction in the rate of inflation but also an increase in the rate of unemployment. During the 1974 to 1978 period, the Canadian economy was sliding back down the short-run Phillips curve. Unfortunately, however, the effects of the OPEC price shock had shifted the curve to the right. As a result, by the time the rate of inflation returned to 1972 levels, unemployment was 2 percentage points higher. Moreover, just as inflation had moderated and price controls had been removed, OPEC once again started to exert its market power. As a result, the price of oil more than dou- bled in 1979.

In the wake of the second OPEC oil price shock, the Canadian economy was faced again with a much higher rate of inflation and the threat that expectations of inflation would remain high. In 1980, after two OPEC supply shocks, Canada had an inflation rate of more than 10 percent and an unemployment rate of 7.5 percent. This combination of inflation and unemployment was not at all near the tradeoff

Figure 21-9

THE SUPPLY SHOCKS OF THE 1970S.   This figure shows annual data from 1973 to 1980 on the unemployment rate and on the inflation rate (as measured by the GDP deflator). Increases in the world price of oil in the early 1970s and again in 1979 caused large jumps in the rate of inflation and caused the short-run Phillips curve to shift to the right. In between these two oil price shocks, tight monetary policy and wage and price controls caused Canada to slide down a temporarily stable short- run curve.

SOURCES: SEE FIGURE 21-6.

"Remember the good old days when all the economy needed was a little fine-tuning?"

that seemed possible in the 1960s. (In the 1960s, the Phillips curve suggested that an unemployment rate of 7.5 percent would be associated with an inflation rate of less than 1.0 percent. Inflation of more than 10.0 percent was unthinkable.) With the misery index in 1980 near a historic high, the public was widely dissatisfied with macroeconomic performance. Something had to be done, and soon it would be.

QUICK QUIZ: Give an example of a favourable shock to aggregate supply. Use the model of aggregate demand and aggregate supply to explain the effects of such a shock. How does it affect the Phillips curve?

THE COST OF REDUCING INFLATION

In October 1979, as OPEC was imposing adverse supply shocks on the world's economies for the second time in a decade, the Bank of Canada decided that the time for action had come. As guardian of the nation's monetary system, the Bank of Canada had little choice but to pursue a policy of *disinflation*—a reduction in the rate of inflation. There was no doubt that the Bank of Canada could reduce inflation through its ability to control the quantity of money. But what would be the short-run cost of disinflation? The answer to this question was much less certain.

THE SACRIFICE RATIO

To reduce the inflation rate, the Bank of Canada has to pursue contractionary monetary policy. Figure 21-10 shows some of the effects of such a decision. When the Bank of Canada slows the rate at which the money supply is growing, it contracts aggregate demand. The fall in aggregate demand, in turn, reduces the quantity of goods and services that firms produce, and this fall in production leads to a fall in employment. The economy begins at point A in the figure and moves along the short-run Phillips curve to point B, which has lower inflation and higher unemployment. Over time, as people come to understand that prices are rising more slowly, expected inflation falls, and the short-run Phillips curve shifts downward. The economy moves from point B to point C. Inflation is lower, and unemployment is back to its natural rate.

Thus, if a nation wants to reduce inflation, it must endure a period of high unemployment and low output. In Figure 21-10, this cost is represented by the movement of the economy through point B as it travels from point A to point C. The size of this cost depends on the slope of the Phillips curve and how quickly expectations of inflation adjust to the new monetary policy.

Many studies have examined the data on inflation and unemployment in order to estimate the cost of reducing inflation. The findings of these studies are often summarized in a statistic called the **sacrifice ratio.** The sacrifice ratio is the number of percentage points of one year's output lost in the process of reducing inflation by 1 percentage point. Macroeconomists have found it difficult to obtain a precise estimate of the sacrifice ratio. Typical estimates of the sacrifice ratio for Canada fall over quite a wide range of between 2 and 5. That is, for each per-

sacrifice ratio

the number of percentage points of one year's output lost in the process of reducing inflation by 1 percentage point

---

Figure 21-10

DISINFLATIONARY MONETARY POLICY IN THE SHORT RUN AND LONG RUN.   When the Bank of Canada pursues contractionary monetary policy to reduce inflation, the economy moves along a short-run Phillips curve from point A to point B. Over time, expected inflation falls, and the short-run Phillips curve shifts downward. When the economy reaches point C, unemployment is back to its natural rate.

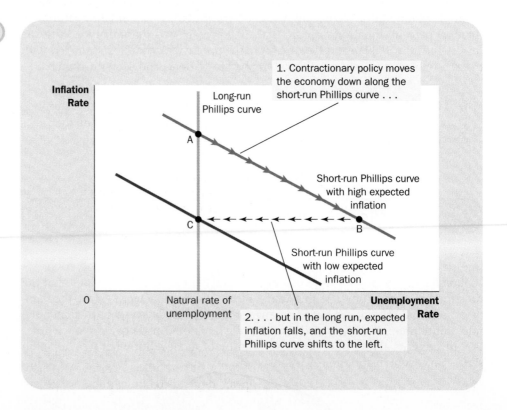

centage point that inflation is reduced, between 2 and 5 percent of one year's output must be sacrificed in the transition. We can also express the sacrifice ratio in terms of unemployment. For this purpose we need an estimate of how much a 1 percentage point fall in output translates into an increase in unemployment. **Okun's law** provides such an estimate. Okun's law suggests that a change of 1 percentage point in GDP translates into a change of 0.5 percentage points of unemployment. Therefore, the range of estimates for the sacrifice ratio suggest that reducing inflation by 1 percentage point requires a sacrifice of between 1 and 2.5 percentage points of unemployment.

Such estimates surely must have made the Bank of Canada apprehensive as it confronted the task of reducing inflation. In 1979, inflation was running at 10.0 percent per year and the unemployment rate was 7.5 percent. To reach moderate inflation of, say, 4 percent per year would mean reducing inflation by 6 percentage points. If the true size of the sacrifice ratio were at the top end of the range of estimates, so that each percentage point cost 5 percent of one year's output, then reducing inflation by 6 percentage points would require sacrificing 30 percent of one year's output. By the same token, it would cost 15 percentage points of unemployment.

According to studies of the Phillips curve and the cost of disinflation, this sacrifice could be paid in various ways. An immediate reduction in inflation would depress output by 30 percent and increase the unemployment rate by 15 percentage points in a single year. That outcome was surely too harsh even for inflation hawks. It would be better, many argued, to spread out the cost over several years. If the reduction in inflation took place over five years, for instance, then output would have to average only 6 percent below trend during that period to add up to a sacrifice of 30 percent. Similarly, reducing inflation by 6 percentage points over a five-year period would mean the unemployment rate would need to rise by only 3 percentage points and remain at 10.5 percent for the five-year transition period. An even more gradual approach would be to reduce inflation slowly over a decade, so that output would have to be only 3 percent below trend. Whatever path was chosen, however, it seemed that reducing inflation would not be easy.

Okun's Law
the number of percentage points the unemployment rate increases when GDP falls by 1 percentage point

RATIONAL EXPECTATIONS AND THE POSSIBILITY OF COSTLESS DISINFLATION

Just as policymakers were pondering how costly reducing inflation might be, a group of economics professors was leading an intellectual revolution that would challenge the conventional wisdom on the sacrifice ratio. This group included such prominent economists as Robert Lucas, Thomas Sargent, and Robert Barro. Their revolution was based on a new approach to economic theory and policy called **rational expectations.** According to the theory of rational expectations, people optimally use all the information they have, including information about government policies, when forecasting the future.

This new approach has had profound implications for many areas of macroeconomics, but none is more important than its application to the tradeoff between inflation and unemployment. As Friedman and Phelps had first emphasized, expected inflation is an important variable that explains why there is a tradeoff between inflation and unemployment in the short run but not in the long run. How quickly the short-run tradeoff disappears depends on how quickly expecta-

rational expectations
the theory according to which people optimally use all the information they have, including information about government policies, when forecasting the future

tions adjust. Proponents of rational expectations built on the Friedman–Phelps analysis to argue that when economic policies change, people adjust their expectations of inflation accordingly. Studies of inflation and unemployment that tried to estimate the sacrifice ratio had failed to take account of the direct effect of the policy regime on expectations. As a result, estimates of the sacrifice ratio were, according to the rational-expectations theorists, unreliable guides for policy.

In a 1981 paper titled "The End of Four Big Inflations," Thomas Sargent described this new view as follows:

> An alternative "rational expectations" view denies that there is any inherent momentum to the present process of inflation. This view maintains that firms and workers have now come to expect high rates of inflation in the future and that they strike inflationary bargains in light of these expectations. However, it is held that people expect high rates of inflation in the future precisely because the government's current and prospective monetary and fiscal policies warrant those expectations. . . . An implication of this view is that inflation can be stopped much more quickly than advocates of the "momentum" view have indicated and that their estimates of the length of time and the costs of stopping inflation in terms of foregone output are erroneous. . . . This is not to say that it would be easy to eradicate inflation. On the contrary, it would require more than a few temporary restrictive fiscal and monetary actions. It would require a change in the policy regime. . . . How costly such a move would be in terms of foregone output and how long it would be in taking effect would depend partly on how resolute and evident the government's commitment was.

According to Sargent, the sacrifice ratio could be much smaller than suggested by previous estimates. Indeed, in the most extreme case, it could be zero. If policymakers made a credible commitment to a policy of low inflation, people would be rational enough to lower their expectations of inflation immediately. The short-run Phillips curve would shift downward, and the economy would reach low inflation quickly without the cost of temporarily high unemployment and low output.

DISINFLATION IN THE 1980s

As we have seen, when the Bank of Canada at the beginning of the 1980s faced the prospect of reducing inflation from its peak of about 11 percent, the economics profession offered two conflicting predictions. One group of economists offered estimates of the sacrifice ratio and concluded that reducing inflation would have great cost in terms of lost output and high unemployment. Another group offered the theory of rational expectations and concluded that reducing inflation could be much less costly and, perhaps, could even have no cost at all. Who was right?

Figure 21-11 shows inflation and unemployment from 1980 to 1988. As you can see, the Bank of Canada did succeed at reducing inflation. Inflation came down from almost 11.0 percent in 1980 and 1981 to about 2.5 percent in 1985 and 1986. Credit for this reduction in inflation goes completely to monetary policy. Fiscal policy at this time was acting in the opposite direction: The increases in the budget deficits of the provinces and the federal government were expanding aggregate demand, which tends to raise inflation. The dramatic fall in inflation from 1981 to 1985 is attributable to the equally dramatic anti-inflation policies of the Bank of Canada. From 1979 to 1982, the money supply, as measured by M1,

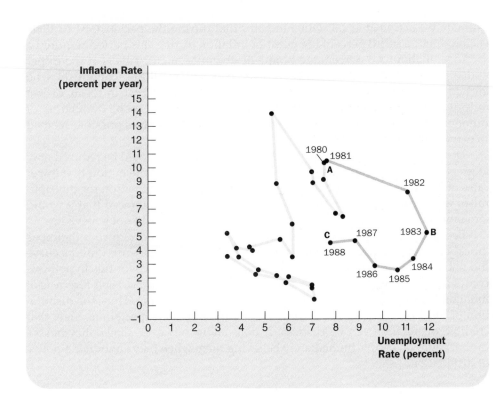

Figure 21-11

DISINFLATION IN THE 1980S. This figure shows annual data from 1980 to 1988 on the unemployment rate and on the inflation rate (as measured by the GDP deflator). The reduction in inflation during this period came at the cost of very high unemployment from 1982 to 1985. Note that the points labelled A, B, and C in this figure correspond roughly to the points in Figure 21-10.

SOURCES: SEE FIGURE 21-6.

shrank by an average of just under 6 percent per year. Economists David Laidler and William Robson suggested that monetary policy during this period was "excruciatingly" contractionary. The description certainly seems appropriate.

Figure 21-11 shows that disinflation did come at the cost of high unemployment. In 1982, 1983, and 1984, the unemployment rate was more than 11 percent. At the same time, the production of goods and services as measured by real GDP was well below its trend level. (See Figure 19-1 in Chapter 19.) The disinflation of the early 1980s produced the deepest recession in Canada since the Great Depression of the 1930s.

Does this experience refute the possibility of costless disinflation as suggested by the rational-expectations theorists? Some economists have argued that the answer to this question is a resounding yes. Indeed, the pattern of disinflation shown in Figure 21-11 is very similar to the pattern predicted in Figure 21-10. To make the transition from high inflation (point A in both figures) to low inflation (point C), the economy had to experience a painful period of high unemployment (point B). At the beginning of this transition period (point A), the unemployment rate was 7.5 percent, approximately equal to the natural unemployment rate. By 1988, which marked the end of the transition period (point C), unemployment was again close to the natural unemployment rate. (As we showed in Figure 14-4 in Chapter 14, the natural unemployment rate is generally viewed as having increased during the 1980s; by 1988 it was roughly 8 percent. We use the estimates of the natural unemployment rate presented in Figure 14-4 in our calculations below.) If we add up the number of percentage points the unemployment rate remained above the natural rate and divide that amount by the number of percentage points inflation was reduced over this period, we arrive at an estimate of the sacrifice ratio defined in terms of sacrificed employment. The estimate we arrive at is 2.3. This indicates that during the period 1981 to 1988, each reduction of 1.0 percentage point in inflation during this period required a sacrifice of about 2.3 percentage points of unemployment. This is at the upper end of estimates of the sacrifice ratio suggested by those economists who argued that reducing inflation could come only at great cost in terms of lost output and high unemployment. For those economists, then, the claims of rational-expectations theorists that less costly disinflation was possible seemed to carry little weight.

Despite the evidence supporting the view that inflation could be reduced only at great cost, many economists felt it was too soon to reject the notion that lower rates of inflation could be obtained at smaller cost. The main reason for this optimism was the fact that even though the Bank of Canada announced that it would aim monetary policy to lower inflation, much of the public did not believe it.

Because few people thought the Bank of Canada would reduce inflation as quickly as it did, expected inflation did not fall, and the short-run Phillips curve did not shift down as quickly as it might have. Some evidence for this hypothesis comes from the forecasts made by commercial forecasting firms: Their forecasts of inflation fell more slowly in the 1980s than did actual inflation. Thus, the disinflation of the 1980s does not necessarily refute the rational-expectations view that credible disinflation can be costless. It does show, however, that policymakers cannot count on people immediately believing them when they announce a policy of disinflation.

THE ZERO-INFLATION TARGET

The latter half of the 1980s was a period of strong economic growth. By 1988, the unemployment rate had fallen by 4 percentage points from its high in 1983. Toward the end of the decade, however, this strong economic growth led to an increase in the rate of inflation. In 1988 the governor of the Bank of Canada, John Crow, made a speech known as the Hanson lecture. In that speech, Crow offered a clear statement defining the future direction of monetary policy in Canada. He asserted that the sole goal of the Bank of Canada would thereafter be to achieve and maintain a stable price level and zero inflation (for technical reasons that have to do with how inflation is measured, 1 percent inflation is generally accepted as being "zero").

The purpose of the Hanson lecture was to define a clear target for monetary policy and to announce this policy widely. Many macroeconomists believed that, because the new monetary policy target was so clearly and firmly stated by such a well-known inflation hawk as John Crow, the public ought to believe what he was saying and quickly adjust inflation expectations downward. In this way, inflation might be reduced to the targeted level with a smaller sacrifice in terms of unemployment and lost output than had been experienced previously. The Bank of Canada began contracting the money supply in 1989 and continued to do so in 1990 and 1991. Figure 21-12 shows that the unemployment rate increased from 7.5 percent in 1989 to 11.4 percent in 1993, while inflation fell from 4.5 percent to 1.5 percent. The inflation target was thus reached very quickly (the Bank of Canada's target for inflation is based on the "core" rate of CPI inflation, a rate slightly lower from that calculated here using the GDP deflator). From 1993 to 1999, the inflation rate averaged just over 1 percent, so that the target was successfully maintained.

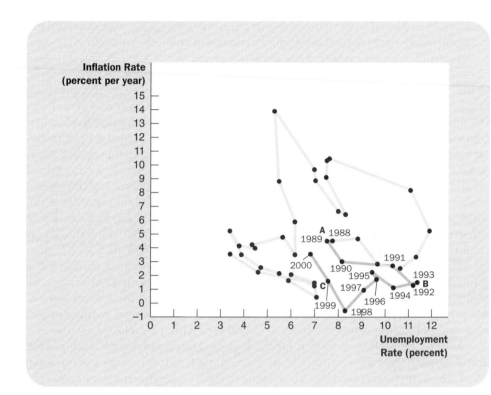

Figure 21-12

THE ZERO-INFLATION TARGET.
This figure shows annual data
from 1988 to 2000 on the
unemployment rate and the
inflation rate (as measured by the
GDP deflator). In 1988 the Bank
of Canada announced its zero-
inflation target, and in 1989
monetary contraction began. The
Bank's target was reached in
1992, by which time the
unemployment rate exceeded 11
percent. Note that the points A, B,
and C in this figure correspond
roughly to the points in Figure
21-10.

SOURCES: SEE FIGURE 21-6.

By the end of 1999, the unemployment rate had returned to what it was in 1989, a level generally regarded as roughly equal to the natural rate.

Just as it did in response to the Bank of Canada's effort at disinflation in the early 1980s, the economy adjusted toward a lower rate of inflation from 1989 to 1999 in a way that closely corresponds to the pattern shown in Figure 21-10. If we label 1989 as point A, 1992 as point B, and 1999 as point C, the data in Figure 21-12 appear to show that inflation expectations were slow to adjust downward. As a result, it appears that the economy adjusted along a given short-run Phillips curve (from point A to point B) before inflation expectations adjusted, shifting the short-run curve to the left (to give us point C). If we add up the number of percentage points the unemployment rate remained above the natural rate and divide that amount by the number of percentage points inflation was reduced over the 1989–99 period, we arrive at an estimate of the sacrifice ratio equal to 5.0, an estimate twice as large as our estimate for the 1981–88 period. The experience of this most recent attempt to reduce inflation has confirmed the opinion of those macroeconomists who believe that inflation can be reduced only at great cost. The Bank of Canada clearly defined its intention to contract the money supply so as to reduce inflation to zero, and yet the cost of reducing inflation seemed to be larger than ever before.

Despite this evidence, many macroeconomists are still not ready to reject the notion that lower rates of inflation can be obtained at smaller cost if the central bank makes a credible statement of its intention to deflate. They maintain their optimism by pointing to a number of factors in the transition to zero inflation that may have prevented inflation expectations from falling as quickly as they might otherwise have. One such factor was that the deficits of the provinces and the federal government remained very high throughout most of this period of transition.

Concern over these deficits culminated in 1995, when credit agencies lowered the rating on federal government debt. High deficits and credit downgrades may have caused people to doubt whether the Bank of Canada could reach its target of zero inflation, and thereby caused people's expectations of inflation to remain high. Critics of the Bank of Canada argue that it should have foreseen this problem, because the main reason government deficits were increasing over this period was the tight monetary policy of the central bank. These critics argue that the Bank of Canada's credibility was in doubt because of its decision to launch a tight monetary policy before the federal and provincial governments reduced their deficits. A second reason inflation expectations may not have fallen as quickly as was hoped when the Bank of Canada announced its zero-inflation target was that the federal government, in preparing its budgets, was using a forecast of 3 percent inflation. Thus, at the same time that the Bank of Canada was announcing its intention to achieve zero inflation, the federal government was in effect announcing that it was doubtful that the target could be reached. Once again, the lack of a coordinated effort by the central bank and the federal government may have conspired to cause individuals and firms to adjust their inflation expectations more slowly than they might otherwise have. Perhaps in recognition of this problem, the federal government issued a news release in conjunction with its 1998 budget reaffirming its commitment to supporting the Bank of Canada's inflation target.

Another possible explanation for the high costs associated with attaining the zero-inflation target may be that the sacrifice ratio is larger at low rates of inflation. Macroeconomists who hold this view argue that the reason the move to zero inflation proved so costly had less to do with the failure of inflation expectations to adjust and more to do with the short-run Phillips curve becoming much flatter at low rates of inflation. As a result, the cost of lowering inflation from 3 percent to 1 percent may be substantially greater than the cost of reducing inflation from 5 percent to 3 percent. Our calculations of the sacrifice ratio involved in reducing inflation from 10.5 percent in 1981 to 4.5 percent in 1988 (a sacrifice ratio of 2.3) versus the sacrifice ratio involved in reducing inflation from 4.5 percent in 1989 to 1.5 percent in 1999 (a sacrifice ratio of 5.0) seem to offer strong evidence in favour of this view. These macroeconomists also point to the recent experience of the United States to support this view. From 1984 to 1997, the inflation rate in the United States has fluctuated between 3 and 5 percent, with relatively small changes in the unemployment rate. In Canada, it was the reduction in the inflation rate below 3 percent that seemed to incur the greatest cost. The relative success of U.S. monetary policy in the 1990s may therefore be due to the Federal Reserve being satisfied with a higher rate of inflation than the Bank of Canada.

What does the future hold? Macroeconomists are notoriously bad at forecasting, but several lessons of the past seem clear. First, our interpretation of the evidence concerning the rates of unemployment and inflation since 1956 suggests that the existence of a short-run tradeoff between inflation and unemployment is well established. While policymakers may be able to influence output and unemployment, they can do so only temporarily. Second, those who claim that inflation can be reduced without increases in the unemployment rate face a good deal of contrary evidence against which they must present their case. Third, the possibility always exists for the economy to experience adverse shocks to aggregate supply, as it did in the 1970s. If that unfortunate development occurs, policy makers will have little choice but to confront a less desirable tradeoff between inflation and unemployment. Fortunately, while oil prices increased quite dramatically in 2000 and remained high in 2001, because the Canadian economy is far less dependent on oil than it was in the 1970s, the tradeoff does not seem to have worsened as it did earlier. Fourth, as long as the Bank of Canada remains vigilant in its control over the money supply and, thereby, aggregate demand, there is no reason to allow inflation to heat up needlessly. Fifth, many macroeconomists remain convinced that the costs of disinflation can be minimized if the Bank of Canada clearly announces its intentions, so that people and firms have the opportunity to adjust their inflation expectations before a monetary contraction. Certainly the Bank of Canada remains convinced of this, and for this reason it continues to make clear statements of its intentions. Finally, the debate continues over the question of whether the costs of disinflation increase at lower rates of inflation.

Figure 21-12 stops with measures of unemployment and inflation for the year 2000: 6.8 percent and 3.5, percent respectively. On the one hand, the observation that inflation has returned close to what it was in 1988 when the zero-inflation target was announced is discouraging. It suggests that the years of high unemployment between 1989 and 1999 were all for nought. On the other hand, the fact that unemployment has fallen below 7 percent for the first time since 1974 is encouraging because it suggests the possibility that the natural unemployment rate is falling in value. If so, then the possibility exists that policymakers now face a more attractive short-run tradeoff between inflation and unemployment. Thus, for example, while the rate of inflation in 2000 was roughly equivalent to that in 1990, the unemployment rate in 2000 was 1.4 percentage points lower. If this represents a fall in the natural unemployment rate, then Canada's productive capacity has increased significantly.

CASE STUDY   IS THE PHILLIPS CURVE NOW SHIFTING TO THE LEFT?

Figure 21-12 shows that since 1956 Canada's short-run Phillips curve has shifted to the right. In this chapter we highlighted the role oil price shocks played in causing these shifts. In the early 1970s and again in the late 1970s rapid increases in oil prices shifted the Phillips curve to the right and thereby worsened the short-run trade-off. We referred to these oil price shocks as adverse supply shocks. (Recall that a supply shock is an event that directly alters firm's costs and prices. An adverse supply shock shifts the short-run aggregate-supply curve to the left, lowering output and raising prices. It therefore increases both unemployment and inflation and shifts the short-run Phillips curve to the right.) Many economists stress another reason why Canada's Phillips curve shifted to the right: adverse supply shocks in the form of higher taxes and higher government debt. Increases in tax burdens increase the costs to firms both directly, if corporate taxes are increasing, and indirectly, if personal taxes are increasing and firms must consequently offer higher wages to attract workers. To the extent that increased government debt causes interest rates to be higher, firms similarly face higher costs to finance capacity expansions. In both of these ways, then, the rising tax burden and rising levels of government debt Canadians faced during the 1980s contributed to the rightward shift of the Phillips curve.

Although it is still too early to be sure, the last three observations in Figure 21-12 suggest that the Phillips curve may be shifting back toward the left. Some economists suggest this may be happening because of a number of *favourable* supply shocks. By reducing a firm's costs and prices, a favourable supply shock shifts the short-run aggregate-supply curve to the right, raising output and reducing prices. The shock therefore reduces both unemployment and inflation and shifts the short-run Phillips curve to the left. In particular, these economists identify the following as causing favourable supply shocks:

◆ *Debt reduction*: Since the mid-1990s, Canadian federal and provincial governments have made great strides in eliminating their deficits and most are now regularly reporting budget surpluses. The result has been a reduction in the level of government debt and falling interest rates. Reduced interest rates lower the financing costs firms face for expanding capacity and thus represent a favourable supply shock.

◆ *Tax cuts:* In 2000, the federal government announced a major set of tax cuts. Most provincial governments are also making efforts to reduce taxes, and many are emphasizing cuts to corporate taxes. Tax cuts reduce

IN THE NEWS

The Moving Short-Run Tradeoff between Inflation and Unemployment

WHEN HAS THE UNEMPLOYMENT RATE fallen too low? The answer depends on how far one believes the economy is from the natural unemployment rate. In the following article, former Bank of Canada Governor Gordon Thiessen (who has since been replaced by David Dodge) expresses concern that strong growth and a falling unemployment rate might be signalling that the rate of inflation is about to increase. Economist Tim O'Neill discusses how the Bank of Canada is uncertain about when inflationary pressures might arise because it is uncertain about the effects produc-

tivity gains have had on the economy's ability to grow without inflation. In other words, the Phillips curve may be shifting to the left, allowing unemployment to fall further without inflation. If so, the Bank of Canada may be able to delay raising interest rates in an effort to prevent inflation.

Rate Rise Warning Flag Raised by Thiessen

BY JILL VARDY

OTTAWA—Gordon Thiessen, the Bank of Canada's governor, raised a warning flag yesterday that the economy may need a cooling dose of interest rate hikes to take some of the heat out of inflation.

But the point at which the economy overheats may be higher than it once was, and so the bank can afford to be less aggressive in its efforts to cool things down, Mr. Thiessen suggested.

Speaking to the Canadian Society in New York, he said Canada's economy is expanding faster than expected. That could spark higher inflation, something

the Bank won't tolerate. "We continue to see strong momentum in our economy so far this year," he said. "By some calculations, we could be operating at full capacity.

"The Bank is now monitoring a wide range of indicators for early-warning signs of pressure on capacity and prices. Up to now, our inflation performance bodes well for the continued expansion of the Canadian economy."

He said even the unemployment rate appears to have room to drop further before higher wage demand starts to push up inflation.

The Bank of Canada has been grappling to define the noninflationary rate of unemployment for Canada. Productivity gains make it difficult to gauge how much further the jobless rate can fall, Mr. Thiessen said.

The Bank of Canada is expected to follow an anticipated 25-basis-point interest rate hike in the United States after that country's Federal Reserve meets on March 21. That will be the fifth jump in U.S. interest rates in eight months.

producers' costs and in this way act as a favourable supply shock for the economy.

◆ *Technological advances:* Some economists believe that the Canadian economy has entered a period of more rapid technological progress. Advances in information technology, such as the Internet, have been profound and have influenced many parts of the economy. Such technological advances increase productivity and, therefore, are a type of favourable supply shock.

◆ *Free trade:* Exposing Canadian firms to greater foreign competition provides them with an incentive to minimize costs and adopt the latest technology. For both of these reasons, many economists judge free trade agreements as a type of favourable supply shock.

Economists debate whether the Phillips curve is in fact shifting back to the left, and they debate which, if any, of the explanations listed above is responsible for this shift. In the end, the complete story may contain elements of each.

"I think the bank has been signalling they're ready to move and they will likely move if the Fed moves on the 21st of this month," said Tim O'Neill, chief economist at the Bank of Montreal. "On the other hand, other comments in Mr. Thiessen's speech suggest there is not a sense of urgency or panic here, that the moves will be gradual rather than very aggressive."

The Bank of Canada has increased its trendsetting bank rate twice, in November and February, following similar hikes in the United States.

Certainly Canada's economy is growing by more than expected. Real gross domestic product rose at a 4.6 percent annualized rate in the fourth quarter of 1999. Strong growth has pulled the unemployment rate down to just 6.8 percent, its lowest level in almost 25 years.

Despite that, Canada's inflation performance to January has been better than expected, Mr. Thiessen said, with Canada's core inflation rate remaining around 1.3 percent, at the bottom half of the 1 percent to 3 percent target the central bank has set.

"The job of the Bank of Canada is to keep inflation in Canada low and stable," Mr. Thiessen said. "Without that, we will be risking both the economic expansion and the potential productivity gains."

The risk of inflation grows as the economy nears its peak capacity, because that's when workers start demanding higher wages and producers can pass on higher prices to consumers. But no one is sure now just what is Canada's potential capacity, Mr. O'Neill said.

The U.S. economy has shown remarkable improvements in its productivity, and in its capacity for noninflationary growth, thanks largely to investments in machinery, equipment, and technology. That appears to be happening in Canada, too—but no one knows to what extent.

"We're prepared to be less aggressive than we might have been previously, because we're not as confident about what precisely are the capacity limits on the economy. So we don't want to be overly aggressive here. The U.S. has

done remarkably well by not overreacting to strong growth. The limits may be higher than they thought," Mr. O'Neill said.

Canada's capacity utilization rate— which measures actual production against the amount of production of which the economy is capable—rose to 86.8 percent in the fourth quarter, from 85.5 percent in the previous quarter.

"That suggests there may be more room for error here without dire consequences and I think it's that more balanced interpretation that I would give to the speech today," Mr. O'Neill said. "The situation is different and so the way in which the bank conducts monetary policy must be different."

SOURCE: *National Post*, March 10, 2000, National Edition, p. C1/Front.

Keep in mind that none of these hypotheses denies the fundamental lesson of the Phillips curve—that policymakers who control aggregate demand always face a short-run tradeoff between inflation and unemployment. Canada's experience with this tradeoff suggests, however, that it changes over time and can worsen or improve.

QUICK QUIZ: What is the sacrifice ratio? How might the credibility of the Bank of Canada's commitment to reduce inflation affect the sacrifice ratio?

CONCLUSION

This chapter has examined how economists' thinking about inflation and unemployment has evolved over time. We have discussed the ideas of many of the best economists of the twentieth century: from the Phillips curve of Phillips, Lipsey, Samuelson, and Solow, to the natural-rate hypothesis of Friedman and Phelps, to the rational-expectations theory of Lucas, Sargent, and Barro. Four of this group have already won Nobel prizes for their work in economics, and more are likely to be so honoured in the years to come.

Although the tradeoff between inflation and unemployment has generated much intellectual turmoil over the past 40 years, certain principles have developed that today command consensus. Here is how Milton Friedman expressed the relationship between inflation and unemployment in 1968:

> There is always a temporary tradeoff between inflation and unemployment; there is no permanent tradeoff. The temporary tradeoff comes not from inflation per se, but from unanticipated inflation, which generally means, from a rising rate of inflation. The widespread belief that there is a permanent tradeoff is a sophisticated version of the confusion between "high" and "rising" that we all recognize in simpler forms. A rising rate of inflation may reduce unemployment, a high rate will not.

Summary

◆ The Phillips curve describes a negative relationship between inflation and unemployment. By expanding aggregate demand, policymakers can choose a point on the Phillips curve with higher inflation and lower unemployment. By contracting aggregate demand, policymakers can choose a point on the Phillips curve with lower inflation and higher unemployment.

◆ The tradeoff between inflation and unemployment described by the Phillips curve holds only in the short run. In the long run, expected inflation adjusts to changes in actual inflation, and the short-run Phillips curve shifts. As a result, the long-run Phillips curve is vertical at the natural rate of unemployment.

◆ The short-run Phillips curve also shifts because of shocks to aggregate supply. An adverse supply shock, such as the increase in world oil prices during the 1970s, gives policymakers a less favourable tradeoff between inflation and unemployment. That is, after an adverse supply shock, policymakers have to accept a higher rate of inflation for any given rate of unemployment, or a higher rate of unemployment for any given rate of inflation.

◆ When the Bank of Canada contracts growth in the money supply to reduce inflation, it moves the economy along the short-run Phillips curve, which results in temporarily high unemployment. The cost of disinflation depends on how quickly expectations of inflation fall. Some economists argue that a credible commitment to low inflation can reduce the cost of disinflation by inducing a quick adjustment of expectations.

Key Concepts

Phillips curve, p. 501
natural-rate hypothesis, p. 510

supply shock, p. 512
sacrifice ratio, p. 516

Okun's Law, p. 517
rational expectations, p. 517

Questions for Review

1. Draw the short-run tradeoff between inflation and unemployment. How might the Bank of Canada move the economy from one point on this curve to another?

2. Draw the long-run tradeoff between inflation and unemployment. Explain how the short-run and long-run tradeoffs are related.

3. What's so natural about the natural rate of unemployment? Why might the natural rate of unemployment differ across countries?

4. Suppose a drought destroys farm crops and drives up the price of food. What is the effect on the short-run tradeoff between inflation and unemployment?

5. The Bank of Canada decides to reduce inflation. Use the Phillips curve to show the short-run and long-run effects of this policy. How might the short-run costs be reduced?

Problems and Applications

1. Suppose the natural rate of unemployment is 6 percent. On one graph, draw two Phillips curves that can be used to describe the four situations listed below. Label the point that shows the position of the economy in each case.
   a. Actual inflation is 5 percent and expected inflation is 3 percent.
   b. Actual inflation is 3 percent and expected inflation is 5 percent.
   c. Actual inflation is 5 percent and expected inflation is 5 percent.
   d. Actual inflation is 3 percent and expected inflation is 3 percent.

2. Illustrate the effects of the following developments on both the short-run and long-run Phillips curves. Give the economic reasoning underlying your answers.
   a. a rise in the natural rate of unemployment
   b. a decline in the price of imported oil
   c. a rise in government spending
   d. a decline in expected inflation

3. Suppose that a fall in consumer spending causes a recession.

   a. Illustrate the changes in the economy using both an aggregate-supply/aggregate-demand diagram and a Phillips-curve diagram. What happens to inflation and unemployment in the short run?
   b. Now suppose that over time expected inflation changes in the same direction that actual inflation changes. What happens to the position of the short-run Phillips curve? After the recession is over, does the economy face a better or worse set of inflation–unemployment combinations?

4. Suppose the economy is in a long-run equilibrium.
   a. Draw the economy's short-run and long-run Phillips curves.
   b. Suppose a wave of business pessimism reduces aggregate demand. Show the effect of this shock on your diagram from part (a). If the Bank of Canada undertakes expansionary monetary policy, can it return the economy to its original inflation rate and original unemployment rate?
   c. Now suppose the economy is back in long-run equilibrium, and then the price of oil rises. Show the effect of this shock with a new diagram like that in part (a). If the Bank of Canada undertakes

expansionary monetary policy, can it return the economy to its original inflation rate and original unemployment rate? If the Bank of Canada undertakes contractionary monetary policy, can it return the economy to its original inflation rate and original unemployment rate? Explain why this situation differs from that in part (b).

5. Suppose the Bank of Canada believed that the natural rate of unemployment was 6.0 percent when the actual natural rate was 5.5 percent. If the Bank of Canada based its policy decisions on its belief, what would happen to the economy?

6. The price of oil fell sharply in 1986 and again in 1998.
   a. Show the impact of such a change in both the aggregate-demand/aggregate-supply diagram and in the Phillips-curve diagram. What happens to inflation and unemployment in the short run?
   b. Do the effects of this event mean there is no short-run tradeoff between inflation and unemployment? Why or why not?

7. Suppose the Bank of Canada announced that it would pursue contractionary monetary policy in order to reduce the inflation rate. Would the following conditions make the ensuing recession more or less severe? Explain.
   a. Wage contracts have short durations.
   b. There is little confidence in the Bank of Canada's determination to reduce inflation.
   c. Expectations of inflation adjust quickly to actual inflation.

8. Some economists believe that the short-run Phillips curve is relatively steep and shifts quickly in response to changes in the economy. Would these economists be more or less likely to favour contractionary policy in order to reduce inflation than economists who had the opposite views?

9. Imagine an economy in which all wages are set in three-year contracts. In this world, the Bank of Canada announces a disinflationary change in monetary policy to begin immediately. Everyone in the economy believes the Bank of Canada's announcement. Would this disinflation be costless? Why or why not? What might the Bank of Canada do to reduce the cost of disinflation?

10. Given the unpopularity of inflation, why don't elected leaders always support efforts to reduce inflation? Economists believe that countries can reduce the cost of disinflation by letting their central banks make decisions about monetary policy without interference from politicians. Why might this be so?

11. Suppose Bank of Canada policymakers accept the theory of the short-run Phillips curve and the natural-rate hypothesis and want to keep unemployment close to its natural rate. Unfortunately, because the natural rate of unemployment can change over time, they aren't certain about the value of the natural rate. What macroeconomic variables do you think they should look at when conducting monetary policy?

12. Figure 21-13 plots data on the unemployment rate and the inflation rate for two periods: 1956 to 1968 and 1989 to 1997. Observe that these two sets of observations span the same rates of inflation, from less than 1 percent to 5 percent. The two sets of observations also span a similar range of unemployment rates, from a low of 3.4 percent to a high of 7.1 percent (a range of 3.7 percentage points) for the early period, and from a low of 7.5 percent to a high of 11.4 percent (a range of 3.9 percentage points) for the later period. These two sets of data therefore define two very similar short-run Phillips curves. Explain why the 1989–97 curve lies to the right of the 1956–68 curve. If the government has the goal of permanently lowering the rate of unemployment, how should it do so?

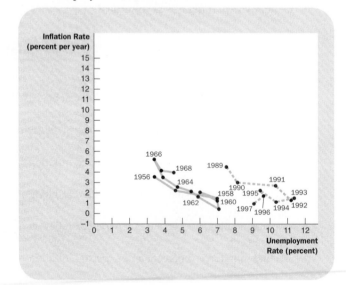

Figure 21-13

THE PHILLIPS CURVE, THEN AND NOW

SOURCES: Data on the unemployment rate for the period 1966 to 1997 are from Statistics Canada, *Historical Labour Force Statistics*, Catalogue No. 71-201; data for 1956 to 1965 are from F.H. Leacy, ed., *Historical Statistics of Canada*, 2nd ed.(Ottawa: Statistics Canada, 1983), series D233; data on the GDP deflator are from Statistics Canada, *National Income and Expenditure Accounts*, Catalogue No. 13-001, and CANSIM.

Nine

FINAL THOUGHTS

22

FIVE DEBATES OVER
MACROECONOMIC POLICY

IN THIS CHAPTER YOU WILL . . .

Consider whether policymakers should try to stabilize the economy

Consider whether monetary policy should be made by rule rather than by discretion

Consider whether the central bank should aim for zero inflation

Consider whether fiscal policymakers should reduce the government debt

Consider whether the tax laws should be reformed to encourage saving

It is hard to open up the newspaper without finding some politician or editorial writer advocating a change in economic policy. The federal government should use the budget surplus to reduce government debt, or it should use it to increase government spending. The Bank of Canada should cut interest rates to stimulate a flagging economy, or it should avoid such moves in order not to risk higher inflation. Parliament should reform the tax system to promote faster economic growth, or it should reform the tax system to achieve a more equal distribution of income. Economic issues are central to the continuing political debate in Canada and other countries around the world.

The previous dozen chapters have developed the tools that economists use when analyzing the behaviour of the economy as a whole and the impact of policies on the economy. This final chapter presents both sides in five leading debates over macroeconomic policy. The knowledge you have accumulated in this course provides the background with which we can discuss these important, unsettled issues. It should help you choose a side in these debates or, at least, help you see why choosing a side is so difficult.

SHOULD MONETARY AND FISCAL POLICYMAKERS TRY TO STABILIZE THE ECONOMY?

In Chapters 19, 20, and 21, we saw how changes in aggregate demand and aggregate supply can lead to short-run fluctuations in production and employment. We also saw how monetary and fiscal policy can shift aggregate demand and, thereby, influence these fluctuations. But even if policymakers *can* influence short-run economic fluctuations, does that mean they *should*? Our first debate concerns whether monetary and fiscal policymakers should use the tools at their disposal in an attempt to smooth the ups and downs of the business cycle.

PRO: POLICYMAKERS SHOULD TRY TO STABILIZE THE ECONOMY

Left on their own, economies tend to fluctuate. When households and firms become pessimistic, for instance, they cut back on spending, and this reduces the aggregate demand for goods and services. The fall in aggregate demand, in turn, reduces the production of goods and services. Firms lay off workers, and the unemployment rate rises. Real GDP and other measures of income fall. Rising unemployment and falling income help confirm the pessimism that initially generated the economic downturn.

Such a recession has no benefit for society—it represents a sheer waste of resources. Workers who become unemployed because of inadequate aggregate demand would rather be working. Business owners whose factories are left idle during a recession would rather be producing valuable goods and services and selling them at a profit.

There is no reason for society to suffer through the booms and busts of the business cycle. The development of macroeconomic theory has shown policymakers how to reduce the severity of economic fluctuations. By "leaning against the wind" of economic change, monetary and fiscal policy can stabilize aggregate demand and, thereby, production and employment. When aggregate demand is inadequate to ensure full employment, policymakers can boost government spending, cut taxes, or expand the money supply. When aggregate demand is excessive, risking higher inflation, policymakers can cut government spending, raise taxes, or reduce the money supply. Such policy actions put macroeconomic theory to its best use by leading to a more stable economy, which benefits everyone.

CON: POLICYMAKERS SHOULD NOT TRY TO STABILIZE THE ECONOMY

Although monetary and fiscal policy can be used to stabilize the economy in theory, there are substantial obstacles to the use of such policies in practice.

One problem is that monetary and fiscal policy do not affect the economy immediately but instead work with a long lag. Monetary policy affects aggregate demand by changing interest rates, which in turn affect spending, especially residential and business investment. But many households and firms set their spending plans in advance. As a result, it takes time for changes in interest rates to alter the aggregate demand for goods and services. Many studies indicate that changes in monetary policy have little effect on aggregate demand until about six months after the change is made.

Fiscal policy works with a lag because of the long political process that governs changes in spending and taxes. To make any change in fiscal policy, a bill must go through Cabinet committees, and then parliamentary committees, and then pass both the House of Commons and the Senate.

Because of these long lags, policymakers who want to stabilize the economy need to look ahead to economic conditions that are likely to prevail when their actions will take effect. Unfortunately, economic forecasting is highly imprecise, in part because macroeconomics is such a primitive science and in part because the shocks that cause economic fluctuations are intrinsically unpredictable. Thus, when policymakers change monetary or fiscal policy, they must rely on educated guesses about future economic conditions.

All too often, policymakers trying to stabilize the economy do just the opposite. Economic conditions can easily change between the time when a policy action begins and when it takes effect. Because of this, policymakers can inadvertently exacerbate rather than mitigate the magnitude of economic fluctuations. Some economists have claimed that many of the major economic fluctuations in history, including the Great Depression of the 1930s, can be traced to destabilizing policy actions.

One of the first rules taught to physicians is "Do no harm." The human body has natural restorative powers. Confronted with a sick patient and an uncertain diagnosis, often a doctor should do nothing but leave the patient's body to its own devices. Intervening in the absence of reliable knowledge merely risks making matters worse.

The same can be said about treating an ailing economy. It might be desirable if policymakers could eliminate all economic fluctuations, but that is not a realistic goal given the limits of macroeconomic knowledge and the inherent unpredictability of world events. Economic policymakers should refrain from intervening often with monetary and fiscal policy and be content if they do no harm.

QUICK QUIZ: Explain why monetary and fiscal policy work with a lag. Why do these lags matter in the choice between active and passive policy?

SHOULD MONETARY POLICY BE MADE BY AN INDEPENDENT CENTRAL BANK?

As we first discussed in Chapter 15, the Bank of Canada determines the rate of monetary growth in Canada. On the basis of an evaluation of current economic conditions and forecasts of future conditions, the Bank of Canada chooses whether to raise, lower, or leave unchanged the supply of money in Canada. The rate of monetary growth is set so as to meet a monetary policy goal. Since 1988, the Bank of Canada has asserted that its goal would be to achieve and maintain a stable price level and zero inflation. In 1991, the Bank made this goal more specific by announcing its intention to conduct monetary policy in such a way as to hold inflation between 1 and 3 percent. In May 2001, the Bank announced its intention to extend this target band for inflation to the end of 2006. At that time the federal government and the Bank will determine whether this will remain the long-run target for monetary policy or whether a new target needs to be announced.

The relationship between the Bank of Canada and the federal government has evolved in such a way that the Bank has almost complete discretion over the conduct of monetary policy. The laws that created the Bank gave the institution vague recommendations about what goals it should pursue. However, they did not tell the Bank how to pursue these goals, nor did they indicate whether some of these goals might be more important than others. These choices have largely been left in the hands of the governor of the Bank. The Bank has used this independence to adopt a monetary policy rule: The rate of growth in the money supply will be sufficient to maintain a rate of inflation between 1 and 3 percent. This target rate of inflation was achieved in 1992 following two years of monetary contraction that caused considerable economic pain in the form of high unemployment.

Some economists are critical of the Bank of Canada's independence. Our second debate over macroeconomic policy, therefore, focuses on whether the Bank should be allowed to conduct monetary policy without being directly answerable to the electorate or to elected officials.

PRO: MONETARY POLICY SHOULD BE MADE BY AN INDEPENDENT CENTRAL BANK

Allowing elected officials influence in conducting monetary policy has two problems. First, when given this power, politicians are sometimes tempted to use monetary policy to affect the outcome of elections. Suppose that the vote in an upcoming federal election is based on economic conditions at the time of the election. Politicians who are able to influence monetary policy might be tempted to pursue expansionary monetary policies just before the election in order to stimulate production and employment, knowing that the resulting inflation will not show up until after the election. In a small open economy with a flexible exchange rate, like Canada, monetary policy has very large effects on aggregate demand. As a result, the temptation to use monetary policy for political ends is even stronger. Thus, to the extent that politicians influence monetary policy, economic fluctuations may come to reflect the electoral calendar. Economists call such fluctuations the *political business cycle*.

The second, more subtle, problem with allowing elected officials a say in conducting monetary policy is that such influence might lead to more inflation than is desirable. Suppose that policymakers, knowing that there is no long-run tradeoff between inflation and unemployment, announce that their goal is zero inflation. Economists believe that zero inflation is more likely to be achieved if the central bank is independent of political influence. Why? Economists believe that, once the public forms expectations of inflation, policymakers face a short-run tradeoff between inflation and unemployment. They are tempted to renege on their announcement of price stability in order to achieve lower unemployment. This discrepancy between announcements (what policymakers say they are going to do) and actions (what they subsequently do) is called the *time inconsistency of policy*. When policymakers act in a time-inconsistent manner, people become skeptical about policy announcements. As a result, people always expect more inflation than policymakers claim they are trying to achieve. Higher expectations of inflation, in turn, shift the short-run Phillips curve upward. This not only causes the rate of inflation realized in the long run to be higher than it would otherwise be, but also causes a less favourable short-run tradeoff between inflation and unemployment. Since elected officials face a greater incentive to try to exploit the short-run tradeoff in order to curry favour with voters, the rate of inflation realized in the long run and the sacrifice ratio measuring the short-run costs of disinflation will always be higher than they would be if monetary policy were conducted by an independent central bank.

One way to avoid these difficulties is to conduct monetary policy independent of political influence. Because the governor of the Bank of Canada is not elected, the governor faces little incentive to try to exploit the short-run tradeoff between inflation and unemployment for political gain. In addition, because people know that the governor faces little incentive to exploit the short-run tradeoff, they are more likely to believe the Bank of Canada's announcements of low- or zero-inflation targets. In the long run, therefore, the rate of inflation will be lower. Empirical evidence seems to support this conjecture: When economists have compared average rates of inflation across countries, those countries with the most independent central banks tend to have the lowest rates of inflation.

CON: MONETARY POLICY SHOULD NOT BE MADE BY AN INDEPENDENT CENTRAL BANK

Although there are pitfalls in allowing elected policymakers a say in conducting monetary policy, there is also an important advantage: accountability. Giving central banks complete independence in conducting monetary policy is a problem because it does not limit incompetence and abuse of power. When the government sends police into a community to maintain civic order, it gives them strict guidelines about how to carry out their job. Because police have great power, allowing them to exercise that power in whatever way they want would be dangerous. When the government gives central bankers the sole authority to maintain economic order, it gives them no guidelines. Instead, it gives monetary policymakers undisciplined discretion and does not make them answerable for mistakes. In a small open economy with a flexible exchange rate, monetary policy has a large and lasting influence on aggregate demand. Since changes in aggregate demand translate into changes in employment and income, it is important that someone be accountable for monetary policy choices.

Moreover, the practical importance of time inconsistency is far from clear. Despite clear and forceful statements by the Bank of Canada, it is not obvious that enhancing the credibility of inflation targets has reduced the short-run cost of achieving lower inflation. The sacrifice ratio associated with the Bank of Canada's effort at disinflation in the early 1990s was not made obviously smaller by repeated announcements of a zero-inflation target. In fact, evidence suggests that the sacrifice ratio involved with this effort at disinflation was *larger* than that associated with earlier efforts. The supposedly enhanced credibility of monetary policy announcements that comes from central bank independence therefore seems to yield few dividends.

Finally, the idea that elected policymakers might use monetary policy to generate political business cycles seems at odds with the concept of rational expectations and the incentive people have to understand the implications of policy announcements. If people understand that reductions in unemployment before an election are temporary and will be followed by increases in unemployment following the election, it seems difficult to understand how elected policymakers can benefit from manipulating monetary policy. What's more, monetary policy influences inflation and nominal interest rates. It is difficult to direct the benefits of changes in inflation and interest rates to any but very broad interest groups (for example, unexpectedly higher inflation benefits borrowers at the expense of savers). Thus, elected policymakers would not find monetary policy to be a very useful way of trying to influence voters. Fiscal policy seems much better suited for this purpose. Changes in government spending and tax laws can be more easily targeted to very specific interest groups with whom a policymaker might want to curry favour. Despite this, the fact that fiscal policy decisions are determined by elected policymakers has not been deemed a serious problem. On the contrary, political accountability with respect to fiscal policy decisions ("no taxation without representation") is a cornerstone of democracy. Why should this not also be true of monetary policy? Economists Lars Osberg and Pierre Fortin, editors of the recent book *Hard Money, Hard Times,* argue forcefully that

> it is inappropriate that major economic decisions, with implications for many aspects of Canadian life, are outside the influence of the democratic political process. As the legal mandate of the Bank of Canada recognizes, a complex market economy has a real need for macroeconomic stability. The Bank of Canada is rightly assigned the duty to "mitigate by its influence fluctuations in the general level of production, trade, prices and unemployment, so far as may be possible in the scope of monetary action, and generally to promote the economic and financial welfare of Canada." The citizens of a democracy also have a right to expect that their views will matter in major issues of public policy, such as the balance which is struck among these objectives. (page xv)

▌ **QUICK QUIZ:**   Should the governor of the Bank of Canada be elected? Explain.

SHOULD THE CENTRAL BANK AIM FOR ZERO INFLATION?

One of the *Ten Principles of Economics* discussed in Chapter 1, and developed more fully in Chapter 16, is that prices rise when the government prints too much money. Another of the *Ten Principles of Economics* discussed in Chapter 1, and developed more fully in Chapter 21, is that society faces a short-run tradeoff between inflation and unemployment. Put together, these two principles raise a question for policymakers: How much inflation should the central bank be willing to tolerate? Our third debate is whether zero is the right target for the inflation rate.

PRO: THE CENTRAL BANK SHOULD AIM FOR ZERO INFLATION

Inflation confers no benefit on society, but it imposes several real costs. As we discussed in Chapter 16, economists have identified six costs of inflation:

◆ shoeleather costs associated with reduced money holdings
◆ menu costs associated with more frequent adjustment of prices
◆ increased variability of relative prices
◆ unintended changes in tax liabilities due to nonindexation of the tax code
◆ confusion and inconvenience resulting from a changing unit of account
◆ arbitrary redistributions of wealth associated with dollar-denominated debts

Some economists argue that these costs are small, at least for moderate rates of inflation, such as the 1.5 percent inflation experienced in Canada during the 1990s. But other economists claim that these costs can be substantial, even for moderate

IN THE NEWS
Central Bank Independence

THE BANK OF CANADA ARGUABLY CONTROLS the most powerful tool of macroeconomic policymaking: monetary policy. Yet the governor of the Bank of Canada is not elected. In this article, Andrew Coyne suggests that Canadians be allowed to vote for the governor.

The Vote Standard

BY ANDREW COYNE

Sometime in the next few weeks, the government will appoint a new governor of the Bank of Canada. The decision is supposed to be made on the recommendation of the Bank's board of directors; at the same time, they are not likely to recommend anyone not to the government's liking.

This saw-off is in keeping with the Bank's ambiguous, quasi-independent role. Yet of late the Bank's independence seems more quasi- than ever. Not only is it under pressure from the finance department to allow faster economic growth than the present governor thinks wise, but the former deputy minister of finance is reputed to be a leading candidate to replace him. [Author's note: Mr. Coyne is correct. David Dodge, a former deputy minister of finance, was appointed governor of the Bank of Canada in February 2001.] The erosion of the Bank's autonomy that began with the forced departure of John Crow is in peril of becoming a wholesale takeover by Finance.

Once again, the age-old debates over central bank independence resur-

face. It is a battle that never seems to be resolved. The roundheads in this conflict, invoking democratic principle, insist central banks must be accountable to some elected authority. The royalists defend the divine right of central banks to set policy independently. Monetary policy, on this view, would inevitably lean to inflation if left to the vagaries of democratic politics. A politicized central bank would find it harder to take unpopular but necessary steps to maintain price stability.

Royalists argue an independent central bank is still accountable, in the end. Central bankers are, after all, appointed by elected officials. Still, this ought to give democrats some pause. The analogy is frequently drawn with the Supreme Court, which is also "unaccountable." But that's because the Court must often protect minorities from the tyranny of the majority. The implication here is rather that the majority must be protected from itself.

Must we choose between democracy and stable prices? Isn't there some middle ground here? Yes there is: Elect the governor.

The whole issue of whether the Bank should be "independent" or "accountable" stems from a failure to define our terms: Accountable to whom? Independent of what? Let's not blame the people for the sins of their leaders. It isn't democracy that monetary policy must be protected from, but government. It's perfectly legitimate that something as critical in its effects on the economy as monetary policy should be subject to democratic control. But it should be direct control.

The case for keeping the money supply out of government hands is grounded not in aristocratic distrust of democracy, but in the classical liberal ideal of separation of powers—in this case, fiscal and monetary. The historic reason for this was to prevent the government

from welching on its debts by debasing the currency in which they are to be repaid. To deny government this power is in keeping with our oldest democratic traditions: Inflation is a tax that can be levied without consent, even without warning.

Or at least, it could. In theory, the Bank can do this by engineering a larger amount of inflation than bond markets anticipate—as it did for a time in the 1970s, when real interest rates actually fell below zero. To fool the markets again, however, would take some doing: These days, bond prices drop like mine canaries at the first whiff of inflation. And of course, to achieve any lasting reduction in real rates, the Bank would have to go on fooling them, over and over and over again.

This may seem to indicate inflation is no longer a threat. The simultaneous judgement of millions of investors around the world imposes a ruthless discipline on national monetary policies. But just because a thing is impossible doesn't mean governments won't try it. And so long as there is any doubt about the authorities' intentions, the potential for damaging missteps remains. In a world of "rational expectations," the case for central bank independence is stronger than ever. This bears some explanation.

Bond markets are not the only ones that make bets on inflation. Monetary policy engages the whole of society in an intricate exchange of expectations. The public scrutinizes the authorities, trying to guess future policy moves; the authorities in turn try to factor the public's response to policy changes into their own economic projections. If economic agents expect higher inflation, they will ask for higher prices, wages, and interest rates to keep pace. If policy instead tightens, and inflation falls, it will catch the public offside. Lower inflation plus higher nominal wages and interest rates means real wages and interest rates jump. Result: higher unemployment, and recession.

So if governments wish to reduce inflation without recession, it's vital that people understand the policy they intend to pursue. Just as important, they must believe the announced policy will really be carried out. This is the central paradox of monetary policy. The greater the public's conviction that the authorities are determined to tighten policy, no matter what the costs, the less those costs are likely to be: Inflation expectations would adjust to keep wages and prices in line.

On the other hand, if the public knows, or suspects, that the monetary authorities will do anything to stave off a recession, they will be encouraged to behave in ways that invite one. Wages and prices would spiral, on the calculation that, whatever it might say to the contrary, the Bank would always stand ready to pump up demand enough to accommodate them. Expectations of ease would in this way prove self-fulfilling: until at last, with inflation spinning out of control, the Bank was forced to disappoint them.

It's important, then, not to let the Bank's credibility become an issue in the first place. Why would an independent Bank be more credible than one more directly accountable to government? Because, royalists have always answered, it bears no responsibility for the fiscal consequences. It would not then be tempted to use the printing press to escape its debts. But this is only another way of saying that it is not democratically accountable. Which in the end is not, well, credible.

It's all very well just to pass a law stating that the central bank is autonomous. But if true, this is undemocratic, and if false, it is worthless. In practice, the latter has more often been the case: Central banks have proven not

to be so independent as all that, easing policy in election years and tightening afterward. It could not be otherwise. No central bank, however independent it may be on paper, has the legitimacy to defy a democratically elected government determined to get its way. The issue, then, is not whether the central bank should be "independent" or "accountable": If it's not accountable, it won't be independent.

The same applies to all those other means proposed from time to time to tie central banks to the straight and narrow: steady-growth rules, gold standards, fixed exchange rates, even privately issued currencies. All of them, without exception, beg the question of political will: Any government that could summon the nerve to put itself on the gold standard, much less privatize the mint, would have no trouble running a stable monetary policy.

Political will derives from popular will. The express preference of the people for stable prices is ultimately the sole assurance of the authorities' resolve. For that matter, inflation is not only a matter of meddling by wastrel politicians: Historically, it has often been unclear whether the central bank itself is wholly devoted to stable prices. Central bank independence is therefore a necessary but not sufficient condition for honest money. A clear, unambiguous mandate for stable prices would be as instructive to the Bank as to the government.

The solution follows. Put monetary policy, not on the gold standard, but the vote standard. Elect the governor.

I hear the skeptics. Would the people vote for honest money? Or would they be swayed by a sweet-talking soft-money salesman? Maybe they would—once. But the best advertising in the world won't sell a bad product a second time. Monetary policy is undoubtedly a complex issue. But if you want voters to

make responsible choices, you have to give them responsibility. They'll educate themselves soon enough.

A democratic Bank would have to talk openly with the public, making less likely any miscalculation as to its intentions. And the public could in turn speak more clearly. Inflation does not usually become an election issue until it is already out of hand. In an election strictly on monetary policy, the public's preferences would be known from the start.

Moreover, this conversation would be eavesdropped by a third party: capital markets. If a candidate promising loose money were leading in the polls, interest rates would rise sharply; if the tight money candidate then pulled ahead, they would immediately ease. The lesson, that the way to lower interest rates is through low inflation, could not be brought home more forcefully.

Perhaps people would still vote for the loose money candidate, notwithstanding the markets' alarm. But I doubt it. The evidence is that inflation, like protectionism, is not the vote-getter it is imagined to be. That's why, when inflation began to climb exponentially in the late 1970s and early 1980s, the public in country after country turned to politicians with the will to control it. The process was painful. But the same leaders were re-elected time and again.

It comes down to this: Either people want honest money, or they don't. If they do, they haven't had much of it, and they won't until they have the means to tell both governments and central bankers that that's what they want. If they don't, if what they really want is inflation, let them have it. That, after all, is democracy.

SOURCE: *National Post*, September 19, 2000, National Edition, p. C15.

inflation. Moreover, there is no doubt that the public dislikes inflation. When inflation heats up, opinion polls identify inflation as one of the nation's leading problems.

Of course, the benefits of zero inflation have to be weighed against the costs of achieving it. Reducing inflation usually requires a period of high unemployment and low output, as illustrated by the short-run Phillips curve. But this disinflationary recession is only temporary. Once people come to understand that policymakers are aiming for zero inflation, expectations of inflation will fall, and the short-run tradeoff will improve. Because expectations adjust, there is no tradeoff between inflation and unemployment in the long run.

Reducing inflation is, therefore, a policy with temporary costs and permanent benefits. That is, once the disinflationary recession is over, the benefits of zero inflation would persist into the future. If policymakers are farsighted, they should be willing to incur the temporary costs for the permanent benefits. This is precisely the calculation made by the Bank of Canada in the early 1980s and again in the early 1990s when it introduced monetary contractions designed to reduce the rate of inflation.

Moreover, the costs of reducing inflation need not be as large as some economists claim. If the Bank of Canada announces a credible commitment to zero inflation, it can directly influence expectations of inflation. Such a change in expectations can improve the short-run tradeoff between inflation and unemployment, allowing the economy to reach lower inflation at a reduced cost. The key to this strategy is credibility: People must believe that the Bank of Canada is actually going to carry through on its announced policy. Parliament could help in this regard by passing legislation that made price stability the Bank of Canada's primary goal. Such a law would make it less costly to achieve zero inflation without reducing any of the resulting benefits.

One advantage of a zero-inflation target is that zero provides a more natural focal point for policymakers than any other number. Suppose, for instance, that the Bank of Canada were to announce that it would keep inflation at 1.5 percent—the rate experienced during the 1990s. Would the Bank of Canada really stick to that 1.5 percent target? If events inadvertently pushed inflation up to 4.0 or 5.0 percent, why wouldn't they just raise the target? There is, after all, nothing special about the number 1.5. By contrast, zero is the only number for the inflation rate at which the Bank of Canada can claim that it achieved price stability and fully eliminated the costs of inflation.

CON: THE CENTRAL BANK SHOULD NOT AIM FOR ZERO INFLATION

Although price stability may be desirable, the benefits of zero inflation compared with moderate inflation are small, whereas the costs of reaching zero inflation are large. Estimates of the sacrifice ratio suggest that reducing inflation by 1 percentage point requires giving up between 2 and 5 percent of one year's output. Using the midpoint of this range of estimates, to reduce inflation from, say, 4 percent to zero requires a loss of 14 percent of a year's output. At the 2000 level of gross domestic product, about $1000 billion, this cost translates into $140 billion of lost output, which is about $4600 per person. Although people might dislike inflation, it is not at all clear that they would (or should) be willing to pay this much to get rid of it.

The social costs of disinflation are even larger than this $4600 figure suggests, for the lost income is not spread equitably over the population. When the economy goes into recession, all incomes do not fall proportionately. Instead, the fall in aggregate income is concentrated on those workers who lose their jobs. The vulnerable workers are often those with the least skills and experience. Hence, much of the cost of reducing inflation is borne by those who can least afford to pay it.

Although economists can list several costs of inflation, there is no professional consensus that these costs are substantial. The shoeleather costs, menu costs, and others that economists have identified do not seem great, at least for moderate rates of inflation. It is true that the public dislikes inflation, but the public may be misled into believing the inflation fallacy—the view that inflation erodes living standards. Economists understand that living standards depend on productivity, not monetary policy. Because inflation in nominal incomes goes hand in hand with inflation in prices, reducing inflation would not cause real incomes to rise more rapidly.

Moreover, policymakers have recently taken steps to reduce many of the costs of inflation. In the fall of 2000, the federal government indexed income tax brackets to prevent inflation from pushing taxpayers into higher tax brackets. Policymakers can also reduce the arbitrary redistributions of wealth between creditors and debtors caused by unexpected inflation by issuing indexed government bonds, as in fact the Bank of Canada did in 1991. Such an act insulates holders of government debt from inflation. In addition, by setting an example, it might encourage private borrowers and lenders to write debt contracts indexed for inflation.

Reducing inflation might be desirable if it could be done at no cost, as some economists argue is possible. Yet this trick seems hard to carry out in practice. When economies reduce their rate of inflation, they almost always experience a period of high unemployment and low output. It is risky to believe that the central bank could achieve credibility so quickly as to make disinflation painless.

Indeed, a disinflationary recession can potentially leave permanent scars on the economy. Firms in all industries reduce their spending on new plants and equipment substantially during recessions, making investment the most volatile component of GDP. Even after the recession is over, the smaller stock of capital reduces productivity, incomes, and living standards below the levels they otherwise would have achieved. In addition, when workers become unemployed in recessions, they lose valuable job skills. Even after the economy has recovered, their value as workers is diminished. Some economists have argued that the slow speed with which Canada's unemployment rate falls following recessions is the result of workers losing job skills while they are unemployed and thus finding re-employment difficult.

Why should policymakers put the economy through a costly, inequitable disinflationary recession to achieve zero inflation, which may have only modest benefits? Economist Alan Blinder, a former vice-chairman of the U.S. Federal Reserve Bank, argued forcefully in his book *Hard Heads, Soft Hearts* that policymakers in countries like Canada and the United States—countries that typically experience moderate rates of inflation—should not make this choice:

The costs that attend the low and moderate inflation rates experienced in the United States and in other industrial countries appear to be quite modest—more like a bad cold than a cancer on society. . . . As rational individuals, we do not volunteer for a lobotomy to cure a head cold. Yet, as a collectivity, we routinely prescribe the economic equivalent of lobotomy (high unemployment) as a cure for the inflationary cold.

Blinder concludes that it is better to learn to live with moderate inflation.

QUICK QUIZ: Explain the costs and benefits of reducing inflation to zero. Which are temporary and which are permanent?

SHOULD FISCAL POLICYMAKERS REDUCE THE GOVERNMENT DEBT?

Perhaps the most persistent macroeconomic debate in recent years has been over government finances. Throughout most of the 1970s, 1980s, and 1990s, Canadian federal and provincial governments spent more than they collected in tax revenue and financed the resulting budget deficits by issuing government debt. As we discussed in Chapter 13, the result was an accumulation of a startling amount of government debt. In that chapter we saw how budget deficits affect saving, investment, and interest rates. Recently, however, most governments in Canada have taken measures to reduce and even eliminate their deficits. In February 1998, the federal government announced its first balanced budget since 1970. In October 2000, it predicted large budget surpluses—an excess of tax revenue over government spending—were possible to at least 2006. At that time, the federal government announced that it planned to use these projected surpluses to introduce a combination of tax cuts, spending increases, and debt repayments. Similarly, almost all provinces now regularly forecast budget surpluses and have announced plans on how they plan to use these projected surpluses to reduce taxes, increase spending, and repay debt. Our fourth debate concerns what fiscal policymakers should do with projected surpluses: Should they use projected surpluses to reduce the debt they steadily accumulated over the past quarter-century, or should they eliminate the projected budget surpluses by cutting tax rates and increasing spending on social programs?

PRO: POLICYMAKERS SHOULD REDUCE THE GOVERNMENT DEBT

From the mid-1970s to the mid-1990s, governments in Canada spent substantially more than they received in tax revenue. At the federal level, the resulting budget deficits caused the federal debt to rise from $24 billion in 1975 to a peak of $583 billion in 1998. While some debt has been repaid since 1998, by 2000 it remained very high at $565 billion. If we divide that debt by the size of the population, we learn that each person's share of this debt is just under $19 000. If we include the debts

"My share of the government debt is $27 000."

of provincial and territorial governments, the level of government debt in 2000 increases to about $821 billion, or about $27 000 per person.

The most direct effect of government debt is to place a burden on future generations of taxpayers. When these debts and accumulated interest come due, future taxpayers will face a difficult choice. They can pay higher taxes, enjoy less government spending, or both in order to make resources available to pay off the debt and accumulated interest. Or they can delay the day of reckoning and put the government into even deeper debt by borrowing once again to pay off the old debt and interest. In essence, when the government runs a budget deficit and issues government debt, it allows current taxpayers to pass the bill for some of their government spending on to future taxpayers. Inheriting such a large debt cannot help but lower the living standard of future generations.

In addition to this direct effect, budget deficits also have various macroeconomic effects. Because budget deficits represent *negative* public saving, they lower national saving (the sum of private and public saving). Reduced national saving causes the real exchange rate to rise and net exports to fall. Large and persistent budget deficits, and the accumulation of debt, also increase the default risk that lenders perceive when they consider buying Canadian debt. This causes the real interest rate in Canada to remain above the real interest rate in the rest of the world. Because higher real interest rates cause investment to fall, the capital stock grows smaller over time. A lower capital stock reduces labour productivity, real wages, and the economy's production of goods and services. Thus, when the government increases its debt, future generations are born into an economy with lower incomes as well as higher taxes.

There are, nevertheless, situations in which running a budget deficit is justifiable. Throughout history, the most common cause of increased government debt is war. When a military conflict raises government spending temporarily, it is reasonable to finance this extra spending by borrowing. Otherwise, taxes during wartime would have to rise precipitously. Such high tax rates would greatly distort the incentives faced by those who are taxed, leading to large deadweight losses. In addition, such high tax rates would be unfair to current generations of taxpayers, who already have to make the sacrifice of fighting the war.

Similarly, it is reasonable to allow a rise in government debt during a temporary downturn in economic activity. When the economy goes into a recession, tax revenue falls automatically because the income tax and payroll taxes are levied on measures of income. If the government tried to balance its budget during a recession, it would have to raise taxes or cut spending at a time of high unemployment. Such a policy would tend to depress aggregate demand at precisely the time it needed to be stimulated and, therefore, would tend to increase the magnitude of economic fluctuations.

The budget deficits incurred by the federal and provincial governments since the mid-1970s are difficult to justify. The major culprit seems to be the failure of fiscal policymakers to take advantage of periods of strong economic growth to pay down the debt incurred during recessions. For example, the federal government's debt increased quite substantially as a result of the 1980–81 recession. This recession, the worst experienced in Canada since the Great Depression, caused a large fall in tax revenue and necessitated a large increase in spending on programs such as Employment Insurance. Not surprisingly, the federal government's deficit was large during this period and its debt grew. From 1983 to 1988, however, real output grew by an average of 4.5 percent per year. During this period, the rapid growth in incomes caused tax revenue to grow quickly and expenditures on programs such as Employment Insurance to fall. This was the federal government's opportunity to run budget surpluses and pay down the debt incurred as a result of the recession. Instead, the federal government continued to run large deficits and to add to its debt. Indeed, in 1985, despite real output growth of 5.3 percent, the federal government announced a deficit in excess of $31 billion (equivalent to $44 billion in 2000 dollars). It is hard to see any rationale for this policy. Although governments need not commit themselves to a balanced budget as an inflexible rule, the budget should be balanced over the course of a business cycle. This requires budget surpluses during good times to offset the budget deficits that naturally arise during bad times. If the federal government had been operating with such a plan in place since 1975, today's university and college graduates would be entering an economy that promised them greater economic prosperity.

It's time to reverse the effects of this policy mistake. A combination of fiscal prudence and good luck has left the federal government and most of the provinces with budget surpluses now and into the near future. We should use these surpluses to repay some of the debt that our governments have accumulated. Compared with the alternative of cutting taxes or increasing spending, repaying the debt would mean greater national saving, investment, and economic growth.

CON: POLICYMAKERS SHOULD NOT REDUCE THE GOVERNMENT DEBT

The problem of government debt is often exaggerated. Although the government debt does represent a tax burden on younger generations, it is not large compared with the average person's lifetime income. The debt of the federal, provincial, and territorial governments is about $27 000 per person. People who work 40 years for $25 000 a year will earn $1 million over their lifetime. Their share of the government debt represents less than 3 percent of their lifetime resources.

Moreover, it is misleading to view the effects of government debt in isolation. The government debt is just one piece of a large picture of how the government chooses to raise and spend money. In making these decisions over fiscal policy, policymakers affect different generations of taxpayers in many ways. The government's budget deficit or surplus should be considered together with these other policies.

For example, suppose governments use their budget surpluses to pay off government debt instead of using it to pay for increased spending on education. Does this policy make young generations better off? Government debt will be smaller when they enter the labour force, which means a smaller tax burden. Yet if they are less well educated than they could be, their productivity and incomes will be lower. Many estimates of the return on schooling (the increase in a worker's wage that results from an additional year in school) find that it is quite large. Reducing government debt rather than funding more education spending could, all things considered, make future generations worse off.

Single-minded concern about the government debt is also dangerous because it draws attention away from various other policies that redistribute income across generations. For example, the federal government recently increased the payroll tax used to finance Canada Pension Plan (CPP) payments to elderly people. This policy will redistribute income away from younger generations (who are paying the payroll tax) toward older generations (who are receiving the CPP payments), even though it does not affect the federal debt. Thus, government debt is only a small piece of the larger issue of how government policy affects the welfare of different generations.

To some extent, the adverse effects of government debt can be reversed by forward-looking parents. Suppose parents are enjoying the benefits of low taxes and high government spending on social programs but are worried about the impact of the resulting government debt on their children. Parents can offset the impact by using the income they are saving as a result of low taxes to leave their children a larger bequest. The bequest would enhance the children's ability to bear the burden of future taxes. Some economists claim that people do in fact behave this way. If this were true, higher private saving by parents would offset the public dissaving of budget deficits, and deficits would not affect the economy. Most economists doubt that parents are so farsighted, but some people probably do act this way, and anyone could. Deficits give people the opportunity to consume at the expense of their children, but deficits do not require them to do so. If the government debt actually represented a great problem facing future generations, some parents would help to solve it.

Critics of budget deficits sometimes assert that the government debt cannot continue to rise forever, but in fact it can. Just as a bank officer evaluating a loan application would compare a person's debts with his or her income, we should judge the burden of the government debt relative to the size of the nation's income. Population growth and technological progress cause the total income of the Canadian economy to grow over time. As a result, the nation's ability to pay the interest on the government debt grows over time as well. As long as the government debt grows more slowly than the nation's income, there is nothing to prevent the government debt from growing forever.

Some numbers can put this into perspective. The real output of the Canadian economy grows on average about 3 percent per year. If the inflation rate is 2 percent per year, then nominal income grows at a rate of 5 percent per year. The government debt, therefore, can rise by 5 percent per year without increasing the ratio of debt to income. In 2000 the federal government debt was $565 billion; 5 percent of this figure is $28 billion. As long as the federal budget deficit is smaller than $28 billion, the policy is sustainable. There will never be any day of reckoning that forces the budget deficits to end or the economy to collapse.

If moderate budget deficits are sustainable, there is no need for the government to maintain budget surpluses. Let's put this excess of revenue over spending to better use. The government could use these funds to pay for valuable government programs, such as increased funding for education. Or it could use them to finance a tax cut. In the late 1990s taxes reached a historic high as a percentage of GDP, so there is every reason to suppose that the deadweight losses of taxation reached a historic high as well. If all of these taxes aren't needed for current spending, the government should return the money to the people who earned it.

QUICK QUIZ: Explain how reducing the government debt makes future generations better off. What fiscal policy might improve the lives of future generations more than reducing the government debt?

SHOULD THE TAX LAWS BE REFORMED TO ENCOURAGE SAVING?

A country's standard of living depends on its ability to produce goods and services. This was one of the *Ten Principles of Economics* in Chapter 1. As we saw in Chapter 12, a nation's productive capability, in turn, is determined largely by how much it saves and invests for the future. Our fifth debate is whether policymakers should reform the tax laws to encourage greater saving and investment.

PRO: THE TAX LAWS SHOULD BE REFORMED TO ENCOURAGE SAVING

A nation's saving rate is a key determinant of its long-run economic prosperity. When the saving rate is higher, more resources are available for investment in new plant and equipment. A larger stock of plant and equipment, in turn, raises labour productivity, wages, and incomes. It is, therefore, no surprise that international data show a strong correlation between national saving rates and measures of economic well-being.

Another of the *Ten Principles of Economics* presented in Chapter 1 is that people respond to incentives. This lesson should apply to people's decisions about how much to save. If a nation's laws make saving attractive, people will save a higher fraction of their incomes, and this higher saving will lead to a more prosperous future.

Unfortunately, the Canadian tax system discourages saving by taxing the return to saving quite heavily. For example, consider a 25-year-old worker who saves $1000 of her income to have a more comfortable retirement at the age of 70. If she buys a bond that pays an interest rate of 10 percent, the $1000 will accumulate at the end of 45 years to $72 900 in the absence of taxes on interest. But suppose she faces a marginal tax rate on interest income of 40 percent, which is typical of many workers once federal and provincial income taxes are added together. In this case, her after-tax interest rate is only 6 percent, and the $1000 will accumulate at the end of 45 years to only $13 800. That is, accumulated over this long span of time, the tax rate on interest income reduces the benefit of saving $1000 from $72 900 to $13 800—or by about 80 percent.

The tax code further discourages saving by taxing some forms of capital income twice. Suppose a person uses some of his savings to buy stock in a large Canadian corporation. When the corporation earns a profit from its capital investments, it first pays tax on this profit in the form of the corporate income tax. If the corporation pays out the rest of the profit to the stockholder in the form of dividends, the stockholder pays tax on this income a second time in the form of the individual income tax. This double taxation substantially reduces the return to the stockholder, thereby reducing the incentive to save.

In addition to the tax code, many other policies and institutions in our society reduce the incentive for households to save. Some government benefits, such as Old Age Security pension payments, are means-tested; that is, the benefits are reduced for those who in the past have been prudent enough to save some of their income. Colleges and universities grant financial aid as a function of the wealth of the students and their parents. Such a policy is like a tax on wealth and, as such, discourages students and parents from saving.

There are various ways in which the tax code could provide an incentive to save, or at least reduce the disincentive that households now face. Already the tax laws give preferential treatment to some types of retirement saving. When a taxpayer puts income into a registered retirement saving plan (RRSP), for instance, that income and the interest it earns are not taxed until the funds are withdrawn at retirement. There are, however, limits on the amount that can be put into an RRSP each year; currently, the limits are the greater of $13 500 and 18 percent of income. A small step toward encouraging greater saving would be to increase the maximum amount households can contribute to RRSPs.

An important step the federal government took to encourage greater saving was to introduce the Goods and Services Tax (GST) in 1991. The great majority of federal tax revenue is collected through the personal income tax. Under an income tax, a dollar earned is taxed the same whether it is spent or saved. The GST is a consumption tax. Under a consumption tax, a household pays tax only on the basis of what it spends. Income that is saved is exempt from taxation until the saving is later withdrawn and spent on consumption goods. For this reason, a consumption tax increases the incentive to save. Because of this, economists were generally in favour of adding the GST to the federal government's tax mix, and many would favour an increased emphasis on consumption, as opposed to income, taxation.

CON: THE TAX LAWS SHOULD NOT BE REFORMED TO ENCOURAGE SAVING

Increasing saving may be desirable, but it is not the only goal of tax policy. Policymakers also must be sure to distribute the tax burden fairly. The problem with proposals to increase the incentive to save is that they increase the tax burden on those who can least afford it.

It is an undeniable fact that high-income households save a greater fraction of their income than low-income households. As a result, any tax change that favours people who save will also tend to favour people with a high income. Policies such as RRSPs may seem appealing, but they lead to a less egalitarian society. By reducing the tax burden on the wealthy, who can take advantage of these plans, they force the government to raise the tax burden on the poor.

Moreover, tax policies designed to encourage saving outside of RRSPs may not be effective at achieving that goal. Many studies have found that saving is relatively inelastic—that is, the amount of saving is not very sensitive to the rate of return on saving. If this is indeed the case, then tax provisions that raise the effective return by reducing the taxation of capital income will further enrich the wealthy without inducing them to save more than they otherwise would.

Economic theory does not give a clear prediction about whether a higher rate of return would increase saving. The outcome depends on the relative size of two conflicting effects, called the *substitution effect* and the *income effect*. On the one hand, a higher rate of return raises the benefit of saving: Each dollar saved today produces more consumption in the future. This substitution effect tends to raise saving. On the other hand, a higher rate of return lowers the need for saving: A household has to save less to achieve any target level of consumption in the future. This income effect tends to reduce saving. If the substitution and income effects approximately cancel each other, as some studies suggest, then saving will not change when lower taxation of capital income raises the rate of return.

There are other ways to raise national saving than by giving tax breaks to the rich. National saving is the sum of private and public saving. Instead of trying to alter the tax code to encourage greater private saving, policymakers can simply raise public saving by increasing the budget surplus, perhaps by raising taxes on the wealthy or by restraining government spending. This offers a direct way of raising national saving and increasing prosperity for future generations.

Indeed, once public saving is taken into account, tax provisions to encourage saving might backfire. Tax changes that reduce the taxation of capital income reduce government revenue and, thereby, lead to a budget deficit. To increase national saving, such a change in the tax code must stimulate private saving by more than it reduces public saving. If this is not the case, so-called saving incentives can potentially make matters worse.

QUICK QUIZ: Give three examples of how our society discourages saving. What are the drawbacks of eliminating these disincentives?

CONCLUSION

This chapter has considered five debates over macroeconomic policy. For each, it began with a controversial proposition and then offered the arguments pro and con. If you find it hard to choose a side in these debates, you may find some comfort in the fact that you are not alone. The study of economics does not always make it easy to choose among alternative policies. Indeed, by clarifying the inevitable tradeoffs that policymakers face, it can make the choice more difficult.

Difficult choices, however, have no right to seem easy. When you hear politicians or commentators proposing something that sounds too good to be true, it probably is. If they sound like they are offering you a free lunch, you should look for the hidden price tag. Few, if any, policies come with benefits but no costs. By helping you see through the fog of rhetoric so common in political discourse, the study of economics should make you a better participant in our national debates.

Summary

◆ Advocates of active monetary and fiscal policy view the economy as inherently unstable and believe that policy can manage aggregate demand to offset the inherent instability. Critics of active monetary and fiscal policy emphasize that policy affects the economy with a lag and that our ability to forecast future economic conditions is poor. As a result, attempts to stabilize the economy can end up being destabilizing.

◆ Advocates of an independent central bank argue that such independence guards against politicians using monetary policy in an attempt to influence voters. They also assert that a lower rate of inflation and a more favourable short-run tradeoff between inflation and unemployment is possible when the central bank is independent of political influence. Critics of central bank independence argue that because monetary policy has large and lasting influences on aggregate demand, and hence on output and employment, citizens should have a say on the conduct of monetary policy, just as they do on the conduct of fiscal policy.

◆ Advocates of a zero-inflation target emphasize that inflation has many costs and few, if any, benefits. Moreover, the cost of eliminating inflation—depressed output and employment—is only temporary. Even this cost can be reduced if the central bank announces a credible plan to reduce inflation, thereby directly lowering expectations of inflation. Critics of a zero-inflation target claim that moderate inflation imposes only small costs on society, whereas the recession necessary to reduce inflation is quite costly.

◆ Advocates of reducing the government debt argue that the debt imposes a burden on future generations by raising their taxes and lowering their incomes. Critics of reducing the government debt argue that the debt is only one small piece of fiscal policy. Single-minded concern about the debt can obscure the many ways in which the government's tax and spending decisions affect different generations.

◆ Advocates of tax incentives for saving point out that our society discourages saving in many ways, such as by heavily taxing the income from capital and by reducing benefits for those who have accumulated wealth. They endorse reforming the tax laws to encourage saving, perhaps by switching from an income tax to a consumption tax and increasing the amount people can contribute to an RRSP. Critics of tax incentives for saving argue that many proposed changes to stimulate saving would primarily benefit the wealthy, who do not need a tax break. They also argue that such changes might have only a small effect on private saving. Raising public saving by increasing the government's budget surplus would provide a more direct and equitable way to increase national saving.

Questions for Review

1. What causes the lags in the effect of monetary and fiscal policy on aggregate demand? What are the implications of these lags for the debate over active versus passive policy?

2. What might motivate a central banker to cause a political business cycle? What does the possibility of a political business cycle imply for the debate over whether monetary policy should be conducted by an independent central bank?

3. Explain how credibility might affect the cost of reducing inflation.

4. Why are some economists against a target of zero inflation?

5. Explain two ways in which a government budget deficit hurts a future worker.

6. What are two situations in which most economists view a budget deficit as justifiable?

7. Give an example of how the government might hurt young generations, even while reducing the government debt they inherit.

8. Some economists say that the government can continue running a budget deficit forever. How is that possible?

9. Some income from capital is taxed twice. Explain.

10. Give an example, other than tax policy, of how our society discourages saving.

11. What adverse effect might be caused by tax incentives to raise saving?

Problems and Applications

1. The chapter suggests that the economy, like the human body, has "natural restorative powers."

   a. Illustrate the short-run effect of a fall in aggregate demand using an aggregate-demand/aggregate-supply diagram. What happens to total output, income, and employment?

   b. If the government does not use stabilization policy, what happens to the economy over time? Illustrate on your diagram. Does this adjustment generally occur in a matter of months or a matter of years?

   c. Do you think the "natural restorative powers" of the economy mean that policymakers should be passive in response to the business cycle?

2. Policymakers who want to stabilize the economy must decide how much to change the money supply, government spending, or taxes. Why is it difficult for policymakers to choose the appropriate strength of their actions?

3. Suppose that people suddenly wanted to hold more money balances. For simplicity, assume Canada is a closed economy.

   a. What would be the effect of this change on the economy if the Bank of Canada followed a rule of increasing the money supply by 3 percent per year? Illustrate your answer with a money-market diagram and an aggregate-demand/aggregate-supply diagram.

   b. What would be the effect of this change on the economy if the Bank of Canada followed a rule of increasing the money supply by 3 percent per year *plus* 1 percentage point for every percentage point that unemployment rises above its normal level? Illustrate your answer.

   c. Which of the foregoing rules better stabilizes the economy? Would it help to allow the Bank of Canada to respond to predicted unemployment instead of current unemployment? Explain.

4. The problem of time inconsistency applies to fiscal policy as well as to monetary policy. Suppose the government announced a reduction in taxes on income from capital investments, like new factories.

   a. If investors believed that capital taxes would remain low, how would the government's action affect the level of investment?

   b. After investors have responded to the announced tax reduction, does the government have an incentive to renege on its policy? Explain.

   c. Given your answer to part (b), would investors believe the government's announcement? What can the government do to increase the credibility of announced policy changes?

   d. Explain why this situation is similar to the time inconsistency problem faced by monetary policymakers.

5. Chapter 2 explains the difference between positive analysis and normative analysis. In the debate about whether the central bank should aim for zero inflation, which areas of disagreement involve positive statements and which involve normative judgements?

6. Why are the benefits of reducing inflation permanent and the costs temporary? Why are the costs of increasing inflation permanent and the benefits temporary? Use Phillips-curve diagrams in your answer.

7. Suppose the federal government cuts taxes and increases spending, producing a budget deficit equal to 12 percent of GDP. If nominal GDP is rising 7 percent per year, are such budget deficits sustainable forever? Explain. If budget deficits of this size are maintained for twenty years, what is likely to happen to your taxes and your children's taxes in the future? Can you do something today to offset this future effect?

8. Explain how each of the following policies redistributes income across generations. Is the redistribution from young to old people, or from old to young people?

   a. an increase in the budget deficit

   b. more generous subsidies for education loans

   c. greater investments in highways and bridges

   d. indexation of Old Age Security benefits to inflation

9. Surveys suggest that most people are opposed to budget deficits, but these same people elected representatives who in the 1980s and 1990s passed budgets with significant deficits. Why might the opposition to budget deficits be stronger in principle than in practice?

10. The chapter says that budget deficits reduce the income of future generations, but can boost output and income during a recession. Explain how both of these statements can be true.

11. What is the fundamental tradeoff that society faces if it chooses to save more?

12. Suppose the government reduced the tax rate on income from savings.

    a. Who would benefit from this tax reduction most directly?

    b. What would happen to the capital stock over time? What would happen to the capital available to each worker? What would happen to productivity? What would happen to wages?

    c. In light of your answer to part (b), who might benefit from this tax reduction in the long run?

GLOSSARY

absolute advantage—the comparison among producers of a good according to their productivity

aggregate-demand curve—a curve that shows the quantity of goods and services that households, firms, and the government want to buy at each price level

aggregate-supply curve—a curve that shows the quantity of goods and services that firms choose to produce and sell at each price level

appreciation—an increase in the value of a currency as measured by the amount of foreign currency it can buy

automatic stabilizers—changes in fiscal policy that stimulate aggregate demand when the economy goes into a recession without policymakers having to take any deliberate action

balanced trade—a situation in which exports equal imports

Bank of Canada—the central bank of Canada

bank rate—the interest rate the Bank of Canada charges on loans to the commercial banks

bond—a certificate of indebtedness

budget deficit—a shortfall of tax revenue from government spending

budget surplus—an excess of tax revenue over government spending

capital flight—a large and sudden reduction in the demand for assets located in a country

catch-up effect—the property whereby countries that start off poor tend to grow more rapidly than countries that start off rich

central bank—an institution designed to control the quantity of money in the economy

ceteris paribus—a Latin phrase, translated as "other things being equal," used as a reminder that all variables other than the ones being studied are assumed to be constant

circular-flow diagram—a visual model of the economy that shows how dollars flow through markets among households and firms

classical dichotomy—the theoretical separation of nominal and real variables

closed economy—an economy that does not interact with other economies in the world

collective bargaining—the process by which unions and firms agree on the terms of employment

commodity money—money that takes the form of a commodity with intrinsic value

comparative advantage—the comparison among producers of a good according to their opportunity cost

competitive market—a market in which there are many buyers and many sellers so that each has a negligible impact on the market price

complements—two goods for which an increase in the price of one leads to a decrease in the demand for the other good

consumer price index (CPI)—a measure of the overall cost of the goods and services bought by a typical consumer

consumer surplus—a buyer's willingness to pay minus the amount the buyer actually pays

consumption—spending by households on goods and services, with the exception of purchases of new housing

cost—the value of everything a seller must give up to produce a good

cross-price elasticity of demand—a measure of how much the quantity demanded of one good responds to a change in the price of another good, computed as the percentage change in quantity demanded of the first good divided by the percentage change in the price of the second good

crowding out—a decrease in investment that results from government borrowing

crowding-out effect on investment—the offset in aggregate demand that results when expansionary fiscal policy raises the interest rate and thereby reduces investment spending

crowding-out effect on net exports—the offset in aggregate demand that results when expansionary fiscal policy in a small open economy with a flexible exchange rate raises the real exchange rate and thereby reduces net exports

currency—the paper bills and coins in the hands of the public

cyclical unemployment—the deviation of unemployment from its natural rate

deadweight loss—the fall in total surplus that results from a marked distortion, such as a tax

demand curve—a graph of the relationship between the price of a good and the quantity demanded

demand deposits—balances in bank accounts that depositors can access on demand by writing a cheque or using a debit card

demand schedule—a table that shows the relationship between the price of a good and the quantity demanded

depreciation—a decrease in the value of a currency as measured by the amount of foreign currency it can buy

depression—a severe recession

diminishing returns—the property whereby the benefit from an extra unit of an input declines as the quantity of the input increases

discouraged workers—individuals who would like to work but have given up looking for a job

economics—the study of how society manages its scarce resources

efficiency—the property of a resource allocation of maximizing the total surplus received by all members of society

efficiency wages—above-equilibrium wages paid by firms in order to increase worker productivity

elasticity—a measure of the responsiveness of quantity demanded or quantity supplied to one of its determinants

Employment Insurance—a government program that partially protects workers' incomes when they become unemployed

equilibrium—a situation in which supply and demand have been brought into balance

equilibrium price—the price that balances supply and demand

equilibrium quantity—the quantity supplied and the quantity demanded when the price has adjusted to balance supply and demand

equity—the fairness of the distribution of well-being among the members of society

excess demand—a situation in which quantity demanded is greater than quantity supplied

excess supply—a situation in which quantity supplied is greater than quantity demanded

exports—goods and services that are produced domestically and sold abroad

externality—the impact of one person's actions on the well-being of a bystander

fiat money—money without intrinsic value that is used as money because of government decree

financial intermediaries—financial institutions through which savers can indirectly provide funds to borrowers

financial markets—financial institutions through which savers can directly provide funds to borrowers

financial system—the group of institutions in the economy that help to match one person's saving with another person's investment

Fisher effect—the one-for-one adjustment of the nominal interest rate to the inflation rate

foreign exchange market operations—the purchase or sale of foreign money by the Bank of Canada

fractional-reserve banking—a banking system in which banks hold only a fraction of deposits as reserves

frictional unemployment—unemployment that results because it takes time for workers to search for the jobs that best suit their tastes and skills

GDP deflator—a measure of the price level calculated as the ratio of nominal GDP to real GDP times 100

government purchases—spending on goods and services by local, provincial, and federal governments

gross domestic product (GDP)—the market value of all final goods and services produced within a country in a given period of time

gross national product (GNP)—the market value of all final goods and services produced by permanent residents of a nation within a given period of time

human capital—the knowledge and skills that workers acquire through education, training, and experience

import quota—a limit on the quantity of a good that can be produced abroad and sold domestically

imports—goods and services that are produced abroad and sold domestically

income elasticity of demand—a measure of how much the quantity demanded of a good responds to a change in consumers' income, computed as the percentage change in quantity demanded divided by the percentage change in income

indexation—the automatic correction of a dollar amount for the effects of inflation by law or contract

industrial product price index—a measure of the cost of a basket of goods and services bought by firms

inferior good—a good for which, all things equal, an increase in income leads to a decrease in quantity demanded

inflation—an increase in the overall level of prices in the economy

inflation rate—the percentage change in the price index from the preceding period

inflation tax—the revenue the government raises by creating money

interest rate parity—a theory of interest rate determination whereby the real interest rate on comparable financial assets should be the same in all economies with full access to world financial markets

investment—spending on capital equipment, inventories, and structures, including household purchases of new housing

job search—the process by which workers find appropriate jobs given their tastes and skills

labour force—the total number of workers, including both the employed and the unemployed

labour-force participation rate—the percentage of the adult population that is in the labour force

law of demand—the claim that, other things being equal, the quantity demanded of a good falls when the price of the good rises

law of supply—the claim that, other things equal, the quantity supplied of a good rises when the price of the good rises

law of supply and demand—the claim that the price of any good adjusts to bring the supply and demand for that good into balance

liquidity—the ease with which an asset can be converted into the economy's medium of exchange

macroeconomics—the study of economy-wide phenomena, including inflation, unemployment, and economic growth

marginal changes—small incremental adjustments to a plan of action

market—a group of buyers and sellers of a particular good or service

market economy—an economy that allocates resources through the decentralized decisions of many firms and households as they interact in markets for goods and services

market failure—a situation in which a market left on its own fails to allocate resources efficiently

market for loanable funds—the market in which those who want to save supply funds and those who want to borrow to invest demand funds

market power—the ability of a single economic actor (or small group of actors) to have a substantial influence on market prices

medium of exchange—an item that buyers give to sellers when they want to purchase goods and services

menu costs—the costs of changing prices

microeconomics—the study of how households and firms make decisions and how they interact in markets

model of aggregate demand and aggregate supply—the model that most economists use to explain short-run fluctuations in economic activity around its long-run trend

monetary neutrality—the proposition that changes in the money supply do not affect real variables

monetary policy—the setting of the money supply by policymakers in the central bank

money—the set of assets in the economy that people regularly use to buy goods and services from other people

money multiplier—the amount of money the banking system generates with each dollar of reserves

money supply—the quantity of money available in the economy

multiplier effect—the additional shifts in aggregate demand that result when expansionary fiscal policy increases income and thereby increases consumer spending

mutual fund—an institution that sells shares to the public and uses the proceeds to buy a portfolio of stocks and bonds

national saving (saving)—the total income in the economy that remains after paying for consumption and government purchases

natural-rate hypothesis—the claim that unemployment eventually returns to its normal, or natural, rate, regardless of the rate of inflation

natural rate of unemployment—the rate of unemployment to which the economy tends to return in the long run

natural resources—the inputs into the production of goods and services that are provided by nature, such as land, rivers, and mineral deposits

net exports—spending on domestically produced goods by foreigners (exports) minus spending on foreign goods by domestic residents (imports)

net foreign investment—the purchase of foreign assets by domestic residents minus the purchase of domestic assets by foreigners

nominal exchange rate—the rate at which a person can trade the currency of one country for the currency of another

nominal GDP—the production of goods and services valued at current prices

nominal interest rate—the interest rate as usually reported without a correction for the effects of inflation

nominal variables—variables measured in monetary units

normal good—a good for which, all things equal, an increase in income leads to an increase in quantity demanded

normative statements—claims that attempt to prescribe how the world should be

Okun's law—the number of percentage points the unemployment rate increases when GDP falls by 1 percentage point

open economy—an economy that interacts freely with other economies around the world

open-market operations—the purchase or sale of government bonds by the Bank of Canada

opportunity cost—whatever must be given up to obtain some item

perfect capital mobility—full access to world financial markets

Phillips curve—a curve that shows the short-run tradeoff between inflation and unemployment

physical capital—the stock of equipment and structures that are used to produce goods and services

positive statements—claims that attempt to describe the world as it is

price ceiling—a legal maximum on the price at which a good can be sold

price elasticity of demand—a measure of how much the quantity demanded of a good responds to a change in the price of that good, computed as the percentage change in quantity demanded divided by the percentage change in price

price elasticity of supply—a measure of how much the quantity supplied of a good responds to a change in the price of that good, computed as the percentage change in quantity supplied divided by the percentage change in price

price floor—a legal minimum on the price at which a good can be sold

private saving—the income that households have left after paying for taxes and consumption

producer surplus—the amount a seller is paid for a good minus the seller's cost

production possibilities frontier—a graph that shows the various combinations of output that the economy can possibly produce given the available factors of production and the available production technology

productivity—the amount of goods and services produced from each hour of a worker's time

public saving—the tax revenue that the government has left after paying for its spending

purchasing-power parity—a theory of exchange rates whereby a unit of any given currency should be able to buy the same quantity of goods in all countries

quantity demanded—the amount of a good that buyers are willing to purchase

quantity equation—the equation $M \times V = P \times Y$, which relates the quantity of money, the velocity of money, and the dollar value of the economy's output of goods and services

quantity supplied—the amount of a good that sellers are willing to sell

quantity theory of money—a theory asserting that the quantity of money available determines the price level and that the growth rate in the quantity of money available determines the inflation rate

rational expectations—the theory according to which people optimally use all the information they have, including information about government policies, when forecasting the future

real exchange rate—the rate at which a person can trade the goods and services of one country for the goods and services of another

real GDP—the production of goods and services valued at constant prices

real interest rate—the interest rate corrected for the effects of inflation

real variables—variables measured in physical units

recession—a period of declining real incomes and rising unemployment

reserve ratio—the fraction of deposits that banks hold as reserves

reserve requirements—regulations on the minimum amount of reserves that banks must hold against deposits

reserves—deposits that banks have received but have not loaned out

risk premium—a positive or negative differential between domestic and world interest rates that compensates lenders for the risk of exchange rate depreciation or appreciation

sacrifice ratio—the number of percentage points of one year's output lost in the process of reducing inflation by 1 percentage point

scarcity—the limited nature of society's resources

shoeleather costs—the resources wasted when inflation encourages people to reduce their money holdings

shortage—a situation in which quantity demanded is greater than quantity supplied

small open economy—an economy that trades goods and services with other economies and, by itself, has a negligible effect on world prices and interest rates

stagflation—a period of falling output and rising prices

sterilization—the process of offsetting foreign exchange market operations with open-market operations, so that the effect on the money supply is cancelled out

stock—a claim to partial ownership in a firm

store of value—an item that people can use to transfer purchasing power from the present to the future

strike—the organized withdrawal of labour from a firm by a union

structural unemployment—unemployment that results because the number of jobs available in some labour markets is insufficient to provide a job for everyone who wants one

substitutes—two goods for which an increase in the price of one good leads to an increase in the demand for the other good

supply curve—a graph of the relationship between the price of a good and the quantity supplied

supply schedule—a table that shows the relationship between the price of a good and the quantity supplied

supply shock—an event that directly alters firms' costs and prices, shifting the economy's aggregate-supply curve and thus the Phillips curve

surplus—a situation in which quantity supplied is greater than quantity demanded

tariff—a tax on goods produced abroad and sold domestically

tax incidence—the study of who bears the burden of taxation

technological knowledge—society's understanding of the best ways to produce goods and services

theory of liquidity preference—Keynes's theory that the interest rate adjusts to bring money supply and money demand into balance

total revenue—the amount paid by buyers and received by sellers of a good, computed as the price of the good times the quantity sold

trade balance—the value of a nation's exports minus the value of its imports, also called net exports

trade deficit—an excess of imports over exports

trade policy—a government policy that directly influences the quantity of goods and services that a country imports or exports

trade surplus—an excess of exports over imports

unemployment rate—the percentage of the labour force that is unemployed

union—a worker association that bargains with employers over wages and working conditions

unit of account—the yardstick people use to post prices and record debts

velocity of money—the rate at which money changes hands

vicious circle—cycle that results when deficits reduce the supply of loanable funds, increase interest rates, discourage investment, and result in slower economic growth; slower growth leads to slower tax revenue and higher spending on income-support programs, and the results can be still higher budget deficits

virtuous circle—cycle that results when surpluses increase the supply of loanable funds, reduce interest rates, stimulate investment, and result in faster economic growth; faster growth leads to higher tax revenue and lower spending on income-support programs, and the result can be still higher budget surpluses

welfare economics—the study of how the allocation of resources affects economic well-being

willingness to pay—the maximum amount that a buyer will pay for a good

world price—the price of a good that prevails in the world market for that good

CREDITS

Photos and Cartoons

Page 7 © CP Picture Archive

Page 9 © 1990 from *Wall Street Journal*. Reprinted by permission of Cartoon Features Syndicate.

Page 11 © Corbis Images/Bettmann

Page 14 © 1978 Wayne Stayskal and *Chicago Tribune*

Page 20 © The New Yorker Collection, 1986 J.B. Handelsman from cartoonbank.com. All rights reserved.

Page 30 © The New Yorker Collection, 1981 James Stevenson from cartoonbank.com. All rights reserved.

Page 58 © Corbis Images/Bettmann

Page 73 © 2001 Dick Hemingway

Page 83 © 1995 *Washington Post, Non Sequitur Survival Guide for the Nineties*

Page 89 © PhotoDisc

Page 89 © The New Yorker Collection, 1972 Robert Day from cartoonbank.com. All rights reserved.

Page 102 © Ann & Carl Purcell/Words & Pictures/PNI

Page 110 © Gary Trudeau and Universal Press Syndicate. Reprinted with permission.

Page 120 © Owen Franken/Corbis Images

Page 156 © Robert Ginn/PhotoEdit

Page 162 © The New Yorker Collection, 1970 J.B. Handelsman from cartoonbank.com. All rights reserved.

Page 169 © Tom Hanson/CP Picture Archive

Page 170 © Stock Montage

Page 193 © *Berry's World*. Reprinted by permission of Newspaper Enterprise Association, Inc.

Page 197 © Donald L. Miller/International Stock

Page 218 © PhotoDisc

Page 228 Photo courtesy Nokia Corporation

Page 231 (top) © *Wall Street Journal*. Used by permission of Cartoon Features Syndicate.

Page 231 (bottom) © The Kobal Collection

Page 247 Photo courtesy of Honda Motor Corporation

Page 255 © Stock Montage

Page 258 © Andromeda Interactive

Page 266 © Frank Gunn/CP Picture Archive

Page 268 © 1994 *Arlo and Janis* reprinted by permission of Newspaper Enterprise Association, Inc.

Page 274 © The New Yorker Collection, 1994 Mick Stevens from cartoonbank.com. All rights reserved.

Page 282 © The New Yorker Collection, 1989 Robert Weber from cartoonbank.com. All rights reserved.

Page 294 © PhotoEdit

Page 307 © The New Yorker Collection, 1970 Allen Dunn from cartoonbank.com. All rights reserved.

Page 311 © 2001. *Dilbert* reprinted by permission of United Feature Syndicate, Inc.

Page 313 © Corbis Images

Page 322 © 1984 from *Wall Street Journal*, Art Pine.

Republished with permission of Dow Jones and Co. Inc. Permission conveyed through Copyright Clearance Center, Inc.

Page 323 © The New Yorker Collection, 1998 Lee Lorenz from cartoonbank.com. All rights reserved.

Page 325 © 2001 Dick Hemingway

Page 328 © The New Yorker Collection, from cartoonbank.com. All rights reserved.

Page 336 © The Kobal Collection

Page 343 © The New Yorker Collection, 1978 Frank Modell from cartoonbank.com. All rights reserved.

Page 363 © The Kobal Collection

Page 373 ©The New Yorker Collection, 1992 Mort Gerberg from cartoonbank.com. All rights reserved.

Page 375 © Paul Conklin/PhotoEdit

Page 390 © Corbis Images

Page 426 © The New Yorker Collection, 1990 Robert Mankoff from cartoonbank.com. All rights reserved.

Page 446 National Archives of Canada/PA68220

Page 450 ©Marc Ribaud/Magnum Photos

Page 515 © The New Yorker Collection, 1983 Dana Fradon from cartoonbank.com. All rights reserved.

Page 533 © The New Yorker Collection, 1983 Frank Modell from cartoonbank.com. All rights reserved.

Page 542 © Karen Carleton

Articles

Page 33 © 1992 Richard M. Alston, J.R. Kearl, and Michael B. Vaughn, "Is There Consensus among Economists in the 1990s?" *American Economic Review*, May 1992. Reprinted by permission.

Pages 56–57 © 1999 Douglas A. Irwin, "Lamb Tariffs Fleece US Consumers," *Wall Street Journal*, July 12, 1999. Reprinted by permission of Copyright Clearance Center.

Pages 88–89 © 2000 Reprinted with permission from *The Globe and Mail*

Page 103 © 1996 *Washington Post*. Reprinted with permission.

Page 121 © 1999 Terry L. Anderson and Clay J. Landry, "Trickle-Down Economics," *Wall Street Journal*, August 23, 1999. Reprinted by permission of Copyright Clearance Center.

Page 124 © David Gratzer

Pages 156–57 © 1992 by The New York Times Company. Reprinted by Permission.

Page 174 © Jonathan Chevreau/*Financial Post*

Page 187 © The Toronto Star Syndicate. Reprinted with permission.

Page 197 © 1996 by The New York Times Company. Reprinted by permission.

Pages 198–99 © 1997 Jagdish Bhagwati, "Free Trade without Treaties," *Wall Street Journal*, November 24,1997. Reprinted by permission of Copyright Clearance Center.

Page 217 © Kathryn May/*Ottawa Citizen*

INDEX

Note: Page numbers in **boldface** refer to pages where key terms are defined.

SUGGESTIONS FOR SUMMER READING

*If you enjoyed the economics course you have just finished,
you might like reading more about economic issues in the following books.*

■ **DOUBLE VISION: THE INSIDE STORY OF THE LIBERALS IN POWER,** Edward Greenspon and Anthony Wilson-Smith, Toronto: Doubleday, 1997. Written by two journalists, this is the inside story of how the Liberal party, elected in 1993 on a platform of a high level of social spending, was forced to slash spending to restore fiscal stability.

■ **THE GREAT CANADIAN DISINFLATION: THE ECONOMICS AND POLITICS OF MONETARY POLICY IN CANADA, 1988–93,** Policy Study 19, David Laidler and William Robson, Toronto: C.D. Howe Institute, 1994. Two of Canada's leading monetary economists take a critical look at the economics and the politics of Canadian monetary policy.

■ **HARD MONEY, HARD TIMES: WHY ZERO INFLATION HURTS CANADIANS,** Lars Osberg and Pierre Fortin, eds., Toronto: James Lorimer & Company, 1998. This book is a collection of essays by economists who question the wisdom of the tight monetary policy adopted by the Bank of Canada in the early 1980s and again in the early 1990s.

■ **THE WEALTH AND POVERTY OF NATIONS: WHY SOME ARE SO RICH AND SOME SO POOR,** David S. Landes, New York: Norton, 1998. The most important question in economics is the one originally asked by Adam Smith in 1776: What are the causes of the wealth of nations? In this landmark study of world economics, David Landes argues that culture is the key to understanding why some nations are rich and others are poor. Without certain cultural traits, industrialization is impossible to sustain.

■ **GETTING IT RIGHT: MARKETS AND CHOICES IN A FREE SOCIETY,** Robert J. Barro, Cambridge, Mass.: MIT Press, 1996. In this collection of essays based on his *Wall Street Journal* columns, conservative economist Robert Barro offers his view about the workings of the economy and the proper scope of economic policy.

■ **HARD HEADS, SOFT HEARTS: TOUGH-MINDED ECONOMICS FOR A JUST SOCIETY,** Alan S. Blinder, Reading, Mass.: Addison-Wesley, 1987. How should government policy-makers balance economic efficiency and social compassion? Alan Blinder, who has served as an economic adviser to President Clinton, offers his answers in this wide-ranging book.